D1288170

Nationalist in the Viet Nam Wars

CHINA

Ha Giang
Lao Cai
Camp Cong Troi
Pingxiang
Lai Chau
Lang Son
Yen Bai
Son La
Vinh Yen
Dien Bien Phu
Ha Noi
Dao Cai Bau
Hoa Binh
Ha Dong
Haiphong
Hong Gai
Nam Dinh
Thai Binh
Ninh Binh
Bui Chu
Dao Bach Long Vi
Phat Diem

LAOS

Thanh Hoa
Camp 5
Thanh Phong
Ky Son
Nghe An
Quynh Luu
Dien Chau
Camp 6
Vinh
Ha Tinh
Ron

Gulf of Tonkin

Hainan

Vientiane

Dong Hoi

North 17th Parallel

DMZ
Dong Ha
Quang Tri
Hue

South China Sea

THAILAND

Da Nang
Cu Lao Cham
An Diem
Tam Ky
Cu Lao Re
Dak Pek
Quang Ngai
Dac To
My Lai
Bong Son
Kon Tum
Phu Cu pass
Pleiku
An Khe
Plei Me
Qui Nhon
Phu Bon
Song Cau
Xuan Phuoc
Tuy Hoa
Ban Me Thuot
Ninh Hoa
Nha Trang

Bangkok

CAMBODIA

Gia Nghia
Da Lat
Loc Ninh
Cam Ranh
Dong Xoai
Phan Rang-Thap Cham

Gulf of Thailand

Phnom Penh
Mekong
Tay Ninh
Thu Dau Mot
Bien Hoa
Sai Gon
Phan Thiet
Ham Tan

Chau Doc
Cao Lanh
Tan An
My Tho
Vung Tau
Ha Tien
Long Xuyen
Ben Tre
Rach Gia
Vinh Long
Dao Phu Quoc
Can Tho
Tra Vinh
U Minh
Soc Trang
Mekong Delta
Ca Mau
Bac Lieu

Con Son
(Poulo Condor)

VIETNAM

- Ho Chi Minh Trail
- International Boundary
- Road
- River
- ★ National Capital

0   50   100 Kilometers
0   50   100 Miles

Nationalist

in the Viet Nam Wars

MEMOIRS OF A

VICTIM TURNED SOLDIER

Nguyễn Công Luận

INDIANA UNIVERSITY PRESS

Bloomington & Indianapolis

Publication of this book is made possible in part with the assistance of a Challenge Grant from the National Endowment for the Humanities, a federal agency that supports research, education, and public programming in the humanities. Any views, findings, conclusions, or recommendations expressed in this publication do not necessarily reflect those of the National Endowment for the Humanities.

This book is a publication of

Indiana University Press
601 North Morton Street
Bloomington, Indiana 47404-3797
USA

iupress.indiana.edu

Telephone orders   800-842-6796
Fax orders   812-855-7931

© 2012 by Nguyễn Công Luận
All rights reserved

No part of this book may be reproduced or utilized in any form or by any means, electronic or mechanical, including photocopying and recording, or by any information storage and retrieval system, without permission in writing from the publisher. The Association of American University Presses' Resolution on Permissions constitutes the only exception to this prohibition.

♾The paper used in this publication meets the minimum requirements of the American National Standard for Information Sciences—Permanence of Paper for Printed Library Materials, ANSI Z39.48-1992.

Manufactured in the United States of America

Library of Congress Cataloging-in-Publication Data

Nguyễn Công Luận, [date]
  Nationalist in the Viet Nam wars : memoirs of a victim turned soldier / Nguyễn Công Luận.
    p. cm.
  Includes bibliographical references and index.
  ISBN 978-0-253-35687-1 (cloth : alk. paper) — ISBN 978-0-253-00548-9 (e-book) 1. Nguyễn Công Luận, [date] 2. Vietnam (Republic). Quân lực—Officers—Biography. 3. Political prisoners—Vietnam—Biography. 4. Political refugees—Vietnam—Biography. 5. Indochinese War, 1946–1954—Personal narratives, Vietnamese. 6. Vietnam War, 1961–1975—Personal narratives, Vietnamese. 7. Vietnam—History—1945–1975. 8. Vietnam—History—1975– I. Title.
  DS556.93.N5215A3 2012
  959.704'3092—dc23
  [B]
                                    2011024044

1 2 3 4 5 17 16 15 14 13 12

In memory of warriors from all sides who were killed, wounded, or recorded as missing while fighting the wars they believed would bring freedom and prosperity to Việt Nam

CONTENTS

FOREWORD

As it was being fought, the Việt Nam War was the most thoroughly documented and recorded war in history. It is, therefore, especially ironic that more than thirty-five years after the fall of Sài Gòn, Việt Nam remains one of the most misunderstood of all American wars, shrouded in a fog of misconceptions, bogus myths, and distorted facts. One of the most cherished of those many false beliefs centers on what was supposed to have been the complete operational ineptness and combat ineffectiveness of the Army of the Republic of Việt Nam—the ARVN. The seemingly stark difference between the ARVN of the South and the People's Army of Việt Nam—the PAVN—of the North prompted many pundits at the time and since to ask why "our Vietnamese" couldn't fight, but "theirs" obviously could.

Even the leaders of North Việt Nam believed the common wisdom about the ARVN being little more than a house of cards. One of North Việt Nam Defense Minister Võ Nguyên Giáp's key assumptions when he launched the 1968 Tết Offensive was that the ARVN would collapse on first contact. But it didn't collapse. It fought, and it fought well. The ARVN again put up a stiff and largely successful fight during North Việt Nam's 1972 Easter Offensive. And when the North Vietnamese again attacked with overwhelming force in the spring of 1975, some ARVN units finally did collapse under the crushing onslaught, but many other South Vietnamese units went down fighting. Most of the ARVN soldiers who survived then paid the terrible price of years of brutal treatment in the forced "reeducation camps" established by the victors.

Most Americans who served in Việt Nam had some contact with the soldiers of the ARVN. Those who served in Special Forces units or as Military Assistance Command, Việt Nam (MACV) advisors had almost daily contact with the South Vietnamese military, and consequently they developed a more in-depth understanding of its particular structural and institutional problems, as well as the intricacies of the broader South Vietnamese culture from which the ARVN was drawn. For those GIs who served in the conventional U.S. units, the contact was more sporadic, and what understanding of their allies they did develop did not run very deep. Thus, while some Americans had positive experiences and still hold fond memories of their South Vietnamese comrades, many others had experiences with the ARVN that were frustrating at best.

In the past ten years, memoirs written by former ARVN officers and soldiers have contributed immensely to our understanding of that military force. Most have been written by South Vietnamese who either escaped after the fall of Sài Gòn or were allowed to immigrate to the Unites States following their release from the camps. So far, no accounts written by former ARVN soldiers who remained in Việt Nam have appeared in English, if indeed the current Vietnamese government has allowed any to be published at all. One of the most important of those volumes published in the United States is this book, *Nationalist in the Viet Nam Wars: Memoirs of a Victim Turned Soldier,* by Nguyễn Công Luận.

Major Luận starts his narrative by detailing his childhood in North Việt Nam under Japanese occupation during World War II and through the subsequent French phase of the Việt Nam War in the late 1940s and early 1950s. After his family fled to South Việt Nam in the mid-1950s, Nguyễn attended one of the first graduating classes of the Republic of Việt Nam Military Academy and was then commissioned an officer in the ARVN. He served just short of twenty years, right through the collapse of South Việt Nam in April 1975. Nguyễn then endured almost seven years in the reeducation camps. He finally was allowed to immigrate to the United States under the Orderly Departure Program.

Most of this book is devoted to Major Luận's service and experience as an ARVN officer. This is one of the most compelling and thoughtful ARVN accounts ever published. Nguyễn's view of the ARVN from the inside offers a perspective that few Western readers will ever have an opportunity to see. Along the way he also provides fascinating accounts of Vietnamese village life and social culture, the French colonial occupation, the communist government of the North, and the U.S. forces in Việt Nam during the second phase of Việt Nam's thirty-year war.

This book is an unblinking, unflinching account, and it will be received with serious reservations in many quarters. Some readers among the French most likely will object to Luận's portrayal of the French military during the period of the colonial occupation. The current government of Việt Nam quite likely will not be pleased with his descriptions of the corruption and brutality of the communist system, both in the North after the French defeat and in the South after the fall of Sài Gòn. Some members of the former South Vietnamese government and the ARVN likely will object to Luận's frank assessments of the weakness and political corruption systemic to South Việt Nam. And some American veterans might take umbrage at his "warts and all" portrayal of the U.S. military and of his severe criticisms of the U.S. government's overall handling of the war. Nonetheless, everything that Major Luận writes rings true. He calls it like he saw it, but he does not take cheap shots. Despite his well justified descriptions of the cultural blindness exhibited by too many Americans during the war, it is very clear that he still has a great deal of sympathy and admiration for the typical American soldier and a genuine affection for what is now his adopted country.

Although he never served above the rank of major, Luận was for three years the director of the Reception Directorate, the largest of the three directorates of the RVN Chiêu Hồi Ministry, which included the National Chiêu Hồi Center. He was responsible for evaluating former Vietnamese communist soldiers and training them to be integrated into South Vietnamese society. He also served several years as chief of the strategic study and research division of the General Political Warfare Department. The Chiêu Hồi program was widely misunderstood and generally underappreciated. Major Luận's unique perspective and his discussion and evaluation of the program constitute one of the book's most valuable contributions.

The author's integrity comes through on every page of this brutally honest account. Major Nguyên Công Luận was above all a patriot who loved his country and was willing to make any sacrifice for it. When the North Vietnamese army started its final attack on the South in the spring of 1975, he was in the United States, a student at the U.S. Army Infantry School. Even as the doom of South Việt Nam seemed all but certain, Major Luận chose to return to share his country's fate. He didn't have to go back. Senior-ranking U.S. military officers were urging him to stay and offering to help him get his family out. But Major Luận remained true to the end to his soldier's oath. Eventually he did leave Việt Nam, and in the long run that country's loss was America's gain.

Maj. Gen. David T. Zabecki, PhD
Army of the United States, Retired
Editor emeritus, *Vietnam* magazine
Second Battalion, Forty-seventh Infantry,
Việt Nam, 1967–68

PREFACE

In my early childhood, "war" was one among the first abstract words I learned before I could have the least perception of its meaning. It was when World War II began. When I was a little older, I saw how war brought death and destruction when American bombers attacked some Japanese installations near my hometown. But it was the wars in my country after 1945 that resulted in the greatest disasters to my people.

Particularly, the 1955–75 Việt Nam War has been the most destructive in Việt Nam history and the most controversial in the United States as well as in many countries in the world. The debate seems endless, the arguments contradicting.

Before and since April 1975, there have been conferences, teach-ins, books, reports, and movies about the Việt Nam Wars after 1945. I realized that many of them contained incorrect and insufficient information, one-sided and superficial arguments, and erroneous figures. There have been conferences held outside Việt Nam about the war, but among many hundreds of participants, there was not a single Vietnamese from either side.

Besides, most books in English about the Việt Nam War were written by presidents, ministers, congressmen, generals, scholars, journalists, or U.S. fighting men, not by common Vietnamese who were victims and participants of the wars, who saw the wars from the bottom, not the top, and from inside, not outside. Most of these individuals can't write well even in Vietnamese, let alone in English. Many who are fluent in English would prefer to do something else rather than write about wars.

Only a few works by pro-South Việt Nam writers can be found in bookstores and libraries in the world, whereas the communist regime in the North spent great effort and a hundred times more money than South Việt Nam to inundate foreign libraries with its propaganda publications. The voice of the nationalist Vietnamese was rarely heard by the world outside, and they were slandered and humiliated without the fair opportunity to defend and tell the truth. The nationalists in South Việt Nam did not spend much of their taxpayers' money for the costly propaganda operation, as the communist North Việt Nam did.

As a member of the South Vietnamese Republic Armed Forces, I have an obligation to contribute my little part to the protection of the honor of our military servicemen and my fellow nationalists. The Vietnamese nationalists, the Republic of Việt Nam (South Việt Nam) and its armed forces were the undeniable entities representing a large segment of the Vietnamese people and their wishes. They deserve recognition in world history, however good or bad they were.

I was just a nobody in Việt Nam, only a common person of my generation in the two wars. I was serving the South Việt Nam Army with all my heart, but I have not contributed anything great to my people nor to my army. I have never strived to make myself out to be a hero, and I have never been one. I've done nothing important, either good enough to boast about or bad enough to write a book to justify.

This is not an academic study, so there are no lengthy references. I only compiled my experiences from my memory concerning the conflict between the pro-communists and the anticommunists to write these memoirs with my best effort at honesty and impartiality.

It is my great hope that these stories might give a little more insight into the very complicated ideological conflicts in my country, into how the many millions of Vietnamese noncommunist patriots like me were fighting in the wars, and why we believed we were on the right side. Truthful and sufficient perception of events in history can be attained from common people's personal experiences and stories, not only from what the big wheels of the time were doing or saying.

These memoirs were written not to nourish wartime animosity but to help the coming generations, particularly those of Vietnamese origin, have a clear look into what life was like during the wars that killed millions of my dear compatriots and left the country with the scars that deeply divide the Vietnamese people.

I also would like to touch upon the roots of the war begotten from social traditions, nature, and conception, without which a deep understanding could hardly be achieved. Therefore, I go into details at some points to help clarify the related aspects or circumstances in question and construct the overall view of the wars as I saw them. So please read them with patience.

These memoirs are based mostly on facts and events I experienced as a child and as a young man that are imprinted on my memory, although I did not try to remember. I could not understand many of them during the early years of my life. But as I was growing older and my general knowledge developed, I recollected each of them and found the explanations by people around me and even by myself.

Other experiences came later in my life. During my time serving in the South Vietnamese Army in the 1955–75 war, I happened to be serving in various jobs that helped me have a close look at the war, especially at the rank and file, at the peasants living between the anvil and the hammer, and at the horror of war from both sides.

A NOTE ON VIETNAMESE NAMES

Vietnamese names generally consist of three parts: family, middle, and given, used in that order. In writing or speaking, a respected old man or a despicable bastard is referred to by his given name, and this is correct in any case, be it formal address or colloquial dialogue.

Highly respectable men of celebrity who are considered old are referred to by family name, as a mark of respect. For example: Phan Bội Châu, a revolutionary, was called Cụ Phan (Cụ = old Mr.), and nobody called him Mr. Châu. Usually such men were born before 1900. This rule is applied when the person cannot be mistaken for another in a text or a speech. If that is not the case, the full name must be used instead. Hồ Chí Minh was called President Hồ or Mr. Hồ because he was the only famous person who carried the family name Hồ. Nguyễn Tường Tam, the famous writer and a Việt Nam Quốc Dân Đảng leader, was not called Mr. Nguyễn because there are other famous personages with this very common family name. Instead, he went by a pen name, Nhất Linh. A pen name is usually a two-word noun and inseparable in any text or speech.

No one addressed Hồ Chí Minh as Mr. Minh, or ARVN General Duong Văn Minh as General Duong, or Nguyễn Văn Thiệu as President Nguyễn. Ngô Đình Diệm, born in 1906, was simply Mr. Diệm or President Diệm. A number of his supporters called him President Ngô, probably because he was born in the pivotal era at the beginning of the twentieth century.

PART I

A Grain of Sand

ONE

A Morning of Horror

It was a cool summer morning in 1951 in my home village, a small and insignificant place on the Red River delta, some sixty miles south of Hà Nội, in the north of Việt Nam. Under the bright sunlight and the cloudless blue sky, the green paddy in front of my grandma's house looked so fresh and peaceful. It would have been much more beautiful if there had not been war in my country.

I was surprised that I was still able to perceive beauty when the whole village was filled with horror. At about 5 AM, African soldiers of the French Army arrived, took position in the pagoda area, and began searching the village houses at sunrise.

Sitting by the doorway of our brick house beside my grandma and a cousin, I was waiting for the worst to happen to me. The village was very quiet; even birds seemed to be aware of impending dangers. At that hour of a day in peacetime, the air would have been noisy with voices, children babbling, birds chirping, and the rice fields active with farmers working.

We three sat still for hours. At times we spoke, but only in clipped words as if a complete phrase would precipitate disaster. My chest was heavy, my mouth dry, and my mind blank. Occasionally I cast a quick glance at my eighty-two-year-old grandma and my fifty-year-old third cousin. Their eyes were expressionless, their faces tense, and those only heightened my fear.

I turned my eyes to the horizon far away. Beyond the winding canal a mile from my village was a hamlet where columns of black smoke rose high behind the bamboo hedge. The French Army soldiers must have been there and set the houses on fire. Fortunately, my village had been spared fire and destruction after many raids in four years of wars. I loved my village so much. It was small with the population of about 300. Since 1950, my village had been under French military control. A village chief was appointed along with members of the village committee working under King Bảo Đại's administration, the noncommunist government that sided with France against the Việt Minh.[1]

However, our submission to the French military authority did not protect us from being looted, raped, tortured, or killed by French soldiers. Every private, whether he was a Frenchman, an African, or a Vietnamese, could do almost anything he wanted to a Vietnamese civilian without fear of being tried in a court or punished by his superiors. It was safer in the cities where higher military officials and police authorities could exert their judicial power.

In 1950, my mother brought my two little sisters and me back to Nam Định (our provincial city, only six miles from my village), where I would attend high school. The French military forces had controlled the city since early 1947, a few months after the war broke out on December 19, 1946.

During the summer of 1951, I came to see my grandma as I always did whenever there was a day or two open from school. Although life in the countryside was full of danger, she refused to come live with us in the city. Despite every hazard, she was happy to remain in the house where many generations had lived and died, full of memories of her life with my grandpa. They had eight children, of whom my father was the fifth.

She loved me more than anyone else in the world, as I was her only grandson. She always worried about my safety. A bruise on my knee or a cut finger would move her to tears.

As if she happened to remember something, she handed me a bowl of warm rice she had cooked before dawn with a chunk of fried fish. She whispered, "You eat something. You should not be hungry."

She did not say what I knew she really meant: she wanted to be sure that I would not be a hungry ghost in case I should be killed. I was always willing to please her, but I found it impossible to swallow even a small bit as fear choked my throat and dried my mouth.

Long hours of waiting drained my energy. I wished that the soldiers would come sooner if the calamities were unavoidable.

When the sun had climbed high above the bamboo row, I heard the black soldiers shout loudly about 300 feet away. Often we could tell how near they were by the sound of their heavy boots and the smell of the tobacco they smoked, which could be detected from a mile or more away.

The noises of household objects being broken and the cries of women and children drew nearer and nearer. After a while, four tall black soldiers appeared, rifles on their shoulders. The area so far had been free of activity by the Việt Minh, so it was not necessary for these soldiers to be ready for combat. They kicked open the gate of my cousin's house across a small garden and a low wall from my grandma's and walked in. In a few minutes, they came out, after breaking a few jars and earthenware.

They walked across the garden, entered my grandma's house by a side door, and searched every nook and cranny. They didn't find anything worth stealing. How could anything of value be left after so many raids during the previous years? One of them broke the rice pot with his rifle butt; the other swept the altar with his machete and shattered a joss-stick burner. On the way out, the tallest soldier took a small bottle of rice wine left on the altar and emptied it in just four or five gulps.

The tallest soldier approached the doorway where we were sitting. He stared at me for a few seconds, then motioned for me to stand up. I rose slowly, trying to find out from his countenance what he would do to me. It was a blank face, hard and savage, and it frightened me much more than his rifle and machete did. He grabbed my arm and pushed me toward the gate. I felt his big hand tightening around my upper arm like an iron vise. As I only came up to his chest, he had no difficulty keeping me in his hand without any fear of my escape. I produced my student ID card, but he refused to look at it.

My grandma burst into tears. She rose to her feet, clasped her hands together, bowed low before the soldiers, and implored them in Vietnamese to set me free, although she was well aware that the African soldiers did not understand her language. One of them turned and, without a word, hit her in the upper back with a big bamboo stick, knocking her down on the ground beside my cousin.

The soldiers brought me to a place beside the dirt road where there were about twenty villagers, all the men and teenage boys, who were crouching under the soldiers' rifles. I sat down beside one of them. Each glanced at me, then looked away. I felt calm, not from any courage but from the utmost despair that numbed my feelings and perhaps from seeing that there were many others suffering along with me.

Whenever I was in great danger, I used to ask myself what would happen to me the next minute and hope that it wouldn't be worse. In doing so, I could calm down a little by nourishing a flickering hope of getting through a perilous situation.

When a soldier arrived with two villagers, the three soldiers beside us flew at the two and beat them violently while laughing. It was obvious that they tortured the villagers for pleasure, not out of anger. The tallest soldier hit a fifty-year-old villager in the lower back with a wooden club. The man collapsed with a short, loud scream. Some of us were about to help him, but a soldier stopped us with his rifle. The blow didn't kill the man, but he could never sit up or stand again.

Suddenly, the tallest soldier turned to me. He pulled me up and led me to a fruit garden about thirty yards away beyond the thin bamboo hedge. He asked if I spoke French. My French at the time was very poor, hardly enough to exchange anything more than very simple ideas. It was a risk to speak that kind of French to the Africans, whose French wasn't much better than mine, so I shook my head. He asked, "Where are the Việt Minh?" Again I shook my head.

The soldier flew into a rage. He slapped my face, and I almost fainted. I felt warm blood trickling down my lips and chin. He yelled at me in French and held out a book, demanding to know whether the book was mine. That was my French textbook with my name, the date of purchase, and a small photograph of me glued on the flyleaf. It was foolish to say that it wasn't mine, so I nodded.

He slapped me again and asked me why I didn't speak French to him. I could only say that I was afraid of speaking with my poor French vocabulary. In fact, my language was no worse than what was taught in the textbook, but it was useless to explain to him.

"Where are the Việt Minh?" he asked, his eyes red with anger.

"I don't know any Việt Minh," I said, trying to make every syllable as clear as possible.

"You liar! You swine!" He shouted at my face, so close that his breath made me feel queasy. Again he slapped me several times and pointed at a piece of paper on which two names were scrawled. The names were of two villagers in their twenties who had joined the Việt Minh and left home two years earlier.

The soldier took a piece of rope about two yards long and pushed me down, my face on the ground. He then tied my arms together on my back from my wrist up, so hard that the elbows nearly met, my shoulders pulled back, and my chest tightly drawn. Then he led me to the paddy nearby and showed me two little boys sitting on a grassy bank. Because their faces were badly bruised, it took me take a few seconds to realize that they were my cousins.

The soldier showed them the paper, pointed at me, and shouted, "Parler! Parler!" (Speak! Speak!) One boy told me that the soldier had beaten them, given them paper and pencil, then asked them, "Việt Minh? Việt Minh?" Therefore they had to write the only two Việt Minh names they knew. I was surprised that the African soldiers also applied a Việt Minh intelligence technique: drawing information from children and old people in their dotage.

I tried my best to explain to the soldier that the two men had left the village, but he kept shouting at me. I really didn't know whether he understood me or not with such pidgin French, his and mine. He began hitting me hard, punching my chest and my face, and kicking my ribs and stomach. His wall-eyed face convulsed. He clenched his teeth, and saliva dribbled from his mouth while he was beating me madly.

I held my breath with all my strength to bear the blows that landed all over my left side. For minutes I didn't feel any pain. The great fear probably turned me numb to every blow. I closed my eyes to undergo the agony.

When he stopped, I opened my eyes and had a faint hope that it was all over. I was wrong. He picked up the submachine gun that he had hung on a small tree nearby while beating me, and before I knew what would be happening, he kicked me hard in the chest. I lost balance and fell over on the soft soil.

Lying on my elbows, I could see the soldier cocking his French MAT-49 submachine gun and pointing it at me with one hand. And it flashed with something deafening but so quick that I could hardly hear it.

The whole thing happened in no more than a second. I didn't have enough time to feel fear, to close my eyes, or to turn away. I was still able to reckon that only one or two rounds were shot, then the magazine was empty. I also realized that the bang of his gun was less dreadful than one shot at a longer range of about 50 to 100 yards that I had experienced previously. The bullets hit the soil beside me, sending dirt high above and then down on my face and chest.

I lay there not frightened yet, only wondering if any bullet had hit my body. Seeing no way to escape death, I kept still, waiting for what would happen. The soldier angrily replaced the empty magazine with another one. "It must be full with thirty rounds," I thought.

As he was about to cock the gun, an African sergeant ran up. He snatched the gun from the soldier, spoke to him in his language with a rather loud voice, and shoved him away to the roadside. The sergeant took the end of the rope and pulled me up.

Only in that very minute did I feel a great fear. Horror seized me, and my knees trembled. My legs were paralyzed. In five seconds or so, I wasn't able to move when the sergeant told me to step forward onto the dry ground.

I still thought that I must have been wounded somewhere. I had heard that one might feel nothing in the first few minutes after he was shot. So I tried to look at my legs but was unable to bend my head as the tied arms pulled my neck backward. When I finally could make a few steps to the pathway, I turned back to see if there was any blood on the soil. No blood, so I had not been shot.

The sergeant told me to sit down in front of him and talked to me in soft voice. He told me that if he had arrived a few seconds later, I would have been dead. I thanked him with the best words I could summon from my wretched vocabulary. What surprised me was that the sergeant spoke French with the formal grammar we were taught at school. Despite my poor French, I could understand him, at least the main points.

I answered his questions about the two Việt Minh, and he seemed to believe me. I also told him about my family and that I was a high school student on summer vacation. He glanced at my student ID. After a moment, he told me to stand up. He untied the rope from my arms and tied it around my left wrist to keep me from running away. Then he took me to a high ground down the road and away from other soldiers, where we sat.

Encouraged by this unexpected behavior, I told him that his French was perfect. He replied that he had been a junior high school graduate in Senegal and that he had volunteered for the army, not for money but because something very sad had happened to him. When I asked why he was not promoted to officer rank, he only said, "The French," and pointed his thumb down.

At last, I asked him if he could release me. He looked at me for a few seconds and sighed. "In this war, every private can arrest anybody but none of them has the right to release, even if he finds out it was an error a few minutes after that." What he said has been and still is partly true in Việt Nam.

When I asked him for help, he said, "I can't release you, and I can't help you overtly. But there is something I can do. In about an hour, the units operating in this area will move back on this road. I'll let you see if there is anyone you know who can give you some help." Then he led me up the road to the pagoda area near his mortar section.

It was about 9 AM. Passing by a white brick wall under the bright sunshine, I looked at my silhouette and I could see how my face was swollen. It must have been badly deformed.

The soldiers and the captives were still there, but I saw no more beating. The sergeant and I sat under a big fig tree. About an hour later, a green cluster-star flare was shot into the air far to the south. The sergeant nodded to me. It was a signal for the troops to withdraw.

From a village half a mile from mine, a long column of troops slowly approached. Most of them were Vietnamese along with Senegalese and Moroccans marching as if on a pleasant hike, not like warriors. Some drove cows or buffaloes; some carried chickens dead and alive and other household objects that they had looted from the area.

The sergeant and I stood a few yards from the road. My left wrist was still tied to one end of the rope, the other end held fast by the sergeant. After hundreds of troops had passed by, I had seen no one I knew. There were some who looked familiar, but I dared not claim acquaintance. If by mistake I should choose a "death informer," it would be my certain death. A death informer at that time was a former Việt Minh who had surrendered to the French Army and was used to identify other suspected rebels. Anyone identified by such an informer as a Việt Minh would be shot on the spot, unless he might be a good source of intelligence. These informers were envoys of death all over Việt Nam during the first few years of the 1946–54 war.

Then came a group of French officers with golden stripes on their shoulder straps. I knew they were part of the operation's mobile command post. Among them was a stout Frenchman in military shorts, his shirt unbuttoned, a Vietnamese conic hat on his head, and a pair of rubber tire sandals on his feet. He wore no insignia, but his manner displayed unmistakable high dignity and authority. Two majors and many captains and lieutenants were around him.

When he came nearer, I recognized him easily. He was a lieutenant colonel from the Southern Zone Headquarters of the French Việt Nam North Command.

We students all knew him well, as he appeared sometimes at ceremonies that we had to attend in Nam Định City. As he passed in front of us, the sergeant snapped to attention and saluted. Just on instinct, I drew myself up and said, "Bonjour, mon Colonel." Within a split second, I was filled with fear: I didn't know if I had done the right thing. In war, anything could turn out to be a mistake, sometimes a fatal one.

The colonel stopped and responded gently with a refined language. The sergeant briefly reported my case to him in favor of my innocence. The colonel turned to me and asked, "Why do you know me?"

"I saw you several times in the city, sir," I said.

He said something to the tall major, who then stepped forward and took my ID card from my chest pocket. Looking at it for a few seconds, the major asked me softly, "Who is your principal?" I told him my principal's name and description. When he saw a twenty piaster bill in my pocket, he asked me, "Did the soldiers take anything from you?" I said no. That twenty piaster bill is equal to about US$30 today. I was lucky: none of the soldiers had searched me for money.

The colonel nodded, and the major himself untied the rope from my wrist. He asked me if I felt much pain from the beating. I said, "Very much, sir. But I can stand it all right."

All the French officers stood in silence and looked at me attentively. Then the colonel spoke to me very slowly: "In this situation, unlucky civilians are like grains of sand falling into a machine of war. A cogwheel can't stop to save you while the others are turning. By good luck you might not be caught by any part of the running machine and safely escape the machine unharmed. Otherwise, you'd be crushed. Now you may go home. Take care of yourself."

I bowed to salute and thanked all the officers. I paused with the sergeant, shook his hand, looked him in the eyes for a moment, then walked away. The troops kept moving north, while I used another path away from the road to get home, lest some crazy soldiers far behind in the column should arrest me again.

At the gate, my grandma was waiting. Someone had told her that I was dead. When the troops withdrew from my village, she asked two neighbors to go fetch my corpse with a pole and a hammock. They were about to depart when I got home. My grandma wept for joy and mumbled a prayer as I ran to her arms. She said, "Pray Buddha protect you!" She was still feeling great pain in her back, but the blow from the bamboo stick had not broken her spine.

I found out that all my neighbors who had been arrested early that morning had been released, probably by order of the colonel. Many young captives from other villages were brought to the prisoner camp in Nam Định and locked up for over two years as war labor serving French combat units. Some were killed on the battlefields.

That afternoon I packed and left for the city. I was treated with herbal medicine and anything handy that we could afford, such as a kind of bitterroot soaked in rice wine and sugar, raw blood of a terrapin, and juice from mashed crabs. For a month, I just stayed home. How could I risk running into some of my girl classmates with such a bruised and swollen face?

My mother said to me several times, "It could have been worse, darling." In war, anything less than death makes a victim feel lucky.

This encounter with the French soldiers was one of the many dangers and pains I was to experience.

TWO

My Early Years and Education

MY FAMILY

I was born into a lower-middle-class family in 1937, not long before Japan waged war against China, beginning with the Marco Polo Bridge crisis in Beijing, which my father used to refer to when talking about my birth.

My grandparents had not been rich farmers when they married in 1884, having nothing more than a small wooden house and a few acres of farmland. My great-grandfather was poor, but he managed to send my grandfather to school for ten years. My grandfather didn't obtain a degree, but his education was enough to give him a decent position in the village. My grandparents had to work hard to raise their eight children and to send all their sons to school. Their eldest son was born in 1887. They gained respect from most of the villagers and also from people of the neighboring villages, and they had no enemies.

My grandmother was a strong-minded woman who sometimes was more obdurate than my grandfather. When I was still a young boy, my aunts and uncles used to tease me, saying that I took after my grandpa and that I would be a henpecked husband. (They were right.)

My grandma had a perfect memory. She could remember exact dates of all events in her family and in many others' since she was seven. She could recite by heart 3,254 lines of *Truyện Kiều*, the famous verse story by the great poet Nguyễn Du. I inherited her good memory, which helped me in school and especially in writing these memoirs. But sometimes I wished I didn't have any memory at all, so that I would have been much less concerned about the events in war and the hardships of our people and lived a much happier life.

My grandfather was one of the many supporters of Kỳ Đồng (Child Prodigy), real name Nguyễn Văn Cầm, the young man in our neighboring province who led a struggle against the French at the beginning of the twentieth century. Some of my grandfather's cousins and a few villagers joined the fight and were defeated after a short clash. They brought back a battle drum and a large conch, which were later displayed in the village temple for worship. When I was a child, I often came to look at them and to conjure up some heroic images of the people from my village who had fought desperately but bravely against the French. I was very proud of them.

My father was born in 1904 and was his parents' favorite son. At age six, he was sent to a private teacher's Chinese characters class along with two elder brothers and some other children in the village. In the early 1900s, Chinese was still the official written language in Việt Nam. It was gradually replaced by quốc ngữ (national language), Vietnamese written in the roman alphabet. This form of written Vietnamese had been in use since the mid-nineteenth century, but was not officially taught and prescribed as the language of administration in Việt Nam until 1905. By the time my father was born, many families in Việt Nam still refused to let their children go to the new schools established by the French colonial government for learning quốc ngữ.

In 1912, my father's uncles persuaded my grandfather to give up his passive resistance against the French and to let my father and my uncles attend the new school for quốc ngữ and French language. After months of thinking it over, my grandfather took their advice. As any other in their generation, my grandfather and his sons were greatly influenced by Confucianism. They wanted their children to be well educated more than to earn big money. My grandpa died when I was two years old.

In 1925, my father participated in some anticolonialist activities in Hà Nội. In 1927, he joined the Việt Nam Quốc Dân Đảng (Việt Nam National Party), abbreviated VNQDĐ.[1] The VNQDĐ, well known in Việt Nam as Việt Quốc, launched a bloody uprising in several provinces close to Hà Nội in 1930 but was crushed after a few days.

The VNQDĐ revolt was an anticolonialism military action by the first well-organized revolutionary party in the French colonies. French authorities mobilized its forces to suppress the patriots' movement, which resulted in hundreds of death sentences and thousands of prison terms for VNQDĐ members. Nowadays, the revolt is referred to as the "Spirit of Yên Báy," named for the province where the fiercest fighting took place on February 10, 1930. The situation became even more serious to the French when the communists led the farmers' protest, the so-called Nghệ Tĩnh Soviet. It was a violent movement against the French in the "Soviet" style that led farmers from several villages in Nghệ An and Hà Tĩnh provinces to stage mass protests for months after May 1930. My father's friends were among the communists who participated. The Nghệ Tĩnh movement lasted longer than the Yên Báy uprising, but it drew much less attention in Việt Nam and France at the time.

After the February 10 uprising, my father was on the French Security Service's blacklist. With help from some bribed officials, he changed his name and moved to a northern province for a teaching job to escape arrest. After two years, those officials managed to have his police records cleared so he could come back home safely. The bribery took away two acres of my grandparents' property.

In 1931, he applied for a government job. Until September 1945, he was serving magistrate courts in many different districts in Tonkin, far from Hà Nội. My father and my mother married in 1935.

* * *

I was born two years later in the provincial town of Vĩnh Yên, thirty miles north of Hà Nội. In 1942, when I was five and could understand simple things in life, my father often met with his comrades in secret gatherings. At times, strangers came to see my father at night, then disappeared quietly after an hour or two. My grandma and my mother were worried, but found no way to stop him. It was such a serious matter that they dared not interfere.

As I was growing up, my father became more involved in revolutionary activities. He devoted much of his spare time to meeting with comrades in villages far from main roads. Although he and his friends kept it a secret, my mother was somewhat aware of what he was doing. How could a man conceal everything from his wife, especially when he had to ask her for help that no one else could provide?

He used to bring me along to the meetings as if we were visiting friends. My father and his comrades played cards to disguise their real purpose, and I was allowed to play with other kids around the place. "Don't worry, mama," my father once said to my grandma. "The French secret police won't think I'm going to do anything big when my kid is with me." That seemed to be true. And he taught me to keep what he was doing a secret from the security agents in case they should interrogate me about him.

From the age of six, I was often permitted to listen to many of his conversations with his friends. Therefore, I knew about war and politics in a childish way much sooner than I should have.

At seven, I was interested in matters that didn't bother most children of my age. I was proud of that, but when I grew up after years in the war, I wished that my father hadn't brought me along with him to his secret meetings and let me learn such things so early. If he hadn't, my life might have been much different, maybe much better in a sense. So I am not surprised to see teenagers in some countries fighting real wars with automatic rifles as volunteers. I know it's not a difficult task to teach kids to hate and to kill with less fear of death.

Many of my father's comrades were teachers and public servants like him. A large number of the patriots serving different revolutionary parties before and after 1945 were teachers, probably because the teaching profession engendered fervent patriotism in them.

One of my father's best friends and comrades was Hoàng Phạm Trân, pen name Nhượng Tống, a founder of the VNQDĐ and a close assistant to the national hero Nguyễn Thái Học. After 1930, he was arrested and sentenced to many years in the well-known prison camp on Poulo-Condore Island. He was released on probation sometime before 1940. He often visited with my father. He told us stories of Poulo-Condore, of how the French guardians had tortured political prisoners, and of heroic struggles against the French authorities in jail. His stories hardened my abhorrence of the French colonialists.

My father served the district magistrate court headed by the district governor, a mandarin. Many people who were defendants or plaintiffs attempted to bribe him, but he never accepted their money or gifts. Several times I saw him show the door to those who came to offer him bribes. In his time, receiving bribes was considered the privilege of a public servant, but he often taught us, my cousin and me, that bribery was immoral and that if we became public servants, we should never take bribes. That's what I liked most about him.

Whenever my father had a vacation, he brought me with him on trips to scenic mountains, rivers, and historic spots, along with his friends. On the trips, my father often told me stories about how we should love nature, love the fatherland, and do everything possible to help the poor. Sometimes we rode in a boat under the full moon while my father and his friends were reciting poems, chatting, and drinking. Too young to wholly understand the poems, I could only appreciate the melodious sound under the bright moonlight on the immense body of water that spread to the darkened shores far away.

Those trips created in me a deep love for rivers. Any river is beautiful to me: the Mekong in Cần Thơ, the Perfume River in Huế, the Dak Bla in Kontum, and especially the Red River near my home village.

Many afternoons my friends and I went to the Red River to watch it running swiftly to the south—much larger and swifter in autumn, the flood season. Right there was the place where the king's soldiers and men in our district had fought a desperate battle with flintlocks and spears against a French warship on its way to the first attack at Nam Định City in the late nineteenth century.

FIRST EXPERIENCES OF WAR

I began learning to read and write at home. At the same time, World War II escalated with the attack on Pearl Harbor. In the following school year, 1942–43,

I was six years old and was admitted to the first grade by permission of the school district inspector. Before that, my father had been teaching me.

It takes a child about two years to learn to read Vietnamese well, even words that he or she does not understand. At age seven, I could read some parts of newspapers and magazines that my father brought home. Every day I read about the war in China and Europe, learning about guns, warplanes, aircraft carriers, destroyers, cruisers, submarines, and V-1 and V-2 rockets before I was taught science, math, history, and geography. My second cousin, who was ten years older than I and was living with us, was always eager to explain to me anything I didn't understand.

As a child, I had a vague notion that war was an action whereby people killed to get something they wanted, such as money and land. Once I overheard my father discussing war with his friends. He said, "Since kids everywhere in the world still love to play with toy guns, pistols, swords, and daggers, wars will never end."

To most working-class Vietnamese at that time, World War II was something still far away. In the village, peasants didn't care that the war was going on in other countries. The war only affected the middle class and above when imported goods such as gasoline, mechanical spare parts, bikes, medicine, cloth, milk, fruits, or toys ceased to come in. At school, there was a great shortage of paper, pens, pencils, and chalk, even of the worst quality manufactured by domestic industry. Students were asked to write in lines of a half space. I had to wrestle with my pen to write in narrow lines on rough paper. People of my generation could write letters with characters only one millimeter high.

Sometime in my first year at school, Japanese soldiers stopped by our town. Children in our neighborhood rushed to the roadside at the marketplace to watch them. We had not seen or heard of anything to be afraid of. We had heard of no crime or savage maltreatment done by Japanese soldiers.[2]

It was a Japanese platoon of about forty soldiers and one officer with a sword at his side. They stopped at a fruit stall, bought some oranges, and paid generously. A man in the candy store near my school told us that the Japanese sword was extremely sharp: a hair blown against its edge would be cut in half. We believed him because he had been a sailor who traveled to many ports. He also told us that when the blade was unsheathed, one head must be decapitated. So we looked at the officer's sword with great fear and admiration. Whenever he touched the handle, we were ready to run. Fortunately, he did not draw the blade out. The man became a propaganda team member after the Việt Minh ascended to power in August 1945.

When I was in second grade, American bombers began pounding away at bridges and Japanese military installations in our province. Every day before 9 AM, the time for American planes to reach our area from their bases in the Pacific, rich families left the city for the rural areas nearby, returning after dark. Others who stayed would be ready to rush to bomb shelters when the siren wailed. Most elementary schools were moved to nearby villages.

A few months later, the planes began bombing also at night. In the city, the sound of the siren was frightening, especially when the whole city was drowned in darkness of the blackout. During each air raid, a number of civilians were killed or wounded.

Once I followed my cousin to a place a mile from home where American bombs hit not the bridge but a street close by. There we saw a dozen dead bodies soaked in blood, limbs chopped off, stomachs torn open. It was horrible, and for the first time I realized what war really was.

One noon while we boys and girls were playing in the large schoolyard, a plane suddenly popped out over the tall bamboo grove on the other side of the river several hundred yards away. It roared in fast and so low that we could see the pilot. We all cried, and the teachers shouted to stop us from running. We had been taught to stand still when a plane came so that the pilot would not notice us. A few seconds later, another plane followed. Its gun barked noisily and frightened us much more than the first. We dared not move, even a minute after both had disappeared in the horizon. Our teacher said that the first was an American bomber and the chasing plane was Japanese.

FROM VILLAGE TO CITY

My home village was only twenty miles from the district town where my father was working. I always spent my holidays (summer, Christmas, Tét, and Easter) in my village with my grandma, my aunts, and my uncles, who all loved me and coddled me much more than my parents did.

During my first eight years of life, Việt Nam was a French colony. French colonialists imposed oppressive measures to exploit the colony. However, life in my village before 1945 was calm, and people were living peacefully with each other. The peasants had to work ten hours a day almost 365 days a year to produce enough food for their families. One-tenth of the population owned no land at all and worked as sharecroppers.

In most villages, every man, at age eighteen, rich or poor, was allocated an equal portion of village-owned land, usually about two-tenths of an acre, free or at a very low rent. In villages like mine, which owned a large common property, land was allocated also to women.

In a good year for crops, farmers usually had enough rice to feed their families. In years with bad harvests, their meals might consist of only 70 percent rice, the 30 percent rice substitute being sweet potato, manioc, or Indian corn, which were considered far inferior to rice. In some very bad years, they had only 30 percent rice. In some extreme cases, they had to live on thin porridge for days while waiting for the next crop.

The richest landlord in our area owned about 90 acres. There were only two landlords in our neighboring districts who owned more than 100 acres. Most, as far as I knew, did not impose brutal exploitation on their tenants. Traditional relations between villagers and religious teachings somewhat restrained them from being too avaricious. Land rent was usually about 30 percent, including government tax. In years of severe weather that caused a sharp drop in production, landlords usually postponed rent collection and would let it be paid back with the next crop. In some cases of good friendship or close relation, the debts could be remitted. As a matter of course, there were many avaricious landlords who paid low wages, imposed high land rent, and lent money at high rates. Their avarice led peasants to resentment but rarely to profound animosity. I heard of some wicked landlords who demanded exorbitant rent from tenants. Some even tortured farmers who failed to pay rent and treated peasants roughly as if they were slaves. But there were not many such landlords in my district. Their atrocities were often dramatized in fiction, especially in the propaganda materials of every revolutionary party at that time, nationalists and communists alike.

When I got older, I learned from books and the grownups that the plight of poor farmers in my home province was not the worst. Wicked landlords in China ruled their immense family farms of thousands of acres with cruel exploitation and heartless laws, as if they were emperors. Farmers were beaten, tortured, and even killed.

A MANDARIN IN EACH VIETNAMESE

In old-time Việt Nam, according to a 1,000-year-old system of regional power distribution, the village had been autonomous. Each had its own written or unwritten "charter" that stipulated special customs and regulations that were to be abided by. Some of these might have been contrary to common rules as stated by the proverb "King's laws sometimes are second to village's customs."

The village charter determined the ranking order of the notables—whether by seniority or by degree of education. In some villages the charter fixed the marriage fee that a groom had to pay in cash or in kind. In a village up north, the groom was required to go naked into a pond (usually in winter) to catch one fish of any size as a symbol before the village committee approved the proposed wedding. The required task was a trick just to make sure that his genitals looked normal. The rules might be harder on grooms from outside the village.

When the French occupied Việt Nam in the second half of the nineteenth century, they maintained the ancient Vietnamese system, as it had proved its efficiency to facilitate their rule.[3]

For 1,000 years until 1945, Việt Nam had been ruled by the notables, who were mostly landlords and rich farmers, with deep-rooted customs as their instrument of rule. As leaders of rural Việt Nam, most of them gained respect from the peasants not by coercive measures but by the tradition of paying reverence to educated persons. It should be noted that the educated notables in the old Việt Nam lived right in the midst of the poor peasants. Therefore, good relations between them and the poor, as well as their leadership role, were maintained and consolidated.

At the same time, Việt Nam strongly adhered to 1,000-year-old traditions in which honors from an official title were highly regarded. However rich a man could be, he would gain little respect if he bore no title. Everyone seemed to be born with a thirst for fame and power more than for riches. A name should always be preceded with some title, even one denoting an insignificant position. Mr. Ba, a clerk of a private small business, loved to be addressed as "Mr. *Clerk* Ba." Bón, a soldier, would be pleased with the title "Mr. *Private* Bón." Mr. Nam, a Trương Tuần (chief watchman) was called "Mr. *Trương* Nam." With the title so shortened, Keo, a communist cadre, would prefer being called "*cadre* Keo," not plain Keo.

People born into the old Việt Nam society were highly conservative and regionalistic, which is true to some extent even today. Some people would do anything possible to reach and to preserve a higher position in the village, sometimes in a fierce or even bloody competition. And once in power, many could be very authoritarian. Some bad traditions were therefore maintained. Family feuds divided many villages. Fighting for a more decent seat at village feasts at the communal house sometimes led to heated arguments and even to physical assaults and vendettas in extreme cases.

This traditional ruling class in the countryside was the primary target of the communist revolution. The Vietnamese Communist Party doctrine asserted that the absolute "cleansing" of that ruling class must be accomplished in order to seize power in the countryside. Even so, the current officials of the communist infrastructure, the leaders and cadres of village and district party committees, are not much different from their pre-1945 predecessors, although their authoritarianism may be concealed under better-coined titles and melodious rhetoric on behalf of "the Revolution."

A village chief or a village committee member was usually given the right to farm a piece of village-owned land, the size of which depended on the property. But he worked hard in his job, sometimes to ruthlessness, impelled only by his title and the power he was vested with.

My village chief carried his brass seal in his pocket day and night. Along with his signature, it was of first importance in every paper, such as an ID card, certificate, notarized document, and laissez-passer. He was free to accept a little money or gift as legal fees from applicants when he signed and sealed their papers.

As a basic unit of administration, my village, like any other, had a council of the notables or the legislature, headed by the Tiên Chỉ (first notable). This council supervised the elected village committee, the executive, which was headed by the Lý Trưởng (village chief), who actually ran local affairs. The French rulers established this form of village government in Tonkin and Annam, their protectorates; in Cochinchina, form was modified to reflect that region's status as a colony and other local geopolitical concerns. The Tiên Chỉ was not paid and had little execu-tive authority, but he functioned as the head of the village, especially in rites at the temple, during annual festivals, and at banquets. He also presided over the council conference to decide the village budget. When some family offered the village notables a boiled chicken, he was given the chicken's head, a formal indication of his status. Drumsticks, wings, and breast were shared by the lower-ranking offi-cials: the chief of village, the deputy chief, the watchmen chief, the registrar, and the land surveyor.

The village watchmen, though equipped only with bamboo canes, were very efficient in enforcing the law. Taxes were collected to the penny. Violators were properly dealt with. If we children removed rocks from railroads, we would be severely reprimanded, even punished by rods, and our parents would have to pay a fine. It seemed that village leaders after 1945, both in South and North Việt Nam, inherited such behavior from colonial times. And indeed, local Communist Party and government officials have proved themselves much like their predecessors.

At the bottom of a village hierarchy there was a man who served as the mõ, or village crier. His principal job was to make public announcements after strik-ing a "mõ," a wooden instrument similar to one that a Buddhist monk used in the pagoda. His secondary job was to serve every other villager whenever help was needed, usually to invite guests, to run errands, and to wash dishes at an-niversary parties. The mõ's status put him in the lowest rank; everybody was above him and had the right to request his services when he was available. No one ate at the same table with him. Mõ was a special institution of the old Việt Nam society. Thanks to his status, no other commoner in a village had the feel-ing of being at the bottom of society. No one other than his son would succeed the mõ when he became disabled or died, although farming land given to a mõ was relatively large in some villages. In the old Việt Nam, the mõ and the king were the only two titles that were hereditary.

Above the village was a canton, which was a subdivision of a district. The canton chief had some power of inspection and was usually rich. However, he did not play a very great role in the colonial administrative system.

At the next echelons, the mandarins ruled provinces and districts. They served under the French colonial government of the so-called protectorates of Tonkin and Annam and also under the king of Việt Nam in Huế. The mandarin was taken for "the people's father" by tradition. The mandarin who was the governor of our district was a good one. He owned the only car in the district. Peasants bowed when seeing him ride in his shiny black French sedan.

I was a friend of his two sons, one four years older and the other two years younger than I, and of his daughter, who was my age. The older brother used to lend me books, mostly fiction and biographies of world heroes. Once in a while, he called me into his closed room or even into a large restroom in his home to read some books that the colonial authority had banned. His mother soon found out why we often occupied the restroom for too long, but she never forbade us or told his father. As a governor, his father would not let us read such prohibited publications, which featured wicked mandarins and village officials; the authors dared not directly attack the French colonialist rulers yet. But they indirectly encouraged some kind of revolutionary ideology.

After 1945 this friend of mine joined the Việt Minh and became a communist ranking cadre, and his father returned to Hà Nội to serve the nationalist government. In the 1960s, his younger brother became a South Vietnamese Air Force pilot. His sister and I were in the same third-grade classroom, and we liked each other. At eight years old, for the first time in my life I felt her charm attracting me for what might be called love, a vague sympathy, pure and pristine, of a little boy for a friend of the opposite sex. It was my first school romance. Her elder brother told me that he would ask his parents to marry her to me when we grew up so I would become his brother-in-law.

The district governor had under his command a squad of ten local guards, who were equipped with French muskets and wore green puttees as part of their uniform, to keep the 100,000 people in good order. A gang of twenty bandits always took to flight when they confronted a single soldier with that three-round-clip, nineteenth-century Mousqueton rifle. Though living under the oppressive colonialist regime, our people enjoyed true peace and order.

In the old time Việt Nam, a student went to school so that he would become a mandarin. Everyone, regardless of his family origin and background (except for children of actors and actresses, singers, brigands, thieves, and prostitutes), who passed the king's examinations held every three years in some major cities would be nominated a mandarin with full privileges. Many famous mandarins in our history were children of poor farmers. In the king's strictly supervised examinations, no bonus mark was given to any candidate because of his family background, his merits, or the services he or his parents had rendered to the king or the nation.[4]

There were many mandarins and village officials who were notorious for their brutality and inhumanity. The colonial government obviously condoned their wrongdoing up to a point to maintain an efficient system that kept the whole of Indochina well under its control. The oppressed people had no way to resist or seek protection. Tonkin was nominally under the king in Huế, although the people were actually living at the mercy of the mandarins in provinces and districts and of the village officials who carried out the draconian orders given by the colonial government.

In the cities, life was better. The colonial regime allowed a large gap between life in the cities and life in the rural villages. The city population had electricity, running water, paved streets, movies, imported goods, and medicine. In cities, people did not live under direct oppression. To some extent, the city bourgeoisie enjoyed the advantages of a modern society, which included better justice. However, poor workers led wretched existences in murky slums and were pitilessly exploited by French employers in large factories and by Vietnamese owners of small firms. Several times I witnessed savage beatings of rickshaw drivers who had failed to pay their day's rent to the owner of a rickshaw-rental house. Policemen kept the city in good order. Fines for littering were rather heavy, so sidewalks were always clean. A kid back from school would hold his bladder full to soreness until he got home because he dared not urinate at the wrong place on city streets.

At the top of my province was the French administrator, known as the "résident Française," not the Vietnamese provincial governor. The mandarins, although having great authority over Vietnamese peasants, only played the secondary role. Complete authority was in the hands of the French colonialists. In Tonkin, the top French official was the "résident supérieur," who also carried the title of viceroy of the king of Việt Nam. Thanks to the mandarin hierarchy and the village administrative system as instrument of repression, the French colonialist regime exerted a highly oppressive power upon the Vietnamese people in order to exploit all resources available in the colony.

Rice wine and opium were sold on a forced consumption basis. Each month, every village had to buy compulsory quantities of rice wine and opium, the production of which was the monopoly of French firms. Those products were so bad and expensive that their consumers preferred rice wine illegally distilled by peasants and opium smuggled in from Chinese border areas.

The arrival of the French customs officers always brought fear to my village and others. Hiding rudimentary distilling tools on someone's private land and then reporting it to the French customs house was one way to bring trouble to one's enemy, sometimes sending him to jail for months and costing him a heavy fine.

Taxes were high, especially the poll tax and rice production taxes. Many poor men in my village were unable to pay the taxes and were jailed for weeks. In extreme cases, they were flogged by village watchmen and even by district local guards.

Democracy, freedom, and human rights were unknown to poor peasants in my village and others who were living in a way not much different from that of 100 years earlier. Only men's clothing and hairstyles had changed, and Vietnamese in the roman alphabet was taught instead of Chinese characters in public schools. Women were considered inferior. Many were ill treated and had almost no rights at home if they were not able to get along well with their in-laws. Polygamy was legal.

Under the French, educational, medical, and social services were meager. My province had a hospital of about 200 beds, a small maternity hospital, and a few dispensaries. Only the middle and higher classes knew preventive medicine. The majority of the Vietnamese still relied on traditional herbal medicine. Once when I was six years old, cholera broke out in my village. On the first day, it took away a dozen lives. Local authorities did not provide much aid to control the epidemic.

REVOLUTIONARY STIRRINGS

In 1945, a large proportion of the population was illiterate. Only half of the children in my village went to one of a half dozen elementary schools in my district when I was a first-grader. Five of those children later completed fifth grade and passed the examination for a primary school diploma in the only six-classroom primary school of my district.

Our province had only one junior high school of about 200 students; a few of those who wanted to attain higher education would have to go to Hà Nội to attend one of the three senior high schools in the whole of Tonkin. Also located in Hà Nội was the university, which enrolled students from all over Indochina.

At school, we were taught subjects common to that of any other country, with the exception that French was a compulsory language. We started learning French in first grade. By third grade, I had to know by heart all tenses and moods of the two auxiliary verbs, *être* (to be) and *avoir* (to have); it would be several years before we were taught how to use them. From fifth grade on, everything was taught in French and, ridiculously enough, we were given history lessons in which we read, "Our ancestors were the Gauls." We were taught that France, as the mother country, brought civilization to her colonies and would bring them up to mature like a tree bearing fruit: "When fruits have ripened, they'll leave the tree and grow up by themselves." However, what I knew from my father and my cousin was much different. "The French were only leeches," they said.

Subjects relating to anticolonialist or patriotic movements against the French were not mentioned, of course. But in history classes, my young teacher, a new graduate from the teachers school in Hà Nội and a fervent patriot, found the best time to teach us patriotism, independence, liberty, and equality in a simple form so that a child might comprehend them. From my father, my uncle, and my cousin, I learned about anti-French movements and celebrated patriots like Phan Chu Trinh, Phan Bội Châu, Đề Thám, and Nguyễn Thái Học. Many other teachers who were friends and comrades of my father did the same with students at higher grades but more aggressively. Years later, those teachers and many of their students became passionate fighters on both sides in the long wars from 1946 to 1975.

When I began school, many patriotic songs had been composed praising our ancestors' achievements and victories in wars against Chinese aggressors. Although not mentioning the French, the songs indirectly evoked patriotism and fostered Francophobia.

As I entered first grade, the colonial government launched a nationwide sports movement. Every school had to promote sports activities. Each district had to build a soccer field, surrounded by a running track, where matches were held regularly. Sometimes we boys were lined up along Highway 1, a few miles from our school, to cheer bicycle riders on the Indochina Tour. The adults in my family said that the sports movement was only a plot of the French to attract Vietnamese youth and deflect them from nursing rebellious patriotism. Meanwhile, my father took advantage of the movement for his party. He was appointed president of the district sports club, under the smoke screen of which he recruited and trained new party members, as I learned soon thereafter when his activities were no longer secret following the 1945 Autumn Revolution.

THE RICH AND THE POOR

During the time I was in second and third grades, the French Security Service arrested many people in the district town where my family was living. Some of them were said to be criminal gang members, some communists. I believed that the communists were doing something against the French, as was my father, and that possibly some of the people arrested were his comrades, but he wouldn't tell. To me, they all were heroes because they had the courage to stand against the French in Việt Nam.

I didn't really know what communism was, but my eight-year-old heart felt sympathy with it when my cousin explained to me that the communists took money from people who were too rich and gave it to the poor. Like any other child in the world, I was always fascinated by the stories of Robin Hood, Jesse James, and other outlaws, and I thought that what they did was not wrong but done in the name of social equality. I lived close enough to the poor farmers to be aware of their miseries and the large gap between social classes.

My family was Buddhist. Since I was very young, I had been much influenced by my parents' teaching about good and bad, cause and effect, benevolence, and destiny. Sometimes I asked my parents whether my grandparents had done anything dishonest to build up their property. My parents assured me that they had not and that our inherited estate came only from my grandparents' hard work and savings. As for my parents, they only added to the family's property some three or four acres purchased with savings from my father's salary and my mother's occasional trade business.[5]

My father once told us the story of some landlords in Nghệ An province who dedicated all their farmlands to organize their villages into co-operatives where poor peasants worked collectively and shared the crop according to their labor. My father supported the idea, but my uncle said, "It sounds like communism," to which my father replied, "It is. But anything that minimizes the misery of our poor peasants is acceptable."

Living in easy circumstances, I always felt somewhat embarrassed when I noticed that I was better dressed and fed than many other children around the district town. Several times a week, beggars of all ages stopped at our gate to ask for food and money. If I had an opportunity, I would give a beggar a full bowl of uncooked rice.

"It was too much," my mother said. "With 100 families each giving him a handful of rice, he'll be richer than a middle-class farmer." I knew that she was right, but I always gave beggars more than others did.

THREE

1945: The Year of Drastic Events

THE FAMINE

The winter of 1944 was the coldest in many decades in the Red River delta, my grandma said. Temperatures dropped to a little above zero degrees Celsius (32 degrees Fahrenheit) as a bitter north wind brought death to some old people in the villages near mine. The winter harvest was the greatest failure in a century, according to the old villagers. Rice production at some villages was less than 30 percent of a normal crop in many fields, my uncle told my father. Panicles of rice in many rice fields bore only empty chaffs. Even children my age realized that a serious famine was looming on the horizon.

After Tết, hungry peasants in overpopulated districts of my province began moving to other areas and Nam Định (the provincial city), where they hoped they would find food. Before leaving, they sold everything they could. A thatch roof could be sold as kindling for a few pennies. In many hamlets south of my village, parts of poor neighborhoods were gone; only earthen walls remained. Some villages that had been verdant with live bamboo fences were devastated. Skinny bodies in rags wandered all over the country roads and city streets. Then corpses began to appear along roadsides and in pagoda yards, church grounds, marketplaces, city parks, and bus and railway stations.

Groups of hungry men and women with babies in their arms and other children at their sides invaded every accessible field and garden to search for anything they thought edible: green bananas, cores and bulbs of banana trees, bamboo shoots. They even ate oilcakes, used for fertilizer, which caused many deaths.

My villagers had to defend their land with force. Every night, strong men patrolled the fields to chase away trespassers. Sometimes there were clashes and injuries. Hungry crowds attacked rich landlords' homes and looted their granaries. In many cases, law and order was not enforced. It was widely said in my town that some people, including the four-year-old son of a Chinese businessman, were killed for meat. My parents and others in the neighborhood were scared by the rumors. They kept their children in sight at all times and didn't let them play outside the gate.

One day, my three-year-old sister was standing at the front door ten yards from the gate opening to the street, eating a rice cake. The larger part of the cake was in her right hand. An emaciated young man stopped at our gate. He looked like a ghost in ragged clothes. At one jump he reached the doorstep. He held my sister's jaws with his left hand, squeezing her mouth open. His right hand scooped out the bite of cake from her mouth, then he stuffed it into his, snatched the remaining cake from her hand, and he tore away like a flash. My mother stood dumbfounded. It happened too quickly for me to have any idea how to react. My mother soothed my sister and said nothing, but I saw tears in her eyes and on her cheeks.

Every morning I saw some oxcarts, each carrying several gaunt bodies on the way out of town. They were buried without coffins or any cover in mass graves already dug beforehand in a narrow strip of land beside the main road. Public cemeteries were already full. Sometimes when I got up at 6 AM, I found one or two corpses along the roadside in front of my home. They were stiff and so thin that I could see every rib and bone. For the first time I knew that the picture of a human skeleton hung in my third-grade classroom was accurate.

Newspapers reported that there was a great surplus of rice in Cochinchina that couldn't be sent north because U.S. bombs had destroyed most bridges and railroads.

I didn't suffer much. My little sister and I were the only two in my family of nine who were fully fed. The others, including my grandmother, only got two bowls of rice in two meals a day—instead of the usual six—to save some rice for starving people, a dozen of whom could be found at any time on our street. All other middle-class families in my neighborhood did the same.

That summer the harvest brought a good crop. The new rice was reaped a little earlier and saved a lot of people who were about to collapse. Still, a dozen people in the area died, not from hunger but from eating too much after gathering the first few bushels of newly collected grains. After the disaster, I learned that from 2 to 3 million peasants had died in the 1945 famine. People said that the famine was caused not only by the failure of rice production but also by the French and the Japanese, who had commandeered an immense amount of rice in Tonkin for their own military food reserves.

I will never forget the emaciated victims of that famine.

THE FORMIDABLE JAPANESE

While millions of Vietnamese were suffering from hunger, the Japanese forces overthrew the French colonial government. On March 9, 1945, after a short nighttime clash of barely an hour, the Japanese took control of the city, and that meant they controlled the whole province. The next morning, I saw leaflets and posters everywhere. One declared martial law; others proclaimed independence for Việt Nam and praised the Greater East Asia Co-Prosperity Sphere.[1]

A few days later, a large meeting was held at the district soccer field to celebrate the great event. The district town was decorated with the king's flags, Japanese flags, banderoles, and posters. A thousand young men from the villages and students of all ages sang "Tiếng Gọi Thanh Niên" (Appeal to the Youth) as the flags were raised on the tall masts. This song was written by Lưu Hữu Phước, and it later became the national anthem of the RVN (Republic of Việt Nam = South Việt Nam). It was composed years before 1945 with the title in French "L'appel aux étudiants" (Appeal to the Students); there were other lyric versions in Vietnamese praising the Vietnamese heroes and victories in fighting for the country's independence that we used to sing in class. The crowd chanted patriotic slogans loudly after each speaker concluded his speech with "Long live Việt Nam!" "Down with French colonialism!" "Defend our Fatherland to our last drop of blood!" Patriotism swelled in every soul, even my third-grade classmates and me. It was our great pleasure to see that there was no more French occupation and oppression, that our fatherland was independent, and that our people had freedom, even when the Japanese still dominated.

Teachers were now free to tell us stories of how the French had tortured and massacred our patriots; treated our workers ruthlessly in rubber plantations, factories, and mines; brutally exploited our country with heavy taxes; robbed us of priceless treasures; and ruined our society by encouraging consumption of rice wine, opium, and legal prostitution.

All of what we learned about colonialism planted in our minds a profound hatred for the French. Once I saw a group of about ten French former officials doing hard labor—digging ditches, pulling heavy carts—under the surveillance of two Japanese soldiers. I felt pleasure in seeing the Japanese doing what the French had done to our compatriots. To me, every Frenchman in Việt Nam was guilty and deserved severe punishment.

Although they were also members of an army of occupation, the Japanese soldiers gained some respect from the Vietnamese common people. They showed their iron discipline in the barracks and on the streets. They may have been arrogant and somewhat authoritarian, but I never heard of Japanese soldiers raping or looting. They were pitiless with thieves, robbers, and swindlers.

The Japanese officer in charge of my district caught a renowned burglar stealing a woman's money. With his bare hands, the officer beat the burglar to death in the marketplace. The next day, all thieves in the area reported to the Japanese officer, asking for mercy and promising to abide by the law.

A rumor circulated that there was a woman who sold rice bran to the Japanese for food for their horses. One day some horses died because they had eaten sawdust mixed in with the bran. We heard that the Japanese cut open the belly of a dead horse, put the woman inside, sewed it up, and buried her alive. No one knew for sure if the story was true or not, but it was well known in Việt Nam, and it frightened away every scheme to cheat the Japanese.

In the area around my village and the dry land section nearby, the Japanese ordered large fields that had been used for food production to be set aside for growing jute to make supply gunnysacks for the Japanese army. Severe punishment was inflicted on those who failed to meet the required production goal. This imposition provoked animosity toward the Japanese but not as bitter as that toward the French. What the Japanese did in the Philippines, China, Korea, and Malaysia was not known widely in Việt Nam at that time. Not until I was twenty did I learn about the Japanese brutality in those countries. In fact, among the foreign soldiers who were once in Việt Nam—including the French, the Russians in the 1980s, the Chinese in 1945, the Red Chinese in North Việt Nam in 1965–73, the Australians, Koreans, and Americans in 1961–73—the Australian and the Japanese soldiers received the highest regard from the common Vietnamese.

As a child, I liked the Japanese, especially the captain who often came to see the father of a friend of mine. He taught me Japanese and gave me pens, pencils, and notebooks. He showed special affection for children. However, my father hated the Japanese. He said that they were also our people's enemies and always avoided meeting any of them. His party and other patriotic movements opposed the Japanese occupation.

During the summer vacation, news of war that reached our home foreboded some great event in my country. My cousin, who used to explain the news to me, said that after having won the war in Europe, the Allies had now turned to Asia to defeat Japan. He also said with an air of importance that an enormous aircraft carrier of the U.S. Navy would enter the Gulf of Tonkin before long, and all of Indochina would be "shaken" into pieces. Then we learned that Japan had launched a campaign of kamikaze attacks. All my classmates admired their heroism. The war was coming closer and closer.

There was more bombing in the area. It was the first time I ever heard about an American. After an air raid, an American pilot was shot down somewhere north of Hà Nội. A friend of my father's who had been at the scene told my father that the pilot wore a jacket with "solid gold buttons." He also said that that "American money is in gold coins" and that "many things in America, including some household utensils, are made of gold." I believed his stories. For a long time in Việt Nam, people had the expression "spending money as extravagantly as an American." I would find out the truth of his words only several years later.

The more bombing there was, the more we were worried about war, but no one had the least idea about what would really happen if our area became a battlefield. My mother said that if war came, we would have to move to the hills three miles from our home. She prepared many jars of powdered grilled rice for the family to use in case of emergency. She didn't know that life in war wouldn't be so simple. Meanwhile, my father became much busier with his comrades. Since 1944, many of his VNQDĐ activists in the area had been cooperating with members of other movements, including the Việt Minh Front. He and his comrades were working hard to prepare for the general uprising. Sometimes my uncle helped him hide pistols and rifles, circulate indoctrination materials, and gather support for his party. I overheard the adults in my family saying that the Việt Minh were recruiting new members and training them in secret bases. It seemed that the Việt Minh organization was active everywhere.

Although my cousin and I didn't know much about my father's friends, we could tell who among them belonged to which group. Only years later did I realize how they did not have a proper concern for security measures when the threat from French and Japanese secret police was hovering not too high over their heads.

GENERATION GAP

In 1945, my years at school were the most beautiful time in my life, so beautiful that since then I have long dreamed of living just one day from that time again. Millions of Vietnamese of my generation must have the same wish.

We were trained, as our forefathers had been, under the influence of Confucianism. Textbooks on morals emphasized being a good member of the great family and an Asian-type gentleman—a man of moral integrity and generosity, who honored duty and despised riches. The lessons went along with numerous examples taken from Chinese and Vietnamese books.

In the traditional society, students were supposed to pay higher respect to their teachers than to their parents. The more a teacher punished his students, the more their parents gave him grateful thanks, and better gifts would be presented to him during the Tết season (Lunar New Year).

For many years before 1945, students had been taught the same subjects from the same textbooks. I shared with people fifteen years older the same image of our school life, the same emotions about contemporary culture. After 1945, we were motivated by the same causes that drove us to serve one side or the other in wars, and we fought each other fiercely under the same slogan of patriotism.

Romantic literature existing in the old Việt Nam was enriched with that from France. Introduced into the country in the 1920s, it greatly influenced middle-class Vietnamese, even kids like me. The image of a handsome young man, rucksack on his back, walking on a lonely road over the green mountain slope leading to a secret base in the border areas where he would fight for the lofty objectives of the Revolution, leaving behind his beloved and a luxurious life and worldly pleasures, had long been tempting hundreds of thousands of young Vietnamese into joining heroic struggles for the independence of the country.

This romanticism has played an important role in the psychology of generations of Vietnamese.

THE NEW PAGES

Although declaring independence for Việt Nam, the Japanese had merely replaced the French as the sovereign power. The mandarin administrative system was kept intact. The event of March 9, 1945, created a new political atmosphere, but the lives of the common Vietnamese changed only a little.

We children did feel something new and worth welcoming: independence. At home, we hung the new flag. By order of the new cabinet under His Majesty Bảo Đại, the national flag was three short red stripes at the center of a yellow background; the stripes were one-third the horizontal length with the center stripe broken in two at its middle. The stripes represented the *Li* symbol of the Chinese *I-ching* (Book of Changes).[2]

A very small number of city people owned radios, but their tuning mechanism was locked at a specified frequency by order of the Japanese authorities to keep people from listening to foreign stations. So news from other sources took time to travel to our district town. We heard that the Japanese had lost all of their important strongholds in the Pacific. My father told my uncle that Japan would be defeated in a matter of months and that Việt Nam would have the best chance to recover its independence.

In early August 1945, the two atomic bombs destroyed the Japanese cities of Hiroshima and Nagasaki. It was awful to everybody to learn that many thousands of Japanese, more than sixty times the population of our town, had been killed in a second. The word *atomic* was heard for the first time. In Vietnamese, *atomic* is *nguyên tử*, known only to junior high school students or higher. People were frightened by the idea that if Japan did not give up, Việt Nam could be a target for that horrible weapon.

On August 14, a group of about ten men armed with muskets gathered on the main street of the town. They asked the district governor and the local guard squad to surrender. Seeing that they represented nobody, the governor refused. The group withdrew silently. Then we got news that Japan had unconditionally surrendered to the Allies. Everyone was delighted but was too afraid of the Japanese to have any kind of celebration. As for me, I didn't fully understand what "democracy, liberty, independence" would bring us, but I felt glad that the war had ended, so we wouldn't have to worry about death or about shortages of food, goods, medicine, and especially toys.

On the morning of August 18, another group of about twenty men armed with rifles, pistols, swords, and spears appeared in the town. One hundred unarmed young men followed, yelling strange political slogans. They said they were Việt Minh guerrillas. They waved a red flag with a yellow star, then surrounded the squad of local guards and disarmed them. They invaded the governor's mansion to arrest him and brought him to the schoolyard. They tied the governor to the flagpole and declared that he was given a death sentence because he was a *Việt gian* (Vietnamese traitor). This word has since become a label for years of uncountable political persecutions and executions in the new Việt Nam.

The guerrilla group ransacked the district warehouse and took away anything they could. They said that they would execute the governor that morning. My third-grade teacher and some of the public servants openly supported the Việt Minh guerrillas but begged them to drop their intended execution. Many other respectable old men in the town and my father followed suit, strongly opposed to the guerrillas' intention. They proved that the mandarin had always been nice to the people and said that they were ready to protect him. In the afternoon, he was set free. The next morning, the governor and his family quietly left town. No one was permitted to see them off.

My father said the raid by the Việt Minh guerrillas was a surprise to him and his comrades, who were still waiting for orders from their party leadership. Members of other revolutionary parties in the area, besides the Việt Minh, who cooperated with my father's group such as the Đại Việt,[3] the Tân Dân, and the Duy Dân, were also standing by. I knew all about this because my father received many guests during that time. They argued and overtly discussed almost everything in the heat of the quick-changing situation, and we children could feel free to listen. They blamed the Việt Minh activists for the premature uprising before being ordered to take action as had been agreed upon by the parties' leaders at their joint command somewhere in China. For months before August 18, the Việt Minh members in the district—including friends of my father—often met with my father's group at many places, sometimes at my home.

As I still remember, a month before the August 18 event, one of the Việt Minh gave my cousin a copy of a Việt Minh song and taught him how to sing it. I learned the song from my cousin. It was the marching song "Tiến Quân Ca" (Troops' Advancing Song). The song began, "Đoàn quân Việt Minh đi chung lòng cứu quốc" (The Việt Minh troops are marching with their common struggle for national salvation). Later, the words *Việt Minh* were changed to *Việt Nam,* and after Hồ Chí Minh claimed ruling power, he made the song the national anthem of the communist regime.

The true Việt Minh cadres in the district area may have been no more than a dozen or so. In the next few days, the Việt Minh recruited a large number of young peasants for their support. Many were hoodlums and vagabonds who served the Việt Minh alongside well-bred youth. The Việt Minh said they were revolutionaries and that they would redistribute land and other kinds of property to poor peasants, that there would be no taxes under the new regime, and that people would be equal—no one higher than the other. With guns and support from the new recruits, the Việt Minh organized the revolutionary government. They appointed the chairman of the provisional administrative committee of the district and its members. Specialized public servants were retained in their jobs.

According to my father and his comrades, on August 18 in Hà Nội there was a great meeting of tens of thousands of students, public servants, and workers held to proclaim Việt Nam's independence. It was sponsored by nonpartisan activists in the League of Civil Servants. Two dozen Việt Minh cadres sporting their party's colors, the yellow star on red, managed to join the crowd. They pushed their way to the podium and snatched the microphone. They delivered speeches, appealing to people to fight to recover independence. In no time, the communists took control of the meeting under the nationalist label. Their comrades in the provinces followed suit, each led by a small band of greenhorn Việt Minh members. The viceroy gave up his power easily. It was the reluctance to act on the part of noncommunist forces before receiving orders from their top leaders that helped the Việt Minh to gain power. My father said, "It was like playing an easy local sport and winning the national prize."[4]

After many decades of hunger for national independence, people didn't care who led them. Anyone was just fine, provided that he was fighting for national freedom. In such an atmosphere, the Việt Minh consolidated power quickly and easily, "with little trick and ready mind, not with real strength," said my father's comrades.

The meetings that my father, his comrades, and Việt Minh activists held at my home months before August 18, 1945, proved to me that the allegation of the nationalist side was true: there had been a plan of joint action between the nationalists and the communists and a break of that promise by the Việt Minh. However, I also realized years later that besides "little trick and ready mind," the Việt Minh were more successful than the other parties in organizing and motivating their members. From the very beginning, communist leaders relied on the class of the most unprivileged people for power. At that time the nationalists said that local communist leaders, not Hồ Chí Minh, made the quick decision on the August 18 uprising. In 2000, former Tonkin Communist Party Committee member Nguyễn Văn Trấn confirmed that Hồ was somewhere outside of Hà Nội at the time and that Hồ was unaware of the decision for the August 18 uprising.[5]

The days that followed were deeply imprinted in my memory. The town was red with Việt Minh flags. People went to meetings held every other day to support the new revolutionary government. Young men and students painted banderoles and posters, and women made flags. At meetings, we children loudly chanted slogans along with the adults; many of those words we didn't understand. Although my father's Việt Quốc party did not get along well with the Việt Minh, he often encouraged my cousin and me to join the meetings. Sometimes the meetings lasted long into the cool autumn nights with long speeches in which the orators showed their deep love of using enigmatic words newly introduced to the common people's ears only a few days earlier. Not until attending high school could I fully understand most of those political terms.

In some remote areas the Việt Minh recruits conducted raids against a number of landlords, village officials, and mandarins who had been well known for their atrocities and authoritarianism. Some were killed; the others were beaten, their houses destroyed, and their property looted. All of them were labeled "Việt gian." Greatly attracted by meetings and promises of the new rulers, few people cared how those traitors were treated and took for granted that they deserved severe punishment. But before long, they knew that many of the victims were not traitors at all.

When I grew up, I learned that the killings took place everywhere in August and September 1945, and the Việt Minh got rid of many well-known men. Among the victims was Phạm Quỳnh, a distinguished writer and a mandarin who supported moderate construction of an autonomous regime in Việt Nam under France's protectorate. He was charged with being a traitor and was killed not long after Bảo Đại's abdication on August 25, 1945. Other victims whose names were known to Vietnamese patriots included Tạ Thu Thâu and Phan Văn Hùm, members of the Fourth International.

My father worked hard to serve the new regime. He and his comrades said that, Việt Minh or not, they were also patriots. Some argued that the Communist Party manipulated the Việt Minh Front, but the others objected to the idea that the communists would do anything harmful to the noncommunist movements. In early September 1945, Vietnamese revolutionaries in China returned to Việt Nam by the thousands. Among them was Nguyễn Hải Thần, the prominent leader of the Việt Nam Cách Mệnh Đồng Minh Hội (Việt Nam Revolution League), who became Hồ's rival a short time after he and the league had been back in Hà Nội. The Revolution League, or Việt Cách, was founded in 1942. Member parties of the Việt Cách included the VNQDĐ, the Việt Minh, and other smaller parties for the highest joint effort to restore Việt Nam's independence in the last years of World War II.

One of my father's friends was a communist in the Việt Minh Front. In those days, he often visited us and had my mother and her friends in the neighborhood make many hundred Việt Minh flags for his committee. He was friendly to every one of my father's comrades. But some of his comrades were not. One morning, a young man who was a probationer clerk working in my father's office as a subordinate came to see him. His mother was about two years older than my mother and her friend. He used to call my mother "aunt" and my father "uncle" as dictated by the Vietnamese traditions. He had just joined the Việt Minh ranks a few weeks before the August event. That morning, he stepped into the front yard where my mother was washing clothes. He greeted my mother with "Hello, sister. Is my brother home?" Everybody in the house was surprised to hear him call my mother "sister" and my father "brother." I couldn't believe my ears. It was impossible in Việt Nam. It was very rude and was also an insult in a certain environment. Three times he repeated the words; three times my mother ignored him. At last he gave up and asked, "Hello, aunt, where is my uncle?" to which my mother said, "He is out and will be back in an hour or so." The incident taught me at my age how Việt Minh followers misunderstood "equality."

Back in my village, things were the same. A few days after August 18, two Việt Minh cadres carrying their flag and two unsheathed swords came and summoned all the village officials to the communal house beside the pagoda. There they confiscated the seals of the Tiên Chỉ, the village chief, and the registrar, as well as all documents and records. The old village committee was dismissed and the new provisional administrative committee was quickly appointed. One of the notables was appointed chairman of the new committee, and the *mõ*, the bottom citizen of the village, was appointed "committee member for information." After the appointment, the former mõ announced that from then on, he was equal to everyone in the village, that people should pay him respect because he represented the people, and that he was no more a mõ. Not long after August 1945, he became one of the first Communist Party members of my village.

That was what went on at the bottom of society. At the top, we heard for the first time the name Hồ Chí Minh. His declaration of independence brought a great pride to everyone.[6] After sixty years bearing the dishonor of being under foreign domination, we had our president and a declaration of independence like any other free country in the world. The new name, Democratic Republic of Việt Nam, and its accompanying motto, Independence—Freedom—Happiness, sounded so sweet to our ears. It was in no way inferior to the French Republic and its motto, "Liberty—Equality—Fraternity." And we were proud, as if just having that title and motto printed on every official letter made us equal to France in every aspect. Months later, I found in an article of the Việt Quốc newspaper that the motto "Independence—Freedom—Happiness" derived from the "Three Principles of the People" of China's Sun Yat-sen.

The Việt Minh cadres extolled Hồ's patriotism to the skies. They said that he himself wrote the most beautiful sentence, "All men are created equal," in his declaration of independence. Of course, I believed the story for a long time until the day I found out that the sentence was taken from the U.S. Declaration of Independence. They also said that Hồ spoke fourteen languages.

In the beginning of September 1945, Hồ Chí Minh's portraits, printed in black-and-white and in various sizes, were sold everywhere. Each of us schoolboys tried to buy one to hang in the best place of our homes if the adults had not done so. We were hungry to have a national hero to worship. That the king, Bảo Đại, had abdicated made few people feel sorry for him.

The majority of our peasants had never been photographed; photography was a product of civilization enjoyed only by the middle class and higher. So in the rural areas, not the cities, the Việt Minh cadres said to the peasants that President Hồ had "two pupils in each of his eyes, a sign of his saintly talent." The peasants were easily convinced when they saw his picture in which two bright spots appeared in each eye. They were reflections of the floodlights in the photographer's studio, as in any other portrait taken in studios under artificial light at the time. It had been my first lesson that humans easily fall for lies. And after the truth is revealed, they are ready to fall for new lies.

THE REPUBLIC BRINGS CHANGE

In September, every kid of school age of all social classes was admitted into the Young Children for National Salvation or the Teenaged Children for National Salvation troops. We wore a uniform with hat and scarf and had a few hours of close order drill every night and on Sundays. We were taught simple political lessons about colonialism, patriotism, and Hồ Chí Minh and his merits and were taught to sing many martial songs as well as to play games, to our delight. The town and the surrounding villages were filled with the sound of drums, children's laughter, and marching music. Young men and women participated in the activities of their appropriate leagues, attending basic military and political courses at night. Once a month, they held cultural entertainment on makeshift stages with songs and plays. Everyone talked politics. Everyone was eager to show off his or her patriotism. Even old men and women acted with enthusiasm in their senior citizens' association meetings.

People were looking for changes for the better. To many young men, "revolution" meant abolishment of the old to build the new order. In some places, Việt Minh cadres ordered people to burn all "remnants of colonialism and feudalism," such as honorary title certificates bestowed by the king, medals and citations awarded by the French, and even school diplomas and certificates of birth, marriage, and death. Opium dens, gambling dens, and red-light districts were closed.

Evening classes for illiterate adults attracted students. Altogether, the revolution brought the countryside a new face. It could be said that the August 1945 Revolution had the strong support of people from all walks of life. Women's rights became a topic of discussion, and an unusually high number of divorces occurred.

In early September 1945, Hồ Chí Minh declared the "Gold Week," in which he appealed to the people to make a contribution in gold to purchase weapons for national defense. Everyone was eager to respond to the call. My mother and other ladies in the neighborhood donated jewelry. My grandmother also supported the appeal, persuading her friends to take part in the contribution. She said that it was the greatest contribution she had ever known. The total gold contribution came to 370 kilograms (13,000 ounces), the Việt Minh later acknowledged.

Meanwhile, my father was feeling more and more uneasy working under some young Việt Minh cadres. They had little education, but they were tricky, greedy, and even insolent. After a few weeks during which they learned how to do different jobs, they began to discharge the former key public servants one by one. Capability and anticolonialist background were disregarded if you were not loyal to the Việt Minh. In late September, my father resigned. He wanted to give up his job before they fired him.

A week later, my family moved to Nam Định City. We lived in a rental house, and I was admitted into a fourth-grade class of a primary school right on the main street. As the new school year began, we did not have to study the French language any more. Our load of school tasks was reduced. Using alphabetic written Vietnamese, a third-grader of my generation was expected to write and to read Vietnamese without spelling mistakes. Children at my age could read most writings, although they were unable to grasp all the meanings. At nine years old, many of my classmates often discussed simple matters of adult concern, such as patriotism, democracy, and social affairs, even if at a childish level. That helped the mental capability of kids of my age to develop earlier, but it also made them easy prey for propaganda and demagogues. Besides, as I learned when I was much older, their mental strength faced a limit in study at a university, where they would attain excellent degrees in technology, but failed to succeed at business management courses and other areas of education that required synthetic mental ability. If they joined communist cadres, they could be prone to talk big in politics and simply parrot what they had been told.

* * *

The main street was the best-looking one in my city. Flags, streamers, and paper banners of the world's five major powers were displayed on the front and inside of every public building, as well as restaurants, theaters, shops, and private homes. In the military barracks, Japanese, though already disarmed, still maintained good order and discipline. They worked and played as if they were still in power, and they always were very friendly to us schoolboys.

The Chinese soldiers who had come to disarm the Japanese looked ugly and emaciated. Coming from Yunan with wives and children, they took up quarters in any good home they liked, which they then littered with all kinds of waste. Often drunk, quarreling, and fighting, many of them refused to pay for goods they bought. After a few months, new Chinese regular army units came to replace them and things were better. The new Chinese soldiers had better equipment. Their military police conducted patrols all over the city.

In a short time, Japanese troops left my city for their homeland. But many Japanese deserted and stayed in Việt Nam. Some joined the Việt Minh; others served the Việt Quốc and the Đại Việt. On either side, they did their best. The Việt Quốc had an army officer training school in Yên Báy with a board of Japanese instructors who helped produce many brilliant military commanders for both Vietnamese sides in the post-1945 wars. The brave Japanese soldier was taken as a good example for Vietnamese warriors. "Do like a Jap soldier!" and "Practice Japanese discipline!" were the mottoes of the time.

The Việt Minh government main force, the Vệ Quốc Đoàn (National Defense Force), was weak and ill-equipped, incapable of fighting against the Chinese Kuomintang army units. (In 1949, the Vệ Quốc Đoàn was renamed Quân Đội Nhân Dân Việt Nam, or the People's Army of Việt Nam.)

Once or twice every week, all students in the city had to attend meetings in the central park. Children were always delighted to have a free morning, even though they had to stay in line and chant slogans once in a while. Speeches from the big wheels didn't concern us, though we were brought there to yell support for the resistance against the French reoccupation of Cochinchina.

As the situation in Sài Gòn developed into war, my whole city was in a fever, clamoring for armed resistance to drive the French away. Hundreds of young men went south each month to fight beside their southern compatriots. They belonged to many groups, nationalist and communist. At the railway station, people, including groups of students from various schools and grades, waved red flags to wish the men victory. It was one of the unforgettable images of my childhood.

Stories of bravery performed by fighting men in the South incited more people to join the crusade for independence. Besides, many women joined military and guerrilla units, mostly in paramedic groups. Every week men in the Association of Youth for National Salvation painted slogans and mottos on any wall or surface they found blank: "We're determined to claim our independence," "Let's not join the French Army," "Let's not supply food to the French," "Long live President Hồ," "Long live Việt Nam," "The Resistance shall gain final victory." My cousin and I joined them to help with trivial tasks. We were happy to take part in such revolutionary activities in which we felt we were somewhat useful.

THE FIRST SPARKS IGNITE THE CIVIL WAR

Since my family moved to Nam Định in early 1945, my father had devoted all his time to his party. A few blocks from my house was the VNQDĐ local headquarters, in front of which was a large flag, a five-pointed white star in a blue disk on a red background. A unit of several hundred VNQDĐ troops known as "Thiết Huyết Quân" (Iron and Blood Soldiers) was billeted in a building of the city railway station.

At first, people seemed to live peacefully with each other. The Việt Minh military force was a battalion of the Vệ Quốc Đoàn (National Defense Force) garrisoned in the barracks of the former colonial administrative guards. They were lightly equipped with weapons of several makes. The militias of the Quốc Dân Đảng Front, an alliance of the Đại Việt and the Việt Quốc, were stronger than the Việt Minh military. Đại Việt clandestine cells had militia bases in many areas around the country in 1945, while the Việt Quốc maintained a powerful force with cadres trained and organized in China and in the provinces of Việt Nam adjacent to China. Between them, the two parties held an overwhelming military strength in late 1945 and 1946.

The Quốc Dân Đảng Front militias had control over the northern parts of Tonkin, or North Việt Nam. Their strongest base was in Yên Báy province, where bloody battles had occurred on February 10, 1930, and where thirteen VNQDĐ heroes had been guillotined four months later on June 17. They had other strongholds in the port city of Hải Phòng and in the provinces sharing a common border with China, in Nam Định and Thanh Hóa. Much smaller VNQDĐ forces were also present in smaller provinces of Vietnam Central (Quảng Trị, Thừa Thiên, Quảng Nam, Quảng Ngãi, Bình Định) and in Sài Gòn.

Not long after my family moved to the city, the conflict between the Việt Minh and opposing Minh forces began to rise steadily. There were shootings around the city, especially at night. People were arrested. Assassinations and massacres committed by both sides occurred more frequently.

In many other places, especially north of Hà Nội, brief skirmishes had been going on since September 1945 and were causing more and more loss of life on both sides. This conflict had actually begun long before 1945; it became more open less than a month after the August Revolution. I think it's not wrong to say the Việt Nam wars in the late twentieth century actually began in September 1945. My cousin and I read reports in the newspapers of both sides that my father brought back home from his party office every day. What I learned from my father and his comrades, as well as from reliable political accounts in later years, gave me a rather clear picture of the long story.

MORE BLOODSHED

That story dated as far back as the late 1920s when the Communist Party and the VNQDĐ initiated their revolutionary activities in Việt Nam. Before 1925, there had been many movements for the independence of Việt Nam, and all were brutally suppressed by the French. The Việt Nam Thanh Niên Cách Mạng Đồng Chí Hội (League of Vietnamese Revolutionary Young Comrades), the first communist movement in Indochina, and the VNQDĐ were among the first few revolutionary parties that were better organized and had a doctrine to follow. The Vietnamese communists gained advantages over the others by having a well-drawn doctrine, experience, and support from the Russian communists.

The VNQDĐ emerged as a sheer patriotic movement, organized by a group of young patriots without any support or influence from outside. They were certainly inspired by China's 1911 revolution and Sun Yat-sen's Three Principles of the People when they named their party after the Kuomintang. However, the VNQDĐ had absolutely nothing to do with Generalissimo Chiang Kai-shek or the Chinese Kuomintang during that period, as confirmed by all of my father's comrades whom I met and asked later in my life. The Việt Quốc members were mostly devoted to the struggle for national independence and didn't care much for political doctrines and global revolution.

From 1927 to 1930, there were rumors among the ranks of the Việt Quốc that the communists had sent the French Security Service a list of noncommunist parties' members and their activities, particularly concerning the planned Việt Quốc uprising. However, most of the Việt Quốc leaders saw the betrayal not as a deliberate plot by the Communist Party to eliminate its prospective opponents but rather as individual denunciations pried out of others by the French secret police.

On February 10, 1930, the Việt Quốc launched a large-scale uprising in many provinces in Tonkin. The decision was made after French security raids destroyed many Việt Quốc secret cells. The leaders had to do something before the whole movement was eradicated. "Không Thành Công Thì Thành Nhân" (loosely translated as "If we do not succeed, we will have constituted a good cause"), declared Nguyễn Thái Học before the decision to launch the putsch, a phrase that was to become famous. The uprising failed. Many Việt Quốc members fled to China, where they got little help from the Kuomintang. They reorganized the Việt Quốc in southern China and made contact with their comrades who were still free and active inside Việt Nam.

The Việt Quốc's activities subsided until the early 1940s, when it gathered momentum during World War II. Its glorious fame from the bold uprising and numerous heroic deaths under the guillotine gained it much respect and support from the Vietnamese people. It can be said that the 1930 Việt Quốc uprising greatly encouraged young Vietnamese to stand up to fight for the independence of Việt Nam in many revolutionary parties and movements, including the Communist Party.

There must have been some influence from the anticommunist campaigns of the Chinese Kuomintang that aggravated the hostility between the communist and noncommunist Vietnamese revolutionaries in China. Information about the hostility had not been widely known in Việt Nam until September 1945. Before that, most nationalists took communists for friends—maybe not good friends, but not foes. To my knowledge, good friendship between my father's group and the Việt Minh supporters in our area before August 1945 strongly confirmed those sound relations.

After August 1945, more and more Vietnamese of different parties began to return from China, and many facts were revealed. As early as the 1920s, it was said, the Vietnamese communists in China under Nguyễn Ái Quốc (who later changed his name to Hồ Chí Minh) conducted a secret plot to get rid of eminent young Vietnamese exiles in China who refused to join them. The Việt Nam communists sold information concerning those Vietnamese patriots to the French Security Service so that the French could arrest them as soon as they reentered Việt Nam. In the same way, Nguyễn Ái Quốc and his comrade Lâm Đức Thụ informed the French of the exact whereabouts of the celebrated Phan Bội Châu in exchange for many thousand Hong Kong dollars. Phan was captured in China and brought back to Việt Nam for trial in a French colonial special criminal court.

At first, my father and my uncle didn't believe the story. It was too much to be true. However, a friend of my father from Thái Bình province who was, as far as I could remember, a close relative to Lâm Đức Thụ, confirmed it after Lâm was shot and thrown into the Red River by a communist death squad to stop him from talking about the story. Further information from my father's friend Nhượng Tống also supported the allegation. In 1971, I got a similar confirmation from Ba Liệu, a respectable revolutionist, who was well known for his impartiality and held in high esteem by all patriots, including Hồ Chí Minh. His version about the Phan Bội Châu scandal was not far different from allegations by many other authors.

In the early 1940s, Hồ was imprisoned by order of Chiang Kai-shek. Almost no one discovered that Hồ was the very same communist Nguyễn Ái Quốc who had committed unpardonable crimes against other Vietnamese nationalists in China. It was Nguyễn Hải Thần, a respectable Vietnamese revolutionary and a famous general in the Chinese army, who used his influence to intercede with Chiang for the release of Hồ Chí Minh.[7] He did so against the advice of many others who believed that it was Nguyễn Ái Quốc under another name. Had he not, Hồ would have perished in jail.

Also released at the same time thanks to Nguyễn Hải Thần's intercession was Nguyễn Tường Tam[8]—pen name Nhất Linh—a Việt Quốc leader locked up by order of the local Chinese governor.

As World War II was coming to the end, Vietnamese revolutionary parties in China gathered in a unified front called the Việt Nam Cách Mệnh Đồng Minh Hội (Việt Nam Revolutionary League, known by many Vietnamese as Việt Cách, shortened the same way as Việt Quốc and Việt Minh). Nguyễn Hải Thần led the Việt Nam Cách Mệnh Đồng Minh Hội. Its member organizations included the Việt Quốc and the Việt Minh. Hồ Chí Minh reorganized the Việt Minh (Việt Nam Độc Lập Đồng Minh Hội) to be his own after its founder, Hồ Học Lâm, passed away.

My father's comrades who had worked closely with Nguyễn Hải Thần asserted that his league had appointed Hồ to come back to Việt Nam to study the situation and report back to the league so that a plan for a general uprising could be formulated and executed with the participation of all parties. Hồ solemnly swore before the league's colors to carry out the mission. Hồ then slipped back into Việt Nam and seldom reported the situation there to the Việt Cách. He managed to seize power with his own Việt Minh members, or to be more exact, his communist members. Because of the lack of timely communications, the Việt Cách in China was not aware of what Hồ was doing in Việt Nam in 1945 until it was too late. Việt Cách was waiting to repatriate along with the Chinese army corps, which was going to invade Việt Nam to disarm the Japanese troops.

A large number of noncommunist parties' members were sent back separately to Việt Nam, especially after Japan had surrendered. The Việt Minh murdered many of them at the border. Some of my father's friends were among the victims. When Nguyễn Hải Thần and his Việt Cách, the Việt Quốc, the Đại Việt, and others arrived in Hà Nội with their small armed forces, the Việt Minh had already established their administrative system; it was not strong, but it had spread to most of the provinces. It was not that the people preferred the Việt Minh to the other groups. There is an old saying in Việt Nam: The one who strikes first gains the upper hand.

At the time, the Indochinese Communist Party led by Hồ Chí Minh declared its dissolution, and only a Marx-Engels Study Group remained. The Việt Minh in my district persistently denied that they were communists. Its public security office put some in my district area in jail because they had said that Việt Minh and Hồ were communists.

EARLY DAYS OF THE FRATRICIDE WAR

In Hà Nội, the noncommunist parties were fiercely opposed to the Việt Minh government. Nationalist parties rallied in an anticommunist coalition. Nguyễn

Hải Thần, chairman of the VNCMĐMH, became the leader of the coalition. My father said that Nguyễn Hải Thần was a brave, honest, and capable commander, an ethical revolutionary. But, according to my father, on the political battleground he was not a politician who could gain an upper hand over Hồ Chí Minh, who was the most sanctimonious and artful national leader in the history of Việt Nam.

The nationalists published newspapers with articles strongly criticizing Hồ and the Việt Minh Front. The two renowned anticommunist newspapers I used to read were the *Việt Nam Daily*, the official paper of the Việt Quốc, and the *Chính Nghĩa* (Right Cause) of the VNCMĐMH. Việt Minh security cadres tried every way to stop those papers from reaching readers in the countryside. The Việt Quốc had to escort their papers on buses with rifles. Every afternoon, my father and his comrades received the papers from a bus coming from Hà Nội, then redistributed them to different routes, a part of them going on main bus lines to the district towns, under armed escort most of the time. From these papers, readers learned many things that the Việt Minh wanted to conceal. What I liked most was a column in the *Việt Nam Daily*, written by the novelist Khái Hưng. He attacked Việt Minh and Hồ Chí Minh with ironic humor and ardent satire so simple that, at nine years old, I was able to understand most of his articles.

In one of their campaigns, the opponents of the Việt Minh argued that the yellow star flag represented the Việt Minh, not the national colors. They proposed that a contest be held and that the National Congress would select one of the best entries for the national banner. The dispute lingered for many months until December 1946, when a hastily called session of the National Congress voted that the communist flag and the Việt Minh hymn were now the national banner and anthem. Only communist and pro-communist members were present at the session, while most of the nationalist members and many of the neutralists were absent because they had been eliminated or imprisoned.

At that time, the two sides attacked each other more and more vigorously in the newspapers and on loudspeakers. In a few weeks, more street fighting with rifles and pistols followed. A number of the Việt Quốc were arrested and tortured or killed. To retaliate, the Việt Quốc did the same thing to the Việt Minh. In my city, skirmishes took place almost every week, and nine out of ten times, the Việt Quốc gained the advantage until the Chinese military police arrived to stop the fighting and restore order.

The Việt Quốc was recruiting new members after August 1945 (including some bad ones, according to my father). My father and his comrades regularly held open meetings and handed out their party's newspapers and booklets, introducing its policies and criticizing the Việt Minh. At the time, with the limited perception of a fourth-grader on such matters, I understood that the two sides were using very different ways to build and maintain power. The nationalist parties were recruiting key members from among middle-class people who had some education. With those members they built a solid core for their parties, but they did not take effective steps to organize and train a large number of individuals who would become the frontline soldiers.

Meanwhile, the Communist Party recruited new members from people of the lowest class, many of whom were illiterate. They were indoctrinated with communist ideology and employed as low-level leaders. They were fanatical elements in the infrastructure of various fields whom the party needed in order to take effective control.

Gradually, the support from the Chinese army decreased. It appeared that the Chinese commanders were not as interested in backing up the Vietnamese nationalists as people had expected. It was well known later that Hồ Chí Minh had bribed the top commander of the Chinese forces, General Lu Han, with a lot of gold from the "Gold Week" so that he would withdraw all support to the Vietnamese nationalists. My father's comrades asserted that one of the gifts given to Lu Han was an opium pipe set made of solid gold; all of the gifts may have amounted to several dozen kilograms of pure gold.

In the last months of 1945, the Việt Minh public security force arrested more people, including my uncle and one of my father's best friends. One morning, my mother and I visited them in the city public security bullpen. While the jailer was busy examining the gifts my mother had brought, my father's friend held me tightly and whispered into my ear, "Tell your dad they're beating me every day." My uncle was released a few months later, but it was the last time I saw my father's best friend. The Việt Minh got rid of him, leaving no trace for his family to track down his corpse. I was sorry to learn that, about the same time, his eldest son had joined the Communist Party against his mother's wishes. He had his own reasons, I thought. In 1954, he became a high-ranking Việt Minh, possibly a regimental commander.

In December 1945, the Việt Cách, Việt Quốc, Đại Việt, and other nationalist parties were about to go to war against the Việt Minh. These anticommunist parties, especially the Việt Quốc, were militarily much stronger than the Việt Minh, with bases in the northern Tonkin provinces and commando units in other provinces. My father and his friends believed that it would take the nationalists a few days to overthrow the Việt Minh government at all levels in Tonkin and a few weeks to establish a new administration all over the country. Later in life, I thought they had been rather optimistic.

Before 1945, facing this dangerous situation, the VNQDĐ and the Đại Việt had merged into an alliance called the Quốc Dân Đảng Front. The Đại Việt Quốc Dân Đảng's brilliant leader, Trương Tử Ahn, was elected to head the alliance. From the time the Việt Minh had seized power, the alliance had continued to fight against them. The alliance ended after the Việt Minh's political cleansing campaign came to a peak in late 1946.

The nationalist opposition demanded that Hồ Chí Minh reorganize the government so that every political disposition could be represented before the election. The Việt Minh refused. The dispute continued, and the Việt Minh leaders delayed a definite settlement to buy time and to wear out their enemies' patience. The opposition strongly protested against the Việt Minh's "scheme of holding a fraudulent general election," they said. "Down with the fake election" was seen in newspapers of the opposition and on walls and banderoles where the opposition took control. Children and younger brothers of the Việt Quốc activists lent their hands in painting posters. I loved to work with them at menial tasks such as running errands, cleaning brushes, mixing paints, and fetching objects for the elders.

Sometime in December, the tension became extremely high. The opposition threatened to resort to violence to settle the conflict. Nguyễn Hải Thần rejected Hồ Chí Minh's proposal to form a coalition government. On the propaganda front, Hồ appealed to the people for the "Great Solidarity."

An anecdote ran that on a day in December, Hồ came to see Nguyễn Hải Thần and spent the whole afternoon and evening trying to persuade him to approve his plan. Nguyễn, under pressure from the other parties' leaders, kept saying no. According to a version from many of my father's comrades, the two old men talked far into the night. Finally, Hồ hugged Nguyễn and burst into tears.[9] Sobbing, he said that Nguyễn would be fully responsible in history for his unyielding position, which could lead the country to a catastrophe both from colonialist aggression and from civil war, and that the Vietnamese people would never forgive Nguyễn's mistake. Nguyễn accepted Ho's proposal. My father and his comrades held Nguyễn in high esteem. They all said that he was an outspoken respectable old leader but not Hồ Chí Minh's equal in politics. He was afraid of being held responsible, and he took fighting the French as his first task and neutralizing the Việt Minh as the second. Hồ took him and the nationalists as his primary enemies.

Consequently, they reached an agreement to share power. Newspapers reported that 50 out of 350 seats of the National Congress would be reserved for the Việt Quốc. The Việt Cách and other minor parties would get 20. All those 70 seats were to be appointed, not voted for. With a stronger armed force, the Việt Quốc accepted the concession made in that agreement as a victory. Many of them, probably my father included, were somewhat ostentatiously conceited, as if they could eliminate the Việt Minh in a single day. They believed that even though the Việt Minh would play all sorts of tricks to have its men elected, there were a large number of renowned noncommunist candidates who would win a significant number of the remaining 280 seats and would possibly stand by the Việt Quốc in Congress.

FOUR

On the Way to War

GENERAL ELECTION

The new government of the Democratic Republic of Việt Nam was officially founded after the general election on January 4, 1946. Nguyễn Hải Thần became vice president to Hồ Chí Minh in the first so-called coalition government. Other nationalist leaders were appointed ministers, such as the famous writer Nguyễn Tường Tam, pen name Nhất Linh, of the Việt Quốc, as minister of foreign affairs, and Vũ Hồng Khanh of the Việt Quốc, vice chairman of the Resistance committee, beside Võ Nguyên Giáp.[1]

Although I was only nine, I did feel happy to see the sign of peaceful co-operation and reconciliation between the two sides. But the election itself left a deep scar in my soul. In my village, primary school kids who had good hand-writing were assigned to write ballots for illiterate citizens because the Việt Minh government could not afford printed ballots. The village committee said that it appointed kids to write ballots because they didn't have political partiality. I was one of the selected kids. The evening before the election, a village official gave us a list of many names that we would have to learn by heart. When we were asked to help, if we could be sure that a voter was really illiterate, we would just write down those listed names disregarding the name the voter told us. In fact, most of the voters said to us, "Please write whatever names you think suitable. I just don't know who is who." It was apparent that they voted because they had to, not because they wanted to. That was the first time I experienced a fraudulent election and knew it was a fraud despite all propaganda efforts made to praise it. And before I left for the United States in October 1990, I had never seen a fair election in Việt Nam, whether under the communist or non-communist regime.

After the election, two of my father's comrades in the Việt Quốc provincial standing committee became congressmen. They were given congressional immunity, but the local Việt Minh Public Security kept harassing them; my father had to leave home and go to Hà Nội to live with a friend to avoid trouble. Only those comrades who were armed remained to run the downtown office.

The conflict between the Việt Minh and the nationalists drove the Vietnamese people into a widening division and then ignited a war of ideology. Some joined a party because of its doctrine of which they had only a vague notion, even a misunderstanding. Many others only followed in their relatives' or friends' footsteps. There were also many who took one side only because their foes favored the opposite. As the struggle was going on, more bloodshed and animosity accumulated.

In late 1945 and early 1946, my father's circle and a number of his friends on the Việt Minh side were still friendly to each other despite the fact that the number of small clashes between the two sides was escalating. Sometimes they got together at our home to discuss various subjects, and they usually ended up arguing about politics. One of those subjects was education. Some of the men, both Việt Minh and Việt Quốc, contended that formal education was not necessary for a revolutionary to fulfill his duty well and that he could learn more from his activities. One of them even said, "Why do we have to learn algebra and geometry? We don't need them. They are for clerks and cashiers."

My father and others from both sides disagreed. They said that formal education, though having some defects, was indispensable to leadership in any situation because it provides general knowledge that could help in making more effective decisions. Still a youth, I did not have any ideas about education and leadership. Not until many years later during the war could I see how communist and nationalist leaders were ruling the country.

FRIENDS OR FOES

While the internal conflict was going on, the French increased pressure on Việt Nam with demonstrations of military power along with peace talks in which the French produced unreasonable demands. News from the South indicated that fighting around Sài Gòn was escalating. My schoolmates had to join more demonstrations against the French aggressors. Everyone saw the country as being on the brink of war. Most of my cousins were among the young men and women who received basic military and first aid training. Some kids were taught to be messengers for combat units.

The nationalist parties were unflinching against the French. They criticized the Việt Minh for being soft on the French in order to have a free hand to eliminate nationalist activists. About mid-1946, the French and the Việt Minh forces attacked many Việt Quốc military units on both sides in the border area. In the

Hải Phòng coastal area, extending to the common border with China near Móng Cáy City, newly arriving French navy ships bombarded a Việt Quốc battalion, while the Việt Minh launched a massive attack on the other flank.

Việt Quốc forces in the province of Lào Kay fell into a similar situation. French remnant troops in Chinese territories crossed the border, assailing the Việt Quốc units, which were confronting a much larger Việt Minh force.

One of my cousins who served the Vệ Quốc Đoàn (national guard corps, or Việt Minh army) was fighting in the battle to overrun a Việt Quốc base northwest of Hà Nội. The Việt Minh command told my cousin and his fellows that the base was held by "ethnic Thái rebels." The fighting lasted several days, and a Việt Minh force of five times larger decimated a Việt Quốc battalion. My cousin met my father and related the story. He said that only after seizing the base did he discover that the "Thái rebels" were Việt Quốc troops.

As for the French, it was apparent that they found it more difficult to talk with the nationalists than with the communists. Meanwhile, the Việt Minh preferred the presence of the French to the Chinese. According to many books and reports concerning Việt Nam, Hồ Chí Minh once said that he'd rather "smell French shit for five years than eat Chinese shit for the rest of his life."

Some might think it an indication of Hồ's Sinophobia, but my father and his friends took it differently. They said that Hồ was only referring to the Kuomintang Chinese, not to all Chinese. They said this was Hồ's way of winning people's support for his strategy of allowing the French forces' presence in North Việt Nam to replace the Chinese Nationalist Army. The Chinese nationalists were more dangerous than the French to his existence at that time. He meant to incite a streak of Sinophobia in the common Vietnamese people, who always remembered the brutal domination by the Chinese for more than 1,000 years and by the French for nearly 100 years. The explanation was obviously true, as Hồ and the Vietnamese communist leaders slavishly adhered to Chinese communism at least until 1975. He was a Sinophile and a faithful Maoist.

THE FRENCH RETURN

In early March, a French force entered the Gulf of Tonkin and threatened to attack. Then Hồ Chí Minh, Vũ Hồng Khanh, and the French representative Sainteny signed the provisional agreement of March 6, 1946. According to the agreement, the French Army would be stationed in the major cities north of the 16th parallel, including my beloved city of Nam Định, to replace the Chinese Army.

News about the agreement shocked every patriot. An old mandarin, a patriot and a most respected teacher of my father, my uncle, and many others, heard the news while he was playing cards with my father and three other gentlemen. In high dudgeon, he fell down mumbling, "Traitors! Traitors!" and died of a stroke within minutes.

The nationalists strongly criticized Vũ Hồng Khanh for signing the agreement. He was one of the top leaders of the Việt Quốc, holding the seat of vice premier in the coalition government at the time. He later admitted that he was duped into endorsing the covenant. The provisional agreement dealt a deadly blow to the nationalist parties. They would have to fight both French and Việt Minh forces alone. As for the communists, they might claim it as their victory. It should be noted that although the Chinese army was siding with the Việt Quốc as a policy of the Chiang Kai-shek government, the support was merely in terms of politics and was probably limited in financial and military aid.

If the Chinese stayed, the nationalists would soon bring an end to the Việt Minh. If the French returned, Hồ would have to fight just one enemy, whereas the nationalists could hardly survive attacks from both the French and the Việt Minh. As the top leader of his party, Hồ had his reasons for signing the agreement, probably to buy time to consolidate his power and strengthen his party, at all costs, a price that his compatriots would have to pay.

Not long after the agreement was signed, French soldiers arrogantly moved into my city. People were resentful at seeing them riding in Jeeps and trucks on the streets of Nam Định City. They clashed with our self-defense group frequently. Hồ again called for national unity to defend the Fatherland.

The Việt Minh propaganda machine justified the agreement by saying that those newly arriving were the "good new French," not the "bad colonialists." As far as a nine-year-old boy could tell, very few people would believe that.

One day, my father and two comrades, members of the Việt Quốc Provincial Standing Committee of Nam Định, were granted a private audience with Hồ to complain of being menaced by the local Việt Minh. Hồ received them warmly and had his aide send directives to Nam Định Public Security Service to stop annoying the three men, whom he referred to as "my brothers" and said that "you may have a different political position, but you are patriots who should be helped, not hindered." He assured the three men that they would be completely safe, so there was nothing to worry about.

My father offered my family his hope that since Hồ assured them of their safety, there was no need for further worry. He came back home as soon as he was sure that local authorities had received orders from Hà Nội to leave him and his friends alone. In the following months, there was no harassment. My uncle, however, did not think that the threat would come to a full stop.

HỒ CHÍ MINH'S BIRTHDAY

Some events weren't interesting to many children, but I always felt them worth memorizing. On May 19, 1946, my mother and I were in Hà Nội visiting some family friends. In the early morning, without previous notice, Việt Minh cadres went from home to home telling people to display flags in front of their houses. Only later in the afternoon did they explain that it was Hồ Chí Minh's birthday. Over the next few days, the opposition revealed that it was not Hồ's birthday and that the flag display was ordered only to welcome Admiral Georges Thierry d'Argenlieu, a French representative, on his official visit to Hà Nội.[2]

Today, there is no concrete evidence to prove that May 19, 1880, was his birthday, and written materials found in the last decade firmly alleged that Hồ was not born on that date. Archives found in at least three institutions confirm the allegation: In his petition for enrollment in the French Colonial School on September 15, 1911, he claimed he was born in 1892. At the Paris Police Department on September 2, 1920, he claimed the date January 15, 1894. At the USSR embassy in Berlin in June 1928, his application for a visa listed his birthday as February 15, 1895.

THE 1946 PURGE

In June 1946, Hồ and a Vietnamese delegation departed for France for further negotiation. In September, when Hồ signed an agreement that was a disservice to Việt Nam, all the nationalist parties protested.

While Hồ was in France, the Việt Minh launched a raid against the nationalist parties. They staged a scene at a house on Ôn Như Hầu Street in Hà Nội to justify the raid. It had been the office of a Việt Quốc agency that the Việt Minh had overrun days earlier. The Việt Minh authorities held a press conference and displayed a number of corpses of men they said had been assassinated by the Việt Quốc. They also charged the Việt Quốc with robbing and raping passers-by. The Việt Quốc denied the allegations, of course. The communists used the brazenly staged event for months as a source of propaganda with which to attack their enemy.

When I asked my father whether or not the Việt Quốc did such horrible things, he said, "The Việt Quốc did kill many Việt Minh somewhere else, but they were not so stupid as to do the killing and looting and raping right at their office in the heart of Hà Nội. I know some of the men there. They are not the type that can do such shameful things." Sometime in 1949, a French Army unit captured one of the agents who had participated in the setup of the Ôn Như Hầu scene. He confessed that the Việt Minh had been behind the slanderous plot.

In the Việt Minh's summer 1946 raid, the Việt Quốc and other nationalist parties suffered heavy losses. Some important cadres were arrested, and many were murdered. Their military bases were attacked and besieged. The Việt Quốc fought back bravely and were not completely wiped out as their enemy had expected. In September, when I entered fifth grade, the attacks on the nationalist parties increased. The bloody "cleansing" campaign was conducted while Hồ Chí Minh was in Fontainebleau to negotiate with France. He arrived there on

May 31. He signed the modus vivendu of September 14 with French minister Marius Moutet and came home on October 20. It was alleged by the nationalists that his top aides with Võ Nguyễn Giáp as executor were running the cleansing campaign while Hồ was away so that he would not be fully blamed for masterminding the plot.

More bad news came to my father every day. He became obviously nervous. A Việt Quốc member narrowly escaped death when the Việt Minh security agents brought him and half a dozen others to the riverbank for execution. He told my father the horrible story and concluded, "The Việt Minh selected their victims carefully." Thanks to darkness, he escaped a minute before he was to be executed. According to him, a cool-headed young Việt Quốc calmly asked the executioners, "I'm only a low-ranking cadre of the Việt Quốc. Why do you kill me, not my high-ranking superiors?" He was a former seminarian, a talented violinist, and a fervent Việt Quốc member. Whenever he visited with my father, he gave me some basic music and singing lessons. "Good question before you die," a Việt Minh executioner replied. "You are low-ranking, but will be dangerous in the future. Your bosses will not." A moment later, his head was smashed into pulp.

There may be something to be said for this macabre strategy. From the founding of the Republic of Việt Nam in the South, following the 1954 Geneva Accords, until it collapsed on April 30, 1975, the nationalist side seriously lacked a class of medium- and high-ranking patriotic anticommunist leaders. The communists had systematically massacred the majority of them, and the survivors were not sufficient to fill all key jobs in the administration and the armed forces.

During the atrocious cleansing campaign in mid-1946, many nationalist leaders had no option but to flee Việt Nam. Former king Bảo Đại did not return after a diplomatic mission in China in late March; Nguyễn Hải Thần escaped to China a month later. Nguyễn Tường Tam, Vũ Hồng Khanh, and many Việt Quốc members followed suit in May and June. Other leaders stayed to fight and to share the fate of their comrades.

The notorious communist prison camps such as Đầm Đùn and Lý Bá Sơ were constructed at that time, and many thousands of Việt Quốc, Đại Việt, and Duy Dân quickly filled those camps to the maximum capacity.

NATIONALIST PARTIES WIPED OUT

In the second half of 1946, many of my father's comrades fled to their bases in the provinces north of Hà Nội. The Việt Quốc strongholds in the delta provinces were harassed and besieged.

When going out during these critical months, my father often carried a .25 caliber pistol. He taught me how to take care of the little thing that looked like a toy but could kill. I loved it. He showed me how to disassemble, clean, and use it.

He said if a child knew how a pistol or a gun worked and how it might cause fatal wounds, he would be scared away from curiosity and from dangerously tampering with it. Although I was not allowed to shoot a real cartridge because ammunition was in short supply, handling a real pistol was the greatest thing to a child; it made me feel important. During wartime, as I had to keep my pistol at home, I trained my two sons and two daughters ages five to twelve the same way. I allowed them to shoot at objects like bricks or coconuts to see how dangerous a gun could be.

My father planned to bring me with him to China if the situation forced him to flee. To prepare for my future in the foreign land, he had his remote cousin teach me Chinese characters. This teacher crammed my head with three to five characters a day. In three months, I could remember about 200 words; that didn't help me much except for better understanding a few Vietnamese terms derived from ancient Chinese.

One evening, my father's close friend, who was also a Việt Minh Public Security cadre, stealthily dropped by. He disclosed to my father, "My agency was well aware of your plan to flee to China with your son. You just can't do that." My father asked him, "Do you know why the Public Security did not get rid of me as they killed some of my comrades?" His friend said, "Although you are considered a kind of dangerous Việt Quốc like some of your dead comrades, because you are a member at the provincial level, you've earned significant prestige and popularity in this area. They don't want to make the people feel bad. So you'll be safe unless you do something and they feel it's dangerous to let you flee." So my father gave up his plan to escape.

In autumn 1946, there were more clashes between French soldiers and the Self-Defense Corps in Hà Nội, Hải Phòng, and my city, Nam Định. War was impending, and many families left the cities for rural areas.

At that time, Việt Minh units already routed many nationalist units. Most Việt Quốc and Đại Việt strongholds were overrun by Viet Minh's ten-to-one attacks. The Việt Quốc newspaper office in Hà Nội was overrun, although both sides suffered losses. We did not receive the *Việt Nam Daily* anymore. Only the Việt Minh's *Cứu Quốc* (National Salvation) was available in my area.

My father and his friends realized that Việt Quốc organizations in all other provinces in Việt Nam, large and small, were being brutally repressed. The Vệ Quốc Đoàn or national guard of the Việt Minh grew rapidly in personnel strength and won several battles where the Việt Quốc militia units were willing to fight but were seriously outnumbered. The Politics and Military Training School of the Quốc Dân Đảng Front north of Hà Nội suffered heavy casualties after powerful surprise attacks by the Việt Minh with a force five times larger. Most captured instructors and students were killed and thrown into the Red River.

Many prominent leaders of the nationalist parties were abducted and assassinated. The most brilliant among them was Trương Tử Lê Khang, a genius central committee member of the Việt Quốc. By the end of 1946, the nationalist opposition parties were practically wiped out. Hundreds of nationalist leaders at all levels lost their lives or just disappeared. Thousands of other members were incarcerated. Those who survived the terrorist campaign fled to China. Those remaining stayed in the hope of surviving the brutal cleansing campaign. In December 1946, people were feeling that war was coming near. While tension was rising, the cleansing campaign continued at a higher rate.

My father's two friends who had been assured of their safety by Hồ Chí Minh were arrested. Their Congress member's immunity and Hồ's promise could not save them. One of the two, and a dozen other dissidents, were killed in a rice field a few miles north of Nam Định City. A witness related that the victims were buried alive up to their necks and a harrow drawn back and forth by two water buffalo tore off their heads. My father's other friend was taken away and never seen again.

When I was older, I asked many persons who had reliable knowledge of the matter about which side had started the bloody feud and should be held responsible for the fratricidal war. Carefully and candidly analyzing their opinions, I concluded that both sides should be blamed. However, it is certain that the number of victims done away with by the Việt Minh was many times higher than those put to death by the nationalist parties. Searching farther into the twentieth-century history of Việt Nam, it is reasonable to assert that the early communists of the 1930s started the killing in southern China. The victims were noncommunist revolutionaries whom the communist leaders classified as their future dangerous rivals.

PART II

The War of Resistance

FIVE

Take Up Arms!

When a company-sized unit of French soldiers arrived in Nam Định City not long after the March 6 agreement, the city population was nervous but not in a panic. Neither side concealed its hostility. However, there were no organized firefights. Every week, newspapers reported sporadic exchanges of fire by small units in the three largest cities of North Việt Nam (Hà Nội, Hải Phòng, and Nam Định). But the joint control teams quickly halted them.

Tension rose. In late November and early December, the French soldiers in my city consolidated their defense in the large concrete building of the former Indochina Bank, situated on the main street, and in the silk factory nearby. Street fights between individual soldiers took place more often. The government once again advised people who had no job in the city to move to the countryside, and ordered the military to be ready to confront any threat by French forces.

On the morning of December 19, 1946, French soldiers became more aggressive. They used their half-tracks and armored cars to clear redoubts, breastworks, and barricades that had been erected on most of the streets by the city's self-defense corps. With little provocation, they opened fire on Vietnamese militiamen and civilians. At noon, my mother, my father, my cousin, my sister, and I left the city for our home village with what we could carry by hand.

Later that evening firefights exploded, starting the real war. The bad news spread far and wide in less than an hour. Most villagers were up all night. Many said that battles would be fought in the city until one side won control, but not in the countryside. They would soon realize they were wrong.

Early the next morning, thousands of city people were seen walking on the main road with all kinds of portable belongings. Many were heading for their home villages or the villages of relatives, and many were fleeing to any place at all. About ten of my villagers whose houses were rather large offered to lodge those who had no place to go.

Soldiers, militiamen, and public security cadres were busy preparing for war. Everyone worried about what would happen next. Việt Minh authorities set up checkpoints on roads and bridges and in marketplaces; one of them was right at my village's gate. Men passing by were ordered to show their identification. Those who failed to present such papers were detained for investigation, sometimes for a day or two. In some places, many people who had books, papers, letters, or tags in their clothes, or almost anything with blue-white-red marks, the French national colors, were suspected of being traitors or spies. They got little trouble, and all were freed. But I heard that there was one beaten to death somewhere in my district.

The war did not keep the Việt Minh from intensifying its cleansing campaign. A few days after the war broke out, the famous novelist Khái Hưng, a founding member of the Self-Strength Literary Group, was killed and dumped in a river about ten miles from my village. News of his death came to my father in three or four days. Later in the month, my father learned that many more of his comrades had been murdered.

The French soldiers were hemmed in by thousands of Vietnamese fighting men. Some were armed with rifles and pistols, others with hand grenades and cold steel. Every week there were attacks on the French positions. The soldiers and militiamen fought hard and suffered heavy casualties. For months, the French weren't able to break the siege around their two compounds.

Everyone, pro- or anticommunist, was eager to do something for the brave fighters on the front line. Every appeal of the Việt Minh government was responded to quickly and enthusiastically. My father devoted all his time to the task of promoting support for the Resistance, especially for the wounded warriors.[1] He urged his friends to cooperate with the Việt Minh government to fight the French, whom they should consider their archenemy.

HIGH MORALE

In January, Việt Minh authorities announced the implementation of scorched-earth tactics. Farmers were to deliver loads of straw or dry wood to fill city houses that were away from the French positions. Then one night, the whole city was set on fire. In the morning, from three miles away, we could see smoke rising high above my beloved city, the third largest and second best-looking city of Tonkin. People said a large number of public buildings and private houses were reduced to rubble.

Many large brick houses in the countryside far away from the city shared the same fate. The authorities said that if the French came, they could take quarters in them. Our family's brick house in the village survived the policy because it was not large enough for such a purpose, but a smaller, two-story house in the nearby village was torn down. The decision depended on the opinions of local government officials. In this case, the district officials decided that the French would be using the two-story house as an observation post. Rumors had it that the tactics were aimed at a hidden objective to harm the rich rather than to obstruct the French.

The people's morale was very high at the outbreak of war. A great many youths in my city joined the self-defense corps and fought bravely around the French positions, while many young men and women in the villages volunteered for military service in regular army units and the militia. I could see them in military basic training everywhere before they were sent to the city to reinforce the self-defense corps, even though they were poorly equipped.

There were examples of heroism on the front line by young men of every origin. One carried an antitank explosive and plunged onto a French armored car to destroy it and himself. Others slipped into heavily defended French installations around the silk factory at night armed only with daggers, killed several enemies, and slipped out unscathed. And a hundred similar stories encouraged more young men to join the fighting.

Many kids of my age were also admitted to combat units as messenger boys. We all learned the story of a boy in his early teens who had sacrificed himself on a messenger's mission. I used to look at those boys with great admiration because I knew I would never be brave enough to do such a job.

One of those messenger boys had been my classmate. When he dropped by to visit his family for a day or two, all the kids in the village came to say hello and claimed their friendship with him, including those who had always bullied him a few months earlier. He told us combat stories, which we listened to with our eyes and mouths wide open. I didn't know that many of his stories were just lies until many years later. However, the desire to become a hero took root in our little hearts and stayed there for a long time.

Early in 1947, the war was fought only in a part of the city where the French were surrounded in the two separate areas. They could find no supply of water or receive food from the outside. Although well equipped with modern weapons, the French were not able to make a sally to control the city and to link up with French forces in Hà Nội. Therefore, life in villages far from the city was still somewhat peaceful. The presence of thousands of city people in the countryside had a significant impact on the rural areas.

The city people brought with them their modern way of living, which greatly influenced the peasants and altered the appearance and society of the countryside. Many rural locations became busy centers of commercial and cultural activities where a young villager could enjoy a cup of coffee with a cigarette or a bowl of *phở* at reasonable prices. In a prosperous village of my province, which attracted a lot of war refugees from the city, people could even listen to romantic or patriotic songs presented by pretty singers in coffeehouses. In this way, the provincial city was broken into a dozen rural towns with almost everything left from prewar days from city life except for paved streets, running water, and electricity.

Besides fighting, the cultural front was similarly important. Since August 1945, many songs, poems, and plays had been composed to promote the people's willingness to fight for national independence. Nothing was more attractive to the young than songs. My classmates and I were delighted to learn a new song every week or two, songs that I will never forget because they have become a part of the childhood of my generation. Their lyrics and tunes planted a lively seed of patriotism in our hearts. Patriotic songs played a role in building the extremely high morale that induced people to fight the better equipped enemy with almost nothing more than a few outmoded rifles, their bare hands, and courage.

One day in January 1946, a fighting unit managed to acquire a 75 mm howitzer, although it had just three shells. It was the only thing bigger than an automatic rifle in the whole province of Nam Định. The cannon was brought to a riverside about a mile from the Indochina Bank where the French were besieged. Without any indirect fire training, gunners aimed the cannon at the building. The first shot missed the target; the next hit the building; the third misfired. We got the news in the afternoon that "our brave artillery unit blew off one-fourth of the building and eliminated scores of French soldiers." That evening, a meeting was held at the pagoda to celebrate the great feat.[2]

Tightly besieged in the two narrow areas without food and water resupplies, the French would have had to surrender if the Vietnamese forces had been able to maintain the siege for one more month, people said later. But one day, some French airplanes appeared and dozens of parachutes bloomed in the sky. The French airborne reinforcements quickly drove the Vietnamese out of the city and established a new defense line along the city perimeter.

After a week or so, French ships from Hà Nội and Hải Phòng were able to reach the city river quay safely. With nothing bigger than automatic rifles, the Vietnamese could conduct only harassing fire at French warships moving on the Red River, not enough to do them any kind of serious damage. By mid-1947, the French had consolidated their defense system around the city and expanded their control over adjacent villages.

From their outposts around the city, French soldiers frequently raided the areas outside with squad or platoon-sized operations. What the Vietnamese force could do was lay some mines or set up sniper fire to harass the enemy before withdrawing. In no way could they directly clash with the French for more than thirty minutes. People in my district composed satirical poems deriding our force for always "withdrawing safely," the term often used in news reports of the Việt Minh government's newspaper.

The French forces did not widen their control over a larger area until November 1947. In the meantime, the countryside of the province was still safe, and I was able to continue my education in the district primary school that I had attended since autumn 1946.

At school and at home, we students all participated in any task we could perform to support the Resistance. Local governments offered courses to instruct us in politics, combat skills, first aid, and propaganda techniques. A batch of new Communist Party members in every village strengthened their party. Although their activities were supposedly covert, people could easily tell who those new members were by their manner of speaking.

In the village election, my father became the chairman of the village Ủy Ban Hành Chính Kháng Chiến (Administrative and Resistance Committee), a village chief with a new title. More than 90 percent of voters wanted him to have the job. The job was too low for him, but he accepted it as a tacit compromise with the Việt Minh provincial government. Later, he was elected vice chairman of the district Liên Việt Front (Vietnamese Alliance Front, later known under the new title Mặt Trận Tổ Quốc, or Fatherland Front), which consisted of members of different noncommunist parties, some Buddhist monks and Catholic priests, and prominent notables of the area, nominally representing the various political and social groups. In truth, it was solely a figurehead under the strict control of the Communist Party.

In his jobs, my father took charge of some campaigns supporting the Resistance. Not only did he devote all his time to the tasks but he also encouraged my family to participate in them. During "Disabled Veterans' Week," he had me print thousands of paper stamps using a wooden seal. I had to do it until late at night so that the stamps could be ready early in the morning for schoolchildren to sell to raise money for disabled veterans. I was tired, and my right palm was sore. My uncle asked my father if he was eager to do such tasks just to please the Việt Minh. He was not offended as I expected, but in his usual soft voice he made it clear to my uncle that he accepted the task only for the benefits of the brave disabled to whom he was grateful. He also told me that I should do the same whenever I was required to.

"When the Việt Minh decide to do me harm," he said to my uncle, "they will do it and will never spare me even if I lick their boots a thousand times."

TERRORISM

In 1947, most of the French soldiers were rather friendly to Vietnamese civilians they met in their operations. They paid generously for what they bought and were very polite to the aged. They gave medicine to villagers who were ill and sometimes candies to kids. But that friendliness didn't last long. More soldiers came from France—the French and the North Africans—and more Vietnamese were recruited from the French-controlled villages. During combat operations, the French soldiers began raping and looting more frequently. There was no competent administration governing the French-controlled villages, and therefore laws were not enforced. The French commanders only cared about military affairs.

On August 18, 1947, my mother gave birth to my second sister while villagers were preparing to celebrate the second anniversary of the Revolution. Much of what a newborn needed was unavailable.

Three months later, the French launched a company-sized operation in the area two miles north of my village. All the villagers moved south along with thousands of others swarming the country roads. Each of my family members carried a rucksack containing the most valuable and necessary objects, and my mother carried my baby sister. We all scurried away while machine guns were barking closer and closer.

After the operation, the French Army established three forts along the wide dirt road one mile north of my village. Most villagers in the French newly controlled area returned home. Subsequently, my village was under the crossfire between French soldiers and Việt Minh troops, and the strip of about ten villages along the wide dirt road became a disputed area where people had no ID card of either side but suffered brutality from both.

Both sides were utilizing terrorism to attain their objectives. The French soldiers would burn a village to the ground if one of them got killed by sniper fire or an antipersonnel mine. In the most serious case, villagers would be shot, hanged, or beheaded and their bodies would be eviscerated or dismembered. Victims of French terrorism rose: five in my village, five to ten in the ten nearby villages in six months. On the Việt Minh side, right after the war broke out, the terrorist campaign conducted against the nationalist dissidents since mid-1946 continued, peaking in late 1947 and 1948. Many members of nationalist parties who had survived the earlier campaigns were imprisoned or assassinated. Anyone who was suspected of having relations with the French or one who was thought to be dangerous to the regime was eliminated. Several times we kids found corpses. Some were eviscerated, chopped up, or beheaded, while most had been shot or stabbed to death.

But the most horrible to see were victims who were buried alive up to the neck in wet soil, their mouths stuffed with rags, and left to die a slow death under the hot sun that burned their swollen faces. No one dared to rescue them, and no one knew who they were as no identification could be found. The owners of the rice fields would have to bury the corpses.

I could say there were probably three people in every village around mine who were imprisoned for months or years by the Việt Minh authorities. Death squads executed a smaller number of villagers.[3]

Since the August 1945 event, I heard that communists would play rough with their opponents according to their motto in the early 1930s: "Trí, Phú, Địa, Hào, đào tận gốc, tróc tận rễ" (Intellectuals, rich farmers, landlords, wicked lords must be grubbed up, all their roots and stumps). However, I didn't believe it at the time, as it seemed to be a slanderous propaganda scheme by the anti-communists. The Communist Party had allegedly proclaimed the motto during the 1930 Nghệ Tĩnh Soviet Movement, an uprising of poor farmers in Nghệ An and Hà Tĩnh provinces led by the communists.

Only when the cleansing campaign in 1947 expanded did I see that what common people had said about merciless communist policies was true.

SIX

My Dark Years in War Begin

THE FIRST TASTE OF WAR

In January 1948, my family and many villagers moved to a village about three miles to the south. My school moved to a pagoda just a mile away, so I could continue fifth grade. My father continued his jobs in the Liên Việt and as the village chairman in exile. Although he performed his duty well, sometimes he was summoned to the district Public Security Agency to answer questions concerning his suspected anticommunist activities. His job in the Liên Việt led him to make the acquaintance of Catholic priests and Buddhist monks, some of whom were in the anticommunist organization known as the Mặt Trận Liên Tôn Chống Cộng (Interreligious Anticommunist Front). Probably his relations with those individuals alerted the Public Security Agency.

In January 1948, the French military authorities formed many anti–Việt Minh militia units in selected villages under their control and armed them with hand grenades and rifles of WWI vintage (.30 caliber Remingtons and Springfields). At that time, to the common people, a group equipped with ten rifles was a formidable force, more fearful than a battalion would be twenty years later.

Although most Vietnamese people supported the Resistance, a number of those who escaped from the Việt Minh's massacre campaigns had only one way to go. That was to flee to the French side or even to join the French Army or the anti–Việt Minh militias. Between the two enemies, one has to live with the less life-threatening one.

One day in February 1948, a friend of my father from a village in the French-controlled area came for a short visit. He handed my father a letter from the French military authority in Nam Định. The French officer who signed the letter promised my father a job as district chief or provincial deputy chief if he left the

Việt Minh and moved to the French-controlled territory. If my father accepted the proposal, a small-scale operation would be conducted on our village area to bring my whole family to the city. The French soldiers would pretend to capture my family—we would have been tied with ropes, our home ransacked—so that the Việt Minh could have no good reasons to harass our relatives who stayed. At that time the French were looking for a political solution, and they needed a Vietnamese administrative system to assist them in various civil affairs.

My father discussed the proposal with my uncle and my mother, who both supported a positive answer. After a week of pondering, my father decided to say no. He drafted a letter in French and had my most confident cousin and me make it into a clean copy without bearing my father's name or address to avoid any risk to my father in case the letter should fall into the hands of the Việt Minh Public Security Agency. The letter was sent to the French commander through the same friend.

In the letter, my father said that he would not accept the offer because until then, the French were fighting the war only to reestablish colonialism in Việt Nam. As a patriot, he had gained some respect from the population of the area. So he wouldn't betray them by joining the French despite the fact that if he stayed with the Việt Minh, his safety could be endangered at any time.

So we stayed. The two other former public servants in the area who had received similar letters accepted the offer. The French sent a platoon to bring them with their families back to the city, and both were appointed as district chiefs. For years, my family members regretted my father's decision. But I thought he was right when acting according to his heart and his ideals.

In February, I experienced an air raid for the first time. Two black French fighters (later known as the Hellcats) suddenly appeared in the sky and circled the area. Then they began strafing every brick house in the village for about five minutes. At last, they dropped four bombs near the concrete bridge and the pagoda. In those five minutes I was horribly frightened. Each time the planes dived, I prayed that bombs and bullets would hit somewhere far from me. When I saw the four black objects—the bombs—falling from the planes, I was panicked and ran to a bigger stack close by. The bombs hit a rice paddy 100 yards from my home.

When the planes disappeared over the horizon, we found out that only two women had been killed by machine-gun fire. The four bombs dug large craters in the rice field, killing no one. A big bullet hit the floor of the house my family was living in, only a few inches from my aunt, slightly wounding her.

It was my first lesson that bombing and shelling scared people more than really injuring them, except in a carpet-bombing. It also taught me that people could be less afraid of being killed after undergoing numerous attacks by bombs and artillery shells and that with some courage, a soldier could withstand such bombing firmly.

POOR DADDY!

In March 1948, the Liên Việt Front (Vietnamese Alliance) assigned my father the task of founding the Red Cross Association in our district. My cousin and I helped him with some of the paperwork. In a month, hundreds of people registered for membership. Some of them were my father's comrades in the Việt Quốc.

"It's unusual," my uncle warned my father. "The Việt Minh are always sensitive to such matters. You must be careful, though. You don't mean to do anything against them."

On a morning of April 1948 when my father and I were talking about my homework and my mother was holding my baby sister, four Public Security cadres came and produced a search warrant. My father, in an imperturbable manner, invited them into the house and showed them the part of the house my family occupied in a village where we had lived since after the French air raid in February 1948.

They began searching the house carefully, inspecting every object and looking at every piece of paper for more than an hour, but found nothing special. They asked my father a couple of questions, then declared that my father was under arrest. My father quietly put some clothes, a blanket, and a towel into a small bag. My mother slipped a few twenty-piaster bills into his pocket before he followed the four Việt Minh to their office about four miles away.

No one worried much because my father had been summoned many times to that office and held there for a day or two. But I felt something much different this time. By the way the two Việt Minh cops behaved and my father's sad look at me, saying only three short words, "Be brave, son!" I knew that he was in serious trouble. Two days later, my mother and I went to the Public Security office to give him food and medicine, but he was not there. We were told that he had been transferred to the higher agency for interrogation.

The situation gave me a feeling that this time my father would be treated roughly and that his way home would be very, very long, possibly never. It was the first time since he came back to live in our village in December 1946 that he was brought to a security office higher than district level.

My mother spent the whole month of May 1948 trying to find out where my father was being detained, leaving my little sister under the care of my father's older sister. At last, she was permitted to visit him in a provincial jail in the seaside village twenty miles from where we were living. The jail moved every two or three months to a new place. Locating it among a dozen provincial prisons was difficult, and sometimes it was dangerous for a woman frail and meek like my mother.

One of my remote uncles, who had joined the Việt Minh army in 1945 and been promoted to platoon leader, was discharged in late 1947 when the Việt Minh army conducted a political purge to get rid of any military cadre suspected of having contact with the nationalist parties. He wasn't a Việt Quốc member, but he had often visited with my father and discussed politics before he volunteered to join the Việt Minh regular army. A month after my father was arrested, my uncle fled to the French-controlled area one night when the Public Security men came to arrest him. He was then admitted into the anticommunist militia newly founded by the French, although he hated the French no less than my father did.

There is no statistic available on how many nationalist patriots who had been truthfully serving the Resistance but were not anticommunists had to leave the Việt Minh to join the French side because of communist crackdowns on them. But I am certain that it must have been no less than 1,000 as of 1950 in my province.

Toward the end of 1948, the Public Security arrested many people in the villages. Some of them were my father's comrades. Many others were only victims of suspicion. Việt Minh Public Security sent many of those to the prison camp Dam Dun, the frightening name that was well known to kids and most illiterate persons in the lower Red River delta provinces.

On the French side, things were in no way better. The French Deuxième Bureau (G-2, or Intelligence Service) was not second to the Việt Minh Public Security in atrocious interrogation of suspects. To draw information, the French G-2's applied numerous torture techniques to force their prisoners to talk. The most common was to tie the prisoner down on his back, put a towel over his face, then slowly pour water or a mixture of fish sauce, vinegar, and hot pepper into his nostrils. The other ways were to pinch him with a red-hot pincers, to burn his fingers, or to apply electric shock by cranking a small generator or a field telephone.

The Việt Minh Public Security outdid the French G-2 in some torture techniques. For the first time after 1945, people in Việt Nam heard of "to go by air" (hanging the victim upside-down and beating him) and "to go submarine" (to tie up the victim and submerge him in a pond or water tank), performed by the Việt Minh along with many other interrogation methods.

The Việt Minh and the French interrogators often invented new ways of torture that gave victims the most painful feeling without leaving marks on their bodies. One such method was beating the soles of the victim's feet with the blunt edge of a flat piece of wood. This left no mark but caused such pain that the victim was unable to stand or walk for many days.

A villager who was close to my family was one of those who experienced the sole beating. The place where he was locked up in the district Public Security interrogation office was a small brick house, situated in the middle of a large rice field without any other house within 300 yards, half a mile from where I lived. About twenty prisoners were held there at the time, kept by half a dozen Public Security agents. The office was off-limits to the public. But if the agents caught us children wandering near the house, they would shoo us away without causing us any trouble. Some kids occasionally sneaked into the garden surrounding the house and climbed into the trees to watch the interrogation through an open window. I followed them just once, and it was so horrible to me that I dared not come back to watch it for the second time. The sight of an emaciated prisoner who was beaten with a bamboo stick terrified me. However, childish curiosity prevailed, and we stayed for a few more minutes. When the victim was tortured with some sharp object pushed into the quick of his fingernail, he let out a long, deafening scream that made me fall to the ground. I tore away at full speed. Out in the open field, the ear-splitting scream still echoed in my ears, and I felt pain in my own fingernails as well.

Every week a few prisoners were released. Some of them were unable to walk, and their relatives came to carry them back home. The story of one of them is still in my memory. He was fifteen years old and the son of a Việt Quốc member. His father escaped in time when the Public Security came to get him. The boy was detained and interrogated for information about his father's activities. As a young man detained there at the same time with the boy later related his story to my family, he suffered torture bravely.

When the interrogators asked him whether he knew who encouraged his father to join the Việt Quốc subversive movement, he said, "The sublime interests of the Vietnamese people urge him to fight against you, the communists." To the question "Do you know who are your father's most faithful comrades?" he said he did but he wouldn't tell. The interrogator pushed a needle into his finger quick. He shrilled in pain but said to the interrogator, "Even if you continue at my other nine fingers, I won't tell the names." He was released about a month later. He was carried home and died after many bedridden weeks.

At that time, many others serving the Việt Minh behaved in the same heroic way when suffering French Army interrogation. Some died as a result of torture. They endured unbearable pain but still refused to talk until passing away in agony. Many suspected Việt Minh died during interrogation, and others walked out of detention with deformed bodies. I witnessed such barbaric torment while living a short time in a French fort.

Patriotism at the highest degree gives to some an almost unimaginable will to survive, but it also encourages people of the same forefathers to kill their compatriots more eagerly and savagely. That is a reality of the armed conflict from 1945 to 1975 in Việt Nam.

LIFE IN THE CROSSFIRE

In the summer of 1948, my family returned to our native village. As a farming family, we had to cling to our land, although our village was under the constant danger of war.

Until 1948, there were not many Vietnamese soldiers serving the French side. In the area about five miles around my village, four of some twenty villages had anti–Việt Minh militias. Three of those were composed of Catholics, and one consisted of Buddhists (or non-Catholics, to be more exact). The militias were armed with bolt-action rifles and received no salary or any assistance from the French. While fighting the Việt Minh, they were always friendly to villagers—no looting, no abuse, no unscrupulous killing.

The so-called partisans were different. They served as Vietnamese hirelings and were paid a relatively decent salary. Many of them would behave well to peasants, but others felt free to loot, to rape, and even to kill without being sanctioned and punished by their French commanders. Their atrocities were second only to the North Africans and the Legionnaires in the French Army.

By the end of 1948, a considerable number of Vietnamese had returned to the city to live under the French military authority. Many ran out of money and were not able to continue living in the Việt Minh area; the others fled to avoid being killed or imprisoned, and former officers and NCOs of the French Army returned to the city to reenlist for active duty.

Every village in the area outside French control had a team of about ten men and teenagers who each in turn took sentry duty at the top of a tall tree. The sentry would sound the alarm, usually with a gong, when the French Army soldiers moved southward in the direction of our villages. It was easy to detect movement of even one soldier across the wide rice field separating the French-controlled area and my village, but at night it was a difficult task. One day, about fifty French Army soldiers raided my village. They came under cover of dense fog at 4 AM, and none of us had time to escape.

They ransacked every house and took away everything they liked. In my house, they found some hundred books in Chinese characters, in French, and in Vietnamese, left by my grandpa, my uncle, and my father. They destroyed all of them, tearing them up or burning them to ashes. They were happy to find some antiques we had hidden underground and a wall clock. I was held prisoner and brought to the fort. An hour after my arrival, a Vietnamese sergeant in the French Army heard that I was captured. A son of my father's friend, he had lived with my family from 1935 to 1937. The sergeant immediately called on the French lieutenant, commander of the fort, and interceded with him for my release, to which the French lieutenant agreed.

A sergeant in 1948 might have had the power of a viceroy in the Middle Ages. While a private could kill and rape almost anyone in a Việt Minh–controlled area, a sergeant could do more than that. People addressed him as "Ngài," a word equivalent to "Your Excellency," only used in connection with gods and mandarins. So the fact that I was a close relative of a sergeant earned me respect from people in the fort. The sergeant told me to stay in the fort for a time so that he could arrange to send me to a school newly established in the city.

In the fort, there were three Frenchmen: the second lieutenant, the sergeant in charge of the African platoon, and the corporal operating an 81 mm mortar. The Vietnamese personnel consisted of two sergeants, two corporals, and about forty troops. The soldiers, Africans and Vietnamese, all lived with their Vietnamese wives and children inside the fort.

The French lieutenant had a new wife. She was a pretty girl about twenty years old from a noble family. The family had been captured while returning to the city from the Việt Minh area and had been brought to the fort to be interrogated. She was a ninth-grade graduate and a fluent French speaker. Not many female citizens earned education degrees that high at the time. The lieutenant asked her to be his wife, but she refused. So he had her and her family sit on a bench against a thick brick wall in front of a French-made automatic rifle FM 24/29 and its gunner. On the other side was a Vietnamese corporal of the French Army. He had been caught working as a spy for the Việt Minh. He was tied to a bamboo pole in front of another automatic rifle and a gunner.

When the two gunners were ready, the French lieutenant told the girl that if she said no to his marriage proposal, all her family would suffer the fate of the convicted corporal. At his sign, the machine gunner pulled the trigger, and the bursts of many dozen rounds chopped the corporal up into bloody pieces. The young lady immediately accepted the lieutenant's proposal. A wedding ceremony was held, and she became his legitimate wife. Her family was released and helped to find good jobs in the city.

Although he had a lovely and well-educated wife, the French lieutenant still kept a harem in the basement of the main building, formerly the house of a rich mandarin. About ten young women captured in operations were living under armed guard. They were well fed and clothed and had nothing to do except serve the lieutenant any time he wished. When he captured some new girls during his operations, those who had been in the harem the longest would be released and given a gift of about 200 piasters (about US$300 in 2005).

Every day, the villages around the fort had to provide some fifty men to do chores at the fort such as repairing the bamboo and barbed-wire fences, cleaning the yards, and filling the water tanks. Those villages also had to provide laborers for military operations. Failing to provide the required laborers, a village would be fined a cow or several pigs.

The fort had a small room in which to interrogate prisoners. They were often tortured for information by a Vietnamese soldier. Sometimes at night I was unable to sleep because of the prisoners' cries of pain. My room was close to the interrogation room.

A few weeks later, the sergeant who had interceded for my freedom took me to Nam Định City. We rode on a military truck. The road was rather safe, but houses along the two sides were vacant. There were no people, and moss and grass grew freely all around. Clashes in the area had driven the inhabitants away. At last we reached the city after crossing the river by ferryboat beside the headquarters of the southern subsector, commanded by a French first lieutenant. He also had a little harem and sometimes held girls captive for a night or two. He was also famous for his sanguinary passion. Spies and stiff-necked prisoners did not live long under him. Sometimes he himself handled the executions, usually with his dagger.

In the city, we visited a friend of my family who had just returned from the Việt Minh area three months earlier. The population was in the thousands, much less than one-fifth of that before the war. The city market had revived, and one primary school was to open in September. Curfew was imposed from 8 PM to 6 AM. Many blocks had no residents, and after 8 PM they looked like a ghost town.

After three days, I followed the sergeant back to the fort. The family's friend tried to persuade me to stay so that I might continue my education, but the atmosphere of the city frightened me. Moreover, as my father was still in a Việt Minh prison, I was afraid that my staying would cause him more trouble.

In the next few days, I moved to a village close to the fort to live with the uncle who had fled my village a few months earlier. He didn't want to let me live in the fort, where I had to see many things injurious to a child's mind. This was a typical village armed by the French Army to fight the Việt Minh.

RELIGION

Since August 1945, the Catholics had been overtly anticommunists. In Hồ Chí Minh's appeal for "Great Solidarity," the Catholic population was one of the principal objectives. In the 1946–48 terrorist campaign, a number of Catholic priests were killed or imprisoned.

After 1946, the French Army treated the Catholics carefully to win them over to their side. In military operations, ones who could say a few prayers fluently were usually taken as friends. So many non-Catholics wore the cross when the French soldiers came. One of them was a friend of mine who couldn't recite a word of any Catholic prayer when a French Army Vietnamese soldier asked him to. He was shot right away, but the bullet only slashed his belly slightly; the wound bled a lot without killing him.

The Việt Minh, on the other hand, were doing everything to create hostile feelings against the Catholics, and they were successful, owing to their skillful propaganda techniques to exploit the differences between the religions.

The southern area of my province was one of the first sites the European missionaries visited in the sixteenth century. In the mid-nineteenth century, the kings ordered the ban on Catholicism that resulted in the execution of thousands of its followers. Despite the massacre, non-Catholics in our area lived peacefully with the Catholics without any clash, large or small. In the 1850s, by order of the king and the province governor, each non-Catholic village in our area had to execute leading members of Catholic parishes who refused to step over the cross, an act to affirm their decision to renounce their faith. The district governor ordered my village to perform some of the executions. But instead of killing them as instructed, the village notables decided to save them and secretly hid them after killing some pigs and spreading their blood over the riverside to prove to the district authority that those Catholics had already been put to death and thrown into the stream. Years later when the ban was lifted, those Catholics returned home safely. After that, in every Tết (Lunar New Year) season, their relatives came to visit my village and offered gifts to villagers. The practice continued until the fighting spread to our area in 1947.

Most of the Catholics in our area (Bùi Chu diocese) had been converted before the French occupied Việt Nam in the 1880s. When the French established its colonial regime over all Việt Nam, the Catholics won the French government support and their priests gained some power. Under the French colonialist regime, a part or all of some villages were converted only because some Catholic priests had helped them win lawsuits against other individuals in the same villages or in other villages. But that did not create any serious rancor.

Until 1945, the number of Catholics who joined the movements for national independence was rather small compared with other religious groups. Việt Minh propaganda exploited that fact as much as possible, along with their usual Marxist indoctrination, to instill hatred against the Catholics. When the French returned to Việt Nam, it was easy to see why many Catholic villages sided with them, founding militia units and fighting the Việt Minh.

Besides defending their villages, the militia units sometimes were given tasks to reinforce the French Army soldiers' raids in other areas. The village where I was living temporarily with my remote uncle had about fifty young men with basic military training, but only sixteen were armed with Remington rifles and lots of hand grenades. They fought bravely and beat off many Việt Minh night attacks. In raids, they showed good discipline.

They had a lot of friends and acquaintances in the operation area not very far from their village. The militiamen had to do farm work for their living. They got no pay from the French Army even when they were wounded or killed.

After a month, I asked my uncle to let me go back to my home village, and he agreed. On a morning when farmers were working in rice fields, I slipped through the strip of uncultivated land separating the two areas and walked back home. My mother held me for a minute and cried. She had just come back from a trip visiting my father, who had been moved to another prison camp.

IN THE VIỆT MINH–CONTROLLED AREAS

At the beginning of the 1948–49 school year, my uncle sent me to a school farther south. I had to walk three miles to school and three miles back every day from the home of my first cousin's husband, where I lived. Held in two classrooms located in a large pagoda, school began at 10 AM and closed at 2 PM so that students from far away could attend.

By that time, the French had more bombers. From their base in Hà Nội, the planes made air raids in my district more frequently. The students sitting in the last rows of the classroom had to alert the school when they heard the sound of the approaching airplanes. At the sound of the alarm gong, teachers and students rushed to take shelter in foxholes all around the pagoda. In any alert, I was always calmer than my classmates, not because I was brave but only because I had been in similar situations.

In 1948, the Resistance was in high spirits. The Resistance army units began reacting actively against the French Army raids. Some ambushes were laid successfully, killing a number of French soldiers. The French Army soldiers also suffered casualties, more from land mines than other weapons. The Việt Minh produced the largest number of land mines in the world, according to some friends of my father.

At the same time, the Việt Minh government did its best to consolidate the infrastructure in the villages under its control. Political courses were held for members of mass organizations of men, women, senior citizens, and teenagers. Many more young people became Communist Party members. I could tell every one of them by listening to them talk. A communist neophyte always liked to talk of something big such as Darwin's theory of evolution: "long ago, a monkey living on the shore of the Danube . . ."

In 1948 and 1949, the Communist Party local committee was recruiting illiterate young men from the poorest families, particularly those violent and ill-mannered characters who had had problems with the pre-1945 colonialist local authorities.

In the village where I stayed, there was a class for propaganda cadres from many villages of the district given by instructors coming from the provincial office of information. Although I was not old enough to be a student, I was permitted to listen to the lessons because I had helped the village official in charge of the class. He let me sit in the last row of the twenty-student classroom, actually a thatched roof earthen-walled house measuring eighteen by thirty-six feet.

The students were taught how to practice the technique of "three-together" (eat together, live together, work together with the targeted family) to persuade the family to support the Việt Minh government. They learned how to speak to an audience, to run an armed propaganda mission, to print leaflets and booklets by lithography, to write slogans on walls, and to use bullhorns to deliver antiwar messages to the French Army soldiers at night. Most of the students had a second-grade education; only a few had graduated elementary school. So the instructors gave model speeches that they had to learn by heart so they could use them in different situations. Some trainees were very clever in writing slogans on large walls in darkness that looked neat and beautiful as if they had been done by professionals in daylight.

Cultural activities in 1948 reached their peak with hundreds of songs, poems, plays, and novels. The best songs, especially patriotic songs in Việt Nam, were composed during this period. They still move millions of Vietnamese hearts today. In my opinion, the composers of those songs (Phạm Duy, Văn Cao, and some others) contributed the best and greatest parts to the Vietnamese culture, far more than all of the Vietnamese politicians and statesmen after 1945 both in North and South Việt Nam.

I will never forget the evenings when the district cultural group entertained the Resistance units with songs and plays a few hours before they departed for the night attacks on the French forts. One of the plays presented the story of a Resistance soldier coming home to find his house burned and his wife gone insane after being raped and seeing her baby stabbed to death and thrown into the flames, all done by the French soldiers. The actress performed her role so well that many people cried and forgot to applaud for a few seconds after the curtain dropped. Such propaganda work was successful because the audiences were mostly simple-minded peasants whose imaginations made up for the lack of supportive scenes and costumes. With talented actors and directors performing on a makeshift bamboo stage, any clothing and any instrument could deeply move such audiences. Days later, I learned that the attack that night, actually a harassing operation, had been fiercer than ever.

The địch vận action (enemy proselytizing) was one of the successful efforts of the Resistance. Spies were planted everywhere. Many women were assigned to such a mission in the French military outposts or headquarters, where they had to get married to the French, African, or Vietnamese soldiers. In most cases, they only collected military information. But in some forts, they were successful in persuading the soldiers to surrender to the Resistance or to help the Resistance attackers overrun the fort.

By 1948, there were many great changes in the rural society. Young men and women eagerly endorsed the new way of life in which they had more freedom and new values and backward traditions were done away with. Although they were not in a majority, many women claimed equality with men and their reasonable status in the husband's family.

People learned several new words, mostly Sino-Vietnamese political terms. Cadres working in government agencies and members of mass organizations were fond of discussing politics and of calling each other *đồng chí* (comrade). I heard many young, ill-educated peasants who were communist neophytes saying, "One is equal to every other, even to his or her parents." Some even said that they had no reason to be grateful to their parents because they were born solely out of their parents' sexual pleasure. They dubbed that attitude "revolution."

THE LAST TIME I SAW MY FATHER

In December 1948, my mother and I visited my father. The moving prison camp was then in a seaside village fifteen miles south of my home village. My mother, my first cousin, and I went on foot for nearly ten miles before we could hire a small bamboo boat to complete the remaining five miles. The next morning we were permitted to meet my father in the local Public Security office for only half an hour. The Public Security cadres carefully examined the food and medicine we brought for my father.

During the precious thirty minutes we were permitted to spend with him, my father held me tightly on his lap while talking to my mother. A Việt Minh Public Security guard sat beside us. When the guard went to do something outside for half a minute, my father quickly pulled up his pants and showed me his knees. In a low voice he said to me, "They have been beating me here for the last few weeks." It was why he had been hobbling along the small road from the small prison camp to the office to see my mother and me.

His knees were black and blue. I couldn't hold my tears, though I had promised myself that I wouldn't cry. He looked at my eyes and said quickly when he saw the guard returning, "Try to complete a university degree, and you should become either an engineer or an officer in a good army to work for the bright future of our country." I did not have enough time to ask him what would be a good army as the guard took his seat beside us again.

Five minutes later, the cadre showed us the door, and that was the last time I saw my father. Sometimes, in my dreams, I still see him in brown clothes trudging along the country dirt road and looking at me without a word, his pants pulled up showing his knees, bruised and swollen.

Not long after the visit, my father's friends in the area managed to have all the families in the village sign a petition asking the Việt Minh authority to release my father. One of my father's friends, my uncle, my mother, and I went to see the district public security office one morning with the petition. A man who must have been a high-ranking cadre received us. After reading the petition, he said, very softly with a refined language, that my father was a man dangerous to the Democratic Republic regime in time of war, although he had done nothing wrong after 1946. Therefore, he would be released only when the war ended.

On the way back home, my father's friend told us that he was very disappointed. "As far as I am concerned," he added, "you should bring your family to the city so that the kids can go to school for a better education." My uncle and my mother kept silent, but I didn't think it was a good idea. In the Việt Minh area we had freedom, although living conditions grew worse and worse and French troops and bombers occasionally caused some danger. In the French-occupied area, people had better living conditions, but they were under permanent threat from the French soldiers and the French Security Service.

My family still had a faint hope that my father would be released, so we weren't thinking of doing anything against the Việt Minh.

By the end of 1948, many more people were leaving the Việt Minh for the French-controlled areas or Phát Diệm, a small town under Bishop Lê Hữu Từ, who had declared his diocese to be autonomous from both the French and the Việt Minh. But my family stayed put.

THE CRUMBLED IDOL

I was still attending school but at a new location in a temple large enough for forty students. Textbooks were not available, so the teacher had to dictate lessons to students. Every week, we had an hour or two for citizenship lessons, in which we were taught to worship Hồ Chí Minh. Once while the class was singing a song praising him, I looked out the window at a beautiful rainbow. At the end of the hour, a girl whose father was a Việt Minh big wheel rose and bitterly criticized me for showing no respect to "President Hồ" by looking at something outside the window and singing reluctantly. Some others supported her opinion, but many stood by me, saying that my inattention for a few seconds was not a good ground for such severe criticism. My classmate from my village whispered to me when we were walking back home, "I know you don't like him as much as I do, but you should conceal your thoughts as much as possible."

After August 1945, Hồ Chí Minh had been my great idol. In him I saw not only a national hero but also a god, omnipotent and polyvalent. It seemed that every kid of my age was always yearning for someone of greatness to idolize, and that was Hồ. But that didn't last long. Since I learned more about Hồ and the contemporary personages from my cousin, my father, and other sources, my idol crumbled without anyone to replace him in my heart. The noncommunist side was making no effort to deify any of its leaders. Even though I was a kid, I couldn't stand the cheap propaganda schemes vigorously praising Hồ, such as about his having "twin pupils," as I have mentioned.

The Việt Minh propaganda agency also released a poem reportedly composed by Hồ in which he compared himself to the thirteenth-century hero Trần Hưng Đạo, who drove away the Mongolian aggressors in a great battle on the

Bạch Đằng River. Comparing oneself to a heroic ascendant is in no way the manner of an educated gentleman, let alone a national leader.

Worse than that, in the poem he addressed Trần Hưng Đạo as "*bác*" and called himself as "*tôi.*" In Vietnamese, *bác* (uncle, or you) in pairs with *tôi* (me, I) is used between two people who are equal in age and in rank. However great Hồ Chí Minh could have been, his words addressing Trần Hưng Đạo in the poem sound extremely insolent to the ears of a Vietnamese. Realizing that such arrogance hurt the people's feelings, some Việt Minh cadres said that someone else, not Hồ, might have composed it. Even if this were so, I thought, Hồ should not have permitted his subordinates to circulate that poem if he was really as modest as his Việt Minh propaganda agency always asserted.

After the 1946–48 cleansing campaign, I hated him much more when I heard of people killed or saw someone buried alive by the Việt Minh, especially after my father was imprisoned. Meanwhile, the Viet Minh continued to disseminate a lot of stories idolizing Hồ as if he were the god of Việt Nam. The propaganda was very successful with the peasants because of its simplicity and sensationalism. In a few years, Hồ ascended to the throne of a wise king in the minds of many Vietnamese and of some of his ill-informed opponents as well.

Since then, I have rarely taken anyone as my idol. I have never trusted anyone to be a national hero and have always been skeptical about great personages of other nations. Sometimes I ask myself if what has been written in history books about George Washington, Abraham Lincoln, Napoleon, Lê Lợi, and Quang Trung is true, or if their stories are just big lies like those about Hồ.

IF THE FRENCH . . .

One of the provincial Resistance military units in charge of our area was the Seventy-seventh Company. It was conducting guerrilla operations to hinder the French Army's activities, and whenever possible, it laid small ambushes to cause some loss to the enemy soldiers in a group of three or four. They frequently shot at the French platoons.

Several nights, the company gathered in the large brickyard near where I was living to conduct night sessions, and I was one of the teens who were always present. We were not members of the company, but we offered them assistance even when the company was in action, such as carrying the routine messages, cleaning weapons, and hauling ammunition.

I didn't like the Việt Minh leaders, but I sympathized with the soldiers who were friendly to everyone, very brave and patriotic, especially with a French lieutenant who deserted to the Việt Minh side and served in the Seventy-seventh Company as an advisor. I liked to talk to him with my little French. His name, which I have forgotten, appeared many times in French-language newspapers before 1954.

It should be noted that a great number of the brave small unit commanders were sons of the middle and upper classes. They were bold in fighting and brilliant in other tasks directly supporting the war.

In my district, there were a few cultural groups whose members were high school students from bourgeoisie families. They moved from village to village, performing programs of music and plays that attracted an audience of several hundred people every night, thus enhancing public enthusiasm for the Resistance.

In the French-controlled area, life was under the iron hands of the French soldiers. After 7 PM, no one could stay outside the village. At night, no light was permitted. A lamp of any kind had to be partially covered so that no light could be seen from the fort; otherwise, a few mortar shells might be fired at the place as punishment.

In late 1948, the Việt Minh forces were stronger, as they had had time to be intensely trained. The people's morale was higher after some victories on the Lô River and in the northern border area. Propaganda supporting the Resistance produced the largest effect. More songs, the best patriotic songs in the history of music in Việt Nam, were on the lips of men, women, and children. However, there was no big battle in my district area, because the Việt Minh forces were not equipped well enough to confront the French, and the French did not try to expand their control beyond the line they had established in late 1947.

After 1954, in books I was reading, some military historians wrote that if the French forces had concentrated their efforts to pacify all North Việt Nam delta provinces in the first two years (1947 and 1948) instead of wasting time trying to control the northern border areas, they could have won the war or at least ended the war more in their favor. After almost two years of fighting, the French had left the large region of Nam Định and Thái Bình provinces intact. The region was the granary of North Việt Nam, which supplied the Việt Minh not only with food but also with manpower. Therefore, the Việt Minh gained much time to establish control over the population, train and consolidate their units, and organize an effective system of food supply for future battles in North Việt Nam.

I think the French could have won the hearts and minds of the population if they had conducted the war with an adequate effort to take care of the people's welfare and safety, particularly prohibiting their soldiers from committing war crimes and treating the Vietnamese so savagely.

SEVEN

Between Hammer and Anvil

CAMP #5

In 1945, the Việt Minh established several prison camps and named them Trại Sản Xuất (production camps). In 1954 they were renamed Trại Cải Tạo (reeducation camps).

In February 1949, my father was moved to Camp 5 in Thanh Hóa province. It was the most notorious prison camp in all of the areas under Việt Minh control. It still exists today. It was also known as Camp Lý Bá Sơ, named after its chief jailer. Hồ Chí Minh himself selected Lý Bá Sơ and other jailers.

According to sources from the Communist Party history books, among the first things Hồ did after ascending to power in August 1945 was to appoint his most faithful party members to be provincial public security chiefs, who were the backbone of his regime, and then to select the chief jailers of important prisons. Lý Bá Sơ was an illiterate who was said to be a most formidable Việt Minh official for the rough way he treated prisoners. He quickly became the Việt Minh jail chief known for his iron fist. Every adult in the northern lower delta provinces knew his name.

The inmates were given complex labor tasks and were severely punished if they failed to fulfill them. In such cases, their daily food allowance was reduced, and in more serious cases, they were even beaten or tortured with newly invented techniques.

After my father was moved to Camp 5, my mother had to go visit him every three or four months to provide him with dry food, medicines, and clothes. Camp 5 was about seventy miles from my home village. It took my mother nearly a week to walk there, and a few more days to finally see my father for just half an hour. Then it was another week to get back home to prepare for the next visit.

She had to travel through many lonely roads and forests, some dangerous with poisonous snakes and even tigers. She used to go along with two or three women whose husbands were detained in the same prison camp. Each had to bear about seven certificates to get through a dozen checkpoints of Việt Minh Public Security. My mother and her friends could obtain only five of these certificates from local authorities. The other two were unavailable, so she had to pay bribes to get the sixth certificate. I helped her with a fake copy of the seventh.

On one visit, my father told my mother that the camp guardians beat him with a bamboo stick for several days in a row. His right side was so badly hurt that he wasn't able to move his right arm for months. He failed to fulfill the given tasks because he was too injured to work. The turnkeys didn't think so and said that my father was a malingerer.

Upon coming back, she didn't tell the story to the family. She told it only to me and asked me not to share it to anyone, especially my grandma, who was ill, because such a story would make her health worse. My mother was exempted from other work at home so that she could prepare dry food and procure medicine for the trips. My father's elder sister, who was a childless widow, took care of my little sister, so my sister was closer to her than to Mom until our aunt's death in 1979.

LIVING UNDER FEAR

In February 1949, my family moved to a place three miles from my home village. My mother and my aunt had to find any work available to earn a living. I helped them spin processed cotton into thread using two sets of spinning wheels. Thanks to our dexterity, the thread we produced drew a lot of textile weavers. We could earn some money; it was scant, but we could make ends meet with it.

I came back to my home village often after school to be with my grandmother. At her age, she preferred staying at her home with the ancestors' altar. Her ten-year-old great-niece was taking care of her.

My village was located about a mile from the French-controlled region where a row of three French outposts marked the disputed line between the two sides. French soldiers frequently made raids in our area and also into the area from which the Việt Minh launched harassment attacks.

Beginning in mid-1948, my village came under attack from both sides. Babies were born, young men and women got married, and people died without being registered. We had no ID cards from the French or from the Việt Minh, children had no school to go to, and wounded and sick people were treated with herbal medicines. The nearest aid station was 5 miles to the south, and no better medical facility existed within the whole region of about 150 square miles. The French authorities didn't have any humanitarian or charitable program to help the Vietnamese population under their rule. The provisionary administrative authority, made up of Vietnamese civil servants under French military command, had no adequate budget to provide health care. There was one medium-size hospital with limited capacity for the whole province of a million people.

In mid-1949, via news from the French-controlled area and some leaflets dropped by French airplanes, we learned that King Bảo Đại had established the national government and signed a covenant with the French president that recognized the independence of the state of Việt Nam.

My villagers did everything during the day. After 7 PM, we all had to stay inside the village bamboo hedge. The French forbade light. For their part, the Việt Minh did not allow us to keep dogs because their barking could help the French detect guerrilla movement. So at night we had to keep our only dog inside and train him not to bark at anything, and he obeyed. War affected even animals' instincts. Every night, from 7 PM until 6 AM was the time of fear during which I had to speak softly and make no loud noises. My gate to the road outside the bamboo hedge was closed at 7 PM, and it seemed to be the boundary between safety and danger. The darkness outside the hedge was full of risks that frightened me whenever I had something to do near the gate.

After so many years, I still dream about getting back to my village in the time of war, probing my way in darkness at the wooden gate, while something frightful is wandering outside. Great fear wakes me up.

I used to get up early, summer or winter, and stay in until there were people on the road, walking and talking. I would dash to the gate, open it, and run outside to do some exercises and breathe the sweet morning air. Then the day's work of every family began.

Human beings and animals alike got used to life in war, and their senses also developed to adapt to the safety of every living soul around them. Day or night, most healthy villagers were ready to flee whenever an alert was sounded. Some single men and women without children or elderly parents to take care of always kept a bag of clothes and a little food while working in the field, in case they should have to run away without having time to get back home.

Whenever the French soldiers came, all kinds of sounds subsided. Even domestic animals—beasts of burden, pigs, and dogs—seemed to try to make the least noise. All kept quiet and acted frantically as if they could apprehend fear conveyed by the behavior of panic-stricken villagers. Most dogs ran about to find a nook of safety in dense bamboo groves. Some pigs sneaked into concealed holes when their owners yelled, "French coming!" Two of the dozen buffaloes in my village would act accordingly to the shout "Lie down!" when they were under fire while fleeing the village. When the French soldiers were gone and the villagers returned to their normal activities, all those animals became lively again and made their usual noises and sounds.

Several times I was met by gunfire from the French Army soldiers at a range of only 300 to 500 yards, and I had to run for my life, crossing the dry field so fast that I thought I could have achieved some national track records. Other times I hid in any safe place I could find. Once, running under fire from four or five French soldiers from less than 100 yards, I saw a thick bush in the dense fog. With all my strength, I plunged into it, leaving everything to fate. It was a little brook about four yards wide, covered with dense briars. Thorny branches ripped my pants and shirt and scratched my skin all over my body. Cold winter water made the scratches more painful. Mosquitoes bit my face, and leeches clung to my legs. An hour passed before the French soldiers withdrew. It took me only a second to plunge into the brook, but I was able to get out of it only after about five minutes with some more painful scratches on my legs and arms. Such confrontations with imminent death taught me that it is not easy to kill an escaping person and that it is not very difficult to be a guerrilla.

Although I had never had any intention of becoming a guerrilla, the few guerrillas in my village taught me how to use booby traps, spike pits, and antipersonnel mines. We had a dozen ways to fool the enemy with spikes and traps combined with mines, well camouflaged in places that the enemy could hardly expect. But we never placed them in the vicinity of the village.

WHITE TERROR

After two years of fighting against the guerrillas who hit and ran like ghosts, the French Army turned to more *terreur blanche* (white terror). A mine found in a village would cause all houses to be burned. If a French soldier was killed in a hamlet, the whole population could be subjected to ruthless retaliation.

One day, an antipersonnel mine in a small hamlet a mile and a half from my village went off and killed two African soldiers. After the soldiers had burned down all the houses and left, we teens and young men gathered at the killing field to offer help as we often did when a raid was over. In the large brick yard of a rich family, forty-eight heads of men, women, and children of all ages, including some newly born babies, had been placed in line on the house veranda. Strewn all over the yard and the garden were the forty-eight bodies without heads, all naked, some eviscerated or impaled by bayonet. Blood covered the entire brickyard. The odor of blood and the sight of goggling eyes struck great fear into my heart and I felt faint. Only the scores of hamlet people who had fled before the soldiers came survived the massacre. The survivors brought the corpses of their relatives back home to bury. They could recognize the heads, but many could hardly tell whose trunk was whose.

Once a guerrilla laid a wire-controlled mine on the road leading to a neighboring village. When the French soldiers reached the place, the guerrilla pulled the wire, but the mine was a dud, so he ran away with the remaining wire on a reel. He dropped the reel in the garden of an old man and ran to safety. The French Army soldiers found only the reel, but they tied the old man on his bed and cut his throat, catching his blood in an earthenware basin.

Beside killing and looting, raping women of all ages was common. Some victims were sixty years old, some twelve. A few of those were then killed. Therefore, when the French soldiers came, young women were the first to run away. Some smeared their bodies with anything dirty or stinking, even dung or human waste.

One early morning I went to the neighboring hamlet to trade rice for some chicken. A platoon of African soldiers surrounded the area, and we had no way to escape. They came searching the houses, not for Việt Minh but for women. They found us five teenagers in a house, kicked two of us, and then left us alone without saying a word. The only young woman who failed to escape was caught and brought to a house only ten yards from where we were sitting in fear. The black soldiers punched and kicked her until she collapsed. One tore up her clothes, and all the seven soldiers raped her in turn for about fifteen minutes. When they left, she lay unconscious on the floor, her abdomen swollen. As there was no healthy woman around, we five embarrassed teens had to carry her back home. Some old women took care of her. She was bedridden for weeks.

The scene shocked me greatly, and since then I have always taken it that rape is the worst crime in war. I said to myself that if I were an officer, I would blow out the brains of any soldier who committed rape.

In war, killing in a fight was not as gruesome as the way a man was put to death. The longer the war went on, the dirtier and bloodier it became. One summer afternoon, a few Vietnamese soldiers of a French unit conducted a patrol far to the east of my village. The Việt Minh guerrillas encircled them, and in half an hour they killed two and captured one. The captive had two gold teeth. A guerrilla stabbed him with a spear and tried to pull out his gold teeth. He failed to do it by hand, so he ran to a nearby home to get a pair of pliers, and a minute later he had what he wanted.

I had seen many corpses beheaded, dismembered, eviscerated, even scalped, but nothing more disgusting than the sight of that guerrilla holding the two gold teeth, his face beaming with savage contentment.

THE VIỆT MINH'S WATCHFUL EYES

Meanwhile, the Việt Minh government strengthened its security system. The Public Security Service employed many informers in every village, including many teens. They were to keep watch over some persons or families by order of the security agents and report everything those persons and families were doing: how much rice they cooked, what they ate, meat or fish or vegetables, what they were selling and buying.

My family was one of a dozen families in the village under such close watch. I knew that every night there were some spies who sneaked inside our fence and watched us cooking, eating, and talking. My uncle was summoned to the district security service almost every month or two to be interrogated about almost anything that the service could have suspected him of doing. He was usually detained for a day, sometimes three or four, but never more than a week.

My father's elder brother had no children, and he adopted me. Since I was very young, he took care of me much more than my parents did. The spirit of great family was rather strong in him. After my father was imprisoned, my uncle seemed to love me much more. He always worried about my safety and the dangers from both sides, the Việt Minh and the French.

One evening in May 1949, a group of five former members of the village notables council met to have a dog meat dinner. While they were drinking and talking, a Việt Minh squad surrounded the house and attacked. Four men escaped; one was killed. It was known later that the Việt Minh district Public Security got a report from an undercover informer saying that those men were discussing a scheme to form a village council that would serve the French authority and receive rifles to arm the village's anticommunist militia. I knew that it was a lie.

That was when the campaign of "destroying the French-supported village councils and eliminating the traitors" came to a peak. A tip provided to the Việt Minh security authorities reporting someone as a collaborator of the French military intelligence might have brought him or her serious trouble, even death. The Việt Minh guerrilla units were always eager to perform a feat of valor, and eliminating unarmed traitors was their easiest task.

CAUSE AND EFFECT

In July 1949, French Army soldiers caught me again when I got back to my village for a few days. A French corporal picked me out of a group of old men and women and told me to carry a heavy bag in which he had placed some antiques he had looted from some homes. I followed him with the bag.

Three other men were also taken captive. The clothes of one were stained with a few streaks of yellowish clay. The French corporal interrogated them with help from a Vietnamese soldier as interpreter. Although the man said the clay was from his work repairing the wall of his house, the French corporal decided that the man had laid an antipersonnel mine that morning on the road crossing the wet clay area about 500 yards from my village. My village was on sandy soil, not clay. He pushed the man against the brick wall at my small garden and raised his Tommy gun, slowly aimed it at the man just ten feet away, and pulled the trigger. After a short but loud bang, the man collapsed onto the row of onions in the garden. Blood spurted from his head. I was filled with compassion for the victim, who was my neighbor. But I was not shocked, as my emotions had become hardened after seeing so many killings.

When the corporal went off to search the other parts of my village, he told me to stay at the gate and wait. A few minutes later, a Vietnamese sergeant, an interpreter NCO of the French Army, came in from the main road. In 1949 a Vietnamese interpreter sergeant was someone to whom people had to pay their high respect, as I have described. Unlike the partisans, most of the interpreters were disciplined and treated the people kindly, as they were servicemen of the French regular army with official status.

He asked me my name and my parents' names. After I told him, he held me tight and said, "It happens to be you. I'm lucky to come here this very minute to save you. An order was given to shoot every young man and teenager suspected as Việt Minh in this village after a mine was detected. I can't intercede for your release, but I have another way."

When I asked him who he was, he told me his name. My father, who was his father's good friend, had brought up and sent his eldest brother to school for three years when his family fell into serious financial trouble in 1934. Owing to my father's help, his brother completed primary school and could get a good job in a rubber plantation in Cochinchina.

With a decent income, his brother brought him up and sent him to school. For many years they had not seen us, so he and I weren't able to recognize each other.

"I'm very grateful to your family," he said. "If your father hadn't helped my brother, I would be no more than an illiterate common laborer. So I will do everything I can to save you."

He told me to leave the bag at the gate and hide in a large straw stack in the garden corner. He covered me with a thick layer of straw and ordered a Vietnamese private to sit on it so that the French and other soldiers would not pay any special attention to the spot.

The soldier did exactly as he was told. For more than an hour, I lay there quietly. Although I felt itchy all over my body, I dared not scratch or budge. When a signal for troop withdrawal was given, the soldier reminded me to stay there until I was sure that all the troops were actually out of the village. "Sometimes they turn back after having pulled out for a few minutes," he said.

That morning, two men of the three taken captive were also shot after becoming drunk on the rice wine that the soldiers forced into their stomachs.

A little help my father had given his friend's son was thus repaid. What happened that morning of 1949 has greatly affected my behavior. I believe that if you help others, you will get help later in your life, possibly help much greater than what you have given.

MY BABY SISTER

In September my school moved ten miles farther south. It was too far for me to follow, so I had to drop out. I stayed home with my mother, my aunt, and my sisters in the home of a distant relative who lived three miles from my village.

When my mother was away visiting my father, I had to help my aunt take care of my twenty-month-old sister. My most difficult task was to feed her rice porridge or soup. Babies of her age are disinclined to eat. I spent a lot of time trying to have her consume a regular meal.

One day, I brought her back to my home village so my grandma could see her. At about 5 AM, the alert sounded and I hastily carried her piggyback to join the other villagers on our way south. With a piece of cloth, I tied her to my shoulders the way Chinese women carried their babies.

On the country road narrow and muddy, there were hundreds of people along with a dozen cows and water buffalo jostling against each other on their way to safety. I fell several times but still tried to keep my baby sister from getting wet. Under early daylight, I could see a long line of people and domestic animals moving on the road. My sister was awake, and she cried, asking me for food. Suddenly, machine guns from the village about 500 yards to our left barked deafeningly at us.

At that time, most kids my age could tell whether a gun was shooting at us or not by its reports. Under the rain of fearsome whizzing bullets, two men and a buffalo fell dead on the roadside. Three men and an old woman hobbling along the road were wounded, and their clothes were stained with blood. I put my entire mind to the road with a belief that I would be lucky not to get hit. We reached a small river. It was not more than twenty yards wide, but the stream was rather swift. The bridge had been destroyed in the 1947 scorched-earth campaign; only its middle concrete pier remained, on which two pairs of rails were laid for a footpath about two feet wide.

While the hundreds of people were slowly crossing the slippery makeshift bridge, mortar fire followed. A dozen shells whizzed over our heads and exploded somewhere in the villages and the fields around them. The crowd panicked. Crossing the river with my sister was my only concern. The swift river frightened me, as I couldn't swim. When I got scared, I saw a young woman with her baby in her arms fall into the river. In a few seconds, they were carried away, and no one tried to rescue them.

While I was sitting on a stump and weeping, I heard a voice calling my name. It was a friend of mine who was with his buffalo. He said he would help us cross the river. Without delay, I rose and followed him. He rode on top of the animal and I held fast to its tail. At his sign, the buffalo waded into the water and swam. I could hear my sister getting choked with water, but I was unable to do anything more than pray for our safety. In only half a minute, we got to the other side. My good friend quickly took my sister from my back, and without knowing any emergency technique or CPR he held her upside down by the legs and shook her violently. A lot of water poured out of her mouth, and she cried. "Thank God," I said to myself. "So she is not dead." Twenty-two years later at her wedding party, memories of this scene moved me again to tears when I told her husband to take care of her at least as I had done.

UNDER TWO YOKES

News about the victory of Mao Tse-tung in China came to my village and encouraged the Việt Minh and its supporters. Before 1950, the Việt Minh had been very careful when referring to the Chinese Communist Party; now they were overtly praising "the Red Orient" and "the great Chairman Mao Tse-tung." But Mao's victory offered very little hope to our peasants, who only wished for peace of any kind.

As the war began a sharp turn, French soldiers became more and more brutal to the innocent civilians, driving most of the fence-sitters over to the Việt Minh side. However, as the Việt Minh also became more heartless toward the people, their measures drove more Vietnamese to the French side as well.

In spring 1949, news of the birth of the nationalist government under King Bảo Đại reached our village. At first, the people had hope, but the new government appeared unable to change their miserable plight.

The French side utilized almost no psychological warfare. A small number of leaflets dropped from airplanes had far less impact than the Deuxième Bureau and the wicked French soldiers, who scared more people away from the newly established Bảo Đại government. From the rice fields north of my village, we could see the Bảo Đại nationalist government banner, three red stripes on yellow, streaming on the pinnacle of a Catholic church in the French-controlled area. But most people did not expect much from this government, which seemed to have very little power beside the French terrorizing army.

If the French or the Bảo Đại government had been able to afford anything similar to the RVN civic action program in the Việt Nam War (1955–75), and without so many war crimes done by French Army soldiers, the Việt Minh would have been wiped out long before 1954, despite the fact that the majority of the people hated the French. And the nationalist government was slowly drawing to its side a number of Vietnamese who could not live under the Việt Minh for one reason or another.

Meanwhile, the Việt Minh was trying hard to control the countryside. Its secret service successfully classified the population into categories and closely watched individuals whose loyalty was felt to be uncertain. More suspects were arrested, but there were fewer murders, as most dangerous persons had already been eliminated.

Still, life in the buffer zone became more and more difficult and risky. In every village, there were some people who worked as spies for either side. In my village, a man of thirty years old volunteered to play a double agent to protect the village from both French and Việt Minh terrorism. With help from some villagers, he regularly reported military intelligence information to the French by a "secret letter box," an intermediary, in the adjacent village. At the same time, he provided the Việt Minh intelligence service with what he collected in the French-controlled area. Sometimes the French paid him money for his information.

Among the teens, I was the only one he trusted. He told me about some of his tasks in exchange for my help in writing short messages for reports. I was sure that my village had some others who worked for both sides. Owing to those spies, my village was not terrorized in the second half of 1949.

On the bright side, those years of fear and hardship taught me many useful things. From mortar shelling, I was taught that there never were two shells or two bullets that hit the same place. So under artillery attacks I felt totally safe in a new shell crater. From the French habits, we learned several ways to escape their raids. When French soldiers came, we moved aside from their advancing route and waited. When they passed, we followed them. Staying behind the enemy was the best way to be safe, except for the case of a cunning French commander who left behind a squad to lie in wait for us.

Some of my cousins and I dug a secret underground hideout below the thick bamboo grove. It was about six by ten feet, and three feet under the surface. There were several small bamboo tubes leading to the surface for air, and a narrow opening leading to the nearby pond below water level. To get in, we had to be very careful not to trouble the water and mud for fear that the French soldiers would detect the hideout. They could do so by observing the bubbles and unusual pattern in the duckweed. I hid myself only once in that hideout along with another man for an hour or so. It was a horrible experience to stay in the stuffy narrow space in total darkness while the French soldiers sounded as if they were right over our heads.

In only one year, I learned most of the guerrilla techniques to survive and to fool the enemy. Once I followed a propaganda team to a place already cleared and protected by armed guerrillas where they used tin speaking trumpets to read newsletters and propaganda materials and to sing to the French Army soldiers in the fort. Team members used Vietnamese only, as none of them could speak French or an African language. The speaking trumpets were made into periscope shape so that the speakers could hide deep in foxholes while speaking. And as no light was allowed, they had to learn the texts by heart before departure.

The French Army soldiers in the fort often answered our call by opening fire with machine guns and sometimes mortars. Free to move in the wide field, we were not scared much by their firepower, and it became our game to tease them. The more they fired at us, the more we felt delighted as if winning a game.

The village guerrillas invented several ways to make the enemies nervous. One of the tricks was to twist dry straw into a big rope to be used as a slow fuse that would ignite gunpowder in a container in half an hour. The explosion or even just the flame of the fuse would draw a torrent of bullets from the French soldiers.

I was allowed by the guerrillas to join those activities only a few times without permission from my family, as none of my relatives would let me go on such risky adventures. It was on one of those nights that a guerrilla let me shoot a real cartridge for the first time. Each guerrilla squad was armed with only one or two old French rifles, each with about twenty or thirty cartridges, so it was a great favor they did me. I felt as great as when I received the beautiful toy car my father bought me during the Tét season when I was six years old. We were half a mile from the fort, but I aimed the rifle at the fort and pulled the trigger. A large dazzling flame burst out at the muzzle, and the rifle kicked my shoulder so hard that I thought I had broken my collarbone.

On the night of August 19, the fourth anniversary of the 1945 revolution, under the protection of darkness and a dense fog, a group of men in the village east of mine skillfully pitched a small bamboo arch of triumph, colorful with paper flags, flowers, and posters, only 500 yards from the fort. I could never do anything so bold. Another night, a team from a neighboring village went into a village in the French area for armed propaganda tasks. One of the boys in the team, a year older than I, was caught by French troops who lay waiting on the pathway. The others in the team weren't aware of his absence until they got home. The next morning the African soldiers hung his head on a long bamboo pole erected in the middle of the road. Rumors had it that he was very brave, refusing to say any names before he was tortured to death.

Because of these experiences, in the later years of the war, I was not surprised that guerrillas or sappers could sustain their enemy's dreadful firepower and conduct hit-and-run attacks or sniper fires so skillfully. In war, man and animal easily find the best way to survive. Under permanent pressure of war, well-seasoned guerrillas find the enemy's firepower less frightful. Harassing French Army soldiers was a risky but playful game. The guerrillas were afraid of bombs and artillery, but not so much as western people might have guessed. Most Vietnamese believe in destiny. They think that no one can avoid his fate. Life or death, good luck or bad, all are unavoidable. Like many others, in a dangerous situation, I always ask myself, if I am about to die, what do I have to be afraid of? If that belief doesn't give me any courage, at least it helps me maintain my composure in combat. The guerrillas were no different.

EIGHT

The Shaky Peace

YELLING AT THE EARLY MORNING SUN

In December 1949, the French Army launched a large-scale operation in the southern area of my province. While foot soldiers penetrated the Việt Minh sanctuary further toward the seashore, the French river force sent its boats patrolling the main rivers and attacked the Việt Minh from the rear.

My mother, my first cousin, and I decided to go back to our village. We hired a man to take us up the small river on his sampan. At a high price, he accepted. But when we reached the concrete bridge that had been left intact after the scorched-earth campaign, the French soldiers in a nearby hamlet opened fire.

The man pushed all three of us onto the muddy shore and dashed away with his sampan without waiting to get paid. We three slowly followed the river to cross the main road. In the twilight of a late winter afternoon we could see many mines tied to the piers of the bridge exposed by low tide. On the road, there was a mine crater about three feet in diameter and, nearby, blood and pieces of flesh, the biggest of which was a human leg clean cut at the knee. A battle between the Việt Minh and the French had ended only an hour earlier. The two opposing forces had withdrawn to take position in the two small villages away from the river.

We dared not cross below the bridge, as it was too risky with unseen mines and traps, so we decided to cross the road instead. We chose the portion of the road that we thought the safest near the bridge, worrying that it might have several live mines under the surface. Although the scene and the odor of blood frightened me, I had to take the lead. My mother knew nothing about traps and mines, nor did my cousin, who was two years older than I.

When it was dark enough to cover us from the French but we could still see the ground, we started to go on all fours, very slowly and carefully. I felt the ground to avoid the mines with all my senses. My mother and then my cousin followed, putting their feet and hands exactly at the places I had put mine. It took us almost five minutes to cross the road of about 40 feet and we all were sweating. In darkness we went on for three miles to reach the rice fields of my village. We slept in a vacant fisherman's hut because no one in the village would open the gate for us at night.

In the morning, we were told that the French Army soldiers had raided the area the day before and declared their permanent control over the large region previously in the Việt Minh's hands. All members of my family were safe and returned to our home to live together as before. I disliked the French, but a little peace under them was better than none, even one day or one month.

The next morning, a Vietnamese sergeant and fifteen soldiers in the Bảo Chính Đoàn, a paramilitary corps of the newly established Bảo Đại government, came from the district headquarters. On behalf of the district chief, the sergeant conducted a quick election of the village committee that would represent the village under the nationalist government and informed the villagers of some new rules and regulations.

After concluding the meeting, the sergeant and his troops dropped by my home to chat with my uncle. I was sitting in a corner of the room. At a point, I rose and asked him, "Am I permitted to yell loudly when I wake up early in the morning?"

He turned to me and said, "Why do you ask? Of course you are, if you don't bother your family. But why?"

I knew he wasn't able to understand what I was yearning for. The next morning, I woke up at about 6. I ran to the gate, opened it, and yelled at the early morning sunlight to the east.

Some farmers on their way to their paddies and peddlers to the market all looked at me as if I were insane. But this was the first time in almost two years that people could go out so early in the morning without fear of being shot.

In the first week of January 1950, after our village came under the nationalist government's control, my mother and I went to the city to visit with our relatives and friends. The city was then much better than it had been when I was there in 1948. Streets were crowded, and electric lights brightened the noisy avenues. The central market was busy.

My mother gave me some money. The first thing I did without a second thought was to buy five red apples, the only thing that I had been hungering for since 1942 when imported fruits stopped coming from France. I ate two and carefully wrapped the other three as gifts for my sisters and my eight-year-old cousin. Sitting comfortably on a bench in the city park under the morning sun of midwinter, I relished the sweet smell and taste of an apple, something that I had enjoyed only in my dreams.

* * *

In the first few months under French control, my village and others in the area recovered most of what we had had before the war. Religious ceremonies could be conducted even at night; children went to schools; country markets re-opened. Rice production increased, and goods from Hà Nội, Sài Gòn, and some foreign countries reappeared in stores.

My mother, however, was facing much more difficulty going into the Việt Minh area with dry food and medicine for my father. She faced much more danger as war escalated and French bombers attacked suspected areas more frequently.

My father suffered all kinds of maladies and became weaker. My mother and I lost the tiniest hope of seeing him back home, but we never spoke our thoughts. My uncle used to be more optimistic, but he also saw nothing better for his brother. Only my grandmother was always confident that her son would be home someday.

As for my aunt, the first thing she did in January 1950 was to buy a woolen coat for me and new clothes for my sisters. My uncle didn't wait long to send me to school.

Because the provincial government wasn't able to establish its education system down to district level and below, we had to rely on private schools. So I was sent to a teacher who was my father's friend and who lived in a village two miles north of our home. My uncle went with me. I brought my clothes and a few of my belongings, all stuffed into a leather bag my aunt had bought me. I would be boarding in the teacher's home and would be permitted to return home for a short visit on Sundays.

Before I left, I said good-bye to everybody in the family including my paternal great-uncle, who always saw in me the honor of the Nguyễn family. My grandmother held me tightly in her arms. Her eyes were full of tears. Although I was going to a place not far from my village, everybody knew that it was the first step that would take me farther and farther from home.

For a minute, my uncle, my aunt, my mother, and my grandmother kept silent. At last, my grandmother said to my uncle and the family: "You all say, as your father always did, that we'd better give the kids a good education than riches. So I'm not against sending this only grandson of mine to school. However, if I were to decide this matter by myself, I would let him stay home to do farmwork instead. Because of your medium degree of education, you [she pointed at my uncle] and your brother [my father] have already been in great trouble. Illiterate farmers have to work hard to make a living, but they live a peaceful life, and no one cares about them."

My uncle strongly protested, saying that it had been the greatest hope of my grandfather to have his grandson well educated. As for me, what my grandmother said that Sunday afternoon would never be forgotten.

Years later, I met some people who had fled North Việt Nam long after the 1955 Land Reform Campaign. They told us that the reform had resulted in the execution of tens of thousands of landlords and notables after summary trials. According to the communist theory, the Revolution had to get rid of the land-lord class, which had been the ruling class for thousands of years, in order to establish the proletarian dictatorship. Most members of the landlord class were educated. Naturally, they had been holding the leading jobs in a society where 80 percent of the population was illiterate.

Consequently, after the Land Reform, many rural families did not send their kids to school beyond the third grade and decided to let them do farming jobs instead. They had had the same opinion as my grandmother, especially when most communist leaders from village, district, and higher were third-grade dropouts. But contrary to my grandmother's guess, illiterate farmers were not "living in peace" and were suffering a lot of hardships under the communist regime.

So in Việt Nam, education brought calamity, not happiness, to a segment of its population.

THE NORMAL LIFE RETURNS

The large area south of Nam Định province enjoyed a rather peaceful life after the Việt Minh withdrew farther south to Thanh Hóa province, leaving it in French hands. However, the nationalist government was too weak to maintain peace. It had very limited power to protect its citizens from war crimes and mistreatment by French Army soldiers, especially in remote villages. The propaganda front was weak and inef-fective, probably because of the lack of money, faith, right cause, and motivation.

The war had been too horrible to everyone, so common people had some hope that the Bảo Đại government might do something to ease the disaster. I didn't see in Bảo Đại a hero or a good national leader or a rival to Hồ Chí Minh, but I still expected him to contribute something to the independence of Việt Nam. The Bảo Đại government formally wielded the ruling authority over the entire country, but in the North it actually controlled only the cities and some rural areas of the Red River Delta provinces. North Việt Nam, formerly Tonkin, one of the three autonomous regions of Việt Nam beside the Central and the South (Annam and Cochinchina), was under a governor.

In 1950, a Bảo Chính Đoàn platoon of forty soldiers and a sergeant replaced the French Army unit in the fort near my village, assuming control of the area. One or two battalions were assigned to each province to be in charge of security in the territory controlled by the nationalist government, occupying the small forts that dominated many villages.

The Bảo Chính Đoàn were armed with World War I weapons, mostly British .303, U.S. 1917 Remington rifles, Springfields, and .30 caliber Browning automatic rifles, commonly known as BARs. They had no machine guns or mortars and no communication equipment. However, they fought the Việt Minh with great courage and success.

Most members of the Bảo Chính Đoàn were volunteers. Unfortunately, they were not sufficiently trained and equipped to confront the Việt Minh, who were gaining more military assistance from Red China. People were well aware that to win the war, the nationalist side had to improve its appearance by promoting psychological warfare. But any attempt to win the people's hearts was nullified by the French Army soldiers' crimes and the way they treated people.

Meanwhile, the coastal region of my province came under control of the Catholic paramilitary force. Dozens of Catholic villages were armed to defend themselves. Their diocese of Bùi Chu became the area of responsibility of the anticommunist Catholic forces and later was officially reorganized into the new province of Bùi Chu, which began from two miles south of my village to the coastal villages of the Gulf of Tonkin.

In 1950, the area enjoyed full security. People could go anywhere at night, and market activities were normalized. Under the Catholic militias, Bùi Chu had an air of an independent country without French soldiers terrorizing innocent people. Both currencies of the French Indochinese Bank and of the Việt Minh Bank were officially accepted in Bùi Chu province.

Since the first days of the Việt Minh in power, many Catholics were overtly anticommunists. After the war broke out, the Catholics in Bùi Chu and Phát Diệm dioceses didn't officially collaborate with the French, although many Catholic villages were armed by the French as early as summer 1947. After Bảo Đại government was formed, following the agreement signed by King Bảo Đại and French president Vincent Auriol on March 8, 1949, Phát Diệm officially sided with the nationalist authority and Bùi Chu followed suit. Catholic militias fought the Việt Minh successfully and two infantry battalions in the new regular army were activated, mostly with Catholic recruits. The Eighteenth BVN (French for Battalion Vietnamien) in Phát Diệm and the Sixteenth BVN in Bùi Chu were once dreadful foes of the Việt Minh forces.

The Catholic militias behaved well toward the people. There might be killing by mistake, but no rape or looting. So they got support from the Catholics as well as the Buddhists to some extent. Until late 1951, life was peaceful.

THE CITY IN WARTIME

In 1950, my mother and my uncle decided that I should be sent to the city for better schooling. For the first several months, I lived with the family of my father's best friend, who had been assassinated by the Việt Minh in 1946.

After many years in war, we had lost most of our belongings. I spent the winter with inadequate warm clothes and was given very little money to spend for what a kid would need. For months, I didn't go to the movies because I couldn't afford the cheapest ticket.

I quickly succeeded at school and had many new friends. We had devoted teachers. Some of my teachers as well as many of my classmates were Việt Minh sympathizers.

The city was a strategic military stronghold of the French Army Southern Zone (south of North Việt Nam). It had many camps, an airfield, and large prison camps. Thousands of French Army troops—Frenchmen, Africans, and Vietnamese—from several corps (infantry, Legionnaire, armored, amphibious, airborne, engineer, artillery) roamed the streets day and night.

Nam Định had the greatest number of bars and nightclubs in Việt Nam. Brothels were legal and could be discerned by red lights hung above front doors. Bar girls wearing strong perfume and heavy makeup and flashy thin clothes occupied a few blocks of a downtown side street. Drunken soldiers made the streets noisier, and several times a week there was fighting between troops of different units, sometimes with guns. Bars and restaurants were covered with wire mesh to prevent hand grenade attacks by the Resistance secret cells in the city.

Although curfew was not imposed before 11 PM, young women were seldom seen on the streets after 7 PM. It was okay for teens like me to go out on the few main streets after dark, but not for my female classmates. Aside from these challenges, life in the city was fine. Once a month, my closest friends, who were sons of affluent families, would take me to a coffee shop for a glass of strong black coffee and cigarettes, usually the popular brands 999, 555, or Phillip Morris. We also enjoyed listening to music from a new hi-fi record player. That was the little happiness we could have in a country at war. Clad in cheap nylon raincoats, we loved to walk in a cold drizzle along bright sidewalks with close friends at night just to talk. It was such little pleasures that would beget many writers and poets of my age many years later in South Việt Nam and now in the United States, Canada, Australia, and Europe.

MY DADDY GONE

My mother came to the city to see me once every month to resupply me with rice and money to pay for my boarding and a little pocket money. One day, on the way to the ferry station, she stopped me and said, "I don't want to tell you the bad news, but I love you so much that I can't keep it my secret anymore."

I knew right away that what I had been anticipating had come true. She continued with a choked voice and quick words as if she were afraid she couldn't complete the sentence. "Your Daddy is no more. He died a week before I came to visit him last month."

She handed me his cigarette lighter, the only thing the prison returned to her after my father had passed away from exhaustion. She told me not to let my grandmother and other members of my family know the bad news. However, she could not keep it from them more than a few weeks, as she knew she wouldn't be able to lie to them forever. It was the greatest shock in my life.

I knew how much my mother suffered from the death of her husband. During the Vietnam War a decade later, I saw many soldiers of our side, Vietnamese and Americans, killed in action. Their bodies were to be brought back home. They always made me think of my mother and other women like her on both sides whose sons and husbands died in battle and in jail but who were not able to view the bodies even once before they were buried. Those women suffered a great deal from war.

OUR POOR NEIGHBORS

In summer, my mother and my two sisters moved to the city and we rented a tiny ten by twenty foot room, wide enough to put a bed for my mother and the two sisters, my folding cot, and my small table with a chair. I often came back to see my grandmother, and once I got into trouble with the African soldiers, as I related in the first chapter of these memoirs. After that, I only returned to see her in daylight and left before 3 PM to get to the city before 6 PM, half an hour before the ferry boat stopped operating.

My nine-year-old sister went to a girls school. Sometimes during the month, French Army units whose rear bases were not nearby came to the city after operations to rest. They often displaced the students to bivouac in the school for two or three days or even a week.

Every morning, my mother went to the open market to sell fruits and vegetables she had procured the previous afternoon at low prices. She often earned enough money to provide us with rice, boiled vegetables, and a little meat or fish. Once a month, she went back to our village and got some rice, which helped us for many days, in addition to the money she could earn from her vegetable stall. Sometimes she even traveled as far as to Hà Nội, fifty miles away, to do some trading.

One day, she wasn't able to get back because of a heavy battle that interfered with civilian transportation on Highway 1 from Hà Nội to Nam Định for three days. My sisters and I ran out of rice after the second day. We were so hungry that my youngest sister, who was four, cried all day long. My older sister was old enough to understand our problem. She didn't cry, but she looked miserable. At lunch and dinner times, my nose was so keen that I could smell a pot of rice being cooked in a home twenty yards away. I decided not to ask for any help from our neighbors, although they were friendly. I thought that doing so was shameful.

On the fourth day my mother came back. That evening I ate until my stomach was full and went to bed early. I hadn't done my homework, and the teacher gave me four hours of detention on Sunday. I didn't tell him the story, although I knew for sure that he would have forgiven me if I had.

The place we were living was a poor neighborhood, a slum area in every way much worse than what I learned later in books describing the workers' quarters of the nineteenth-century Marseille, London, or New York. Before that, I had been familiar only with the life of poor farmers. After three years of war, my family became one of the city workers and shared with them the poverty and hardships of war. People in my new neighborhood were mostly workers in the large textile mill in the city. The others were cyclo drivers, peddlers, carpenters, masons, and petty traders, including balloon and ice cream vendors. However, there were no prostitutes, hooligans, or thieves.

The people in my neighborhood were mostly honest and friendly. Poverty bound the poor together. Sometimes they were indelicate and unrefined, but they became the best friends we have ever had. I learned many good lessons from them.

WHEN PRISON WAS TAKEN FOR A SAFE HAVEN

The city of Nam Định had two large prisoner camps controlled by the French military. Only a small part of each camp was reserved for prisoners captured on the battlefield. The rest was for healthy male civilians apprehended in operations and brought to the camps as war labor. Many were only my age, fourteen years old.

Civilian prisoners had to do manual labor to support the troops in military operations such as carrying food and ammunition or building forts and bunkers and cleaning barracks. Sometimes they were killed or wounded in operations. Their regular tasks at the camps were hard, but not as toilsome as farmwork. They were well fed with rice galore and raw or dried fish and meat. The meals were in no way luxurious but much better than scanty bowls of rice in their villages. Most of them were burly and much healthier than at home.

The war laborers who stayed there the longest would be released when new prisoners were brought in from operations to replace them, usually after one year. They were given release certificates so that the French Army would not capture them again. Once a week on Sunday, their relatives were permitted fifteen-minute visits. Some of the prisoners were from my village, so I often visited them when their relatives asked me to help them in handing out little gifts. Many times I heard parents saying to sons something like this: "Sonny, they said you'll be released in three months, so try your best to stay here. I'll pay the bribe if it is not too much. Try not to be sent back home. Our village is between hammer and anvil; you won't be safe from either side." So I understood why very few prisoners here tried to escape. Only years later did I realize that the French treated their prisoners not as brutally as the Vietnamese did to their compatriots. It made me sad to see our people suffering so much from war that prison became a little paradise to them. Back at their villages they might be killed or wounded, and they would certainly be hungry unless they volunteered for the Việt Minh or the nationalist army or French combat units. Any place to avoid early death was alright.

One day, a large-scale operation named "Mandarin" searching for Việt Minh units was conducted in Thái Bình, the most densely populated province in Việt Nam (more than 1,500 persons in a square kilometer). Thái Bình was also the granary of North Việt Nam. Unable to do any quick screening on the spot to separate Việt Minh suspects from common peasants, the French headquarters ordered a roundup of all villagers from newborn babies to octogenarians with one foot in the grave. Several thousand people were transported to Nam Định by trucks and dumped onto the large tarmac yard of a prison camp. Many died on the trucks because of dehydration, as no water was supplied even though the temperature was over 90 degrees Fahrenheit. On the tarmac yard, heated by the scorching sun, more old men and children died.

A quick relief program was set up. Contributions in cash and kind were given in an hour. Responding to the call of some charity groups, my classmates and I took part in the emergency actions to help the victims, but we were not allowed to enter the camp.

When bread was delivered, we made sandwiches stuffed with meat, ham, canned fish, sausage, or anything people brought to us, tied them with rubber bands, and threw them to the crowd. At the same time, many car-washing stations brought in their powerful pumps to spray water over the victims and conic hats were thrown to them. With the conic hats they collected water to drink.

The work continued from noon until curfew at 9 PM, and yet scores of prisoners died. Although I had seen much death in war, the scene was still a great shock to me.

THE NEW PHASE

While attending school, I still had contact with some friends serving the Việt Minh in my village area. Although I hated the communist leaders, I still sympathized with the Resistance against the French occupation. In the ranks of Việt Minh units and agencies, there were so many brilliant and respectable people who stayed to serve the Resistance, despite having to suffer hardship and privation.

Many other civil servants, former employees of the colonial government, left for cities where they could find jobs in the nationalist government. A reliable nationalist source asserted that Hồ Chí Minh himself gave a directive to his subordinates that those civil servants should be allowed to go wherever they wanted. Hồ contended that those people were a burden to his government, and their joining the French side would cause little harm to the Việt Minh. I knew he was right only when I was older.

Meanwhile, the Việt Minh became more active in 1951. After Mao Tse-tung took complete control over mainland China, the Việt Minh got his direct and overt support, and the political atmosphere in the Việt Minh areas changed significantly. Việt Minh cadres returned to my village in daytime to reorganize the party system and reactivate guerrilla cells. There were no clashes with the French or nationalist forces, but behind the bamboo fences, the Việt Minh actually controlled the population. I could see how things were going every time I went back to my village for a short visit.

The Vietnam Communist Party under the name of Indochina Communist Party, which had declared its dissolution before 1945, then officially reappeared with the title Lao Động Party (Workers' Party). Communist teachings were given overtly; Mao and Stalin were worshipped beside Hồ Chí Minh as if they were omnipotent. New terms, such as the "Uncle and the Party," were heard from every Việt Minh cadre and soldier and quickly became a kind of political prayer. Most speeches at villagers' meetings began with "Thanks to our Uncle and the Party." It irked me to read or hear that phrase. It was against what I learned at school and from my family. It eroded the remaining sympathy I had for the Việt Minh.

TURNING THE TIDE

It was well known to us high school students that many Việt Minh units were sent to China for training and to be armed with better weapons. Some young men in my village who joined the groups going to China to transport military supplies told me many stories of their trips. Troops were newly equipped with recoilless rifles and bazookas, which greatly assisted in attacks on bunkers and fortified positions and against light tanks and obsolete armored personnel carriers, the half-tracks.

A Việt Minh offensive campaign was conducted along the Đáy River south of Nam Định and along the defensive line north of Hà Nội. Cities in the North were shaken; many rich families moved to Sài Gòn. Then General Jean de Lattre de Tassigny appeared on the scene. I read reports about him in newspapers at the city Public Information Office almost every day. De Lattre ordered heavy bombardments during fierce battles even at objectives where soldiers of both sides were engaging in close combat. Thus air firepower killed many of his troops, but the tactic also caused heavy losses to the Việt Minh units. Soldiers from my village came back and told me how dreadful the battles had been.

The Việt Minh forces everywhere became much more aggressive. Many bold attacks were launched at hard-to-reach objectives.

Since 1950, French local military authorities had formed several commando units, most at company size. The soldiers of those units were Vietnamese volunteers who served with auxiliary status just like the partisans in previous years. They signed in, were briefly trained, were given weapons, got paid, and walked out any time they felt like doing so. They fought well, but they were often brutal to civilians and POWs.

The most renowned unit was the Black Tiger Company in Nam Định, activated in 1950. Most of the company soldiers were former Việt Minh troops born in Nghệ An and Thanh Hóa provinces who were captured by the French Army. They were recruited from prison camps to serve the company as mercenaries and were paid on a monthly basis. The company's NCOs were Vietnamese from the French Army, and a French lieutenant known for his courage was appointed company commander. The company conducted many successful commando raids deep into the Việt Minh areas. Black Tiger troops disguised themselves as Việt Minh regulars to sneak into selected objectives, using Việt Minh tactics to get rid of their enemy and then withdrawing quickly before the Việt Minh could react. Because all of the soldiers had been Việt Minh soldiers, their disguise was usually a great success.

The company commander was Roger Vandenberghe, twenty-three years old in 1950, who had been directly commissioned to lieutenant from sergeant after a famous battle in Ninh Bình province in 1950. He was then a favorite of many French top commanders and became a very haughty officer.

His soldiers went into restaurants, bars, and cinemas with rifles and submachine guns or even .30 machine guns, and often won in fighting against troops from other units, owing to their boldness and brutality. One night, a mutiny occurred. The revolting soldiers broke into the company commander's room and riddled him and his pretty mistress with bullets before the couple knew what was happening. The company barracks was on the outskirts of the city, not far from the zone headquarters, but the mutiny was so quick that nothing could be done before the mutineers withdrew to the Resistance zone, leaving only some dead soldiers who refused to join them.

After the event, curfew began at 9 PM. Business in the city was greatly affected, the streets were deserted too early at night, but students seemed to achieve more in school than their fellows in Hà Nội.

THE MASS CHANGING SIDE

Because the communists overtly controlled the Resistance, many people changed sides. In 1951, I did not need to be a statistician to see that the number of people who left the Resistance zone increased at a very high rate. Many had long been active anticolonialist activists, skilled specialists, and military cadres. The nationalist bloc took on a better appearance with more respectable figures joining its side.

The population of the major cities of North Việt Nam grew much faster than in the previous two years. More shops opened, as well as more private schools. The city of Nam Định recovered some of its prewar aspects, except for the ugly appearance resulting from the war. Military track vehicles and tanks cracked the main roads. In winter, streets were muddy, and in summer, winds blew dust into every house. Most homes destroyed in the scorched-earth campaign in 1947 were not rebuilt. Buildings of the water supply company were still large heaps of rubble, so people had to live on river water from man-drawn carts.

Once my mother and I went to Hà Nội, the former capital of the French Indochinese colonies, to see some acquaintances for information about her mother, brothers, and sisters, with whom we had lost contact in 1946. I knew very little about the relatives on her side.

Hà Nội was still colorful and peaceful as ever because the scorched-earth campaign had not been actively implemented there. Many rich people seemed to be unaware of the war going on a dozen miles away. Streets were as beautiful as before the war with restaurants, theaters, nightclubs, bars, and dance halls flourishing. Drunken soldiers fighting and assaulting women were seldom reported. There was no curfew, and it felt great to go out at night. Việt Minh attacks near its outskirts were almost impossible. But there were a lot of secret pro–Việt Minh cells, a fact that everyone knew.

I had come back to the capital after almost five years and felt at a loss. The war had thrown me out of the middle class and turned me into another kind of boy: a skeptical, sarcastic, and somewhat gloomy teenager.

THE NATIONALIST GOVERNMENT

Like anyone else, my school days were the best time of my life, full of memories and unforgettable fancies. Most of my classmates were older than the age supposed for the grades because of delay by war. A great number of us were interested in politics. At breaks, we often talked about world events, and before long we found ourselves on opposite sides.

My class consisted of twenty-nine boys and sixteen girls. Four of us were sons and brothers of ranking Việt Minh officers and officials; six were children of nationalist public servants of different ranks; five were from families who suffered from Việt Minh's atrocities one way or another. About ten of my classmates were pro-Việt Minh, openly or not, and about twelve (including me) opposed the Việt Minh and French colonization. The remaining students, including the girls, were fence-sitters.

It was apparent that most children of rich families in the city didn't care much about anything besides enjoying their easy lives, except for some who were pro–Việt Minh. On the other hand, many from the countryside bitterly hated both the French and the Việt Minh. The two sides in my class and probably in every other class at that time had something in common: we all were supporting the struggle for a better life for the poor and to build a prosperous and independent Việt Nam after driving the French aggressors out of the country. Although we knew we had different points of view—the politics of teenagers—we never had any quarrels.

On the propaganda front, the nationalist government under King Bảo Đại was nothing more than an underdog. Bảo Đại himself, in the fourteen-year-old boy's eye, was in no way Hồ Chí Minh's equal. Many people considered the members of his government and his army officer corps to be French collaborators. Only a few were renowned patriots. Most civil servants had been employees of the pre-1945 colonialist administration and were not strongly anticommunist patriots. They did good work in administrative affairs but did little to help in politics. Corruption, a remnant of the colonial era, continued to undermine the credibility of the regime. There were many civil servants who were members of some nationalist parties, but they could do very little in the administration without independent authority.

The government was just a noncommunist administration and nothing more. Beside the cabinet, there was neither a legislative body nor a supreme court. It didn't advocate any ideology or call for any specific policy attractive enough to us young people to serve our country.

Many nationalist army officers I knew had joined the French colonial army before 1945; others volunteered for French officer candidate schools after 1946. They were mostly good gentlemen, but I only saw a few of them as patriots. Many took bribes. Some even were famous torturers in the French Deuxième Bureau. I had a feeling that many were against the Việt Minh not because of any ideology but because the Việt Minh treated them badly. Besides, they saw the Việt Minh as rebels fighting against the formal and legitimate authority, even though that authority was the French colonialists.

Even so, a significant number of the officers were genuine patriots who fought the communists as if in a crusade, but none could make great changes in the general makeup of the nationalist army. Because of a personnel shortage, the army assimilated a small number of members of the French colonial army (the Régiments Infanterie Colonial, Régiment Artillerie Colonial, and others) and even employed some French officers to command its units. It had to apply the French-styled organization, training, and administrative management. However, as more and more Vietnamese officers graduated, they began to some extent to contribute to incorporating Vietnamese specialties into the nationalist army.

The military academy in Đà Lạt and the officer candidate schools in Hà Nội, Huê, and Sài Gòn, training Vietnamese officers for the nationalist army, began introducing new individuals into the anticommunist front. The proportion of true patriots in the nationalist administration and the army began to grow—but not quickly enough.

In late 1951, the nationalist government issued a decree drafting young men into the army. Students above eighteen years old who had graduated ninth grade were called to the reserve officers school in Nam Định, where they were trained for nine months and graduated as second lieutenants of the Army of the State of Việt Nam. Draftees with less education were trained in four NCO training centers and four boot camps in each of the four military regions.[1] They brought a new face to the NCO corps. Until 1952, the reserve officers school was located at one end of my city. Many of the cadets were friends of my cousin, some four to eight years older than me. They represented a young generation that had grown up in war and lived in the areas under French control. Most of them had an equal dislike for the French and the Việt Minh.

MUSIC AND WAR

The year 1951 saw a lot of changes on both sides of the conflict. One of them was in music. As I have said, songs played a significant role in the wars. Such a change was one of the landmark events in the history but rarely noticed by researchers' and writers' works on the wars in Việt Nam.

On the anti-French front since 1945, patriotic songs, poems, plays, and novels were written to support the fighting for independence, promoting contribution to the war, and even urging prompt implementation of government policies. By 1951, patriotic songs composed in the Việt Minh area were written with only anti-French lyrics. In the French-controlled areas, we were not allowed to sing them in public, but we were free to sing them with modified or rewritten lyrics.

Sometime in 1951, the Việt Minh banned many of the love and patriotic songs we liked to sing because they were not compatible with the new Lao Động Party's policy concerning cultural activities. The ban aimed specifically at music with themes of love and patriotism composed before 1951 not asserting support for the party's cause. The banned songs were by different composers, including the famous Phạm Duy, who left the Việt Minh to return to Hà Nội in 1951, and Văn Cao, author of the communist national anthem.[2] Ever since 1951 in the Việt Minh areas, the communist cultural branch introduced many new songs to praise Stalin, Mao Tse-tung, Hồ Chí Minh, the Communist Party, and the "noble" objectives of the party. Most of these new pieces sounded Chinese. Many were set to Chinese tunes.

In general, the new cultural policy of the Communist Party upset the spirit of the Resistance that encouraged people to support the fight against the French. Literary works smacked of Chinese communist teachings. Besides songs, the Red Chinese group dances found their place in cultural presentations and weekly get-togethers of young men and women in villages in the Việt Minh areas. It could be said that in 1951–52, a great many cultural and literary works of the Việt Minh side began to imitate Chinese communist style to an unacceptable extent. That was why many Vietnamese believed that Hồ Chí Minh and his assistants were true Sinophiles. Hồ was no more a devoted patriot than a faithful communist as some of his admirers claimed.

Besides cultural reform, the Việt Minh launched a remarkable change in education. The new ten-year education system replaced the twelve-year system, which had been in place since the colonial era and was still maintained in the nationalist-controlled regions.[3]

CATHOLIC MILITIAS' FAILURE

The area from my district to the coastal region of Bùi Chu diocese had enjoyed peace since winter 1949. However, peace didn't last long after renewed attacks by the Việt Minh. They also launched a skillful propaganda campaign against the villages' militiamen, who were mostly Catholics. As in any war, once they got their hands on guns, some men seemed drawn to excesses of power, and abuses were thus committed. A Catholic militiaman killing another Catholic civilian was a pure homicide, but a Catholic militiaman killing a Buddhist was labeled "religious oppression" by the Việt Minh. There were also reports of Buddhist pagodas burned, statues broken, and sacred objects looted and blasphemed by some militiamen. Such incidents were rare and might have happened in any country in any situation. However, exaggerated by the Việt Minh propaganda, the events stirred resentment among non-Catholics. Though calling for "great solidarity," it was the Việt Minh that covertly fostered a feud between Catholic and non-Catholic people.

At the same time, Việt Minh secret agents slipped back into the area after more than a year since they had withdrawn to their security zone in Thanh Hóa province. In many villages, guerrilla units were reorganized to conduct skirmishes and sniper fire against Catholic militiamen.

Meanwhile, as far as I could understand the situation with my little knowledge of military affairs, the militias had very little training and were commanded ineptly. The priests gained their highest obedience, but clergymen were not supposed to be good military commanders. Under enemy high pressure, the militia units in Bùi Chu diocese had to reduce their territorial control, and they gradually lost their ground to the Việt Minh. At last, most militias could only control their villages in daylight. At night, militiamen gathered in the church or chapel fortified with earthen or sandbag walls and bunkers where they staged the defense.

After a year, the situation deteriorated quickly. French Army units were sent to the diocese areas to control growing Việt Minh activity. There were many better fortified villages built with thick bamboo quick hedges, thousands of blind ditches and foxholes, and numerous bunkers, trenches, and systems of tunnels to be used for safe withdrawal from the villages. But there was no hope of reestablishing the favorable situation. Bùi Chu soon became the fiercest battleground in all of Indochina, according to national newspapers.

NINE

Bloodier Battles

THE SHORT PEACE ENDS

In 1952, after only two years under the nationalist government, the peaceful period in my village area came to an end when the Việt Minh took control. I was still able to come back to visit my grandma and my uncle during the daytime when there was no military operation, and the Việt Minh guerrillas were still friendly to me.

The Việt Minh returned to the region with more weapons, especially new antitank recoilless rifles and bazookas. Ferro-concrete bunkers were no longer safe shelters for soldiers in forts and barracks. Armored cars and tanks lost their superiority. Việt Minh soldiers in my home district were equipped with more weapons from China. In addition, specialists of all classes, most of them from the bourgeoisie, helped the Resistance government produce materials that had previously been imported, greatly improving the war effort of the Resistance. One such effort was the local production of low-grade TNT to supply the Việt Minh with small mortar shells (40 mm), antitank and antipersonnel mines, hand grenades, and explosive packets.

In the countryside not under French military protection, the Việt Minh introduced more harsh measures to control the peasants. The patriotic atmosphere of 1947–48 now blended with the darker side of communism. More new propaganda schemes were devised to idolize Hồ Chí Minh and his Workers' Party with a language too cheap for my ears. Agricultural taxes were raised, much higher for those who owned half an acre and more. Tax assessment was carried out mainly to do harm to rich farmers and landlords. Security agents were increasingly snooping around at night to find out how much targeted families spent and what they ate.

My mother had to pay the Việt Minh tax even though she was not living in the village anymore, while my two sisters and I weren't allowed to be claimed for a reduction in her taxes. In the garden of our home in the village, we had twenty betel nut trees. For years since the war broke out, we hadn't taken care of them, so they yielded little fruit. The five grapefruit trees, eight jackfruit trees, and five custard apple trees were in the same situation. But the tax assessor from the Việt Minh district tax agency estimated the production five times higher than the best trees could ever yield. My uncle had to sell something else to pay the tax on the imaginary fruit production.

Farmers who failed to pay taxes would be severely punished. A handful of Việt Minh cadres in a village held supremacy over the population and had become the most proficient tax collectors. The peasants quickly noted that taxes were much higher and more brutal than under the colonialist regime.

The Việt Minh security service proved to be similarly adroit. Political indiscretion seldom escaped the agents' notice. Spies and many suspects were more harshly treated. A barber was chopped up by machete with his death sentence written on a piece of paper pinned to his hat. He was charged as a traitor for giving information to a nationalist soldier who had been an old friend of his when both had been barbers at the same shop. His other close friends asserted that he had nothing to do with such reckless behavior. The two old friends ran into each other in a market and just said hello. But that was enough to bring him a violent death only a few days later.

Death squads executed many wicked village chiefs who served the French too faithfully and treated the people heartlessly. One in a village two miles from mine was notorious for killing Việt Minh cadres. He stayed home during the day and slept in the French fort after 5 PM, only coming back the next morning at 8 AM. The Việt Minh death squad failed to reach him several times.

One night, members of a death squad sneaked into a corner of his garden and hid in a thick bamboo grove. They dug a small underground hiding space, concealed by a bush, and left a squad member behind to wait. At noon the next day when most people were taking siesta, the death squad member with a pistol approached his victim, who was sleeping on a hammock. He kidnapped him and hid him in the secret underground. Even the chief's two bodyguards weren't aware he was missing until late afternoon.

That night, he was brought out of the village as quietly as when he was abducted. He was then beheaded, eviscerated, and dismembered at a place under a big tree not far from his village. A paper sheet stating his crimes was pasted on the tree close by.

Not only wicked lords but also many village chiefs who had been compelled by the local nationalist government to take the job and had done nothing willingly harmful to the Việt Minh were also accused of imaginary crimes and assassinated. One of the cadres in my village told me that the "anti-traitors campaign would eliminate every village chief until no one dared to take the job."

The Việt Minh gained on the propaganda front when they got rid of the wicked lords. But when more innocent persons were done away with, they turned more people against them. Such acts did, however, frighten many people away from collaborating with the French or the nationalist government. Blood always calls for more blood, and it was one of the incitements for the expansion of the war after 1954.

South of my village, the Việt Minh forces overran a large number of Catholic self-defense villages. Only villages near cities or forts survived these attacks. A half dozen newly organized nationalist units were sent to the area. But the Việt Minh could still do what I thought was their highest priority: control rice sources to supply other areas and to store for future campaigns.

A new fort seven miles south of my village had been besieged since late 1951. For six months, the French soldiers were trapped in their underground defenses. The only way to resupply food, ammunition, and even water was by parachute. The Việt Minh force made several attempts to destroy the fort, but all failed because the underground defense system was very effective against bazookas and the like. It had a surrounding ditch about thirty feet wide and ten feet deep with steep banks, mines, and underwater spikes that frustrated every attempt to capture it. After six months, the French Army unit in the fort quietly withdrew. The Việt Minh pursued, but only captured the commander.

BLOOD CALLS TO BLOOD

The war drove more young men to take sides. Some in my village joined the Việt Minh regulars, and others volunteered for the French Union units or the nationalist army battalions. As far as I could find out, the first thing that impelled most of them to become soldiers was not ideology or patriotism. The countryside in war was full of danger from both sides. Just earning a living had become more and more difficult. The young men decided that they would rather be soldiers than stay at home to suffer from war and hunger. Many of them picked up arms primarily because they thought they could lead a better life as a soldier. If they had any loftier reason, it would come to them later, if at all.

A number of men joined the French or the Việt Minh side to take revenge on individuals who had killed their parents or relatives. A good example was a Vietnamese sergeant of the French Army unit, Trần Văn Loan. (His actual rank was unknown, but people called him sergeant.) He was a brilliant high school student in Hà Nội while his only elder brother stayed home in a rural area. His brother had raised him since their parents had died many years before and now supported him at school. One day a Việt Minh death squad assassinated the brother as a suspected spy, something that his villagers knew he was not. After the burial of his brother, Loan enlisted in a French "partisan" unit and asked to be assigned to the fort a mile from his native village. Although his formal education could secure him an officer's position in the French Army after training, he only wanted to be able to fight the Việt Minh as soon as possible, even as a private. Of course, the French were pleased with him, and he was assigned to serve at Fort Núi Gôi, a company-sized stronghold built on a hill, seven miles southwest of Nam Định City.

One day, a few months after his arrival at the fort, he armed himself with a pistol, a submachine gun, a lot of ammunition, and grenades. Without telling anyone, he went into a village a few miles from the fort looking for the guerrillas who had butchered his brother. The French force would never enter that village with less than a platoon. Surprisingly, none of the guerrillas noticed his coming. In less than fifteen minutes, he used up all his ammunition, killing many surprised guerrillas—maybe a dozen—and left unscathed, with only a few pistol cartridges set aside for committing suicide if he were captured.

After that, he became a bloodthirsty demon. If he captured an enemy who was a Communist Party member, he would cut his or her arm to get a glass of blood to drink; then he left the victim to bleed out. My friends in the area said they could not forget his eyes, which were always bloodshot. He killed many communists that way until the French commander decided to get rid of him. In a fake ambush, the French killed him, or at least that was what people speculated had happened.

Except for the case of the nationalist army and administrative guards who had some ideological motivation, most of the French Union units' will to fight was very low. No political indoctrination taught them why they had to fight, and little discipline on behavior toward the people was enforced. It should be noted that most of the soldiers from Africa were fighting the war reluctantly. They were brutal to civilians, raping women and even young boys, but they seemed to have very low morale. Sometimes I saw them hiding deep in foxholes when facing the Resistance forces and firing carelessly with their heads down.

The French soldiers themselves were better, and the Legionnaires fought bravely, but they, too, were brutal to both their enemy and civilians. Some of the nationalist battalions known in French as Bataillion Vietnamien proved to be more efficient combat units that caused heavy losses to the Việt Minh regulars. But their morale was not high enough to neutralize the effects of the enemy's propaganda. However, they were not committing serious crimes during operations.

HOW TO KNOCK OUT A BURLY FRENCH SOLDIER

On April 30, 1952, the French Legionnaires celebrated their anniversary of Cameron, the heroic battle fought by Legionnaires in 1863. Those whitecap soldiers were cut loose in my city. Three of them entered a barbershop on my street and used a hatchet to cleave the skull of the barber while he was giving a haircut to a customer, who was then killed with the same hatchet. The three Legionnaires took money they found in the barber's till, which was not a great sum.

From early in the morning until late in the afternoon, hundreds of Legionnaires raided the city, looting shops and houses. More civilians were killed, but we heard of no rapes. Every door was closed and bolted. Many people ran into the countryside near the city. French military police patrols that had been cruising the streets day and night completely disappeared from sight.

At around 5 PM, hundreds of Vietnamese soldiers from French Union and Nationalist Vietnamese units garrisoned in the city gathered in the market area on whose instructions no one knew. About half an hour later, two Legionnaires attacked a Vietnamese policeman guarding the police department and destroyed some office equipment and a window. Like a spark igniting a fire, the event started violence against the Legionnaires. Vietnamese soldiers at the police department beat one Legionnaire to death, whereas many others attacked them on the streets.

My four classmates and I followed the Vietnamese troops. At first we just watched, but later we joined the fight. We stopped a Legionnaire who was trying to get back to his barracks along with many others on a side street. The strongest Vietnamese soldiers flew at him and hit him with stick and rocks. Although he was rather burly—no less than six feet and 180 pounds—he could not stand for half a minute. As he collapsed, a torrent of rocks and other objects found at hand fell on him. I felt furious when an old woman told me that the Legionnaire had broken a shop window to loot and hurt the owner badly. So I snatched a club from one of the men and hit the Legionnaire on his chest and legs, aiming at the parts that were the most painful. He was unable to resist; his hands covered his bloody face. Of course, I could hit him only because he was drunk and had already suffered a savage beating.

Images of the hundreds of war crimes committed by French soldiers I had witnessed came to my mind, clear and provocative. I didn't feel anything immoral in my act or any compassion for the man lying there unconscious and soaked in blood. I just drained my animosity on him, beating him with all my strength while people around me were doing the same.

When a French Army ambulance arrived at the scene, the poor man was nothing more than a red rag. I thought he was dead. A few French stretcher bearers carried him into the ambulance and drove away without a word.

Everywhere in the town, scores of Legionnaires were beaten, and some died. Only when the situation became serious did the French military police appear in their patrol cars to evacuate the injured Legionnaires.

From then on, some of my classmates and I often joined the Vietnamese soldiers we knew to conduct hit-and-run attacks aimed at French soldiers, especially the Legionnaires and the Africans. We selected ones that were dead drunk on whom to vent our fury. How could my classmates and I, no more than five feet three inches tall and around 100 pounds, have beaten them if they had not been under the influence? We lured them into dark streets by playing pimps and promising to bring them to nice prostitutes. Many others of our group laid in wait and hit them without a bit of compassion.

The best time for us to do so was on festive occasions such as Christmas, New Year's Day, Tét, or July 14 (Bastille Day) when many soldiers were drinking like fish. Once we stopped a tall French soldier staggering on a dark corner. When we flew at him, we quickly realized that he was not drunk. In a second, I found myself at the other end of the block, running for dear life and having no time to think where my friends were. Years later, I still felt ashamed of having acted so cowardly.

Although I hated the French Legionnaires, one of them was a good friend and helped me with my language study. In March 1951, the French Army sergeant whom my father had fed and helped to continue his primary education (mentioned in the first chapter) invited my family to move into a home next to his so he could take better care of me and my sisters. We moved into a better house. Across the street was the barracks of a Legionnaire unit. After a few weeks, I noticed a Legionnaire corporal who was very friendly to us boys and girls in the neighborhood. Before long the corporal and I became friends. He told me that his mother was British and his father was German. He had been born in England and lived there until he was eighteen, when he and his family moved to Germany before the start of World War II. He later became a German officer. He was captured before the war ended, and his parents died in Germany during an air raid.

After the war, he joined the Legionnaire corps and was sent to Việt Nam in 1950. He laughed a lot when I read my English lessons. My pronunciation was mostly incorrect, neither British nor American, he said. During my time in high school, our teachers rarely met any native English speakers.

So he began teaching me English. Though he was not a professional teacher, he did help me much. On my birthday, he gave me a pocket dictionary and began talking to me only in English while encouraging me to do the same. My pronunciation improved a lot, but my grades in the English class dropped. My English teacher once scolded me for "incorrect" pronunciation—the way my Legionnaire friend had taught me.

Six months later he was killed in an outpost up north in the Tu Vũ battle (Hòa Bình Province, west of Hà Nội). I only got the news a month later. I remain thankful to him for initiating me into a language that opened my eyes to the world and led me to some successes in later years.

IDEOLOGICAL DIFFERENCES GROW

As the war went on, my classmates were splitting into sharper divisions on ideological matters. We used to discuss politics, and pro–Việt Minh arguments always seemed to gain an upper hand. Communist theories appeared to be reasonable in every topic of social life. The Việt Minh produced solid evidence to prove that capitalism exploited the working class of their plus-value. In the same way they accused the Americans and their allies of "creating war to foster war" for the interests of arms brokers or warmongers, whereas the Soviet Union and Red China were appreciated as true friends of the poor and of the oppressed peoples. They said that the United States often supported corrupt regimes and only helped poor nations with consumer goods, whereas the USSR gave the people of these nations the means to produce on their own.

One of the best-selling Vietnamese detective stories at that time introduced the lead character as a hero who fought social evils and did marvelous acts against corrupt officials to help the poor. At the conclusion, he turned out to be a revolutionary who was struggling for the international cause of the oppressed peoples. It was the ideal of fighting for social equality and the better life for the poor that charmed us teenagers. Not only the Việt Minh but almost all of the noncommunist revolutionary movements in Việt Nam also advocated some kind of socialism, although the nationalists were much less fanatical.

In the countryside Việt Minh areas under the sign of revolution, the Lao Động Party (Workers' Party) overtly exerted oppressive measures against the middle-class farmers and the upper classes, measures that were sometimes unreasonably crude and brutal. They apparently were aimed at pleasing the poor to win them over to the Việt Minh side when more and more people of all kinds left the Việt Minh–controlled areas fed up with—and frightened by—communism.

Little by little, I realized that communism was not as beautiful as it was eulogized. The Việt Minh were becoming more and more attached to the Soviet Union and China. What I learned from anticommunist books was actually happening on the Việt Minh side. The factual comprehension brought me some new light: communist leaders disguised as patriots became an internal enemy, more dangerous and perilous to Việt Nam and more difficult to get rid of than French colonialists, the enemy from outside.

In another aspect, communist propaganda also proved how illiteracy and ignorance contributed to the growth of the Communist Party. Thus a large portion of the common population accepted pro-communist arguments. In such an environment, my conviction against communism was not convincing to my friends. It lacked concrete and obvious supporting evidence until many years later.

At the time, I only had a simple opinion, which was that a tricky and brutal dictatorship is always harmful to the people and only promotes the interests of a small group of leaders. Moreover, building a better society by violence will eventually destroy everything successfully constructed.

MOURNING STALIN

The death of the Soviet Union leader Joseph Stalin did not make big news in the nationalist government areas. However, to us students, a poem mourning Stalin we received months later from the Việt Minh areas drew more interest. It was written by Tố Hữu, a talented and renowned poet, known to the nationalists as "the genius verse maker" of the Việt Minh Front. He mourned Stalin with the tone of a child to a father at the funeral:

> *Vui sướng thay khi nghe con học nói,*
> *Tiếng đầu lòng con gọi "Xít-ta-lin."*
> *Xít-ta-lin ơi! Xít-ta-lin ơi,*
> *Hỡi ơi ông mất Đất Trời có không?*
> *Thương cha thương mẹ thương chồng,*
> *Thương mình thương một thương ông thương mười.*

> *How happy it is to listen to my baby learning to speak.*
> *In the first word of his life, he called "Stalin."*
> *Oh! Stalin, Stalin!*
> *Oh! You have gone! Are there Heaven and Earth?*
> *My love for you is ten times greater than*
> *my love for my parents, for my husband, and for myself.*

He was the first and only Vietnamese who has ever cried his heart out over the death of a foreign leader. The poem was widely circulated in Việt Minh publications, but it was withdrawn at the start of the Khrushchev era. It has not appeared again, either in Tố Hữu's recent biography or in any publication out of Hà Nội. The poem was so servile that even my pro–Việt Minh classmates had to admit that it could be considered an indelible black mark in Tố Hữu's career, although he wrote many excellent poems supporting the national struggle and the communist ideology.

VNQDĐ ACTIVIST

I met several of my father's friends who had fought against the French and later against the Việt Minh. They were working for the reorganized Việt Nam Quốc Dan Đảng (VNQDĐ, or Việt Quốc) in cities all over North and Central Việt Nam and some in the South. I came to see some of them every week to ask questions about the VNQDĐ's struggle, which had always been the most beautiful image in my heart since I was quite young. From them I found something lofty, heroic, and attractive. They were rather poor, but their exemplary lives won my highest respect and easily led me in their way.

Growing up in war and amid ideological conflicts, many boys were tempted by the romantic image of a warrior devoting his life to the nation, disdainful of luxuries. In early 1953, I became a member of a Việt Quốc's student organization in the city. There may have been some other Việt Quốc cells operating in the province, but we were not permitted to know about them. We also knew that other nationalist parties were operating in the area.

Because of the party's Francophobia, the French authorities did not always tolerate the Việt Quốc in the French-controlled area. The French-backed nationalist government did not ban its activities, but gave it no support, and its Public Security Agency would take us into custody and try us in court if we were caught distributing anti-French leaflets. The Việt Minh secret inner-city cells posed another threat. If we proved to be an obstacle, our lives would be in danger.

Restricted by the situation in a French-controlled city, we couldn't do much. We gathered at a different place every week, holding formal sessions in which we exchanged opinions and received indoctrination. A part of each session was devoted to criticism and self-criticism. These sessions looked like those of any revolutionary organization including the Việt Minh, but we tried to conduct them differently. We discussed an issue cordially in an informal tone and criticized one another with a friendlier manner. However, the communists proved that their way was more effective than ours because theirs was associated with "iron discipline." Sometimes we were ordered to distribute leaflets to the people and even to the French Army soldiers. We were trained to safely hand propaganda materials to people on the streets or in their homes.

Once I sneaked through a thin barbed wire fence around a temporary barracks of a French Army Moroccan unit under total darkness. The few electric bulbs in the kitchen area were not strong enough to scare me. The leaflet called on the Moroccan soldiers to treat the Vietnamese peasants with humanity. A Moroccan corporal friend of ours wrote the text in his language, and we printed it with help from a small printing house. We paid the corporal 100 piasters ($3 in the early 1950s) for his help. I quickly dropped dozens of leaflets around the kitchen backyard. Two minutes later, I was out again.

My two comrades completed their tasks at the other barracks and a private school. We met at the other end of the main street, reported on our work, then were about to go home when I realized that I had dropped my student ID card along with the leaflets when I took them from my breast pocket.

Getting into the barracks the first time was in no way a pleasant game. Getting into it the second time to search for my ID card in darkness with the possibility of being caught was really horrible. It was in early winter, but I felt sweat trickling along my backbone as I searched for the ID. I found it and sneaked out without being discovered. During my nineteen years in South Việt Nam military service later on, nothing ever frightened me more than that.

Owing to high motivation, we quickly expanded our organization to nearly twenty members. Two were schoolgirls of my age and older. Although it looked small, an organization advocating anti-French nationalism made up of so many teens in my city was significant. Among our group members, the most fanatical were the two from pro-Việt Minh families. Their brothers were high-ranking Việt Minh cadres, and their fathers covertly supported the Việt Minh side.

We had a monthly publication for internal indoctrination and also for propaganda, printed secretly in jellygraphy (a printing technique similar to lithography, but the printing surface is gelatin instead of stone). We produced about 100 copies of each issue (40 pages, half letter size) and distributed them to our cells. Some were sent to the province chief by mail and even to the prime minister's office in Sài Gòn, although I didn't expect that those big wheels would ever glance at it. Nothing has ever excited me as much as what I did to have that clandestine publication circulated. We were sorry we couldn't sneak it to the Việt Minh areas.

Like in any other urban area at that time, there was at least one secret Việt Minh student organization in my city. Those students were fervent patriots, and we were certain that most were serving the Việt Minh because of sheer patriotism, not communism. Their activities were merely in propaganda.

Some of my comrades were skillful in gathering intelligence. They infiltrated a Việt Minh student group and supplied our superiors with a list of its members. We were also informed of some of its activities, sometimes a few days ahead. One of my comrades was approached by a nationalist government secret police agent who asked him to provide the police department with the list of Việt Minh students. We didn't know why the police knew that we had the list. My comrade categorically denied his knowledge. With help from one member's brother, who was also working for the national police, we were safe. "If we want to eliminate them, we would do it ourselves, but we don't because they are only patriots," we said, showing that we would rather play gentlemen, or Wang Tao (the Way of the King), rather than Pa Tao (the Way of the Lord).

Although we decided not to harm any Việt Minh students, whenever possible we neutralized their activities. A few times Việt Minh activists slipped into the classrooms of a school at night and put leaflets into student table compartments. About one hour later, our comrades would slip into the same classrooms to collect their leaflets and replace them with ours.

We were very proud of what we did, even though they were insignificant deeds as trifling as a high school romance. However, such acts would contribute a great deal to our political and social behavior years later.

THE AMERICAN FIGURE

After the war in Korea broke out, we began to learn more and more about the Americans. Every week, the information service of the city showed outdoor news and documentary movies in a large schoolyard, and I was one of the free moviegoers in the neighborhood. The pictures of war always attracted kids like me.

However, the news of war did not help my side. It only showed that Red China was growing stronger and the Americans were unable to defeat it. At that time, Việt Minh propaganda praised Mao Tse-tung as Red Asia's hero. Lin Biao, his general, was called a "military genius" who had invented the tactic of "one point two sides."[1]

American aid began to trickle in with some health programs, such as one to cure trachoma among students. Colorful and funny cartoons were being used successfully to teach people how to prevent diseases. U.S. aid came in many projects: housing, water wells, and food with the sign on the containers in which the American and the Vietnamese flags were joined under the overlapping French tricolor in the middle. It meant U.S. aid was controlled and redistributed by the French. After 1954, the French colors were removed from the logo.

There were the American and British information services in Hà Nội that did not exist in my city. However, we still could find several books published by the two services. Stories and pictures about the United States attracted me more than anything about France, probably because I had suffered too much from the brutality of the French Army. At sixteen, I was old enough to appreciate the value of French culture and the peerless spirit of liberty in France, but images of war crimes were still vivid in my mind.

There was an argument at the time for supporting better relations with the United States among those who were against both communism and French colonialism. Some said that if we had no way to avoid being someone's younger brother, we had better accept the more generous one. I objected to the idea because I didn't want my people to be anyone's servant. We must be independent, and if we struggled hard, we would certainly achieve our goals. Like any other boy of my time, I believed in the moral strength with which our ancestors had driven off powerful enemies from China. We should find a friend—maybe not a very good friend, but not a boss. And that could be the United States.

From the books I read, I believed that the Americans might be at least better than the French. First of all, the United States didn't advocate colonialism and had reestablished independence in the Philippines. It had fought bravely in the two world wars for the freedom of its allies. I was sure that like any other country, the United States must have had some interests when it helped its allies, but such interests might have been reasonable. The Americans seemed to be generous and not too miserly in assisting poor countries.

It could be said that, at that time, more and more Vietnamese who didn't side with the Việt Minh looked across the Pacific hoping for some assistance from the States. Those who truly supported the French were just a minority. We also praised Great Britain for having granted independence to many of her former colonies after World War II.

After 1946, people who opposed the communists and were against French colonialism found themselves at the crossroads. Which of their two enemies did they have to fight first: the communists or the French? Some said the French had to be driven out first, whereas matters concerning the Việt Minh, who were our fellow countrymen, could be handled as an internal affair. The others disagreed, saying that the French were easier to defeat and less dangerous and that the communists posed a greater threat to the nation with their tempting theory and tricky but brutal politics. They felt that communism would bring havoc to our people and to our culture, particularly under the disguised domination of the Red Chinese.

A friend of my uncle, a member of the Đại Việt Party, said to me that the French would leave Việt Nam sooner or later because the movement of the oppressed nations for independence grew stronger every day. The United States and Great Britain would certainly support the movement. Therefore, the nationalist Vietnamese should fight the communist forces first to eliminate the greater threat to the nation. Then they would struggle peacefully and persistently against the French for independence, which we would eventually win.

THE VIỆT MINH GAIN GROUND

News from Korea about the Chinese human wave attacks strengthened Việt Minh propaganda. No one thought it was possible to win a war against China, where the loss of a few hundred thousand lives meant little to its leaders. Even when the Chinese advance was checked, Việt Minh propaganda claimed the Panmunjom cease-fire as a victory of its giant ally. I found no way to deny that.

At that time, the war in my area entered a new phase, with more ground yielded to the control of the Resistance forces. There was no successful antiguerrilla campaign to tip the scale. In some forts, French Union and nationalist army soldiers set up intelligence networks and laid ambushes at night. They also disguised themselves to conduct surprise attacks deep into the Resistance area or night raids far from their bases, frightening their enemy and keeping the area under control. But such operations required soldiers with high morale and firm anticommunist convictions. Unfortunately, those soldiers were not easy to find.

While the French and the nationalist forces relied on strongly constructed fortifications with dense barbed-wire fences and mines, they conceded the areas outside their forts to their enemy at night. The Resistance forces were free to select the battleground and time of attack. The militias who concentrated their defense in forts or churches were eliminated one by one. Only militia units that dispersed their men all over the villages and defended every inch of their ground with booby traps, spikes, and alert systems could beat off attacks, even of battalion size.

The fort next to my village was attacked one day from 9 PM until 4 AM without being overrun. The militia unit in a village half a mile from it provided good protection to the west side. In the morning, the enemy withdrew, leaving more than fifty bodies at the fence.

The next morning, three companies of the French Army and the administrative guards were ambushed one mile from the fort. A Resistance company half-naked and armed only with machetes emerged from underground hiding places and killed half of the spearhead company and captured most of its other half in about five minutes. The other companies escaped. A few hours later, the soldiers and the militiamen withdrew to the city.

Underground ambush, which required extreme courage and strength, was a successful Việt Minh tactic. It depended on accurate intelligence information to select the exact location of the ambush, usually along a road. When everything happened as planned, the ambushed side would hardly survive the engagement. It worked best against enemy soldiers who did something habitually, such as patrolling at the same time along the same road every day. If the enemy were moving even fifty yards away from the predicted pathway, the whole thing would certainly wind up in a total disaster for the ambushing side.

After 1951, the Resistance forces conducted more and more bold attacks against the French side. Sappers infiltrated enemy forts or barracks, or even the French air base near Hà Nội, to cause heavy losses to the French personnel, military equipment, and morale. In other places, sappers penetrated into fortified positions across many yards of barbed wire and mine fields under powerful protective fire to inflict heavy casualties on the defenders.

Back in 1949, I was allowed to watch a training session given to sappers who were required to crawl through a dense barbed-wire network with simulated mines, flares, and other devices. They moved about a foot per minute, carefully cut the wire, defused the mines and flares, and deactivated the alarm system. However, it was not the technique that counted. I could sneak into a barrack to drop leaflets. Although it was a less risky operation that any Vietnamese peasant could perform, what counted in performing such dangerous tasks was very high morale and a strong will to fight.

At the same time, in an attempt to obstruct and to harass surface communications, the Resistance troops launched a campaign to attack their enemy's convoys, trains, and ships. Every morning, soldiers from the forts along the main roads had to send troops to clear mines with mine detectors and to search for enemy ambushes or snipers before normal traffic was allowed. Every month during the campaign, civilian buses were blown up by land mines, killing dozens of innocent people. The guerrillas laid mines deep below the roadbed, and only heavy vehicles could activate them. Sometimes as many as three buses were destroyed in one day, with so many dead and wounded that the city hospital was unable to take care of them. Volunteers had to be called in to help victims lying in hospital hallways.

National Highway 5 from the port city of Hải Phòng to Hà Nội was called "the bloody road." Several Việt Minh attacks were directed along this highway, the backbone of the logistic system supporting all the French forces in North Việt Nam via the port of Hải Phòng, but the French still held it firmly. National Highway 1B from Nam Định to Ninh Bình was a similar objective. The village of Hào Kiệt, seven miles from Nam Định, stretched about one-third of a mile beside the highway; it was a place where French units were ambushed many times. All French efforts to maintain security in the area failed. Finally, the French brought in bulldozers and razed the village.

Many other roads were abandoned, and waterways were relied on instead. The Resistance force could harass but was incapable of controlling the rivers.

WAR LABORERS

Since 1952, my villagers had to pay heavy taxes to the Việt Minh authority. They also had to provide the so-called *dân công* (people's laborer; in effect, war laborer).[2] Each month, the village had to provide some 2 to 3 percent of its labor force (healthy men and women ages eighteen to forty-five) to the people's labor program. The policy was part of the "People's War" and has since become one of the key efforts of the communist regime to support wars in Việt Nam.

The war laborers would have to transport supplies—mainly rice—to the battle areas up north. Each carried about fifty-five pounds of rice to a place about 100 miles away in the mountainous area northwest of Hà Nội. The round-trip took them about twenty-five days, and each consumed some thirty-three of the fifty-five pounds of rice, leaving only twenty-two pounds at the food storage site on the front lines. Each village also had to provide laborers for three-month and six-month tasks to transport weapons and ammunition from the border with China to logistic stations inside North Việt Nam.

Although my mother had already moved to the city, her name was on the war laborer list of my village after the Việt Minh returned. When her turn came, my family had to pay a fine for her absence.

Many villagers knew that they were on the Việt Minh authorities' blacklist, so they would have to go anyway. In the village meetings to select war laborers, they quickly asked to put their names on the list instead of waiting to be chosen. Eventually, almost all of the war laborers had registered; some of my villagers called them "compulsory volunteers."

Life in my village lost its usual atmosphere. No one trusted anyone. Some could be in trouble because of something they said or rules they didn't follow as required. Some who were convicted of having intended to join the French or nationalist armies could be severely punished. The Việt Minh security agents would chop off their right index finger so "they could not pull the trigger," they said. In more serious cases, the hand or even the head would be the price.

THE NEW TERROR

After Tết 1953, the Resistance force conducted an attack on the boot camp where draftees selected for technical branches were given basic training. The camp's barbed-wire fence was no more than 300 feet from where my family was living.

At 1 AM, a deafening explosion was followed by bursts of submachine-gun fire and yelling. In less than ten minutes all was over. The French armored units and infantry reinforcements came too late; the attackers had already withdrawn without any casualties. Only a handful of draftees were injured; however, 100 rifles in the warehouse were stolen.

The French pursued with no luck. The Resistance force dispersed quickly, leaving no trace. On the nationalist side, many more army units were activated and more Vietnamese officers were appointed commanders of battalions and higher units. A few "mobile groups," tactical units similar to the U.S. army's separate brigades with embedded artillery, armored, and engineer elements, were commanded by Vietnamese colonels.

With hundreds of newly graduated officers, the appearance of the nationalist army gained some public favor, although it was not enough to win significant popularity. Psychological warfare was taken into consideration with some effort to win the people's hearts and minds and to promote the troops' willingness to fight. But it appeared to be too weak in comparison with the Việt Minh's.

Before 1953, I had only heard of the communist class struggle in which landlords and rich farmers were treated as enemies. In 1953, the Việt Minh declared the Movement of Mass Motivation, but my friends and I were unable to tell what the movement would actually do. The Việt Minh started the land reform campaign as part of the Mass Motivation. Later, it was said that the campaign started in December 1953, when Hồ Chí Minh signed a decree to activate it. But I knew it had been carried out a short time before that in the "experimental phase."

At that time, the situation for the people in the Việt Minh areas became critical. Farmers were controlled by the tax system. The village tax collectors did not spare even trivial farmers' products, such as a bunch of vegetables or a pound of small crabs. Trading of other stuffs of higher values such as poultry and pork were under the monopoly of the state-run trade agency. Farmers began showing bitter dissatisfaction. Inflation galloped. Prices were so high that a pack of cigarettes cost a bag of Việt Minh bills. People suffered from the severe shortage of medicine, even medicinal herbs. Wounded Việt Minh soldiers and civilians relied only on miracles to survive. The nationalist hospitals in cities had to provide treatment for many injured peasants evacuated from the Việt Minh–controlled areas.

Not long before the land reform began, I returned to my village to see my grandmother. While walking across a cornfield, I found a leather bag. At first I thought that it belonged to some low-ranking communist cadre because there was nothing special in it except for a few notes vaguely referring to "land reform." I told the story to a cousin who was a Communist Party member. He still had good but discreet relations with me, as he owed my family much for its help during the 1945 famine. He said that from the notes, an insider could tell that the bag must have belonged to a high-ranking party member. He explained to me that "land reform" would soon deal a hard blow to the landlords. That was what he had heard from a reliable source of his party cadres, and it was also confidential.

Upon his advice, I returned the bag to the place I had found it. An hour later, the guerillas in my village were ordered by the Việt Minh district security agency to search for the bag with the highest priority, exactly as my cousin had anticipated.

From the event, my cousin also taught me a lesson that would be useful many years later. He told me that if high-ranking cadres had to cross an area under enemy control with only a few paths to take, they would rather move on a route closer to the enemy position. Should they be captured, the enemy would certainly think that they were just unimportant privates.

The policy of eliminating the landlord class started in mid-1953. According to people who fled the Việt Minh areas, the policy was activated first with the so-called Land Rent Reduction Movement, although at the time nearly all landlords had reduced rent to the lowest rate possible or had simply given up the land. So the reduction movement was solely an initial step that had to be launched before other phases followed as the Việt Minh land policy dictated. The second step was the organization of all farmers into "mutual aid groups," a foundation for agricultural co-operatives after 1954 in North Việt Nam. At almost the same time, the Lao Động Party also carried out "Thought Reform" with intense indoctrination in communist ideology and the implementing of a cultural cleansing.

These programs were actually taking place in areas deep in the Việt Minh–controlled territory (in Ninh Bình, Thanh Hóa, and Nghệ An provinces to the south of my home province). My home village, too close to the French-controlled areas, only experienced a little bit of the campaigns.

The land reform campaign was launched in many villages in Thanh Hóa province, and the campaign then spread over a larger area in what was called an "oil-stain tactic." News from Thanh Hóa reached my city, but the details about what was happening were very confused. Many people in my city believed the stories of brutality, but others didn't, because it seemed too excessive to be true. I heard a lot about the campaign, but I had only a vague notion of what was actually happening.

Victims who fled the Việt Minh areas in Ninh Bình and Thanh Hóa reported horrible scenes of the so-called *tố khổ*, or denunciation. The denunciation session was often held in the evening in a large yard of a rich family's house or in a pagoda. Almost all villagers as well as landlords were forced to attend. Poor farmers were brought forward and compelled to denounce the landlords' crimes before the "people's court" presided over by a Việt Minh cadre. A session might last far into the night and over several evenings. The people's court had power to pronounce death sentences, and a firing squad would carry out the execution right away. In some places, those convicted were stoned to death, hanged, left to die of thirst and hunger, or even buried alive.

I finally believed the reports when I met many victims of the campaign. Among them were the two brothers of my next-door neighbor who fled their native village in Ninh Bình province in June 1953. Each had owned about ten acres inherited from their parents. Both were eager Việt Minh supporters working in some district agencies and had given up most of their land to the Việt Minh local government in 1947. When their village was selected as an experimental site for the land reform campaign, they didn't know that they would be among the accused. Their family, including old parents and babies, were brought to the people's court. They were charged with many counts; most of the charges were completely fabricated. During the "denunciation," hundreds of farmers accused them and abused them with the worst language, whereas they were not allowed to enter a plea.

When the defendants argued that they had "supported the revolution" and handed over to the government all their land, the presiding judges simply told them that "all your land was of the people; we don't need you to hand it over. The trial tonight has nothing to do with your land, only with the crimes that you, your parents, and your ancestors have committed against the poor farmers for thousands of years."

Some landlords were given death sentences, but the two brothers along with their wives and parents were ordered to kneel on pebbles with a bamboo pannier full of rocks on their heads for three consecutive days and nights. One of the two women, who was in her third month of pregnancy, miscarried the child on the spot and was released when she collapsed. She died from hemorrhaging a few days later. After that, they were allowed to stay home waiting for further decisions from the district land reform office. The landlords were so frightened that some committed suicide. One night, with help from a few close friends and relatives, the two brothers, the surviving wife, and the children fled to the French-controlled area. One of the brothers then volunteered for the nationalist army. In April 1975, they were among the first to flee Sài Gòn.

The land reform campaign caused great shock among people of all classes. It drove many people serving the Việt Minh to the opposite side. Many had been fervent patriots and active Resistance cadres. Consequently, the nationalist government was reinforced with many enthusiastic new anticommunist citizens. Some of my cousins who had been serving the Resistance in military and civilian agencies returned to the city to find jobs in the private sector or in public services or in military units.

The realities of the land reform campaign were too horrible for the common people to believe. Anyone who wasn't assured by a witness he or she trusted would certainly discount the stories as French propaganda. Even my villagers who had suffered so much from communist brutality didn't believe them, let alone my classmates, who were just city boys and girls with no experience of rural life.

For the first time I learned that truth is not easy to find, even though it is in front of you, and that lies are often welcomed instead.

The barbaric land reform was the last blow that drove me definitely to one side of the line. I hated the sight of children joining hands in collective dances and singing about the Chinese communist style. Furthermore, I couldn't hold my anger when talking to poorly educated Việt Minh cadres who loved to use big nonsense political terms and Chinese words and phrases when Vietnamese already had more than one simple way to express similar ideas.

So 1953 saw another sharp turn of the conflict. Eventually, it was the communist atrocities that reinforced the nationalist side and promoted stronger anticommunism.

*   *   *

In late 1953, the war reached a new level with several heavy battles fought in areas around my city. But to my own observation, the most important development was the logistic campaigns of the Resistance. The Việt Minh was collecting great amounts of rice from the southern parts of Thai Bình and Nam Định provinces, the rice granary of Việt Nam North. Every month, war laborers from both sides of the Red River transported hundreds of tons of rice along the Việt Minh–controlled corridor to the mountainous locations in the northwest.

My villagers who came back from serving in the labor force told me that rice was stored in many caches all over the large areas close to the common border with Laos and China. On the way carrying rice from the Red River coastal areas to the mountainous region, many were killed by French ambushes, air raids, and artillery attacks. I was certain that the French headquarters must have known that a major battle was being planned.

Sometimes the French forces won sporadic victories. Once, a French task force conducted a deep thrust into a heavily defended Việt Minh logistic base in Lạng Sơn province near the common border with China. The French destroyed a large quantity of weapons and ammunition before withdrawing unharmed. However, a single victory seemed too little to affect the military situation that was increasingly favoring the Việt Minh.

LUCK COMES TO MY FAMILY

In the summer, my family fell into much narrower circumstances. My mother used all of her money for a trading business between the city and the Việt Minh areas. The profits she made were barely enough for the four of us to live with scanty meals. She had built up a small capital of some 7,000 piasters (US$200 at the time), which ensured her a larger profit, when one night she lost all of it. A French patrol accidentally discovered the bales of goods on the way to the Việt Minh areas and destroyed them. The next morning, when a friend of hers came with the bad news, my mother almost fainted.

In the following months, she could do very little to support us. The small amount of money that we relied on was no more. Now she had to return to a small stand in a corner of the city central market, selling vegetables and collecting pennies to feed us.

Then one of my father's friends located us and offered help. He had been close to my family when working in the same district office with my father before 1945, but we had lost contact with him when war broke out in December 1946. He searched for a year before he found us. He helped me get a part-time job coaching some children in the third and fourth grades. He also gave us some extra money to pay our house rent. Thanks to his help, we could manage with less difficulty. But he was not wealthy enough to help us more than that.

Life in a city in war became harder as fighting intensified every month. We couldn't keep up with the high cost of living. Many times I thought of dropping out of school to find some menial work to help my mother. One night I wrote a letter bearing the name of my mother to the North Việt Nam governor (nationalist government), explaining our plight and asking for assistance. When mailing the letter, I had almost no real hope. After a week, I nearly forgot it.

About a month later, a police officer came to see my mother to ask her questions concerning her biography and political background. She was frightened at the idea that he came to investigate her trading with the Việt Minh. Only after fifteen minutes did she find out that the officer came just to complete her security clearance for a job in a government office.

We learned later that an assistant to the North Việt Nam governor, the mandarin who had been my father's boss before 1945, found my letter in a clerk's desk by chance, about to be discarded. He immediately asked the personnel branch to give my mother a job. He said to my mother and me when we visited his home that he never forgot my father and others who had actively raised their voices to protect him when the Việt Minh militia threatened to execute him on August 18, 1945.

One month later after training, she was employed as a correctional officer in the city jail, in charge of a dozen women prisoners. With her pay equal to that of an army sergeant, she could take better care of the family. My sisters and I were given more food and better clothes. And I didn't have to worry any more about whether to continue my education. My happiness was equal to that of a man who had won the lottery. I taught my two sisters to pray to Buddha and God for help. I believe that when we live honestly, are helpful to others, and do nothing harmful to anyone, we will be rewarded by a divine power.

In the city jail, there were more than 100 prisoners; half were Việt Minh who had been arrested not as prisoners of war but as members of clandestine organizations operating in the nationalist government's areas. Many of them were hard-core communists. The nationalist government intentionally recruited individuals whose close relatives had been killed by the Việt Minh. The government expected those officers to treat the communist prisoners with strict discipline. My mother, however, was doing her assigned duties with her kind heart. As any pious Buddhist, my mother said she would treat the prisoners well to soften their suffering, including the communists whose party had brought peril to her family. To return good for evil was what she always told me to do.

In a few months, she was highly appreciated by most of the prisoners. On weekends, she checked out some inmates, who would stay the whole day in our home, helping us with some chores, having lunch with us, and getting paid generously—more than jail regulations required.

LOOKING TO THE SOUTH

As the war went on, we boys were drawn farther to one side or the other. My comrades and I were yearning for a territory where we could fight both Vietnamese communists and the French. Then we heard of General Trình Minh Thế in Tây Ninh province, Việt Nam South.

The war in South Việt Nam before 1954 was not as intense as in the North, and communism did not prosper well in the South, where people were leading easy lives. However, since 1945, the Resistance in South Việt had produced numerous heroes. The most famous was General Nguyễn Bình. Many of us teenagers knew his reputation.

Nguyễn Bình had long been a nationalist revolutionary, a VNQDĐ member before joining the Communist Party. After the Việt Minh took power, he became one of its talented military leaders who fought against the French. He quickly became a famous military commander of the Resistance Southern Theater of Operation. He planned and conducted many successful attacks, including one on the large ammunition warehouse in Sài Gòn, next to the zoo. A legend ran that he had notified the French about the attack several days ahead.

His popularity was rising in the South and that brought him trouble.

Later the story circulated that in 1953 he was ordered to go north to receive the highest commemoration from Hồ Chí Minh. His journey was made known widely, and there were ceremonies honoring him along his way to the North through Cambodia. That was what the French were looking for. Not long after he entered Cambodia, he and several of his bodyguards were killed in an ambush. His diary, which the French found among his belongings, was published in *Paris Match* magazine. And people who had had experiences with Hồ Chí Minh's tricks knew the scheme. To many students, Nguyen Bình had been their favorite hero, especially after he was killed.

General Trinh Minh Thế of the Cao Đài sect was renowned as another young hero of the South. He led the Cao Đài militia from a base near Núi Bà Đen (the Black Virgin Mount) in Tây Ninh province. Several friends and I used to listen to the radio programs of the National Allied Front of General Trình Minh Thế. Although the signal was rather weak, we could still listen to the broadcast when the weather was fine. Besides, the father of a friend of ours, who was serving in General Trình Minh Thế's small army, came back to visit his family. He told us hundreds of anecdotes about how the general's forces were fighting the French as well as the Việt Minh.

We heard that Trình Minh Thế's troops were generously supported by the people in the region and that they conducted many commando-type raids, causing serious losses to the French and the Việt Minh. Some also said that the forces were backed up secretly by the United States.

After my friend's father left for South Việt Nam again, I heard that some young men in my city had followed him to Trình Minh Thế's secret bases in Tây Ninh province. And there grew my dream of going to join his forces.

TEN

The Geneva Accords

ĐIỆN BIÊN PHỦ

One night in February 1954, the Việt Minh forces made a bold attack deep inside Nam Định City. They infiltrated the city by several routes. Some disguised themselves as pilgrims joining the annual religious procession to get into the suburban neighborhoods.

At midnight, they opened fire on a security patrol and attacked an outpost in the suburban area to lure French reinforcements out of the city into their ambush. Việt Minh soldiers positioned themselves on the roofs of several houses in my block. However, a nationalist army armored unit frustrated the Việt Minh scheme by encircling them from behind, directing powerful gunfire at the rooftops, and sealing off their way to retreat.

The attack was a Việt Minh military failure, but it was a forceful blow to the French morale. It proved to the people that the Việt Minh could thrust their spear deep into the French inner defense systems. On the nationalist side, the battle was an indication of the nationalist army's better combat capability, even though it was not a very big victory.

In mid-March, the French suffered a stunning reversal at Điện Biên Phủ when Việt Minh artillery decimated the French command and set up a siege around the isolated French forces. Fierce fighting would continue until May 5, when the Việt Minh overwhelmed the remaining French troops. Điện Biên Phủ became the major battle that drew international attention. We students knew that there would be another sharp turn in the course of war. An already large number of war laborers in the area of my native village who had been activated several months earlier to support the battle were now augmented by two to three times. More were killed on the way to the front line.

Some distant relatives from my village who had come back from the battle areas told me that many Chinese communist military cadres disguised as Việt Minh officers were present around Điện Biên Phủ. They were advisors to the Việt Minh staffs and artillery units, even commanding some Red Chinese artillery batteries directly supporting the Việt Minh units. The Chinese never spoke to people when they were away from their units. The presence of the Chinese was confirmed by other sources in my area. Unfortunately, the mass media did not report the information. The presence of Red Chinese military in Điện Biên Phủ was ignored until the 1990s, when some Red Chinese generals confirmed the allegation.

While delegations from all parties were negotiating in Geneva for an end to the fighting, other battles were being fought elsewhere. My friends and I all felt that the French would have to concede much ground to the Việt Minh under pressure from the French people. There was no possibility that they could win the war.

NATIONALIST GOVERNMENT POWER

I had mixed feelings about the nationalist Vietnamese government under King Bảo Đại. It seemed to be a legal institution with formalities and titles. But it was too weak to have a decisive voice against the French. I felt ashamed being under a government that was too dependent on the French, a feeling that I shared with many people. Besides, the nationalist government was not able to get rid of the corruption that made it more and more unpopular. Meanwhile, the Việt Minh appeared as a patriotic organization and gained sympathy as well as support.

Under King Bảo Đại were his prime minister and a cabinet that governed with limited power. Foreign affairs, national defense, and currency management were still in the hands of the French High Commissariat. France provided little economic, medical, educational, and social aid to Việt Nam under the Bảo Đại government in addition to the support necessary to maintain 150,000 nationalist army soldiers. At that time, U.S. aid was scanty. However, the French did not impose harsh measures on the Vietnamese people as they had done before 1945 to exploit the country. The citizens under the nationalist control had to pay taxes only to the Bảo Đại government, and the tax was very low. The government had very little money to cover public expenses.

A governor was appointed by Chief of State Bảo Đại, the king not called a king, to rule each of the three regional governments of Việt Nam: North, Central, and South. Each consisted of several provinces. There was no national parliament. The press was under strict censorship, and nationalist opposition and criticism were not permitted.

As I have mentioned before, we students were not as proud of our top leader as the Việt Minh supporters were of their idol, Hồ Chí Minh. To the average

Vietnamese, Bảo Đại was more or less a French puppet. The nationalists sided with him only because they had to fight the communists for survival, not because they supported French neocolonialism in disguise. The situation was a great dilemma to many nationalists. The government had no clear and acceptable policies to end the war and to rebuild the country, let alone an ideology. Its control over the population was superficial, allowing some degree of freedom to the Việt Minh for various activities, especially in the propaganda domain.

Public health care was poor, and social services were extremely inadequate. However, education efficiency was maintained at all levels up to the university degree, although the primary and high school systems were not large enough to admit all eligible students. Private schools filled part of the gap.

To consolidate the administrative system at village level, the nationalist government launched several Quân Thứ Lưu Động groups (mobile administrative operational groups). They were supposed to help villagers in the government-controlled areas organize the village governing authority, the self-defense corps, health care, and educational services. This was all done with limited success. The campaign could have worked well if there had been adequate moral and material support. U.S. aid was just for show, and France spent its money only for military purposes.

After four years, the nationalist military was better organized and somehow asserted its identity. Better-trained personnel joined the armed forces. However, the French still held a decisive role in military operations. A small number of commanders were French officers. The French control of the nationalist military at this time probably contributed to the misperception—encouraged by communist propaganda—that American officers were in command of ARVN units during the Việt Nam War between 1955 and 1975.

By 1954, the anticommunists gained more momentum in their cause after the Vietnamese communists overtly exercised their control over the people, culminating in their effort to terrorize the masses with the Land Reform Campaign. The lives of the people in the Việt Minh areas continued to deteriorate. Besides the shortage of food and basic consumer goods, cultural and educational values were deteriorating. For years after 1947, there was no university education. High school curriculum dwindled into the ten-year system like the one in Red China; even textbooks were translations from the Chinese originals.

For half a century, students had been pronouncing the music scale "do re mi fa sol la si do." Since 1951, people in the Việt Minh areas had to say "*to le* mi fa sol la si *to*" as did the Chinese, who could not pronounce the consonants *d* and *r*. To many of us students in the city, local communist leaders were behaving in a servile way with their constant flattery of their Chinese comrades.

The patriotic atmosphere of 1945 had once pervaded every walk of life in the Việt Minh–controlled areas in the first years of war. That atmosphere waned after many years of terror, poverty, and dictatorship, especially after the Lao Đồng Party overtly claimed total power. The new Việt Minh personnel policy brought many ill-educated party members into important jobs. Well-educated cadres and public servants from the middle class and higher, who had previously contributed greatly to the success of the Resistance, were employed in subordinate positions. It was the first time in the history of Việt Nam that the intelligentsia were serving under a class of ignorant bosses.

As nationalist parties in North Việt Nam suffered heavy losses after the Việt Minh's great terrorist campaign, the party members who survived the campaign and fled to the French-controlled areas reorganized their parties and resumed their activities. However, they were not as strong as they had been.

Most nationalist parties were divided into smaller groups, each claiming the same title. Some leaders became ministers in the Bảo Đại government; some refused to cooperate with it. But none of them was prominent enough to gain large support from the people while they had to confront both the French and the Việt Minh. Various nationalist movements and parties failed several attempts to establish a strong, unified anticommunist front to win the right cause over to their side and to claim total independence from France. It seemed to me that such a task was impossible, although I couldn't say why.

I was proud of being a Việt Quốc, of having the right to claim relation to the 1930s glory. I was hoping that my party would be gaining power so that it could lead the great struggle of our people not only to independence but also to liberty, democracy, and prosperity. At eighteen years of age, I had more dreams than reasons.

Almost all of the nationalist parties in Việt Nam adopted some kind of socialism, even though they never claimed the title "socialist." Besides independence and freedom, millions of people were hungry for a better life where the poor wouldn't be too poor and the rich not too rich. So every party more or less supported the idea of a welfare state in a noncommunist style.

THE GREAT RETREAT

In early May 1954, Điện Biên Phủ fell as we had expected after several fierce battles. The Việt Minh victory shook confidence in the French power. However, the Việt Minh suffered heavy losses in exchange for the triumphant victory. No accurate figure was given by the press, but from what we were told by war laborers and Việt Minh wounded soldiers coming back to my village, we could say that many thousands of the attacking forces were killed and a much larger number were wounded. Until May 1954, I still had contact with my villagers, those of my age in particular. They found no difficulties in visiting the city. Civilian travel to and from the Việt Minh areas was not prohibited.

Furthermore, the economic situation in the Việt Minh areas was in an incurable crisis. Rice production, the key factor of the rural economy, was too low, while the Việt Minh required a large quantity to supply the army units and, as some of my villagers asserted, to supply the Chinese in the districts bordering Việt Nam, who were on the verge of a famine as well. A large number of war laborers transported rice across the border into China and then carried military equipment back to Việt Nam.

Tension rose high in the cities of North Việt Nam. A lot of rich people sold their homes in the cities to move south to Sài Gòn. As for my friends and me, we praised the victory of Điện Biên Phủ. Although we were anticommunist, we saw the victory as a great feat achieved by the heroic sacrifice and courage of our compatriots. The Communist Party's leadership played a significant role, but it was not the absolutely indispensable factor of the victory.

After Điện Biên Phủ, I was certain that some big event would be coming soon. Since June 20, the French Union army and Vietnamese nationalist units in Nam Định began dismantling their heavy equipment and moved them to Hà Nội. The population was shaken by the idea that the French forces would withdraw from Nam Định. However, the French headquarters was still preparing for a large military review and parade in the city on July 14, the national holiday of France. On June 24, large-scale movement started with logistic supporting units. Hundreds of trucks headed for Hà Nội, leaving several barracks empty. Military cargo airplanes took off every ten or fifteen minutes, moving personnel and equipment to Hà Nội.

It was no longer a secret that the French forces were about to withdraw from the southern part of North Việt Nam. People from all walks of life filled every bus going north to Hà Nội. In a few days, bus tickets were sold at a price several times higher than normal. Other city people who didn't see anything wrong with living with the Việt Minh worried about these events but remained in the city to wait and see.

Minutes before 7 AM, June 30, five large civilian trucks and a military truck with a squad of the government administrative guards reported to the city's prison. The squad leader, a sergeant, carried a written message from the top military authority of the city that ordered all members of the prison staff and their families and all prisoners to move to Hà Nội. The trucks had to be at the city checkpoint at exactly 7:30 AM. And we knew this time the French military police would be extremely punctual.

A second after receiving the message, we were in a hurry to pick out what we should take along with us. It was a difficult task because everything seemed to be indispensable. At last, when everything was in a few suitcases, we still had fifteen minutes.

I asked my mother for permission to go see my "friends" living a kilometer from us for a minute, "just to say good-bye to them." My aunt said no; she was afraid that I would be late. But my mother calmed her and told me to go as quickly as possible. She knew where I was going. I got my bicycle and rode it at full speed, almost hitting some pedestrians and bikes and a truck on my way.

In less than five minutes, I stopped at the corner about fifty yards across the street from the home of the girl I loved. She was my classmate, and I had fallen in love with her the previous summer. I had never said a word to her, but I was sure she knew what was in my heart. In the traditional society of the early 1950s, it took time and a circuitous path for a young man to approach a girl and declare his love, even when everybody knew his feelings.

On the small French-style balcony of the second story, she was sitting on a chair drying her long black hair in the morning breeze. In anticipation that it would probably be many years before I returned, or even that I would never see her again, I felt pain in my heart. Gathering all my courage, I blew her a kiss, to the surprise of some passers-by. And without seeing whether she was aware of it or not, I beat a hasty retreat.

Five minutes later, I was on the truck with my family, who had been nervously waiting for me. And in exactly five minutes, the small convoy of six trucks began the trip to Hà Nội. It was a miracle for many Vietnamese to observe such punctuality.

The convoy, along with many others, covered the fifty-one miles to Hà Nội in two hours. The highway was rough with puddles, the best speed-limiting device since the scorched-earth campaign in 1947. Road security was taken care by a large force seen every few hundred yards. Mines had already been laid on all bridges, which would be blown up when all withdrawing convoys passed, the engineer soldiers told us.

Only later did I learn that it had been a marvelous retreat under French Army colonel Paul Vanuxem (who was promoted to general a short time after the operation), with extremely precise timing, perfect secrecy, and surprisingly few losses. Vanuxem was one of the French celebrities who supported an independent and prosperous noncommunist Việt Nam. Nearly twenty-one years later, he witnessed the last days of Sài Gòn in April 1975, when there was no way for his Vietnamese friends to continue fighting and had to flee in panic after the communist forces overran South Việt Nam.

That night of June 30, the foremost part of a Việt Minh force sent from the northern region to cut off the retreating route of the French forces launched its bloody attacks at Phủ Lý, a small town thirty miles south of Hà Nội. The fighting lasted all night and destroyed a large part of the town of tens of thousands of inhabitants. When the French Army and the nationalist government and military hurriedly withdrew, they left behind many militiamen in anticommunist villages without giving them the order to withdraw to safety. A number of those betrayed combatants fled on foot, but many others were captured, and some were later executed by the Việt Minh.

WAITING FOR AN UNKNOWN FUTURE

Before leaving the city, I had too little time to do anything for my Việt Quốc comrades. I could only give some of them my address in Hà Nội and advice about how to ensure the safety for our members who stayed. In a week, about half of my comrades contacted me in Hà Nội. The party hierarchy temporarily assigned us to serve on the Hà Nội Party committee. We got orders from our leaders to consolidate our organization and to stay fully alerted. We were to be prepared for actions required to cope with any special situation.

I had to report to my party bosses for orders once every evening and sometimes early in the morning. Now and then, my group was assigned a leaflet mission. Such missions had long been duck soup for my fellows and me, so they were usually given to the greenhorns as a primary exercise. The leaflets conveyed nothing great, just appeals to the population and Vietnamese soldiers to heighten their vigilance and be ready to support our party in the struggle for total independence from the French and against the communists.

During the first weeks of July, Hà Nội was bubbling with rumors. A lot of anticommunists were happy to hear that Ngô Đình Diệm would be prime minister of the Bảo Đại nationalist government. We didn't know much about that former mandarin, but still believed that as a well-known patriot, he would be capable of doing something for the country. Many thought that he would possibly be a rival to Hồ Chí Minh. Such was the attitude of many people in Hà Nội when they stood along a boulevard to welcome Diệm on his visit to the old capital a few days after he was appointed.

Meanwhile, it was said that there would soon be a cease-fire and that each side would hold on to its territory until nationwide elections could be held. That seemed impractical, because in 1954 many places around the cities were under the control of the French and nationalist government during the day and of the Việt Minh at night. Such a situation would make any cease-fire almost impossible to be implemented.

Another rumor that frightened many nationalists was that Việt Nam would be divided into two parts after the cease-fire. No one liked that idea. It meant we would have to leave the North for the South. Diệm established the Committee for Defense of North Việt Nam with instructions to continue defending the North should the French and the Việt Minh decide to divide the country. Police forces in Hà Nội and other northern cities were armed with military equipment and prepared for actual combat. All nationalist parties supported Diệm's decision.

Since the last days of Điện Biên Phủ, rumors were circulating that the U.S. Seventh Fleet—some of its warships already in the Bay of Hạ Long—might give direct support to the nationalist army to defend its territories in North Việt

Nam. Some of my friends laid hope on the American intervention. The others did not believe that U.S. involvement would be the solution when the French still held full power. But all agreed on one point: it was unlikely that the Americans could save the French from defeat.

The French Army celebrated Bastille Day with a large-scale military review and parade in Hà Nội. Posters displayed the picture of a clenched fist along with the information that the French withdrawal from the five provinces south of Hà Nội was a new strategy intended to concentrate military forces for more powerful offensive actions. The strategy was compared to a clenching fist instead of spreading fingers. This propaganda ploy seemed weak and unconvincing. There was no way to make anyone believe that the French would gain anything more than what they were presently holding. Việt Minh popularity was already at its peak, and no propaganda could harm them significantly.

For many consecutive nights, we dropped leaflets all over Hà Nội, especially near the French barracks, including those of North African soldiers, calling for support of our nationalist cause. Personally we knew it was a hopeless task unless the Americans intervened. But we had to do it anyway, at least to show the readers of our leaflets that there were true nationalists who were more patriotic than the Việt Minh.

Obviously the French were aware of the nationalist intentions. Heavily armed North African soldiers were deployed at many key military and civilian installations for safeguarding.

THE PAINFUL NIGHT

On July 21, four of my friends and I heard Radio Hirondelle, the French Army radio station in Hà Nội, announcing that France and the Việt Minh had signed the Geneva Accords. The Vietnamese nationalist government and the United States did not sign the pact.

Although we had expected that the French and the Việt Minh would come to some agreement and that the nationalists had no way to affect their decision, we were still shocked at the news. For more than a minute, we fell into sorrowful silence. We knew we were witnessing an event that would change our lives forever.

According to the agreement, Việt Nam would be temporarily divided into two areas by the Bến Hải River at the 17th parallel north. The two opposing forces would have to evacuate to their sides within three hundred days. The Việt Minh would take over Hà Nội in October 1954 and Hải Phòng in May 1955.

That night, two friends and I stayed up late. We went to the historic Lake of the Sword, sitting on the grassy bank until midnight, talking. One of my friends wept. We returned to my home and did not sleep that night. The painful feeling of leaving my beautiful native land for a long, long time, possibly forever, kept me awake.

So the war would come to an end. We didn't know for how long, because the situation in Việt Nam in no way ensured a cease-fire forever, but we hoped it would last, the longer the better. Our discussion came to another topic: if there had not been the communist Việt Minh, what would the Resistance have become? We didn't come to any firm conclusion at the time.

* * *

Only many years later when I had learned more about different matters did I have an answer for myself. If there had not been a Communist Party, or if the Resistance government had been run by the nationalists, we could have won the war sooner with greater victory and much less death and destruction. I always believe that a noncommunist Việt Nam would have gained total independence from France with much less bloodshed, difficult but peaceful like India and Indonesia. The free world and the United States would have supported Việt Nam, and France would have had to give up recolonizing Indochina. The high morale of our people would have enabled any leadership to lead them to victory. It did not need to be the Việt Minh. I guessed that with such a scenario, Việt Nam would have become a democracy like Thailand, or even the Philippines— not very stable politically, perhaps, but with greater economic development.

* * *

In the last week of July 1954, the nationalist government in Sài Gòn announced a program to help the northerners who wanted to go south. My mother asked a friend of the family to return to my village and bring my grandma, my uncle, his wife, and his adopted son to Hà Nội in order to join us in moving to Sài Gòn. She said she would pay him a lot of money, almost all of what she had saved after eight months on the job.

Once the Geneva Accords took effect, moving from Hà Nội to the Việt Minh areas and back was relatively easy. The Việt Minh forces could not impose strict control over the large areas and the great number of people who were crossing the line between the two warring sides every day.

Our friend shuttled between Hà Nội and Nam Định every week and had succeeded in getting out many people who lived deep inside the Việt Minh areas. But he failed to bring the four members of my family to us. My uncle was under the close scrutiny of the Việt Minh village authorities, and there was no way to get him out. My grandmother would have been able to join us, but she refused to leave. She said she was too old for anything, so she would rather stay and die where she had lived as a good wife and mother and be buried beside my grandfather. Furthermore, she wanted to be with my uncle, as she felt that he would surely be in trouble.

In Hà Nội, my mother and my aunt feared for the safety of my two sisters. Việt Minh agents kidnapped the children of some families they wanted to keep from leaving. So my aunt and my mother never let my sisters out of their sight for more than a few seconds.

While we were preparing to leave, many former Việt Minh cadres came to urge us to stay. They had known my mother while they were imprisoned in the Nam Định city jail and were grateful for her help. They had been released in early July in an amnesty. They assured us that as they had rejoined the Việt Minh ranks and held medium-level jobs, they could protect us at any cost, so we should not worry. But nothing could change our minds. In the Land Reform Campaign, we knew many "good" landlords who contributed the best of what they had to the common cause of fighting the French and whose children served as high-ranking Việt Minh cadres, and yet they had been executed. Any sympathy with the Việt Minh had long faded away.

A few days before my scheduled departure for Sài Gòn, some of my first cousins on my mother's side visited with us. They were all Việt Minh cadres and had come to persuade us to stay. My mother firmly rejected their proposal that our family should move and live permanently with them in my mother's native village where they would protect us. The husband of my mother's eldest sister, however, advised us to go south. He had served in the Việt Minh for more than twenty years in another area. He said to my mother, "You should bring the kids to the South. You wouldn't be safe if you stayed anywhere in the North. I say so because you are my wife's blood sister. I have to stay because I am a Communist Party ranking member, otherwise . . . but you know what I mean."

MY LAST DAYS IN HÀ NỘI

By the end of July, a large number of people left Hà Nội for South Việt Nam at their own expense, while official announcements were made that North Vietnamese who wanted to leave would be helped with transportation and resettlement, beginning in a few weeks.

In early August, men in my group were ordered by the Việt Quốc leadership to join the government social services. We would be sent to Sài Gòn to help with the refugee program, establishing and running reception centers for the refugees from the North. My mother and the family would depart for Sài Gòn a month later.

I spent the last days in Hà Nội visiting my favorite places. The streets were crowded with people from everywhere, including many Việt Minh cadres. The nationalist army and police didn't bother to control the enemy infiltration unless someone did something excessively unacceptable.

Early one morning my two friends and I were relishing hot black coffee at a small street cafe beside Thiền Quang Lake in the southern part of the city. Since people had begun leaving Hà Nội in large numbers, the streets in that area had become open marketplaces where people were running collective "sidewalk sales." Those who were about to leave were trying to sell everything they wouldn't be able to take with them. Almost anything could be found on the sidewalks, from a broken sewing needle to a brand-new bicycle. The sellers were trying to collect every penny possible for their new homes far away.

My two friends and I were the first customers of the street cafe, located at one end of the "sidewalk sales" area. It was 6 AM, the blue sky was waiting for the rising sun, and the air was cool. Peddlers from the suburbs carrying loads of goods with poles on their shoulders were on their way to the inner-city markets. And the sidewalk sellers had already displayed hundreds of miscellaneous articles.

When daylight came, people around the corner from the cafe noticed that a Việt Minh flag was hanging from the top of a low tree. Some men and women yelled, "Get that dirty rag down and destroy it!" A boy of my age responded to the call right away with a loud "Yes sir." He climbed the tree with ease and reached the flag in half a minute. At the same time, a French officer in his khaki uniform passed by.

When the boy came down from the tree, he laughed heartily and began to tear up the red flag while others cheered. The French officer snatched the flag away while shaking the boy by his collar, saying something loudly. People standing nearby told us that the officer said the flag represented a government and should not be humiliated. The poor creature must have had very little background about the situation in Việt Nam, especially about the people who were selling their junk along the sidewalks. His actions—siding with the communist Việt Minh and accosting the boy—ignited the crowd.

At one cry, a dozen men flew at the French officer with whatever they could get—sticks, locks, carrying poles, and especially rocks from a pile on the sidewalk that a public works contractor had prepared for road mending. Within seconds, women and children joined in the mass beating. I also flew into a rage but tried to restrain myself. I didn't know which way to react, so I just stood watching. After a minute, the crowd stopped beating the Frenchman. They returned to their places, leaving the poor man lying on the sidewalk. His face was bruised, and blood tainted his uniform. When a French Army ambulance came to pick him up a few minutes later, he was still unconscious.

On the afternoon of August 11, my friends and I visited our favorite shrimp fries kiosk on Cổ Ngư Avenue beside Lake Hồ Tây (West Lake) for the last time. That avenue was filled with romantic couples strolling along every summer and autumn afternoon. While we were eating, a few boys, ages ten and younger, approached and asked us for money. I gave them some and told them that they should have done something more decent to earn money instead of begging. To my surprise, the youngest looked straight at me and said, "The Việt Minh will come here before long. We poor people will be given property, you dirty rich people will be felled, and you'll beg us for money."

His saucy manner drove us to red-hot anger, and one of my friends was about to give him a good slapping when I pulled the kid to my side to protect him. I softly told him that I also came from a poor family and that he had learned the wrong lessons about the communists. He talked back, saying that he knew only the Việt Minh. Apparently he didn't know what a "communist" was. "Poor little brother," I said. "You're too young to tell right from wrong. But if you are brilliant enough, you'll see for yourself what the Việt Minh really are after a few years living under them. When you've grown much older, remember what I'm telling you today."

When I let him go, he walked about ten yards, then stopped to look at me, a look so deep and dark that I would never forget and that would help me recognize him fourteen years later in Sài Gòn.

* * *

That night, I stayed up until 1 AM, writing twenty-two pages to the girl I loved who was still in Nam Định. This was the first love letter in my life and the longest one I have ever written. I asked one of my cousins who was going back to Nam Định the next morning to hand my letter to the girl personally. In the letter I promised that I would never forget her and that I would come back someday in triumph. In fact, her image was so strong in me that I didn't fall in love with any other girl for years.

In 1992, two years after I had resettled in America, with help from an old classmate, I located the girl and we exchanged letters occasionally. She was now a widow and had many children and grandchildren. One day in 2001, I talked to her for the first time by telephone about my last days in Hà Nội. I couldn't help asking if she had received my long good-bye letter. She was silent for about five seconds and then said that she had not. My cousin had never handed my letter to her. After our long conversation, she sent me an email in which she admitted, "If I had received your letter, I would have joined you in the South, and our lives would have been greatly different." I replied that it was because of the war. She flashed back, "That's our destiny, you and I."

FAREWELL, HÀ NỘI, HELLO, SÀI GÒN!

At 6 AM, August 12, I said good-bye to my family and reported to the Gia Lâm Airport near Hà Nội for a flight to Sài Gòn. While I was waiting to board a military plane, a young French first lieutenant came to talk to our group of twenty Social Services cadres. We told him our objectives and our future plans in the

South. When we were about to leave, he shook hands with all of us and said: "I know France has made many mistakes that caused endless tragedies to you Vietnamese. Your trip today is a consequence of those mistakes. I can say only that I regret it. I wish you good luck and great success in your struggle for a better Việt Nam." Although I was nursing dislike for the French, his words, delivered with obvious emotion, moved me very much.

So at 8 AM, we boarded a French C-47 for Sài Gòn. I've never forgotten the last sight of Hà Nội when the plane circled over the ancient city before heading south. A gray shroud of clouds hung low over the city we loved so much. From about 3,000 feet, I saw the best part of Hà Nội through an opening in the clouds: the Hoàn Kiếm Lake (Lake of the Sword), the Red River, and the Long Biên Bridge. My friends and I had tears in our eyes. A man sitting next to me said the image made him think of a gray mourning scarf around the face of a young woman. We all nodded without saying a word.

We arrived in Sài Gòn three hours later. I could see canals and rivers with coconut trees along their banks bordering green fields and gardens. The landscape, slightly different from that of my home province, made me feel both homesick and excited.

After reporting to the Ministry of Social Services, we were assigned jobs receiving North Vietnamese who began arriving in the Sài Gòn area, about 100 persons a day at first, then more than 1,000 a day at Tân Sơn Nhứt Airport. Airplanes of all kinds, military and civilian, were landing every ten or fifteen minutes from 11 AM until 9 PM. Meanwhile, ships from many nations, including the U.S., British, and French navies, brought in thousands of refugees.

Many of our teams had to work late and as much as ten hours a day, including weekends, to welcome the refugees and give them initial assistance. The others had to prepare paperwork for refugees in reception camps, sometimes all night long, so that they could be paid as early as possible after their arrival. Although exhausted, we all felt happy to serve our compatriots.

All schools in Sài Gòn and Chợ Lớn areas were used to lodge the newcomers. Each refugee was paid every week or at five-day intervals an allowance of VN$12 per day, half for a child of twelve and younger. In 1954, VN$12 was equal to 30 cents but was enough to buy decent meals for one day. One could even save a little by cooking for oneself. (Minimum wage was about VN$500/month.)

Although distributing the allowance was handled with simple procedures and very little paperwork, which made stealing quite easy, very few of us were dishonest. Most of us were still too idealistic to commit such shameful misdemeanors.

On the first weekend when we could be free from work, my two friends and I went to Tây Ninh province seeking more information about Trình Minh Thế's army. If things appeared to be fine, we would join the force. In the first few hours of our visit, we learned that Trình Minh Thế and his army would soon join Ngô Đình Diệm's government. The dream we had been nursing since 1953 came to an end.

THE FIRST MONTHS IN SÀI GÒN

On trips to places around Sài Gòn, we felt happy to see people leading an easy life. Unlike the North Vietnamese, who worked so hard to earn a scanty living, people in the South enjoyed life in a carefree manner. I liked their way of living.

However, all of us newly arriving from the North shared the same concern about what the working class in the South had learned about the communists. During the war of Resistance, Việt Minh forces in South Việt Nam were rather weak. Many Việt Minh policies in the North were not applied in areas in the South and only the southern part of Central Việt Nam under its control. Many of the South Vietnamese knew very little about the true Việt Minh. To them, Việt Minh was a patriotic movement and had nothing to do with communism. Some who associated the Việt Minh with communism believed simply that communism would make the poor wealthy. Some were even credulous enough to ask us why we had gone south when the North was "independent." Right in Sài Gòn, there was some overtly produced propaganda. In many villages, pro–Việt Minh activists showed their attitude without fear of being arrested.

South Việt Nam in 1954 was not far different from the time it had been a French colony known as Cochinchina. Administrative papers were in French. Streets were named after celebrated French personages, including notorious colonists and their Vietnamese collaborators. In the North and the Central, all of those remnants of colonialism had disappeared since March 1945.

One of my friends was right when he predicted that the situation would cause much difficulty for the incoming struggle against the communists. He was afraid the South Vietnamese would only learn from the experiences of their brethren in the North when it was too late.

Beginning in late August, the flow of North Vietnamese refugees increased, and more social cadres were recruited to handle the situation. Intellectuals, experts, technicians, skilled workers (especially mechanics), and middle-class people from northern cities and towns left for the South. Some decided to leave forever; some just planned to go south for a few years and return after the elections were held as stipulated in the Geneva Accords. Some of the refugees were poor peasants who came with nothing in their pockets. Many had to walk for hundreds of miles to reach the French-controlled areas. Some even fled the Việt Minh areas on risky boat trips.

The Việt Minh employed every trick to stop people from leaving. On Highway 5 between Hà Nội and the port city of Hải Phòng, they forced hundreds of peasants, especially women, to act as human obstacles, lying in front of civilian buses and military trucks. Some pulled the refugees from vehicles or away from their walking groups to order them not to go. There were clashes resulting in bloodshed.

Although Catholics formed less than 10 percent of the population, they made up half of the refugees. Most came from the dioceses of Phát Diệm and Bùi Chu. And because of the cease-fire agreement, an important number of noncommunists serving the Resistance could flee to the South. They would later play significant roles in the South Việt Nam administration and armed forces.

Almost all North Vietnamese refugees were looking to the United States for material and moral support. The Americans seemed to be better friends, offering us generous aid.

The first time I talked to—or argued with—an American was in late August 1954. He was a captain in charge of the newly built tent city in Phú Thọ area next to the Sài Gòn racetrack. The camp was built with American funding and reserved for refugees coming on two U.S. ships, the *Marine Serpent* and the *Marine Adder*, as I recall.

On a rainy evening, a French ship brought in more than 1,000 refugees. Someone in the Ministry of Social Services, our headquarters, told the truck drivers to make for the Phú Tọ tent city. The Americans there refused to let them in, simply because they were not brought to the South by U.S. transportation. When news came, two cadres and I, who seemed to be the only ones capable of speaking "some" English, were sent to Phú Thọ "to do something," as we were told.

We tried our best with our poor vocabulary and accent to talk to the U.S. captain. We showed him the people standing on roofless trucks under the heavy rain. We patched our sentences with anything that came to mind, trying to make him agree to let those poor compatriots of ours into the camp, at least overnight, until we could find some other place in the morning.

The argument went on for about two minutes. After looking up words in a pocket dictionary for almost every sentence, we failed to move the captain's heart. At last we gave up, not because we were exhausted but because we had exhausted our vocabulary and grammar as the dialogue went into more complicated areas. Then came an English teacher who was a Vietnamese working for the U.S. embassy. He handled the affair in about two minutes, and everything went fine: the refugees were welcomed into the tent city at midnight.

My mother, my aunt, and my sisters arrived in Sài Gòn in early September. My mother worked as a corrections officer at the Sài Gòn Central Prison. In December, I came back to live with them and reentered school. Meanwhile, my comrades and I continued doing what our Việt Quốc Party required.

The Ngô Đình Diệm government had to face strong opposition right from the beginning. The nationalist army chief of staff, General Nguyễn Văn Hinh, son of the former prime minister, Nguyễn Văn Tâm, openly opposed Diệm. Every day since October 1954, the two had waged war not on the streets but on the radio. The war of words frustrated many young men of my age. We longed for stability in the South, a basic requirement for the construction of an effective anticommunist regime.

The crisis came to an end after weeks of a heated war of words. General Lê Văn Tỵ was appointed joint general chief of staff, replacing General Nguyễn Văn Hinh. The remnants of the French supporters lost their foothold in the nationalist army. Meanwhile, I joined the student-led campaign for new street names honoring Vietnamese heroes. The campaign was an instant success. Within a month, most of the street names related to colonialism disappeared after a quick resolution by the Sài Gòn City Council. Names of great patriots, including those who had fought the French colonialists, were now seen on the city street corners.

ELEVEN

The Year of Changes

ADVANCE TO THE NORTH

When the Reverend Hoàng Quỳnh, a Catholic priest and ardent anticommunist activist, founded a new regiment with the name Bắc Tiến (Advance to the North), my group was ordered by the Việt Quốc leaders to join it as a part-time psychological operations team. The regiment included ethnic North Vietnamese soldiers who had deserted from nationalist army units. Most of them were Catholics, rallying under the command of a brilliant officer, Colonel Trần Thiện, who was said to have been trained by the United States somewhere in the Pacific.

The regiment was sponsored by General Lê Văn Viễn, leader of the Bình Xuyên forces, once a powerful gang that had joined the Resistance before returning to Sài Gòn to collaborate with the French. The Bình Xuyên was then given control of the territory of Rừng Sát, south of Sài Gòn, and the right to run two famous gambling dens and a well-managed brothel.

By agreement between Lê Văn Viễn and Reverend Hoàng Quỳnh, the Bắc Tiến became an autonomous part of Bình Xuyên forces. It was supposed to be a spearhead in the future national liberation of North Việt Nam.

The regiment's morale was rather high. Once every week, our cultural group of a dozen students visited the companies, giving them general information briefings and political indoctrination and entertaining them with a show that usually lasted two hours with songs and skits. Many times the troops rose to join us in patriotic songs. The atmosphere was much like that of 1947–48, when the heroic resistance reached a high pitch in my district area, with brave warriors setting out for battle after being entertained in almost the same way.

We served the Bắc Tiến regiment with much enthusiasm but less confidence. We felt that our Việt Quốc leaders were not as clairvoyant as we had thought. How could they do anything with a poorly equipped regiment having no reliable sources of support?

In early 1955, relations between the Diệm government and the armed sects in the South turned sour. The Bình Xuyên was more and more against the government. The various sects were counting their last days. A good friend of ours who was a Bình Xuyên officer told us to leave when armed conflict seemed to be inevitable. The Diệm government ordered that the two gambling dens and the brothel should be closed. The purpose was to strangle the Bình Xuyên by taking away its greatest financial sources.

Some of my friends in the cultural group, who lived in the Bình Xuyên area on the other side of the Y Bridge connecting the Bình Xuyên area with Chợ Lớn, fled to Sài Gòn on the afternoon of April 27, only a few hours before fighting erupted between the national army and the Bình Xuyên forces. The Bắc Tiến regiment had disintegrated weeks before the clash.

The days that followed saw fierce battles in eastern Sài Gòn with hundreds of casualties and a large neighborhood burned to the ground. Within a week, the Bình Xuyên was crushed and its leaders were arrested or forced to flee the country. In some aspects, the fighting appeared to me to be the last attempt of the French to overthrow Ngô Đình Diệm.

It was in this battle that General Trình Minh Thế was assassinated by sniper fire. All my friends and I attended his funeral. The general was a devoted supporter of Ngô Đình Diệm. In February 1955, he had moved his regiment to Sài Gòn and integrated it into the national armed forces. Many people believed that his regiment protected President Diệm's government from a coup. Trình Minh Thế was gaining significant support from a lot of people from South Việt Nam.

Rumors circulated that Diệm was behind the plot to eliminate the general. Many people believed the story. In the early 1970s, a Frenchman admitted in a Paris newspaper that he had done the killing on orders from the French military in Việt Nam. I can't say which story is true.

According to one estimate, the fighting between the army and Bình Xuyên caused at least 100,000 North Vietnamese to change their minds about going south.

THE CHALLENGE

During the first half of 1955, the Diệm government continued to be confronted by fierce opposition. Diệm needed to be tough and resolute to survive, as we students could see. A few months after he became prime minister, two nationalist parties began to actively oppose him. The Đại Việt held the Ba Lòng war base in Quảng Trị province; the Việt Quốc had established an independent territory in the west of Quảng Nam province in early April 1955 and had already clashed with local military units.

As a Việt Quốc member, I had to support our comrades in Quảng Nam. My group was given the task of distributing leaflets and other propaganda supporting the uprising. However, our comrades were unable to withstand fighting longer than a few months. They were in no way comparable to the government army in strength and logistical support. In January 1956, the Việt Quốc ended its armed revolt.

In any case, Diệm's government was facing the greatest threat from the militias of several sects in the Mekong Delta region. Since early 1955, Diệm and his newly established government had been attempting to neutralize the different sects that had been in control of territory in the southern part of the country since 1946. With the consent of the French authorities, these sects had raised and supported their own armies with taxes collected from people in their areas. The French tolerated the sects' militias for the purposes of fighting the Việt Minh. In fact, they were the Việt Minh's bitter foes. Some of these militias were popular and consisted of good fighters such as the Cao Đài of Trình Minh Thế and the Hòa Hảo of Lê Quang Vinh, alias Ba Cụt.

After Trình Minh Thế sided with the government and the Bình Xuyên were eliminated, smaller sectarian lords surrendered, except for the army of Ba Cụt. He was from the Hòa Hảo Church, a branch of Buddhism. The Hòa Hảo followers had been the most fanatical anticommunists ever since the Việt Minh massacred many thousands of their people in 1947. The government had to spend much time and effort to get rid of Ba Cụt in 1956.

Although not siding with the sects, most of the noncommunist parties also opposed Diệm and his political movement, the Phong Trào Cách Mạng Quốc Gia (National Revolutionary Movement). I was too young to understand the complexity of politics, but I was allergic to anything that resembled communist propaganda. Diệm's courtiers began idolizing him with legends and a hymn, praising him as a national hero. My friends and I had been fed up with Hồ Chí Minh, so we wouldn't accept deifying Ngô Đình Diệm in the same way.

THE REFUGEES PROSPER

After the last refugees left Hải Phòng and the iron curtain covered all of North Việt Nam, there had been almost 1 million refugees from above 17th parallel resettled in the South. According to official records, the figure was 868,000. But that figure did not include the thousands moving to their new homes by their own transportation and those who did not register as refugees. Some authorities said that if the Việt Minh had given people a green light to leave the North as they wished, there would have been another half million North Vietnamese going south.

The refugees produced great changes all over South Việt Nam, especially in the cities. They competed with ethnic Chinese in many businesses, particularly by running restaurants, stores, and groceries. Before 1954, the Chinese con-trolled the major part of the South Việt Nam economy. The presence of so many North Vietnamese refugees disturbed the calm and easy life in the South. There was conflict between the newcomers and the native South Vietnamese, but it was much less serious than some had expected. The differences between the two groups created no major problems, and most were settled without much difficulty.

TERRITORIAL SECURITY

In late 1954, people traveling in many remote countryside areas of the Mekong Delta encountered some security problems. It was not uncommon that rich people in those areas sometimes received four-inch nails from some bandit group along with letters demanding money. The letters also carried a message: the nails would be driven into the victims' ears if they failed to meet the bandits' demand.

In only one year, the appearance of Sài Gòn changed a lot. Streets flour-ished with new small businesses and many more people. Thanks to the cease-fire, I could join my new friends in visiting villages far away from Sài Gòn. Most routes were safe, day and night.

TAKING OVER FORMER VIỆT MINH AREAS

When the last Việt Minh troops left their staging areas for North Việt Nam, the Diệm government's military and administrative elements took control of the territories. There were only about 100,000 Việt Minh troops and civilian sup-porters in the South who went north.

Beside the troops, the government also sent many administrative teams to establish local governments in those territories. Among them were the Công Dân Vụ (citizens affairs teams). The teams tried to win the hearts and minds of the people who had been misinformed by Việt Minh propaganda for a decade. They were hostile to the nationalist troops and civil servants.

A number of my friends joined the campaign, serving in the citizens affairs teams in the Mộc Hóa area, about seventy miles west of Sài Gòn. With extreme enthusiasm, they came into the hostile land and vowed to do something great for the poor people. Other friends and I sometimes visited them in the villages.

We met a team when its members were working with district medical work-ers and the village youth in a vaccination program. As the team members re-lated, for the first two weeks, villagers didn't talk to them. They even refused to let the members sleep in their yards. They didn't allow them to get water from their wells and didn't give them a light to kindle their wood for cooking. The cadres patiently went on. They approached children by teaching them new games to play and songs to sing, giving them candy, and training them to take care of their own health. Whose kids could resist candy and games?

The villagers were moved when they saw the young men from Sài Gòn in black pajamas, taking good care of their children, holding them in their laps, washing the dirty kids as if they were their own brothers and sisters. The villagers realized that the young men were in no way "puppets of the French and Americans" who came to reestablish the colonialist regime, as the Việt Minh had taught them. The teams provided great help to the poor and proved to be devoted public servants, in many aspects better than the Việt Minh.

Two months later, when the team moved to another location, all the villagers signed a petition asking them to stay for one more month. And when the team finally had to leave, many women and children cried while saying good-bye.

The campaign was a great success for various reasons. The most important of all was that many members were enthusiastic young men of the nationalist parties who were motivated to do their jobs. Many were high school and college students who temporarily quit school for one year to enroll in the teams just for idealistic purposes. Later, during the war, teams working in the countryside did achieve some success, but there were several obstacles that hindered such programs. The largest was the government's management of the campaign. We used to say that if things had gone smoothly the same way as the first teams did, we would have won the war right from the beginning.

ONE YEAR AFTER THE GENEVA ACCORDS

On July 20 1955, a great anticommunist demonstration was held in front of the two Sài Gòn hotels, Metropole and Gallieni, where members of the International Commission for Control and Supervision (ICCS) and a Việt Minh delegation were staying. I was in the crowd at the Gallieni with my comrades. The crowd of a few thousand people was in order and acted peacefully during the first fifteen minutes.

Suddenly, the crowd became angry, swarming into the hotel, smashing anything they could reach, and attacking anyone they thought was Việt Minh. A similar incident took place at the Metropole on Catinat Street (later Tự Do Street).

A policeman told me that a French soldier in a team providing protection for the ICCS hit a student who had arrived at the commission office to present a declaration. The soldier beat the student with a pistol, leaving a deep gash in his scalp. The sight of the student with a blood-soaked face and shirt may have been the spark that ignited the anger in the crowd.

The hotels suffered considerable losses in furniture and equipment. A few persons were injured, but there were no deaths. Members of the Việt Minh delegation escaped before the mob began the raid. After that incident, the Việt

Minh delegation did not appear in public until they were called back to Hà Nội after the South Vietnamese government strongly protested their presence. It was not a glorious feat to achieve, but in our late teenage years we loved participating in any action against the enemy, just like we had done several times against the French soldiers in my hometown.

The ICCS, which consisted of delegations from India, Canada, and Poland, was in Việt Nam to make sure that the terms of the Geneva Accords were being followed, but it was powerless to deal with violations of the agreement.

My close friend, a lieutenant in the nationalist army who had been captured by the Việt Minh after an ambush that defeated the Sixth Battalion in Ninh Bình province in March 1954, was not returned in the POW exchange as stipulated in the accords. He happened to meet a relative who was on his way to flee North Việt Nam while he was working in a forest near the prison camp where he was being held in Quảng Bình province, near the 17th parallel. He sent a short note with the name of the camp, its location, and his prisoner serial number. His family complained to the ICCS. In early 1955, the commission sent a team to the camp to investigate, but the communist authorities denied his family's allegation and would not allow the team access to the camp's records.

In the school year 1954–55, several high schools in the North moved south. Some schools well known to the students were Chu Văn An, Trưng Vương (for girls) from Hà Nội and Hồ Ngọc Cẩn from Bùi Chu. I enrolled in a South Vietnamese high school to continue my education.

In the first few months, there was little friendship between the North Vietnamese and local students. Some cavils occurred, but mutually positive relations eventually developed.

In mid-1955, there was a fight between a group of students and the French soldiers who were waiting to return to France, stationed in Camp Petrus Ký, Sài Gòn. The fight prompted a larger clash that drew crowds of students both from the North and the South. One French soldier died.

The summer of 1955 was my last time at school before I dropped out.

BASIC REFORMS

One year after the cease-fire, South Việt Nam began to progress. The new nationalist government under Ngô Đình Diệm continued to consolidate its power. More new administrative regulations were enacted and proved to be effective. Complicated and time-consuming paperwork was reformed, reducing a lot of red tape. Many kinds of notarized and certified paperwork that previously required one month to complete could now be done in a day or a week.

The government's efforts to control social evils succeeded significantly. Until mid-1955, hundreds of opium dens, gambling dens, and brothels could be found in the capital city. The Bình Xuyên gang was running two legal casinos and a house of prostitution in Bình Khang. All were very well managed, attracting a large number of customers. The closing of the two large casinos and the brothel, as well as largely reducing the number of small whorehouses, casinos, and opium dens, earned the government strong approval from the common people.

In a bold move, Diệm enacted the most striking decree forbidding aliens to work in eleven trades; eight of these had been almost monopolized by Chinese nationals and the others by East Indians and the French. The decree also banned foreign ownership of land in Việt Nam. In 1955, all Chinese living in the South retained their alien status. After the decree, most began to apply for naturalization. Although my party leadership opposed the Diệm government, many of my comrades and I supported Diệm's policy toward foreigners living in Việt Nam. We thought that it was the best way to restore control of the country's businesses to the Vietnamese people, especially restaurants and groceries.

Also in mid-1955, the French authorities handed over to the South Vietnamese government the remainder of the institutions still under their control, including the currency issuance institute and the military supreme command. French military units left South Việt Nam one after another.

U.S. military officers began training major Vietnamese units along with the remaining French instructors. They received a hearty welcome from anticommunist people who had hope that the Americans would be true friends to us Vietnamese. They said that the French came to Việt Nam with no lofty cause and they were our enemy, while the Americans were not. Those who supported the French didn't think so. They didn't expect the Americans to do anything better than the French. And many others who were ingrained xenophobes predicted that the Americans could only destroy Việt Nam before they would fail at last.

My mother was working at the Sài Gòn Central Prison in charge of one of the female prisoner groups. Since the Ngô Đình Diệm government assumed power, there had been significant changes at the Central Prison. The inmates were no more under the rough-handed rule of the "kings," the heads of the gangs who actually governed the prison wards. The prison officials under the French authority had relied on the "king system" to maintain order in the wards.

My mother was doing her job with her kind heart, as she had done previously for the inmates in the Nam Định prison.

PART III

The Cogwheel

TWELVE

To Be a Soldier

THE MILITARY ACADEMY

As my father had been a public servant and had died in the communist prison camp, and I was my mother's only son, I was exempted by conscription law from the military draft. If I had applied for a scholarship abroad, I would have been on the priority list. My mother and my aunt hated the idea that I would be in the military. They wanted me to be a doctor or an engineer.

Some of my friends thought that we should not join the army because it was spoiled by corruption and had too many incapable officers who impeded the army's progress and spoiled the young officers' efforts to improve the organization. My friends thought that young men with above-average intelligence, like some in our group, would be better able to help the country if they became doctors or academics. Besides, the salary of armed forces officers was rather low.

Other friends had a different opinion. They said in a world where the conflict between communist powers—especially China—and the free world was becoming more and more serious, another war in Việt Nam would be inevitable in the next few years. In such a situation, we should be serving in the army to defend our stronghold of freedom.

Another argument was that in almost all small, underdeveloped countries, military leaders held ruling power because they had discipline and could perform their tasks much more effectively than civilian politicians. Therefore, the best path for a patriot like me would be to serve the country as an army officer.

To my question about corruption and ineffectiveness in the army, some of my friends contended that because of such shortcomings, we young patriots should be in the army to clean it up and to build it to defend South Việt Nam and to liberate North Việt Nam some day. This argument was the most persuasive to me. Furthermore, I knew I was a lazy boy. I believed that I could be successful if I served under any kind of discipline that compelled me to fulfill my duty. And so army life would be better for me, I thought.

When there was an announcement that the Joint General Staff was recruiting cadets for Class 12 of the Đà Lạt Inter-Arms Military School, I decided to enroll. I talked to my mother and my aunt for hours before they reluctantly accepted my idea. As I was under twenty-one, my mother had to consent to my application before the military could accept it.

My aunt never wanted me to leave home, especially to be in the military. She had reminded me many times that I was the only son of her brother and also the only great-grandson of her grandfather. She couldn't bear the thought that I would be sent into battle, even as an officer, and she cried a lot at that.

My mother only said that she didn't like the idea either. But she assured my aunt that if I really wanted to join the army, she would let me go because "everyone has his own destiny." She reminded my aunt of the fortune teller who looked into my horoscope one day in 1945 and said that I would be in the military. She also repeated what my father told me when I visited him the last time at a prison camp: I should become either an engineer or an army officer.

I barely passed the entry examination, ranking 108 of the 110 eligible candidates from the First Military Region (South Việt Nam territory including Sài Gòn). The result disappointed me, but my friends encouraged me to go on. So on October 5, 1955, I said good-bye to my mother, my aunt, whom I loved most, and my two sisters before boarding the morning train to Đà Lạt.

THE CADET'S LIFE

No soldier ever forgets the first days in military life. There were a lot of things to be done from early morning reveille until 9 PM taps, much more than I had expected. But everyone was happy. My classmates were mostly from middle-class families who shared with me almost the same opinion about why we chose a military career. Half of my platoon members were from cities and provinces north of the 17th parallel. All had high morale.

On October 23, 1955, a referendum was held in which people were asked to vote either for King Bảo Đại or for Premier Ngô Đình Diệm to be the chief of state. We cadets were sent to hang banderoles and posters on streets and public sites to encourage people to vote. Influenced by my Việt Quốc Party leaders, I didn't like Diệm. However, between the two, I surely preferred him to Bảo Đại.

We witnessed some tricks by government and military officials in an attempt to bring Diệm the largest number of votes. I felt rather bad about the tricks, as did many of my classmates. We knew that Ngô Đình Diệm would win with a great majority in any fair election. Most people were fed up with the king. Why did the government have to rely on such dishonest practices?

By October 1955, the Diệm government had recovered full national sovereignty from the French (in national defense, foreign affairs, currency administration, and so forth). By the time we arrived at the academy, most of the French officers had departed, except a few who remained in the joint training teams, which also included some American officers. The academy had been reformed to follow the pattern of the U.S. Military Academy at West Point, while retaining some training concepts of the French Military Academy at Saint Cyr and of the Vietnamese military ways and traditions.

The experimental curriculum of my class gave us a broad knowledge of various arms, especially combat arms. The approach was probably borrowed from the French academy. Đà Lạt Inter-Arms Military School was established in 1948 by the French Command in Việt Nam. In 1960 it became the Việt Nam National Military Academy.

The two-month basic training program was tough. All day long, we were running from class to class, from dormitories to the mess hall, and tired by all kinds of exercises. Many of my classmates found it difficult to eat meals with so little time allowed. Some were unable to consume half their food before the bugle sounded the end of chow time. Their friends in the same platoon had to store food in the kitchen, with help from some friendly cooks, so that those poor fellows would not be hungry. They soon caught up. In only a month, they were able to finish everything they had on the table in less than fifteen minutes.

We were so pressed for time. We spent our free time very carefully down to the minute. Because the experimental curriculum required much more time than usual, we had to work eight hours a day and sometimes spend extra hours in night classes as well. That included combat, tactics, weaponry, combat arms, physical training, and general education (math, physics, history, geography, law, and English). We seldom had more than ten minutes after 6 PM to have a quick cup of coffee. Still, everyone appeared to be very happy with the new life. I seldom wrote home, but I often sent presents to my sisters.

After basic training, we had the first preliminary test, which only 1 of my 153 classmates failed. The next thing we had to do was conquer the peak of Mt. Lâm Viên, or Lang Biang, at an elevation of about 7,500 feet (4,900 feet from the surrounding valley). It became a tradition that the greenhorns would be recognized as cadets only after reaching that peak.

There were a half dozen U.S. officers in the combat arms training organization serving the military academy. The last French officers left a month after we arrived. The Americans were nice to us, except for one thing. That was the pith helmet of their uniform. It has been widely used in Việt Nam. But the pith helmet in khaki on a westerner reminded people of the French colonialist officials in Việt Nam, especially French customs officers with batons or whips in their hands, who sowed terror and hatred among villagers before 1945. The Americans' pith helmet was not a big problem, but to me it indicated something more important: the Americans were disregarding the psychological effects of their actions.

One incident almost caused serious trouble to Vietnamese-American relations in the academy. It occurred in a training session when some American officers conducted a one-hour presentation of U.S. military close-order drill on a terrace just outside the main gate. An American captain was briefing my class along with the company officer class, which consisted of some fifty lieutenants from a training school nearby. We were all sitting on the ground. While speaking, the captain noticed that a cadet in the front row close to him was nodding. Every cadet would doze off a few times a day, especially around noon. But the captain looked annoyed. He used his briefing stick to knock softly on the cadet's helmet to wake him up. Elsewhere in Việt Nam or in the United States, such an act was quite common. But for a foreigner to do so to a Vietnamese was different. After many decades under western colonialism, to a Vietnamese, such action meant a contemptuous attitude. The reaction was quick. A first lieutenant from the airborne brigade, well known for becoming involved in fights, rose to his feet. He was ready to hit the American, while some of his classmates tried to assuage his anger. Colonel Nguyễn Văn Thiệu, the academy commandant, who became RVN president in 1967, and other school officers attending the session quickly calmed him down. The event was resolved peacefully.

It seemed that in every Vietnamese—and probably everyone in other former Western colonies—there was a dash of jingoism. Even though we all appreciated the help and presence of the Americans, tough reactions against individual Americans who treated us with disdain were always highly praised.

At that time, an anecdote spread far and wide in the Vietnamese military about a similar incident. The story was that Colonel Lam Sơn, the commanding officer of a Vietnamese Light Infantry Division, had once visited one of his battalions along with a U.S. weapons inspection team. An American captain poked his forefinger into a rifle that a Vietnamese soldier had displayed on the inspection table. The rifle was so dirty that it blackened the captain's finger. He wiped his finger on a medal on the soldier's chest, the anecdote continued. Another version had it that the captain wiped his finger on the soldier's cheek. Colonel Lam Sơn, bubbling over with wrath, slapped the captain in the face. A few hours later, the captain was sent back to Sài Gòn.

The story, told again and again in various versions, was very pleasant to our ears. Many years later, however, I found out that the incident had not been so. Col. Lam Sơn himself told me that the story had been greatly exaggerated.

A PEACEFUL YEAR

The year 1956 started with radical changes in the RVN government as well as in the armed forces. New military rank insignias of gold and silver flowers were introduced to replace the French Army stripes. We were trained in American-style close order drill, modified by Vietnamese innovations. New administrative procedures were applied.

We spent the first three months in intensive military training. In April, the newly recruited Class 13 arrived. Class 12 cadets became "seniors," the first in the new system of command of the cadet corps. My class was put in charge of leading the juniors in morning workouts and conducting a weekly inspection of their rooms. The task at the time was easy, but it developed into a more strictly imposed system in subsequent classes.

Now we had more spare time, as the intensity of training was reduced. We were able to write more letters, especially love letters. On Sundays, many of my classmates could be seen strolling along downtown Đà Lạt streets with their girl-friends, while others were chatting in coffee shops and restaurants. The white cadet uniforms seemed brighter on the green landscape of the beautiful city.

For fun, many cadets played practical jokes on their buddies. One morning when I hastily inserted my left foot into a boot, I felt something wet and slimy in it. As my platoon was already in line in front of an instructor, I had not even five seconds to clean the darned thing, which bothered me until noontime break. A frolicsome fellow had put a rotten banana into my boot.

THE FIRST HINT OF DICTATORSHIP

In the first semester exam, I ranked top in my platoon, and my platoon was given the title of "honors platoon" as its members scored the highest of the class. My platoon was often given the task of honor guard to welcome President Diệm and chiefs of state from foreign countries visiting Đà Lạt. As the honors platoon leader, several times I escorted Diệm while he reviewed troops and the groups of people rallying to welcome him. Diệm's voice was energetic, his looks were dominating, and his manners were authoritarian, all of which made many people cower before him. I saw many high-ranking civilian officials and military generals who seemed fearful when they talked to him.

He was terrifying to us, too. Sometimes I felt disconcerted before him. But my platoon mates and I found our own way to calm ourselves by looking straight at him while thinking that "under his suit, he looks just like us." It helped us maintain self-control.

President Diệm paid much attention to the academy. Once at a breakfast table he told us, "This academy is for those who want to become generals, ministers, or even presidents one day. If you wish to be only a major or a lieutenant colonel before retiring, you should not be here."

While we were at the academy, there were great changes outside. The new government was undertaking several reforms in the administrative system, military reorganization, and other renovations necessary for the independent South Việt Nam. Many patriots supported Diệm, but others were against him.

It was obvious that Diệm's inner circle intended to use his Cần Lao Nhân Vị Cách Mạng Đảng (Labor Personalism Revolutionary Party) behind their newly established Phong Trào Cách Mạng Quốc Gia (National Revolutionary Movement) to rule South Việt Nam as a counterbalance to the Communist Party, which disguised itself under the title Workers' Party in North Việt Nam. Military servicemen and public servants were asked to join. The Cần Lao was thought to play a key role in Diệm's regime. In fact, it lost its practical power several years before the coup in November 1963.

The movement members, many of whom were enlisted men and officers in the academy (and probably in many other military units), caused trouble in the chain of command as they abused their members' rights by bitterly criticizing their superiors in the movement meetings. Some members among the cadets even caused their peers to feel uneasy.

Many of my friends and I refused to join the Cần Lao when we were invited by some classmates. We knew that such a refusal might have brought us disadvantages, but we just didn't like the idea. We said that as long as military regulations forbade political activities in the armed forces, we wouldn't go against the rules. During a casual meeting with the cadets a few months later, President Diệm affirmed that military regulations must be respected: "No politics in the military academy." The Cần Lao became less bothersome, but it still covertly admitted servicemen, especially officers.

Ngô Đình Thục, archbishop of Vĩnh Long, and Ngô Đình Nhu, President Diem's two brothers, were the active supporters of the new doctrine of Nhân Vị (Personalism). They asserted that the Nhân Vị ideology would be a powerful anticommunist tool. There were intensive training courses in Vĩnh Long and in Sài Gòn, but the doctrine was not convincing with its abstract theories that required the reader to have a profound background in philosophy to grasp its basic ideas. In the end, they failed to attain the lofty objectives of Nhân Vị.

In the election for a constitutional assembly held in early 1956, my fellow cadets and I again witnessed old-fashioned tricks to gain advantages for pro-government candidates. Besides the October 1955 referendum, this was the second general election I knew in my life. In 1946, I had already seen a framed election. In 1956, I saw it done once again.

During my teenage years, I yearned for true democracy, and what I saw made me angry. Although I did not have much knowledge of politics, I did contend that true democracy was the best way to fight communism. So I didn't cast my ballot that morning, though I had been eager to vote for the first time. After carefully looking around the booth, I discarded the ballots and dropped an empty envelope into the box.

The year 1956 also saw the large-scale campaign "Tố Cộng" (Denouncing the Communists) rise to a new height. It was primarily a propaganda scheme aimed at indoctrinating the South Vietnamese people about why we should fight the communists. Another objective was to detect communist secret cells. In the military academy, we were required to attend classes discussing communist ideology and what the communists had done and would be doing to their people. In some parts of South Việt Nam, the campaign was primarily directed at former Việt Minh cadres who were suspected of working secretly for North Vietnamese communists. Worse than that, there were reports of people whose close relatives had joined the Việt Minh in North Việt Nam and who were being badly treated. Some illegal executions of suspected communist secret agents were reported.

After the start of Tố Cộng, the term denoting the Vietnamese communist organization and its members became "Việt Cộng," replacing "Việt Minh," the old term that was no longer appropriate to its actual nature.[1] At that time, the Ba Cụt rebels were still fighting against government forces in the Mekong Delta. Ba Cụt, also known as Lê Quang Vinh, was a charismatic leader of a group of Hòa Hảo sect followers. He was also a talented military commander who led the fighting that helped his men survive fierce attacks by the government forces when the other rebel groups were unable to last more than a few months under military pressure of the national army.

One day, the government announced that Ba Cụt had been ambushed and captured. But rumors were that the government had invited him to a formal negotiation, then had broken its promise to let him go safely and arrested him on his way back to his base area. Not long after that, he was sentenced to death and guillotined. His execution has since become a controversial topic of whether or not President Diệm should have commuted his sentence.

ECHOES FROM THE NORTH

On the other side of the 17th parallel, the Communist Workers' Party restarted a nationwide Land Reform Campaign in 1955, which lasted until mid-1956. The South Vietnamese mass media published many stories about the campaign, but it seemed that the reports of barbaric brutality were not credible to people who had had no experience with communists. Many South Vietnamese said the Sài Gòn government made up the stories for propaganda. However, according to eyewitnesses who left the North in 1956, what really went on was more horrible than was reported by the media in the South.

A cousin of mine fled North Việt Nam along with a few friends and arrived in Vientiane in March 1956 after a fifteen-day journey on foot. He resettled in Sài Gòn and used to stop by to see my family. He also visited with me on a Sunday at the academy, telling me about terrible persecutions in the Land Reform Campaign during its most macabre phase, which resumed in early 1955 after a moratorium in early 1954, a few months before the Geneva Accords were signed in July.

Many fled the North on foot and by boat, including a lot of communist cadres. Ironically, two of them were former inmates who, in July 1954, had tried to persuade my mother to stay in the North. Seeing us again after living under the Việt Minh regime for more than a year, they realized that the governing power in the North was totally different from the Resistance government, which they had served prior to 1951 before they were incarcerated by the nationalist authorities.

The stories they told us were much more horrible than what I had known before leaving the North. Had they not been recounted by those friends, I never would have believed that they were true.

After we arrived in Sài Gòn in August 1954, we sent a few postcards to my uncle and my friends. The form and size of the special card were approved in an agreement between the two Việt Nams; each card allowed a message of about fifty words. Both sides imposed strict censorship on the messages. Very little longed-for information could get through, including the death of a close relative. We received a few replies, and then everything stopped as the Land Reform Campaign came to its peak. My mother and my aunt could do nothing more than pray.

Another remote cousin of mine who escaped from the North in mid-1956 recounted to my family the horrible scenes that took place in my home village in late 1955. My grandmother was brought to the "people's court" along with a dozen old men and women. The court's presiding judge was a young communist who had only a first-grade education. My grandmother was humiliated and charged with crimes she had never committed. She refuted the charges with a tough language that angered the "court." At eighty-five, she didn't care about death or prison, nor did other victims of her age.

The people's court didn't sentence her to a prison term but put her under house arrest. Given only 200 grams of food a day during a year of being isolated, she would have starved if some poor farmers had not secretly fed her. Five women in turn covertly slipped into the little hut where my grandma was locked up to supply her with a little food, usually sweet potato and manioc. They did the same for three or four other old ladies.

My uncle, who was brought to the same trial, got a sentence of ten years in prison. On the way to a prison camp, he snatched a hand grenade and killed himself, along with one of the guards.

The massacre of tens of thousands of landlords during the Land Reform Campaign was horrible, but it was the compulsory denunciation that begot this incredible barbarism. In my village as well as in others, by orders of the Land Reform group, many young women accused their fathers (even their grandfathers) of having sexually assaulted them. The women had to do what they were told in the people's courts in order to avoid harsh punishment (at least three years in prison) that would result from refusing the group's order requiring them to denounce their fathers.[2] Under any label and for any objective, however lofty it might be, these extremely barbarous measures would never have been acceptable.

Such unimaginable immorality left a deep scar in people's hearts and marked the darkest page in Việt Nam's history. It was the dirtiest crime of the communist dictators in Việt Nam.

GENERAL ELECTION

July 20, 1956, came and went without the general election as scheduled in the 1954 Geneva Accords. The faint hope of many people for a peaceful unification was dashed. President Diệm responded to an official letter from the North Việt Nam prime minister and turned down Hà Nội's proposal for a general election as suggested by a clause in the declaration attached to the 1954 Geneva Accords.

From what I had learned about the North, I thought the South Việt Nam government was right when it refused to join general elections. In the North, the bloody Land Reform Campaign in 1955–56 had created an extreme fear of communist power among the common citizens. The fear was so great that "people dared not speak in loud voices at night, friends would not meet for casual talk," and "acquaintances would not nod to each other when running across each other on village roads," as related by people coming from the North between mid-1955 and mid-1956. They asserted that no one would dare to cast a vote for anticommunist candidates in an election at any level, and no noncommunist politician would be so stupid as to participate in an election in which his defeat was certain, even before ballots were cast.

Much later, communist literature and many foreign books and articles would claim that Ngô Đình Diệm's refusal to participate in a general election caused the 1955–75 war. I supported Diệm's position. Diệm was not so stupid as to accept an election under the current situation, even if international observers had been assigned to every polling station. Communist leaders in North Việt Nam must have known that and made the proposal merely for propaganda purposes.

TRUE HEROES

On July 6, the cadets' battalion went to Sài Gòn. At the Independence Palace, we welcomed Vice President Richard Nixon, He was visiting on the occasion of Diệm's second anniversary of assuming top government powers as prime minister. The next morning we joined the parade at Phú Thọ racetracks, where I learned the first lesson about how a soldier could become a hero.

Prior to the parade before the president and tens of thousands of spectators, there was a skydiving demonstration by paratroopers and an airborne supply demonstration. When we began marching, a C-47 flew the last circle over the area and dropped a large crate of simulated military supplies. We concentrated on marching, trying our best to keep perfect lines, unaware of what was going on. We heard the spectators screaming and thought they were cheering us, although they didn't sound happy. So we kept marching in good order.

Only after the large crate—at least a ton—hit the ground about twenty yards from the right side of my company bloc did we realize what caused the people's panic: the three parachutes on the supply crate had failed to open, and the crate was falling free above us. The crate broke and shook the ground like a small shell, spraying us with sand, dirt, and bits of wood, but no one was hurt.

The people gave us a thunderous applause, this time really praising us. One hour later, we received a handwritten note from the president and notes from the minister of defense and chief of the Joint General Staff, highly commending the "extreme courage" of the corps of cadets, "who were keeping perfect parade discipline, without any sign of fear and disorder under the imminent danger." We all were happy with that, but privately we confessed that if the visors of our cadet caps hadn't kept us from seeing the falling crate, we might have acted differently.

THE QUỲNH LƯU REVOLT

News of another important event reached us in October 1956. South Việt Nam media reported the "rectification of errors campaign" in the North. Hà Nội officials in charge of land reform had resigned, and General Võ Nguyên Giáp delivered a speech admitting that errors had been made.

The Hungarian Revolution broke out in late October. The Soviet crackdown on the streets of Budapest and the brave actions of leader Imre Nagy lent spiritual support to the anticommunist Vietnamese. Thousands of North Vietnamese Catholics in the Quỳnh Lưu area joined a bloody protest for religious freedom and their right to resettle in the South. The brutal crackdown was a shock to us all.

At the same time, the dissenting movement, the so-called Nhân Văn—Giai Phẩm, reached a new height after the rectification campaign was begun. It gained momentum late in the year but was soon suppressed. Information about the movement and its fate was insufficient for us cadets to have a clear view of the actual situation in the North until years later. It was a spontaneous movement founded by scores of famous writers who published two special magazines, *Nhân Văn* (Humanism) and *Giai Phẩm* (Selected Works). Many articles, short stories, and poems indirectly criticized the communist regime and Hồ Chí Minh. The communist regime cracked down on the movement with a heavy hand. The writers were sentenced to two years in prison and then lived under house arrest, some until 1985. The famous songwriter Văn Cao, author of the Hà Nội national anthem, was a member of the group.

A SURPRISE FAVOR

One night in early October 1956, my class was greatly surprised by a message from the Joint General Staff: by order of the president, we would be sent to attend the company officer course at the U.S. Army Infantry School at Fort Benning, Georgia, right after graduation. When the academy headquarters duty officer broke the news to us at 10 PM, five minutes after the message arrived on the academy commander's desk, we all went wild singing and yelling—with the permission of the duty officer. We would graduate six months early and attend the infantry school for nine months in Georgia. Great!

On October 26, the corps of cadets participated in a magnificent celebration when President Diệm officially promulgated the constitution of the Republic of Việt Nam. In white uniform, the five company-sized blocs of cadets marched while the air filled with martial music and the endless applause from people gathered on the sidewalks to watch. Our corps of cadets was at the head of miles of parade troops and vehicles.

Most of us seemed to share the same opinion that the establishment of the republic and the creation of the new laws and regulations of an independent nation brought us pride and confidence. We were no longer under French domination. Although I was not a Diệm supporter, I thought he was at least a respectable leader for us to serve and obey without shame.

We had a secondary task when showing up in public: to attract young men to join us in the academy. After the ceremonies for October 26, we toured several military and civilian installations. Whenever possible, we were introduced to the local communities to promote better relations between the armed forces and the civilians, which had not been close so far.

In the third week of November, we completed the fifteen-day final exams that covered a staggering variety of subjects. Many of us lost one or two pounds during those two weeks. In the afternoon of the last exam, we were so tired that many skipped dinner, plunged into bed, and fell into a deep sleep without washing and brushing teeth.

A week later, we gathered in the large auditorium to hear the results. I ranked fourth out of the 147 graduates, a great success that would please my family very much. I felt regret that I had no girlfriend to share the pride with me. The girl I loved was still somewhere in the North. I hadn't heard from her since that morning of June 30, 1954, and I still couldn't forget her.

The graduation on December 2 was great with pompous ceremonies presided over by the president. We would never forget the very minute when the cadet battalion commander gave the order, "On your knees, cadets!" Then the school's officers slipped the epaulets with second lieutenant insignia—a golden flower—on our shoulder straps. We took the oath "to be loyal to the Fatherland and the people of Việt Nam." At last, the academy commander shouted, "Stand up, officers!" Pride could be seen on every face: we were on the first step of the career ladder.

That night, after the formal dinner celebrating our commission, we all went downtown for the first time as officers. Đà Lạt streets seemed brighter for the brand-new second lieutenants. The scenes made me sad again. If only the girl I loved were here with me.

Tough training had armed me with a great deal of military knowledge, mostly of conventional warfare. I still felt our training lacked something important, which was how to win a war in which guerrilla terrorist tactics and propaganda tricks were the most effective weapons of our enemy.

EXPLORING AMERICA

After a fifteen-day leave, we were all busy preparing for schooling in the United States. Selected by my teacher as one of the top ten students in English fluency, I was in the first of three flights to depart on a PAA Super Constellation. I left Việt Nam on December 27.

We stopped by Honolulu for twenty-four hours, staying at the Edgewater Hotel on Waikiki Beach. The first American I met at the swimming pool asked me, "Where are you from?" and I didn't understand her question until she used her wetted finger to write the words on dry tiles bordering the pool. When I told her I came from Việt Nam, she didn't know where Việt Nam was. It was my turn to draw a map of Asia to give her a faint idea of the location. I then failed to understand her second question, if I was a pilot, until she moved her hand imitating the plane diving and soaring. That was how well one of the top ten in English fluency could really communicate with an American.

We spent New Year's Eve in San Francisco while staying in the Oakland Army Terminal. Everything was so beautiful: the Japanese Tea Garden, the Golden Gate Bridge, Chinatown, and Fisherman's Wharf. We departed by train on January 3, 1957, and arrived in Columbus, Georgia, on January 6, crossing the various landscapes across the U.S. continent, including many vast plains covered with snow, which we saw for the first time.

Our course began on January 7. As we were still fresh from training, we had little difficulty with the course. Moreover, we were assisted by a group of interpreters. Most of our attention was directed toward the American way of life.

That was the era of Nat King Cole, Louis Armstrong, Elvis Presley, Pat Boone, Frank Sinatra, Elizabeth Taylor, Marilyn Monroe, and other bright stars. We saw color TV, recently introduced, and freeways. Everything was new to us. I spent most of my spare time traveling. My friends were Americans and officers from other nations. Most of what I learned came from outside the school. However, my English capability was still very limited, so I would have to learn much more.

Before leaving Việt Nam, we had heard much about life in the States. In a briefing in the military academy, a Vietnamese officer just returning from the United States told us how great freedom was over there. He said American citizens had the right to buy any kind of weapon, and so pistols, machine guns, howitzers, mortars, tanks, and rocket-launchers were sold in department stores and gas stations. I believed what he said without question. But during the first few months at Fort Benning, I hadn't seen any such gun sales until the 1957 Army Day, when I went downtown and discovered the truth. On this occasion, the army displayed almost all kinds of weapons in various places, including department stores, gas stations, and used car lots. A few Vietnamese had mistaken the exhibition for a sale. Years later, many Americans would fall into similar errors while visiting and serving in Việt Nam or writing about the war.

Among my new friends were two Japanese officers. My Vietnamese friends and I often met and talked with them. But we were surprised that many officers from Korea, the Philippines, Taiwan, and Malaysia objected to our friendship with the Japanese. For the first time we were aware of the hatred of other Asian peoples toward the Japanese.

On another occasion, some Japanese and even some Koreans officers advised us not to watch *Sayonara* with Marlon Brando, the movie we had heard about before going to the States. They said, "It's not Japan and Japanese. You'll feel embarrassed at the scenes." Of course, I didn't feel embarrassed when I went to watch it, as I knew little about Japan.

A few months later, it was our turn to advise them not to watch *China Gate* with Nat King Cole. Except for the song "China Gate" and a few scenes of Vietnamese peasants running away from battle areas taken from some newsreel clips, the film presented nothing that was Vietnamese. That really embarrassed us. It was the first lesson I learned about how images of a country can be distorted by a foreigner's camera.

When I was still in North Việt Nam, I had read many books about the history and geography of the United States, about the Pilgrims, the Founding Fathers, George Washington, Abraham Lincoln, and the Civil War translated into Vietnamese and the monthly magazine *Free World* printed in Vietnamese by the U.S. Information Service. Therefore, it was fascinating to see the States with my own eyes, to visit Peachtree Street in Atlanta and the Panorama, and to learn more about the area that I had only known from *Gone with the Wind*.

We gradually got acquainted with America and were affected by its way of life. We put much confidence in America and its democracy, as well as the "Spirit of 1776."

On February 22, 1957, a young man attempted to take President Diệm's life at the Ban Mê Thuột economic fair. The bullet missed the president but seriously injured his agricultural minister. The assassin, later revealed to be a communist thug, used an automatic weapon (French-made MAT-49 submachine gun) in the attempt, but the gun jammed after the first shot.

In the TV news reports a day later, I was surprised to see the president's reaction. He remained perfectly calm, without a sign of panic. Although I was still against his authoritarianism, I began to hold him in higher esteem for his courage. Very few leaders could act like him in such an extremely dangerous moment. The assassin was held for years in a guarded room at the National Police Headquarters until the military junta released him after November 1, 1963. The president ordered the police to treat him well and to send him to a court of justice only when he broke his silence in an official investigation session.

In May 1957, President Diệm visited America. President Eisenhower welcomed him in a pompous ceremony, and he delivered a speech to a joint session of Congress. I felt certain that the United States would back South Việt Nam with determination, because it was in the interests and it was also the obligation of the American republic to defend freedom in Southeast Asia.

My close friends and I visited many places in the Deep South, from Tallahassee, Mobile, and Pensacola to New Orleans on Mardi Gras 1957. On every trip we brought along a map of Asia to give people we met some idea of the country we came from.

In nine months at Fort Benning, we learned many differences between Việt Nam and the United States, from wall power outlets and screw-in light bulbs to ways of life. In the first days, we were really frightened by so much abbreviation in travel orders and related papers. But after a few months, we got used to them and began to experience some American red tape.

What I couldn't get used to was racism. I always felt uneasy on a bus where the rear section was for "colored people" or in front of tourist sites where there were two separate entrances, one for white and another for colored. We Asians were not classified as "colored people," but we still felt like we were being treated as not equal to whites. Once I intentionally walked to the "colored" entrance of a state park in Florida. A security guard stopped me and said, "You aren't a colored person. You're an Asian." He refused to give me further explanation even when I pointed to my skin, saying I was "yellow." He shook his head. "I don't care, but it's the law, sir, and I won't let you in that gate."

We left Fort Benning in early August but had to stay in San Francisco for more than four weeks waiting for a flight to Việt Nam. It was when PAA planes were grounded by a big strike. So Market Street and Golden Gate Park became a deeply imprinted part of my memory along with the 1957 Asian flu epidemic, which caught a dozen of us at Honolulu. We landed at Tân Sơn Nhất, Sài Gòn, still exhausted from the flu but happy to be home and looking forward to the military career awaiting us.

BOOT CAMP

A week before our graduation from the Việt Nam academy, we were asked to select the branch of service we would like to serve. All but one of us chose Combat Arms. Airborne and Marine corps were the most preferred. The next were Infantry, Ranger, and Armor. We were all eager to do something great.

Upon our return from Fort Benning, many of us were assigned to Quang Trung Training Center, a boot camp some eight miles from Sài Gòn. We were to be instructors giving basic training to the new draftees. Being an instructor was nothing great, but it was a pleasant job that I really liked. I spent my time encouraging the greenhorns to learn anything that would help them survive a battle if not to defeat the enemy. Most of them were about my age, so we had no difficulty in building mutual understanding.

THIRTEEN

Progress and Signs of Instability

In 1957, South Việt Nam was at peace. Anyone could see economic progress not only on the streets but also in the hamlets, with better houses and clothes. I used to visit friends in villages, in some cases in remote areas where the only way to go was on foot. Security was of little concern. After crushing all hostile armed sect groups and integrating the friendly ones into the national army, the government imposed its control in the immense Mekong Delta, which quickly recovered its peaceful life. Local authority was once again established in the areas previously under Việt Minh control.

The peacetime economy bloomed, and although postwar problems existed, I could see a better life for everyone. Prices and the currency were relatively stable. New industries flourished. The countryside prospered. Many foreign observers predicted that South Việt Nam would be highly successful in economic development and would become one of the dragons in Asia before long.

One of my concerns was that the government insufficiently supported our military servicemen. Compared with a civil servant of the same capability, level of education, and training, a military serviceman was paid much less.

Việt Nam was developing in peace. However, I already sensed something ominous below the surface. Anti-Diệm attitude built up in the country. In Sài Gòn and other major cities, dissension was growing among intellects and members of many nationalist parties' factions. The president and his family members were targets of bitter criticism.

It was obvious that the president did not accept any kind of opposition. Moreover, people heard the rumor that the president preferred Catholic candidates for government jobs and military command positions. Many high-ranking officers and administration officials did convert to Catholicism. And many Catholic priests became powerful because of friendly relations with the president's family.

Diệm's brother Ngô Đình Thục became a powerful archbishop. Another brother, Ngô Đình Cẩn, was given the title of advisor for guidance to the political organizations in Central Việt Nam. A third brother, Ngô Đình Nhu, was a member of Congress and a political advisor to the president. Nhu's wife was also a member of Congress. A fourth brother, Ngô Đình Luyện, was appointed ambassador to Great Britain.

Except for Ngô Đình Luyện, who kept himself out of the political arena, the president's family brought him more disservice than help, certainly as far as his popularity was concerned. The president and his government could gather strong support from a large number of Catholics, especially those from North Việt Nam, but not much among other people.

Many of my fellow officers shared my opinion about the president. We respected his personality as a patriot but not his mandarin style of ruling. However talented his family members may have been, he should have forbidden them to overtly get involved in the administration's affairs, particularly in things that would bring them personal gain.

As early as 1954, when Ngô Đình Diệm claimed presidential power, the Sài Gòn government propaganda machine launched a campaign to promote Diệm's popularity, the sort of eulogizing of the leader usually seen in communist countries and many despotic regimes. The campaign intensified after he won the referendum on October 23, 1955, and by 1957 it was approaching idolatry. Although this idolization was weaker and less brassy than that of Hồ Chí Minh in the North, my friends and I felt unable to support what we called "cheap" tactics. We had fled the North partly because we detested the shameless actions used to idolize Hồ.

The Vietnamese people were always sensitive to corruption. For many years living under oppression and corrupted government members, they were yearning for freedom and democracy and were very suspicious of political and state leaders. Without experience of a democratic regime, they were easily confused about freedom and social order. Besides, they were extremely credulous to rumors concerning administration officials' shady affairs.

A rumor about Madam Ngô Đình Nhu was a good example. In 1953, fire destroyed a neighborhood in Khánh Hội, a suburb of Sài Gòn, leaving thousands of people homeless. It was said that the arsonist, who was arrested later, confessed to the police that he had been hired by an import company to start the fire. This company did so to make large sums of money from the sale of metal roofing sheets. The wife of a former prime minister, Nguyễn Văn Tâm, was said to have shares in this company. When another fire broke out in a nearby area in 1959, the rumor was that Madam Nhu was behind the plot so that she could purchase that piece of land for the construction of a great apartment building. The building, the rumor went, would be rented to the American officers who were coming to Việt Nam in large numbers. She would make millions a year from that venture, it was said. The story was taken for granted by many people as they felt that it was plausible: Madam Nhu was doing some kind of business as Madam Nguyễn Văn Tâm had done. Until Madam Nhu was in exile, nothing for American officers was built on this land except for a public housing project funded by the central government to resettle the victims of the fire.[1]

THE COUNTRYSIDE

While serving in boot camp, I had several opportunities to visit the countryside, as we instructors had a week of open time between the two-month basic training courses. I learned much about the living conditions in the rural areas not far from Sài Gòn from which the draftees came.

Having lived a peasant's life in war, I hated to see that in many places in South Việt Nam, local officials were very authoritarian. They were not elected by villagers but appointed by the province chiefs, and many had been former village council members under the French colonialist regime. They may have been reliable in doing administrative jobs, but not in anticommunist tasks and serving the people in a democracy that required a strong will and the ability to confront a sly, fanatical enemy. It was apparent that there were a lot of excellent administrators at every level of the government, but few were the anticommunist civil servants that we needed so badly. To many of those, communism was unacceptable only because their interests were endangered, not because of anything idealistic or patriotic. In the army, the situation was better, but not much.

My friends and I supported the idea that local government leaders should be young men who could confront the communist insurgency. The Sài Gòn regime did not seem to trust the capability of the young in the government. I felt certain that if the young had been promoted to leading roles after 1955, South Việt Nam would have followed a much more favorable path.

At the age of twenty, I easily kindled new hopes. However, I was also easily shaken by dissatisfaction. I hated to realize that the national situation was not improving as it should. The administrative system, an offspring of the colonial era, was still slow and sometimes ineffective, though there had been several reforms. It became a hindrance to every progress necessary for rebuilding a better South Việt Nam.

Although there was much more freedom in the South than in the North, my friends and I wished that we had the total freedom of press that we had seen in the United States. During the Ngô Đình Diệm era, almost no one dared to criticize the president and his brothers, the armed forces, or the generals in any kind of publication. The true democracy we were longing for came only piecemeal. So we hoped for a great change to build a free South Việt Nam that could survive the communist invasion that would certainly come, sooner or later.

I still had close relations with the Việt Quốc—or actually, one of its factions. All Việt Quốc factions were against the regime. In 1958, preparation was under way for a coup to overthrow Diệm. The plot was uncovered, and many of the notables and nationalist party members were arrested; there were reports of mistreatment. If the coup had not been nipped in the bud, I would have had the smallest part in it. I supported the idea that full democracy was the best way to fight the communists, and the new leadership in a new regime without corruption and nepotism should be in power to defend South Việt Nam and make it a wealthy nation.

ON PROPAGANDA

The imminent danger, I thought, was the communist propaganda that was slowly undermining the regime. Communists in general were good at propaganda; Vietnamese communist leaders were even smarter. In their hands, everything seemed to be easily turned into an ornament for the communist regime or a powerful slanderous blow against their enemy.

For example, sometime in 1957, the Sài Gòn public health service first introduced an injection machine that released a strong jet of liquid vaccine to inoculate students. It would replace traditional syringes. But the communists quickly spread a rumor that the government was using this sophisticated machine to draw blood from schoolchildren to pay the Americans for military aid. Elsewhere in the world such nonsense might have been ignored, but not in Việt Nam. Within an hour or so, parents were rushing to schools to prevent vaccinations.

Communist propaganda was directed against every effort of the government. When the Sài Gòn–Biên Hòa four-lane highway was constructed, communists initiated the hearsay that the highway was mainly for military purposes: U.S. jet fighters would use it as a runway in a future invasion. Thousands of rumors were freely invented to slander the regime; most were based on exaggerated trivial facts. Furthermore, rather tricky schemes were aimed at President Diệm and his family.

The communists called the South Vietnamese and American leaders by the sauciest names. The determiner *thằng* before a man's name expresses disdain or inferiority. A rule of the communist regime compelled people under its control to refer to Diệm as *thằng* Diệm. The same rule applied to Dwight D. Eisenhower and subsequent U.S. presidents. According to Vietnamese ethical traditions, this word should not be used when addressing seniors, however bad they might be in society. Although Hồ Chí Minh was our archenemy, we were not permitted to use the term or its synonyms to refer to him.

Officials in the Information Ministry told us that President Diệm once rejected a proposal by their ministry to launch a propaganda campaign directly against Hồ Chí Minh. In many aspects, Hồ's personal life was no less vulnerable than Diệm's to such attacks, as resources were available to publicize his infamies. But Diệm said that his regime should not lower itself as to use the same ignoble scheme of slanderous propaganda.

To adorn themselves, the communists also gained some success in their scheme of boasting their achievements. Their propaganda machine projected a bright picture about life in the North, where they said there were daycare centers in every village, nursing homes taking good care of the decrepit in every district, land that had been equally redistributed to villagers, and private factories that had been turned into collective possessions.

They boasted that there were no more haves and have-nots. So the dream of the poor peasants and workers for many thousands of years had been realized in North Việt Nam. A considerable number of people in the South believed them.

To the question of the bloody Land Reform Campaign, however, the facts were undeniable. Communist propaganda, while admitting to some atrocities, claimed that "errors" had been corrected. It was difficult to explain to the communist sympathizers that their rectification of errors campaign was only intended to calm the people's anger.

Many of us North Vietnamese refugees knew for sure that the proposed childcare and nursing homes were big lies except for some in certain locations specially designed to welcome visitors. However, it was difficult to convince credulous people when the Sài Gòn government neglected to provide the necessary resources for an active propaganda campaign.

LAND AND POOR FARMERS

"Land to farmers" was the principal concern of those who were interested in social and political matters. Naturally, new members of a revolutionary party like the teens in my group also were keenly interested in such matters.

Land reform was a major part of the Sài Gòn government's social policy. It was the best way to win people's hearts and minds in any poor country where peasants had little land to farm. North Việt Nam availed itself of the situation to claim credit for being on the side of poor farmers. The Diệm government, therefore, had to do something. So it initiated the Land Reform Campaign in 1955.

Actually, Sài Gòn was buying farming lands from rich landlords, paying them in cash and in government bonds, and redistributing the land to poor farmers at very low prices with budget assistance from the U.S. government. The program seemed to produce some humble successes, as I learned from a few farmers in the Mekong Delta in 1957.

The program was not as radical as what the communists did in the North and promised to do so in the South, and a lot of red tape slowed down the process. The procedures of the Sài Gòn land offices required an official survey before approving any paperwork for land transfer. Such a task couldn't be done as quickly as scheduled under the administrative system left by the colonial regime and because of the lack of survey capability.

The Sài Gòn Land Reform Campaign was not a success. It had several defects, and only a few landless farmers were granted land titles. Although they had graduated with honors from French universities, the administrators had never worked with the peasants to understand their problems and had little compassion for the poor farmers. The decree allowed a landlord to retain 100 acres of his land. The common people considered this to be too large a favor that the government awarded to the landlords to pacify them. That made what the South Vietnamese government was doing a travesty. The communists just promised a free land distribution without paying a penny to landlords, just as they had done in areas under their control in 1953. By 1955, the Việt Minh had confiscated all the farming land of rich and middle-class landlords in areas under its control in South Việt Nam to distribute to poor farmers at no cost. Poor farmers did not have to pay rent. But agricultural taxes were higher than the rent they had had to pay to landlords in the colonial era.

In the late 1950s, very few South Vietnamese understood that the true goal of land reform in the North was to eliminate a whole class of rural landlords and middle-class farmers. Beginning in 1958, farmers' lands previously distributed became collective property in co-operatives. The cloak was discarded.

The RVN government made several attempts to promote the rural life. Dispensaries and schools were built in remote villages. Programs to help peasants were supported by the United States and other western countries. In visits to the countryside far from Sài Gòn, I could observe considerable progress in hamlets, which was a better situation than in 1955. The peasants in remote areas, however, did appear grateful for the government's assistance. The smear campaign against the newly established regime was so powerful that it almost overrode the government's efforts. A poorly educated population is always fertile soil for the elaborate obscurantism that turns propaganda nonsense into an effective tool for agitation.

CLEANSING THE COMMUNISTS

The communists did not stop all guerrilla activities after the Geneva Accords were signed in 1954. They only kept it at low profile by conducting terrorist attacks in remote areas.

In the Việt Minh–controlled areas, the Communist Party had conducted a clever campaign for maintaining future contact with the South after they withdrew their men to the North. A few weeks prior to their departure, the party's local leaders persuaded single males and pro-communist female villagers to get married. The women would remain in South Việt Nam as legitimate wives waiting for their men to come back. The women were law-abiding citizens whom the Sài Gòn government had no reason to detain unless they committed some crime. Moreover, there were other men who had never had any obvious relations with the Việt Minh, but they were true communists. The police could keep them under surveillance but had no legal reason to act against them.

Beginning in 1955, a denunciation campaign became an effective tool for uncovering communist agents. About 500 hard-core clandestine communists were arrested and imprisoned without formal trial. In some areas, local authorities treated the suspects with rough hands and in certain localities took revenge for what the Việt Minh had done since 1945. Innocent people may have been victims in such circumstances, but not at the exaggerated figures later stated by communist propaganda. I believe that no more than a few hundred communists were killed during the communists' denunciation campaign, although the pro-communist literature claimed that Diệm and the Americans executed more than 300,000 South Vietnamese patriots.

What I thought was a serious error was the way the government treated the former Việt Minh cadres. As many of us nationalists knew, a large number of those who served in the Việt Minh ranks were not communists, although they may have been ardent anticolonialists and advocates of social reforms. Many of my fellow officers and I never supported the idea of getting rid of suspected communists by detention, because no one could be able to keep them in jail for all their lives. Experience proved that prisons were the best places for the Communist Party to train neophytes to become its hard-core supporters.

We contended that noncommunist Việt Minh followers should be treated as friends, not foes. There may have been some risks, but it was better to accept such risks than to create more enemies. It seemed to me that many administration and high-ranking military officials chose the easiest way to deal with the problem without considering what was in the best long-term interests of the country.

Beginning in late 1957, there were insurgent attacks in distant corners of South Việt Nam where government security forces were unable to respond in time. Hundreds of village and hamlet officials and common citizens were kidnapped and murdered. In 1958, terrorist attacks increased. Nationalist opposition also became more active. Many politicians and intellectuals raised concerns about the growing communist insurgency. They criticized the government's despotic rule and called for changes in national policies to stop the communist subversion. A large number of anticommunists among the dissidents were detained. The first newspaper that overtly protested the government, *Thời Luận,* was closed.

What the government was doing disheartened me a great deal. I thought we couldn't fight and defeat a dictatorship by imposing another dictatorship. Only a democracy and cooperation among nationalists could defend the republic against the North, although such politics could face difficulties and troubles from inside.

Being an army officer, I was not permitted to engage in politics as an official party member. However, I served in the Việt Quốc Sài Gòn chapter as a covert member. I had to conceal my participation from the military security services.

THE MILITARY OLD-TIMERS

In the first few years of my career, most officers and noncommissioned officers (NCOs) in the pre-1955 nationalist army were still serving in the new Army of the Republic of Việt Nam (loosely known as ARVN). Before 1955, these officers didn't accept French neocolonialism, although they were fighting the Vietnamese communists with support from the French. Some had served in the pre-1945 French colonial army and had joined the nationalist army as committed patriots. They were respectable officers and NCOs.

However, there were others who had been supporters of the French in Việt Nam, and they seemed to be not at all patriotic, just some kind of mercenaries. Many had also been serving in the French colonial army before joining the nationalist army. These bad old-timers were a hindrance to necessary reforms in the army and the improvement of troop morale. They were sources of evil and depravity as well. So many times I felt that my hope of building a better army, an army of our people and our country, could never be realized.

Once in a while I was at odds with them because they often drove my soldiers to work too hard at something that was not really necessary just to please their superiors. I politely gave my opinion, only to incur their disfavor. I hated to see some of my seniors do their jobs as if we were in the French colonial army, not in the armed forces of an independent and democratic state. My response to the situation was to treat the draftees under my command as well as possible. I granted them favors more than I might, and sometimes that caused me trouble. The living conditions of the draftees in the boot camp were not too bad, though they got very low pay. What they asked for most often was weekend leave. I used to grant leaves to more men in my company than was allowed by headquarters.

Nevertheless, I was promoted to first lieutenant on December 1, 1958, after two years of second lieutenant's service.

PHÚ LỢI SCANDAL

The last half of 1958 saw Việt Cộng insurgent activities increase dramatically. There were VC sapper attacks at remote military installations. At Dầu Tiếng district headquarters, the attackers caused heavy casualties among the Bảo An (national guard).

The Sài Gòn government relied mostly on two local forces for rural security: the Bảo An and the Dân Vệ (People's Defense, or village militia). The national budget supported these forces without foreign aid. The Bảo An were equipped with French infantry weapons and served under the province chief. The Dân Vệ were "village soldiers" of about one platoon per village and were armed with muskets made before World War I.

Lack of training, low morale, and poor organization in the two forces created serious weaknesses and made them incapable of maintaining security in the countryside. This became even more critical in the wake of increased VC aggressiveness on the psychological front, which peaked with the Phú Lợi scandal.

Phú Lợi was one of the two concentration camps where communist insurgents were being detained. The camp, in Bình Dương province about ten miles from Sài Gòn, held 400 to 500 prisoners. Regulations in such camps allowed prisoners to receive raw food from civilian suppliers, which they cooked for themselves in dining hall kitchens.

Political prisoners in camps near the capital were always treated more kindly because they would protest angrily at anything they could, and their complaints would quickly be heard in Sài Gòn. But one day, a score of prisoners suffered food poisoning from tainted meat or vegetables. Some prisoners stayed in the camp's dispensary for a day; others were released to their wards after proper treatment. My mother, who worked in Sài Gòn Central Prison, was on temporary duty at Phú Lợi when the incident took place, and she witnessed the whole event.

On the weekend after the food poisoning incident, when the prisoners' relatives came for weekly visits, word spread that the government had deliberately poisoned the prisoners. Quickly seizing the opportunity, some prisoners staged a protest against the camp authority. The protest drew relatives to larger gatherings outside the camp at night, while the prisoners inside joined in a hunger strike. The protests lasted for a week. After the news reached Hà Nội several days later, North Vietnamese communists launched a large-scale propaganda campaign against Sài Gòn with slogans calling for revenge, accompanied by fabricated reports of the event. Guerrilla units were named after Phú Lợi, and command of the units launched a special military campaign to retaliate for the "Phú Lợi crimes." Workers in many North Việt Nam factories and farms were ordered to work on Sundays to "support the Phú Lợi struggle."

If it had not been for my mother's account, I would have believed some of the communist propaganda. Personally, I was certain that somewhere, in remote areas, torture and killing of communist suspects occurred. But the Phú Lợi scandal was basically nonsense. If the Diệm's government had intended to get rid of those communist prisoners, it could have easily killed them one by one at the district level or below, where no one could confirm the event. The Diệm government was not so stupid as to massacre prisoners in a camp so close to Sài Gòn, which any reporter could reach without difficulty.

FOURTEEN

Mounting Pressure

The war started in 1955, when communist guerrillas began a new program of terror and propaganda in remote areas of the country. The war reached a new phase in 1959, when the communist regime took a more aggressive course of action against the South. The South was following a war policy of defense. In the first few years after the 1954 Geneva Accords, Vietnamese nationalists, especially those from the refugee community, often talked about the liberation of the North. But by the late 1950s, few of them still fostered such a dream.

MY UNFORGETTABLE LOVE

It was in this period of my life that I fell madly in love with a beautiful girl I first met in December 1957 at a wedding party. She attracted me like a powerful magnet, and I found myself unable to resist.

Like most pretty girls, she paid little attention to patriotism and politics. She had dreams that differed from mine. I found nothing wrong when she wished we would have a nice family and a high income, although I had never sought to become rich. However, she did influence me in some ways. I began thinking of other careers, such as studying to become a university physics professor or an engineer. I wished I could do something greater, something that an infantry officer wouldn't be able to realize. Our love grew deeper and deeper. I never expected a breakup.

In January 1959, several days before Tết of the Year of the Pig, her father sharply berated her because she was sometimes going out with me beyond the limit his rule allowed. At the time, single girls were not given full freedom in relationships with boys. I stayed in her home, soothing her the whole day, and forgot to report for duty that evening at Quang Trung Training Center, the boot camp.

At midnight, a large-scale protest erupted—reportedly a communist scheme—by 1,000 draftees opposing the camp's decision to cancel their Lunar New Year leaves. The guards opened fire to stop them, killing half a dozen and wounding several others. The event enraged the president, the minister of defense, and the joint chief of staff. The president suspended a previously approved decree for the promotion of several hundred officers of the armed forces. The Quang Trung boot camp commander and his staff were severely reprimanded, and he vented his anger downward onto his subordinates. A dozen officers and NCOs were punished with various charges, some the most trivial. Absent from duty that evening, I received a serious citation by the JGS along with others in the group.

So I was in trouble. On the second day of Lunar New Year 1959, I was punished with a forty-day detention in a barrack building along with fourteen other lieutenants. The commanding general pressed for this decision, which was too severe for such a trivial violation. The forty-day detention was the fourth harshest punishment for an officer; only a sentence by a court-martial, forced labor at a fortress (by the authority of the minister of defense), and the sixty-day detention were more severe. I didn't feel angry, but quietly accepted the punishment. In the South Vietnamese armed forces, any officer had the right to punish subordinates to a limited term of barrack arrest without recourse to a court-martial. The procedure had been inherited from the French military.

On March 16, 1959, after being released, I was transferred to the Twenty-second Infantry Division in Kontum province as an additional disciplinary measure. My military career and my humble role in the war began a new phase.

THE CENTRAL HIGHLANDS

When I arrived, the Twenty-second Infantry Division had just been created from the merger of two light infantry divisions, the Fourteenth and the Sixteenth. Everybody was working hard to reshape the unit according to the new TO&E (Table of Organization and Equipment). There were not enough officers, so three-fourths of the company commanders were second and first lieutenants, and the remainder were master sergeants. Six of the nine battalion commanders were captains; the remaining three were first lieutenants. Under Diệm's regime, there had been few military promotions. It took an average first lieutenant more than six years to be promoted to captain, and in some cases it took nine or ten years. Most of us officers in the division were first lieutenants.

By 1958, communist secret organizations in the Mekong Delta were conducting limited activities, mostly on the psychological front. In remote areas, which government security forces were unable to fully control, there were assassinations and kidnappings of local government officials. A number of village offices, bridges, schools, and dispensaries were demolished or burned to the ground by communist guerrillas. The wave of killing and sabotage initiated the ever-escalating campaign of terrorism that lasted until 1975, when the war ended.

In areas of easy access in the highlands, it was safe for us to travel day and night. The whole division devoted most of its time to training and reorganization. For the first few months, because of the personnel shortage, I was assigned to the division staff as an assistant to the G-4, a captain, although I was a new first lieutenant. We worked about ten hours a day for two months on logistic projects to make sure that subordinate units of the division were fully equipped with proper equipment conforming to the new TO&Es. Since being assigned to the division G-4, I was working more closely with the Americans. The Twenty-second Division Military Assistance Advisory Group (MAAG) team consisted of fewer than ten officers and some NCOs, living in a small compound at the northern side of Kontum city.

Many of the Americans spoke Vietnamese, some at advanced levels. They often appeared in restaurants and cafés along with the Vietnamese, and they had relatively close relations with their Vietnamese counterparts. I was one of the five officers in the division staff who spoke English, not fluently but well enough for the Americans not to feel uneasy and confused by the sign language we used to define words that did not exist in our vocabulary. Our mutual relations were warm. We often met for dinner parties and went on inspection trips together.

The principal task of the MAAG team was to assist us in training and logistic affairs, especially the end-use inspection, which focused on the proper maintenance of equipment. The inspection of the RVNAF along with American inspectors from MAAG headquarters in Sài Gòn was always a stressful event for units having heavy equipment. Besides, the Americans had no authority to step into Vietnamese-only domains such as personnel, command, and decision making. For people who were not acquainted with military activities, the presence of the American officers might have been confused with the role played by French soldiers before 1954.

AN EXPANDING INSURGENCY

In 1959, after establishing the effective ruling system over North Việt Nam, the Communist Workers' Party in Hà Nội announced one of its ultimate long-range objectives: "taking care of South Việt Nam," communist rhetoric for "conquering South Việt Nam." What I had feared was looming on the horizon.

The media reported more assassinations and kidnappings, especially after some 400 hard-core communists broke out of a prison in Phú Yên province and took to the bush after a daring guerrilla attack. More public facilities such as dispensaries, schools, bridges, and village administrative offices were blown up at night. Farm machinery from state-run agricultural agencies was destroyed. In short, communist insurgents did everything that was the most destructive to the property and popularity of the Sài Gòn government.

VC security pressure increased significantly in some provinces in the Me-kong Delta. In other areas, subversive campaigns were more psychological than overtly terrorist. In some remote Mekong Delta villages, primary schools were built, maintained, and paid for by the Sài Gòn government, but teachers were intimidated into teaching VC materials. On the school flagpoles, the red-stripes-on-golden RVN national colors were still streaming, and on students' tables were books from the Ministry of Education in Sài Gòn. But the teachers were stuffing the kids with communist propaganda and ideology as directed by VC secret cells. Many teachers resigned rather than be killed for failing to act in concordance with orders from clandestine VC agents.

Communist rebels also began a fierce campaign to "strangle Sài Gòn and the capital region," according to their announcement. Ships and barges trans-porting vital food and utility supplies, particularly rice and mangrove coal from the Mekong Delta to Sài Gòn, were attacked, causing some disruption in sup-plies to Sài Gòn and surrounding cities.

In July 1959, while I was on leave in Sài Gòn, VC sappers conducted a sur-prise attack on the MAAG compound in Biên Hòa. I had a feeling that the direct attack against the Americans indicated that the Communist Party leaders in Hà Nội were determined to defy their archenemy. It was an evil omen to people of both the North and the South, foreboding a bloody war for years to come.

The Communist Party relied on its terrorist campaign as the primary tool of subversion in the South. The United States and its allies were to fight fiercely against terrorism in the Middle East many years later; in Việt Nam at this time, they did not approach terrorism with the same concern.

LAW 10/59

Until 1958, South Việt Nam did not have any laws to deal with sabotage and terrorism. In police operations in my division area, many communists were caught keeping guns. Often they did not fire on the police, because they knew that if they did, the police would try them as bandits and they would be subject to a prison sentence of more than five years. Without fighting back, they might be guilty only of illegal possession of firearms. They were right. In court trials, the judges were unable to pass any sentence of more than a few months in jail in such cases. This was why the Diệm regime enacted Law 10/59. For those convicted of assassination, abduction, and sabotage in order to subvert the RVN government, this law would require aggravated sentences more severe than in regular criminal cases. Law 10/59 did not allow for appeal.

The law must have been a hard blow to the communists. From Hà Nội to Beijing and Moscow, in South Việt Nam and in other countries, Vietnamese com-munists loudly accused the South Vietnamese government of using the law as a tool "to massacre patriots" and "drag the guillotine all over South Việt Nam to execute thousands of innocent people." As far as I know, the RVN authorities only executed a dozen communist rebels under the law before 1975. Most of the VC on death row were never executed. Some were released after long years in jail. The others lived to be freed when the Sài Gòn government collapsed in April 1975.

In 1959, the prisoner affair was not a problem to the RVN government. VC soldiers and political cadres were detained in the communist rebel camps. After 1962, Law 10/59 did not apply to prisoners who fought against the government forces as members of an organized military force (the National Liberation Front Army) with discernible uniforms and a military hierarchy. They would be detained in prisoner of war camps, whereas VC terrorists and other communist insurgents subjected to Law 10/59 were incarcerated in regular prisons as criminal convicts.

Most of the insurgent activities at that time occurred in the southern part of South Việt Nam, in remote areas accessible from Cambodia by jungle trails and nearby secret communist bases. Meanwhile, along key national highways crossing unpopulated woodland areas, highwaymen often held up civilian buses and robbed the passengers of their money and jewels. However, military personnel riding on the buses were not harmed, and military vehicles were not attacked. The mass media would naturally report the events as simple robberies. When arrested, the robbers usually pleaded guilty as highwaymen. Only keen intelligence experts would say that they were communist militants who conducted the holdups for dual purposes—to procure supplies and to create security problems for the land communications system.

The highlands and most of the coastal areas in Central Việt Nam were still safe in 1959. The district chiefs controlled almost all of their villages and hamlets. Communist guerrilla activities in my division area of responsibility were at an insignificant level. There were antigovernment leaflets in faraway hamlets or the occasional appearance of squad-sized guerrilla units in the border jungles. However, the division was often ordered to launch company-sized operations to search for small groups of rebels. The companies always came back empty-handed, and the troops were unnecessarily tired and demoralized. Their tasks should have been handled by local paramilitary units, instead, or should not have been done at all because of the harm to troop morale and the waste of manpower and time. Such an unwise use of troops contributed in a significant way to the end of the South Vietnamese armed forces and the republic itself.

"GENERAL UPRISING": A NEW PHASE

In the first week of January, VC insurgents held protests in many places of Kiến Hòa (Bến Tre) province. With villagers on the front lines supported by gunmen behind them, they did overrun some local government militia units. They kept some villages under their control for a few days. Later on, the communist propaganda called the incident Đồng Khởi (general uprising). The mass protest in Kiến Hòa foreboded more serious troubles to the Sài Gòn government's stability. I knew that a bloody storm was brewing.

Due to the peaceful situation in the highlands, our Twenty-second Division commander granted seven-day leave to 50 percent of his soldiers so that they could enjoy a happy Tết season at their homes. While I was in Sài Gòn, communist rebels overran an ARVN military base, which caused a powerful shock to the public. On January 26, 1960, a few days before the Lunar New Year, communist guerrillas attacked Trảng Sụp in Tây Ninh province west of Sài Gòn, home base of an ARVN infantry regiment. The regiment suffered few casualties, but there was a heavy loss of weapons. The guerrilla force, previously underestimated, proved its remarkable strength.

The Kiến Hòa and Trảng Sụp events and the attack at the American MAAG compound in Biên Hòa marked the beginning of the fully armed conflict conducted by the Communist Party in South Việt Nam, carrying out what NVN General Võ Nguyên Giáp had called for: "taking care of South Việt Nam." Every Vietnamese knew that North Việt Nam was behind all of the insurgent activities, but many scholars and foreign news agencies echoed North Việt Nam's assertion that the conflict was just a "civil war" between "the people" and the Sài Gòn government in the South without any support from Hà Nội.

The late 1950s and early 1960s were eventful years in the world. In Cuba, Fidel Castro came to power. The USSR launched the first satellite into Earth's orbit, sent the first man into space, and successfully tested an intercontinental ballistic missile. U.S. space technology lagged behind. These events hurt American pride and gave a boost to anti-American propaganda. Even people who sided with the Americans had to admit that in the course of conducting the cold war against the communist camp, the United States was supporting many dictators in the world. Even though the United States sent large amounts of economic aid to underdeveloped countries, it earned little support from the beneficiaries.

I thought this lack of support for the United States resulted from the lack of proper publicity and ineffective propaganda. And it seemed that many Vietnamese were skeptical about American intentions. Bearing that in mind, I happened to interfere in an incident involving two American civilians.

AN AMERICAN IN TROUBLE

While I was traveling on Highway 19 from Pleiku to Qui Nhơn, the traffic was blocked at a bridge under reconstruction, some twenty miles from Qui Nhơn. A Vietnamese Engineer Corps "low boy" trailer carrying a bulldozer got stuck in the dirt bypass. The tractor driver could not make a turn smaller than the curve, so the rear left end of the trailer slid and sank by two meters to one side of the bypass.

In hopes of freeing the trailer and unblocking the road, two Americans from Johnson & Drake Inc., the company building Highway 19 from Qui Nhơn to Pleiku, brought a heavy crane to the place. They tried to lift the trailer and the bulldozer to road level so that the tractor could pull them onto the highway, but they failed again and again. Every point around the platform where the hooks of the crane were placed broke under the weight of the bulldozer.

At last the Americans gave up. They advised the Vietnamese sergeant in charge and his driver that the bulldozer should be pulled out of the trailer into the river to clear the way for traffic. It meant discarding the bulldozer, a valuable piece of equipment for the land development program at that time and an expensive army property that a sergeant was in no position to get rid of. So the sergeant rejected the proposal, and that made one of the Americans angry. He seized the sergeant by his collar and yelled. About 100 passengers from a dozen buses waiting at the site and people from a nearby village had gathered around as the quarrel between the Americans and the Vietnamese soldiers became heated.

When the American seized the sergeant's collar, the crowd flew into a fury. They rushed to the scene with rocks and sticks and anything else they could find, apparently ready to attack the two Americans. The tractor driver, his face reddened and eyes bulging, quickly loaded his M-1 rifle and pointed it at the angry American's stomach.

It was a matter of seconds before I was only ten yards from the two foreigners. Another army officer, a captain who had just happened to be at the scene, quickly disappeared. So I was the only officer witnessing the incident. The two Americans, obviously frightened by the yelling crowd, turned to me for help. I was no hero, but I couldn't turn my back on them. I expected very serious consequences would follow if the quarrel resulted in deadly injuries, and I would be in trouble with the military if I made no effort to control the chaos.

My driver held his carbine and loaded. With my loud but controlled voice, I told everyone to cool down. After half a minute or so, the angry crowd stopped yelling. Many in the crowd argued with me, saying that I should not side with the Americans and that I must protect the sergeant's honor. I did my best to assure them that I would deal with the case. Every Vietnamese knew that although we needed much help from America, we were always sensitive to even the slightest bit of misbehavior.

Only after I promised to handle the affair fairly did the crowd make way to let the Americans, the sergeant, my driver, and me go to Johnson & Drake's Camp #32 about a mile from the site in my jeep and a J&D Volkswagen. At the camp, we talked to the chief engineer in charge of the camp while 100 hot-tempered peasants were waiting outside the gate. The chief of the camp showed his good heart and understanding in talking with us. We admired his noble manners. At last, the American who caused the incident frankly apologized to the sergeant for what he had done. A Vietnamese civilian interpreter who witnessed his apology went to the front gate and told the crowd what was going on and how I was dealing with the situation. After his explanation, the crowd dismissed and they all seemed pleased.

I said to the Americans in Camp #32, "If you did that in America, it would not prompt any public anger. But right here, it is a big problem. Everyone in the third world countries is a jingo." Although the immediate situation had been defused, the people at the bridge area were still angry. The bulldozer blocked more than twenty buses and several military trucks all that afternoon and possibly another day. So after the sergeant's proposal, we decided to try to clear the road. Although I wasn't an engineer, I came up with a plan with what I had been taught at the military academy.

I called drivers of buses and trucks to assist and soldiers to lend their hands. About forty of them responded. I gave each a job. We used four strong lifting jacks placed on thick wooden boards arranged above the wet ground and strived to lift the trailer up to the level of the road. We succeeded on the third try. The trailer was lifted to the road level and propped up with many wooden beams borrowed along with the boards from a nearby hamlet.

The driver started the tractor engine while I was standing beside him. The sergeant directed the driver to make a quick, forceful pull with a well-timed engaging of the clutch. The heavy steel monster jumped from the beams onto the narrow dirt road and over to the main road as planned. So the bypass was cleared at last, as hundreds of people cheered and applauded. It took us two hours with great personal effort to complete the task. The experience proved that men with high volition can perform some incredible tasks.

MY NAMELESS JOBS

In early 1960, I was assigned to a special job. On personnel records, my job was listed as "liaison officer" working directly under the chief of staff of the division. However, my actual responsibility covered a wide range of tasks that couldn't be given a specific title. The chief of staff and the division commander gave me any tasks they thought I could complete, big and small. Although I didn't like the job, it gave me a chance to learn much more about the armed forces and military activities.

A part of my job was to read all the incoming papers, including top-secret documents, directives, and military plans, to direct important materials to the proper units and offices, and to follow up their processing paths. My office was to provide the chief of staff and the division commander information they needed concerning where to look up certain documents, military plans, and directives. Four senior NCOs and a lieutenant assisted me in these tasks.

I was to read and follow up most of the important outgoing documents. Sometimes I was sent to hand-deliver operational orders or directives to various commanders and to convey verbal instructions that would help clarify the true intentions of the division headquarters.

On many occasions I visited battles and locations of special concern to observe and report on events to the chief of staff and the division commander and to express my personal opinion. I carried out the tasks as if I were a war correspondent or a special researcher for the division staff. In some battle situations, I joined the operations by doing anything I was requested to do, such as taking the role of an artillery forward observer, setting up special emergency radio communication networks, and even assisting with some trivial logistic affairs while waiting for the competent and responsible personnel to take charge.

ARVN units had for a long time adopted the French approach to creating red tape, and they had invented some for themselves. Reorganization according to a different concept took too much time and energy. The chief of staff at every level had to sign hundreds of documents a day, even though his deputy chief of staff had signed large numbers of less important papers for him already. Compared with the Americans, the Vietnamese must have created five times as much paperwork, most of which had to be done by hand. We tried to cut down on the red tape, but succeeded only in reducing paperwork inside the division by about 30 percent, and that was taken as a great success. Years later, the JGS solved most of the problems, but some lingered until April 30, 1975.

Because the mail system was slow and unreliable, the quantity of radio messages rose rapidly. Networks were so overloaded that sometimes it took two days for a message to reach its destination. In many main stations, officers in charge had to forward messages by written texts through army postal services. That led to dangerous negligence of radio communications security, one of the major flaws of the ARVN.

THE PEOPLE'S WISHES

Experiences from my childhood in my small home village during the 1946–54 war directed my concerns more to the bottom than to the top of a system. I was interested in matters related to enlisted men and poor peasants more than to what presidents and ministers declared.

I had lots of opportunities to travel in my division's responsible area along the coast. Sometimes I stayed overnight in a poor peasant's home and talked to villagers, old and young. Their wishes were simple—no different from those of my villagers in North Việt Nam years before—merely to have three rice meals a day with some meat or fish and vegetables, simple clothes, and a solid thatch-roofed shelter to live in, nothing great.

But what they needed most was security. Some old men told me outright what they thought after I had won their confidence: many governments after 1945, including the Việt Minh, claimed that they strived for the highest interests of the people when actually they did not. The old men said the Việt Minh used skillful propaganda and behaved as if they were peerless patriots, but they provided little more than lip service to really helping people get out of poverty. They supported division of classes, were very authoritarian, and were always ready to kill. They gave nothing, but people had to pay extremely heavy taxes.

The old men also said the nationalist government brought them many things—such as schools, dispensaries, agricultural aids—but corrupt village officials really ruled the countryside with rough hands. Many corrupt officials siphoned cash and other aid from the central government, letting little drip through their filter to reach the bottom level of society. And the rich enjoyed economic privileges over the poor.

Ironically, some old men argued that they were living a life not much better than before 1945, when the country was not independent and the French colonialist regime imposed oppressive policies on the Vietnamese. Some even said that if they were allowed to make a choice, they would rather live under the French in peacetime.

BLOODSHED BETWEEN SIBLINGS

The two coastal provinces of Bình Định and Phú Yên had been under Việt Minh control prior to the 1954 Geneva Accords. The population had suffered heavily from war and poverty, and the communist influence ran deep in a lot of people, especially in the secluded hamlets of the foothill areas. Years under deceitful communist propaganda left some psychological problems that could hardly be solved.

In some areas, when the nationalist army moved in to establish authority after the Việt Minh forces withdrew to North Việt Nam by the end of 1954, the troops had to confront hostility. In some places, poor peasants were taught by Việt Minh cadres that all of the nationalist army tanks and armored vehicles were "made of heavy-duty cardboard," not steel, and they did believe that. Sometime in 1954 when the war was still blazing, Việt Minh cadres ordered hundreds of local peasants to attack French armored units with crossbows, machetes, and sticks. The troops failed to stop them with any warning. The poor peasants stormed their positions, attempting to break and burn the "cardboard combat vehicles." At last, in some places, the surprised peasants just swore and yelled, "They are the real things, not cardboard," and withdrew. But other attacks were so fierce that the troops had to open fire, and several peasants were killed.

In later years, that coastal area would become a bloody battle ground for the armed conflict between the two Việt Nams and the scene of fierce battles in which many U.S. servicemen fell for a cause they didn't comprehend.

By 1960, there were ominous signs that a savage fratricidal war would take place before long. In a number of families, brothers joined opposite sides. Some fought on the communist side as guerrillas and assassinated their blood brothers who held jobs on village committees. Others who served the village militias shot and killed their siblings who came back from secret guerrilla bases in the greenwoods.

HOME OF THE MONTAGNARDS

The highland provinces in our division area, meanwhile, were rather quiet. We officers were all aware of communist efforts to influence the tribes and to have tribesmen prepare supply routes for future battles. Under President Ngô Đình Diệm's regime, the Montagnards (as the tribesmen in the Central Highlands were called) enjoyed some good development programs and tribal minority protection.

Since 1959, when I first arrived in Kontum, their living conditions had been improving greatly. The Montagnards learned to use fertilizers and gave up bad medical practices, taking modern health care advice. However, they continued to live in extreme poverty and were always in danger of famine. Montagnards were honest and industrious. They were not brave warriors, except for the Sedang ethnic group in the northern districts of Kontum.

Immense dense virgin forests covered the areas along the common border between Laos and Cambodia and Việt Nam. Once I joined a party of the local forestry service and Engineer Corps specialists surveying the terrain and the lumber in that area, as well as inspecting the preparation of emergency landing zones for helicopters on some dozen dominating hilltops.

The area was a no man's land with high mountains running north and south on the western side of the Trường Son (Long Mountain). This is a chain of mountains running along the common border of Việt Nam with Laos and Cambodia, also known as Annamite Range. Kontum and Pleiku provinces are on its western side. However, to my surprise, the terrain in many parts on the common border with Cambodia and Laos could permit movement of trucks without much difficulty. Along 100 miles, there was only one ARVN border outpost at Ban Hét. The troops would open fire on anyone they saw in the forest, because any human near the outpost was assumed to be an enemy gunman. The jungles beyond the observation of the outpost were free of enemy movements.

The infantry troops at Ban Hét were resupplied twice a month. They had to save food for emergency storage in case supply convoys were delayed. They read out-of-date newspapers a portion a day, saving the remaining for the following days of the week. For fun they tuned their radios to the Postal Service long-distance telephone frequencies to monitor people talking, and they laughed at conversations between lovers hinting at sex and other intimate exchanges.

Many ethnic Vietnamese communist cadres were assigned to work in remote tribal hamlets, learning the language and living with the Montagnards to indoctrinate them with communism under patriotic label. Many other cadres operated the strategic logistic system to procure food and to build food caches along the footpaths connected to the system of trails in the Long Mountains.

They did their tasks silently, never engaging government troops that were conducting search operations, until one day in October 1960.

THE NORTHERN KONTUM CAMPAIGN

It was the first battalion-sized attack that the communist forces conducted against the ARVN in the South Việt Nam highlands since the 1954 cease-fire and eight months since the Trảng Sụp raid on January 26, 1960. A well-armed communist unit with reportedly more than 500 men overran a dozen platoon and squad-sized outposts in the mountainous region about 60 miles north of Kontum city or 250 miles north-northeast of Sài Gòn.

In the area, there were ten small hamlets of about 200 tribal people each. Contrary to communist reports and books that claimed the event was an "uprising," not a single soul among the population joined the communist side in the campaign.

The outposts were defended by units of the Bảo An , which was very poorly equipped with old French rifles and had almost no proper training. It took the communist forces only a few hours to destroy those strongholds, killing a dozen national guardsmen and burying alive the deputy chief of province for ethnic affairs.

As first reports reached the division headquarters, the division commander, Colonel Nguyễn Bảo Trị, with his forward command post of a few officers, rushed to the area to see how his two battalions were executing a search operation. I joined him twenty-four hours later.

The offensive drew much attention from Sài Gòn and Washington. Generals and colonels from Sài Gòn and from the II Corps HQS went to Kontum, all meaning to do something great. The division forward CP, headed by the division commander with only seven officers, moved six miles on foot to set up a command post on top of a hill with limited communications and support. We commanded an operation in an isolated area with two infantry battalions and one airborne battalion coming from Sài Gòn.

Although the enemy suffered more than 100 KIAs and a half dozen POWs, their main force escaped and disappeared into dense forests as quickly as it had attacked the national guards. The first four POWs captured by one of our pursuing battalions confessed that they had been in South Việt Nam prior to July 1954 before moving to North Việt Nam in 1955. They were trained in various northern camps before infiltrating the South in mid-1960.

The POWs were presented at a press conference in Sài Gòn, along with captured weapons and written documents as evidence. North Việt Nam communist leaders, of course, denied the charge that they had violated the Geneva Accords by sending troops and by conducting subversive activities. Two members (India and Canada) of the International Commission for Control and Supervision for the 1954 Geneva Accords endorsed Sài Gòn's allegation. The third member, Poland, objected to it.

Every Vietnamese could verify the allegation of the South Vietnamese government after listening to the accent of the POWs and the vocabulary they used. However, those in the world who were supporting Việt Nam communists loudly echoed Hà Nội's theory that the conflict in the South was just a civil war without any material and personnel support from Hồ Chí Minh and his party. That was how partiality and stupidity lent support to the wrong side from the first days of the war.[1]

The offensive in Kontum province was one of the communists' nationwide campaigns to introduce the new political tool of the Việt Nam Communist Party in the South. On December 20, 1960, the communist side declared the birth of the so-called National Liberation Front of South Việt Nam (NLF). The new label of the Communist Party chapter in South Việt Nam did not surprise my friends and me or most South Vietnamese people. But it became a theme for the communist propaganda front until May 1975, when the NLF was silently discarded and forgotten by its own creators.

GREEN MOUNTAINS

The Central Highlands in South Việt Nam has only two seasons, the dry and the monsoon, which occur at the same time of year with Sài Gòn, as opposed to the Central Coastal provinces. Kontum is the only area in the Central Highlands with bright soil, whereas the others are covered by red dirt.

When I first arrived in Kontum, I felt a great despair at being in a small city without electricity or running water. I was trying to be transferred back to Sài Gòn or somewhere else, but every effort failed. Without a good connection, such attempts would always end in failure. However, only a year later, I began to develop a warmer feeling for the place. The mild climate and the green mountains one after another with purple crests in late afternoon were enough to attract me. How exciting it was to see silver clouds floating above mountains with white fog covering the foothills in early mornings and golden sunlight in dry winter afternoons.

Moreover, the friendly atmosphere in the unit I was serving especially won my heart. An American or Western soldier may have not experienced the same thing, as ways of life were different. In a division far from Sài Gòn and in a small town with limited conveniences, officers and enlisted men all were closer and very friendly. We had nothing to envy or to compete with one another. Without many places to go for leisure time, we spent more time together, always ready to help. Enlisted men who were with a unit for five years since it was established made it their family. They knew the date and every detail of many events, big and small. There were artillery NCOs who were with the same howitzer for five years and could recite by heart the firing range table, and sergeants in the tactical operation center who could tell six-digit coordinates of every major terrain feature—bridges, sharp river elbows, road junctions—from memory.

So I was integrated into the unit where I could find something closer to my ideal. I felt more enthusiastic about the tasks I was given.

THE 1960 COUP ATTEMPT

In 1960, the Sài Gòn government was facing more protests from the opposition. The crackdowns in 1958 continued through 1960 on a smaller scale. A remarkable event in spring 1960 was the press conference of the "Caravelle Group," so called because the group met with many foreign correspondents at Hotel Caravelle in Sài Gòn Central. The group released a letter asking President Diệm to stop crackdowns on nationalist dissidents and to revoke undemocratic policies. It also proposed radical reforms in many fields—political, social, military, and economic—to effectively defend the republic from communist insurgency.

The group consisted of eighteen renowned intellectuals; two of them were VNQDĐ leaders: the lawyers Trần Văn Tuyên and Lê Ngọc Chấn. In the following months, many nationalists, including some of my VNQDĐ comrades, were incarcerated without court trials. The Caravelle crackdown strengthened my support for a coup to overthrow the president's government and establish a new democratic ruling system.

My comrades and I believed that it was necessary to bring new leaders to power so that South Việt Nam could deal effectively with the communists and become a place of full freedom and democracy like the United States. We were encouraged when South Korea's president, Syngman Rhee, had to resign under pressure from a strong opposition. We believed that if our side showed enough resolution and strength for a coup attempt, the Americans would have to support us. "You should not defeat a dictatorship with another dictatorship," one of my VNQDĐ leaders had taught me.

On November 10, 1960, I received a letter from my Việt Quốc comrade in Sài Gòn, in which he informed me by prearranged code that I should get back to the capital as soon as possible to join my comrades in a coup d'état planned by military field grade officers with whom our VNQDĐ group cooperated. No specific date was set in the short letter.

Early the next morning, when I was about to receive a travel order and get on the manifest for a military flight to the capital, news reports from Sài Gòn Radio announced that the coup had already been launched in the capital city. All air communications were canceled. I regretted missing an opportunity to participate. The letter came to me two days later than usual.

The coup was a hard blow to the regime. When President Diệm announced his decision to open talks with the coup leaders for a peaceful compromise, most of the high-ranking officials and military officers gave no sign against the revolting officers. We knew that by monitoring the army and government security radio networks. However, my fellow officers and I all felt something was wrong with the poorly coordinated and contradictory announcements over Sài Gòn Radio. So we kept quiet. The division commander sat on the fence, admitting to his close aides that the government committed certain errors in how it treated the nationalist dissidents, but he gave strict orders to the units under his command to stay away from political matters and to concentrate on fighting the communists.

Hà Nội was obviously taken aback. Hà Nội Radio reported briefly on the coup. Not until the coup had been over for days did it broadcast a long editorial strongly denouncing both sides in South Việt Nam as American puppets who were competing for "their master's favor."

The coup ended, as many could have guessed, two days after it broke out. Its leaders fled to Cambodia; other officers stayed and were arrested. Many of the officers in the coup were well known for their virtue and capability.

For the first time, rumors spread quickly all over the country that the U.S. Central Intelligence Agency (CIA) had supported the coup just to threaten Diệm, and when it had built as much pressure on him as Washington needed, the Americans turned off the green light and let the coup leaders run for their lives.

I didn't believe the whole story, but that was not the problem. For a very long time, rumors had been playing a more and more important and even decisive role. It was not a question of whether the rumors contained some truth; what counted was that so many people, especially the troops, believed them.

Since the early 1960s, the CIA had been the ghost behind every important event in Việt Nam. Unfortunately, the legend—that the invincible CIA was playing every trick to start and end the war in Việt Nam—had some unfavorable impact on the psychological warfare effort of the South. From then on, anyone could be dubbed a "CIA informant or operative."

After the failed coup d'état, the government cracked down on the opposition. The police detained many well-known people and prosecuted them.

ON CULTURAL LIFE

The year 1960 saw a brightening of the cultural life in South Việt Nam. As I mentioned above, cultural activities of all kinds contributed to the war effort. Before 1954, in the resistance against the French, the people's high spirit was greatly promoted by songs and plays, not only by political indoctrination. The middle class, the bourgeoisie, played the key role on the cultural front. The proletarian leaders were in no way capable of such tasks, though they began to occupy key jobs in the ranks of the Việt Minh. And the cultural front was so important that any writing about the Việt Nam War without properly treating cultural activities would be deemed insufficient.

Most musical works were songs and ballads. Other types of music (instrumental and operatic) were extremely rare. Most South Vietnamese people, however, preferred the Cải Lương, a type of traditional musical opera in pentatonic scale. It was characterized by strong sentimental tunes and lyrics closely associated with the spoken language, simple and intimate. The Cải Lương art prospered along with "modern music" or heptatonic scale musical works. In the war of resistance, nine out of ten songs called for fighting colonialists and defending the motherland. Many of the songs had artistic value in both lyrics and melody that warmed the hearts of the younger generation.

Before the 1954 Geneva Accords dividing Việt Nam, cultural activities in the nationalist areas were passive. Almost all songs were about love, natural beauties, and the like. There were some works eulogizing the combat soldiers produced by the National Army Morale Action Bureau and the Information Ministry. A few of those martial songs had artistic value. But none was directly against communism or against the French. Probably the artists in the nationalist areas had a complex of siding with the French and were also afraid of getting into trouble with the French Security Service. After South Việt Nam became totally independent and the French Expeditionary Forces had withdrawn, cultural circles and the mass media went in a new direction. Songs, plays, books, and newspaper and magazine articles dealing with positive anticommunist themes began to appear boldly. The government cultural and psywar agencies produced some; a larger number were private and spontaneous contributions.

Artists who were anticommunist felt free to compose anything to support their ideals. Some anticommunist movies were produced. But South Vietnamese were also free to sing tunes composed before 1954 praising the war against the French and calling for patriots to fight for independence. The South Việt Nam government tacitly affirmed that cultural works composed during the war of resistance that did not have content praising communism, Hồ Chí Minh, or his party were legal. All patriotic songs by any composer—even those who were serving the communist regime in North Việt Nam—were considered to be national assets, and anyone might sing or play them freely. At the military academy, officer candidate schools, training centers, and units, martial songs from the pre-1954 era could be selected as the official songs of platoons, companies, and higher.

Meanwhile, on the communist side, most songs composed before 1951 were interdicted. Many were treasures of patriotic music. After 1951, new rules were imposed on music composition by the Workers' Party, dictating to composers how to write to be strictly compatible with the party line. These rules also applied to writing poems, novels, and other literary works.

In North Việt Nam after 1954, every piece of music called for socialist struggle, fighting enemies, and praising the party, Uncle Hồ, and the big communist brothers, the Soviet Union and China, especially Mao.

Tố Hữu, the well-known poet of the Communist Party who wrote "Mourning Stalin" in 1953, composed other "steel and blood" poems. His typical work promoting the Land Reform Campaign in 1955 was the following:

> *Giết nữa! Giết nữa đi! Bàn tay không phút nghỉ,*
> *Cho ruộng đồng lúa tốt thuế mau xong.*
> *Toàn Đảng toàn dân chung sức chung lòng,*
> *Thờ Mao Chủ Tịch, thờ Xit-ta-lin bất diệt.*

> *Let's kill, let's kill more, the hands rest not for a minute.*
> *So that rice fields thrive and [agricultural] tax is quickly collected,*
> *All people and the Party share the same effort and willingness*
> *To worship the undying Chairman Mao and Stalin.*

There were some love songs, but their themes also aimed at praising the Communist Party leaders and promoting the fighting spirit. Besides, love songs and stories from other origins were classified as taboo and were labeled "golden music," a North Vietnamese communist term for romantic love songs. Anyone singing or playing "golden music" might wind up in jail. Those who disseminated the "golden music" would face capital punishment. A court in Hà Nội pronounced one such death sentence in 1968.

After 1954, North Vietnamese produced hundreds of songs supporting the communist revolution each month. According to many North Việt Nam songwriters, almost everyone might compose songs praising the revolution, the party and its leaders, and the patriotic soldiers. Many songs were played on the radio or the stage just once or twice. Most of those amateur songwriters were not able to read musical scores and had no perception of basic rules of musical composition.

Impartially speaking, it was true that some of the North Vietnamese communist martial songs had a certain artistic value and intense patriotic effect that produced a high degree of public motivation. Besides, communist artists in the

North were contributing folk songs, which were the abundant traditional cultural assets in the rural North Việt Nam. They also wrote a lot of songs for children, especially songs promoting loyalty to the party and support for the war.

In South Việt Nam, there were thousands of songs, ballads, poems, and books of all categories and other cultural works coming into existence by the end of Sài Gòn regime on April 30, 1975. After seizing South Việt Nam, communist authorities ordered the eradication of all cultural works of the South, but only a part of the works were destroyed owing to the people's efforts to preserve them. Many are still the favorites of Vietnamese of every living generation, in South Việt Nam, in Vietnamese communities living abroad, and North Việt Nam as well.

In the two decades of South Việt Nam being separated as a nation, the contribution of South Vietnamese artists and writers—including those in the military—to the nation's culture was at least ten times that of the North Vietnamese. However, the volume of cultural works serving the political and military struggle made by South Việt Nam was one-hundredth of that made by North Việt Nam.

In a rare exception, both North and South Việt Nam governments and armed forces—including the Vietnamese émigré communities in Western countries today—have been playing the same hymn for the commemoration of their war dead in public ceremonies. People say the souls of the dead warriors on both sides may find some mutual consolation in the underworld when they listen to the tune, and they are the only ones who are actually reconciled.[2]

THE PRESIDENTIAL ELECTION

Being in charge of screening all papers including top-secret operation plans and reports sent to the division from higher headquarters, I had an opportunity to learn more about the national situation and accurate information in other areas.

The communist forces in South Việt Nam increased their subversive campaign over almost all remote countryside areas with ambushes, bold attacks, kidnappings, and assassinations. Nor did they conceal their intention to get rid of every village government. Communist activities increased dramatically in our division area, especially in the foothill villages of Phú Yên and Bình Định provinces.

At that time—until 1965 when American troops arrived—the two northernmost provinces of South Việt Nam, Thừa Thiên and Quảng Trị, were extremely quiet. Apparently North Việt Nam Army avoided making noise and smoke too close to its home.

The second term presidential election was held in early 1961. The campaigns weren't interesting because everybody knew that it would be a walkover for President Diệm. The other candidates had no hope of winning an election in such a political environment.

As I understood from a foreign news report, in an interview President Diệm strongly supported the viewpoint that the great majority of Vietnamese peasants accepted the traditional political concept of living under a wise and benevolent king assisted by honest and capable mandarins. The people's interests were best served in such a system, he argued. In a sense, I agreed with him. After talking to all kinds of people I met in poor hamlets, I had gained some understanding. The peasants really didn't care about what was going on in Sài Gòn or Washington. All they needed were scanty meals every day and peaceful sleep at night without fear of being killed or arrested.

Once in a while, on leave in Sài Gòn, I visited the old revolutionary Nguyễn Thế Truyền, one of the most renowned anticolonialists, whose wife had been a royal princess of Belgium. He treated me as if I were his nephew, and I loved to listen to him talk about the struggle for independence before 1945. He knew most revolutionary personages in the different movements, especially Hồ Chí Minh. When Hồ first landed on French soil, it was Nguyễn Thế Truyền, then a well-known activist, who helped him to be admitted as a member of the French Communist Party and to get Hồ's first book published. He had graduated as a chemical engineer in France, but his manners were of an Asian gentleman. He admired Hồ as a talented politician, but he looked down on him because Hồ was a "crafty old fox."

Nguyễn Thế Truyền ran for vice president along with Hồ Nhựt Tăn for president in the 1961 election. So in this period, when I dropped by the small wooden house in a poor neighborhood where Truyền lived by himself, I had to take a few safety measures to prevent myself from being blacklisted by the secret police.

MY SISTER PROTECTS ME

My nineteen-year-old sister devoted much time to serving Nguyễn Thế Truyền's political campaign, although she knew there was very little hope for him to win.

But one morning my mother called me on the post office radiotelephone line. With a choked voice she told me that my sister had been killed in a traffic accident. I almost fainted but tried my best to calm my mother.

I took the first cross-country bus that afternoon to get home the next morning after a sleepless night. My two sisters and I had been always close. By Asian family tradition, I had had a greater moral responsibility to them since our father died.

At my sister's funeral, my mother and my aunt sobbed endlessly. My younger sister and I wept silently.

A week later, I returned to Kontum by bus. At a rubber plantation about sixty miles north of Sài Gòn, a squad of VC guerrillas stopped our bus. I was in extreme danger because the ID card that everyone must have while traveling specified my occupation as "military." Since 1959, communist guerrillas had begun capturing military servicemen and police in civilian clothes riding on buses and sometimes on trains. They had different ways to pick out soldiers besides checking their ID cards—many soldiers had IDs listing anything but military as their occupation. Sometimes the VC ordered male passengers to get off and show their bare feet. The rebels could easily tell who the soldiers were by examining the skin on their upper instep. If the skin was hardened and darkened, he must have been a soldier because his foot showed the impact of wearing jungle boots for a long time. Sometimes the VC told people to fall out in lines and then unexpectedly shouted, "Attention!" Nine out of ten times, men who were military servicemen or policemen would draw themselves into stiff posture, giving themselves away. Often the enlisted men were brought to the jungle for a few hours or more, given a political lesson, then released. The officers were different. The rebels usually brought captured officers to their secret bases deep in the border areas or even in Cambodia. Many RVN officers were killed when the guerrillas were unable to bring them along.

There were three other servicemen on my bus: a first sergeant and an old sergeant major and a second lieutenant. Two were sweating in fear. Only the old sergeant major seated right behind me retained his composure. I knew that sergeant major was a wonderful creature in many armies, but I hadn't expected one so brave. He knew me when he served in Kontum.

When the six guerrillas began inspecting the passengers' identification, we all knew that our end would come soon. I have never experienced anything so tense. In fighting, death might hover over my head, but I had a weapon in my hand to do something before getting killed. I couldn't bear the idea of confronting the enemy with virtually nothing to defend oneself.

At that desperate moment, I began praying: "Help me, little sister. Lead me to safety." The prayer damped down my fear and seemed to enlighten my mind when confronting the guerrillas.

A guerrilla locked the bus doors before checking everybody's ID card through the windows. I had no idea of how to lie to him as he glanced at my ID. He looked me straight the eye and asked, "Are you a soldier?" As if I were in a dream, I replied, "Yes, I *was*." Right then, idea after idea flashed in my head, and I went on talking to him in a cool voice without the least sign of panic.

He asked me about six or seven questions, and I lied to him that I was a draftee just discharged from the army after two years' service. He smiled at me, saying that he had been in Quang Trung Training Center in 1957, Company KA, Thirty-eighth Battalion. Oh, my God! His company was fifty yards from the company under my command at the same time. Thank God! He did not recognize me. He asked me many questions about the camp. All my answers were compatible with existing facts. At every question, something prompted me to give the proper answer. The lies convinced him. I was surprised at my own reactions.

A minute later, another guerrilla began checking the luggage. Opening the first suitcase he found a khaki shirt with an army unit insignia. He immediately ordered all passengers to come out and to stand beside their suitcases. The old sergeant major winked at me in an imperturbable manner. He quietly slipped beneath my seat a switchblade and told me in a low voice, "Lieutenant, no way to hide our uniforms in the suitcases. Everybody dies sometime. So just watch me. When I fly at one of them, try to get another son of a bitch that is nearest to you with this knife before they get rid of us." I knew I would have to do that when he showed me a shortened carbine bayonet in his sinewy hand and said, "I have this."

Suddenly as if from nowhere, two British-made armored vehicles of World War II vintage and troops of a district patrol noiselessly appeared not more than fifty yards from us. The troops opened fire, and the guerrillas began running into the dense vegetation beyond the rubber trees. It took me a few seconds to unlock the bus door and kick it open. But the sergeant grabbed my arm and held me back: "No, sir. It's too late to get them. Our soldiers might mistake us for VC." I admired his quick mind. He was a truly a tough sergeant major.

To this day, I don't know how I would have acted if the troops had not come and the sergeant major had done as he intended. Probably I would have finished off the shortest guerrilla standing ten feet from me, a rifle hanging on his shoulder. I never thought I could be so brave. But I think when driven into a corner with some brave fellows beside you to lend some courage or esprit de corps, you might become some kind of hero. In my case, it was the sergeant major who commanded the lieutenant.

When my mother and my aunt heard the story, they agreed that my dead sister had saved me. In the minutes of danger, a wrong word could have brought me death. And my sister prompted me to say the right words, my aunt said. My lies flashing in my mind fit one another into a well-organized story, credible and reasonable like a jigsaw puzzle. Probably extreme danger incited quick and reasonable reactions by intuition.

The incident intensified what I had been thinking for years about how to provide full security protection to highways and other means of communication. The military academy and the U.S. Infantry School hadn't taught me any effective tactic to deal with the issue; neither had the Joint General Staff. So far, to protect the roads, our military units were just doing what they had been doing for years even during the 1946–54 war, which was clearing roadbeds of mines and searching roadsides for ambushes or snipers in early morning, deploying troops on dominating positions along the road, and withdrawing at sunset. At night, the guerrillas had free access to the roads in the surrounding area.

ALARMING SITUATION

In the latter half of 1961, communist guerrilla activity in the deltas rose to an alarming level. The guerrillas laid several successful ambushes and overran several military forts. In the highland provinces, they avoided contact in the dry season and became very active in the monsoon season, which always lasts from May to October.

VC activities in 1961 brought the conflict to a new phase. There were debates at high levels in Sài Gòn and Washington concerning the war. Different arguments were freely reported in newspapers and radio in Việt Nam. To most people, including the troops, a fact reported in Vietnamese newspapers was just a report that drew little attention. But a lie told in a foreign publication and in radio broadcasts was taken for the truth. Such an attitude became much more poisonous in later years.

In July 1961, a company of the Fortieth Infantry Regiment of my division suffered heavy losses in an operation to rescue the Toumorong district headquarters, about twenty-five miles north of Kontum. The headquarters on the slope of a mountain more than 3,000 feet in altitude was overrun after a fierce attack that lasted two hours. A dozen provincial troops were killed, and a dozen others were wounded. The attack drew every major command into action. Corps and division headquarters all got involved. It seemed to me that the commanders acted to show the JGS and especially the president that they were doing their jobs more than to serve the ultimate goals of the army and the nation.

The Fortieth Infantry had to send a battalion to pursue the fleeing enemy in the dense jungle area. On the way to the objective, a company fell into an ambush. About forty ARVN soldiers were killed, fifty were wounded, and the remaining two dozen were captured. Learning the bad news, Corps II headquarters sent a marine battalion to reinforce our infantry battalions for a pursuit operation that lasted a week but produced little success. Until late 1961, our infantry units in operations were seldom supported by firepower other than mortars. Air support, if any, was used only for resupply, because there was no air base for fighters in the area. The 105 howitzers were often unavailable because the few roads were not always negotiable in the monsoon, while the 4"2 mortars were too heavy to be moved quickly.

An operation usually lasted from fifteen to twenty-five days. In that kind of terrain, operating troops would find no enemy if they marched five days into the dense forests. But whenever they did make contact with the enemy, only a few shots were exchanged before the enemy melted into the green foliage. Casualties on both sides were usually light, with one or two dead or wounded. The enemy seldom engaged in unanticipated firefights unless they had no other options.

The division and regiment headquarters were well aware that many operations were not necessary. Such actions mostly rendered no harm to the enemy but did cause the troops unnecessary fatigue, resulting in low morale and a distrust of command. However, they had no way to object. Headquarters higher than the division ordered many a company-sized operation.

Our army had been trained in tactics for conventional warfare, and that was where the Americans could help. But what we needed was training in how to conduct antiguerrilla warfare, and that wasn't being taught at training centers or by the U.S. Army field manuals. Many local and low-level commands invented rather effective ways to deal with the enemy, but these tactics were never compiled into general directives, let alone into a coherent training program in antiguerrilla warfare.

After the communist general uprising in late 1960, and the emergence of the National Liberation Front of South Việt Nam, many bold attacks of platoon and company size were launched against remote forts. The number of civilian officials assassinated by communist terrorists sharply increased. In many instances, the victims included the officials' families. VC guerrillas even attacked antimalarial teams that were visiting hamlets to spray insecticide; the guerrillas accused them of spying.

Night travel over portions of highways and the railway connecting the two ends of South Việt Nam was made dangerous by ambushes or land mines. Military vehicles were harassed by sniper fire even in daylight. VC guerrillas missed no opportunity to attack military ambulances and medics on roads and battlefields, killing physicians and medics to seize medical supplies. The TO&E provided medical personnel with pistols only. After strenuous complaints from the medical personnel, the division was forced to seek permission to arm them with rifles, carbines, and hand grenades.

The Twenty-second Division area of responsibility included 100 kilometers of common border with Cambodia to the south and with Laos to the north. Most communist forces had their safe camps on the Cambodia side of the border. They would retreat to those camps, and ARVN units were not allowed to pursue them into Cambodia. One night in late 1961, my division was alerted of the infiltration by two unidentified airplanes into the airspace of Pleiku province. The radar station in Pleiku discovered their signals on the screen. As there had been no fighters stationed at Pleiku's new airbase at the time, RVN Air Force fighter bombers from Sài Gòn's Tân Sơn Nhất airbase were scrambled. But when the interceptors arrived at the coordinates, the clandestine planes had fled to the North. Later in the day, we received reports that the planes were of a Soviet model and had dropped by parachute several cases of weapons and radio equipment on a marked site in Cambodian territory, a few kilometers from the common border between Pleiku province and Cambodia.

REMAINING IN THE ARMY

Summer 1961. I missed my last chance to go for schooling in the United States to study for a university degree in physics, for which I had a special talent. I was

FIFTEEN

The Limited War

MACV: STEPPING UP THE WAR

In his first year as president of the United States, John F. Kennedy brought a lot of hope to the South Vietnamese anticommunists. These feelings were so strong that some Vietnamese began having concerns about the elections, which could remove Kennedy from power.

In early 1962, the Military Advisory and Assistance Group (MAAG) was transformed into the Military Assistance Command in Việt Nam (MACV). This change marked another step in the American war effort. The U.S. Air Force came with fighters, and several U.S. Army helicopter units were deployed in every key area.

That year, along with more aid from the United States, the Vietnamese armed forces were largely restructured. In the late 1950s, many province chiefs were civilians; only some were military officers. Later on, most were army majors and lieutenant colonels. Similarly, most district chiefs were army lieutenants and captains. Presidential Decree 7 of 1959 vested large powers to the province chief. A province chief, as the representative of the president in the province, had the power to mobilize military personnel and units of any size or any rank stationed in the province and to implement tasks concerning the maintenance of social and political order, provided the province chief promptly reported his actions to the president of the republic.

The infantry divisions, supposedly mobile units, were given territorial responsibility, namely, Division Tactical Areas (DTA). A DTA supervised a number of sectors, each of which was the military territory of a province. As 99 percent of province chiefs were military officers, they were also sector commanding officers and virtually under control of the division CO. Similarly, the four corps commanders were also COs of the Corps Tactical Zones (CTZ), and each included two or three DTAs.

A military officer serving as the province chief with powers vested by Decree 7/59 and cumulating the authority of a territorial military commander was in fact a powerful official in the domains of administration, political and military. The RVN armed forces' strength increased. The Airborne Brigade became the Airborne Division. The RVN air force and navy received more personnel and equipment. U.S. aid began to pay for and equip the Bảo An Đoàn (national guard), whose salaries had previously been covered by the national budget and whose members were equipped with ordnance left by the French Army. Bảo An units and officers' corps were also reorganized to take care of territorial security responsibility. After this reorganization, it was much easier to coordinate the war effort with other government activities. In later years, however, it would help constitute a kind of militarism. On the plus side, we staff officers had opportunities to learn and to run our shops with knowledge beyond the military domain.

As more Americans arrived after MACV was established, people began to talk about the larger involvement of the United States in Việt Nam, especially when there was a demand from the American side to place their advisors at lower levels. Previously, American military advisors were assigned only down to regiments and civilian advisors to provinces; now the Americans were asking that advisors be assigned to battalion and district levels. A directive my division received from the Presidential Palace ordered that, in any talk with the Americans at our level relating to the matter, we should say no. But sometime later, the Americans got what they wanted.

Some friends of mine were concerned about the possible presence of American combat troops fighting the communist forces in Việt Nam. Their presence would certainly aggravate Sài Gòn's existing weak spot on the propaganda front.

The short peaceful period after 1954 in South Việt Nam thus came to a definite end. From then on, life would never be the same, and most Vietnamese peasants began to lose what they had gained in the previous years.

ONE OF THE FORGOTTEN HEROES

After 1961, more and more battles were fought and more and more soldiers became heroes, but most were not well known to the public. Among those who fought and suffered heroically in the Twenty-second Division, Second Lieutenant Phạm Văn Châu was forever in my memory.

Châu graduated in 1958 from Thủ Đức Reserve Officer School as an "aspirant" (above sergeant major and below second lieutenant) and served in the engineering corps. In 1961 he was promoted to second lieutenant and commanded an engineer company of the Twenty-second Division Combat Engineer

Battalion. He was a good friend, and I helped him with paperwork for his marriage approval, as military security regulation required. At the time, his company was opening a new road into a military site in a jungle area some ten miles north of Pleiku City.

When his wedding was approved by the Ministry of Defense, he asked his parents to arrange a wedding party in Sài Gòn. The division commander awarded him a fifteen-day leave for his wedding. A few days before the wedding ceremony, he left his company road construction site for Kontum to take a flight to Sài Gòn. He was traveling in a three-quarter-ton truck along with ten of his soldiers. Midway to Pleiku, they were ambushed. A company-sized VC unit opened fire on the truck. In a minute all of the soldiers were killed or wounded. Châu was slightly injured but still able to move around and fight.

According to wounded soldiers who witnessed the scene, Châu kept fighting with his M-1 carbine for possibly fifteen minutes. He spent all his ammunition and some taken from the injured troops around him. He only stopped when enemy bullets crushed his legs and one arm and he ran out of ammunition. A VC charged at him with a machete. Châu raised his unhurt arm to protect his body and the machete chopped off his forearm. The VC believed Châu was dead. When they left, some wounded soldiers helped him with emergency bandages before he was evacuated to the hospital in time to save him.

Châu regained consciousness at Cộng Hòa Military General Hospital in Sài Gòn after doctors tried their best to save his life from the extremely critical wounds. However, all his limbs were amputated.

His fiancée dropped by the hospital to see him just once or twice and never returned. Of course, no one would talk about the wedding. I couldn't blame her. She was a pretty girl. Who could do otherwise in her case except for some characters in a novel?

I've always remembered Châu as a handsome man who had never been expected to fight like a tiger in that battle.

SECRET OPERATIONS

When I first came to Sài Gòn in August 1954, some members of a secret service approached a very close friend and me to insist that we join their secret plan against North Việt Nam. That meant we had to go there to live under false names and identities for a long term, possibly forever if efforts to bring us back failed.

The agents contacting us promised no big money but only said that we should join them out of patriotism. Assistance to our families would not be much. After a week, my friend and I decided that we would not go, only because we were not skillful or brave enough to be spies. The agents asked us to keep the story a secret. They did not specify for whom they were working, but we guessed that they might be from a CIA branch.

In 1957, high-ranking officers I knew in the army spoke in a private meeting about South Vietnamese spies operating in North Việt Nam, Cambodia, and Laos. The Office of Political and Social Research under the legendary Dr. Trần Kim Tuyến was said to be sending spies.

As early as 1959, rumors about secret operations in the communist-controlled territories were spreading in the military. I heard of at least two or three agencies with disguised names such as Topography Service and Observation Group 77, which were sending *biệt kích* (commandos) into territories outside South Việt Nam. Their activities were for intelligence purpose in Cambodia, Laos, and also in North Việt Nam, according to my two classmates who were serving at the *biệt kích* training center.[1]

On another occasion in 1959, one of my chums and also a classmate in the military academy serving those secret services asked me to volunteer for the mission. Again, I refused his proposal.

Another friend was a pilot who flew several missions over North Việt Nam for such operations. One night, his C-47 with a special force team crashed at a rush farm near Phát Diệm, the town of the famous anticommunist Catholic force before 1954, about seventy miles south of Hà Nội, according to unofficial information from friends and from a Hà Nội Radio report.

Hà Nội claimed that its antiaircraft unit shot the plane down, but some RVN Air Force officers told me that the pilots informed the radar station that they were having engine trouble and would have to land. The men, including the copilot, were alive and captured. My friend was not mentioned in Hà Nội news reports. He was probably killed or missing or had escaped to safety in some secret location.

Military servicemen of Mường, Thái, and Nùng ethnic groups in my division were the best to be sent back to their native areas. They were brave, loyal, highly opposed to the communists, and familiar with the mountainous regions. In a year, a large number of the Twenty-second Division enlisted men from the three groups were transferred to the special unit for missions over the North.

In those years, Hà Nội Radio often broadcast reports about South Vietnamese special operation teams captured and tried in North Việt Nam courts-martial. Sometimes, special operation units returning from Laos crossed the common border to enter our division territory and return to Kontum. So operations in North Việt Nam and Laos were no longer absolute secrets.

THE SPECIAL FORCES

After MACV was established in early 1962, more Americans came to serve in our division area. Many of the new faces were soldiers from the U.S. Fifth

Special Forces group in their green berets. They represented the Americans who were eager to do something extraordinary in Việt Nam.

The ARVN also overtly created its own Special Forces. A half dozen camps were established along the trail used by the North Vietnamese Army to infiltrate men and supplies into our DTA. At the time, the Special Forces operation, a new concept of limited war, was welcomed as an effective strategy for the unconventional warfare being fought overtly in the South and covertly in the North.

The Special Forces built camps in the areas where military actions were launched to control the enemy's routes of infiltration. In a short time, a great number of tribesmen from village militias were trained and armed with WWI rifles such as .30 bolt action Springfield and Remington models, shotguns, WWII M1 carbines, and even M2 carbines. The Special Forces brought radical changes to the tribesmen's lives while training them to use weapons, equipment (telephone, radio transceiver), and military tactics.

However, the arms allocation created a great concern for Vietnamese authorities, as there would be no way to control the possession of weapons in the Montagnard hamlets, particularly in the Twenty-third Division area (HQS in Ban Mê Thuột).

Three years later, the FULRO,[2] a movement for autonomy of the highland tribes, once suppressed in 1958, rose again in Ban Mê Thuột with hundreds of militants, all armed with light weapons provided by Special Forces camps in 1962 out of local authorities' control.

Most of the tribesmen preferred the Green Berets to their Vietnamese Special Forces brothers. They were recruited and paid by the U.S. Special Forces, without being on the Vietnamese government's payroll, to serve in counterinsurgency units or Mike Force (Mobile Strike Force). They were under the sole control of the Special Forces camps, operating without the Vietnamese military or paramilitary status. However, they were taught that they were fighting the communists to serve the noble cause of the Vietnamese people and the Free World.

Running each camp was a Vietnamese team and a U.S. A-Detachment team; each U.S. team included two officers and ten NCOs. The Montagnards troops were organized into companies. Company commanders and platoon leaders were mostly ethnic Vietnamese civilian volunteers. The western media sometimes referred to these tribal militiamen as mercenaries. Although the term seems nothing special to Western ears, it sounds extremely disdainful in Vietnamese, much worse than "hireling," its synonym. In the propaganda warfare, the communist side always used "mercenary" to denote troops coming from Australia, Thailand, South Korea, and New Zealand, who were fighting the war beside the South Vietnamese and Americans.

The Special Forces camps spent a lot of money paying for various services, which included building fortifications and clearing vegetation along the roads leading to the camps.

At the same time, the new Combat Research and Development Center of the ARVN Joint General Staff/J-5 began its tests for new weapons and equipment in cooperation with MACV counterparts. The Center's special teams often came to work in my division, bringing samples of AR-10 and AR-15 rifles, M-79 grenade launchers, personnel radar detectors, field antennas for portable radios, lightweight flame throwers, and several others for testing in combat. I heard that many sophisticated weapons and equipment were being tested in other areas. The new military ordnances did enhance of the troops' fighting spirit, particularly in the Airborne, Marine, and Ranger units.

In the same year, a special program of defoliation began spraying chemicals to clear brush along highways and on VC bases. Communist propaganda service in Hà Nội and Beijing loudly protested the program, claiming that the Americans and South Vietnamese were employing chemical warfare, spraying poisonous substances to kill communist troops, and causing death to thousands of innocent people. At first, the communists did not say that it was a defoliation agent. A few years later, the communist side made loud noises against the so-called Agent Orange. In the recent campaign, Hà Nội released a list of victims; most of them were North Vietnamese soldiers.

Troops in my division and others even carried hand-pump sprayers in operations at VC bases to destroy their food plants. Ten of thousands of other troops spent long years living or operating in sprayed areas. They should have outnumbered the NVA troops in that list if Agent Orange really caused such serious health problems.

In Việt Nam, many people believe that the chemical did contain some toxic ingredients that may have caused harmful health effects, but not so severe. Reports about the use of Agent Orange seem to be exaggerated. No soldiers in units I knew who had been in longtime contact with the defoliant ever suffered cancer or reproduction defects. It should be noticed that for decades, North Vietnamese farmers were using insecticides containing harmful ingredients to excess. These were among the possible causes of the health problems in North Việt Nam since 1955.

THE PRESIDENTIAL PALACE BOMBED

After the failed coup on November 11, 1960, I still had contact with my Việt Quốc comrades. The party was still divided into at least three major groups. The groups did not get along well with one another, despite the fact that all the factions suffered from the government's oppression after the 1958 attempted coup. However, they didn't fight or take any action harmful to the others.

It was that disunity of the party that made me feel extremely disappointed. The Việt Quốc had been the most powerful rival of the Communist Party, but after being defeated by Hồ Chí Minh and his Communist Party leaders, the Việt Quốc had lost a large number of its prospective capable leaders. The 1946–48 political purges by the Communist Party proved its long-term effects.

The other parties in South Việt Nam were mostly in the same situation. Under repression, most went clandestine. Since 1955, almost none of the noncommunist parties had been getting along with Diệm's supporters because the Sài Gòn leadership was consolidating a powerful one-party regime, denying participation by the major political parties to confront the Communist Party. What we were wishing for was a true democracy, a true freedom in which we wouldn't have to deify anyone or join any party to have a good job. Furthermore, the "personalism" introduced by President Diệm's Cần Lao Party was too complicated and abstract even for officers to understand, let alone the enlisted men and the common people.

On February 29, 1962, two South Vietnamese Air Force Skyraider fighters attacked the Independence Palace (Presidential Palace) in Sài Gòn. President Diệm survived the bombing. One of the two pilots, Lieutenant Phạm Phú Quốc, was shot down and arrested. The other, Lieutenant Nguyễn Văn Cử, flew his plane to Phnom Penh, Cambodia, for political asylum.

Nguyễn Văn Cử's father, Nguyễn Văn Lực, was a Việt Quốc leader and a friend of my family. In August 1954, he appointed me leader of a social cadre team going to Sài Gòn to help the local social services receive North Vietnamese refugees.

After the failed attempt, Nguyễn Văn Lực went into hiding until November 1963, when President Diệm's regime collapsed. I was not informed or asked to participate in the plot this time. If I had been ordered, I would have joined the scheme in some way. However, unlike the 1960 coup, I felt that it was not the right time for such an attempt. The military situation was so critical that stability in Sài Gòn was indispensable to the war effort. Eventually, the air attack was another powerful blow to the popularity of the regime.

THE BEST AMERICANS IN VIỆT NAM

I believe that the 1961–64 period was the best time for Vietnamese-American relations at intermediate and low levels. It may not have been the same at the ambassador-to-president level, but I was too low in rank to know about that. The Americans serving as advisors were always polite and never poked their noses into our affairs. They were absolutely different from the pre-1954 French. Actually, the Americans came to Việt Nam for a much loftier cause. The publication of letters of an American captain to his wife before he was killed in Việt Nam had a favorable effect on public opinion about the Americans and the war, both in Việt Nam and in the United States. We welcomed the American officers as true friends, although sometimes we felt hurt by the irresponsible and ignorant American political leaders in Washington, D.C., for their baseless criticism against our nationalist side.

Although the Americans lived independently with their own system of supply that provided them with almost everything, they still had to maintain good relations with us. Many of them went to downtown Kontum at night to have a cup of coffee or in the morning to eat a large bowl of *phở* (Vietnamese noodle soup). It was those early American servicemen who built the best understanding between the Americans and the Vietnamese.

The relations between us and the Americans at division level and lower was next to perfect. Whenever they needed help, they came to us the same way we came to them. So Vietnamese officers rarely considered themselves to be "American puppets," as communist propaganda labeled them. I know that the advisors would report to their bosses in Sài Gòn if they found something incorrect in our unit. The U.S. top ranks in Sài Gòn would talk to our superiors, who then took some action to correct us. But that was not a matter of our concern. They might remind us about implementing military directives on the unit management, material maintenance, and training that had been issued by our channel of command, and they never interfered in our tasks even when there were disagreements between the two sides. We were aware of the fact that when the Americans assisted us with millions of dollars a year, they had the right to monitor our activities to make sure that their dollars were spent for appropriate purposes.

We Vietnamese officers were not well paid. Naturally many people in countries where U.S. military units were stationed liked to buy something from the American PX stores, and the Vietnamese did, too. Some had American friends buy them liquor, radios, or watches, which they then resold for profit. That bothered some Americans.

Although the American senior advisor and Lieutenant Ludovinsky, the officer in charge of the PX, allowed me to buy anything I wanted from the small store in the compound with Vietnamese piasters, I only bought some ammunition for my .22 long rifle, which was not available in Việt Nam. But I understood why some Vietnamese didn't act like me and also why some Americans felt uneasy when being thus bothered.

One day, a Vietnamese second lieutenant of a battalion logistic section asked an American captain serving the regiment advisory group to buy him a carton of cigarettes. The American replied slowly so that the lieutenant couldn't miss a word: "I am sorry, sir, but I am not a supply officer." The Vietnamese lieutenant was a friend of mine. It took me minutes to make him accept my opinion that in American society, there was nothing incorrect in the way the captain acted.

Months later, the captain and the lieutenant were at the battalion command post (CP) in an operation. The American captain was in great confusion while firefighting broke out at a company close by. Vietnamese who spoke English were all busy in radio communications and other emergency activities. The captain ran into the lieutenant and anxiously asked: "What's going on?" The lieutenant slowly replied in English: "Sorry, sir, I'm no S-2 or S-3."

That the Americans respected our sovereignty satisfied the Vietnamese side. But sometimes I wished they had been allowed to exert more competent authority in the expenditures of American aid.

Danger promoted comradeship between servicemen. That was why we Vietnamese officers felt a close relationship with the Americans serving beside us, and certainly they felt the same. Many times in operations, I saw how lonely the American advisors must have felt among their Vietnamese fighting fellows.

While fighting was going on and everybody at the command post was busy with reports and orders, sometimes under the enemy's fire, no one had enough time to talk to the advisors who were apparently perplexed and nervous. It would have been much easier for the advisors if there had been something for them to do, such as communicating by radio with American pilots on supporting helicopters, fighters, and observation planes.

Advisors in MACV Team 22 at Vietnamese Infantry battalions were under strict regulations. They had to be with the battalions all the time. They shared daily meals with the Vietnamese officers when their battalions were on operations. The meals were prepared by the troops themselves. Certainly they were not at all attractive to the American taste. I knew many Americans who lost ten to fifteen pounds after a few months with the Vietnamese battalions in continual operations. Many came back to the Kontum MACV compound after three months and found they had trouble digesting their American food. Captain Weil, who was my advisor in his second year in the Twenty-second Division, was one of them. But on the brighter side, he really enjoyed Vietnamese meals at my home.

The first Americans who died in our division were shot down over a hamlet some fifteen miles from Kontum. One of them was Lt. Colonel Anthony J. Tencza, the acting senior advisor, who won the sympathy of every Vietnamese who knew him.

ASPECTS OF MILITARY LIFE

The newly established MACV brought in more weapons of all kinds. Communications was greatly enhanced with advanced military technology such as the tropospheric scatter network. Military effectiveness was improved, but not as much as one would have hoped.

The high rate of deserters damaged the performance of infantry units. Operational strength of a battalion was often below 400, sometimes as low as 350 soldiers. The only two battalions of my division that crossed the line of departure in an operation with more than 600 out of its 650 troops were the Mường 3/40 Battalion and the Thái 1/42 Battalion. Mường and Thái are the two largest and most developed ethnic groups in North Việt Nam. Soldiers deserted mostly because living conditions in the army were so harsh, and they left the units for somewhere but not to join the VC side. In fact, most of the deserters went AWOL (absent without leave) for a few months to get back home and to give themselves a time of rest.

A directive for my division required its subordinate units to award their troops fifteen-day leaves each year, but because of the shortage of transportation for soldiers' private travels, not all units could carry out the directive. Most deserters were AWOL for months before they enrolled in a different unit. The problem of desertion and its related consequences lingered until 1975.

The soldier's pay virtually was lower than the lowest government civilian employee's. Meanwhile, many soldiers, private to corporal, were married with children. Their families were living near their units or in many cases in a part of the barracks. The soldiers should have been paid enough to provide their relatives with a decent living. So the South Vietnamese unit commanders had more responsibilities that included the welfare of their subordinates' dependents, a task that never bothered their counterparts in North Việt Nam and was only a little problem in the United States.

Since 1954, the government had tried to help improve the soldier's family life with social services for military dependents. The service was similar to the American Red Cross but more involved. The services included housing, daycare, kindergarten, and medical assistance. However, as the budget was limited, such help did not meet the required demands. After 1961, when the United States increased military aid to South Việt Nam, some efforts were made to improve the social services system, especially to establish a network like the U.S. Army Post Exchange but on a much smaller scale. Unfortunately, the problems of transportation and the government's red tape limited the results.

As high-level headquarters used to send troops to chase the enemy on the basis of any information at all and against almost every one of the enemy's actions, combat troops had less time to rest than they should have. The infantry units operating in the highland areas seldom had an operation that lasted less than fifteen days. In some instances, a battalion might be in an operation for twenty-five days in a row without rest. There is nothing that impairs the willingness of soldiers to fight more than marching for days through rough terrain and bad weather, suffering from fatigue and hunger for twenty days a month, and feeling certain that there will be no enemy to fight. Even when no fighting occurred, soldiers confronted other dangers. In many operations, VC spikes made of bamboo and iron wounded soldiers. The spikes lay underground in pits. Spikes rarely hit a soldier at his sole but often at his calf. The rusty iron or the dirty bamboo that had been immerged in cow droppings for days caused deadly infections and slowed down the unit movement as two soldiers had to carry one injured fellow.

Although many reforms were made to the RVN armed forces units with great help from the United States, the core problems of the military system were not resolved radically. One of these problems, I believe, was the role of the non-commissioned officers. The South Vietnamese sergeant had much less authority than one in Western armies. In the RVN armed forces, there were no clubs for the NCOs or chiefs. The sergeants were respected more in boot camp than in regular units. So the South Vietnamese units did not have a strong backbone, the NCOs, as was the case with the U.S. armed forces.

NCOs who were specialists and technicians performed their tasks as well as any American at similar jobs, sometimes better. They were especially skillful mechanics and technicians in the army technical corps (ordnance, engineer, signal, and medical) as well as in the air force and the navy. They have been contributing to the development of basic technology in Việt Nam, even in the "market economy" under the communist regime today.

AMERICAN NONMILITARY AID

Washington provided more and more assistance to South Việt Nam in various programs relating to national education, public health care, road and bridge construction, administrative reform, and economic development. The best known to the poor Vietnamese was the Food for Peace program. American Public Law 480 allocated a quantity of surplus food production (powdered milk, oatmeal, wheat flour, butter, soybean oil, bulgur wheat) to South Việt Nam. When the United States committed more actively in Việt Nam in 1962, more aid items arrived, including used clothing and small articles such as toothpaste, shampoo, soap, writing tablets, and pencils.

Unfortunately, anti-American propaganda and donations from the United States accompanied by little supporting publicity partly dampened the expected success. Although the Vietnamese people were happy with American aid, many didn't feel grateful for the assistance. Anti-American folks claimed that the United States sent to Việt Nam as aid only discarded materials and surplus products that were useless in the States. Most poor people receiving assistance from the Food for Peace program didn't know the nutritious and monetary value of these products. They would have preferred flour and oil only, although some liked butter, powdered milk, and oatmeal. But none of them liked bulgur wheat, as they did not find it tasty and didn't learn the recipes. Many of the program recipients fed the oatmeal and bulgur to their hogs.

While fighting the bloody war, South Việt Nam successfully imported American and Western technology and business management styles by mutual contact and cooperation. Such technology and skills of doing business did help the country a great deal even after the war.

LAND DEVELOPMENT PROGRAM

The land development program, created in 1955 and supported partly by American aid, was intended to move poor peasants from overpopulated areas—mostly in Central Việt Nam coastal provinces—and resettle them in new villages in the uncultivated lands along the common border with Cambodia. Those villages were called "land development centers." The soil was fertile but sparsely populated. The land development center was supposed to carry out a dual-purpose program. Its primary objective was to create self-sufficiency in food production by growing rice and corn. At the same time, the farmers started growing cash crops as a secondary, long-term objective—rubber, kenaf, coffee, and the like. Besides, the government also hoped that the new settlements would be the Vietnamese "kibbutzim," a belt of outposts to control the border region.

The government established about ninety land development centers through-out the border provinces. In my division's area of responsibility, there were more than thirty such centers that I often visited. Twenty-five were in Pleiku province, where the red soil promised high agricultural productivity, and five were in Kontum.

In the beginning, only volunteers were sent to those newly established land development centers in Pleiku where the program seemed to have significant success. The volunteers included a number of discharged ARVN soldiers. President Diệm frequently visited the centers and devoted every affordable resource to the program, which was claimed to be a national policy of first priority. However, when the program expanded, things went awry. After a time, there were no more volunteers. I didn't know whether by directives from Sài Gòn or not, but in some districts where people were supposed to be persuaded to volunteer, local authorities actually compelled people to be resettled in the land development centers without their consent.

Villagers who had relations with Việt Minh cadres going to North Việt Nam after the 1954 Geneva Accords—usually their parents and siblings—were ordered to move to the land development centers. In some cases, their close friends were ordered to move as well. People at one of those resettlements told me that one night district soldiers surrounded their home village in the coastal area and gathered villagers in an open field. Some were forced onto trucks and sent to a land development center in Pleiku province where more people were needed. Several families were divided. I met an old man who was sent there along with his daughter-in-law, her baby, his single daughter, and his unmarried youngest son, while his wife and his eldest son remained at home.

The Vietnamese communists were directing propaganda efforts against the program. They did not miss anything that could be used to blacken the Diệm regime, describing the land development program as "brutal, vengeful, and done by orders of the American Imperialists." The few illegal compulsory resettlements of people that occurred in some districts provided the communist propaganda with stark evidence for attacks against the Sài Gòn government. Some foreign news reports and articles echoed communist allegations asserting that the Sài Gòn government had seized farming lands of the Montagnards in order to resettle the 900,000 North Vietnamese 1954 refugees. These reports also claimed that thousands of Montagnards rallied in protest. However, they were completely wrong, having been based on one-sided information and ignorance. Most of the 900,000 North Vietnamese refugees melted into the local communities, doing every trade except farming. Only a few land development centers for refugees—fewer than five, as far as I knew—were located in Montagnard areas. The majority of land development resettlers were ethnic Vietnamese from the Central Việt Nam coastal districts.

I knew from my visits to the areas that there were some groups of radical Montagnards, the predecessor of the FULRO front in 1964, who voiced complaints about the land matter, but no mass protests of Montagnards ever took place.[3]

GENERAL NGUYỄN CHẤN Á

Many Vietnamese, even some anticommunists, did not fully trust the U.S. government. They looked at Taiwan as an example. That skepticism could be observed in the attitude of the Nationalist Chinese officers who came as advisors to the South Việt Nam Army.

One of those who expressed his great concern about the Americans was Chinese Nationalist Army general Nguyễn Chấn Á. He was the grandson of the famous Vietnamese hero Nguyễn Thiện Thuật, who led a guerrilla force in the late nineteenth century that fought for a decade against the French colonial rulers before he was defeated and forced to flee to China. His beloved grandson Nguyễn Chấn Á was born in China, fought the Japanese in World War II, and was promoted to brigadier general in the Chinese nationalist army. But his heart was for his fatherland, Việt Nam. President Diệm welcomed him back to South Việt Nam and appointed him advisor to the Joint General Staff.

Once in 1962, he visited my division and talked to the officers. He warned us that if we relied too much on the Americans, we would suffer the same fate as the nationalist Chinese. He told us how Washington forced its opinions and American know-how on the Chinese Nationalist Army during the last years of the Kuomintang on the mainland. In one of his examples, the Americans pressured the Kuomintang government to break up the army political warfare system, reducing it to the role of a public relations service. Such ignorance about the nature of the ideological conflict, along with the rampant corruption of the regime, contributed to the collapse of the Chiang Kai-shek government, he said.

With tears in his eyes, he urged us to do much more and to rely on ourselves first. Moreover, he insisted that corruption (not very serious in 1962), if not quickly controlled, would play the greatest part in the fall of South Việt Nam, should it happen. And he warned us that although mainland China extends more than 3,000 miles from north to south, the Chinese Nationalist Army had lost one piece of land after another in just over three months. The 500-mile length of South Việt Nam wouldn't take that long to be conquered by the communists.

Few in the audience thought that his prediction would come true in the near future.

THE WAR ON ECONOMY AND TRANSPORTATION

The war in the upper highlands came to a new intensity in 1962. Since 1961, troops in my division had had little time to rest during the rainy seasons—from May to October. Most of the objectives of communist attacks during this period were outposts defended by national guard units.

In cities, the year 1962 saw an increasing number of VC bomb attacks on civilian targets. VC sappers threw grenades or bombs at theaters and restaurants of certain owners who failed to pay contributions to communist clandestine gangs. On October 25, the National Day (Declaration of the Constitution, founding the Republic of Việt Nam), VC sappers conducted a bomb attack at the exhibition at a small park in front of the Sài Gòn City Hall, killing nine and wounding twelve, all civilians. The attack took place as I was walking nearby

Meanwhile, the VC directed more effort not only against the military units and installations but also in actions designed to sabotage the economic infra-structure, particularly land and water communications. According to national intelligence reports I read every week, the VC attempted to hinder supply of basic farm products from the rich Mekong Delta provinces to Sài Gòn and other major cities. Rice and coal were among the necessities that VC insurgents tar-geted. They demolished coal kilns that produced the main source of cheap fuel for urban areas and murdered kiln owners. After 1964, mangrove coal stopped coming to Sài Gòn and its market cities in the Mekong Delta. The VC also tried to block the main waterways connecting Sài Gòn with the delta districts. But until 1975, the VC couldn't stop the large barges from reaching Sài Gòn and other major cities except by harassing them with sporadic gunshots.

National highways and provincial routes crossing remote and unpopulated areas became less safe for military vehicles after 1961. Sniper fire increased in late 1961 and came to its peak in 1964. The railroad system that the coastal provinces in Central Việt Nam had to rely on for supply of food and fuel was sometimes mined or destroyed in remote areas. Once in May 1962, I took a night train from Tuy Hòa to Sài Gòn. At 9 PM, the train was stopped by a guerrilla platoon. I was on a sleeping car at the rear. After the incident on the cross-country bus that could have brought me serious trouble in 1961, the Kontum Police Department approved my new ID card, which listed my profession as "teacher."

The guerrillas searched two of the four passenger cars and were about to jump on the sleeping cars when the nearby national guard unit arrived. The guerrillas quickly disappeared into the dark forest. In about five minutes of searching, the guerrillas captured just one soldier. He changed his khaki uniform for civilian shirts and slacks when he heard the guerrillas stop the train. He was captured and brought away only because he had forgotten to discard his fatigue cap with a military unit insignia on it.

Besides attacking military lines of communications, after 1961 communist guerrillas were increasingly harassing civilian transportation on almost every highway in remote areas. The guerrillas often stopped civilian buses and ordered the passengers to get off. After searching for soldiers, they would gather people on the roadside and delivered propaganda speeches, mostly about the "political outlines" of their National Liberation Front. Gunships dared not attack them for fear of killing civilians.

But once a group of communist troops showed their sense of humor.

In the war of words, the two sides used to label each other as practicing "exploitation of people's labor achievement (or property) for personal or class profits." The word in Vietnamese is *bóc lột,* the literal meaning of which is "to peel and to strip off," from which derives the figurative meaning "exploitation" or "squeezing." My fellow officers in the Twenty-third Infantry Division area told me a story that took place somewhere on National Highway 21 between Ninh Hòa and Ban Mê Thuột. One hot summer night, a group of communist troops stopped a cross-country bus of about twenty passengers. As they had often done, the guerrillas gathered the passengers on the roadside to attend a short political indoctrination session. However, after the lesson, the guerrillas' leader said that the Sài Gòn government used to blame them for *bóc lột.* He asserted they had never *bóc lột* anyone.

"So today," he said, "we will really *bóc lột* you as the Sài Gòn puppet regime is saying." The guerrillas then ordered everyone, very young babies to the oldest passenger, male and female, to take off everything except their underwear. Though strongly protesting, at last the passengers had to do what they were told at gunpoint. The guerrillas collected the clothes and melted away. It is not difficult to imagine what took place at the first checkpoint on the outskirts of the town when the bus arrived.

The story was widely circulated in the areas along Highway 21. It was a thin streak of humor in the war that became bloodier.

MILITARY IN SOCIAL LIFE

By 1961, most common people in South Việt Nam had very little contact with the military. The limited draft law inducted into the army a small number of men who had graduated no higher than tenth grade. That was not enough to make military matters a part of people's lives. The newspapers often avoided referring to the military, its policies, or its members. Reports of military activities were based strictly on information released by the JGS. From 1954 to 1960, the characters in fiction were rarely soldiers. In music, military life and warriors were principal themes in many songs, but these themes were not pervasive except in music composed by writers working for the Information Ministry and the military psywar agencies.

When the war became a major threat to the regime, and with more aid being accepted from the United States, a new mobilization law was passed. Under the 1957 law, many young men who graduated high school were not drafted and trained to serve in the military. According to the new conscription act in 1961, all men under twenty-eight holding a high school diploma and higher were conscripted, trained, and commissioned as army reserve officers. The Thủ Đức Reserve Officer School graduated about 7,000 officers before it closed in April 1975.

That a great number of young intellects underwent tough training and became officers contributed greatly to South Vietnamese society. Most people began to get used to military terms and its way of life. At the same time, the intellectual flowers of the nation brought a new atmosphere into the armed forces.

Newspaper articles covered more and more military subjects, so they were no longer peculiar to most civilian readers. More songs and novels were written with themes praising the soldiers in fighting and suffering, their loves, and the hardships of their families. Typical characters and heroes in fictions were brave soldiers. The new sympathy toward fighting men was spontaneous, not something dictated from above and in keeping with a strict party line as in North Việt Nam.

Girls in peacetime usually didn't like to marry soldiers. The mobilization produced changes in the sentimental life of a large segment of the young female population in every concern. Girls took for granted that seven out of ten young men who could become their husbands would be in the armed forces, not for a few years but probably for a very long time.

The military draft also turned millions of Vietnamese people who had been fence-sitters into anticommunists because of what they learned about the war and the communists through their relatives in the army.

THE COMBAT HAMLETS

When the war built up into an alarming stage in 1959, the South Vietnamese government experimented with various measures of counterinsurgency. A dozen experiences and theories were tested. One of these was the "Khu Trù Mật" or wealthy area, or agro-ville, also known to many of us as the "Staley-Vũ Quốc Thúc Plan." The basic theory was that several agro-villes established in remote areas would bring better life to the poor farmers, thus attracting them to come live in those sites under the government's control. The plan, which was carried out in the southern Mekong Delta, was soon aborted. We in the highlands learned nothing from it; the situation in our region developed in a different way.

Beginning in 1962, our Twenty-second Division HQS established the first experimental combat hamlets in northern Kontum province following positive achievements in the coastal province of Quảng Ngãi and in northern coastal areas. The program proved effective. The combat hamlets, and what the British had done earlier in Malaysia, inspired many South Vietnamese anticommunist strategists. The idea also came out of experiences in the pre-1954 self-defense villages, where anticommunist militias were fighting the guerrillas.

In the latter half of 1962, the unofficial Combat Hamlet program was replaced by the Strategic Hamlet program, which aimed at long-range economic, social, and political goals. By that time, the military situation deteriorated quickly, especially in the Mekong Delta and remote villages close to communist guerrilla secret base areas north of Sài Gòn. It was the importance of the struggle at the level of infrastructure that drew my attention to tribal people and their land.

After three years serving the Twenty-second Infantry Division, I accepted Kontum as my homeland. It had a beautiful climate. In summer it rained and was cool. In winter it was dry with mild cold winds, and the blue sky turned purple at sunset. Sometimes I thought it was John Steinbeck's great mountains in Monterey, California. I read his *Red Pony,* and it made me feel the same about this small peaceful town. Besides, the ethnic Vietnamese people in the province were honest and friendly. They came from many lowland areas, mostly from the central coastal districts since the late nineteenth century. The life and people were peaceful.

The tribal population mostly came from a half dozen ethnic groups with different dialects and traditions. Some groups, such as the Sedang in the northern areas, had brave warriors who were frightening to the Vietnamese settlers in the nineteenth century. At the beginning of the twentieth century, when some French soldiers beat and killed one of the Sedang, thousands of their warriors attacked the French squad with spears and machetes. Many tribesmen were killed before the French squad ran out of ammunition. Then the tribesmen overran the post and butchered all the French soldiers.

Under the French colonialist regime, the way of life of most of those tribes was kept intact. The French treated them with smooth hands and won their hearts easily. Tribal leaders seemed to prefer the French to the ethnic Vietnamese.

After 1954, many loyal covert communist cadres were planted in every ethnic group. They learned tribal dialects and trained to live among the tribesmen as the good guys. Some communist cadres even rasped off some front teeth and did anything that helped them look like the Montagnards. In this aspect of the ideological conflict, the communist side prevailed.

However, 1962 suddenly saw a great change. Most of the Sedang and some other tribes broke off relations with the communists and moved to the areas under the protection of the RVN government. Thousands of them quit the remote areas close to the common border with Laos, where the communist cadres controlled them and used them as laborers for the production and storage of rice along the infiltration route coming from North to South Việt Nam.

The reason causing this change of mind was easy to understand. They found the communist cadres cheating them for the sake of the party and often treating them unkindly. Their motives were as simple as their way of living. They didn't put up with communists "because they are liars," many of them told me. To the primitive people anywhere in the world, you cheat them once and they will show you the door for good.

The large number of tribal refugees emptied the rice stock of the province. Sài Gòn had to help by dropping rice supplies from C-47 military cargo planes. In the following months, young men from those tribes were trained and armed to defend themselves. That was when the U.S. and Vietnamese Special Forces arrived.

The idea of arming peasants to fight the enemy proved to be working well. My division helped the province of Kontum organize the tribal militias in key hamlets with weapons provided by the "Johnson Plan," which originated from a confidential agreement between Sài Gòn and Washington. The weapons were World War I Springfield .30 rifles, shotguns, Tommy guns, .38 revolvers, and flare pistols. The Sedang groups have been ardent anticommunists ever since. The Combat Hamlets program in Kontum province worked well. One of my responsibilities was to follow up on the implementation of the plan.

When the Special Forces joined the war, building camps along border areas, it was those ethnic groups that provided the young men to serve the first Civilian Irregular Defense Group (CIDG) units of the camps.

VILLAGE DEMOCRACY

From the early stage of the pro-American regime in South Việt Nam, many young patriots like me inside and outside of the military were eagerly advocating a true democracy at the local level of hamlet and village. They argued that only a true democracy could be the best weapon to fight communists' terrorism and propaganda and to lead the country to prosperity. Having lived close by the poor in various parts of Việt Nam, we all perceived the plight of the villagers who were living between hammer and anvil.

One who strongly supported the idea was Captain Nguyễn Bé, then chief of military command of Bình Định province, who was known years later as chief of the Rural Development Cadres Training Center in Vũng Tàu. Bé had been a farm boy, fighting French aggressors on the Resistance side before becoming an anticommunist nationalist army officer. His fervent wish to fight the enemy and do something for the poor peasants attracted me to him. Many other officers and I met with Bé whenever we could to discuss the situation. We all agreed to the urgent solution of introducing true democracy to villages and hamlets. We supported his opinion, contending that what the poor peasants needed most was safety, and only true democracy could ensure their rights and fuse their will to stand up and fight communist insurgents.

After ascending to power, President Diệm did not allow popular elections for village chiefs as I had hoped he would. Province chiefs approved village chiefs from lists of recommendations prepared by the district chiefs. The village chiefs thus became agents of the government, not of the people, and acted more like cops than representatives of their villagers. A number of the village chiefs were very authoritarian. They treated the population roughly, mainly to please the bosses at the district and provincial level. For thousands of years, the Vietnamese have called such officials "wicked lords," but only a very small number of those were bad enough to generate spiteful rumors far and wide. In such a political environment, sophisticated communist propaganda could turn every small drop of dissatisfaction into a pool of resentment.

In the countryside, communist secret cells ran their business with a policy similar to the "carrot and stick" in the most effective way. On one hand, they cajoled peasants into supporting them, and on the other, they were ready to apply harsh punishment to those who violated their rules. A man accused of being a "dangerous antirevolutionary" would receive a sure and quick death sentence.

I used to visit the hamlets I could reach whenever I had a chance to travel in the rural coastal areas of Bình Định and Phú Yên provinces. Once I asked an octogenarian farmer which side he liked. At such an age, he felt free to say what he wanted without any apprehension. His answer was "Neither."

In late 1962, the situation in the coastal provinces became more and more alarming. Communist insurgents escalated their activities. By the end of the year, hundreds of young men in the government-controlled areas fled to the woods to join the VC.

Many government officials objected to the proposal for free elections at hamlet and village levels, saying that such elections would bring communists into local governments and allow them to covertly and legally undermine the regime. My friends and I agreed with Captain Bé that free elections, with preventive measures in appropriate regulations, could always limit the ability of communist moles to do harm. Along with fair application of law and order, we could at least do something better to promote people's morale and determination. We argued that even if VC sympathizers covertly influenced 10 percent of the hamlets and villages, we would certainly save the remaining 90 percent. We admitted the fact that, in implementing the plan, we would probably have to confront various troubles arising from true democracy in the countryside. But that would be the price for a worthwhile freedom.

Earlier in 1961, Captain Bé put all of those ideas on paper and sent them to Sài Gòn, probably to many high-ranking personages. A few months later, he told me that Ngô Đình Nhu, President Diệm's brother, had accepted the idea. However, the president was opposed to it. We knew the president was under the strong influence of many conservatives around him. Some of them preferred treating the people as if they had been the medieval subjects of a king, and they considered our enemy as nothing more than a large gang of bandits that could be taken care of by sheer military power.

A CHALLENGING JOB

In November 1962, I was appointed to be in charge of the division staff section for the Strategic Hamlet program. This had been officially put into effect that summer. The program had the approval of the president; Ngô Đình Nhu was in charge of the Interministerial Committee for Strategic Hamlets. The new program was an outgrowth of the smaller scale Combat Hamlet projects that had been implemented in some provincial areas. The Strategic Hamlet program assumed full power in October 1962.

The policy was a major effort that had full support not only from the United States but also from Australia, Taiwan, South Korea, and West Germany. Sir Robert Thompson, an anti-insurgency expert in the British Advisory Group, was known to have proposed the idea to President Diệm and his brother Nhu. Thompson became one of the key strategists of the program. The idea behind the new policy was to turn every hamlet into a basic local unit where different national programs would be developed. Economic development was the key goal, and there were also cultural, educational, and social objectives. Military actions against the communist insurgence and a self-defense role for the hamlet, though given top priority at the time, would only be of secondary importance in the long run. Nhu didn't hide his ambition to reestablish the traditional commune (or village) autonomy in the millennium-old society of Việt Nam.

In November 1962, my division commander, Col. Nguyễn Bảo Trị, told me his idea to put me in charge of a newly established component of the division staff, the Office of Strategic Hamlets. I knew it would be a hard job, which would include activities directly related to administration and military as well as nonmilitary matters and which would extend even to social, cultural, educational, and economic agencies to a certain extent. A mistake in this job would invite trouble, as the work was directly under the eyes of the formidable Ngô Đình Nhu.

After thinking it over for a few seconds, I accepted the offer. One of the reasons I said yes was that I had been interested in the issue of pacifying the countryside for a long time. Besides, I felt pride that I had been given a job that some captains had refused and that the division commander had entrusted me with this hard task, though at that time I was not in his favor.

THE ẤP BẮC BATTLE

The first week of January 1963 saw a battle that created much controversy on the role of the American strategy and technology in the war. The central subject was the employment of helicopters.

In 1962, U.S. helicopters helped the ARVN in some encouraging victories. In many areas, Eagle Flight tactic had proven to have a certain efficacy. Combat troops were quickly transported by helicopter (air mobile cavalry) on operations to search, attack, and pursue the enemy—like an eagle hunting. In general, the high mobility of helicopter operations for attack or reinforcement in almost all terrain provided great help to the combat units.

One such large-scale operation, the battle at Ấp Bắc, 100 miles south of Sài Gòn, appeared to be a defeat for the ARVN Seventh Infantry Division. News reports by foreign media that reached Việt Nam depicted the battle as a great failure of the ARVN combat units and of the use of helicopters. According to these reports, some 20 VC were killed while ARVN units suffered 80 casualties; five H-21 helicopters were destroyed. But the JGS reports I read every week, confirmed by many commanders fighting the battle of Ấp Bắc whom I met later, asserted that in fact it was not a serious defeat on our side, if the actual number of enemy killed was taken into account. Total enemy losses could only be known accurately several weeks after the whole battle area had been searched. About 150 of the VC battalion of 500 men were killed. Six years later, many VC defectors (Chiêu Hồi) who had fought in the Ấp Bắc battle on the VC side recounted to me the same figures. Actually, the ARVN side suffered 80 KIAs and about 100 WIAs, plus the loss of five helicopters in exchange for 150 VC KIAs and a similar number of WIAs. People might have said the battle was a draw but not a total failure.

I assumed that the loss of five helicopters was the key factor that drew public criticism of the U.S. military involvement. The fumbled maneuver and the losses of the ARVN units seemed to be exaggerated only to support antiwar arguments against the U.S. government, the principal target. Apparently, noises made in the mass media were much louder than gun reports at the battlefields.

Communist leaders in Hà Nội and their subordinates in the South launched a large-scale propaganda campaign against "Mỹ-Diệm," a derogatory term used by Hà Nội to denote "President Diệm and the Americans." North Việt Nam communist authorities held many gatherings on the "Ấp Bắc Victory," calling on workers and farmers to work extra hours daily and on Sundays to lend support to the victorious VC rebels. A VC unit in the South was named after Ấp Bắc. To be frank, the Ấp Bắc event greatly hurt ARVN morale.

The loss of five H-21 helicopters was a failure of the strategy of relying too much on firepower, new war technology, and American know-how. It also represented a kind of "War of the Rich," requiring the expenditure of millions of dollars each month, sometimes for unworthy objectives.

As I still remember, a few months after the Ấp Bắc battle, the ARVN suffered a serious loss in a jungle operation in Phước Thành province. An airborne battalion, the elite of the South Vietnamese Army, suffered about 60 KIAs and 150 WIAs in a skillful and bold VC ambush. Communist force loss was estimated as "light" (a dozen) and the ARVN Airborne battalion was inoperable for months.

The defeat in Phước Thành would have dealt a more humiliating psychological blow to the RVN army if it had been reported in the press because it was the first time a battalion of the "invincible paratroops" had been routed and so many soldiers killed. But there was no news report in Western media because no reporter was present. If the news had reached Hà Nội, communist leaders in North Việt Nam would have made a propaganda campaign with something like "Phước Thành Glory," no less noisy than the one for Ấp Bắc.

It was apparent that the Western media helped transmit communist propaganda. An electronics engineer once said to me that on the propaganda front, the voice of the Vietnamese communists was really not very strong. They had only weak microphones and a prerecorded tape. But it was the American sophisticated amplifiers and loudspeakers and all modern means of communications as well as media technology that helped the communist voice reach the American public loud and clear.

Washington and Sài Gòn began to rely on more expensive methods of warfare. Helicopters, though most of them were the old H-21 "bananas," were effectively used to help in resupply and for medical evacuation, which directly helped troop morale. But after Ấp Bắc, more helicopters were shot down. The cost of war became higher and higher, and more Americans servicemen were killed and wounded.

Many American helicopter crews faced high risks while making bold attempts to evacuate the wounded ARVN soldiers and even Vietnamese civilians under heavy enemy machine-gun fire. This bravery has been one thing about the Americans that many Vietnamese veterans and civilians greatly admired and appreciated through the years.

I GET MARRIED

On January 23, 1963, I married the girl I had met in 1962. She was an average woman in every aspect. In my years of service, she provided me lots of help relating to the military life and especially in taking care of my troops' dependents. When she was twelve years old, a bomb from a French bomber buried her under twenty inches of dirt and sand. Two bomb fragments scratched her forehead and her back, just an inch from killing her. Her uncle accidentally found her and saved her when he was searching for his son. So she understood war.

Of course, marriage is an important event in any man's life. As for me, it was more important because my mother and my aunt had been very anxious to see me get married. They always wished that they would soon have grandchildren, especially to be sure that my father would have a lot of male offspring before anything should happen to me. In war, anything was possible. The marriage and the new member of the family brought extreme happiness to my mother, my aunt, and my sister.

The night after the wedding party, I asked my wife, "Would you take good care of my mother and my aunt should I be killed or disabled or taken prisoner?" She quickly put her hand over my lips to stop my words and said, "Of course I will." I felt sorrow to realize that war invades every corner of life, even in a nuptial bed and in the very center of loving hearts.

THE STRATEGIC HAMLET

After being appointed to a new job I was very busy, while my newly married life already took up much of my spare time. I had to devote myself to new tasks implementing the Strategic Hamlet program. The enemy concentrated on overrunning as many strategic hamlets as possible. Militarily, the Strategic Hamlet program really created much trouble for the communist insurgents.

The government gave the new policy the highest national priority. Nhu himself took the top post of the Interministerial Committee in Charge of Strategic Hamlets. The infantry division was given the second principal role in the Strategic Hamlet program. The division commander was chairman of the Division Tactical Area Committee in Charge of Strategic Hamlets, composed of province chiefs. So the DTA HQS was working directly with this committee. The Corps Tactical Zone and the JGS were given the responsibilities of inspection and support, but were not in the main chain of command. Province chiefs were chairmen of the Provincial Committee for Strategic Hamlet Construction, with district chiefs as members. Similarly, a district chief was the chairman of his District Committee for Strategic Hamlet Construction, at the lowest level.

The system proved to be the greatest coordinated military and administrative effort of the Diệm regime.

Although I was privately opposed to the regime, I had to admit that the Strategic Hamlet plan would be one of the most effective weapons to fight communist insurgency. I was really convinced that if it were done the same way as in Malaysia, we would probably win the war. The little experience in my home district area years earlier supported my opinion.

Politically, I didn't like Ngô Đình Nhu. There have been many rumors about his brutal and tricky schemes to eliminate his antagonists, as well as his deadly crackdowns on dissidents. I was unable to ascertain the truth of such rumors, which usually contained only a streak of truth, but I hated the way he suppressed the opposition. However, I believed he knew how to run a big shop. Many of his opponents saw him as a brilliant theorist. His weaknesses included his unattractive appearance, and he was not a charismatic leader or an eloquent speaker.

Ngô Đình Nhu asked people in charge of the plan from province level and higher to carefully study the weekly Interministerial Committee meeting records and to do what they had to. Separate directives often were not issued in order to save time and paperwork. Therefore, I had to carefully read every word of the records, suggest to the division commander what needed to be done, and draft plans for his approval. It took me much time and energy.

In the Strategic Hamlet program, the Division HQS was a planning agency. The provincial and district committees were responsible for the execution of plans and directives from the higher authority. At least I agreed with Nhu on this point: in the South Vietnamese system, as an intermediate command, Division HQS was not too high to overlook important realities of the lower levels, but it was high enough to grasp the general situation nationwide. Therefore, a corps commander had no active role, which might have complicated the chain of command of the program, but he carried a symbolic title as the central committee's inspector.

The plan went into full swing in late 1962 and early 1963. Almost every government and military effort was devoted to strategic hamlets. Naturally, as in any dictatorship, when the big boss wants something, everyone will try to please him. In a few months, many districts and provinces around the country reported that 90 to 100 percent of their hamlets were "completed." To be considered completed, a hamlet had to fulfill six criteria, every one of which required months to be implemented. The easiest one was to build "a strong protecting fence," and the most difficult was to organize hamlet people into active groups (men, women, elders, youth, and children).

Many of the hamlets were surrounded with hastily built bamboo fences, so weak and shallow that an average Vietnamese woman could pull up the stakes with her bare hands. To some observers, the strategic hamlets were a joke. In other areas, the hamlet construction progressed smoothly. The most difficult task—organizing the population into social associations—could hardly be successful. Unlike a communist dictatorship, a nationalist regime was unable to exert control over the people by compelling them to serve under a strictly organized system.

One of the government's satellite movements was the Thanh Niên Cộng Hòa or Republican Youth, which mobilized a large number of young men and women into political activity. Most of them were female students and civil servants. Madam Nhu assumed the role of a Thanh Niên Cộng Hòa leader and was active in her position. The organization achieved only limited practical success.

Ngô Đình Nhu's ambitions included the "rural democracy" and the preservation of village traditions. Along with the whole Strategic Hamlet program, President Diệm approved Nhu's plan for the election of hamlet chiefs. But Diệm was still hesitant about villagers electing their village chief. Only in mid-1963 did he approve the village election plan, but it was rather late. The security situation was no more favorable for such policy at that time, when the Buddhist crisis was raging.

Nhu's plan to revive the traditional village charter failed to win public support. The old-time village charter, the "constitution" of every Vietnamese village in written or verbal form, was the supreme law of the commune that helped the ancient Vietnamese maintain their identity, characters, and language through thousands of years under Chinese domination. However, in modern Việt Nam, social conditions did not favor the plan, especially in areas that Vietnamese had settled only in the seventeenth century. Even in villages founded over several thousand years ago, the charter could serve only a spiritual role, not one of a legally binding institution.

ON-THE-JOB TRAINING

The Strategic Hamlet Office was new in the division staff. So there was no established standard of operation procedures. I had to travel a lot. Once a week, I had to visit district headquarters and a number of hamlets along with the district chiefs as we felt it necessary. I would report to the division commander, who paid attention to the plan and everything I had done. He expected me to know as much as possible about all 605 hamlets in the three provinces of Kontum, Pleiku, and Phú Bổn.

After a few months, I learned the maps of the area by heart. Helicopter pilots felt safe with me aboard because I could tell them the way to any of the hamlets and outposts by following the roads and other land features even in dense fog. I installed a large set of aerial photos with accurate details concerning the location of almost every hamlet with map coordinates; information on population, manpower, and general living conditions of the people; and sites of flat ground that could be used as emergency helipads. With the detailed maps of the hamlets, we could conduct air and artillery support more effectively with precision and also avoid friendly fire by mistake.

Until that time, there had not been much cooperation between the local administration and the military. In the strategic hamlet system, however, such cooperation was a must as every branch had to devote its efforts to the same objective, though sometimes they were still lacking in coordination. I also got much assistance from the American side. During the long war, that period saw the best relations between American and Vietnamese servicemen as individuals.

My advisor, Major O'Rahilly, went with me on most of my trips to the hamlets. The division senior advisor, Colonel Woolfolk, appreciated my work. He never said no when I asked to use his UH-1B, the only helicopter assigned to the division. I paid him full respect, only getting confused sometimes by his Texan accent, especially when he got mad. The pilot, Warrant Officer 4 Weaver, whose nickname was "the Montagnard," was the best pilot on a chopper; he had been a helicopter instructor for years, flying more than 13,000 hours. He flew many test flights at night with me aboard, dropping flares over hamlets under attack, guiding gunships to targets, and conducting experimental landings in darkness at LZs marked only with six or seven small bowls of burning gasoline arranged in the shape of an arrow. Sometimes VC snipers shot at us.

One afternoon, I was in Weaver's UH-1B returning to Kontum from Pleiku. As we were approaching Kontum City, we received an emergency call on the district security network. The chief of Strategic Hamlet Plei Towan, nine miles south of Kontum, used his HT-1 Strategic Hamlet walkie-talkie to call for help.

A VC sniper had seriously wounded one of the hamlet Combat Youth. His leg artery was severed. The crew was urged to provide help. It was the chief pilot who would make the final decision. After Weaver received approval from the MACV Team HQS, he landed the chopper at Plei Towan. The site was a safe location. The gunners were eager to help with limited first aid to staunch the bleeding. Then Weaver flew back to Pleiku and landed the chopper at the ARVN Military Hospital to have the brave Combat Youth member rushed into the emergency room. We came back to Kontum at 5 PM.

Many times in the very early morning, the military telephone beside my bed rang. At such early hours, it meant trouble somewhere. I had to get dressed quickly in fatigue uniform with a pistol, an M-2 carbine, and dog tags and jump into my jeep to get to the Division Tactical Operations Center.

In mid-1963, more strategic hamlets were attacked, and three out of ten times a province military HQS needed help from the division. Often I had to join the operation, at least to be at the site for immediate assessment. Sometimes I left home at 4 or 5 AM and wouldn't come back for days, without telling my wife ahead of time.

Once my advisor and I, along with the two pilots and two gunners, all of them Americans, were assigned a mission leading the rescue and pursuit operation after a hamlet ten miles east of Kontum was attacked. After reporting that VC had overrun the hamlet, the hamlet radio operator destroyed the set and escaped. When we reached the area, the infantry company commander on the ground, a second lieutenant, told me on the radio that his company had reached the hamlet without any trouble and made a smoke signal—not by smoke grenade, but by damp straw—for our landing.

We landed right on the roughly prepared helipad next to the hamlet gate. All of us stepped off the chopper. The villagers were still under shelters, and a frightened militiaman appeared from an underground shelter and pointed his finger toward the back gate, saying "Việt Cộng" in a low voice. Meanwhile, our infantry company was not in sight. My heart was beating hard, and I really felt scared. The chopper rotors were slowing down. We wouldn't be able to take off in less than a minute. There was no way to get out quickly.

I asked everybody to be ready for whatever might happen. In such situations, it was better to go on. Fortunately, the VC unit of about ten guerrillas or more fled through the back gate. If they had stayed to fight, we would have been in unpredictable trouble with what we had: three pistols, an M-2 carbine, an M-14, and an M-60 machine gun. When the danger was over, the infantry company came and admitted that they had reached the wrong location. We had landed our chopper beside the small burning hut that had been set on fire by VC guerrillas, not the damp straw used by our troops as a signal. I thanked the company commander and gave him instructions for the operation, while the chopper evacuated some seriously wounded villagers to Kontum.

On another trip inspecting a remote hamlet in Pleiku province, we escaped an imminent attack. Along with Major O'Rahilly, the district chief, and an escort of sixteen soldiers, I went to the hamlet with a feeling of safety, probably because the landscape looked peaceful in the fresh morning air. The district chief did not assure me that the area was "clean."

After we had been working for a few minutes, the district chief happened to ask one of the old men if the Việt Cộng had come recently, to which the old mountaineer nodded yes.

The surprised district chief stopped writing and asked, "How often?" The old man said, "About every two or three days."

We all felt very uneasy, so we all asked him, "When was the last time they came here?" The old man kept calm as if there were nothing to worry about and slowly replied, "This morning." We quickly asked, "How many of them?" The old man looked around, counting, then gave a breathtaking answer: "About three times all of you."

The escort squad leader nervously chipped in: "At what time?" Still in a cool composure, the old man said slowly, "Before you came. They moved to the hill over there when your trucks appeared behind the cornfield." He pointed at the hill about 200 yards from the gate.

I knew the situation was serious, but once coming here, we had to complete our task first. So the district chief, also an army first lieutenant, agreed with me to go on while preparing for a firefight. Twenty minutes later, we decided to leave. The district chief would lead the way on his Land Rover, followed by Major O'Rahilly in his jeep. I would be next in my jeep with the driver and two sergeants, with the truck and escorting troops last.

When we were ready, Major O'Rahilly's jeep failed to start. The starter got stuck to the flywheel, and the jeep could not be push-started or jump-started. All the drivers and some troops lent their hands to roll the jeep to its side, and with a heavy hammer they pounded the starter base hard until it broke loose from the flywheel. Then they pushed the jeep to start.

The convoy returned safe and sound after being shot with a dozen bursts of the VC automatic rifle when we left the hamlet's adjacent cornfield.

I faced many more dangerous situations while visiting the hamlets. The confrontation that scared me a great deal was on an inspection trip I went on with the assistant to the district chief of Dak Sút, Kontum province, along with a national guard platoon. A VC squad opened fire on us while we were crossing a hanging bridge made by tough climbing plants, some fifteen feet above a swift stream with a jagged rock bed. It took us almost a minute—the minute as long as a year—to cross the remaining twenty yards of the bridge. It was a real challenge to direct the troops and control the situation while walking step by step on a swinging hammock, facing two possible fatal injuries: falling on the rocky stream or being hit by enemy fire. Luckily no one was hurt.

A BIG DREAM

The Diệm government planned to complete basic organization in two-thirds of the hamlets in South Việt Nam, such as having capable militias and self-sufficiency in food by the end of 1964. Nhu said he expected by 1965 that the great majority of South Việt Nam territory and population would have been pacified, and the economy—at least rural economy—would be stable and begin to prosper. Nhu eagerly promoted his program and showed confidence in realizing his big dream in both economic and military domains.

Economic development, not military strength, was the principal objective of the Strategic Hamlet program. Hamlets that were located in areas not safe enough to have a long-term economic plan but were armed for self-defense only were named "Ấp Chiến Đấu" (combat hamlets), not strategic hamlets.

Economic annual plans for village, province, and national levels were supposed to be coordinated in the general Strategic Hamlet plan, first in low-level projects, then followed by large industrial establishments. I had to participate a little in this process as the representative of the division area headquarters in Strategic Hamlet activities.

The result was limited partly because economic plans were impractical in some places, and local authorities did not fully comprehend the important issue and its long-run objectives to have the plans well implemented. Besides, all depended on military situations and were facing troubles caused by enemy attacks. But in general the plan did help build a primary foundation of local economy.

Besides my MACV Team 22 counterpart, I also worked closely with the American civilians representing the United States Operations Mission (USOM) offices in the three provinces. One good friend of mine was Dwight W. David in Kontum province. The government approved a lot of small-scale socioeconomic, education, and cultural development projects for the three provinces, but by the end of 1963, only a few had succeeded. Such long-range programs needed years to prove successful or not.

Nhu and his supporters dreamed of a new society in which true democracy would be built, beautiful traditions preserved, and education and national culture elevated. They hoped for economic development and the establishment of a social "new value scale"—on top of which would be the freedom fighters. All would be started from and generated by the Strategic Hamlet program.

In the military domain, clear objectives were set. Despite some military inefficiency, Nhu planned to promote the Bảo An Đoàn to gradually take over the territorial responsibility from regular units, including the Corps Tactical Zones and Division Tactical Areas. His directive required the regular infantry divisions to be prepared to conduct operations "anywhere" with complete mobility after being released from territorial responsibility "sometime after 1964." The military reform was the starting point of his long-range strategy. His ambition went much farther than just pacifying South Việt Nam. His many directives indicated that his dream was a strong South Việt Nam "that is leading Southeast Asian countries." In the weekly meetings of his Strategic Hamlet committee, sometimes he vaguely alluded to his first step toward realizing his dream.

So far, only the village Dân Vệ, or People's Defense Militias, were paid on a regular basis out of the provincial budget, whereas the strategic hamlets' Thanh Niên Chiến Đấu or Combat Youths were not paid, except for irregular gifts and aid from local authorities when there were available sources that came mostly from foreign donations and social contributions. So many military officials supported the idea of paying them on a permanent basis. Nhu and his assistants did not buy the idea. They said that whenever the Combat Youths were on government payrolls, they would lose their capability to fight the guerrillas. They would practice what regular soldiers including the Dân Vệ were doing: getting together at night at a vital location and conducting the defense behind the barbed-wire fences in a fortified compound such as the village office house. In the end, they would lose control of the hamlets after dark.

According to Nhu's concept, militiamen should be paid indirectly by donations on an occasional basis such as food, clothing, household utensils, and health care. They must stay home the whole night while working during the day as any other villager. The enemy would have no specific target to concentrate its firepower, but would face the ubiquitous resistance from small groups of militiamen defending their hamlets. I supported his opinion, because it seemed reasonable to me based on my childhood experiences in my home district in North Việt Nam. In armed villages where militiamen dispersed around the place, the attacking force often failed to cause heavy losses to the defenders and many times even suffered high casualties. In villages where the defense was conducted from a fortified building (church, pagoda, or village office), the militia could hardly stand for a year under intensive attacks.

In a weekly meeting of his Interministerial Strategic Hamlet Committee, Ngô Đình Nhu advised local authorities not to be reluctant to arm the hamlet militias. According to him, a fence-sitter peasant would have to take sides when a rifle was put into his hands. He said that the VC couldn't just walk into a hamlet to get the weapons without firing a shot, and their shooting could inflict some casualties. Thus we would get more friends as the VC earned more enemies.

The weapons to be distributed were of WWI vintage, M-1 carbines and shotguns. Each was allocated only two dozen cartridges, just enough for a militiaman to deny free movement to the enemy and to fight a short time to delay the enemy while waiting for the intervention of nearby government forces. The enemy couldn't rely on using such captured weapons with so little ammunition to fight, as some of our military leaders were concerned. Hà Nội would never be so foolish as to ask China and the USSR to build even the smallest plant just to manufacture ammunition for the small number of WWI vintage weapons.

Actually, most armed hamlets could only play the role of the obstacles that denied the VC free movement. Very few hamlets were able to repel VC platoon-sized attacks without timely reinforcement from the local army or regional forces. Unfortunately, a large number of army and local units were unable to fulfill their designated task, as military tactics and organizations were suitable only to conventional armed conflict. Many of the rescue-and-pursuit operations were just failures. Time and strength were wasted because our troops were not quick enough to arrive before the enemy disappeared. In favorable conditions, the enemy would wait to ambush government forces.

Only local commanders who were actively maintaining high troop mobility and sending troops on night patrol and to ambush enemy lines of approach could control the security situation. The enemy had troubles of their own that they could not overcome, such as choosing pathways to move to and from an area at night. They had to choose among the existing ones they knew well, not at their own will. Grasping their rules was a key factor in maintaining the battle initiative. Not many of our small unit commanders could do so because of problems beyond their capability to solve.

PROBLEMS

A strategic hamlet, as well as a combat hamlet, must be in one block surrounded by fences to defend and to control the population. In the Central Việt Nam coastal areas, most hamlets had been built with homes close to each other as in the North. The program met with little difficulty in organizing a hamlet in one block surrounded by a fence. However, in the Mekong Delta provinces, people lived sparsely in isolated houses or groups of a few houses over large areas. So it was necessary to move many of them to one place to be built into a defensible and controllable hamlet.

No one liked the idea of moving, and few peasants were willing to live in a fenced neighborhood where there were only one or two gates to get in and out under guards' control. Communist propaganda and political opponents called them "concentration camps." The peasants also had to contribute human labor and even money to the construction of their hamlets. That prompted stronger protests from the countryside population.

Reading the weekly meeting records of the central committee, I could see that Nhu was well aware of public anger. But his concept was to admit the protests as natural consequences of a "revolution" to build a new prosperous society. He said that if the peasants were well supported to build a much better life, in a few years they would be angry no more. "The peasants," he said in a briefing, "are quick to get angry and also quick to forget if what we are doing now will bring them a better life with higher rice production and with trees in their orchards yielding better fruit in larger quantity." He accepted the risk of people's discontent. Setting up the strategic hamlets system as soon as possible was his immediate goal to deny the VC sources of food and intelligence from the hamlets and to head off communist counteraction. Quality of life and anything else would be settled later.

Under the Diệm regime, especially in the Strategic Hamlet program, there was corruption but on a scale much smaller than in later years. In my area, I heard about some corruption relating to materials, equipment, and gifts given to different programs including Strategic Hamlet. In the Mekong Delta there might be cases of local officials who threatened to draw the projected fence of the hamlets across private property to pressure homeowners to pay bribes. However, bribery was not a matter of importance in the highlands because the tribal people's demand was low and they were mostly poor.

SUCCESSES

In the most convincing estimation, the hamlet system was posing severe difficulties and high risks to VC logistical and intelligence activities. They couldn't feel free any more to collect food supplies and intelligence information from peasant families living sparsely in the flatland area, especially in the Mekong Delta. The general situation weakened their "fear machines" in the countryside. Such small but significant signs of success encouraged Ngô Đình Nhu and his strategists.

A letter from a communist high command (probably the communist Fifth Military Region HQS) to its subordinate units, captured by a battalion of the Twenty-second Division and reported to the Division G-2 and my office, confirmed the situation. It stated that Việt Cong forces were facing more and more difficulties made by the Strategic Hamlet program in conducting insurgent activities. It predicted that in the near future, if the situation was not improved, the communist side would have to change its war policy radically, and the communist command wanted all its units to be prepared for the possible new deployment. Similar communist reports were captured somewhere in the Mekong Delta area. In my division's area, the conditions were different. A half dozen ethnic minority groups made up most of the population. Among the tribes, only the Sedang up north of Kontum were strong anticommunists and well known for their courage. The tribes all lived in close-knit hamlets. So gathering straggling homes was not a concern.

Many Sedang hamlets with only about 100 people and the militias of 10 men each would fight to the death and seldom surrendered. They resisted moving their hamlets to new locations, offering many reasons, or sometimes for no reason at all, even when President Diệm himself asked some hamlets to move to the roadsides for better protection.

They laid bamboo spikes every day until the ground around each hamlet became an immense spike field of 100 yards wide with secret lanes for emergency exit. However, Combat Youth members in hamlets of other tribal groups (Bahnar, Djarai) were not so brave. Some could stand against the enemy of squad to platoon size for a short time whereas others ran away at the first enemy shots.

There were scores of hamlets in Pleiku province that were moved to locations near the main roads. Many people complained that the movement was not necessary. Nhu ordered the Twenty-second DTA to conduct an inspection in a part of Pleiku to evaluate the actual progress of the program and to see if corruption related to the program was committed. I was to carry out the order. I visited 144 hamlets (of the province's 265) in four weeks, looking into scores of matters designated in Nhu's directives. It was a difficult task that required much traveling to many remote areas where ambushes were possible. I found evidence of petty corruption, but there were certain failures in implementing the criteria.

Lệ Thanh district of Pleiku province, where the Ia Drang battle of the American First Airmobile Division took place in 1965, made remarkable achievements, thanks to the brave and incorruptible district chief. An army captain, he organized the effective security system, turning many land development centers into strong strategic hamlets. I believed that the program was on the right track, providing that the United States and other allies supported the program to the fullest extent. Although I still sided with my Việt Quốc comrades against the regime, I devoted all my energy to performing my tasks. I realized that the hamlet program could lead the war to success, and my division commander had the same opinion.

Sometimes I thought that if the United States had spent a generous quantity of money and materials, let's say $100 million at one time in 1963 to boost the strategic program on the economic projects, it would have saved billions in the war in the late 1960s. Unfortunately, the political atmosphere in Sài Gòn was not so hopeful. It was about September 1963 when the Buddhist protests peaked.

SIXTEEN

The Year of the (Crippled) Dragon

THE BUDDHISTS' ANGER

My family and I were all Buddhists. When I was thirteen, I lived more than a year in a Catholic household when I boarded with my teacher. Although I was not converted, I often joined in the prayers of the family in the evenings and before dawn. Sometimes I went to church with the children. Many friends and remote relatives of mine were Catholics. So I felt no great difference between followers of the two religions and me. At my young age, I believed in something supernatural that I was unable to explain, but I found nothing fully satisfied my questions. Probably that was why I was tolerant of any religion. I couldn't stand any kind of discrimination.

The Catholic Church had been granted privileges since the colonial era, and it was apparent that the Diệm regime granted favors to the Catholics and discriminated against the non-Catholic faithful. The opposition harshly criticized Diệm for backing the discrimination. But two of my military academy classmates, who were among President Diệm's confidential aide-de-camps, Đỗ Thọ and Nguyễn Cửu Đắc, and who were devoted Buddhists, did not think so. They assured me that the president did not endorse such discrimination, and I believed them. However, I was sure that Archbishop Ngô Đình Thục, the president's elder brother, was promoting his favorite Catholics and exerting his influence on the president for the sake of his church. He was behind nearly all of the problems that Diệm had to deal with. Diệm probably didn't know what was actually going on at lower levels. Or he may not have reacted appropriately to improper acts by some Catholic priests and his subordinates.

There were, in fact, cases where conversion to Catholicism was a condition to be granted some favors—a job, a new position, and promotion. And a small number of priests in each area were powerful. Their requests for some kind of local government and military material such as lumber, metal sheets or cement, and military trucks, were always approved. The Buddhist monks, meanwhile, never dreamed of receiving such favors.

In Kontum, a new land development center was built on a large flat high ground. The local government allowed a Catholic church to be built on the best, dominating plot, whereas the Buddhist pagoda was constructed on lower ground beside a small brook. Such favors created unpleasant feelings in the non-Catholic people.

Some priests claimed close relations or connections with Archbishop Ngô Đình Thục or with high-ranking government officials in order to pressure local administrative and military authorities, who in turn exerted their political power to curry favor with priests.

In 1959, Madam Nhu, as a congressional representative, used her family power to force through Congress the Family Law. Its most important clause imposed a strict ban on divorce, except for a few rare cases (impotence and false identity), and on concubinage. Feminists welcomed the new law, but rumors circulated that her only purpose was to prevent her sister's husband from getting a divorce. She also had Congress pass the Morality Law, which banned gambling, dancing, beauty contests, martial arts competition (Kung-fu, wrestling, boxing), and cock fighting. The law reinforced the people's feeling that the government was building a Catholic state. Meanwhile, the fact that there were only Catholic chaplains in military units drew complaints by people of other faiths.

The Sài Gòn government did not recognize any of the Buddhist factions as the official church representing the majority of Vietnamese Buddhists, but only as groups of Buddhists under the status of nonprofit associations. The strength of the Buddhist communities was not in an organization but in their population and their faith. I guessed that the Sài Gòn government underestimated the Buddhists' spiritual power when they acted in unity. If the government leaders had paid due attention to the mass psychology of a large section of the population, they would have acted with an appropriate religious policy to calm down the ill feelings of the Buddhists.

When the incident in Huế burst out on Buddha's Birthday, May 8, 1963, I understood the anger of the Buddhists. I was for the Buddhists and hoped that their struggle would bring more equality among religions. But I became more frightened to see the course of events going in an unpredictable direction.

There have been over a dozen versions concerning what really happened on that fateful day. Many of the accounts were not impartial. The single question relating to the death of the protesters at the Huế radio station received different answers. Some said tanks opened fire on the crowd; others alleged that the eight victims were shot to death by rifles. But many soldiers asserted that only concussion grenades were used. I was confused by the conflicting reports.

However, the "grenade" version seemed to be the most reasonable. Major Đặng Sỹ, who ordered the use of the concussion grenades, claimed at the court trial, several months after the regime was overthrown, that without fragmentation the grenade would not kill. Possibly he didn't know that the grenade explosion created an extremely large expansion of gas. Only a human at a distance of a few feet in a flat open field would be unharmed. But when blocked by obstacles such as the walls or a bunker or a crowd of people, its deadly pressure could destroy the obstacle and crush the victims.

In June 1963, the Buddhist crisis escalated quickly from week to week. Everybody listened to the VOA and BBC for hot news from Sài Gòn and Huế. In July, the situation seemed poised to lead to an unavoidable tragic end of the regime. Personally, I wished a military junta would be in power soon to save South Việt Nam from fratricide and from weaknesses that would wind up in the total collapse of the RVN at communists' gunpoint.

In August, I took a seven-day leave to bring my pregnant wife to Sài Gòn to visit our families. This was the first leave I had taken in eight months. After just forty-eight hours in Sài Gòn, the warrant officer who ran the division's liaison office in the capital city appeared at my door with an air ticket. In a low voice, he said, "It's McNamara visiting, sir! The Colonel [division commander] needs you. You have to be back tomorrow." So the next morning, my wife and I took the first Air Việt Nam flight back to Kontum. The CO said a few words about being sorry to call me back before giving me directives to prepare his briefing for McNamara.

The U.S. secretary of defense arrived in Kontum on an UH-1B with a half dozen escorting gunships. At the Division Tactical Operation Center following the CO's briefing, McNamara asked many questions, most of them directed to the American advisors. Some of those Americans looked like naughty Vietnamese students in front of an austere principal when I was a fifth-grader. I could see sweat on their foreheads and the back of their shirts. In one exchange that embarrassed the G-2 and his American counterpart greatly, McNamara asked them how many of our secret agents were working in the enemy's ranks? The answers were something that meant "none." In the war, such was one of our great deficiencies at tactical medium level. As far as I could tell, our side only planted spies at VC strategic high level and more in intelligence networks at a very low level.

McNamara's visit gave everyone in the division headquarters a good feeling. Although the political situation seemed to be deteriorating, we felt that the Americans would be fully supporting South Việt Nam. Watching McNamara during the discussion at the Twenty-second Infantry Division, I liked his intelligence and his way of handling military problems. I respected him until more than thirty years later.

However, relations between Sài Gòn and Washington were not as smooth as we thought. I felt something ominous. At about the same time, a task force of

ARVN Special Forces and the police launched a large raid against all Buddhist pagodas to crack down on Buddhist activists. The attack brought Diệm's regime a very bad reputation and drove more people to the opposition.

Despite the tension felt at every pagoda, my wife and I kept going to the pagoda as usual. The CO was a Catholic, but he was fair in religious matters. When the city pagoda called for contributions to cast a bell, a holy task all Buddhists were eager to perform, he approved a donation of disposed military copper for the pagoda. In fact, protests and demonstrations were taking place mostly in Sài Gòn, Huế, and other major cities. Smaller cities were comparatively quiet. Meanwhile, some armed hamlets in the Twenty-second Division area were being attacked every week. Many were overrun with casualties and loss of weapons.

One hamlet, Dak Bom in Dak Sút district, suffered one dead and a transceiver HT-1 radio destroyed by its operator during a guerrilla attack. The province chief visited the hamlet only two hours after the event, giving some gifts to the dead militiaman's family. I was in his suite. The hamlet chief and the ten-man militia admitted their responsibility for negligence in defending the hamlet. They vowed revenge and told us, "It won't be like this next time they come. You'll see."

Only two weeks later, the province chief, a nice ARVN major, called me up and asked me to join him in Dak Bom again. The hamlet chief sent a message over the district radio network to invite the province chief and his suite to come and see the militias' victory. That morning a woman had noticed a dozen VC armed with submachine guns half a mile from the hamlet. In minutes, all ten militiamen moved quickly through dense vegetation to confront the enemy. When they saw the VC guerrillas 100 yards away, they charged in one row. The clash ended in five minutes with one militiaman killed. The VC guerrillas left five bodies; the others fled before district soldiers arrived.

The province chief admired the militia. He asked them why they hadn't mounted an ambush for which they had been trained in the Special Forces camp, as the terrain and circumstances were favorable. The hamlet chief replied in a tone that might have been considered racist if he had been in a Western country. "We know that, sir," he said. "But those tricky tactics fit only with the ethnic Vietnamese. We Sedang people are honest and outright. When seeing the enemy, we just assail them face-to-face, not relying on wily plots." On the way back, the province chief told us: "They are brave, and there is no way to change them. I'm only sorry for Major Gaspard and his team's efforts in training these Sedangs." Gaspard was one of the heroes of the U.S. Special Forces who ran the Dak Sút SF Camp where most militias in Kontum were trained.

The Buddhist crises became more serious than I had expected. It was a great shock to me when the Venerable Thích Quảng Đức burned himself to protest the government. Not long after that, the famous writer Nhất Linh, who was also a popular Việt Quốc leader, took his own life when he and several other dissidents were about to be tried at a court-martial for joining a dozen dissenting intellectuals called the Caravelle Club and the coup on November 11, 1960. I always held Nhất Linh in high esteem, not only for his novels, which I had read again and again since I was a teenager, but also as one of the most respectable Việt Quốc leaders. I met him only once in 1958 and was attracted to his personality and manners. The two deaths really frightened Diệm.

The crisis was like a great fire, uncontrollable and raging quickly. It had a strong negative effect on the morale of the officers and enlisted men. There were rumors that some combat units would possibly turn against the government. When Washington threatened to cut all aid to Sài Gòn, my friends and I all knew that the countdown had begun.

After the failed attempt to overthrow Diệm's government in February 1962, I believed that a coup d'état was no longer necessary because the military situation was so critical that a total change of the national leadership would create deadly chaos in the republic. But when the Buddhist protests escalated all over the country, I knew that it was impossible to maintain Diệm's government. My only hope was that after Diệm, power would fall into the hands of a new, competent, and devoted leadership better than Diệm's clan.

THE LOST CHANCE

At noon on November 1, 1963, what most people had been expecting came true. An official message from Sài Gòn informed us of the military coup attempt.

In October, relations between the Diệm regime and the Americans experienced a critical period. Washington threatened to suspend aid to Sài Gòn. Diệm's supporters appealed to people to support a self-sufficient economy, which most people felt was impossible. In the last weeks of October, the arrival of Ambassador Henry Cabot Lodge meant to us that there would be a great change. So news from Sài Gòn about the coup wasn't a surprise to me or even to my wife, who seldom got interested in politics.

The division was alerted. As the division G-3 was in Sài Gòn for temporary duty, I was appointed acting G-3. The G-3 shop was not a good place to serve in those days when the coup was going on. Messages came in a dozen times more frequently than usual. Every subordinate unit asked the division for directives, but few messages came to the division from its superiors in Sài Gòn.

The first thing I proposed and the division CO approved was to order all units under the command of the DTA headquarters to keep alert against communist attacks and to avoid getting involved in political events unless ordered by the CO himself. An announcement warned the public that every criminal action such as looting, destruction of public and private property, assault, and murder would be dealt with by army combat troops to protect innocent people, public properties, and national interests.

From the division CO to us staff officers, all behaved with great discretion. No one liked the idea of supporting the wrong side while the situation was not clear enough to say which side would probably lose. Unlike the coup on November 11, 1960, I received no news from my Việt Quốc comrades, although I was sure they were involved in the plot. Many in the military silently welcomed the first declaration of the coup leaders over Radio Sài Gòn.

Although President Diệm had not been my favorite, I got angry when his death was reported. However, when the military junta finally won the short fight against the pro- Diệm force and announced the military revolutionary government, we officers felt relieved. At least a dictatorship was gone, and the political conflict that had torn the country apart had ended before it could become worse with matters relating to religion.

Everywhere people, especially the Buddhists, celebrated. People were free to dance after more than four years when dancing was banned by law.

I think if President Diệm had made some concession to the Buddhists before the crisis reached the point of no return, the outcome might have been better, even though Washington was still planning to dethrone Diệm and to deploy more combat troops in South Việt Nam.

MY FIRST SON

On the morning of November 3, while I was busy with a stream of incoming messages, my wife called me to announce that she was in labor. I drove home to bring my wife and my aunt to the maternity clinic. My aunt had come from Sài Gòn to take care of my wife.

At 2:50 PM, Ngọc Lĩnh was born. His birth gave me more happiness than I could have ever imagined, and also added some weight to my great expectation for the success of the new regime. At least the military leaders, I hoped, would do something for the more successful fighting against the enemy and promote the troops' living conditions.

I named my son Ngọc Lĩnh after the South Việt Nam's highest mountain in northern Kontum province. In the weeks that followed, I was living in bliss. However, as my son looked better every day, the new regime seemed to be worse and worse.

LEADERSHIP CRISIS

There were indications that the military leaders were not the right men my people and I were looking for. During a week of my job as acting G-3, most of the official mail coming to the division headquarters was about promotions of those who participated in the coup—hundreds of them, all serving in Sài Gòn. Not a word about the new rulers' ideas on the most important national political issues.

Then there were changes that everyone expected. Almost all province chiefs and division and corps commanders were replaced. Many were even demoted or jailed because they were suspected of being involved in crimes that the former regime was blamed for. My division commander was virtually powerless after the military junta claimed victory as he was waiting to be relieved from his command. Only a few officers, including me, visited him before he left for a new, humble job.

After the coup, some national policies generated by Diệm's regime had to be reviewed, and the new national leaders needed to make quick decisions about which of them would be continued. Unfortunately, they seemed not to make up their minds on any of those matters. Many of the generals in Sài Gòn were apparently busy indulging themselves in their victory: dancing, feasting, and even shacking up with courtesans.

The most important policies that needed to be addressed were the Land Development and Strategic Hamlet programs. The Twenty-second Division and the three provinces sent special reports on the rural situation to Sài Gòn's new leaders with proposals that the two programs be continued with some modifications suitable to the new environment after the Diệm regime collapsed. We argued that all blame—true or false—could be laid on the former regime, but the principal objectives of the two programs should be kept unchanged and their achievements should be preserved. The programs had been supported with too much money and effort and were too successful to be dropped.

For three months, after much urging, we heard nothing except that "the generals were discussing the issues." We tried through the American channels without luck. The United States seemed to be too formal in such interventions, although the top Americans in Việt Nam—the ambassador and the MACV commander—occasionally treated our generals less than gently. Worse than that, one of the generals declared in a press conference—apparently without much thought—that as the country was liberated from dictatorship, a citizen could live anyplace and travel anywhere he or she wanted.

Although VC units stayed mostly inactive waiting for reaction from their high command, the local communist guerrillas quickly grasped the opportunity and responded. They sowed rumors that the tribesmen would rise to take back the land the Vietnamese had extorted. At night VC gunmen herded hundreds of water buffalo through large rubber plantations. Buffaloes nibbled the soft twigs, one of their favorite foods, and thus killed the young plants. There was no way to save the saplings.

In a month, among more than twenty-five land development centers in Pleiku province alone, at least ten were completely abandoned by the population.

Thousands of acres of industrial plants were left unattended and quickly ruined, so billions of piasters of Vietnamese taxpayers' and foreign aid money became heaps of waste. Many people who abandoned their centers had been compelled to move in from their home villages in the coastal Central Việt Nam a few years earlier. In other centers, people who had come voluntarily from the same areas stayed and prospered. Better houses and clothes and healthier people proved the success of the program.

The military junta made other mistakes. The most serious of them was the release of hundreds of captured communist intelligence officers and secret agents operating in the South. Some said the release was an exchange for enormous bribes from the communists; others said the responsible generals mistook them for anti-Diệm nationalist dissidents without careful examinations.

Under Diệm's regime, a spy-hunting group was known for its incredible feats, having apprehended a great number of spies sent by Hà Nội. Dương Văn Hiếu, who led the special operations team for about seven years before 1963, had captured 400 to 500 communist spies, ranking from captain to full colonel, sent from North Việt Nam. Anti-Diệm activists dubbed him "the Devil of Central Việt Nam," but his admirers called him the "detective genius."

The new generals seemed to be at a loss for making decisions about national policies and problems. They quickly allowed political cleansing of the national police, punishing those who were said to have cracked down on Diệm's dissidents despite the fact that they had only carried out their superiors' orders. Therefore, the effective counterintelligence network was paralyzed and the public safety system was broken.

I felt that the American leaders in Washington and Sài Gòn did not fully grasp the importance and the success of the Strategic Hamlet program, so they failed to take necessary actions to pressure the Vietnamese generals to continue it, even with greater effort. If they had done so, it is likely the war would have gone in a more favorable direction.

The assassination of John F. Kennedy came as a great shock to many of us. But to the South Vietnamese general public, the news didn't draw much interest, as chaotic events after the coup were still filling most front pages. Of course, I didn't see him as a Democrat or a Republican, but as a friend to our side.

In Christmas 1963, some Catholic priests refused help from our military units with the annual December 25 processions. Previously, we were "ordered" to provide assistance such as floats, public address systems, and various gadgets. In early December 1963, the division staff anticipated that the Buddhists would certainly celebrate the coming 1964 Anniversary of the Birth of Buddha to the best of their ability. So our staff officers had to urge the priests to accept our help for Christmas parade to prevent misunderstandings.

ATTACK ON THE AMERICAN COMPOUND IN KONTUM

On January 30, 1964, came another coup d'état. General Nguyễn Khánh overthrew General Dương Văn Minh and his men. The coup, supported by many of Diệm's followers and some Catholic activists, seemed to be an attempt to revive the former regime and thus created more chaos. Again, military commanders and province chiefs were replaced.

The new government under General Khánh renewed the Strategic Hamlet program and renamed it the Pacification program. A "strategic hamlet" was now known as a "new life hamlet." However, the program received less attention and little support. General Linh Quang Viên, the new commander of my division, approved my proposal of providing more support to the three provinces than we were required to give. I believe that the Twenty-second Division was among the few of the nine ARVN Division Tactical Areas that provided strong support for the program.

After the coup, the South Vietnamese enjoyed a short spell of freedom, but the Sài Gòn press corps was in disorder. Some sixty newspapers were in circulation, each filled with articles attacking certain individuals, usually with slanderous or dubious stories. With its newly gained freedom, the South Việt Nam press corps began an era of unjustifiable "chaos."

One night in early 1964, two VC sappers approached the barbed-wire fence of the American MACV compound on the north side of Kontum City. One of them sneaked into the front of the complex and threw hand grenades into the hall, setting off a fire that quickly spread. An American sergeant on duty happened to confront the two VC in time. He opened fire with his .45. The first VC escaped. The second, who was carrying explosives, was hit by a round, which detonated the explosives, tearing the man to pieces.

The division troops arrived almost immediately and tried to put out the fire to save the compound. But the senior advisor stopped them because the American officers had left many hand grenades behind in their rooms.

FROM BAD TO WORSE

In 1964, the general situation began to deteriorate rapidly.

Days after the fall of the Diệm regime, communist military activities subsided. Hà Nội leaders may have been caught off guard by the new situation. Captured documents from VC units indicated that local communist leaders were awaiting instructions from Hà Nội. But not long after that, communist forces launched an offensive campaign to neutralize strategic hamlet systems in many of the lowland provinces. Fortunately, the system in my division area was intact, except for a dozen land development centers that the population left for their old villages. The principal VC military effort was directed against objectives in the Mekong Delta. We in the highlands bore the secondary pressure. In general, within a few months, VC guerrillas regained their momentum and expanded the areas under their control.

The political events in Sài Gòn had a negative effect on the morale of the armed forces. The desertion rate increased; some battalions in my divisions operated with 250 men instead of the required 500. Protests followed by crackdowns became routine in Sài Gòn. Whenever martial music played continuously on the radio, our soldiers would ask, "Is it a coup again?" The most dangerous events were some minor clashes between Buddhists and Catholics in Sài Gòn. Had religious conflicts spread wider, it would have brought the country the greatest catastrophe.

After November 1963, the Buddhists enjoyed a freedom they had never had. There were many celebrations and preaching services. At regiment level and above, Buddhist chaplains were assigned to the units for the first time. Meanwhile, some Catholic chaplains, who had been powerful personages in the units, then retreated to the more humble positions. In several places, communist agents created tension between followers of the two religions. In Kontum, they almost succeeded in luring the militiamen supporting each side into a gunfight against each other. The district chief reacted quickly enough to head off the potential clash. The suspected communist agent, the author of the plot, fled half an hour before his role was detected.

The coup in 1963 changed South Việt Nam a great deal more, to an extent that few foreigners could have fully understood. On the positive side, the domestic press corps enjoyed more freedom than at any time since 1954 when the Diệm administration assumed full power from the French. Before the coup, government ministers and armed forces commanders seemed to enjoy tacit immunity from criticism by the mass media. Even the newspapers of the opposition that bitterly attacked the regime would never say anything against important personnel in the military. To be sure, when he first assumed power, General Khánh imposed strict controls on the media, but these efforts mostly failed. As the political situation began to deteriorate, he left the newspapers nearly free. They were allowed to express their ideas, to publish almost every kind of news, and to ridicule anyone including General Khánh himself. Not all of the restraints on the press were ignored. Some newspapers got into trouble because of articles that were banned by the censor or by having an issue confiscated by the police for violations beyond what could be tolerated by the regime. It was an easy time for the press corps, which led to more freedom years later, despite the fact that the country was at war with an enemy that gave propaganda top priority.

When the United States increased aid to South Việt Nam in 1961, the soldiers' spirit of fighting was somewhat boosted, but the 1963 crisis brought it down far below the pre-1963 period. Furthermore, political unrest in Sài Gòn discouraged the military so much that I could see it on the faces of the troops without asking them.

PACIFICATION EFFORT

Only the tribes were not affected. A month after the coup, local authorities still tried to avoid telling the tribes about President Diệm's assassination. His popularity among some ethnic groups was so high that no justification for the coup would be acceptable to them until several months later.

Not long after General Nguyễn Khánh assumed power, the Pacification program was activated. The program was a new version of the defunct Strategic Hamlet. But the new Pacification program did not get as much support from our superiors as the Strategic Hamlet program had been given before November 1963. However, General Linh Quang Viên, who took command of the Twenty-second Infantry Division in early 1964, gave the pacification efforts the highest priority. With General Viên's support, my office, now known as the Pacification Office, received three more lieutenants to become inspectors in the three provinces. So my men and I had lots of work to do.

By order of the Corps Tactical Zone II headquarters, our DTA was to form thirty-six Pacification teams to work in the three provinces. Each team, under a lieutenant or a medium-ranking civil servant, consisted of about thirty people, including a squad of popular force members, army soldiers, and an army sergeant. The others were from various provincial agencies—agricultural, public health, information services—and all were armed with light weapons just like the former Combat Youth teams of the Strategic Hamlet program. The mission of the teams was to stay in each assigned area for a month or so to reestablish the hamlets in the area. These were not much different from the previously named strategic hamlets. The squad leader was the chief instructor in training the hamlet militia.

I was running a four-week training course for the teams. After the course, the teams were sent to the provinces where they were assigned areas of operation under direct control of the district chiefs. My office had to send inspectors to visit the teams periodically. Those teams were the forerunners of what would be known two years later as rural development teams, which were better organized, trained, and supported. The teams were trained to perform various tasks in the hamlets, including establishing intelligence networks, training the peasants in simple modern farming and cattle raising techniques, and giving lessons in basic health care. But the most important task was training the peasants with their own light weapons, which would help them survive enemy attacks. In most of the hamlets, the peasants could not rely on much help from the district headquarters a few miles away.

Instructors from the civilian services handled the other topics, but my greatest concern was the military training. It was a matter of life and death for these men, and I had to do my best to help them. The Division G-3 helped me by forming a group of three instructors. We visited with many people to see if they could assist us.

The one who taught me the most useful lesson since my time as a cadet was a man of fifty years old. He had been a sergeant in the French colonial infantry and later served the Việt Minh forces as a battalion commander before he quit the Việt Minh in 1954. He was then living in a land development center in Pleiku. I used to visit him when I went on trips to the area. He talked to us for many hours in a week. The first thing he said was, "You are training your troops in training centers much more than truly necessary. As soldiers fighting under sergeants and lieutenants, they don't need to learn so many lessons that they could not digest or remember."

He advised us that we should teach the troops to do the best in digging foxholes, camouflage, and shooting, and how to execute orders given by squad leaders. He said we needed to teach our troops only three or four tactics about what they would do as a member in a squad or platoon in general situations such as attacking, defending, and withdrawing, and to have the troops drill them into habit. Topics more complicated than that would be taught only to sergeants and officers. He helped us design a basic military training of simple tactics that were practicable in hamlets, where the teams were to live and work beside hamlet people with weak defense capability against VC small units.

The first lesson could be taught in a few sentences. If possible, a team should stay overnight at one of the several prepared locations in a hamlet. A net of individual foxholes was prepared in pairs at each location in a perimeter defense. When the enemy opened fire, every cell of two team members had to take position quickly in one pair of foxholes, back to back within thirty seconds. Then they should finish off every creature moving around their position.

The rule was if all defenders—and villagers in many cases—took their positions quickly enough and kept still in their foxholes, they could easily identify who were the attackers—those who were moving—and gun them down without fear of mistaking team fellows for enemies. The sapper attack was successful only when the defenders panicked, moving around in disorder and unable to tell who was a VC. It was why VC sappers always were half naked and armed with concussion hand grenades or similar devices.

With advice from him and other seasoned combat veterans, the instructors began training the teams with the most practical topics. The key instruction was to have the team members drill the reaction as often as possible so that it would become their quickest reflex after the first sign of danger.

So our thirty-six teams were launched into the campaign. After ten months operating in different areas of each district, local VC guerrillas conducted nineteen attacks of platoon-size or smaller against a number of the thirty-six teams. Our side suffered one death; we lost one carbine, one commercial one-band AM radio, and an amplifier. The enemy left five bodies, along with two rifles, and suffered an unknown number of wounded.

The teams were not very successful in training the Combat Youth. What they could do was to teach them with personal combat actions and how to fight along with others in a squad. Ethnic Vietnamese militiamen were learning and fighting better. But few hamlets could stand up against an enemy force larger than a platoon. In the rare cases, it was some Montagnard militias that made spectacular victories.

A typical militia's feat was in a hamlet about two miles from Polei Kleng outpost, some ten miles west of Kontum. The hamlet was armed with about twenty WWI rifles (bolt action, with a five-round clip) and hand grenades, no automatic rifles or machine guns. A VC company of at least 100 well-armed troops applied the standard communist tactics, opened fire on multiple sides, and blew out an opening through the strong bamboo fences.

Without being trained much in tactics, the militia commander of the hamlet reacted instinctively. When the enemy began to rush into the opening, he quickly gathered all his men to the place, leaving all other sides unguarded and just massacred the enemy freely. The fight lasted half an hour. When I came along later with the district chief, we saw more than forty enemy troops killed by bullets and grenades in a small area about 5,000 square feet outside the opening. The militia side suffered only a dozen wounded.

Since the beginning of the Việt Nam War, communist commanders had conducted many successful attacks against the RVN military units. They often applied the same tactics in assailing the government military outposts. The tactics were simple, despite the communist propaganda machine's praise of it as their invincible military invention. The attack usually began with gunfire from at least two positions outside the post to confound the defenders. Naturally, the defending soldiers dashed to the trenches and faced outside looking for the enemy. At the right time, communist attackers would break an opening in the fences by detonating a string of explosive packs—a makeshift "Bangalore torpedo." Through this passage the main attacking element would quickly storm into the objective area.

The storming troops were armed with light weapons, most times with only concussion grenades, and would move into the center of the defensive area. From there they would spread out attacking the defending troops "from behind." As the tactics dictated, the VC unit had to concentrate two-thirds of its force in the assault element to storm the outpost through the entrance (or "gate," in communist terminology). Most soldiers who died in those attacks, as I found out, were killed from inside, while they were expecting the enemy to attack from the outside. Moreover, the traditional trench around the defense system, where the defenders took their positions, augmented the killing power of the explosives. Concussion grenades used by the sappers were made of small bars or packets of explosives with several kinds of detonators and hand-assembled ignition devices. When they exploded on open ground, the blasts could do no serious harm to men more than a few yards away. Inside a room or a bunker or a wall, the destruction was greater because air escape was blocked and the explosive gas expansion produced pressure high enough to crush a thick concrete shelter into rubbles. Blowing up in a trench where air was blocked by two sides, a small concussion grenade could kill people five yards or more away on each side.

The tactics proved effective, especially against RVN units without intensive combat training. However, if the defenders had all their firepower directed at the "gate" on time, the attackers would suffer heavily and fail to get in because they were armed mostly with concussion grenades and explosives.

In an outpost or similar stronghold, perimeter defense was a matter of course. The rule was that the defense commander should keep a strong reserve. He should be watchful and use all of his reserve to crush the enemy main force at the "gate" in time.

In fact, it was often difficult to know when and where the counterattack should be ordered. But if the defense commander was calm enough to control the situation and to deploy his trained troops as the book says, the unit could have a 70 percent chance of prevailing. So the key factors were the leadership of the fort commander and the troops' fire discipline. If the attackers failed in the attempt to get through the gate, they would certainly suffer very heavy losses, as two-thirds of their strength was to concentrate on storming the narrow opening. And under any situation, the VC attacking commander had to follow the plan with no authority to change it, much less to withdraw his troops even when defeat was imminent.

After being at a loss for an effective way to deal with the VC attacks in the first years of the war (1959–60), ARVN units began to learn from their experiences. In many places, government troops successfully drove the attackers away and inflicted heavy losses on them. The communist tactic seemed unsuitable for attacking ARVN and allied combat units at field positions, especially American ground forces with enormous firepower. In the last years of the war, particularly after 1970, this tactic was applied less and less frequently because the two sides were fighting in a conventional warfare.

MY AMERICAN BUDDIES

While serving the Twenty-second Division in the Strategic Hamlet and Pacification programs, American advisors did their best to help. My requests for assistance were always replied to favorably.

In my job, the advisors working closely with me were all nice and enthusiastic. Lieutenant Colonel Whalen, a Normandy veteran, gave me not only help but also warm sympathy. He had replaced Major O'Rahilly in late 1963. Later he became the senior advisor to Kontum province military command. Lieutenant Colonel Matterson was an outspoken officer. Before transferred to the Twenty-second MACV team, he had gotten into trouble when he criticized his corrupt Vietnamese counterpart in the Sài Gòn area with strong words, stronger than MACV rules allowed. He earned my high respect from that and from his wonderful education; he was a PhD in electrical engineering. Captain Lord was an advisor to the assistant chief of staff for psychological warfare (G-5) and also served as my counterpart. He was a friendly officer and a talented trumpet player.

Captain Weil came to be my advisor during his second tour in Việt Nam. I had met him several times in 1963 when he was with a Vietnamese infantry battalion. The battalion was in a six-month operation providing security for the area ten miles east of Pleiku City. Captain Weil—and every other battalion advisor—had to live on Vietnamese meals along with the Vietnamese officers in the battalion. The Twenty-second MACV team's chopper dropped by twice a week to bring him letters, sweets, cigarettes, and office supplies but absolutely no food. Weil, a brilliant West Point graduate, lost some ten pounds after one year serving the battalion. When he had dinner at my home—Vietnamese food, of course—he acted almost exactly like a Vietnamese at the dining table. Major Chambers, who replaced Weil, was a nice officer who shared some of his booze with me after work.

Later on in the war, many Vietnamese in the military believed that if half of the American officers fighting in Việt Nam had understood the Vietnamese—good and bad—as those typical advisors did, we would have changed the course of events in a few years.

In combat units, most American advisors were welcomed. It was partly because the Americans behaved rather well and also because the troops knew that the advisors could be very helpful to them with air support, medical evacuation, and resupply.The advisors proved to be good friends to the Vietnamese also because of their personal safety. A group of two or three Americans living among the Vietnamese—most of whom didn't speak English—had to be nice. Their behavior proved to our troops that the advisors were totally different from the pre-1954 French, and so communist slanderous propaganda aimed at the role of the U.S. soldiers in ARVN units failed to affect our troops.

ARVN combat troops always expressed their strong appreciation for medical evacuation by American choppers. Their crews often defied enemy ground fire to pick up Vietnamese WIAs with impeccable courage.

Once in Pleiku province, a battalion of my Twenty-second Division was fighting a communist attacking force. At midnight, the battalion headquarters requested emergency evacuation of five wounded—four ARVN and one POW. The senior advisor sent a UH-1B to the mission. The chopper was hit and had to make an emergency landing on safe ground near the regimental command post. A second chopper was sent in. Under strong enemy fire, the medevac team succeeded in landing, but only after some hits, including one that slightly wounded the copilot. However, the team could pick up only three of the five wounded. One of the three was a POW, who was assigned priority 2 of the five. Evacuation of wounded POWs along with our WIAs was very common during the Việt Nam War.

There were some bad Americans, of course. Others were not bad but "too American" in the eyes of the Vietnamese. One of them was a captain who was usually very friendly to us. Every three months or so, he traveled to Hong Kong on R&R or temporary duty. In the early 1960s, the five-band shortwave transistor radio Philips made in Holland was the best-seller in South Việt Nam. Some Vietnamese friends of the captain asked him to buy them the set whenever he went to Hong Kong. He was pleased to buy them and got reimbursed in South Việt Nam piaster at the official rate. Each duty-free Philips radio cost about half the price as at a store in Sài Gòn. Two or three of these Vietnamese friends then sold the radios for a profit and asked him to buy them again on his next visit to Hong Kong. He did so the second time. But the third time he did not come back. A week later, his Vietnamese friends found out that he had been transferred to a new job in the United States. At last, in a letter to another American advisor, the captain informed his Vietnamese friends that he had donated all their money to some orphanage in Hong Kong. A receipt was sent along with the letter.

* * *

In autumn 1964, a communist sapper battalion launched a surprise attack on the Plei Krong CIDG (Civilian Irregular Defense Group) camp. The camp was nine miles west of Kontum City on the west side of Plei Krong River and was home to a CIDG battalion under a U.S. Special Forces team, an ARVN Special Forces team, and a squad of regular soldiers of Nùng origin (a North Việt Nam tribe).

The communist force started the attack with 60 mm mortar shells from a place only 200 yards from the fence, and then blew up a passage across the fence to let sappers into the camp center. Nearly sixty CIDG were killed, but the sappers met strong firepower from five Americans and the Vietnamese squad, who suffered only a few wounded.

As there was a group of armed hamlets in the area, I joined the district chief along with two RF companies in an intervention. When we reached the camp, an enemy rearguard element opened fire on us before withdrawing. The hamlets were safe. The enemy did not attack the hamlet militias, only directed harassing fire at some of them.

HIGHWAY SECURITY

Besides my principal responsibility, I was also in charge of a military area along Highway 14, from five miles south of Kontum City to five miles north of Pleiku City. The division commander assigned me the task because my job in the Strategic Hamlet program could help coordinate security operations in the common boundary area between the two adjacent provinces.

The boundary between Kontum and Pleiku provinces ran east to west across the highway in this area. About twenty miles to the west of Highway 14 was the common border with Cambodia. A few miles into the Cambodian territory was the communist army logistic and communications route along the common border with Việt Nam, extending from the 19th parallel north in Laos to eastern Cambodia, known as the Trường Sơn Trails or "Long Mountain" Trails or Hồ Chí Minh Trails.

North Việt Nam sent personnel and weapons to the communist forces in South Việt Nam by this route, which consisted of a network of trails. All of them were negotiable by trucks with low-tech preparation. From the trails, several footpaths branched into South Việt Nam for NVN soldiers and war laborers transporting military supplies into inner areas. Laborers carried supplies on their backs or on bicycles they pushed along the paths. The trails had been blazed for communications on foot from North to South Việt Nam during the War of Resistance, 1946–54.[1]

From the Trails, at least three to five footpath groups branched eastward across my division area into the inner regions of South Việt Nam. One, of secondary importance as an alternate footpath, went along the boundary between Kontum and Pleiku provinces, crossing my area of responsibility. The other pathways in the Twenty-second DTA were at the northernmost area of Kontum and at the area between Pleiku and Darlac provinces to the south.

The communist high command often installed lines of infiltration and logistical support on footpaths along the boundary between two adjacent provinces and districts. South Vietnamese territorial forces tended to keep away from the boundary line to avoid clashes with friendly forces by mistake, thus leaving the swath of land along the district and province boundaries unpatrolled.

As I have mentioned, communications and logistic routes were the backbone of the enemy's effort in the war. They paid a high price to maintain them. And my division's strategy was to block them or at least to minimize the traffic as much as possible. The Special Forces camps improved the operations later.

So I was in charge of a dual-purposed operation. That was to maintain security for the main link between the two strategic headquarters—the Twenty-second Infantry Division and Army II Corps—as well as to monitor the enemy activities so that the division could deal some blows at their movements of personnel and supplies. As the area covered a part of each province with some armed hamlets, I was assigned to fill in the blanks and to secure better coordination between the provinces.

Road security had been my concern for years, but I had only a faint idea of what should be done to keep the road safe from the elusive enemy. I met with several veterans who had experience in the matter. The best ideas came from some sergeants who had fought communist guerrillas over rural areas of North and South Việt Nam in the 1946–54 war, particularly in road protection.

The division CO gave me three intelligence platoons, and six months later one was replaced by a Regional Force platoon from Kontum province. I asked the three platoon leaders to break down their platoons into teams of three or four soldiers each. One-third of the teams would conduct a twenty-four-hour patrol in assigned areas along the highway, from 500 meters to 1 kilometer off the road. In fact, I just needed them to wander in the areas as much as possible and to shoot rubbish if necessary to confuse the enemy about where the troops could be present. The enemy wouldn't be able to guess when and where my men would appear. After one twenty-four-hour mission, operating teams were given the next twenty-four hours off to stay at home. In the twenty-four hours that followed, they would rest at their platoon bases in different hamlets as reserves.

VC snipers dared to waylay military and civilian vehicles moving on the roads only when they believed they had relative safety of movement and a safe path to escape in the wooded areas bordering the road.

Our new tactics proved to be very effective. In the first month, our men in the two platoons captured two snipers and killed three others in four clashes. From then on until regional units from the provinces replaced my task force eighteen months later, there was almost no sniper fire on this part of the highway.

The division commander in mid-1964 was Colonel Nguyễn Văn Hiếu, a well-known incorruptible officer. One afternoon he told me to join him on a trip to Pleiku for a meeting with the corps staff, and he insisted that we should go by jeep, not by chopper. So we went on with two passenger jeeps and an escort jeep with a mounted .30 machine gun. We departed at 3 PM. At 8 PM, Colonel Hiếu told me that he and I were to go back to Kontum. I was surprised at his unexpected decision but said nothing. On the trip back, I drove the jeep.

At the start of the trip, he asked me if I could call any patrolling team to show up at some place on the road to meet him. "You often said that there are patrols every night in the areas along the highway. Is that right?" he asked. Of course, I gave him a positive answer. So I had my sergeant communicate with the teams by radio via a 24/24 relay station. Half an hour later, Master Sergeant K'But, the Twelfth Intelligence Platoon leader, waved a white handkerchief at the roadside. Colonel Hiếu shook hands with K'But and his three soldiers and gave them a little gift of 1,000 piasters. From then on until his last day commanding the division, he never doubted anything I reported to him. He returned to the Twenty-second Division the second time in 1966 after I had left it. He died a few weeks before Sài Gòn fell on April 30, 1975.

The experience of road security of the Twenty-second Division was reported to the Joint General Staff and other major units. But not many ARVN units appreciated it. I had to admit that the tactics might not be the best for other infantry units because it required special support from their headquarters and a well-defined system of command and communications. Many low-level commanders would not buy it. Such tactics would cost them too much time, effort, and responsibility.

ON THE ROAD TO FAILURE

The second half of 1964 saw South Việt Nam creeping to the edge of an abyss. The political mess in Sài Gòn and the intensity of VC attacks played a role in lowering the morale of not only our troops but our officers as well.

The overthrow of President Diệm and the subsequent political disturbances contributed a psychological factor that was almost ignored in the literature of this war. It was the legendary role of the CIA. Ordinary Vietnamese people seemed to feel the deteriorating situation was so hard to fathom that the only way to explain it was to blame the CIA. "CIA" quickly became the answer for almost every question concerning the actions of the United States in Việt Nam or any other country. Ironically, the CIA conspiracy theory haunted both sides in the Việt Nam War.

The case of Ngô Đình Cẩn, the youngest brother of Ngô Đình Diệm, drew public concerns. He was sentenced to death and executed at the Central Prison in Sài Gòn in May 1964. He had been indicted for many crimes that I didn't believe he had committed. However, he was not accused of religious discrimination. According to credible sources close to Cẩn that I could access, he was a rich peasant, not a politician and much less a feudal lord, although he had some political power over the four northern provinces of South Việt Nam.

Some people blamed the CIA for his death. Rumors spread that the CIA had plotted to eliminate Cẩn, who at one time had been a confidential friend to some Americans. I thought Cẩn might have participated in some of his subordinates' wrongdoing, but doubted he was behind the many heinous crimes of which he was accused. I thought he deserved a lenient sentence because two of his brothers had been killed in the coup.

THE VC OFFENSIVE ESCALATES

During the last months of 1964, the Vietnamese communist forces escalated their offensive. The government side suffered heavy losses in several large-scale attacks. From 1960 to 1963, most of the enemy's activities had been surprise hit-and-run onslaughts at remote forts and hamlets or sapper attacks on heavily defended military installations. The attacks were usually of platoon size and seldom of company size. Since early 1964, communist forces intensified their efforts with many more battalion-sized attacks on selected objectives.

However, the communist side still relied a great deal on terrorism, its basic tactic in South Việt Nam. After 1963, more bomb and grenade attacks were conducted in every major city, including Sài Gòn. The VC objectives were government civil and military installations, American military personnel quarters, and bus stations, theaters, and restaurants whose owners refused to pay protection money to the communist rebels. There were more victims every week in the delta and coastal areas on cross-country buses blown up by land mines because their owners failed to provide such monetary contributions to the VC *kinh tài* agents (economic-financial branch.).

In addition, after 1964 many more village committee members in the lowlands were kidnapped and assassinated. Nurses and civilians on anti-malaria teams spraying DDT to kill mosquitoes faced more danger when they went into remote areas to do their jobs. They were suspected of collecting intelligence for the police and army.

In October 1964, General Nguyễn Xuân Thịnh replaced Colonel Nguyễn Văn Hiếu as our division commander. At the time, the Twenty-second Division Tactical Area included Bình Định Province after the Twenty-fifth Infantry Division moved to its new area of responsibility west of Sài Gòn. My job required me to visit the province's people and to learn the regional peculiarities.

Once I paid a visit to the headquarters of Phù Mỹ district when a killing took place in a hamlet some four miles from the district town. Half of the families in the hamlet had members who had joined the Việt Minh and moved to North Việt Nam. Those were called the *tập kết* (regrouping members). In only three months, four innocent persons were killed in this hamlet. Two unarmed soldiers were stabbed to death on the road running through the hamlet.

Two anti-malaria workers spraying DDT were held and tried before a "people's court," presided over by communist security cadres. They were found guilty of "spying for the Americans and the puppet government." A few minutes later, both were executed by machete.

All attempts to investigate these crimes failed. The hamlet residents said that unknown Việt Cộng rebels came to their hamlet and ordered them to participate in the "people's court" and condemn the men. That was true. The VC was doing everything to compel innocent peasants to attend and participate in such trials and executions. They tried every way to draw the local authorities into unfriendly acts against the people to create animosity between the relatives of Việt Minh cadres who had gone north and the local government and the military.

That day when I was visiting the district headquarters, two nurses were captured and tried in that hamlet. One of the nurses was three months pregnant. Both worked in the public health service. That day they went to the hamlet to perform the inoculation program to protect the population against cholera, which was in danger of spreading in the district area. The two were sentenced to death by the same kangaroo court. When the nurses argued that they were doing humanitarian services, the Việt Cộng rebels replied that their works were done "in the name of the American imperialists and as a propaganda tool supporting their war in Việt Nam." Besides, the VC "court" also charged the two with spying for the police. Therefore, they deserved the death sentence. However, the woman was spared because of her pregnancy. The male nurse was executed in front of her.

Upon receiving the report and talking to the woman, everyone present in the headquarters burned with anger. Some military officials spoke of retaliation. But all knew that the peasants were not guilty when they were forced to vote for the sentences already decided by the local VC security chief. In war, there have been hundreds or even thousands of similar cases when our soldiers tried their best to overcome personal emotion to keep them from blindly venting their anger on innocent civilians. They understood the plight of the poor peasants who had to do whatever the clandestine VC agents ordered.

Many others, who were soldiers' or militiamen's wives and their children, also fell victim to communist terrorists. I knew a regional force sergeant famous for hunting guerrillas. After several attempts to kill him, the local Việt Cộng called on him to change sides and promised not to do him any harm. His remote village was in the VC control area where his wife and their small child were held as hostages. The wife was told to go see her husband and persuade him to surrender. If he refused, the local VC cadres said, her son would be butchered. At last he refused to surrender, and the guerrillas cut her baby's throat in front of her to show that they would do what they promised. I didn't know what happened later to the brave sergeant. I heard that he was transferred to a province far away for his safety after his wife escaped their home village.

Many times, the Việt Cộng forced wives and children of the troops to march in front of the guerrillas as human shields during attacks on forts. Some forts were overrun in a few minutes, but one or two in our area were not. In one of those rare cases, the fort commander himself opened fire on the enemy even though he knew his wife was among the women outside the fence crying and begging them to give up. A few women were killed along with a dozen guerrillas, but the troops in the fort survived the fighting. I admitted to my friends that I might not have had the courage to do the same.

The local troops, of course, retaliated. However brutal the retaliation might have been, it did not outdo the Việt Cộng's atrocity, which was systematically conducted as the major means of war obviously with their top leaders' approval.

Several times I saw human heads hung on the trees—those of the guerrillas who were decapitated for revenge by some militiamen. Of course, there were other violations by local security authorities such as torture and illegal detention that took place at village level.

In remote rural areas, the authorities seldom investigated such crimes, as people took it as a matter of course in war. In the regular army, such atrocities were rarely committed, probably because well-educated officers would seldom tolerate war crimes. It was also because of the presence of American advisors, who were not reluctant to report such crimes to their superiors and to our superiors. Reactions from our Joint General Staff would be quick and severe.

Many foreigners might have been misinformed on the actual situation of the rural life in war. Sometimes communist propaganda was successful in creating false images of the South Vietnamese troops, depicting the typical ARVN soldier as if he were a vampire.

I felt very sorry for the civilian victims of communist terrorism, which amounted to thousands each year. They suffered the same way as any other terrorist victim, but were mostly unknown to the outside world where a lot of people were easily angered because of some trivial crimes committed by troops on our side.

A DEVASTATING FLOOD

The great flash flood in autumn 1964 came at midnight, and the news reached the Division Tactical Operations Center just fifteen minutes later. My telephone rang at 2 AM. My office duty NCO told me to join an emergency meeting at DTOC in which the division CO ordered military effort to rescue the victims.

The two U.S. Army helicopter companies in the division area with scores of UH-1Bs participated in the rescue mission at maximum capability. All my officers, along with many others, were aboard the rescue helicopters assisting the pilots as observers and interpreters. Large and medium-scale military operations were canceled. Even those people having an anti-American attitude had to appreciate the performance of the American crews in such humanitarian missions. I had already witnessed several medevac missions in combat and can attest to the courage of the helicopter pilots who defied the enemy's heavy fire to save the victims.

When I flew over the coastal area early the next morning on a chopper, the whole province looked like a shallow sea or a great flooded marshland with scattered tufts of vegetation. I got lost, although I had been familiar with the area and seldom needed a map to locate a hamlet from the air. All roads and other terrain features were under muddy water.

The massive deployment of military resources resulted in the rescue of 1,000 peasants from high ground, as the surrounding water rose higher and higher. Many victims clung to the roofs of their houses that were drifting on the sea. On several foothills, communist guerrillas shot at rescuing choppers. We had to call in Skyraider fighters to silence them while victims on the ground made signs to indicate the guerrillas' positions, using shreds of white cloth to make arrow figures pointing out the possible location of enemy fire.

Human losses were light, but there was serious property damage in several coastal provinces.

When the flood was over, we had a free hand for military actions. My division CO, General Nguyễn Xuân Thịnh, ordered an operational plan drawn up. The concept was to take advantage of the enemy's great loss of supplies caused by the floods to strike a decisive blow at the VC. We would send out a regiment to destroy the communist forces in mountainous bases west of Bình Định province.

As an assistant chief of staff for pacification, I was in the operation bloc along with G-2, G-3, and G-5 (psywar), instead of in the logistic bloc, as was the case for many other DTAs. So I had to participate in the process of the operational planning. We all predicted that whenever we attacked the Kim Sơn area, the enemy would certainly hit or even overrun some military objectives in the lowland area to divert our effort. General Thịnh approved our proposal that in such a case we would continue our raid to eliminate the enemy's backbone and accept the risk of some loss at other strongholds, even at the price of a few hamlets or a regional force outpost.

What happened in the first week of operation proved that we had selected the right course of action. Information by prisoners and a number of materials captured in objective areas ensured us a victory, not by body count but by reducing enemy capability in the area for a long time. A week after D-day, the enemy conducted a series of fierce blows against two district headquarters, overran some armed hamlets, delivered more sniper fire, and laid more mines on highways in remote areas.

We could stand up to our enemy, but we were not able to resist our superiors. Obviously because of great concern over the losses already predicted in our operation plan, our superiors (Corps HQS or the JGS) ordered the operation halted. The division staff under the best chief I had ever known, Major Tôn Thất Hùng, was unable to persuade the higher command to let us proceed.

After our failed efforts, the military situation in the coastal areas became worse and worse, as communist forces had enough time to reorganize their supply system. Six months later, we captured a report from a VC commander in the area sent to his superior in which he confirmed that if we had continued that operation on the enemy base at Kim Sơn for one more week, the whole communist Eighteenth Artillery Regiment (equipped with 82 mm mortars) newly arrived from North Việt Nam would have been virtually destroyed along with major logistic units and a great quantity of supplies. The report stated that all possible routes for withdrawal from the base and dispersing in the area had been blocked by our ARVN firepower or infantry elements. It was not necessary to be a strategist or tactician to realize that this was a typical mistake of the ARVN in war. High echelon commanders sometimes were so concerned about losing a small battle that they gave up larger probable achievements.

In 1964, there were major reorganizations in the military structure in South Việ Nam. The Bảo An, a provincial force similar to the U.S. National Guard, officially became the Regional Force after it was supported by U.S. military aid and armed with regular army equipment and weapons. The hamlet militias, People's Defense or Dân Vệ and the Combat Youths or Thanh Niên Chiến Đấu created since the Strategic Hamlet program, were reformed into a single corps under the new title of Nghĩa Quân or Popular Forces. They were armed with American M-2 carbines, and M-1 Garand rifles replaced WWI vintage rifles. And exactly as we had expected, in many areas the new Popular Forces partly became low-grade army units after they were paid regular salaries. Although they got better training and equipment, they began assembling in conventional platoons and defending fortifications around the village office, leaving the population at the mercy of the VC at night.

From then on, the RVN armed forces consisted of the Chủ Lực Quân (Regular Forces), Địa Phương Quân (Regional Forces, RF), and the Nghĩa Quân (Popular Forces, PF). Some Americans called the RF and PF collectively the Ruff-Puff, a derogatory term.

PEASANT LIFE IN BÌNH ĐỊNH PROVINCE

Before our Twenty-second Division assumed military territorial responsibility over Bình Định province in late 1964, I often heard that 80 percent of its population was supporting the Vietnamese communists. The truth, however, was different.

Anybody who stayed with the villagers long enough and won their trust would quickly find out the rules of the game in this miserable region. The province was highly populated with farmlands cut up by foothills that limited possible high productivity. Its people were among the poorest in Việt Nam. In the war against the French, people in the province lived under the strict control of the Việt Minh. After the 1954 Geneva Accords, thousands of Việt Minh troops and cadres left for North Việt Nam (the *tập kết,* or regroupers), while many were ordered to stay behind for future actions.

In some districts, RVN local governments moved many close relatives of those tập kết to land development centers in the highlands. The relatives who stayed behind faced some discrimination. Skeptical local security officials in many places treated them as if they were second-class citizens. Probably that ill treatment was a consequence of the nationalist-communist conflict dating back to 1945–50 in the provinces from Quảng Trị to Bình Định.[2]

In most of the other provinces of South Việt Nam, local authorities treated parents, wives, and children of the *tập kết* kindly and let them live normal lives. They were not discriminated against in their applications for government jobs. Many of their sons graduated with university degrees and served as public officials and officers in the army, navy, and air force, even at field grades. I personally knew a dozen of those officers. Of course, there was caution against their possible connection with communist intelligence agents who were very skillful at planting spies in the RVN military and government organizations. But Sài Gòn imposed no strict oppressive policy to control VC relatives.[3]

By the end of 1964, communist insurgents had successfully intimidated a large number of the rural population into supporting them. A cell of two or three Việt Cộng cadres ran a village of 1,000 residents efficiently, even though they appeared only when there were no government troops around.

Throughout the war, the security chief of the clandestine Việt Cộng district committee was the most feared person to the common people. He had the power to issue death sentences to "reactionaries" without any kind of trial. "Reactionaries" included members of the police, the armed forces, civil servants, or any civilian whom the VC viewed as "dangerous" elements or as having a "blood debt to the people." Death sentences were also given to anyone who was found providing intelligence information to the government forces. The executions were usually prompt and certain.

The least serious violation of the VC rules was to sell things such as chicken, pigs, or vegetables to ARVN soldiers during an operation. The punishment for such "crimes" was one to three months of "reeducation" in the jungle about ten to twenty miles away. Violators brought along their own food for the "reeducation course."

When ARVN troops arrived in a village under the Việt Cộng terrorists' control, they might confront groups of protesters—young women, children, old men and women. The groups would shout protests against any action of the government and the armed forces, such as military conscription, military operations in the area, and unlawful arrests. To head off possible crackdowns by government forces, they never overtly supported the Việt Cộng.

The protests might have angered troops who faced them for the first time, but not those who were familiar with the situation. Experienced soldiers would advise their new fellows to ignore the protesters, saying, "These poor peasants are compelled by the VC to do this nonsense. Deep in their hearts, they wouldn't."

In some villages, it was the relatives of those serving government agencies or in the military away from home who went first in such protests. Meanwhile, the VC's relatives would treat the soldiers kindly. That was why outsiders often got confused by the tricks VC clandestine security cadres imposed on villagers.

When the troops wanted to buy food, no one dared to sell it overtly to them. Some who could do it covertly would accept only small bills—the one-piaster bill was mostly preferred—before telling the troops to shoot the chickens or the pigs and to take them away as if the soldiers were looting. The peasants would be in trouble with the Việt Cộng if they were found possessing the large bills (VN$10 and higher) without previously reporting to them how they had earned the money. The practice once caused a very large demand for small bills in the coastal area in 1964–65. Local banks were not able to solve the problem quickly and might not have known why, but our G-2 and G-5 did. Many reporters, Vietnamese as well as foreigners, several times reported the soldiers stealing chickens and pigs in operations. Very few of them knew the truth. In some cases, it was actual looting. In many others, it wasn't, but just a way of "safety-to-seller purchasing."

The peasants had to pay some taxes to the Việt Cộng in rice. The rice was not collected for storage at one location, because such storage would be destroyed or confiscated by the government troops. Instead, taxpayers had to keep the tax rice at their homes and dole it out to the VC guerrillas according to instructions of the VC agent in charge.

If ARVN intelligence agents were looking for some information, the only effective way was to stay overnight in different homes. Some agents staying with families that they thought the most likely to tell the truth would quietly and discreetly ask the adults for information. Those being asked would reveal information only if they felt certain that they were safe. There was always the risk that the sources of information would be leaked to the ears of the VC.

In one of these operations, I visited a village in Phù Mỹ district, north of Qui Nhơn, and spent the night with an old man more than seventy years old. I talked to him the way a grandson talks to his grandfather. Deep into the night, when I felt he trusted me, I asked him who had destroyed the small concrete bridge and dug trenches across the dirt road leading to the village.

"It's me and people in this hamlet," he said. "We know the bridge and the road are useful to us. But when the VC ordered us to destroy, we couldn't refuse. Refusal sometimes leads one to death by VC executioners." He added, "If your troops caught us in the act, we might only be sentenced to no more than six months in jail where we would be fed much better than at home. You dare not kill us, but the Việt Cộng do. So we'd rather live without schools, dispensaries, good roads, and bridges than incur harsh punishment including violent death."

When I asked many others in different places later about whether or not 80 percent of the population was supporting the communist guerrillas, most of them said, "Yes, they do." But they explained to me that only about one-third did so willingly. "The other two-thirds have no choice," they said, "and many of those are even anticommunists. But they could do nothing against orders of the rebels." However, it was true that the percentage of pro-VC in the population of Bình Định (and Quảng Ngãi) was higher than in other provinces.

That situation was too complicated for even a Vietnamese to understand, let alone foreigners who had never lived as a peasant and did not speak Vietnamese. When a foreigner visited part of the country where the communists exerted strong influence, most of the time foreign reporters only met those peasants who were coached by the Việt Cộng secret agents and said what they had been directed to say. That sometimes happened even in the cities under full government control, including Sài Gòn. A peasant from an unprotected hamlet who was interviewed by radio or TV reporters was always scared by the possibility of being in trouble with VC secret agents.

CIVIL DISORDER

The latter half of 1964 saw extremely important events all over Việt Nam. Reports on the *Maddox* crisis followed by an air raid at several military sites in North Việt Nam came amid bad news about VC rising military pressure all over the South.[4] Many of us had a vague hope that bringing war to the communist bases in North Việt Nam would be a solution to the conflict. However, many others doubted that. One of them was my father-in-law, who had been well experienced with the communist regime since 1945. He said to me that it might not be the best way to deal with the Việt Cộng. The communist top leaders were "tough like leeches, and it is the troops and the common people who suffer, not the leaders," he asserted.

In Bình Định and many other coastal provinces, the Buddhist-backed opposition movement launched a campaign of protests that continued into early 1965. The protests also took place in Sài Gòn. The protesters accused the government in Sài Gòn of everything plausible to the public. The war was escalating. Scenes of civilians' death and houses destroyed in the countryside incited antiwar sentiment. I saw it as a natural reaction and felt that, deep in their hearts, the protesters were not doing the wrong thing. But the agitators behind the scenes were to be blamed. The communists made every effort to take advantage of the movement to create disorder and unrest in the populous coastal area where Bình Định was the key target.

The protests were fierce and intense, bringing life in Qui Nhơn City nearly to a standstill. No market or business opened, while an around-the-clock curfew was imposed. The protesters attacked civil servants and the police, but avoided—or even flattered—the military and militias. For a few days, many streets were deserted as if from a devastating epidemic. The province chief's family was short on rice, and he had to call the nearest district chief to help him with basic food supply.

Quickly taking advantage of the situation, communist regular units from North Việt Nam began infiltrating the South on a larger scale. Assisted by local guerrillas, they conducted a series of attacks against key militia positions. Most of these positions fell, while many other militias withdrew to safety in district towns even before being attacked. Consequently, a flow of war refugees filled Qui Nhơn.

The 1/40th Battalion of my division was ambushed on the way to rescue a regional force company under attack at Đèo Nhông Pass on Highway 1 north of Qui Nhơn. A communist regiment attacked with four battalions. Most were fresh troops coming from North Việt Nam armed with better weapons, the AK-47. There was no way to save the battalion.

Our division had no reserve force. The II Corps and the JGS didn't, either. Nor were we given any air support, as all available fighters and bombers, American or Vietnamese, were sent to attack North Việt Nam and participate in more important battles somewhere else. We could communicate with the battalion's radio operators, on waves relayed by the only L-19 observation plane flying high over the area. The two radio operators were hiding on high ground. They sent short messages every few minutes, reporting how their battalion was being eliminated piece by piece until they had to destroy the AN/GRC-9 radio and escape to safety. After about an hour of listening to the special "live report," we left the Division Tactical Operations Center with profound sadness.

The VC offensive intensified and expanded their control over more than half of the population of the province. Several portions of Highway 1, the backbone of all coastal provinces, were in enemy hands. VC guerrillas laid obstacles and dug pits to obstruct traffic.

The An Lao district headquarters suffered heavy losses in fierce fighting. The district headquarters of Hoài Ân blunted the first enemy's attack, killing more than 100 communist troops before midnight. But a few hours after that, a communist reinforcing regiment overran the headquarters. The defending company suffered a dozen KIA before retreating to the nearby foothills. The northernmost district of Bồng Sơn was isolated and had to rely on airplanes for supplies.

Communist forces conducted attacks all around the country that spilled into early 1965. They launched a bold mortar attack on the Biên Hòa Air Force Base, destroying a number of American military planes and killing five Americans and some Vietnamese. Communist sappers infiltrated Tân Sơn Nhất Air Force Base, damaging some planes. Another target was Hotel Brink in the very heart of Sài Gòn close to the RVN Congress building. The hotel housed hundreds of American officers, but only two of them were killed by the timed car bomb.

The communists' attacks greatly affected our morale at the time when the Vietnamese generals were vying for political power. Several coups and countercoups in 1964 continued to push South Việt Nam toward the brink.

In all my years serving the ARVN, the events in late 1964 brought me the deepest despair, only second to that in April 1975. It was in the last month of 1964 that my daughter was born. The cute baby brought me a sense of hope. I named her Tường Anh, "the Bird of Luck."

SEVENTEEN

On the Down Slope

Bad news from battles around the country appeared in newspapers almost every day. The North Việt Nam Army moved its soldiers into South Việt Nam in battalion and regimental size. Intelligence reports confirmed that several NVA regular divisions were already present in the South.

In December 1964, the first NVA division appeared in the territory of my Twenty-second Division after moving on truck or by foot on the Long Mountain Trails (the Hồ Chí Minh Trails) and crossing the Việt Nam common border with Laos and Cambodia. From the border area, the footpath routes branching from the Trails into the Twenty-second Division and Twenty-third Division Areas in northern highland provinces became the main NVA logistic lines to the RVN Corps Tactical Zone II. The NVA sea lines provided only a small quantity of supplies for its troops in the Vietnam Central coastal area.

THE ENEMY TAKES THE UPPER HAND

In the last days of 1964, the communist forces attacked Bình Giả village, near the Sài Gòn Vũng Tàu Highway, where 1,000 North Vietnamese Catholics had been resettled in 1954. ARVN Ranger, Marine, and Airborne battalions were sent to Bình Giả and suffered heavy casualties (about 300 KIA). The fact that the VC was able to fight with its multi-battalion task force was a great shock to our confidence. The defeat of our elite combat units took place when the political situation was badly deteriorating, with unstable governments crumbling one after another every few months.

The national military situation changed quickly with the introduction of North Vietnamese Army divisions, rather well trained and equipped with weapons more suitable to the combat environment than ours, the AK's. We celebrated

Tết 1965, or Year of the Snake, in anxiety as political and military situations were going downhill quickly. The Twenty-second Division units waited for the oncoming multiple divisions of the enemy offensive.

A week after Tết, I got a telephone call from the Kontum district headquarters at 6:30 AM, reporting that gunfire was heard from the area along Highway 14 where I was in charge. I quickly turned the radio on and tried to contact the relay station on a steep rocky hill covering my area of responsibility. There was no response. What I'd anticipated had at last come true. The Eighteenth Intelligence Platoon had been ambushed.

When I reestablished communication with the relay station five minutes later, the 405th Thám Kích Thượng (Mountain Combat Intelligence) Company from the division reserve and an artillery section of two 105 mm howitzers were under my command and soon on the way for an intervention mission. Within twenty minutes we arrived at the junction of Highway 14 and the dirt road leading to the battle area one mile away. We were lucky to detect an ambush of about two NVA platoons on the dirt road and drove them into flight before the howitzers took the firing positions.

After contacting the intelligence platoon under attack, I ordered artillery supporting fire, targeted by the platoon leader. Lucky again, though maps of the area by 1965 were not accurate, we hit the enemy positions at the first salvo, and the enemy main force withdrew further into the dense jungles. An NVA platoon stayed behind to maintain contact with my crippled intelligence platoon, which was holding the ground with only fifteen able soldiers and their leader.

I quickly reported the situation to the division before ordering the 405th Mountain Combat Intelligence Company to intervene. The company and I advanced to the battle area, leaving the artillery section under the protection of another infantry company newly arriving to reinforce the operation. In less than ten minutes, my men and I had reached the attacked platoon from behind. My advancing company then charged the enemy with full firepower from the right side.

Upon seeing me, the platoon leader, Second Lieutenant Hùng, got up and shouted, "Come on, I'll have a K-54 for you." The K-54, a China-made pistol, was the favorite war trophy at the time. Then he ran to a dead enemy about thirty yards away whose hand was still holding a K-54. Like a flash, I saw a bareheaded enemy pop up from a foxhole close by and fell Lieutenant Hùng with a burst of his AK. "The lieutenant's dead," a corporal nearest to Hùng yelled. "Let me finish this son of a bitch."

Before I could react, the corporal plunged forward, while the enemy soldier was still trying to replace his empty thirty-round magazine with a full one. The angry corporal discharged his entire .45 Tommy gun magazine onto the enemy soldier. From about twenty yards away, I could see pieces of the communist soldier's skull fly into the air. The soldier was one of the last three or four enemy troops still in foxholes near our position. All were gunned down after their company disengaged and retreated following a short clash with the reinforcing company.

I knelt down beside Hùng, holding his hand. He responded with a reluctant but bright smile, saying, "I won't die, don't you worry!" before two medics carried him under light enemy fire to the dirt road 100 yards behind us, waiting for evacuation.

Hùng was lucky. Later in the day, a doctor told me that only one bullet got in Hùng's chest between two ribs, got out the same way, and pierced through his upper arm without touching any vital part or breaking any rib or arm bone. After that, he was hospitalized for only seven days. In war there are always incredible lucky cases.

We lost one platoon sergeant and eleven soldiers, and twelve were wounded. The enemy left behind twenty-one dead troops.

After evacuation of the KIAs and WIAs, I led a Regional Force platoon just coming from Kontum province to a stronghold in a strongly fenced hamlet half a mile deeper from the ambush site to relieve the platoon that had been there for a month. This platoon had also been under enemy attack but suffered no casualties. The platoon leader reported to me that the enemy force had withdrawn after defeating and capturing all ten militiamen of the nearby hamlet.

When the troops were ready for a quick lunch, an idea flashed in my mind. I looked around the terrain and suddenly felt a strange anxiety at the sight of the high ground 200 meters away. I always trusted my intuition when I needed to make a quick decision. And when I felt I was going the right way, I would stick to it. I was doing the same thing I had done with geometry problems in high school.

So I ordered the incoming platoon leader to send a squad over to the dominating high ground to make sure it was "clean" before the troops had their lunch. Being attacked during mealtime is one of the worst things for combat soldiers.

The platoon leader was reluctant, saying that the enemy had withdrawn, but I told him that when I felt we must do something, my men had to do it. Should anything happen because we didn't, I would never forgive myself. Without a word, he took two squads instead of one and approached the high ground in two lines. I could see how unpleasant he looked.

When they began advancing uphill, an NVA platoon emerged from the ground and opened fire at the two squads and at my position. The two squads fought back, and the enemy fled, leaving eight dead. We suffered two men killed and four wounded, including the platoon leader. An AK bullet hit his wristwatch, burying its tiny parts in his forearm. His platoon sergeant, of the ethnic Bahnar origin, assumed command.

Only five of the communist troops held their ground in narrow foxholes, less than fifty yards from my troops. The enemy usually left a rearguard team like that to delay our pursuit. My troops were determined to get rid of the five, but it proved to be a very difficult task as far as the terrain was concerned. On the patch of red soil, long and dry grass created a perfect natural camouflage. My troops threw about twenty hand grenades without luck, while the enemy could easily observe our movements and hit us with rifle fire and grenades whenever my troops approached.

I left a platoon of the 405th to take care of the five enemy riflemen, assisting the injured regional force platoons. I sent the three remaining 405th platoons to chase the enemy farther west for half a mile as a security measure, but we had no contact with them.

On my part, I was looking for something much bigger than the five communist troops. I sent the new reinforcing company just coming from the division to pursue the retreating communist unit. The division told me that two more reinforcing companies could arrive soon, on my request, if I felt it was necessary to conduct a battalion-sized operation deep into the jungle area to the west.

All soldiers of the Regional Forces platoon begged me to let them have a chance to finish off the five NVA troops before I assigned them any other task. Weighing the psychological advantages, I gave them my consent.

I had a soldier convert a large piece of thick cardboard from a discarded box into a makeshift bullhorn. Another soldier used it to call the enemy troops "to go chiêu hồi" (rally to the RVN side in the Open Arms program). They must have known, as we did, that they had no way to escape.

I knew my troops never liked a slow solution. But I was reasoning differently. I hoped to save the lives of the enemy troops whenever I could. But after about twenty minutes of calling them, our effort failed. We heard them talking to each other at a very close range. Their voices were audible in the dead silence of the surrounding forest. It seemed that four of them wanted to surrender. But the one in the middle, apparently an officer, threatened to shoot any of his fellows who surrendered.

My troops tried every way possible, even shooting M-79 grenades from tall trees, without any luck. The enemy's foxholes were carefully dug and covered, impossible to detect at fifty yards. When I asked the platoon leader if he could use the two 60 mm mortars from the incoming reinforcement, the troops strongly suggested that we shouldn't because if we pulled back our troops to keep them safe from the mortar fire, the enemy would slip away in a few seconds.

At last, two of the 405th troops, a corporal and a PFC, volunteered for a bold mission. The corporal asked just one thing: to help his wife and two children bring his corpse back to his home near Cần Thơ should he be killed. The PFC, who was a single boy, asked for nothing. The two, a Catholic corporal and a Buddhist PFC, prayed for a minute. Then they stripped to their underpants. When crawling on the ground, dry grass would make no sound on bare skin.

Each man held two M-26 hand grenades in his hands, with safety pins removed, and gripped a carbine bayonet between his teeth. Two BARs at the two sides barked intermittently to cover their maneuver.

Quickly approaching the foxholes by the two curved paths, they lost no time in locating the enemy. At a signal from the corporal, both slid quickly forward and dropped the four grenades into the foxholes. Right after the explosions that resulted in a rain of flesh and bone over the small area, the surviving NVA darted from the middle foxhole and ran. The corporal yelled and reached him in a few leaps, caught his collar, and buried the bayonet deep into his chest from behind. The poor enemy fell to the ground.

His eyes reddened with anger, the corporal searched the dead enemy's pockets and found a few pieces of paper showing that he was a second lieutenant, political officer of a NVA company, Third Assault Battalion of the newly infiltrating 325th NVA Division. The corporal was a timid young man, never made even a quarrel with anyone, but he had turned into a fierce tiger in front of me in a minute.

Once again, I realized that anyone could be courageous at the right time and the right place.

I sent the 405th Company back to Kontum at 5:30 PM, leaving the other infantry company to temporarily control the area. I withdrew my relieved regional force and intelligence platoons at 6:00 PM. Upon reaching Highway 14, I met a hamlet chief who knew me well. He told me that an enemy company was taking an ambush position on my way out, but why they did not attack us was unknown.

I didn't believe him until the next morning, when one of my platoons confirmed the story after searching the location. Enemy troops had been preparing about seventy foxholes, twenty yards from the road, obviously for an ambush. No one could tell why the enemy let us get through safely. If they did, my troops of the two badly injured platoons and I would have been gunned down before we were able to react. Such an unsolved mystery reinforced my belief in destiny. Victory or defeat depends on many unknown factors beyond our control.

Early the next morning, the division assigned a two-company task force to me for an operation searching for traces of the assault battalions of the 325th NVA Division halfway to the border area. The operation lasted four days, and we failed to track them down.

On the same morning, General Nguyễn Hữu Có, Corps II commander, an American general, and my division CO, General Nguyễn Xuân Thịnh, visited the place. As commander of the area, I conducted a simple field briefing in English for the three generals.

At my suggestion, General Thịnh awarded the corporal and the PFC, the two brave men who deserved the reward, with the Gallantry Cross with Gold

Star. I didn't put my name on the proposed list for awards, but at last the general pinned a Silver Star on my chest.

As a consequence of this engagement, we lost fourteen men; the enemy left thirty-five killed including the five found on the enemy's path of withdrawal. We captured about twenty AK-47s, some CKC rifles, and a K-54 pistol. Though the enemy suffered twice as many losses, I admitted that it was not our victory, but only a draw. As an unwritten standard, when the enemy's losses were less than three times ours, we should not claim victory, except for propaganda purposes.

This was the largest and strongest enemy force I ever fought during my nineteen years and six months in the military. I had encountered a dozen engagements with the enemy at company size and smaller in operations supporting the strategic hamlets and other special occasions. But this battle was my first against an NVA battalion whose strength might have been as high as 700 soldiers, while I had no more than 400 in three companies and three separate platoons.

KONTUM AND PLEIKU THREATENED

The military situation in the beginning of 1965 in the highland areas became more and more critical. Large North Vietnamese units kept infiltrating many parts of the region. One of their regiments was detected a few miles north of the Dakto district headquarters, or about thirty miles north of Kontum City, the area where the U.S. Army Fourth Infantry Division would fight fierce battles three years later.

Although air strikes inflicted heavy losses to the North Vietnamese regiment, Kontum was apparently under imminent threat. The population was frightened. Many servicemen sent their wives and children to Sài Gòn. Rumors circulated that whenever officers in key jobs in the division headquarters and the provincial military command moved their families out of the city, it would be a time of danger.

Realizing the psychologically critical situation, my division commander issued a verbal order to all the officers holding key positions in the division headquarters to let their families stay calm. A regional force platoon provided protection for the officers' dependents quarters. The chief of staff told us to get our families' portable belongings packed and ready somewhere inside our homes for emergency evacuation, but to have our living rooms look normal as if nothing special was going on.

"Whenever we decide to evacuate your families," he told me, "the division will ensure transportation to safety by helicopters for wives and children of you and my other assistants while you must stay. In the meantime, your families should act accordingly to calm the city population." He also ordered a secret plan be made to evacuate other military dependents and civilians in case we had to withdraw from the area.

"That's an aspect of war my American fellows in the States could never think of," said an American NCO in the MACV team.

AK-47 AND M-16

In early 1965, our troops fought desperately against the better-armed enemy that had newly infiltrated into South Việt Nam. People in the military and outside were praising the Chinese communist-made AK-47 rifle, and so were my troops. They insisted to me that they should be given some AKs. So I borrowed half a dozen AKs from the G-2 arsenal of captured weapons to please my men.

After three or four skirmishes a month later, all of them returned the AKs. They told me that although the AK almost never got stuck because of dirt, there were some other defects. While running, replacing a magazine was a big problem and couldn't be done quickly; the steel box got rusty easily; sometimes the safety and function switch stuck; and if they fired about three magazines in a row, the bullets wouldn't go farther than thirty yards as the barrel expanded when it got hot.

It was at that time many new weapons were brought into South Việt Nam from North Việt Nam. In remote villages, communist guerrillas boasted much about their "sophisticated rifles" from the Soviet Union. For instance, the Soviet WWI bolt-action, three-round-clip rifle K-44 was described by the VC propaganda cadres as "capable of killing ten enemy at one shot." The peasants, like any common credulous people in the world, believed this. Naturally, they talked much bigger about their AKs when they were first used in the northern region of South Việt Nam. The AK quickly became a legend, but I doubted that its fans had ever fought with it in a battle.

The legend produced significant adversary effect on our troops' morale when ARVN troops were equipped with WWII vintage M-1 Garand, Tommy guns, and M-1 and M-2 carbines. Then the U.S. Army introduced the Colt lightweight AR-15 to the Vietnamese.

In 1962, the first batch of the AR-15 (before becoming XM-16) was allocated to the ARVN Special Forces and later to the ARVN Airborne, Marine, and Ranger units. I scrounged a few of them for the division commando soldiers. The AR-15 was a problem sometimes when the cartridge cases stuck in the dirty chamber and could not be extracted. That frightened the soldiers, and many believed that the American weapons were not as good as those of the communist powers.

Although the M-16 had some advantages, many reports against its effectiveness by the media on our side discouraged the troops to some extent. But they discovered the truth before long. Our troops pointed out some defects of the M-16: if it was fired while water clogged the tube, blocked gas could break it and injure the user; the dirty clamber might cause the spent cartridge case to get stuck in it;

the firing rate was rather high (over 550 rounds/minute), but as a result it was quick to run out of ammunition. The defects were repaired before long.

Among its advantages, the lightweight M-16 had a longer effective range (more than 450 yards); the cooling system kept the barrel from getting hot too quickly; it required simple actions to replace the empty magazine, so that could be done more quickly than with the AK-47; an ARVN soldier could carry about 300–450 cartridges, whereas a communist soldier couldn't carry half as many AK rounds; an M-16 bullet had a more powerful impact due to higher muzzle velocity.

However, the AK had a remarkable feature that most reporters missed: it made a frightening ear-splitting sound that might have frightened some of our troops. But that was like the communist propaganda: its bark was worse than its bite.

CAMP HOLLOWAY ATTACK

One night in February 1965, communist sappers attacked Camp Holloway in Pleiku. When the DTOC called me, the attack had begun about five minutes earlier.

The camp was located a mile from downtown Pleiku, more than a mile from the Pleiku Air Base and the ARVN Corp II HQS. Our division G-2 immediately provided suspected enemy mortar locations, and the artillery unit covering Holloway conducted counter-battery fire but did not seem to have hit the right targets. Everything was late. Combined attacks by mortars, B-40s, and sappers rendered heavy losses: about ten Americans were killed and twenty helicopters destroyed.

Camp Holloway was beside the 1,200-meter airstrip built by the French before 1954. In 1962, a U.S. Army aviation company moved in. Its front gate led to National Highway 19. The aircraft, mostly rotary-winged, were supporting the Twenty-second Division on the highland provinces.

Early in the next morning, division G-2, G-3, and I visited the camp. The scene was terrible. It choked my breath for a few seconds. I felt deeply sorry: If we in the division HQS had taken steps to head off the enemy plot, the VC might have given up Holloway or selected another less important objective.

Sometime in January 1965, a combat unit of my Twenty-second Division captured a piece of paper with simple but enigmatic drawings from a dead communist soldier believed to be the commander of a sapper company. It seemed to contain nothing special at first. But looking at it for a few minutes, our G-2 suspected that the drawings were of a military installation somewhere in the three provinces of our Division Tactical Area. He asked me what I thought, as I had been on hundreds of inspection trips, flying a lot on helicopters around the DTA.

Searching my memory, I thought the drawings looked like the area around Corp II HQS, Pleiku Air Base, and Camp Holloway. There were two straight red lines, one shorter than the other. The longer might be the Pleiku Air Base runway, and the shorter was Camp Holloway's landing strip along with rectangular boxes that might stand for the Corps HQS and the MACV compound. There were no details but a few short lines and dots with letters such as A, B, C, and an arrow reaching what I guessed was the Camp Holloway landing strip.

But that was not enough to be sure about the enemy's intention. The G-2 could only send the information to responsible military authorities in Pleiku with directives to focus security effort in the area to head off "possible sappers' attacks at some airstrips and installations in the area." By some glitch in the intelligence system, such preventive measures had not been implemented.

We could understand the full meaning of the captured notes and map only after the attack. The VC 60 mm mortars were set at a low hillside south of Camp Holloway corresponding to the two red small circles on the note. The arrow indicated the line of approach and the point on the fence where sappers would make a "gate" to storm the base camp. If we had examined the paper with much more patience and taken more active measures, we could have done something to nip the enemy's plot in the bud.

MOVING TO THE COASTAL AREA

In the first week of March, 1965, the Twenty-second Infantry Division HQS was ordered to move to Bình Định province to conduct a long-term campaign, neutralizing the enemy pressure around every key district town and stronghold.

Responding to the American escalated bombing over North Việt Nam, the communist forces launched a vigorous offensive everywhere to diminish government control around our key towns and army bases. Many hamlet militias and members of local administrations, along with their dependents, fled their hamlets for safety in well-defended district towns and Qui Nhơn City, even before the communist guerrillas attacked the hamlets. The 10,000 refugees flooding into Qui Nhơn caused many problems for the city, from housing to food supply and health care.

Meanwhile, political chaos in Sài Gòn continued and dealt a deadly blow to the troops' morale. It looked as if South Việt Nam was counting its weeks and months. The civilian government of Dr. Phan Huy Quát, which had been in power since February, seemed to be unable to restore political stability.

General Nguyễn Xuân Thịnh was relieved, and sources from the JGS in Sài Gòn cited the previous lost battles as indications of his incompetence. I was against such a remark. Under the general, three regiments and some dozen regional force companies were confronting at least two communist divisions and a mortar regiment, all fresh from North Việt Nam, plus two local regiments and several local companies, not including guerrilla squads in villages under communist control. An American fellow officer said to me that in such a situation, even if North Vietnamese army commander-in-chief Võ Nguyên Giáp had been doing General Thịnh's job, Giáp would have suffered the same if not heavier losses.

After six years operating in the three highlands provinces, the division was to begin a new chapter in its history in the coastal areas. I left Kontum with some nostalgia.

The military situation was more critical. Highway 19 between Pleiku and Qui Nhơn was closed after a battalion-sized ambush and many smaller attacks on posts in the area by an enemy division.

In Kontum province, Toumorong district headquarters was overrun one night after fierce fighting. The artillerymen had to lower their howitzers and fire without projectiles as makeshift flamethrowers, repelling the enemy for a short time. By the early morning, the communist force controlled the district HQS and executed all of the artillerymen who were still alive.

The Forty-second Infantry Regiment Light CP and one battalion were ambushed and suffered heavy losses early one morning right outside the small town of Tân Cảnh, a kilometer from the regiment barracks. The regimental commander was killed. They were on the way to rescue the Dakto district headquarters, which had come under attack the previous evening. The district forces escaped to safety that night.

A land development delegation from Sài Gòn visiting Lệ Thanh district some twenty miles west of Pleiku provincial town was ambushed; several civilians and military servicemen were killed or captured. The rescue force was also ambushed and suffered more losses and captives.

We were in a very difficult situation, and the enemy became bolder than in previous years. Although it suffered rather heavy military losses, the communist side gained much more on the propaganda front. It was obvious to the people that we were on the defense and the communists had the initiative.

When my division headquarters moved to the Regional Force Training Center in Phù Cát district, the coastal landscapes in many places along National Highway 1 were tainted with war destruction. Many coconut fields that had been green and cool and clean to the sight a year before were now a mess of trunks and leaves broken and seared by bombs, artillery, and 20 mm cannon shells from our side.

A foreign reporter going on a trip with me in the area said that if a communist poet saw the scenes, he might have had inspiration to write some verses accusing our side of war destruction. What we destroyed in war was easy to notice, but what our enemy was doing was much more atrocious but not as easily seen and reported by foreign reporters.

DIVISION G-5

Before the division headquarters moved to the coastal province of Bình Định, I turned over the security control of Highway 14 area between Kontum and

Pleiku to the two adjacent districts. At the same time, I was appointed assistant chief of staff for G-5 or Psychological Warfare (psywar).

When I assumed the job as division G-5, I was only twenty-eight, a first lieutenant, several years younger and three grades lower than my counterparts in the U.S. armed forces. My Vietnamese counterparts, the other assistants to the chief of staff, were all captains. In 1965, our armed forces still suffered a shortage of officers. Promotions were limited. Among more than 300 officers of the division, nearly 100 were first lieutenants. It was said that first lieutenants created the traffic jam on the road of promotion. I knew I needed more experience, so I sought advice from anyone I could, not only those in the military but any wise man I knew.

Spring 1965 saw the general situation in my division area deteriorating. Troop morale was low, and government popularity was dropping. The enemy was gaining control over more land and people. In such a situation, the psychological front should have been reinforced to the largest extent to confront the unfavorable situation. But the RVN and the U.S. high commands did not elect such a course of action.

In Qui Nhơn, communist terrorists blew up Việt Cường Hotel. Among some two dozen victims, fifteen were Americans. Intelligence information later alleged that the young man who placed a pack of explosives on the counter in the main lobby was a Popular Force soldier. His mother, wife, and children were being held hostage in the VC-controlled area and had been threatened with execution if he failed to do what he was told. Holding the close relatives of an official or army soldier to compel him to conduct bomb attacks aimed at the military, administrative, or economic targets was known all over the country as one of the communist terrorist tactics. He fled the hotel but was killed on the spot, along with a VC sapper escorting him.[1]

PSYWAR ORGANIZATIONS

My job at G-5 related to a domain that was considered by our army and our allied militaries as necessary but not of the first importance. Most of what I learned came from the experiences and practices of the veterans in the psyops front. We had no specific doctrine, no systematic guidance, and training courses and materials were insufficient. The organization of the psywar branch seemed not very effective. Mine was on-the-job training, and I relied heavily on my intuition and initiative to perform my tasks.

From the time that the republic was declared in South Việt Nam, the Psychological Warfare Department of the Ministry of Defense was strengthened, and each military unit from battalion level and higher had its psywar office, known as J-5, G-5 and S-5. Since 1961, a deputy chief of staff for psywar had been appointed to each headquarters to take care of the operation. Some planners in Sài Gòn advocated a system similar to the communist military commissariat with decisive power to lead the soldiers in the war of ideology. Both military authorities who never wanted to share power and liberal officers who hated to see anything that sounded like the oppressive system of the Communist Party applied to the armed forces immediately rejected the idea. So the psywar branch had to be content with a deputy chief of staff in charge of psywar.

The system worked well in some aspects, but rendered no miraculous outcome as people had expected. Psywar activities were supposed to raise the troops' morale, to win the people's hearts and minds, and to undermine the enemy's willingness to fight. Thus psywar tasks were directed at our troops, the people, and the enemy. As a division G-5, I had to supervise the S-5 sections of the three regiments and other separate units. But my heavier loads of psywar tasks came from other various areas, out of the psywar hierarchy.

To attain the first goal, many things needed to be done to enhance troop morale. Taking better care of them and their dependents' living conditions was the greatest concern. Indoctrination was a second priority.

Compared with other countries, military servicemen in South Việt Nam were paid much less. After 1954, more young men with increasingly higher education and training degrees joined the armed forces; however, the military pay rate remained the same. Military salary was considerably lower than civilian employees in the government with the same level of education and much lower than those in the private sector. A PFC received monthly pay about 10 percent less than an unskilled common worker earning minimum wages. After the military leaders took over the government, military pay was increased, but it remained below that of civilian jobs. A soldier's wife and children, therefore, lived a life of poverty in military housing and relied solely on what he got from the payroll. The government and the armed forces did assist families by providing some health care, such as dispensaries, maternity clinics, kindergartens, a PX system, and simple housing facilities. But an inadequate budget limited the results.

Discipline was the G-1's responsibility. I only supported him and dealt with psychological matters. Discipline in our army, as in many noncommunist countries, could be maintained only at a moderate level. Although many Vietnamese praised the "iron discipline" of the Japanese and Korean armies, no one had ever supported a harsh discipline system, which common people confused with authoritarianism.

On the other hand, our people who advocated freedom of thought didn't feel like supporting the idea of political indoctrination in the armed forces as well as in the national school system. In the Vietnamese communist military, iron discipline was strongly supported by political indoctrination that relied on propaganda techniques and the party's "machine of fear." Our side was not good at propaganda and had a much smaller and much less brutal machine of fear.

So the military had to rely partly on the personal characters of low-level commanders to improve troop morale and discipline, whereas teaching and indoctrination played a humble role. I had to admit that as a division G-5, I failed to reach the goals I set for myself in the field of enhancing troop morale. It was a difficult task that required many combined actions from many sides; my action as a G-5 was just one of them.

In the early 1960s, infantry soldiers were fighting with inadequate logistic support. They had to manage themselves to survive in the combat environment. Food was a problem. They could not rely on combat rations, which were rarely allocated. In most units, soldiers had to cook rice once for the whole day in operation. They used to prepare food when their units took a long enough rest or a night position, carefully avoiding detection by the enemy by cooking in a foxhole to conceal the light. In daylight they dug several small furrows, then covered them with dead leaves and twigs to dissipate smoke. The metal helmet was the best makeshift cooker.

On long operations, if resupply—often by air—failed to reach a unit, it would be a disaster. Most troops learned to reduce their meals for a few days before the scheduled resupply just in case. There were times when troops ran out of rice, and they had to search for anything edible in the forests.

Under such hardships, many of them were still fighting bravely enough to deserve appreciation.

THE MILITARY DEPENDENTS

In units at regiment level and higher, there were military social services sections, with Women Army Corp officers and NCOs serving as social workers. They took care of services such as dispensaries, maternity clinics, kindergartens, and primary schools supporting the military dependents. Under favorable conditions, the service could also help the dependents grow vegetables and do handicraft work to earn extra money.

At regiment level or in smaller units that moved infrequently, there were quarters for dependents that made the management of support much easier. However, some combat companies—such as reconnaissance or mountain recon—had greater problems properly serving dependents because the companies were often on the move to distant areas. Sometimes, after the unit moved to a place where it might be in operation for a few weeks, a contingent of wives and children would follow and camp somewhere nearby. If the situation permitted, some dependents even stayed with the soldiers in temporary bunkers.

Of course, the Vietnamese communist military in South Việt Nam and in North Việt Nam allowed its soldiers nothing like that. It ignored the military dependents almost completely. On our side, no leader would be willing to impose such rigid measures because of political and humanitarian concerns.

The military servicemen's wives and children shared with them little honor but much suffering. In the war, what imprinted deeply in my heart were the two typical sights of the soldiers' wives: one was killed while covering the babies with her own body in a pocked bunker under enemy fire; another with white mourning turbans over her head and those of her children, sobbing beside her husband's coffin while tears dried up, leaving her eyes dark red and hollow.

The military dependents created a sizeable onerous problem for the combat efficiency of the ARVN combat units, particularly in critical situations that required quick action and full mobility. During large-scale retreats, many units could not assemble their full strength, as soldiers were busy taking care of their wives and children, and that caused chaotic disorder on roads and docks.

The issue of military dependents represented a significant aspect of the war that was unknown to readers of most writing about the Việt Nam War.

My responsibility as the G-5 partly related to the military dependent affairs by mainly providing advice and support to the Military Social Services Section. However, sometimes I had to handle some operations of this kind myself.

In late spring 1965, my division virtually moved all of its subordinate units to the coastal area, leaving the two highland provinces under the responsibility of the newly established Biệt Khu 24 (Special Zone 24). Dependents of the division troops were stuck in Kontum because a strong enemy force blocked Highway 19 to Qui Nhơn, and air transportation for them was unavailable. One day, about eighty women and children, dependents of an infantry battalion from Kontum, reached Qui Nhơn after a two-week trip. They had traveled about 120 miles: 50 miles on a local bus and nearly 70 miles on foot, crossing enemy-infected jungle areas. They had to beg villagers for food in the last 20 miles of the trip. They had undertaken the journey just to see their husbands in a battalion that was engaged in operations for two months in the coastal area. The battalion HQS had failed to help the troops make contact with their dependents and send them money. I was so sorry to see the emaciated women and children in tattered clothes that exposed their sun-burned skin. It took us several days to arrange for their housing and health care.

A few weeks later, a swarm of other military dependents occupied two U.S. Air Force C-130s at Kontum airfield right after the two planes had discharged emergency supplies for the province. The women demanded that they and their children be flown to Qui Nhơn. Police and MPs found no way to expel them. Thanks to the help of our MACV advisors, we were able to get approval from the U.S. Air Force command in Sài Gòn to use the two planes to move the women and children to Qui Nhơn. Division G-4, G-5, and Social Service, however, had to send their NCOs along on flights to make sure that safety rules were strictly enforced.

PROTECTION OF THE PEOPLE

In many operations, when our combat units were confronted with powerful enemy fire, it was sometimes unavoidable that artillery or air support injured civilians and destroyed their property. Many times we dropped leaflets and used loudspeakers mounted on helicopters to warn the civilians to leave their hamlets before the bombing commenced. But most of the time, communist troops would not let them escape so that they could employ poor peasants as human shields.

Communist troops sometimes directed sniper fire from churches, pagodas, and temples and especially from the ancient Chàm towers, historic temples of the Chàm ethnic group whose ancient nation is today's Central Việt Nam. The guerrillas were certain that in most cases our troops dared not return fire at such places unless the VC force posed a deadly threat to the ARVN troops.

The Twenty-second Infantry Division had a strict policy to control the use of firepower to avoid civilian casualties. Besides, all planned artillery and air attacks had to be cleared by the division artillery command. If the objectives were in a populated area, the division artillery would not approve the fire request if the artillery strikes might cause great losses to innocent people.

My concerns about innocent victims in war originated from my years living under the threat of bombs and shells. In the Twenty-second Division, the G-5 was in the "Operation Bloc," not in the "Logistics Bloc." So I had a role in all operations planning that related to civilian safety and other domains of G-5's responsibility.

In one of the meetings, the G-3 and I argued that the bombing requested by a regiment at the helicopter landing zone would kill at least a score of villagers, while we were not certain whether the enemy would suffer more than fifty casualties. In many similar discussions, the American senior advisor supported our proposals as to call off the operation or to shift the LZs somewhere else. In almost all of the cases, the final results of the operation justified our argument.

Once at 9:00 PM, a district chief near our division Jump CP came to see us for approval of an artillery attack against what he said was a communist battalion in the large cornfield of a village about three miles away. He believed it was preparing for an offensive against his headquarters. An enemy battalion was something not negligible, so the chief of staff held an emergency meeting at 9:15 PM. After a quick check, G-2 people and I found out that the information was probably wrong. Late that afternoon, two informers working for G-2 and G-5 had visited the village and had seen nothing out of the ordinary. But more important was that the village had a population of more than 500, and most villagers sympathized with the government side.

The division G-2, G-3, and I strongly objected to the request. If an artillery attack had been approved as requested, a number of villagers might have been injured because the target area was so close to their homes. So an alternative measure was taken by sending a reconnaissance platoon to the village. The recon platoon made contact with only ten to fifteen VC.

Similar examples were numerous in the Việt Nam War. Based on my own experiences, if artillery attacked the VC troops who were present in a village but accidentally killed some civilians, these victims' relatives would bear little rancor. But shelling where no communist troops were hiding in a hamlet would certainly create lifelong animosity against the government.

To win people's hearts and minds, the Civic Action program brought help to peasants. In 1965, the division tactical area was allocated a Civic Action quarterly budget of VN$100,000 (US$700) to provide peasants emergency assistance such as food, clothes, and public construction repairs. Two Civic Action teams from Corps 2 were assigned to my division. They operated in villages along with Medical Civic Action Program (MEDCAP) teams to help villagers in various tasks. The programs produced favorable effects that could have been more successful if larger support had been provided. Since 1964, peasants in war zones suffered more and more loss of life and property, and no relief was large enough to ease their sorrows.

Toward the enemy troops, our principal tasks were distributing messages through leaflets, radio broadcasts, and loudspeaker airplanes. In addition, the G-5 was to treat prisoners of war with care in matters of food, health, and proper treatment. In 1965, the Chiêu Hồi program began to draw more communist troops to our side and was to become a successful policy in the following years.

THE PRISONERS

My job at G-5 Section required cooperation with G-2 on matters that involved political prisoners and prisoners of war. Until sometime in 1962, Sài Gòn had not classified the captive communist guerrillas as prisoners of war under the Geneva Convention because they were not fighting conventional warfare but mostly conducting terrorist attacks. They did not fight in an organized armed force and had no uniform, as stipulated in the Convention. They were detained as criminal prisoners in the so-called Trại Tù Phiến Cộng (communist rebel prisoners' camps).

After 1962, prisoners fighting in the so-called National Liberation Front were given POW status, and the camps' names were changed to Trại Tù Binh Cộng Sản Việt Nam (communist POW camps). Other communist insurgents, especially terrorists, were held in common prisons and tried as common or special war criminals under Law 10/59. There were International Red Cross representatives working beside the six POW camps.

The U.S. combat units that came and fought in South Việt Nam from 1965 to 1972 did not keep communist POWs. Communist soldiers captured in operations were handed over to the POW camps of the RVN. The policy helped the U.S. armed forces to avoid complicated problems concerning POW matters that had once caused trouble to the American high command in the Korean War, particularly at the negotiation table in Pan Munjong.

In many cases, true communist rebels were arrested without concrete evidence. If tried in any court—including courts-martial—they would be acquitted due to the lack of evidence. Therefore, the Sài Gòn government had to rely on the so-called administrative measure (or detention). The measure existed in several countries as a way to detain individuals who were considered dangerous to the community even though they had not committed any crimes, such as the violently insane.

Under the measure, a communist rebel arrested without the evidence necessary to be tried in court could be classified as an "element dangerous to the community." A committee of administrative measure at the province level would review the case and decide the case by voting. An inmate of this kind could be acquitted or given a term of up to twelve months, renewable once and no more. After the terms, the detainee would be released or tried in court if there was new evidence. In South Việt Nam, a prisoner must be freed on the last day of his or her term. Releasing paperwork must have been completed by that very day.

The Twenty-second Division had a representative in that committee along with others from local intelligence, security, and police services, the chairman of the provincial people's committee, and a judge from the court. Sometimes I attended the session along with the division G-2.

We discovered that many of the detainees were innocent citizens who had been arrested in operational areas as suspects without evidence. Communist cadres outside and in jail could try to persuade those detainees to switch sides after they were released, bearing resentment for unjust incarceration. So our division's representatives always voted to release new captives we had reason to believe were innocent.

Usually only those who were really working for the communists but were not deeply involved in communist activities, and whose cases lacked evidence for formal prosecution, were sentenced. I was opposed to the practice. It caused more harm on the propaganda front, but I could not think of any reasonable substitute policy. Vietnamese and foreigners in antiwar organizations and human rights activists fiercely criticized the South Vietnamese government for the detentions. However, no one ever said anything against the similar measure imposed on the North Vietnamese.

Most North Vietnamese were well informed about Resolution 49 of the North Việt Nam Parliament Standing Committee, 1961. I had access to the text of the resolution in the *Nhan Dan Daily,* the Communist Party's newspaper printed in Hà Nội and collected by the library of the ARVN Psywar Department. I also got more related information from interrogations of the "chiêu hồi" and the POWs. Resolution 49 was an efficient tool for Hà Nội, along with the food rationing system, to keep the North Vietnamese under strict control of the Communist Party.

Under the North Vietnamese measure, a police chief at district level or higher, not a committee, had full authority to send anyone in his district to the reeducation camps (the official title of most prison camps in North Việt Nam) for three-year terms, *renewable unlimited times.* The red tape in North Việt Nam aggravated the prisoners' fate. A prisoner's term began when the prison office completed his or her document, which could take several months after he or she was actually incarcerated. On the date the term ended, the prison office began the release process, and the prisoner would be freed only when the process was completed. The release process could take several months, sometimes one or more years. One of several release documents required confirmation of authorities of the prisoner's village, stating their approval of his or her return. Consequently, an unlucky inmate could stay in jail five years for a single three-year term.

After having served the terms, a North Vietnamese prisoner might return to his home village, but not if the local authorities refused to accept him. He would, in that case, be held in the prison camp waiting for authorities somewhere else who would welcome him into their community. Possibly he might be waiting until the end of his life. I would learn much more about the prisoners in North Việt Nam when I was thrown in a communist concentration camp after South Việt Nam collapsed in April 1975.

AN ARVN MARINES' VICTORY

After more than a year suffering heavy losses to the communist attacks, including ones that overran some district HQS in mid-1965, the ARVN in Bình Định province began to recover and to deal some spectacular blows to the enemy.

The first victory was achieved in May 1965 by an ARVN Marine battalion in operation at a place north of Bồng Sơn, about eighty miles north of Qui Nhơn. Two or three communist battalions launched a night attack on the Marines, whose temporary defense included a simple concertina barbed-wire fence.

The Marines were supported by four 75 mm howitzers from Battle Group CP, collocated with its remaining battalion about a mile to the south. Firing at a direction perpendicular to the enemy axis of attack, the 75 mm was accurate enough to create a fire barrage very close to the defense line to repulse waves of assault.

The attacking force withdrew before dawn, leaving 306 of its troops dead on the battleground, as I saw with my own eyes. The Marines lost about a dozen killed, not including scores of the wounded. Little of the battle was reported in U.S. newspapers.

AMERICAN COMBAT SOLDIERS ARRIVE

The first week of March saw the arrival of the first U.S. Marine combat soldiers in Đà Nẵng. In May, a U.S. Marine division and other infantry units landed in Corp Tactical Zones I, II, and III. A short time later, an amphibious task force consisting of a U.S. Marine battalion and its attached landing craft unit arrived at Phú Thạnh, a few miles south of Qui Nhơn. Then American logistic units arrived, building a large tent city along Gành Ráng, Qui Nhơn City's southern beach.

Coming along with them were noisy military trucks, helicopters, and equipment to provide entertainment and recreation for the young GIs. The appearance of the quiet seaside city changed in a short time. The war was going to a new phase in a province already badly torn by bloody fighting. In this new phase, U.S. forces began to play the major role in the ground war, and the Americans began planning for what they thought they could do with their firepower, money, and technology.

Reactions from our officers and enlisted men varied widely. Some believed that the Americans would win the war and that South Việt Nam would stand on its own feet and develop. Some were not so optimistic, saying that the American presence would undermine our just cause and spoil our society with dollars, bombs, and the American way of life. But almost no one ever predicted that the U.S. forces would be defeated.

Actually, most ARVN officers were optimistic about the future of our side after the statements and promises of the U.S. presidents and statesmen, ensuring assistance to the RVN to preserve freedom and prosperity. But we also were greatly concerned about the apparent expansion of war. To me, the grim sign of more killing was looming on the horizon.

EIGHTEEN

Hearts and Minds

THE MILITARY GOVERNMENT

After the Ngô Đình Diệm regime was overthrown in November 1963, the political situation in South Việt Nam was deteriorating seriously. Under the power of military generals, the consecutive governments headed by civilian politicians were replaced by coup attempts. Sài Gòn was in chaos. After President Ngô Đình Diệm was slain, no political leader of his caliber could restore the central power that could answer the critical situation of a country just delivered from a dictatorship. The danger of war was rising high.

With a population of 18 million in the 1960s, the RVN would have had a large corps of thousands of national politicians and statesmen who could be elected to lead the nation, if there had not been the bloody conflict after 1945. When the Vietnamese nationalist side recovered full sovereignty from the French in 1955, there was a serious shortage of political talents to lead the ruling system in the South, largely because the communist tyrants had successfully run relentless purging campaigns from 1946 to 1954, getting rid of a great number of prospective leaders capable of running a nation. These were the devoted patriots and revolutionaries of my father's age and younger.

Before the first republic was established by Ngô Đình Diệm, Việt Nam had not had a real political arena where young politicians were introduced and trained. That led to the leadership crisis in the years of war. Suffering incessant political cleansing campaigns by the French and the communists, the surviving respectable nationalist leaders did not have the time, conditions, or opportunities to establish strong parties or supporting groups with active and brilliant lieutenants who could construct effective political agendas and carry them out. The South Vietnamese and the U.S. government had very few options among

Vietnamese notables who could lead the country with both popularity and effectiveness.

The nationalist parties that should have had a key role in political and psychological warfare were not strong enough to confront their common enemy. The most powerful of them, the VNQDĐ and the Đại Việt, contributed to the national effort to defend South Việt Nam but not as much as they needed to. After 1954, they continued their presence in the political arena as more political than revolutionary entities. The regime of Ngô Đình Diệm cracked down heavily on both groups.

The VNQDĐ had strong grassroots in Huế and the provinces of Quảng Trị, Thừa Thiên, and Quảng Nam, with many thousands of members serving in the Popular Force and the Regional Force and the ARVN regular units, too. The Đại Việt had its infrastructure in the same area and a smaller number of members in the local military, but this party had a large number of members among the intelligentsia. More Đại Việt than Việt Quốc members held cabinet posts in the RVN government after November 1963.

Although the nationalist parties were not strong enough to greatly influence the war outcome and political stability, they did contribute to the construction of democracy, freedom, and justice for South Việt Nam. Their members elected as senators and representatives in Congress often wielded their voices effectively to influence the executive power. They did not constitute a perfect democracy as people wished, but they contributed a good deal by struggling for the rights and interests of the people. The RVN had many highly qualified scholars, administrators, technologists, and experts, but was greatly short of public leaders and political cadres who paid sufficient attention to the people's concerns to attract active popular support. In fact, we had more ardent patriotic leaders than smart statesmen.

In May 1965, the government of Dr. Phan Huy Quát, the premier, and Phan Khắc Sửu, the chief of state, the two respectable national celebrities, failed to restore national stability and resigned, surrendering ruling power to a military junta. On June 19, Generals Nguyễn Văn Thiệu and Nguyễn Cao Kỳ officially assumed power from the civilian government. After November 1963, consecutive cabinets headed by civilian statesmen had proven themselves incapable of dealing with the troubled situation. Many of us ARVN officers hoped that the military leaders would pay more attention to soldiers' lives, fight administrative red tape and corruption in the government agencies, and promote an efficient anticommunist front. I believed that the two generals, young and energetic, would do something better for the country with strong support from the young officer corps and the troops.

A few months later, the new government held the first RVN Armed Forces Congress. All commanders from company level and higher were to attend. It was a success, as officers eagerly lent their support to the new leaders. Thiệu and Kỳ were free of corruption, attractive, and had good reputations in and out of the military. Only a week after the military government assumed ruling power, a VC terrorist attack killed more than forty people. The famous floating restaurant Mỹ Cảnh was attacked by two powerful directional mines, the DH-10, a Claymore-type antipersonnel mine made in China. Ten of the dead were American soldiers and civilians; more than thirty others were Vietnamese civilians.

The terrorist was captured not long after the crime. Months later at the Sài Gòn court-martial, the judge asked him why he had been so heartless as to bring death to those he knew were mostly Vietnamese civilians. He coldly said, "All civilians who collaborated with the Sài Gòn government must suffer the risk of war."

The Mỹ Cảnh incident took place three months after the car bomb attack at the American embassy. Two Americans and 18 Vietnamese civilians were killed and 150 were wounded. A series of bomb attacks aimed at the Americans gave me a feeling that the VC was determined to confront the Americans, after Red China and the Soviet Union provided Hà Nội with generous support for its war effort in South Việt Nam.

AT THE POLITICAL WARFARE CONFERENCE

About five months after taking over the G-5 shop, I went to Sài Gòn to attend the Armed Forces Political Warfare Conference. The meeting included all leading officers of the newly reformed Political Warfare branch from regiment level and higher. I had thirty minutes to present my opinion as the Twenty-second Division G-5. I had a dozen issues to discuss.

In that kind of conference, people often presented positive accounts of their job performance and favorable information with figures to prove how successful their units had been. I didn't think it was a good way to contribute our opinions to the conference. Speaking to the audience for exactly thirty minutes, I admitted that the situation in my division area was critical. Our soldiers were not well supported, and their wives and children were suffering both from danger of war and their living conditions, which were far lower than that of poor farmers. The troops' fighting spirit was dangerously low. I frankly told the audience that a large segment of the peasants were under firm control of the communist infrastructure, whereas a number of our army units didn't care enough about the safety of the villagers in the operations. I fiercely criticized the "body count" reports that sometimes included civilian victims.

As for the enemy, I reckoned that our efforts to undermine their morale and to persuade them to join our side were not succeeding. I strongly argued that we young officers, the flowers of the nation's youth, should have been ashamed of our inability to defend our land and that the young Americans had to fight and die for us on our own soil.

In a formal conference like this one, few officers would like to introduce such sensitive topics to the audience.

My conclusion was that if the officer corps was not doing its best to defend the country with our own blood, there wouldn't be any land similar to Taiwan in which to take refuge. The audience of about 200 officers stood up, enthusiastically applauded, and yelled to show their approval.

Before saying the last sentence, I reminded the Chinese translator not to translate it into Chinese. But unexpectedly, a colonel from the Chinese Nationalist Army Advisory Team stepped forward and hugged me, saying in Vietnamese: "Thank you for reminding the translator not to let us hear your remark relating to our painful defeat. But I grew up in Hà Nội and was speaking Vietnamese before joining the Chinese Nationalist Army. I do appreciate your speech."

After the conference, General Huỳnh Văn Cao, commanding officer of the Polwar (General Political Warfare Department), and his chief of staff, Colonel Nguyễn Vĩnh Nghi, approved my transfer to their GPWD. But it would take me a long time to persuade the division commander to let me transfer to Sài Gòn. In war, every commander prefers subordinates who have been in a job a long time and are used to the work, even if they have only average capability like me. Personnel rotation was not applied as required by a regulation in the ARVN, and that was one of the major defects of the RVN military management.

OTHER ERRANDS

Unlike in other armies, what the ARVN G-5 would accomplish depended to a large degree on the tradition of the unit and how the unit commander wanted things done. Sometimes personality was also involved. That was why I occasionally did my part to assist other colleagues in fulfilling their duties. At least twice I was running around helping the G-4 do his job as sometimes he did to help me.

Once an ARVN Regional Force company defending an outpost in Củng Sơn, Phú Yên province, thirty miles west of Tuy Hòa (the provincial capital), was in danger of being forced to withdraw because the troops would run out of food in two days. The only way to resupply was by air, but no plane would be available for a week. All helicopters of the supporting U.S. Army Aviation units were tied to operations elsewhere. The division G-4 was trying his best with the official channels, but so far he had failed to solve the problem. The advisory team could do nothing to assist, either. So Captain Arthur P. Carroll, my advisor, and I were asked to help. Anything related to the troops' morale was part of the G-5's responsibility. Moreover, I was one of the staff officers who spoke English not too badly for the Americans' ears and had won their trust.

At that time, a U.S. Marine battalion had just landed and was stationed at Phú Thạnh, a few miles from Qui Nhơn. Soon after the Marines landed, we established good relations with them, assisting them in solving some problems. The battalion CO always welcomed me, even though I was only a first lieutenant. So we turned to him as the last resort.

From the city, people could see a U.S. Navy carrier with a score of H-34 helicopters standing by to support the Marines. If the Vietnamese wanted to use one of those helicopters, a request had to go up to our JGS, then to MACV, then to the Seventh Fleet. The Pacific Command in Hawaii would make final approval. That might have taken a few days, while we had only twenty-four hours to do something before the hungry troops would be forced to leave the outpost.

Captain Carroll and I brought about our problem to the Marine battalion CO. I insisted that the civilians and dependents of the Vietnamese troops knew only that we, American and Vietnamese military forces as allies, had many helicopters standing by while 100 freedom fighters were left in hunger. The Marine colonel was quick to help. He sent a message to the carrier's CO, requesting some H-34s to make a long-range security reconnaissance for his battalion. The outpost was within that security zone. And along with his men on the reconnaissance mission, food supplies were brought to the outpost in time.

At about the same time, Phú Bổn province needed help. The province headquarters requested air transportation for emergency rice supplies to Cheo Reo (provincial town) and the three districts, but all the answers were negative. The Americans at Qui Nhơn Air Base advised us to talk directly to the U.S. Seventh Air Force HQS in Sài Gòn. Our G-5 offered help to G-4 again. After two hours of tiresome communication by telephone, flights from Qui Nhơn to Cheo Reo on USAF C-130s for the purpose were approved.

It was a great success. But a week later, Captain Carroll and I were at a lunch table in Qui Nhơn Air Base with a USAF officer. At the end of the lunch, the USAF officer advised me that the next time I dealt with a request for air supply, I should be careful. He said his staff had evidence that some Vietnamese in charge of the emergency supply had collected tens of thousands of VN$ by smuggling consumer items such as cigarettes and alcoholic beverages on the flights. I was so ashamed that I could not say a word. The American assured me: "Of course, we know for certain that you are not aware of the shady affair. That's why we're disclosing it to you." He also said that his boss reported the wrongdoing up their channels and to the Vietnamese authorities.

AMERICAN FRIENDS

Thus the friendship developed between the fighting fellows, American and Vietnamese. For years in the Twenty-second Division I had many American friends. In 1962, Lieutenant Colonel Anthony C. Tencza, a good friend of mine, was killed in Kontum. In 1965, another American friend died in my arms. He was USAF Major William W. McAllister. He came to serve my division flying the L-19. He and other L-19 pilots, Vietnamese and American, worked hard during that period. There were always large demands for air cover everywhere, and pilots as well as observers were often exhausted. Any time I badly needed an L-19, usually for emergency leaflet missions, he helped, even when he was tired after a long flight.

One morning in April 1965, McAllister volunteered for a mission, providing air cover for an important convoy. That was his last day in the Twenty-second Division. The next morning he would fly to Sài Gòn before ending his tour in Việt Nam. But he volunteered for the mission. He was concerned about the safety of moving a battalion on a convoy without air cover. When he completed the task and landed at the airstrip close to the division CP, he asked me to join him on his L-19 to Qui Nhon, so that we could spend the night in the city with other American and Vietnamese friends of his before his departure.

I told him I would be in Qui Nhơn later in the afternoon, as I had a lot of things to do at the time. So I drove him to the airstrip. A moment later, he started the engine, taxied the plane to the dirt runway, revved up, and took off. At the time, VC guerrillas may have been lurking in the area. Suddenly the plane turned upside down, plunged to the ground, and righted up again. It happened so fast, like a flash of a quick movie clip. I ran my jeep to the crashed plane, removed the extinguisher, and gave it to a soldier who had just come to help, showing him what to do in case of fire. Then I jerked open the cockpit door to reach McAllister.

He was seriously injured, but he was partly conscious. When I tried with all my strength to pull him out before the plane exploded because of the fuel leaking in many places, he recognized me. He whispered my name along with something else I couldn't make out. With my small size, it took me a great effort to pull him out. He died a few seconds later after other Americans of the advisory team rushed to the scene.

In our army there was a myth about many who died on their last day with their combat units before they were to leave for a new assignment, schooling, leave, or checking out of the military. Therefore, old soldiers were very careful on their last day in the war zone.

Deep in my heart, I felt much sympathy for the young Americans who were sent to fight for my country, in a war that was too complicated for them to understand, as some of them told me.

The presence of U.S. troops in Qui Nhơn created various reactions. Civilians who had experienced the war with the French, even suffered from the French colonial military atrocities, were hostile to U.S. troops. They saw nothing different between the French and the Americans in their appearances. During the war, and until now, the Vietnamese communists have been using these outward similarities as the basic strategy in their propaganda, which had had some success. To Vietnamese peasants, French and American soldiers looked the same—eyes, hair, and skin color, high nose, helmet, fatigue dress—so they must act the same way in war, they thought, until months later when they had chances to learn about the GIs' behavior.

There were people who hated communists but did not favor the U.S. presence, whereas many others admitted that the U.S. combat troops were really needed to save South Việt Nam. It was apparent that there were many others who didn't care what the Americans were doing except for the fact that the GIs brought them booming business with large profits.

The first complaints I received from the city people were about the GIs serving in logistic units, stationed in a tent-city along the beach. Rowdy GIs sometimes teased teenage girls on their way to and from school. Not much, just some amorous comments and light slapping on their backs, but that was enough to scare the girls and to make them and other people angry. The GIs apparently were unaware of the unfavorable reaction. They thought it was nothing serious.

Once a group of GIs asked me, "Sir, how come many of the Vietnamese schoolgirls are holding each other's hands and shoulders walking on the streets? They look like lesbians." It took me some effort to explain: "In Việt Nam, boys and girls holding hands of friends of the same sex is a habit, not a sign of homosexuality. Not all social standards in America and in Việt Nam are similar." The questions, however, recalled my first time in America in 1957. A month after arriving at Fort Benning, I found out that many notions I had about America were wrong. I believed many American soldiers had similar experiences after a time in Việt Nam, providing that they had opportunities to have contact with everyday Vietnamese.

The city of Qui Nhơn became highly boisterous after the Americans arrived. A lot of people made good money by running bars, nightclubs, bordellos, car wash stations, and laundries. Swarming whores and rocketing prices angered many city people. A fist-size piece of ice cost three times the price of a bottle of soft drink because GIs in the tent city each paid one dollar for a thirty-pound block of ice and put it under their folding cots to cool down the boiling air in the tents. Before GIs came, the block cost only twenty cents.

In the first few months there were some incidents that damaged the relations between the newly arrived GIs and the local people. One day, at a garbage dumpsite outside Quy Nhon, some GIs were emptying their trucks. A group of Vietnamese in their early teens rushed to the site to save reusable items among the discarded garbage, particularly unopened food cans. Too haunted by the stories of guerrillas' tactics of sending children to attack GIs, the soldiers opened fire, killing some children and prompting strong protests. But similar incidents did not take place in the following years.

Some Vietnamese civilians saw the American GI in a pessimistic light. One of the U.S. Marine companies occupied the top of a barren hill by the seaside. It was always above 90° F and certainly the Americans could hardly stand the scorching sunshine. Every afternoon, the Marines were brought down to the beach by helicopters for bathing. This was something new to the Vietnamese. To them, it looked as if the troops were going on a picnic. I knew an old man who had fought in the Việt Minh ranks against the French before leaving them because they turned out to be real communists. He told me with a tone of desperation that "our American friends will never win the war against the enemy who have nothing to care about, even their own souls."

MUTUAL HELP

Once a USO evening show was scheduled for the U.S. Marine battalion, but at the last minute it was canceled after the troupe reached Qui Nhơn by air. Security was the reason, probably because the troupe was scared by the intimidating darkness of the Qui Nhơn vicinity, which in no way resembled Broadway, and by reports about phantom VC guerrillas.

In any event, the battalion CO was upset. A makeshift stage had been set up and everything arranged for nothing. So I decided to do something to help. That morning a Vietnamese cultural group from the Corp II Psywar Battalion had arrived in Qui Nhơn to support my division for a week. The group was scheduled to rest that evening. I had a quick meeting with all members of the group and asked them to help, and they all enthusiastically agreed. My men also invited a dozen local talents to reinforce the group. In an hour, the Vietnamese group appeared before more than 1,000 Marines. The show was a mixture of songs, dances, and music on Vietnamese and American themes. Many Marines participated in a number of instrumental presentations of contemporary jazz and rock.

When all was over, the Marines opened their temporary PX and offered each of the group one item. The Marines were rather surprised to see that members of the group picked only cheap articles such as cigarettes, lighters, canned food, and candy. A Marine officer told me that the battalion HQS had expected that they would have picked more expensive goods, such as cassettes, radios, watches, and cameras.

When I talked to the cultural group, the members said they didn't want the Marines to think that they had performed in hopes of making a personal profit. I greatly admired their attitude and wished that such good relations would continue to increase.

ARMED PROPAGANDA

In spring 1965, the division's combat reconnaissance companies succeeded in chasing away the enemy guerrillas who had occasionally penetrated into Qui Nhơn suburban areas at night and shelled the city with 60 mm mortars because available provincial forces were not enough to protect the city. Our division head-quarters took care of the problem with its regular forces the way we had done in Kontum: breaking down the units into three-man teams to cover the larger areas.

In a few weeks, we expanded our fully controlled areas far beyond the suburbs and shortened curfew times from midnight to 5 AM, which had been 9 PM to 6 AM previously. Then there was one thing that we had to get rid of.

During the period of the VC's highest military pressure in 1964, when they temporarily controlled the northern part of Thị Nại Bay, they constructed a barbed-wire fence with strong wooden poles protected by lots of mines across the little bay just two miles north of the port of Qui Nhơn. On the fence, they hung a large board made of several dozen metal roofing sheets that read "CẤM MỸ NGỤY VÀO ĐÂY" (Americans and their puppets are not allowed). Militarily, the fence and the sign were not much of a matter. A force of company size or smaller would be reluctant to go into the area, as high risk was expected and no military objective was worth the attempt. But as far as propaganda and psycho-logical warfare were concerned, the board was an insult.

So the G-5 suggested an idea to the division chief of staff. We proposed that something must be done, such as an armed propaganda action. Most Americans had no accurate idea about the so-called armed propaganda, and many Vietnam-ese didn't either. They thought that armed propaganda was an action in which propagandists were sent after combat units had cleared the objective areas to deliver information and indoctrination materials or speeches and cultural enter-tainment.From what we G-5 members had learned, armed propaganda must be an operation—a surprise attack or even a commando raid on enemy soil—for the ultimate purpose of winning the people's hearts by actions of courage. Propa-ganda actions that followed would be of secondary importance. With that in mind, we worked out an operation estimate and got approval from the division commander.

One U.S. Marine platoon on nine "AmTracs," the large amphibious person-nel carriers, was assigned by the Marine battalion CO to support our Vietnam-ese psywar task force, which consisted of a Vietnamese reconnaissance platoon and a psywar/civic action team from the ARVN Second Psywar Battalion. My advisor, Captain Carroll, went with me.

One morning in September 1965, we quietly moved into the area in the AmTracs, which emerged only a few feet above the relatively calm bay water. The enemy platoon lurking in the area fled without fighting. We gathered all villagers, nearly 1,000 people, on open ground. It was the first time they had seen U.S. combat soldiers, and they seemed frightened. We had the Marines hand out gifts from various charitable organizations. Meanwhile, the psywar team talked to people in small groups, and a medical civic action team under a physi-cian's assistant helped sick people with medications.

We handed out various kinds of simple reading materials, newspapers, and agricultural information booklets. We also gave the villagers anti-American leaflets that VC distributed in the Bồng Sơn area, about sixty miles from Qui Nhơn. The VC leaflets described how the U.S. Marines raided the villages in Thị Nại Bay, raping women and killing children. We asked the peasants whether the U.S Marines had come earlier. They all said no and laughed at the VC's shameless lies.

The main point conveyed in the psywar team's message to the villagers was that the barbed-wire fence hindered the free movement of people in the area to Qui Nhơn to make their living by fishing and selling products. We asked the people to get rid of the fence. "In a week from today," the team leader said, "if villagers dare not do so, we will."

"At 6 AM this day next week," he continued, "we will be here with forces like today. Please tell the VC when they come tonight that, if they are brave enough, to be prepared for a fight with any size unit when we come back next week, and to stop sniper fire from villagers' homes, using innocent people as human shields." After five hours, we withdrew.

The division CO, General Nguyễn Thanh Sằng, kidded me when we departed. "Are you crazy making a rendezvous with the VC?"

"Yes, sir," I said. "It is armed propaganda."

A week later, we returned with the same forces. One of the AmTracs stayed midway for radio relay station. When we reached the area the second time, all villagers had fled to the other side of the little bay. The Marines used their AmTracs to crush the whole fence after clearing all mines. Only one VC platoon returned fire, and the ARVN reconnaissance platoon landed to chase them.

After about two hours, we pulled off the shore. We called the villagers back and again gave them gifts and medications, along with more leaflets and propaganda booklets. We withdrew at about 1 PM. One VC was killed; one black American Marine sergeant was wounded in the thigh when a burst of enemy machine gun hit the side of the AmTrac I was standing on and his AmTrac 20 yards from me. On the way back, the task force stopped by the beach where our division HQS was stationed. The division commanding general and the U.S. senior advisor praised them and gave the wounded sergeant the highest RVN Cross of Gallantry, a gold star.

THE PHỦ CŨ BATTLE

September 1965 saw another major U.S. combat unit arriving in Bình Định province, the U.S. Army First Cavalry Division (Airmobile). The ARVN Twenty-second Infantry Division held a military ceremony welcoming them to Việt Nam. Captain Carroll and I were MCs for the reception ceremony held at Qui Nhơn Air Force Base. Also in September, the Korean Meng Ho (Tiger)

Division arrived in Bình Định province and was assigned a tactical operation area in part of the ARVN Twenty-second Division area. The reinforcement by allied combat units somewhat enhanced ARVN morale. In that situation, the Twenty-second Division scored a victory.

In mid-September, a major battle took place at Phù Cũ Pass, south of the town of Bồng Sơn, sixty miles north of Qui Nhơn. The Second Battalion, Forty-first Regiment moved along Highway 1 from Bồng Sơn to the Phù Cũ outpost to reinstate control after a North Vietnamese Army battalion overran the outpost the previous night. On the way to the pass, the battalion met an old woman, the mother of a soldier serving in another battalion of the Forty-first. She was hiding in a bush waiting to inform the troops of the exact location of an enemy ambush. It took no time to have her son confirm her identity.

The battalion commander changed the course of advance. His battalion moved along the hillside overlooking the flat land along the railroad, which the initial operation order had selected as the line of approach. When the enemy at last launched the assault, our troops had already occupied dominant positions.

The fighting broke out in early morning and continued until late afternoon. I had the loudspeaker aircraft fly over the battle area to broadcast messages to enemy soldiers as well as to ours. The battle lasted for two days. The enemy left more than 700 corpses all over the large area, along with hundreds of weapons. More than 20 NVA soldiers were captured, and 5 joined the Chiêu Hồi (Open Arms) program. Our side suffered nearly 70 KIAs, and more than 80 were captured at the outpost.

NVA antiaircraft fire took down a U.S. Air Force F-101, which crashed on a rice paddy five miles away from the battle area. A twelve-year-old boy from the nearby village under VC temporary control bravely led the American pilot to safety, using a sampan to cross the Bồng Sơn River. In an hour or so, a small-scale helicopter operation was launched to rescue the brave boy's parents and siblings from their village. The American side, particularly the pilot's mother, rewarded the boy and his family generously.

Our men in the G-2, G-3, and G-5, as well as the Forty-first Infantry S-2, S-3, and S-5, closely checked figures concerning enemy KIAs. However, we had to increase the enemy loss to 1,200 killed in our press release. With other units always exaggerating enemy losses, we could do nothing much different when our superiors didn't want to; we tried only to be not too far from the actual figures. As division spokesman, I held a press conference attended by two dozen journalists and reporters, Vietnamese and foreigners. The division MACV team provided helicopter transportation for reporters to see the battlefield with their own eyes.

On the second day, an NVA company ambushed a platoon of the ARVN Twenty-third Ranger Battalion that had come to the area as reinforcement. The leader of the encircled platoon, a second lieutenant, told the supporting fighters to strike right at the red smoke from a grenade he was holding when his platoon was engaged in close combat without hope to withdraw. He was killed along with half of his platoon. But his heroic action saved the rest of his company, while the enemy company suffered heavy losses. The story has never been in foreign publications. If he had been in the U.S. Army, the brave lieutenant would have been given a Medal of Honor.

As far as I know, the battle of Phủ Cũ has not been in books about the Việt Nam War, either, although it made an impact on the war efforts of both sides in the region. There were not many battles where the enemy lost more than 700 troops. On the ARVN side, the victory had a favorable effect on our troops' morale in the region after our division was defeated in many battles in late 1964 and early 1965.

With help from local authorities, farmers living nearby buried the NVA dead but only those near the road. They burned the other corpses far away in dense foliation with gasoline. For several weeks, flocks of vultures and crows gathered in the area, croaking noisily all day long. The sounds they made have been the macabre symbol of the horrible war of fratricide that was imprinted deep in my heart.

I had seen many dead communist troops in war, but I had never seen them in the hundreds like in the battle of Phủ Cũ. The sight of more than 150 enemy corpses lying along one side of a pathway on a long hilltop, killed by air strike while they were at rest, was a shock. Some of those young men torn by bombs or bullets, or burned black by napalm, might have been my villagers or even my relatives.

To exploit the victory on psywar front, we often recorded Hà Nội Radio news reports about the battle in which it always boasted of the communist victory along with exaggerated losses on the ARVN side. Then we would replay the tape to people living in the battle area without further comments.

Whenever possible, we would provide transportation for people from communities near and far to visit the battleground with captured weapons and POWs, to see the enemy bodies, and even to attend funeral ceremonies of our dead soldiers. The people would find the answers for themselves.

When we had a big victory like one in Phủ Cũ, we often held an exhibition of captured communist weapons and equipments. There were hundreds of AK-47s, RPDs, B-40s and B-41s, radios, mines, and ammunition. We displayed all the items as they had been collected on the battlefield, still tainted with dirt or blood and shreds of clothing. It was convincing to the people. Many other exhibitions of the kind displayed only carefully cleaned weapons, thus breeding the rumor that they were taken from the military warehouses, not from the fields.

TREATMENT OF PRISONERS OF WAR

In some units on both sides, including U.S. combat units, POWs were tortured by interrogators who tried to wring tactical intelligence information from them.

There was some maltreatment of POWs in South Vietnamese and American units, but it was less cruel than what the communists did to our men in their hands.

On both sides, violent interrogation sometimes occurred in low-level units. In the Twenty-second Division, such interrogation was forbidden. The G-2 did not tolerate it, and I would not hesitate to report to the division commander and Capt. Vũ Viết Sinh, the G-2, when I caught someone violating the regulation. Captain Sinh was among the best interrogators; he relied on interrogating technique and patience, not torture. However, we could not control everything done at lower levels, especially in combat situations.

In the first years of war, many communist soldiers showed not only their willingness to fight but also their persevering resistance in interrogation when they were taken prisoner. To this kind of prisoner, experience sometimes proved that rough measures did not bring in valuable information as much as treatment with velvet gloves. The cases of POWs captured in the battlefield of Phù Cũ were typical.

Among communist POWs, there was a young woman, about twenty years old, who was reported to be a dangerous terrorist and a fearless sapper. On my trip inspecting a psywar and civic action team in Phù Mỹ district HQS where the woman POW was kept, I dropped by to see her. The division's G-5 section had to cooperate with G-2 to closely supervise the treatment of the POWs, not only to comply with JGS directives but also to persuade the POWs to disclose information we needed.

When an MP unlocked the room where she was temporarily kept, she jumped to her feet defiantly. When I asked her a few questions, she replied reluctantly and at last she said, "I don't care if you American puppets torture me or even rape me. Your soldier once raped me and meant to kill me. Some more rapes are not a matter to me. But I won't tell you anything against my comrades."

Only then was I aware of her charm hidden under the long unkempt hair and the dirty black pajamas. I knew she was the type who had bitter animosity toward a soldier or a local government official. Not only did they foster vengeance against individuals who wronged them, but they also laid blame on our army and government.

We decided to give her special treatment. I asked the two female sergeants in the Division Military Social Services to visit her and give her help, especially in women's matters. She rejected help at their first visit with hurting remarks. We were patient, giving her magazines and picture books of natural, nonpolitical topics, and taking her to visit markets, schools, and a hospital under casual dress. In about two weeks she changed her mind, faster than I had hoped.

She wrote her own story and a dozen pages of intelligence information, whose value the G-2 verified. According to her report, she was a daughter of a poor farmer. A few years earlier, while she was living with her mother in her native village, a remote place in Quảng Ngãi province, an unknown soldier raped her several times at gunpoint and meant to kill her, but she escaped. The following year, she joined the "Liberation Front" and quickly became a dauntless warrior in several deadly commando missions. Her attitude, however, changed when she was given treatment that was much kinder than she had expected.

According to our experiences, many communist POWs honestly changed their minds quickly if they were treated gently. Probably because they had been lied to so much by communist propaganda, a single truth on our side could get rid of their resentment. Of course, there were many diehard communists on whom we wouldn't waste our time to try to convince.

In South Việt Nam during the war, once in a while there were soldiers who committed rape, mostly in remote areas. The communist propaganda system was skillfully making use of these incidents for slanderous purposes against the whole army. In the seven years I was in the Twenty-second Division, I knew only two or three cases of sexual assault at gunpoint. The culprits were tried and sentenced to prison terms. The rate of rapes committed by ARVN soldiers was far lower than cases of sexual assaults in the civilian population of the same size.

In some cases, VC local cells ordered their young wanton women to seduce ARVN troops for free or for money. Then the women filed complaints against the soldiers at the unit command post, alleging that the soldiers had raped them. Proofs of actual sexual intercourse including features of defendant's under-clothes noted by the victim could be easily secured on the scene. The responsible commanders could face difficulties deciding whether or not to initiate prosecution. In many cases they were unable to run a quick, successful investigation without help from reliable witnesses. Such events staged by secret VC agents could start nasty rumors if military authorities failed to act properly.

As to allied forces, there were only a few cases of rapes committed by American and South Korean soldiers. But according to credible classified reports I received, rumors seemed to be much worse than realities. Facts were exaggerated in some reports circulated in the foreign mass media and much more in the communist propaganda. I have heard of no rumor or report about similar crimes committed by Australian and Thái soldiers.

A few days after the Phù Cũ Pass battle, a ranger company cornered a NVA platoon in a narrow gorge. About half of them were gunned down; only twelve still fought back from inside a small cave. Instead of using rocket launchers or M-79 grenades to get rid of them, the rangers patiently called on them to surrender for half an hour, but they failed to bring them out. At last, the rangers launched tear gas grenades into the cave and captured them. Most of the captured men refused to cooperate and even resisted furiously during primary interrogations.

The G-2 turned them over to my section for medical treatment, as all of them were wounded, two in critical condition. We sent them to the Qui Nhơn city hospital. Government regulations allowed POWs to receive medical treatment as legal citizens in military or civilian hospitals. My men lent them two small radios with shortwave bands, and I told the guards to let them listen to any station, including Hà Nội Radio, provided that the volume was only loud enough for themselves.

A week later, they asked my men, "How come no American interrogated us?" They said they were afraid of being tortured for information as their political officers had taught them to expect. So on Sunday that week, my men brought the prisoners on a four-hour tour to visit the city and the U.S. Marine battalion, including dinner at a small but nice restaurant. What they saw in a week seemed rather much for them. They were surprised to see civilian patients in South Việt Nam had to pay nothing in hospitals. They enjoyed nutritious free meals at the hospital. They said that nothing was free in North Việt Nam hospitals and schools. Under the communist regime, both before and after 1975, the poorest people had to pay for both.

They were especially impressed by the attitude of the U.S. soldiers. They had learned from their Communist Party's lessons that all American GIs were demons who were killing, raping, and even eviscerating and dismembering prisoners at will. The lessons went along with pictures so skillfully made up by communist propaganda agencies that most communist troops had no doubt at all about the allegations.

A week later, some of them told our G-2 men that they were ready to tell anything they knew. Except for the three POWs who still kept silent, the others gave important information that we could have been unable to obtain without their own free will. The G-2 men carefully interrogated each of them separately for fear of their safety when they should be released back to the North at the end of the war.

Several months after I left the division, I heard that five of these prisoners were among the wounded POWs who were released to North Việt Nam in 1966.

GOOD-BYE TO THE TWENTY-SECOND DIVISION

In the first days of October 1965, I left the Twenty-second Infantry Division, the unit I considered my home. In nearly seven years serving the unit, I had shed no blood but much sweat, and I had faced a lot of danger to contribute to the unit's achievements. I had many friends there, Vietnamese and Americans. Some were killed in action, and some became crippled veterans. My wife and I always hold the Twenty-second Division and Kontum City deep in our hearts. Two of our four children were born there. Anyway, it was "My Division."

The MACV team at the division held a beer party on the last Saturday afternoon of each month. Vietnamese officers in key jobs were invited. At the party, incoming and outgoing American officers were introduced. On the Saturday party before I left, to my surprise, I was given a plaque bearing the name of the MACV Team 22 and words of appreciation. Later in my service, I was against the policies of the U.S. government, but the Americans in MACV Team 22 have always been my best friends.

What I hated to see in the last months serving the Twenty-second Division was the flourishing trade relating to services done to the GIs. Some of our officers joined these trades legally and illegally, including taking part in the sale of consumer goods stolen from the U.S. Armed Forces PX stores. They made very big money until 1970.

NINETEEN

Sài Gòn Commando

AT THE GPWD

My new assignment was to serve as chief of the Organization Study Section, somewhat similar to a G-3 plus a part of G-1 at division level, of the newly established General Political Warfare Department (GPWD). It was one of the three general departments directly under the Joint General Staff. The others were the General Training Department and the General Logistics Department.

Serving in jobs around the capital city, we sometimes called ourselves the "Sài Gòn commandos." Once again, my rank was too low for the job of an ARVN major (or a U.S. lieutenant colonel). It meant more toil, and I was promised no special favors and no early promotion.

My section took care of studies and planning related to general personnel policies and the organization of the Political Warfare Branch. Actually, I was cooperating with a section of the ARVN JGS/J-3 in drafting TO&Es for political warfare branch personnel and equipment in every armed forces unit. Besides, my office took part in staff work and supervision in military ceremonies, reviews, and parades. The fiscal year 1965–66 saw increased U.S. military aid and that brought much change in the organization and activities of our military.

Political warfare wasn't new. The new GPWD was only the enlargement of the existing Psychological Warfare Department under the Ministry of Defense. Under the GPWD there were four departments: Psychological Warfare, Indoctrination, Military Security, and Social Services. Its subordinates included the Political Warfare University and the Special Cultural Group. Working beside the GPWD were the US/MACV Team and the Advisory Delegation from the Republic of China (Taiwan). The GPWD was partly modeled after the general "polwar" department of the Taiwan armed forces. In Việt Nam, the political warfare department was given much less power. Most RVN military ranking leaders would never accept anything like that, although it proved a success in Taiwan. They were afraid that such a powerful establishment might become a bothersome whistle blower under their command and would limit their authority.

The political warfare branch received more advice from the Taiwan delegation than from the US/MACV Team. However, much of the Taiwan advice ended up in our top leaders' desk drawers without being read a second time.[1]

Under MACV there were several U.S. psychological operations battalions, which provided assistance to the ARVN polwar branch, mostly by printing leaflets. They also provided loudspeaker planes or helicopters for broadcasting messages and dropping leaflets aimed at civilians and communist soldiers. At the levels below MACV, many U.S. Army and Marine divisions had their own civic action teams, providing emergency care, general health examinations, and medicines to peasants in their areas of responsibility. The activities won some sympathy from the people. However, the success was not multiplied to the highest degree because of the inadequacy of the effort to bring it to a larger targeted audience.[2] In particular, the Marine Combined Action Platoons (CAP) won praise from the villagers in the I Corps/Military Region. A CAP was made up of U.S. Marines and Vietnamese Popular Forces militiamen, operating as a single unit and stationed in villages of the three northernmost provinces of South Việt Nam (within the III Marine Amphibious Forces' tactical area of responsibility).

As far as I was concerned, the psychological or political warfare objectives should have been a part of the commander's responsibility and made a part of his operational planning, not considered as separate supporting actions. A smile or greeting from a soldier to the Vietnamese civilians in an operation was a simple but very important psychological action, more effective than a formal indoctrination lesson. Unfortunately, many commanders cared more about destroying the enemy than winning the support of people in the area of responsibility. They considered psychological operations as only those activities meant to entertain or to give cultural presentations, to console victims, to distribute gifts and aid, and to spread propaganda through leaflets and radio broadcasts.

My intermediate superiors agreed with me; however, many of our higher bosses did not. The Taiwanese advisors supported my concepts, but their voice was not powerful enough. The American advisors had no specific ideas about this domain. So I had very little chance to implement my ideas in the drafting of the organization of the polwar branch.

In searching for a guiding doctrine of the polwar activities, my top bosses accepted the Republic of China (Taiwan) concept of "Lục Đại Chiến" (six grand aspects of warfare: ideology, public support, psychology, intelligence, stratagem making, and organization). However, the doctrine did not have much influence in the ARVN polwar branch.

I was promoted to captain in April 1966, after seven years and six months at the rank of first lieutenant. I wasn't happy about the news after wearing the two golden flowers for so long and serving as division assistant chief of staff for more than three years.

SÀI GÒN 1966

In 1965 and 1966, American military and civil installations were set up everywhere in the capital city, in addition to others that had been established since 1962. Building contractors and realtors saw a period of booming business. Real estate prices went soaring. Housing rent rose almost every week. Traffic jams were incredible. I spent nearly forty-five minutes making the three-mile drive between my home and my office.

The dollars spent by the large influx of GIs boosted industries that served them even indirectly. On top of the list were nightclubs and snack bars where prostitutes usually operated behind the front hall. Bar girls and other women who officially married the GIs also pumped dollars into the local market.[3] In Sài Gòn and cities near U.S. military bases, bars and clubs serving GIs gathered in blocks of certain streets. Rock music, colorful lights, and noise gave these blocks the appearance of being somewhere other than Việt Nam. In nightclubs and bars, people spoke not English, not Vietnamese, but a dialect mix of both languages plus some slang expressions that were coined by both sides.

Consumer goods stolen from the American military post exchange, known as the PX, began flooding cities and towns, available at low prices everywhere from department stores to sidewalk stalls. I knew many Americans who simply bought PX items such as cigarettes, razor blades, shaving lotion, booze, and the like at sidewalk stalls where they paid only half of PX prices. All over South Việt Nam, prices of consumer goods—food and agricultural products in particular—and services rocketed so high that many became unaffordable to my family. In Tết 1966, watermelon was sold at a price five times higher than six months earlier. A medium room was rented to GIs at an average of VN$2,000 to VN$4,000 a month (US$15 to US$30) at a time when my salary (as a first lieutenant with ten years of service and seven years of rank, married with two children) was a humble VN$12,000. Similarly, a clerk typist without English fluency or a janitor working for the Americans was paid at least VN$20,000.

The unstable market worsened the living conditions of government employees and military servicemen and dropped them into a lower social class. Ironically, a police officer next door to me and I had to wait in a long line to buy a few cans of condensed milk at a black market price more than twice that posted on the price list at the grocery store.

I took it for granted that such a situation was an unavoidable side effect of the sharp increase in demand everywhere in the world under similar situations. But many Vietnamese bore a grudge against the Americans, especially when a number of poor women left their husbands and children for a well-paid trade in the red-light districts. Some of these women were just living with the GIs as wives. Such cases were rare, and it happened anywhere in the world under similar conditions, but the GIs were blamed for the trouble.

Hundreds of sensational stories about GIs were circulating. Most of them were fishy tales with no specific purpose, but some were made up by communist propaganda machines insinuating GI crimes and brutality. One of the stories was about a gang of smugglers who were plotting to steal U.S. military supplies from the warehouses. One day they stole a few containers of what they believed were valuable materials. When they opened one container, they found the bodies of three girls. The poor girls were employees of an American service and had been raped and killed before being stuffed into the container to be discarded.

After 1965, a large part of the general public, especially the lower middle class, didn't like the presence of the Americans in Việt Nam because of their diminished living conditions. The educated middle class was not very sympathetic toward the Americans. Ardent patriots were sensitive to the big brother attitude of the American leaders and statesmen and saw Americans as bad friends.

The Mekong Delta provinces, however, did not experience similar problems because there were no large American units stationed in the region. Besides, it should be noted that Đà Lạt, the most beautiful tourist city in the South Việt Nam highlands, was off limits to GIs, except for servicemen bearing official travel orders. Some Americans asked me as a favor to include them in the official party with specified tasks on trips visiting Đà Lạt City.

U.S. aid to the RVN, on the other hand, enhanced the spirit of the nationalist Vietnamese, but they were concerned about the consequences of the American presence in Việt Nam. Students joined several groups to support the anticommunist efforts but also to promote patriotism. There were songsters' troupes spontaneously founded by Sài Gòn University students who traveled around the country to rally the youth to build the spirit of freedom and self-reliance. My sister was a volunteer in one of these groups.

U.S. military forces built up higher and higher in 1966, with heavier battles in the highlands and in the coastal provinces of Central Việt Nam. The relationship between the ARVN and the allies was a matter for consideration. The idea of putting the ARVN under an allied unified command headed by U.S. generals was rejected right from the beginning. Allied forces (Australia, New Zealand, South Korea, and Thailand) were under MACV and were assigned different Tactical Areas of Operational Responsibility (TAOR). The ARVN was responsible for the larger territory where its leaders exerted full military power.

In comparison with the South Korean military in the Korean War, the ARVN held more military authority beside the Americans. Consequently, ARVN generals could not lay the whole blame for the 1975 defeat on the MACV and the Pentagon.

THE WAR OF WORDS ON RADIO

On the propaganda front, radio was the medium of choice. For years before 1966, the South Việt Nam government lagged far behind the Hà Nội regime in the war of words. Along with the increased military aid, the Americas gave assistance to the RVN radio system so that it could increase the range of its broadcasts into remote areas, North Việt Nam in particular.

In the North, local propaganda broadcasts were conducted with cardboard or tin trumpets and later with imported electronic public address appliances. Loudspeakers boomed day and night with news and articles from communist publications and radio stations to the population in every city ward and village. A news report or story might be repeated a dozen times a day, especially at psychologically prime time sessions, 9 PM and 6 AM.

The nationalist government in the South did not make a similar effort. Officials at the local level could do little without active support from the top levels. Their capability was limited to distributing some materials such as booklets and posters, rebroadcasting news reports from radio stations, and holding public meetings.

As a strategic move, Hà Nội Radio increased its ability to broadcast into the South. The Soviet Union and China helped Hà Nội update its broadcasting system with powerful stations, including one close to the Demilitarized Zone. Many South Vietnamese families owned small transistor radios, and they could easily listen to Hà Nội Radio (Voice of Việt Nam).

Even with aid from Washington, South Việt Nam broadcasting lagged behind. Sài Gòn Radio, the central station of the system, operated with a 100-kilowatt transmitter. The six local stations were weaker (four at 50 kilowatts and two at 20 kilowatts each). The broadcasts covered all of South Việt Nam, but were less effective in reaching the North. A Sài Gòn plan to jam Radio Hà Nội failed.

Special broadcasting programs directed to the North came from the station in the district town of Đông Hà near the Demilitarized Zone. Compared to its rival in the North, its broadcast was like a sparrow chirping against a crowing cock. It was shut down when the powerful Voice of Freedom station (VOF) assumed the task of targeting North Việt Nam in 1964. Official VOF broadcasts were "white propaganda," but a branch of it also included "gray" and "black propaganda."[4]

In the North, very few people owned radios. They could only listen to the state-run stations mostly on the wards' and villages' public address systems. So very little information from outside reached the North Vietnamese general public through radio receivers. Listening to South Vietnamese stations was a crime punishable by imprisonment.

ON THE CULTURAL FRONT

As the communists were paying special attention to the cultural front, with an enormous production of martial songs, South Việt Nam was doing its best to compete. North Việt Nam had numerous cultural groups operating at all levels from village teams to the national troupes. A large number of the groups held musical entertainments for combat units in war zones. The Sài Gòn Ministry of Information had its cultural groups usually at district level and higher. Their targeted audiences were mostly civilian. The ARVN cultural groups were stronger artistically and technically.

Under the ARVN GPWD, there were four military cultural troupes in the four political warfare battalions serving the four corps/MRs and a central special cultural troupe. The troupes presented shows of music and dance to entertain ARVN soldiers and allied soldiers at reserve positions and outposts, as well as the common people in government-controlled localities. The American soldiers and other allies always warmly welcomed the artists. Besides their primary task of entertaining the military, members of the groups also contributed an important part to the national musical art in song composition and presentation. Many famous singers in South Việt Nam were trained and had their debut in these groups.

In the general education domain in North Việt Nam, the communist regime required political indoctrination from the first grade through the university level several hours a week, advocating killing and cramming the kids with bloody and fanatical war stories. The South Vietnamese government had never required teachers to do the same. Educators in Sài Gòn maintained that political and war matters should not be taught to the immature minds. Only lessons of "citizenship" or "citizens' obligations" were taught in the high school curriculum without touching anything about animosity or about killing the enemy. Anticommunist teachings were the task of the Information Ministry and military polwar branch, not of schools.

THE 1966 ANTIGOVERNMENT MOVEMENT

The military leaders took over the ruling power in June 1965 and brought a dim light of hope to the nationalists and members of the armed forces. But one year after the military leaders' government began to rule the country, bitter protests by a Buddhist movement broke out in Đà Nẵng and Huế. Protesting Buddhists in Sài Gòn followed suit, bringing their altars down to the streets to block traffic. The police reacted swiftly. On the way home from the barracks, I sometimes had to drive through clouds of tear gas. What I really feared was a war of religions. However small it might have been, such armed conflict would have been devastating to the nation. Thank God it did not develop so badly.

The protests were put down in a few months, but they left a deep scar in the Huế–Đà Nẵng areas. Furthermore, the suppression of the Buddhist protests greatly hurt the troops' morale and military discipline. People ascribed all of the troubles to the CIA, the ghost behind all events and scandals in South Việt Nam.

BOLD ATTACKS

In mid-1966, considerable effort contributed to the construction of a democratic regime. As political chaos subsided, the military government held the national congressional elections. I didn't vote, although I could see no apparent fraud. My experience as a nine-year-old during the 1946 general election had destroyed all my interest in voting.

In 1966, most ARVN units were assigned to pacification tasks, operating in populated areas to destroy local communist forces and to reinforce the Rural Development program. The teams helped in the defense and development of hamlets and contributed much to the pacification program. So it was a good time for the reorganization of the RVN military structure.

The major battles in border areas were handled by U.S. troops. Despite strong criticism and protests against the war, I saw apparent progress in many parts of the country when I visited them on working trips. American combat units launched many offensive campaigns against communist bases and actually caused heavy losses to the enemy. The situation brought in a wave of optimism, whereas communist forces strived to show their capability of conducting stunning strikes at the very heart of the nationalist territories.

On the anniversary of the coup d'état that brought down the Diệm regime, a marvelous military review and parade was held on Thống Nhất Boulevard in front of the Presidential Palace. About fifteen minutes before General Nguyễn Văn Thiệu, then chief of state, arrived, VC guerrillas attacked with 75 mm shells from the east side of Sài Gòn. A shell hit one of the two belfries of the Sài Gòn cathedral, fifty yards from the main bleacher. Had it missed the belfry, it would have landed on the bleacher where ministers, ambassadors, generals, and other VIPs were sitting.

A second round fell in the front yard of a government office fifty yards from the first block of troops waiting for the opening review and twenty yards from me and other monitors of the ceremonies, but the shell didn't go off. I was there as a member of the board of monitors coordinating support for the event in a building overlooking the bleachers and near the first unit waiting for review. A half dozen shells exploded about 100 to 300 yards away.

The parade commander, General Dư Quốc Đống, a famous airborne commander, remained unperturbed, and the troops near the bleachers showed a little panic in the first few seconds and then restored good order. But the colors guards shamelessly ran for cover.

The security force found the gun location right away. A VC crew had emplaced a 75 mm recoilless rifle on a tree at an unpopulated site east of Sài Gòn on the other side of the Sài Gòn River. Enemy gunners conducted a high angle fire, sending a salvo of high-explosive shells at the gun's maximum range (some three to four kilometers). When our troops arrived, the enemy gunners had safely escaped, leaving the 75 mm recoilless rifle tied to the tree. It was firmly secured to the branches and skillfully aimed for direct fire at the cathedral crosses atop the twin belfries, which stood out clearly above the city skyline.

The shelling killed and wounded some civilians, but it also did damage to the prestige of the military. The communist side won another victory on the propaganda front.

As the Pentagon deployed more combat troops in Việt Nam, VC forces launched the most daring commando attacks. A 60 mm mortar crew, emplaced inside a private home in the crowded neighborhood of Vườn Chuối, sent five or six shells precisely aimed at the old MACV headquarters on Pasteur Street in downtown Sài Gòn. A shell hit the HQS building but caused no considerable loss. Another shell hit an ARVN truck on the street, killing two Vietnamese soldiers. After emergency calls from the neighbors, the police raided the house, but the two VC had escaped, leaving the mortar and an empty home with part of the roof removed for the mortar trajectory.

Even with these daring successes, however, the morale of the VC troops was not as high as I had expected. During the 1946–54 war, French soldiers fought their enemy in small-scaled units, and the Resistance force suffered terrible losses even in victory. In many bloody battles, the Việt Minh force ended with 60 percent of the attackers killed, but failed to seize the French strongholds, leaving heaps of bodies in front of the French machine guns. Twice in 1952, Việt Minh companies attacked two French Army posts in my district at midnight. They overran one and failed to capture the other. But they left hundreds of dead fighters on the barbed-wire fences.

Twenty years later, South Vietnamese and allied soldiers confronted tough NVA soldiers who fought with daring in the fierce battles of Idrang Valley, Hamburger Hill, Khe Sanh, Huế, and Quảng Trị. However, the allied soldiers did not experience bloody battles like those of the 1946–54 war, when Việt Minh soldiers frightened their enemy with their extreme bravery and unbelievable human sacrifice in suicide attacks, including human bombs. Apparently the

NVA troops did not attain a similar level of commitment and resolve in combat during the 1955–75 war. The phenomenon illustrates the big difference between the nationalist resistance of the pre-1954 war and the NVA of the post-1954 war.

I was appointed to a high-ranking job in the Chiêu Hồi Ministry on December 31, 1966, four days after my youngest son was born. I named my son Phi Diên, after the scenic small mountain at Ninh Bình City, the birthplace of my wife in North Việt Nam.

THE CHIÊU HỒI PROGRAM

I will have a lot to say about the Chiêu Hồi program in these memoirs. My years of service were the most interesting of my military service. Moreover, the program was successful beyond question, and it faced the least criticism from war protesters. The program represents aspects of the war effort that may help readers understand more about the profound nature of the conflict.

Chiêu Hồi is a Sino-Vietnamese term that means "Calling the enemy to return to the right cause." Ngô Đình Nhu activated the Chiêu Hồi program in 1963, as part of the Strategic Hamlet program, which had become a national policy in 1962. It continued after the Diệm regime fell and quickly attained greater importance after 1965. The idea of a program to call enemy soldiers to surrender and to be given merciful treatment was nothing new in war. The two warring sides in the 1946–54 war had similar programs. Early in the 1955–75 war, the RVN local government and military leaders tried the same efforts. But only sometime before 1963 did the idea develop into a national program with more compassionate policies. It was known that Sir Robert Thompson, a counterinsurgency expert in the British Advisory Group in South Việt Nam, was the enthusiastic advisor and strategist of the Strategic Hamlet program and its by-product, the Chiêu Hồi program.

The program was known in English as "Open Arms." An enemy taking our side in the program was called hồi chánh (returnee). "Hồi chánh" was officially used in the RVN Prime Minister Directive HT-22 in mid-1968 laying out the basic principles for reception of communist soldiers who defected to our side. I composed the draft and presented it for discussion in a meeting with representatives from related ministries and agencies. The final copy was approved by the Minister of Chiêu Hồi, Nguyễn Ngọc An, and signed into effect by Prime Minister Trần Văn Hương. The US/MACV then issued Directive 381-50, dated February 22, 1969, to apply the HT-22 to American and allied units under its command.

The hồi chánh, returnees [or defectors], are individuals who participated in military, paramilitary, political, or administrative organizations operating in the name of the Việt Nam Communist Party and its disguised organizations in South Việt Nam, North Việt Nam, and abroad, and voluntarily leave the communist side to give themselves up to the government of the RVN and to serve the RVN as its citizens.[5]

The defector would become an RVN free citizen after the first competent interrogator of Vietnamese or allied military unit or national police office confirmed that he or she met all the criteria mentioned in HT-22 and was approved by the provincial reception committee. Nothing that a defector had done to serve the communist side would be prosecuted.

An enemy soldier who surrendered to the RVN side against his or her will to join our anticommunist front would be considered only as a POW. Such POWs could always request a hearing at which they could state their true intention to voluntarily join and serve the RVN side. The hearing board could grant the petitioner the Chiêu Hồi status. This issue created a little disagreement between the Chiêu Hồi side and the U.S. embassy.

THE MINISTRY

On January 1, 1967, I took over the command of the Reception Directorate, one of the three principal directorates of the Chiêu Hồi Ministry. The other two were the Operations Directorate, in charge of propaganda, and the Rehabilitation Directorate, in charge of reintegrating the defectors into the South Vietnamese society, which included vocational training and employment.

Defectors who were communist regular troops of all ranks from North Việt Nam and communist troops from South Việt Nam from platoon leader and higher were sent to the National Chiêu Hồi Center. Enemy squad leaders from the South went to the four regional centers. Privates and guerrillas from South Việt Nam were processed in each of the forty-four provincial centers, where they stayed for two or three months.

The Reception Directorate directly controlled its three services: the National Chiêu Hồi Center, the Service of Classification, and the Service of Indoctrination. The Central Chiêu Hồi Center was across the Thị Nghè Canal from the Sài Gòn Zoo, where ranking and selected former communists who joined our side stayed for months to go through screening and orientation. The Service of Classification was in charge of defectors' identification, intelligence information, and personal records. Actually, the Service of Classification was to supervise all the Chiêu Hồi centers' activities concerning primary screening of the newcomers to be sure they met all criteria as hồi chánh, classifying them into categories, interviewing them for intelligence information, and keeping their personal records.

At the National Center, we performed a passive role in the general intelligence collection system. Interrogations at the National Center were intended to collect information that the defectors had not reported when they were at the provincial level. If we detected some valid information—most was of the strategic kind—we sent reports to the intelligence agencies such as ARVN JGS/J-2, the RVN Central Intelligence Agency, the CIA, and the MACV/J-2. Intelligence information collected at the regional and provincial CH centers, most of which had a tactical nature, was promptly transferred to local units or agencies.

The Service of Training handled the orientation and indoctrination courses on RVN social and cultural life, citizenship and civil rights, and political indoctrination, including the constitution, administrative organizations, and the legal system. The objective was to teach defectors the common rules and laws that they must know to adapt to living in a democratic regime and a free society. In the political area, we presented evidence proving that communism would not be a solution to eradicate inequalities and poverty in the world. On the contrary, the communist revolution would leave irreparable destruction on the spiritual civilization, especially the morality of the humankind. The Service of Training was in charge of indoctrination courses at the National Center, the four regional centers, and the forty-four provincial centers. A number of instructors were communist defectors. Occasionally we held discussion courses with the participation of political celebrities and professors as lecturers.

In every Chiêu Hồi center, the newly arrived defectors were organized into indoctrination classes. Each class consisted of 20 to 200 defectors, who remained for one or two months, depending on the average background of class members. My directorate was in charge of the curriculum and instructors. Along with one or two instructors at a provincial or regional center, my Service of Training had a group of about twenty instructors to take care of the courses at the National Center and to reinforce the lower centers in case of the larger newcomers input.

Training topics were simple, based not on theories but mostly on factual presentation and explanation of events. In class, we allowed them to discuss freely almost all topics, sometimes even the most sensitive ones. I knew that former communist soldiers were fed up with listening and learning by heart the lengthening tasteless political lessons.

Former North Vietnamese regulars might stay longer for vocational training and for resettlement while most South Vietnamese communist troops often left the centers after two months for their home villages in safe areas or rebuilt their new lives elsewhere. Defectors from South and North Việt Nam could be resettled in the Chiêu Hồi villages if they liked.

The political training achieved limited success. We were short of capable instructors who had profound experiences in communist indoctrination and the communist soldiers' psychology, as well as political training techniques. Poor salary was not attractive to capable candidates.

A number of defectors had serious illnesses or wounds when they reported for Chiêu Hồi. Most of them recovered after treatment in VN civilian and military hospitals and U.S. Army facilities.

In 1966, the directorate was not in good order, and the minister needed a military officer to handle that military-civil installation. The military predicted that a large influx of defectors would soon fill the centers beyond their capacity. The ministry also needed its complicated activities and procedures to be organized into a proper system.

I was picked for the job partly because no one else wanted it. Many felt reluctant to deal with people who were former communist troops. On the other hand, my boss in the Twenty-second Infantry Division, General Nguyễn Bảo Trị, had just taken over the Ministry of Chiêu Hồi and Information, and Colonel Phạm Anh, his chief of staff in the division, became underminister in charge of Chiêu Hồi. Both asked me to help them reorganize the Directorate of Reception and the National Chiêu Hồi Center. They picked me because of service requirements more than doing me a favor, they said.

In the following years, my family was living in the three-bedroom upstairs apartment in the French-styled mansion that once belonged to Archbishop Ngô Đình Thục, President Ngô Đình Diệm's brother. The large homestead with many smaller buildings was confiscated by the government after the end of Diệm's government and became the National Chiêu Hồi Center. I had to live beside the hundreds of ex-communists day and night to take care of the odds and ends that might have taken place at any time.

I knew very well that as a thirty-year-old captain, I was too young and rather low in rank for the job, a director of the largest directorate of the Chiêu Hồi Ministry with more than 200 government employees, cadres, and military personnel. Most officers in similar jobs in charge of a directorate in other ministries were lieutenant colonels, some majors, and some full colonels. A Chinese proverb says, "There are three possible perils in a man's life; one of them is being too young with limited capability in a high-ranking position." I repeated this to myself time and time again.

I sought advice from the wise old people. My father-in-law and two of my father's friends said I should respect the ideas of the aged men under my command and be honest to the subordinates. My mother's advice was simple: "Act like your dear father. He never took bribes, and he lived to love, not to hate." Following their advice, I treated my subordinates with respect and democratic leadership. The youngest of the chiefs of services and offices under my command was forty. Every major issue was discussed frankly at the weekly meetings of the chiefs. I would make decisions based on the opinions of the majority of the group of eleven people and me. After I left the ministry, I always attributed our successes to our group's work, and I frankly blamed most failures on myself as the head of the group who made final decisions.

WHY THEY DEFECTED

The program was expanded in 1967 with increased aid from Washington. The direct support came from the office of Civil Operations and Revolutionary Development Support (CORDS), a branch directly under MACV. Contrary to some misunderstanding, the Americans just did their job, giving advice and providing financial and material support to the program. The Americans never took the decisive role in the operation of the Chiêu Hồi Ministry and its agencies. In this pure Vietnamese domain, the Vietnamese welcomed every suggestion or criticism from the American side with smiles of friendship, but it was the Vietnamese who made the final decisions. Naturally, the ones who held the key sources of support often had powerful voices.

It must be said that not every ranking commander or official in the RVN supported the Chiêu Hồi program. Some just performed their assigned tasks as required but without goodwill. They were anticommunist extremists who never trusted anyone who had once served the communist regime. However, they were an insignificant minority.

The communist soldiers, especially the NVA troops, joined South Việt Nam's side for several reasons. Many had ceased to believe in the future of the communist regime and didn't think the communists would win the war. Some were anticommunists. But a large number of the North Vietnamese regular troops reported to our side when they confronted the terrible firepower that could be unleashed, saw the huge loss of lives on their side, and were left alone in a strange land after a battle without food and water.

One remarkable defection happened in 1967. A young NVA private first class, Nguyễn Văn Thanh, surrendered to an ARVN combat unit and was transferred to the National Chiêu Hồi Center. Thanh was suffering from acute malaria. His skin was pale, lacking the tint of a living human. An NVA physician in a communist base in Cambodia who was his close relative had advised Thanh to "go chiêu hồi," where his sickness could be cured, then stay there with the nationalist side. The physician said Thanh would live no more than three months if he stayed in the jungle without proper medical care. So Thanh left the jungle base camp with a Chiêu Hồi "safe-conduct pass" leaflet to report to an ARVN unit. In consecutive interrogations, Thanh did not conceal the true reason for his defection and honestly reported reliable intelligence information.

When he arrived at the National CH Center, his very low hemoglobin count and malaria tests revealed the critical condition of his health. The Nguyễn Văn Học Hospital was not able to treat him at that stage of sickness. At last, the American team of the CMIC (Combined Military Interrogation Center), working beside the National CH Center, went in to help. Thanh was admitted to the

U.S. Army field hospital in Sài Gòn. Everything was okay, except for the large demand for blood that the hospital could not provide beyond a limit. At this point, the Americans provided more help. Along with scores of Vietnamese civil servants and soldiers giving their blood, the twenty Americans in the CMIC team contributed money for blood from a blood bank.

After many weeks, Thanh was released. He looked as if he had only had a bout of flu. He was no longer the pale and skinny young NVA about to die. Not long after checking out of the hospital, he enlisted in the armed propaganda company in Nha Trang city, Khánh Hòa province.

Late in 1969, I went on an inspection trip at Nha Trang. At the main gate of Nha Trang Chiêu Hồi Center, a burly young man in armed propaganda uniform ran to me, hugging me tightly and twittering, "Oh, dear brother. We are so glad to see you again." When he saw that I didn't recognize him, his wife quickly reminded me, "Sir, my husband is Nguyễn Văn *'malaria'* Thanh." I was stunned at seeing how much Thanh had changed. He told me that he was working out every day, lifting weights and running. Not a trace of the Nguyễn Văn Thanh of mid-1967 remained in him.

Thanh insisted that I dine at the small home he had just bought, where he lived with his wife and a newborn son. The Chiêu Hồi agency chief told me that Thanh was serving with enthusiasm and a high willingness to fight. Whenever he recalled how the help of the Vietnamese and Americans at the National Center saved him, Thanh joked, "Long Live Thiệu, Kỳ, and the Imperialist Americans." The only communist he was grateful to was the physician in the secret base who had advised him to go "chiêu hồi."

North Vietnamese soldiers were heavily indoctrinated with political training, and they did not have accurate information regarding South Việt Nam and the free world. Their ethnic South Vietnamese comrades had more chances to learn about life in government-controlled areas. That was one reason there were ten times more ethnic South Vietnamese defectors than those coming from the North. Another reason, of course, was that South Vietnamese communists were closer to their homes, while the North Vietnamese found themselves in an inimical environment.

It seemed incredible that the communist lies could affect common people so profoundly. The case of an NVA second lieutenant still brings a smile whenever I recollect his story. A few days before his infantry battalion left its base camp in Thanh Hóa province in North Việt Nam for the South, he went around the villages nearby to collect usable clothes to be given to the South Vietnamese people as gifts from their North Vietnamese compatriots. The communist propaganda machine in Hà Nội taught North Vietnamese people that each Vietnamese in the South was allowed only 1.5 meter of cloth a year, as the Americans appropriated most of South Việt Nam's textile production to satisfy the U.S. market. At the time, a North Vietnamese's cloth ration was 2.5 meter a year, barely enough to make a nightgown.

The clothes that were donated were made of cheap material and full of patches. But the NVA lieutenant thought that the South Vietnamese must have been suffering a lot more than people in the North from lack of clothing. So he began his journey to the war with a rucksack full of used clothes.

Upon his arrival in the mountainous area of Quảng Ngãi province, he asked local communist cadres to hand out the "gifts," but he received only reluctant responses. One day his battalion commander sent him to a village in the foothill area to collect food supplies. He was surprised to see that no one in the village wore tattered clothing as he had imagined they would. Although they were living in war, the people had no difficulty buying good clothing at cheap prices.

When he returned to his unit, he quietly discarded his "civic action gifts," and a few months later he reported to an ARVN unit for Chiêu Hồi. Relating his story to me, he said he was not an errant blockhead but that communist propaganda was so skillful that anyone could fall for its lies.

THE CHIÊU HỒI APPEAL

Despite the fact that top leaders in South Việt Nam and the United States were not sufficiently interested in psychological warfare, especially in propaganda operations, the limited effort given to the propagation of the Chiêu Hồi program did prove efficacious. The Chiêu Hồi Ministry ran its own radio and TV broadcasts and leaflet distribution calling on enemy soldiers to defect, with support from the ARVN and allied forces. The American side assisted. The U.S. Information Service, later known as the Joint U.S. Public Affairs Office, contributed a great deal in support of the two RVN ministries of Chiêu Hồi and Information covering general psyops objectives and Chiêu Hồi on specific materials aimed at calling communist troops to defect. The U.S. Air Force dropped millions of leaflets over North Việt Nam and along the Long Mountain Trails.

The Chiêu Hồi appeal was broadcast on Sài Gòn Radio, and the United States supported Voice of Freedom many hours a day. However, such messages could reach only a limited number of North Vietnamese as too few of them had commercial radio receivers of their own. Few people dared to pick up and read leaflets in the sight of others. Furthermore, many of the leaflets contained texts that were not convincing to North Vietnamese young men, who had been stuffed with lies by the communist propaganda system since they were in grade school. Some messages were written by someone without writing skills in Vietnamese that a common peasant would find hard to comprehend.

Despite all these limitations, general information about the Chiêu Hồi program had reached the targeted enemy soldiers and produced some significant effects. Almost every former NVA soldier in the centers I talked to asserted that if the true situation in the South and life in the Chiêu Hồi centers in particular had reached NVA troops, most of them would have defected to our side.

The Chiêu Hồi broadcast on various radio stations in the South signed in every day with a tune from the well-known romantic song "Ngày Về" (The Day Returning Home) by Hoàng Giác, which began with "Tung Cánh Chim Tìm Về Tổ ấm" (Beat the wings to return to the warm nest). Although the program had limited listeners, it really enticed many North Vietnamese. The lyrics associated with the Chiêu Hồi emblem depicted a lonely white stork flying from the darkness to the bright blue sky. The sentimental impact of the melody prompted communist authorities to impose strict embarrassing control and close watch for years on Hoàng Giác, who was living in Hà Nội. The composer, his wife, and children suffered ill treatment by the local communist security agency until the 1980s, although he had composed it before 1945.

THE KIT CARSON SCOUTS

In February 1967, the large-scale Cedar Falls and Junction City Operations put the communist elite battalions in the Iron Triangle to rout. About 200 troops of the two sappers' battalions, Phú Lợi I and Phú Lợi II, rallied to the government side in two weeks. As the Bình Dương province Chiêu Hồi Center housing capacity was overloaded by the unexpected influx of defectors, the National Center had to share the burden by admitting 200 VC defectors.

After spending months in the Chiêu Hồi centers, many defectors volunteered to serve in the armed propaganda corps, a group under the Chiêu Hồi Ministry, and they were armed and trained to run psychological warfare activities to support regular military units. They were draft exempt and served as paramilitary soldiers, with the same salary as regular soldiers. Each province had an armed propaganda company.

The number of NVA regulars defecting to our side rose in 1967, apparently due to larger military operations launched against NVA units in many areas. Communist defectors in this period were seasoned fighters who had once caused much trouble to the RVN forces. They were brave warriors even when they had changed sides. Later on, many of them became the best soldiers in the ARVN combat units. Some served as Kit Carson Scouts.

The program was established under an agreement between the Vietnamese government and MACV. It was named after the famous scout in American history. The Rehabilitation Directorate of the Chiêu Hồi Ministry helped allied units recruit the defectors who met the right criteria. Most of these men were ethnic North Vietnamese. They received training in military subjects and English, and then were assigned to U.S. combat units, usually two or three scouts in a company. About 700 defectors fought as Kit Carson Scouts in U.S. combat divisions and brigades. They helped American soldiers identify VC suspects, detect mines and booby traps, and acted as interpreters. A smaller number of defectors also served Australian, Korean, and Thái combat units in similar scout programs under different names.

The scouts fought under the U.S. or allied military command but under Vietnamese jurisprudence. When the U.S. and allied infantry and Marine units were phased out of Việt Nam, the scouts were discharged; most volunteered to serve the ARVN until 1975. A scout who committed a crime would be discharged and remanded to my directorate to be court-martialed.

North Vietnamese defectors also fought in the ARVN long-distance patrol teams. They showed great courage and skill in moving in jungles and rough terrain and in antiguerrilla tactics. Many of them saw me after operations in Laos in the dense jungles along the Long Mountain. According to some of the ARVN officers who commanded these operations, the former North Vietnamese soldiers endured adverse conditions with higher resistance and patience than the regular ARVN troops.

A former NVA underwater sapper was quite helpful to the U.S. Navy. Before joining our side, he had been trained in China for two or three years. The U.S. Navy employed him as an expert on base defense. He was well paid and was frequently sent on trips visiting major naval bases in South Việt Nam for security inspections and to offer related advice. Owing to his keen expertise, a number of communist attempts to attack naval bases in Việt Nam were foiled.

AMERICAN SUPPORT

Thanks to assistance from the American side, the construction of new facilities at the National Chiêu Hồi Center made it look better and be in good order. Besides, we introduced some new regulations regarding procedures of screening, classification, interrogation, training, and security. We were well supported by CORDS, a branch directly under MACV, especially by Ambassador Robert W. Komer, chief CORDS, and Ogden Williams, chief CORDS/Chiêu Hồi. Their sympathy with the Chiêu Hồi was passed on to Ambassador William E. Colby and Raymond G. Jones when Komer and Williams left Việt Nam. Although they showed their willingness to help me personally, I never asked them for any favor or support for myself. Eugene Bable replaced Jones in the late 1969, a few months before I left the Chiêu Hồi Ministry.

We received much assistance from an American liaison officer, Raymond Ytzaina, who could speak fair Vietnamese and was fluent in French. Although he was a master sergeant, he ran his officer's position so effectively that he was a great help to my directorate and me. Most of the defectors liked him, as he spoke to them in a warm and friendly manner.[6]

The Chiêu Hồi Ministry permitted a team of Americans from the Combined Military Intelligence Center to work eight hours a day in the National Center. Its members also helped us significantly, especially the team leaders, Captain Groth and his successor, Captain Snedicker. CMIC was a joint establishment of the RVN/JGS/J-2 and MACV/J-2. Besides, my directorate also worked in close co-ordination with the RVN Central Intelligence Special Department, the CIA, the U.S. Defense Security, the National Police, and various "special warfare agencies" (conducting secret operations beyond the border of the republic). We also worked closely with different agencies responsible for psychological warfare such as the USIS, the RVN Information Ministry, Rand Corporation (a private research institute), the ARVN General Polwar Department, the National Sài Gòn Radio, the RVNAF Radio, and the Voice of Freedom.

Although my job had me deal with many American agencies and units, I always kept my distance. Once they introduced some high-ranking CIA officials to me to discuss the possibility of establishing a separate intelligence network outside South Việt Nam, employing North Vietnamese defectors. If it worked well, my small staff and I would receive monetary support several times our RVN pay. We failed to cooperate. I told them that I was not specialized in intelligence activities and had little talent in that domain. I was concerned because all intelligence plans had specific terms. When a plan expired, an agent who volunteered for the mission out of sheer patriotism might be discarded like a useless object. Deep in my heart, I was afraid of being entangled with the intelligence activities, especially when the rumor was running far and wide about a Vietnamese agent working for the CIA who was done away with when he became a nuisance.

RURAL DEVELOPMENT

The first half of 1967 saw a promising situation all over the country that created more favorable conditions for the Chiêu Hồi program. There was much progress in every aspect of the war as well as in politics. The new RVN constitution was enacted on April 1, 1967. It was a blueprint for democracy that every politic regime needs to have. We would have to wait and see its true values in the years to come. If only its promulgation had not been on April Fools' Day!

One of the key efforts to pacify the countryside also gained popular support. It was known as the Xây Dựng Nông Thôn (Rural Development). The Ministry of Rural Development was in charge of the program, which received U.S. financial support second only to its aid to the RVN military. While serving the Chiêu Hồi program, I had to work closely with this program.

The program was somewhat similar to the former Strategic Hamlet and the New Life Hamlet programs in which economic development and self-defense were among the objectives. A new target included in the Rural Development program was "eliminating the wicked lords." Wicked lords have been a major problem in Việt Nam for thousands of years and still are today under the Communist Party. All revolutionary movements in Việt Nam targeted this group as a primary objective for winning the support of the people. The communist regime began to resolve the problem right after its leaders came to power in 1945 and actually got rid of those local chiefs who were labeled "wicked" during the bloody 1953–56 Land Reform Campaign. After the conclusion of the campaign, many local officials under the Communist Party turned out to be neo-wicked lords that people also referred to as "red wicked lords." They ruled their villages with an iron fist and became excessively corrupted. Their abuses of power became part of people's everyday tales.

Under President Ngô Đình Diệm, a lot of village authorities ruled with rough hands. They incurred the people's resentment and so became good targets for VC terrorist campaigns. One of the Sài Gòn Rural Development program objectives was to introduce true democracy into the rural areas by doing away with the wicked lords through free elections so that younger and more capable people could become leaders of local governments.

In late 1967, I visited the Rural Development Training Center for a week-long workshop. The center ran several training classes for more than 7,000 men, many of whom were under forty years old. They maintained perfect discipline. Besides eight hours of formal training a day including physical labor six days a week, they joined a daily criticism session for one hour at night. For their graduation ceremony, the 7,000 men marched and sang in unison, carrying torches that made the night bright with the light of expectation and patriotism. A British diplomat from the embassy sitting beside me remarked that it was the most splendid ceremony he had ever attended.

The marvelous successes of the center were made possible by the direct assistance from the American side—expenses were all paid in cash by the American financial office without cumbersome paperwork. That headed off any attempt to steal money in the financial process of contracting with private firms to provide necessities for the trainees. The commander of the center was the honest, incorruptible Colonel Nguyễn Bé, whom I met many times to discuss rural democracy when he was deputy chief for military affairs of Bình Định province. He was a talented organizer and had many effective initiatives in running the center.

When teams were sent to do their tasks in the rural areas, their success depended largely on the enthusiasm of the district and province leaders. Not all chiefs were willing to implement the program. Nevertheless, the Rural Development program contributed a great deal to improving the political and social life in the rural areas.[7]

One of the successful movies produced by the Ministry of Information was about activities of the teams. Titled *Ba Cô Gái Suối Châu* (The Three Girls at

Suối Châu), it was about three girls with different family backgrounds who served on a Rural Development team. The scenes and the village people were real. The movie affected the peasants deeply, especially the scenes of communist crimes against innocent victims. When our armed propaganda team showed the movie at one hamlet, many of the peasants were moved to tears. Propaganda by movie easily moved the audience. Unfortunately, the RVN Ministry of Information and the military GPWD lacked budgets for such movie productions. The communists used movies for propaganda to a much greater extent.

The RVN government's tactic to move peasants from the communist-infested villages to safe areas greatly increased the number of war refugees. Their resettlement cost millions of dollars. At the request of local Vietnamese authorities, American soldiers set fire to the peasants' huts in order to force them to move to their new homes. The sight of U.S. troops casually burning the poor rural homes must have caused a bad feeling in most U.S. audiences as well as Vietnamese without knowing the reason for the destruction.

By the end of 1967, the total number of defectors since 1962 reached nearly 30,000. We held a Lunar New Year celebration at the Chiêu Hồi Center five days before Tết 1968, when an all-out communist offensive was launched against major cities all over South Việt Nam.

PART IV

Victory or Defeat

TWENTY

The Tết Offensive

The last days of January 1968 marked a communist large-scale campaign against South Việt Nam that turned the war in an unexpected direction. The communist supreme command named the campaign "General Offensive and General Uprising." It was launched on January 29, 1968. It was Tết's Eve, the first day of the Lunar New Year, the Year of the Monkey. So it was generally known as the "1968 Tết Offensive."

In the last weeks of January 1968, at least ten new defectors in Chiêu Hồi centers reported that communist units had secretly purchased a lot of ARVN camouflaged field dress and field police uniforms to prepare for an offensive. The interrogation section under my command was instructed to pass the information and the sources to the Vietnamese and MACV intelligence services.

However, I wasn't worried. I guessed that what the enemy could do in the cities was some assassinations and bomb attacks. The big party to celebrate Tết for 600 defectors and 300 guests at the National Chiêu Hồi Center went on beautifully.

Tết, the Lunar New Year, Year of the Monkey, was welcomed in every family. Traditional firecrackers were permitted after being banned for many years as the security situation was enhanced. As in previous years, the two sides officially agreed upon a three-day cease-fire.

On Tết, January 30, the first day of the Year of the Monkey, the ARVN JGS alerted military units and installations to possible sapper attacks after the communist units broke the bilateral three-day truce agreement. At night on January 29, communist units launched attacks at Đà Nẵng, several cities in the highlands and coastal areas. But there were no sign of a nationwide offensive. I ordered the armed propaganda troops in charge of security of the National Chiêu Hồi Center to strengthen the guards and security measures.

At about 3 AM, January 31, the Sài Gòn Radio station a mile from my center was attacked. Minutes later, gunshots were heard from the U.S. embassy, about 1.2 miles from us. I had just told my men to be ready for fighting, when we spotted about twenty communist soldiers in ARVN field dress with rubber-tired sandals moving through the Sài Gòn Zoo, only 200 yards from us on the other side of the Thị Nghè Arroyo. They were on their way to attack the RVN Navy headquarters. With a pair of binoculars, we could easily detect their disguise. We were unable to do anything against them with our .30 cal. M1 carbines. We also heard guns in downtown Sài Gòn. Our telephone lines were inoperable. I had only twelve riflemen—one ARVN soldier and eleven armed propaganda troops. The other sixty troops were on leave for Tết. So I could have fought the enemy merely as a squad leader. We had thought that the communist side would respect the truce agreement as in previous years.

The ARVN Marine Support Battalion next to the center had only 80 of its 250 soldiers on hand. Captain Trần Văn Thăng, commander of the Marine Transportation Company and in charge of the battalion barracks, discussed with me our joint defense system and stayed alert waiting for the possible attack. Thăng agreed with me that in case I couldn't withstand the enemy firepower, the entire group in the center would be evacuated to his barracks under protection from his Marines. At the time, there were about 300 defectors and more than 50 unarmed employees with about 150 of their wives and children.

Thăng said to me, "I'm afraid that should they overrun your center, they would kill your family members as they have often done. So I'll send two of my best Marines to protect your family until you have consolidated your defense." And so he did.

I gave my sister my .25 caliber pistol and told her to take care of my children and my aunt along with the two Marines. My mother and my wife, both of whom could use the M-1 carbine, were to help my "squad" with whatever was required. My wife, other female members of the employees' families living in the center, and some female defectors began making rounds with coffee pots every five minutes to keep the guards awake.

The center was located at a narrow property of about 8,000 square meters or two acres, surrounded by the fences on the three sides and the Thị Nghè arroyo on the back. The fences were flimsy and too close to the surrounding private estates. It would be very difficult to defend.

I will never forget the favor Capt. Thăng did for me. What happened later to the family of ARVN Major Nguyễn Văn Tuấn, armored battalion commander in Gò Vấp, a Sài Gòn suburb, proved Thăng's foresight. Major Tuấn's elderly mother, his wife, and two children were executed point-blank by the communists that night. Many similar massacres were reported in other areas during the Tết Offensive.

The next day, we found out that a communist battalion of 200 to 300 troops had been sent to attack my center and the Marine barracks on its way to seize the prime minister's office compound in front of the Sài Gòn Zoo. When the communist advance element reached Hàng Sanh neighborhood (near Sài Gòn New Port), its commander had to ask an old man for the way leading to our Chiêu Hồi Center and the Marine barracks, apparently because they had lost contact with their local guides. The old man intentionally gave them the wrong directions, so they moved to a neighborhood where the Sài Gòn-Biên Hòa Highway began, nearly a mile away from our location. They withdrew to Hàng Sanh at dawn and suffered heavy losses when an ARVN Ranger battalion fixed and destroyed them.

Later in the month, my men secretly met the old man and expressed our gratitude. He refused every reward we offered, only asking that we not make his name known to the public or to the intelligence services. How brutal communist revenge could be was unpredictable.

Communists also launched attacks at the U.S. embassy, at the building facing the back gate of the Independence Palace, and at the RVN Navy headquarters, all ended in early morning. It took hours for ARVN Airborne troops to storm the radio station and eliminate communist sappers fighting from inside. All communist troops, about twenty at each of the three places, were killed or captured.

Fighting by some enemy resistance pockets around Sài Gòn continued for two or three days before the ARVN and police forces destroyed all enemy fighters and restored nearly normal activities in the areas. My directorate lost one of its political instructors. An NVA soldier shot him point-blank in the head when he mistook the NVA soldier for an ARVN soldier.

A GI STRAGGLER

Early on January 31, a U.S. Army Spec-5 was wandering near our gate. He appeared extremely frightened by the situation when the around-the-clock curfew was announced. He had spent the night in some bar or nightclub and had tried to return to his base camp in Nhà Bè (seven miles south of Sài Gòn) after two or three days absent from his unit. No transportation to Nhà Bè was available in such a chaotic situation.

Sergeant Raymond Ytzaina met him and brought him to me. I knew how scared he felt, so I told him to stay with us until my men could help him find transportation back to Nhà Bè. He asked me if he could join the fighting if it should take place. I accepted his proposal and assigned him to operate my military radio AN/PRC-10. He happened to make radio contact with some friend of his who was an MP in the U.S. embassy. That assured me of one more way of communications, just in case.

On the third morning, Ytzaina got him transportation to his unit. When he was court-martialed weeks later for going AWOL, he presented the paper bearing my signature, certifying that he had worked as a soldier in my Chiêu Hồi Center during his absence. An American officer from his unit's summary court came to see me to verify the Spec-5's story. At last he was acquitted.

I didn't sleep for three nights in a row. I tried to hide my fear by showing a normal composure, which I did not really have. I ordered my subordinates to continue scheduled games and plays for Tết celebration so that the defectors could relax a little, as recreation could help them overcome worries. I appointed five political instructors who had been serving the military to lead the defector groups, staying twenty-four hours a day with them to lead them in case of emergency.

I also had the duty officer tune in to Radio Hà Nội so that the whole camp could listen to its news and editorials through the public address system. As we expected, Hà Nội was broadcasting reports based on its imagination. In coverage on the offensive in Sài Gòn, it reported, "Our brave National Liberation soldiers have overrun the National Chiêu Hồi Center." It prompted loud laughter from the listeners.

On the morning of February 1, the deputy MACV/J-2 called me up and asked for our help. He required our assistance for further interviews with the defector who had reported accurately on communist units purchasing ARVN and police uniforms. He said his J-2 needed to see the man. The defector had gone on leave at his home in a village under government control in Chương Thiện province. But communist guerrillas temporarily blocked the road to the village.

I sent the chief of interrogation and Sergeant Ytzaina along with an officer from MACV/J-2 on a special plane to Chương Thiện, where they picked up the defector without much difficulty with full support from local military authorities. MACV/J-2 seemed very nervous, but we didn't dig up more details, because we had already heard that MACV/J-2 had been in some trouble with General William Westmoreland.

I have asked myself many times, "Is it true that MACV and ARVN/JGS were unaware of the communist preparation for such a large-scale offensive?"

It took us two days to return to our regular activities and set up a strong defense system with machine guns, M-79s, and hand grenades, which were the most effective urban defensive weapon. While many people didn't trust the former communist soldiers, I felt only a little danger in living next to their dormitories without special security protection.

Four of those defectors, who were former members of the renowned communist sappers battalion Phú Lợi I and who changed sides during the Cedar Falls Operation, performed an incredible feat during the Tết Offensive. They were serving the armed propaganda squad protecting the Chiêu Hồi installation of Sài Gòn City where vocational training was conducted.

Twenty to thirty regular North Vietnamese soldiers attacked the installation with AKs, B-40s, and RPD machine guns. The four armed propaganda troops with two Tommy guns, two M-1 carbines, and a lot of hand grenades took positions on the roof and repelled the attackers before dawn, killing five of them. The defenders suffered no casualties. Other members of their squad only had to supply them with ammunition. After the fighting, I picked one of the four to be my bodyguard.

The Huế-Thừa Thiên Chiêu Hồi community suffered the highest losses, with hundreds of defectors killed and dumped into mass graves, that were found later around Huế. In other provinces, many defectors were assassinated.

In foreign books and newspaper articles I read after the event, the Tết Offensive in South Việt Nam cities was shown by solid red color spots filling up large parts of the maps around sites of fighting. That might have led readers to the misconception that the enemy had controlled large parts of the cities. In fact, the enemy held only small plots such as an office building, a small residential neighborhood, a portion of a street, a hospital, or radio station. Within each plot, usually not larger than 10,000 square feet, communist forces conducted firefights under siege. It was only in Huế that the two sides fought in an area of several acres in the Inner Citadel for more than three weeks.

TV reports were similarly misleading. Images of bursting spots representing communist attacks were flashing over large areas of major cities of South Việt Nam. They suggested that most of the RVN territories were under communist control.

Sài Gòn was under curfew around the clock for only two days, and from 10 PM to 5 AM in the following weeks. And after two months, the curfew time was from midnight until 5 AM. In most cities, fighting ended after a few hours or in some cases after a few days or even a week. But the twenty-five days of fighting in Huế City resulted in the largest destruction and death.

THE STORY OF MY MUSTACHE

The communist surprise attacks made our soldiers extremely nervous. Security guards at gates of barracks carefully checked incoming personnel and vehicles. They requested that every ARVN and allied officer, even a full colonel they didn't know by face, to show an identification card or paper.

Ogden Williams, chief of COORD/Chiêu Hồi, had to show his identification letter in Vietnamese at a checkpoint held by the ARVN Marines on the street leading to the National Chiêu Hồi Center. The Marines searched the civilian jeep he was riding. They stopped only when my troops stepped out and told them, "Mr. Williams is an American big boss and our best friend." The Marines apologized and explained to my men, "We must be fully alerted in this confusing situation. It is possible that some East European communist could disguise himself as an American officer."

During the first week after the communist general offensive started, I was very concerned about the safety of the 300 defectors, armed propaganda troops, employees, and their dependents living in the National Chiêu Hồi Center. I had to supervise the installation security, including water and food emergency storage, and defense coordination as a unit under the city military command while running routine works regarding tasks of defector reception and interrogation all over provincial and regional Chiêu Hồi centers. I was so busy that I had no haircut or shave for about seven days.

My barber shaved my face clean but left my mustache and trimmed it before giving me some advice. He said, "Shave it off if you don't like it. But you look pretty nice with a mustache. You should wear it."

At the same time, I felt something unusual while visiting some military and police installations. At many gates, the guards would let me along with my troops in my jeep get in without much scrutiny while they made careful security inspection on other vehicles and passengers. My driver quickly noted the exception.

He asked many soldiers guarding installations we visited why they were easy with us. Most of them said, "A communist *đặc công* (sapper, commando) is always able to disguise himself as one of our enlisted men, but not as an officer *with a mustache.* Not everyone could wear a mustache handsomely, especially to grow it in a short time."

While I was wondering if I should take the barber's advice, my driver's chat with the guards supported the idea, and I finally accepted it. So I have worn a mustache since February 1968.

THE OFFENSIVE PHASE 2

The second phase of the communist 1968 offensive was launched on June 5 at many spots around Sài Gòn. In my area, enemy troops crossed wet rice fields by platoons and snuck into the capital city. As in the first phase of the offensive, communist troops got through checkpoints by hiding inside loads of vegetables and other goods on trucks. It was impossible to check every vehicle without causing trouble for innocent people. Despite the risk of enemy infiltration into cities, the government and the military had to maintain normal living conditions for the population. Traffic was heavy despite the war.

An NVA platoon of about forty soldiers took position in a crowded neighborhood 500 yards from the Chiêu Hồi Center. We detected the enemy force a few minutes after they got off a few vegetable trucks. An outpost of troops from the ARVN Marine support battalion and the National Chiêu Hồi Center was deployed on one side of the street and the enemy troops were hiding on the other side. Defending the outpost and successfully repulsing the enemy from crossing the street in three hours were eight Marines and four armed propaganda troops.

At dawn, an ARVN Marine company took control of the area. Only two Marines at the outpost were wounded. The enemy unit of about a company in this area also faced firepower from the National Police line defending the Phan Thanh Giản Bridge where the Sài Gòn–Biên Hòa Highway began.

All communist troops in the area were killed before dawn. The government side suffered half a dozen injuries, including the National Police chief, General Nguyễn Ngọc Loan. He was seriously wounded while leading an assault on a communist platoon only 500 yards from my armed propaganda troops' outpost. I got the news a minute after Loan was wounded through an FM-1 radio of the Gia Định Province Police Department network.

Four months before that, on February 1, General Loan had become known for the picture of his execution of a communist sapper with his .38 revolver. It was published all over the world and set off bitter waves of protest in the United States. Before his capture, the sapper had massacred many family members of RVN servicemen. His victims included ARVN Armor Corps Major Tuấn, his mother, wife, and two children at their home on the first day of the offensive, the fact that ignited the general's bitter anger. A friend who was close to Loan told me that his rage was so great that it moved him to kill, even when he was aware that a camera was aimed at him and that reporters were watching.[1]

I heard that under General Loan, the police eliminated a large number of communist secret cells during the first weeks of the Tết Offensive. A lot of VC agents living as the city common people were feeling that their time and chance were coming when the communist units started the fights right in the inner cities. So they shook off their disguised identities and overtly collaborated with the communist attacking forces. When the communist units were routed, their true roles were exposed and they were either taken prisoner, killed, or forced to flee to the boondocks. I thought that was why the security of South Việt Nam cities was improved a great deal after the offensive.

Communist NVA and local units also infiltrated Sài Gòn and other cities, taking up positions to fight at many sites. RVN security forces in Sài Gòn had to expel the enemy during two more battles at Chợ Lớn (Soái Kình Lâm Chinese restaurant building) and Cây Thị ward (Gia Định provincial town). A communist company took a defensive position at Soái Kình Lâm facing the ARVN Thirty-fifth Ranger Battalion. At Cây Thị area, the communist Đồng Nai regiment fought against ARVN Marines and Airborne special commandos.

Colonel Trần Văn Hai, the commander of the Ranger Corps, called and asked me to send some former communist soldiers who had experience with the sappers' tasks to help his men at Soái Kình Lâm. I assigned a special squad of eleven armed propaganda troops to the job. They had served the VC elite sapper companies in the Communist War Zone D for many years before they defected in 1967.

After carefully studying the interior layout of the building, my AP troops crept into Soái Kình Lâm restaurant where a communist company had held fast to the top floors for twenty-four hours. I came with them and stayed outside to give them moral support.

After ten minutes, they got out and reported the enemy disposition. They said, "The VC strength was more than a full-sized platoon, but there were signs of very low morale because they were in a lot of adversary conditions. We could get rid of them by careful room-to-room commando attacks." All eleven former VC sappers volunteered to perform the difficult task. They expected one to three of them would be injured in the exchange of fire with the enemy force. They told me that we had to pay the least for any victory. What they required were tear gas grenades and gas masks, which the police were ready to provide.

After watching their movement in and out of the building, Colonel Hai told me he would not give the task to the eleven men because, he said, "They are the best fighters and would be needed in battles much more important than this. They did give me valuable information on the enemy situation, and I'll have the Rangers seize the objective tonight. If they fail, I'll call for your sappers." At 7 PM, the ranger battalion stormed into the enemy position and eradicated them within an hour.

While the fighting was going on, an incident occurred that marred American-Vietnamese relations. A dozen field grade officers, Nguyễn Cao Kỳ's political supporters, gathered on the front porch of the Chinese high school Phước Đức. A U.S. Army helicopter gunship, attacking the enemy in a concrete building nearby, shot a rocket at the school gate, killing some of the officers and wounding several others. Immediately a rumor spread far and wide that the group had been planning a coup to overthrow President Nguyễn Văn Thiệu and that the Americans had foiled the conspiracy. I was not able to say whether the story was true.

On the occasion of Armed Forces Day, June 19, 1968, I was promoted to major. The promotion was a direct outcome of the expansion of the RVN military personnel size that allocated more rank slots.

A DIFFICULT TASK

In the last week of June, the ARVN Capital Military Region HQS handed over to the Chiêu Hồi Ministry 159 communist soldiers from the NVA Đồng Nai Regiment who had surrendered to ARVN troops in the Sài Gòn suburb of Cây Thị after fierce house-to-house fighting. More than 90 percent of them were NVA regular soldiers. The Chiêu Hồi Center of Gia Định province was unable to handle the process of the large group of defectors who had not been through primary screening interrogation. NVA Colonel Phan Mậu, their regimental commander, defected a few days later.

The size and the composition of the group usually required specific directives by the minister to determine who would be accepted and who would not. But at the time, the former minister for Chiêu Hồi had left after the cabinet reshuffling, and the new minister had not yet assumed his position. The prime minister's office refused to act on matters of ministerial competence. So I had to make appropriate decisions on the matter as required by the situation and would bear full responsibility for my actions. The case could not be delayed any longer.

Unable to devolve the burden to anyone, I had to rely on my staff's collective responsibility. I called a meeting of office chiefs of my directorate, and all joined in a final decision. We formed three groups of interviewers to talk to every one of the newcomers for about twenty minutes each and completed the task in one week. Finally we rejected twenty-one of them and transferred them to the POW camp. Two weeks later, when the new minister, Nguyễn Ngọc An, took over the ministry, I reported to him in detail what my directorate had done. He appreciated our performance and approved all related decisions.

During the interviews, many of the NVA soldiers were outspoken when responding to questions concerning political opinions. They dared to mention and criticize defects and errors of the RVN government as well as social evils in the South, although they asserted their determination to join our side. Their attitude displeased some members of the board of interviewers, but at last we all agreed to award them the Chiêu Hồi status. We were not sure that our decisions were right until several months later.

In late 1968, many of those defectors decided to enlist in the ARVN and particularly in the Kit Carson Scouts serving the U.S. Army combat units. It was the "outspoken" defectors who proved themselves the most faithful to the anticommunist cause. Many were fighting bravely, and some even treated their former comrades captured on the battlegrounds with rough hands. They contributed their part to the war effort better than those who readily expressed unlimited support to the Sài Gòn government in the first minute at the interrogator's table.

A TOUGH DECISION

After preliminary screening and before moving them to my National Chiêu Hồi Center, counterintelligence and police agents warned my security section that some newly arrived defectors would possibly run away whenever there was an opportunity, although they had met all criteria to be awarded the Chiêu Hồi status. However, we could not determine their names with concrete evidence about their intention to send them to prison according to regulations regarding the processing procedures. (After one's petition for Chiêu Hồi status, any violation of RVN criminal law or pro-communist action would send him or her to a regular prison or to a POW camp by decision of a court or a provincial administrative security committee.)

I was so nervous. On one hand, I had to let the newly arrived defectors go out as free citizens in accordance with the Chiêu Hồi center's regulations signed off by me. They would be able to flee to the communist areas at any time. On the other hand, I didn't want to let those enemy soldiers take back their guns against us.

Taking advice given by my staff and the police and military security representatives in an emergency meeting, I decided to do nothing to stop them. My staff members all supported the decision. It could be a typical case to demonstrate the mercifulness of the Chiêu Hồi program and to assert the noble spirit of the RVN national policies. That afternoon, I delivered a short speech to the newcomers in the center's daily session right after they completed primary paperwork.

"There is always a possibility that some of you are planning to return to the communist area," I said. "We could always apply measures to keep you from fleeing, such as to impose a 24/7 curfew on you for strict control. But we don't want to harm the interests of the majority of you defectors. So we have decided to do nothing special to stop you. There is no way to hold back someone who doesn't want to stay. But this gate will not open to you a second time. We want to prove that the government always treats you with leniency and generosity. And we don't really care about one or two more men going back to the communist side." I also repeated a popular proverb: "You can keep ones who want to stay, not ones who want to leave."

The next day two of the group disappeared while strolling with other newcomers in the Sài Gòn Zoo across the Thị Nghè Arroyo from the CH Center.

For days I was asking myself if we had made the wrong decision. But at last it resulted in an unpredictable little feat. About six months later, two communist riflemen in the same company of the two escapees defected to our side, following advice from the two escapees themselves.

They told the two new VC soldiers who were from the same Mekong Delta village that the Chiêu Hồi program was a reality and that "people there were very kind. You should go *chiêu hồi*. As leaders, we two could live longer. But you the privates could hardly live over one year. Besides, we had close relations and profound sympathy with the comrades' leaders at the front, with Comrade Nguyễn Thị Định (she was commander of the VC Liberation Army) in particular. That prompted us to come back to them. Otherwise we would have stayed there."

Of course, we kept the story a secret at the request of the two newcomers, who later enlisted in an ARVN unit. (In order to protect the two ranking communists, I will not disclose any more details. They may still be alive and serving the communist regime in Việt Nam.)

SOME FACTS ABOUT THE 1968 OFFENSIVE

The Chiêu Hồi armed propaganda troops elsewhere in the forty-four provinces of South Việt Nam were fighting communist invaders bravely in the NVA 1968 Tết Offensive.

The Huế-Thừa Thiên armed propaganda company boldly repelled waves of enemy assaults during the first days of the offensive. A few days later, it was one of the two reconnaissance units that supported the main body of the U.S. Marine battalions moving from Phú Bài to Huế in the battle at the Old Imperial Inner Citadel during the 1968 Tết Offensive. On the other flank was the renowned Hắc Báo (Black Tiger) Reconnaissance Company of the ARVN First Infantry Division. Both were performing the reconnaissance mission successfully.

Far away in the Mekong Delta, the Vĩnh Long armed propaganda company was fighting bravely to get rid of communist soldiers who had seized the municipal hospital. They completed the task successfully, killing almost the entire enemy company, but they suffered some ten deaths. Their task had been very difficult because scores of civilian patients were held hostage in the hospital. With the troops' high morale and patience, only a very small number of patients were injured.

In most Chiêu Hồi centers in the country, armed propaganda units fought bravely, either alone or in supporting ARVN regular and regional forces.

The Tết Offensive brought different effects.

Right after the first phase, many of those who put much confidence in the enormous firepower and the U.S. military technology were stunned and disappointed. But the general population realized that such great efforts of the communists could not defeat the RVN, even when the South was under surprise attacks with little help from the Americans in the first days.

During the first days of the offensive, people noticed that according to news reports, communist forces did not attack any U.S. barracks, units, or installations in Sài Gòn and other cities except for the U.S. embassy. Many communist field commanders and some local Communist Party members, who defected months later, confirmed that they had been ordered not to touch the Americans in the first days of the offensive. Some similar symptoms were noticed nationwide.

When fighting erupted again in late May, there were rumors circulating that "it was the Americans who gave the green light to communist units to move into the cities and let them fight the ARVN." They argued that the sophisticated U.S. electronic intelligence network that could detect the movement of every bird in and out of Sài Gòn must have been intentionally closed down to let the enemy infiltrate the capital city so easily. Some even alleged that U.S. helicopters provided food to communist soldiers in several jungle areas. Another allegation spreading in Qui Nhơn in February 1968 even claimed that U.S. Army trucks were moving communist troops into the city to attack the radio station and other sites. Although the rumors were not credible to all Vietnamese, there are a great many South Vietnamese who still believe them today.

Major General Trần Thanh Phong, then ARVN chief of staff, shared his observation with me when I met him in a closed-door meeting in late 1968. He concluded that based on reports he received, since General Creighton W. Abrams took over the command of MACV, replacing General Westmoreland, the U.S. forces really "decimated" communist troops. General Phong quoted a message from Abrams as ordering any U.S. officer commanding a company and higher to explain why he lost contact with the enemy after a short engagement.

He was certain that the enemy KIAs had increased greatly since then. As to my personal knowledge, the U.S. Army combat units were more aggressive in 1968 with a lot more offensive operations. And consequently, the losses of the ARVN and of the Americans also climbed higher than in the previous years. Although they occurred at a lower rate compared with the communists and the ARVN, American losses intensified the waves of protests in the United States.

Most South Vietnamese units were fighting bravely, and none was severely defeated. The general public could see TV reports of the great number of communist casualties in most of the battles, particularly in Huế, Đà Nẵng, Kontum, Pleiku, Qui Nhơn, and Sài Gòn. The communist defeat was incredible. In many places, entire communist attacking units were eradicated.

At Tân Sơn Nhứt AFB, almost all eighty sappers infiltrating the base were gunned down. The NVA eighty-nine-men company attacking the Kontum Province HQS suffered eighty-eight killed. The only one alive was a young NVA private who had defected for Chiêu Hồi at a hamlet an hour before his unit reached the city.

I could tell how communist units were suffering when I saw more than 50,000 AK rifles captured in battles all around South Việt Nam after the first three months of the offensive. A hundred ARVN soldiers were moving the AKs into warehouses of the Ordnance Corps where a close friend of mine was serving when I stopped by to see him. The number of military recruits could provide concrete evidence of the common South Vietnamese youth's devotion to the defense of freedom. When I visited one of the recruiting centers near Sài Gòn three months after Tết, the officers there told me that right after the enemy general offensive started, the number of male Vietnamese under the age of twenty who enlisted as volunteers to serve ARVN combat units was more than double the planned intake of draftees. All common anticommunists like me were astonished to hear that.

Besides, the number of draft dodgers seemed to lessen. Those young men were arrested and transferred to the military police to be sent to the boot camps for training before serving in the infantry units. How could the foreign press reveal and understand such a meaningful indication?

PEOPLE'S LIFE IN 1968

In 1968, the communist offensive created some trouble to life in cities, but it didn't disrupt the normal activities to the extent that it dealt deadly blows to the people. While fighting was on the rise in many locations, people were moving on streets, buying and selling, doing business in areas not close to battle sites. Life seemed close to normal. Battles were fought in small spaces: a building, a group of houses, or concrete constructions. On streets and neighborhoods nearby, people were busy working as if war had not existed. Curfew hours impeded people's activities but not too much.

However, people in foreign countries who were influenced by partial information might think Sài Gòn was the land of death and violence.

Even better educated and well informed people could have fallen for it. In late 1968, my remote cousin living in Thailand dropped by to visit with my family. At 7 PM she insisted on going back before it was dark to her friend's home where she was staying. We asked her why she was so anxious to leave so soon. She said that she was afraid of traveling in Sài Gòn at night even in a taxi, "Many Vietnamese in Bangkok told me that American soldiers were often sexually attacking young women on Sài Gòn streets."

A few weeks later, a newly arriving American colonel told me that he had been thinking that Sài Gòn was not a safe place for women to live. But after a few days in Viet Nam, he became sure that Sài Gòn was much safer than his home city (somewhere in the midwestern United States) as far as robbery and rape were concerned.

COMMUNIST LEADERS' OPTIMISM

Another question concerning the Tết Offensive was how much the communist top leaders believed that it would bring them certain victory. I think they did a great deal. The first evidence was in a report sent from a VC underground intelligence agent in charge of the Sài Gòn region that the police captured at a private home where a long-distance transmitter-receiver was secretly installed. The Sài Gòn police sent me an account of the case as my men were actively supporting it in the raid.

Captured copies of some reports made by the communist agent not long before the general offensive indicated that an estimate was sent to some high command in the Communist Party hierarchy, probably the Supreme Command in Hà Nội or the VCP Central Southern Command. It assured the high command that "whenever the revolutionary forces launch attacks at the bases of the Americans and their puppets in Sài Gòn, at least 90 percent of common people, 70 percent civil servants and the police, along with 50 percent of Sài Gòn soldiers will join the revolutionary forces to take down the reactionary ruling power and establish the new revolutionary local governments."

At first, I thought the report that contained grossly exaggerated information might be used only for propaganda purposes. However, I later sought the opinion of the former communist colonel Trần Văn Đắc (alias Tám Hà), political commissar of the NVA Fifth Division, who left the communist side to join the Chiêu Hồi in late 1968. He was the most respected NVA ranking officer ever leaving the communists for our side. He affirmed to me that his bosses in Hà Nội believed such a report and decided that a triumphant victory of a general offensive and a general uprising would be unquestionable.

The Communist Party leaders might have believed that they could mobilize the million people of South Việt Nam to join the communist uprising like the thousands of men and women of Kiến Hòa (Bến Tre) province had done in the movement that communist propaganda called "Đồng Khởi" (general uprising). It was the mass protests in December 1960 that overthrew a dozen hamlet and village governments in Kiến Hòa and forced a few posts to retreat to the provincial city.

Actually, none of the smallest uprisings ever took place in 1968 by the common people or the military soldiers, even in Kiến Hòa. After eight years, the war of weapons and the war of words significantly changed the common people's psychology.

In another aspect of the offensive, what I saw in Chợ Lớn (Sài Gòn's Chinatown) could be observed all around the country. Many communist units had been told to infiltrate the cities, not to participate in any combat but just to assume control of the cities as the people had already overthrown the Thiệu-Kỳ government. Apparently communist commanders played their wily tricks just to have their troops reach the inner cities. Once being abandoned in the hostile land, their troops had to fight for the least chance to survive. Such a style of operation—sending troops to the enemy territories just to die—was a daring decision, not a maneuver that was worth appraising.

In Chợ Lớn near Soái Kình Lâm Restaurant, about fifty communist soldiers were walking into the city in three-row drilling formation with AK rifles still hanging on their shoulders. A dozen were killed by the police with machine guns. The rest ran into the restaurant to take up combat positions with their fellows for a day before the ARVN thirty-fifth Ranger Battalion destroyed them.

Similarly, military reports received by my office a few weeks later asserted that many NVA troops found dead near Huế and other battlegrounds had been prepared for "running the local revolutionary temporary governments," not fighting. Some died with khaki dress uniforms ready to take part in some parade celebrating the "liberation."

Communist leaders in Hà Nội obviously were determined to conquer South Việt Nam in a short time. They mobilized the highest possible human resources to reinforce their divisions sent to the South. Draft agencies called upon students, technicians, engineers in vital state industrial firms, and teachers who were at key jobs to serve in the infantry battalions being sent to "War Zone B" or South Việt Nam (War Zone A: North Việt Nam; War Zone C: Laos). Many of them defected to the RVN side at their first opportunity.

During the second phase of the communist general offensive, my National Chiêu Hồi Center received some special defector directly from the ARVN Marine Battalion fighting in a Sài Gòn suburb. They were two talented professional singers, Bùi Thiện and Đoàn Chính, a printing engineer who graduated in East Germany and specialized in offset, and five NVA physicians. They were serving in key jobs at state-controlled installations in Hà Nội and were supposed to be exempt from the draft. But the all-out effort to win the general offensive conscripted them into the last battalions to be sent to the South.

It was estimated that the communist side lost nearly 200,000 troops in the 1968 general offensive. I think the figure might be close to the truth. After 1969, it could be observed that communist units of ethnic South Vietnamese troops had been largely eradicated. NVA troops were sent deeper south to fill up the losses. Meanwhile, younger NVA troops were fighting in most battles.

THE FACTOR OF SURPRISE

Why did the communist units launch the offensive on two different dates?

At Đà Nẵng, Qui Nhơn, Kontum, Pleiku, and Nha Trang, the attacks began on the night of January 29 and the small hours of January 30, the Lunar New Year or Tết's Eve. At Huế, Sài Gòn, and other major cities, communist forces started the offensive on the night of January 30 and January 31 in the early hours, the first and second days of the Lunar New Year. So they did not make use of the most important strategic principle of surprise by synchronized attacks.

Sources from North Vietnamese publications and from interrogations of NVA soldiers affirmed later that in July 1967, the communist government in the North changed its lunar calendar, with calculations based on Seventh Time Zone instead of the Eighth Time Zone as previously practiced in Việt Nam as well as in China, Taiwan, Hong Kong, and Singapore. South Việt Nam still used the old calculation.

Therefore, Tết's Eve in 1968 fell on the night of January 29 in the North and on the night of January 30 in the South. Several months later, I learned from ARVN central intelligence services that the Communist Supreme Command had ordered its units to launch the all-out attacks on Tết's Eve. Apparently the Communist Supreme Command was unaware of the difference between calendars of the South and the North. So communist regional field commands using the North Vietnamese calendar started the fight twenty-four hours earlier than those using the calendar published in the South. Thus the offensive lost the precious strategic factors of time and coordination.

The deadly mistake cost the communist side huge losses of personnel and equipment. If communist forces had started the general offensive at the same hour on the same day, the outcome would have been somehow different in favor of Hà Nội.[2]

THE MASSACRES

The Tết Offensive left a deep imprint on every South Vietnamese heart. For people living at the time, the theme song from the movie *Exodus* still reminds them of unforgettable firefights in that bloody year. For months after Tết, South Việt Nam TV and radio stations were playing the first lines of the song as background music accompanying every battle news report. When my children grew up and had their own families, each time they heard the tune they would say, "Oh, the Tết Offensive."

To many of the SVN adults, the communist top leaders, who broke the truce and started the fighting that killed people on a large scale right on the most sacred holiday of the Vietnamese people, would never be forgiven.

There were hundreds of newsreel clips reporting the burial of thousands of victims in mass graves around Huế. Most were civilians, nationalist parties' members, anticommunists, and unarmed soldiers, killed by gunshots, ropes, clubs, sticks, machetes, and knives or buried alive.

Among the reports concerning the number of victims, the most reliable came from the police department of Huế-Thừa Thiên, which compiled information from the authorities of the village level and records of every mass grave. According to Major Liên Thành, chief of the Huế-Thừa Thiên Police Department in 1968, in his book, there were 5,327 bodies found in twenty-six graves; about 1,200 were reported as missing. There has been no information about the fate of the missing.

Civilians were executed by communist units all around the country, but only in Huế-were they done so systematically and in so great a number. The Chiêu Hồi program lost some dozen employees and hundreds of former defectors in all forty-four provinces during the 1968 Communist Offensive.

The horrible scenes of the carnage delivered a great shock to the general population. The atrocity urged most fence-sitters to take sides with us and consolidated the political conviction of the anticommunists.[3]

The communist officials have always denied the massacres, even saying that the bodies found in mass graves around Huế were victims of ARVN and U.S. soldiers. I myself met 100 of the victims' relatives who confirmed the communists' crimes, and I saw with my own eyes an excavated mass grave. Besides, no photographic technology could fake pictures of the 5,000 remains. A great many of them were identified by their relatives. Seeing is believing.

Nobody can deny that the NVA suffered severe military losses in the Tết Offensive. The ARVN and the U.S. forces actually won the 1968 battles, 10 to 1, but the communist side gained triumphant victories in public opinion in the United States due to one-sided reports, biased comments, unbalanced observation, false information, and misunderstandings.

THE PHƯỢNG HOÀNG CAMPAIGN

The RVN had to fight not only the communist military forces but also the whole Việt Nam Communist Party. Its infrastructure was the main force of the VCP in the war of insurgency in South Việt Nam, which provided support to all communist fronts and organizations. Without such support, the communist army from both the South and the North could do very little in war.

The village party committee is the most powerful organization in the communist ruling system even today. District and provincial leaders are like fifteenth-century viceroys, with powers sometimes overriding the central authority. During twenty years of war, the RVN forces wiped out several communist regiments and even divisions, but only one of the clandestine Communist Party provincial committees in South Việt Nam was eliminated.

Realizing the VC insurgent strategy, the CIA directed the Phoenix Campaign with help from various Vietnamese police, military, and intelligence agencies. Facing strong criticism by the U.S. Congress, who opposed the existence of a U.S. government nonmilitary agency in Việt Nam that infringed on RVN sovereignty, William Colby, chief of CORDS/MACV, asked President Thiệu to sign a decree establishing a Vietnamese agency to take over the campaign in the shortest time.

Sometime before the second phase of the offensive in June 1968, a founding committee for a new campaign replacing the Phoenix was convened. Thiệu ordered the committee to settle the matter with the CIA. General Nguyễn Ngọc Loan, commander of the National Police, was actively supporting the group before he was injured in the second phase of the Tết Offensive. As my directorate was responsible for interrogation and classification of the defectors, I was to participate in the process as the representative of the Chiêu Hồi Ministry.

The official committee was created under the name Phượng Hoàng (Phoenix). The American side provided full support to the Phượng Hoàng Committee. An office of the Vietnamese National Police HQS from national down to district levels was in charge of the secretariat of each Phượng Hoàng Committee to coordinate the operation.

Right from the beginning, the campaign proved a success. After the new Phượng Hoàng system was officially founded, the Classification Section in every provincial Chiêu Hồi office had to work closely with the local Phượng Hoàng Committee. The principal objective of Phượng Hoàng was collecting information relating to the Communist Party infrastructure for the elimination of local cell members.

Former communist soldiers in the Chiêu Hồi program were recruited to serve the Provincial Reconnaissance Units. The PRU served under the National Police branch and supported by the CIA's budget. PRU was a non-status paramilitary institution. PRU soldiers infiltrated the VC-infested areas and eliminated VC local cadres. Sometimes the PRU soldiers were disguised as communist troops to lure out the enemy cells.

Detentions made in the government-controlled areas were conducted without violence. In operations on the enemy-infested lands, there could be firefights that resulted in killing and some rare abuses. The enemy propaganda exaggerated the incidents to label the PRU as assassins. But to my personal knowledge, things happened as in any regular military operation.

The Phượng Hoàng Campaign did achieve its principal objectives. However, the national leadership and military commands failed to exploit the Phượng Hoàng successes, thus wasting the greatest success of the campaign effort.

CHIÊU HỒI STATUS

In mid-1968, an interministerial committee (Chiêu Hồi, Defense, Interior, National Police, Joint General Staff J-1 and J-2) met and discussed a regulatory directive with clauses defining principles and procedures to grant former communist soldiers the status of *hồi chánh*. I presided over the meetings and prepared the original draft. A month later, the committee unanimously approved my draft. The minister of Chiêu Hồi approved the final copy before submitting it to the prime minister, who signed it into an executive order known as Huấn Thị 22 (Prime Minister's Directive 22). US/MACV endorsed the directive and made it applicable to the American and allied units under its command (MACV Directive 381-50 dated February 22, 1969).

The directive was respected by the ARVN and allied units. It facilitated every step of classifying, supporting the defectors as well as prompting them to contribute to the war effort. It asserted the defector's right to RVN citizenship immediately after responsible authorities confirmed that he or she met all criteria to be accepted by the Chiêu Hồi policy. Besides, other clauses of the directive provided their protection from improper treatment even at the interrogator's desk.

Later on, the HT-22 provided lawyers with more specific materials for their arguments at the courts trying cases related to the former defectors. The directive protected the defectors from being prosecuted for crimes, however serious, that they had done by order of their communist bosses or communist rules of action.

But they would be tried at the court of justice if their crimes were committed solely because of personal motivation without orders from their communist superiors.

However, before the directive was signed, we had some problems with embassy officials in charge of American POWs detained in North Việt Nam. Since U.S. combat soldiers began fighting the Vietnamese communist troops, they received enemy troops who had surrendered and captured many POWs. American unit commanders were confused between Chiêu Hồi and POWs. After primary interrogations, the S-2 of some units classified a POW as Chiêu Hồi if he showed willingness to disclose accurate military intelligence information.

In other cases, many communist soldiers were classified as POWs and sent to POW camps, but later were reclassified as defectors when those POWs voluntarily expressed their decision to join the RVN side "after they checked in at the POW camps." This policy was done by agreement among military, police, and Chiêu Hồi people in charge of intelligence, POWs, and Chiêu Hồi, rather than by any regulation. The policy was highly appreciated by the International Red Cross in Geneva. By an official letter, the Red Cross confirmed that the policy of converting a POW into a Chiêu Hồi at his request with free will was in compliance with the 1949 Geneva Convention because the policy gave the POW a chance to have a better life. The letter was a great success, but some in the U.S. embassy didn't think so. They objected to the policy, saying that they were afraid of possible retaliation from Hà Nội. They said the communists might react by compelling the POWs in Hà Nội Hilton to do something likewise against the United States.

The Ministry of Defense, the JGS, the Ministry of Interior, the National Police Command, and the Ministry of Chiêu Hồi, with tacit support from many MACV officers related to the matter, all rejected the viewpoint of those Americans. We had experiences with the Vietnamese communist leaders. They would elect any course of action they felt necessary, and they wouldn't have any concern about the fate of their POWs. Such concern for those Americans was futile, we concluded. The POW conversion took up a few clauses in the drafted directive.

Unfortunately, the officials at the U.S. embassy tried another approach through the RVN Ministry of Foreign Affairs. The ministry, without consulting or notifying other related ministries and agencies, supported the embassy's officials and submitted a drafted executive order to the prime minister's office to forbid the practice of reclassifying the POWs to award them the Chiêu Hồi status. The newly appointed prime minister, Trần Văn Hương, signed the order. However, the Chiêu Hồi Ministry found another way to achieve our goals.

The Chiêu Hồi minister, Nguyễn Ngọc An, got mad about the trick, but there was no way to reverse the decision when the prime minister had signed it. So the government-related agencies silently agreed to conduct an attack with guerrilla tactics. The member ministries and agencies separately instructed their subordinate units and offices to lawfully implement a regulation bypassing the decision.

At last, we found a way to skillfully insert the go-around clauses into Directive 22 to set a rule without conflicting with the prime minister's decision.

According to the clauses, whenever a unit or an agency of the RVN or of the allied forces ran the preliminary interrogation on a communist soldier and found out later that he or she was classified as a POW *by mistake* after having shown a desire to join the RVN side, he or she could be removed from a POW camp and transferred to the Chiêu Hồi center at the recommendation of the responsible unit or agency. Such a proposal was made by the battalion S-2 and higher (G-2, J-2) and approved by the provincial Chiêu Hồi committee with the reason as "a mistake" in the process. It was easy to acquire such justification. The International Red Cross and its teams at the camps did not object to such cases.

The regulation worked well, granting valuable assistance to many young men to become honest and prosperous RVN citizens who would have had to spend their green years in the POW camps if we hadn't helped. The story proved that many responsible U.S. officials cared too much about their own responsibility exceeding a reasonable degree, disregarding the ultimate objectives of the war.

THE POW CAMPS

Sometime in 1969, I visited the POW camp at Biên Hòa to check the cases of reclassification. The POWs were treated better than the prisoners in regular prisons. Food and living allowances were higher. The problems, if any, were created by some of them.

As in any prison with a number of Communist Party members among the inmates, there were at least some agitators who would play malicious tricks to create a disturbance. Sometimes they made electric live wires short-circuit or connected conductors to sheet metal walls, injuring or killing other inmates. They also killed inmates who were suspected of serving as secret informers by strangling or by driving sharpened pieces of barbed wire into the heart.

The Military Police were upset and sometimes dealt roughly with violators. In rare cases, the MPs beat violators. Some died after the beatings. An MP officer told me that anyone working there would do the same to keep the other POWs safe and the camp in order.

The daily food allowance for each POW was nearly equal to that of an ARVN soldier, which was VN$80 in 1968. The U.S. embassy officials proposed raising the allowance up to VN$100, but the ARVN disagreed because it would prompt complaints from our troops. In the first month in POW camps, a POW would consume most of the allowed 21 kg of rice per month. In later months, he would feel full with about 15 kg. In 1971 there was an investigation of some camps' officials for illegally selling the unconsumed rice allowance.

THE UNWRITTEN TASKS

Most people only knew Chiêu Hồi through reports of how many leaflets were dropped over communist lands, how much time about the Chiêu Hồi program was broadcast, and how many soldiers defected to our side. But they didn't know that we treated those former communist soldiers as compatriots.

It's rather difficult to list all that we were really doing in the Chiêu Hồi program. Besides our functions as chiefs of sections or services and employees, we all had to perform tasks that have not been mentioned in any book, decree, or regulation.

The tasks soon became an unregulated tradition, spontaneously carried out by Chiêu Hồi employees at all levels, from district up to the ministry. The following were performed in my directorate.

As my job included promoting the defectors' faithfulness and active support to the RVN cause, I had to act simply and modestly. I used to wear military uniform or plainclothes with a shirt and cheap pants. In my spare time, I went to the defectors' dormitories to chat with them to understand their motivations and aspirations and to study the issues related to the communist regime and the society of North Việt Nam. My subordinates serving in the directorate followed suit. Our informality in manners and the simplicity in style displayed another aspect of the war of ideology.

The most tiresome unofficial task was being a best man in the defector's wedding party. A lot of former NVA soldiers had no relatives in the South, whereas their brides' families always want the grooms' parents or someone representing their parents to co-preside over the wedding ceremonies and parties. I had to attend an average of two weddings a month after having passed some to my assistants.

Sometimes we had to do more than that. Some of the marriages broke down after a time, and the girls' parents or siblings came to us for advice or intervention. The cases were mostly difficult, beyond our capacity to help, and we just tried to do our best, leaving everything to God's disposition.

Most of those who were from North Việt Nam made the Chiêu Hồi centers their homes. As for the defectors who served in the Kit Carson Scouts, when they were on leave or R&R, they spent their time in the National Center. They always brought large bags of candy that their GI fellows had given them to hand out to children living in the Center.

There were more than eighty kids living in the dependents' quarters of the Center, including my four children. They joyfully welcomed the scouts when they appeared at the front gate with bags on their shoulders. One of the bags could be full of sweets.

Young men from the North had been living for years under the Communist Party's tight control so rigidly that it more or less deformed their mentality. They seemed to aspire for personal sympathy. They loved the kids so much that during their spare time, they led our children to the marketplace or downtown Sài Gòn, bought them everything they could afford with their little pocket money, particularly those who had jobs.

Sometimes my kids—nine, six, four, and three years of age—went with a group of defectors during their open time for the whole afternoon until dark. I trusted the men, being certain that they wouldn't do anything harmful to the kids. They found in the kids the images of their own children or siblings, which helped ease their loneliness. Many of the defectors were adopted by old people and became devoted children and brothers in those families.

The security services did not think so at first. After I explained the whole situation, the security agents agreed with me that I shouldn't refuse the defectors' sympathy, but at times they were watching to ensure the kids' safety.

Many times when my kids as well as my other family members were sick, I had the former NVA military physician who was assigned chief physician of the National Chiêu Hồi Center examine and treat them. Many government employees in the Center advised me against it, saying that he had been trained in the Hà Nội Medicine School, which was known for its poor instruction and resources. Most physicians who graduated from Hà Nội had very limited medical expertise.

The physician was reluctant to take care of my family. I told him that I trusted him and I wanted to show my confidence in his expertise. Besides, those were the cases of minor sicknesses. My gestures squelched the complaints against him and lifted him up, too.

REHABILITATION

To help the defectors fully integrate into the South Vietnamese society was the responsibility of another Chiêu Hồi agency, the Directorate of Rehabilitation. But as the National Chiêu Hồi Center was under my direct command, and most former defectors made it their home, I had to contribute a little part to the process.

After the orientation classes, most defectors of South Vietnamese origin returned to live in their hometowns or villages. Those of North Vietnamese origin mostly lived in urban areas, and a small number lived in Chiêu Hồi villages. They joined the labor force and were noted for working industriously and skillfully. There were some who were successful in business and became millionaires. Others inherited fortunes from their brothers, sisters, cousins, and even adoptive mothers.

Among defectors who volunteered to serve in ARVN units, the ethnic South Vietnamese had no difference and knowledge on military life while the ethnic North Vietnamese were facing some of the differences on social, cultural, and general perception. The difficulties quickly disappeared when they had to share common dangers and learn from each other. According to many ARVN unit commanders, their former NVA soldiers were fighting and carrying out their tasks rather well with high endurance and courage.

In coordination with the Military Security Department, in 1968 we began to keep track of the presence of former defectors serving in military units. According to a Military Security Department report in 1972, almost every company of the RVN Army had one former defector. A very small number of former defectors serving the ARVN, the Armed Propaganda companies, and the Kit Carson teams rejoined the communist side, and even a smaller number of them were working in communist secret cells.

South Việt Nam intelligence agencies, the U.S. military, and the CIA employed a number of defectors in many operations, including secret works outside South Việt Nam. My directorate helped them select the candidates and only kept general records about their official identity, the time they were in the Chiêu Hồi centers and their follow-up information, but not about their recruitment by secret agencies and units.

On the darker side were the unfavorable acts of some of these "secret operation" commands. Sometimes they just didn't want to employ some defectors they had recruited from the Chiêu Hồi centers and decided to discharge them. They dropped them at the Center's gate without a piece of paper, let alone any personnel documents. Once more, it was an annoying responsibility that we couldn't entrust to anyone else, though it had never been stated in my directorate's standard operation procedures, either by written documents or by inference.

The defectors were extremely important sources of intelligence information. There were a great many minor military achievements that were made possible by accurate reports of defectors. However, not all of their contributions were fully exploited.

Lots of North Vietnamese defectors had affirmed before 1970 that many Red Chinese infantry divisions and engineer regiments were stationed throughout North Việt Nam during the war. Due to that reinforcement, the Vietnamese communist leaders could send the largest NVA combat forces to the South.

They also reported that there were hundreds of Soviet pilots and nearly 2,000 Soviet soldiers serving in antiaircraft units, and hundreds of North Korean pilots and air force technicians joined the NVA. They heard of many North Korean pilots killed in dogfights over North Việt Nam and saw some Soviet pilots parachuting to safety after their planes were taken down by U.S. fighters. South Vietnamese and U.S. intelligence agencies must have recorded the information. However, none of it was made public by the press corps until the 2000s, when Hà Nội authorities overtly held memorial services for North Koreans killed in the war and confirmed the Soviet and Chinese soldiers' presence in North Việt Nam during the war.

TWENTY-ONE

Defeat on the Home Front

From 1962 to 1975, there were nearly 160,000 communist troops who reported to the South Vietnamese side for Chiêu Hồi. Of these, 15,000 were from regular North Việt Nam units. They included one senior colonel, four lieutenant colonels, about ten majors, three dozen captains, hundreds of lieutenants, a few members of the provincial Party Standing Committees (equal in rank to lieutenant colonel), two capable engineers graduated from Eastern European universities, dozens of engineers graduated from Hà Nội, some college professors, hundreds of teachers, ten army physicians, a talented violinist graduated from the Moscow Conservatory, and two famous novelists.

Typical among the defectors was Colonel Trần Văn Đắc, alias Tám Hà, a rare, well-educated NVA officer who had attained a French high school diploma (baccalaureate). In the early 1940s, not many people graduated with this degree. He had a strong anticommunist conviction, but was never very demonstrative in voicing his opinions about the communist leaders. He always showed his impartiality in his comments about the communist regime.

Also typical were Phan Mậu (Lt. Col. Regiment CO), Lê Xuân Chuyên (Lt. Col., Reg. CO), Huỳnh Cự (Maj.), Phan Văn Xướng (Senior Captain, Armor Corps), Vương Quang Xuân (Senior Captain, Intelligence, an undercover agent), and others. The former NVA officers contributed important tactical and strategic information, according to classified reports from various intelligence agencies sent to my directorate.

Captain Vương Quang Xuân, the intelligence agent, was trained in China and sent to South Việt Nam as the leader of a spy network. He provided valuable information to the RVN and American intelligence community. Lieutenant La Thanh Đồng, a NVA antiaircraft battery commander, who reported to the U.S. Marines at Khe Sanh in January 1968 for Chiêu Hồi, helped the Marines with important reports about the NVA units in the area.

The RVN government assigned many defectors to jobs in and out of the Chiêu Hồi Ministry. Lê Xuân Chuyên was appointed director of the National Chiêu Hồi Center from April to November 1967 and later served as a member of the Chiêu Hồi Ministry advisory board along with Huỳnh Cự and others. Five NVA doctors were serving as doctor's assistants after passing the medical comprehension test.

In 1968, under Chiêu Hồi ministers Nguyễn Xuân Phong and Nguyễn Ngọc An, the Ministry was working on a project to commission dozens of ex-NVA officers. I was a member of the studying board that included other officials from the ministries of Chiêu Hồi, Defense, Interior, Education, the Joint General Staff, and the National Police. General Trần Thanh Phong, the chief of staff/JGS along with the Chiêu Hồi Ministry, was an active supporter of the project. If the board's proposal had been approved, many ex-NVA officers would have been commissioned as ARVN officers: NVA Junior Colonel Tám Hà as ARVN lieutenant colonel in the Political Warfare branch, Lt. Colonel Phan Mậu as ARVN major to serve the Command and Staff College, Senior Capt. Phan Văn Xưởng as ARVN captain of the Armor Corps, and many other captains and lieutenants.

The government rejected our proposal, and the board stopped working. We were unable to convince the old-fashioned conservative anticommunist ranking members of the administration.

The ex-communist defectors also brought true images of North Vietnamese life to the people in the South. The famous writer Xuân Vũ, who had had many novels published in the North, joined the nationalist side in 1968. In South Việt Nam and in America after 1975, his books artfully described life in the North, especially the fate of NVA soldiers on the Hồ Chí Minh Trails and their psychology in the war. His best novel, *Đường Đi Không Đến* (The Route That Failed to Reach Destination) attracted a great number of readers.

On the psychological front, the defectors contributed a significant part to the assertion of South Việt Nam's nationalist right cause. At the same time, as eyewitnesses of true life in the North, they provided a profound comprehension of the communist regime to the South Vietnamese, who by then had only a vague and false knowledge about what was happening north of the 17th parallel.

GROWTH OF THE CHIÊU HỒI PROGRAM

The years 1967 to 1969 saw an increase in the number of communist soldiers rallying to the government side, probably due to military pressure against communist forces and raids deep into the communist-controlled areas. In early 1969, General Nguyễn Đức Thắng, commander of the Military Region IV (the Mekong delta), sent troops far into the remote areas in the delta, creating good opportunities for communist guerrillas to join the Chiêu Hồi program. The new defectors amounted to more than 1,000 a month in the populated provinces in the Mekong Delta. Most of them were ethnic South Vietnamese.

Each of the northern provinces (from Bình Định to Quảng Trị) received from 40 to 100 defectors a month; most of them were NVA soldiers. In some provinces of that region, guerrilla strength dwindled so sharply that local communist security cadres had to employ ethnic North Vietnamese regulars to do the guerrillas' job in communist-controlled remote villages. The solution ran counter to the communist theory of "Three Forces" with guerrillas playing the major role in controlling and motivating the population. Ethnic North Vietnamese failed to do the tasks that only native villagers could perform.

The least busy Chiêu Hồi office was in An Giang province, homeland of the Buddhist Hòa Hảo sect, the most ardent anticommunist people. During the 1955–75 war, An Giang was the only province that imposed no curfew at all, except inside the provincial city of Long Xuyên during the Tết Offensive. In 1968 and 1969 when I was making inspection trips to Long Xuyên, local officials drove me and other friends to faraway villages at midnight for bouts of drinking without worrying about road security.

Very few An Giang people joined the communist side. Communist troops from adjacent provinces seldom came to the Chiêu Hồi program by a route into or crossing the province without prearrangement. They might be killed before their true intention was recognized. An average of five to ten defectors reported to Long Xuyên every month.

The large influx of defectors continued to rise when more civilians were assisting the program. The highest number of defectors was 47,000 in 1969. In 1968, the RVN government launched a campaign of promoting civilians to participate in the Chiêu Hồi effort in the Third Party Inducement program. A person who guided a communist soldier or political cadre to rally to the government side would be rewarded an amount of money, about half an ARVN private's monthly pay. The reward was not large, but it encouraged peasants to cooperate and gave the enemy troops a feeling of safety when there was someone who had arranged for their defection. Although the reward mostly induced communist defectors of southern origin, a considerable number of the NVA took advice from peasants whom they met and decided to join the RVN side.

There were a few cases where true defectors reported the name of intermediaries who led them to our side in order to claim the reward, but the cases appeared later to have been falsified.

THE DEFECTORS' MENTALITY

At the time, rumors were that many of the defectors weren't communist soldiers but civilians claiming fake identity to profit from the program, particularly to be awarded six-month conscription deferment. In fact, such fraud did exist, but it was not as pervasive as some people may have thought. In an investigation conducted by my directorate, reliable records confirmed that only about 1 percent of the Chiêu Hồi population was suspected of not having really served communist military or political organizations. They may have been members in groups of para-guerrilla, labor force, or satellite VC organizations, or just common civilians.

It was difficult to sham being a communist soldier or cadre as far as political background, dialect, and accent were concerned. A faked communist military background could hardly mislead local intelligence interrogators. Besides, it was almost impossible to sham a North Vietnamese accent to claim being a North Việt Nam regular if one was not living there after 1954. Differences in spoken vocabulary relating to political, social, and military subjects between people growing up in the two Việt Nams could be easily noticed. Very few young men coming from remote areas under VC control in South Việt Nam would elect such a risky solution for a draft deferment of only six months. Although there was little discrimination, young people disliked the idea of being known as former VCs.

Some other cases were suspected of relating to corruption. But only a very small number of the responsible officials in military, police, and civilian agencies were found receiving gifts from defectors, usually of little value and mostly for trivial favors. Individuals who had a considerable amount of money would not bribe the Chiêu Hồi officials for being sham former VC because they could do so more safely with officials of other agencies, whatever their purposes may have been.

Skepticism of some RVN officials and commanders was also a small problem. Some extremist anticommunists would never trust former communists; they saw communists everywhere. However, they constituted an insignificant impediment to the Chiêu Hồi policy. And the conflict in Việt Nam had a complicated nature where some common rules were not always applicable.

A large number of defectors coming from North Việt Nam defected mainly because they had no other choice to survive. However, once living in the nationalist South, they quickly changed and integrated into the new society within a year. As they had been crammed with a huge quantity of lies about the South and the anticommunists since they were kids, realities in the South and the freedom they enjoyed gradually taught them the truth. Lies stuffed into their heads by communist indoctrination evaporated quickly after they got used to the ways of living in the South. Of course some were still under communist influence.

Many people may have been concerned about the communist plot to have their men infiltrate into the program. They did, but not many. During the three years I was in the job, there were eleven cases of known phony defectors who had been assigned tasks to harm the Chiêu Hồi centers.

Defectors who joined the communists after returning home were even fewer. It was well known that the Communist Party political security service mercilessly punished their men who joined the RVN government side. Most provinces and districts held so-called Defectors' Reunions once or twice a year as a way to follow up on defectors. Former defectors got together to feast and be entertained. The Chiêu Hồi and police authorities would have a chance to collect related information regarding those former communist defectors.

There were a lot of heroes in the Kit Carson Scouts. I lost the records of their stories after April 30, 1975, but I still remember many of them. One of those heroes fought to the death beside an American platoon leader of the First Infantry Division when all others in the platoon were killed or wounded. The two resisted the enemy to the last cartridge before destroying their PRC-25 radio and committing suicide.

What we had not expected was their attitude toward their former comrades. A number of the defectors fighting in the Kit Carson groups showed their bitterness toward captured communist officers, especially the political officers. Some scouts killed those captives if they made them angry.

U.S. officers in charge of the scouts asked my directorate for help, as they needed intelligence information from the captured communist officers and because regulations restricted them. We tried our best to dissuade them from acting so brutally to hardcore communists when we met with them during visits to allied combat units or when they were on R&R in Sài Gòn. But what we could do was conduct casual heart-to-heart talks, as no formal lesson could actually help.

Most of them said to me, "You would have understood our psychology if you were one of us. Our hatred toward those foolish communist cadres exploded because their behavior prompted our recollection of how the cruel communist regime robbed us of our prime of life and we did not realize that until we enjoyed life in the South. We got upset and saw them as a symbol of oppression, atrocity, and duplicity. In a second of resentment, we got rid of them to vent our animosity, which you would feel hard to perceive."

I failed to follow up the results because only a year after that, the U.S. units discharged the scouts before phasing out of Việt Nam.

A FEW TYPICAL FIGURES

Nguyễn Sơn, a twenty-four-year-old sergeant of a North Vietnamese regular unit, joined our side in 1969. He had great sympathy with my family and frequently visited us. After time in the National Center, he volunteered to join the ARVN and served in the reconnaissance company of the ARVN Fifth Infantry Division. Many times in difficult situations he assisted his company with his knowledge of the enemy habits and was a resolute fighter. He found great happiness when he was on leave to visit with my family and other Chiêu Hồi Center employees' families. He spent little of his salary for himself, giving much of it to assist needy friends and charitable organizations.

In March 1972 he was awarded a one-month leave in Sài Gòn before communist units launched their Summer Offensive at An Lộc where his company came under fierce attack. He asked me to help him get back to An Lộc even though he still had twenty more days of leave, insisting that his company would need him badly at that critical time. I found friends at the Fifth Division rear base who put him on one of the last helicopters flying supplies and troops to An Lộc before the enemy antiaircraft fire sealed off the city to aircraft. After the An Lộc battle ended, I received a letter from his friends telling me that he died a hero in a bloody battle a few days before the enemy attacking forces disengaged and retreated.

Another brave VC defector was Nguyễn Văn Liên, whose village was next to mine in the North. He defected in 1966. In 1967, my family held a wedding ceremony and party for him when he got married to a nice girl who was also a defector from a VC medical unit. Two years later, he enlisted in the ARVN Airborne Division. In a battle in Kontum during the Summer Offensive, he was taken prisoner by an NVA unit. At night, less than twenty-four hours after being captured, he used his cunning and his knowledge of the habits of NVA soldiers to lead ten Airborne POWs to escape. On the way fleeing back to his unit, he was shot in the calf.

He was put on thirty-day convalescent leave. After two weeks at home in Sài Gòn, he asked the Airborne Division rear base to help him rejoin his company, which was fighting in Quảng Trị. He seemed to be happier with his fighting fellows than being at home. The next month he came to see me on his crutches. An AK bullet from a close range had smashed off his left heel. He was discharged with decorations for his courage and his wound.

A TOUGH VC WOMAN COMMANDER

There were hundreds of female soldiers and cadres from the communist side who joined the nationalist government. Most of them were guerrillas, logistic service members, medics, and Party Women Association's cadres. The highest woman combat commander who ever defected to our side was Huỳnh Thị Tân. She fought as the company commander in a communist provincial main force for two years before she defected to the Chiêu Hồi program. She was well known by our troops in the Đồng Tháp area for her courage and combat efficiency.

Her fiancé was also a brave VC company commander. For some reason only known to her superiors, the couple was separated and their marriage permission was denied. The man was killed in a battle a few months later. She decided to defect. She was nearly thirty years old.

In 1969, a few days after arriving at the provincial Chiêu Hồi center, she led a team of four armed propaganda troops to make a surprise commando attack to kill the Communist Party district committee secretary. She riddled his bed with her submachine gun, but killed only his two bodyguards because he was outside in the outhouse.

At a dinner with my family, my mother asked her how she could handle the all-male company. She said, "It's not a big problem, Mom. In communist units, we have the iron discipline. I may put to death any soldier of my company who acts against my order, especially when we are fighting."

"Have you shot any troop who refused to carry out your order?" my mother asked.

The former VC company officer smiled and said, "I have never shot anyone for that purpose, possibly because every soldier in my command knew that I would do it if he went against my orders."

THE PRICE WAS CHEAP

American research proved that the cost to call a communist soldier to defect to our side and to feed, train, and resettle him in the Chiêu Hồi program amounted to less than US$500. Statistically, it was much less than the money the military spent on each enemy killed in action, which might have amounted to several thousand dollars. Some may say that such calculations only have a numerical value, but it did mean something important to us, relatively.

Besides the expenditure calculation, it was apparent that the number of 160,000 former communist soldiers rallying under our flag—equal to more than ten divisions—also saved at least 5,000 of our soldiers' lives if the ratio of our loss to theirs was 1:3.

As far as military intelligence was concerned, the program provided a valuable source of information leading to the elimination of many communist units and disruptions of their schemes. Besides tens of thousands of weapons the defectors turned in, many weapon caches and convoys were destroyed, and numerous enemy plots were nipped in the bud. The monetary value of such successes may have amounted to billions of dollars.

There were a few dozen cases of important contributions made by defectors during my three years serving the Chiêu Hồi Ministry. Some typical cases are still fresh in my memory.

Nguyễn Cao, a teacher in North Việt Nam, was drafted and sent to South Việt Nam in the NVA Fifth Regiment, a new infiltrating unit from North Việt Nam in early 1969. While the regiment was resting near Huế to prepare a surprise attack, he defected and reported what he knew to the ARVN I Corps. As the situation dictated the employment of swift and powerful striking force, the 101st Airborne Division (Airmobile) reacted in no time, landing the troops right on top of the enemy formation. As I still remember, hundreds of NVA soldiers were killed, with a lot of military equipment captured, including 140 crew-served weapons.

Cao was rewarded 2.5 million piasters (US$18,000 at 1969 rate) by the Chiêu Hồi Ministry for the captured weapons. He could have been rewarded up to 5 million piasters for his courageous and meritorious contribution, but he refused, saying that the 2.5 million was enough. He then enlisted in an armed propaganda company stationed in the Sài Gòn area. By the Chiêu Hồi Ministry regulation, he would not be assigned to units in Military Region I to ensure his personal safety. He married a girl in Huế.

In 1971 by a record keeping mistake and at the insistence of his mother-in-law, he was transferred to Đà Nẵng. Not long after that, in 1972, a secret communist death squad member threw a hand grenade onto his bed, killing his pregnant wife. He and his two-year-old son were wounded but survived the attack. Cao was killed and dumped into the Han River (Đà Nẵng) when the communists occupied Đà Nẵng on March 29, 1975.

In 1969, a defector led an ARVN battalion to capture two 82 mm mortars, already emplaced and aimed at the front yard of the headquarters building of Phước Tuy province. Elevation and direction were precisely set, dozens of high explosive shells were prepared for a surprise shelling during the routine Monday 8 AM national flag-raising ceremony that would be attended by 200 soldiers and public servants. The planned mortar attack was foiled less than twenty-four hours before its H-hour. The defector was rewarded about VN$1.5 million. He shared 500,000 with the operating battalion, contributed 500,000 to an orphanage, and kept the remaining 500,000.

The destruction of 100 enemy trucks supplying ammunition on the way along the Long Mountain Trails was made possible by another NVA defector. His information led to an air raid, so successful that he was rewarded about more than 3 million piasters.

During my three years serving the Chiêu Hồi program, there were many rewards to defectors who reported accurate information that helped the police get rid of communist secret financial operation cells and confiscate large amounts of money.

CHIÊU HỒI ARMED PROPAGANDA UNIT OPERATION

The Chiêu Hồi armed propaganda force was under the Directorate of Operation. A company of more than seventy men was under my command to provide security to my directorate and the National Chiêu Hồi Center. The company routinely joined propaganda operations.

Besides being used for training purposes, these twice-a-month operations filled a gap on the psychological front in the region around the capital city. I often went with the company when I had time. Sometimes U.S. reporters and military and civilian officials joined us to observe and report. In the operations, our troops visited villagers, the sick and the senior villagers in particular, performing health examinations, distributing medicine, talking to them about the RVN government policies, holding cultural shows, distributing toys to kids, and collecting intelligence information.

Villages around Sài Gòn, as we found out, were on the last lines of the target lists of various government programs and projects. The villages were close enough to the city to be aware of social evils and corruption of the urban life but rather far from getting government assistance.

The population in those areas around Sài Gòn and other large cities were easy targets for communist propaganda. For years, VC secret cells actively operated in the area, although VC military activity was very low. So in an agreement with Gia Định province, I appointed the company to join a task force to do the psywar job.

In many operations, my armed propaganda company cooperated with a company or a platoon from the American 199th Light Infantry Brigade. Along with the ARVN Fifth Ranger Group, the 199th was responsible for security to the capital city. My armed propaganda company consisted of many ex-communist soldiers who were born and brought up near Sài Gòn and served the local communist units in the areas for years. The appearance of those ex-VCs proved to the peasants that, contrary to communist propaganda, defectors were well treated and were serving just like any other ARVN soldier. The peasants' sympathy would bring us valuable information that had never been expected previously.

A company of the 199th, an ARVN Medical/Civic Action team and a platoon of our armed propaganda troops started the first operation of this kind in early 1969 in the villages near Chợ Đệm, only a few miles from the 199th HQS at Bình Điền, the southern boundary of Sài Gòn. The GIs showed up for the first time and brought great fear to the villagers. In the previous years, no U.S. combat unit had ever visited the area of a dozen hamlets bordering Bình Chánh district.

When we approached the village, young women ran away in panic out of the hamlet upon seeing the Americans, and we knew why. The old women told us that they saw the GIs for the first time and were scared to death. They said, "In the hamlet three kilometers from here, five women died after being raped by several dozen American black soldiers." The young women only returned to their homes after our troops stopped them and assured them of their safety. We knew that story was nothing more than a VC propaganda trick to evoke images of abuses by French soldiers two decades earlier. We sent several trucks with Vietnamese soldiers to the hamlet. There we conducted an operation with a MEDCAP team, inviting women from a nearby hamlet as well. The women were given health examinations and medicines and some gifts that included toys for their kids.

When my men asked the women from the nearby hamlet about the alleged "rapes," they gave the same story about the "five women." But they said the incident had happened "here" and added that the American troops had never been to their hamlet. The women from both hamlets shared their stories and changed their opinion about the GIs. Their pale faces turned pink with smiles as if light bulbs had just turned on.

One of my men remarked: "The truth can't reach a place three kilometers away. How could it reach newsrooms in New York City 20,000 km from here?"

In a nearby village, there was a respectable eighty-four-year-old man who drew our attention. He welcomed us to his home every time we came to see him, but he never let us take his picture. His face was so beautiful, expressing the classic facial features of an aging Vietnamese. He said he didn't want his pictures to be displayed by American officers in their living rooms to show their American friends how barbarous the Vietnamese were and to justify why they could kill them without remorse. We knew that at his age, there was no easy way to shake his conviction. But we visited him about every two weeks. He kept calling us "Americans' puppets" and praised Hồ Chí Minh without fear of being arrested. The Sài Gòn regime never arrested senior citizens who just talked against the government.

He was angry about an air strike that had destroyed a small pagoda 500 yards from his home during the Tết Offensive while "there was no VC in it." We took pains to explain to him that it must have been a mistake. He kept dismissing our explanation until an officer showed him a photomap and asked him to pick out his house and the pagoda sites from the map. He accepted our argument when he couldn't tell a house from a temple on the aerial photo.

One morning about two months later when I was walking on the dirt road in front of his home, he called me in. It was the first time he had invited anyone in my group to come in with such a friendly manner. After a minute giving some directives to my officers, I stepped in. He welcomed me with hot tea.

Unexpectedly, the old gentleman asked me, "Major, you always tell me that you in the Republic Army are not American puppets. Could you prove that by telling the two American soldiers there to climb up my coconut tree and pick two coconuts for our refreshment?"

I stepped out and talked to the two GIs guarding the road leading to their company command post. It was not a problem to have the GIs do such a nonmilitary task, but climbing was difficult for the two GIs. If only they had been Hawaiian natives! Seeing the two Americans failing to get more than two yards up the coconut tree, the old man laughed and asked me to thank the two GIs for their effort. Then he called his ten-year-old grandson. The slim boy reached the treetop, climbing with the ease of a monkey, and brought down four large coconuts to his grandpa.

The old man became more pleasant and friendly. "Major, now I believe in what you said. What I asked you to do today is just to see how American soldiers react to a Vietnamese officer. Last week when you were here, I saw an American captain coming in to meet you for something. I didn't know what he was talking with you about. But the way the tall American captain saluted and talked to you, a short Vietnamese major, all showed full respect. So I was convinced. No explanation can, but just that," he said with gleeful smile while offering me a glass of coconut milk.

However, he complained forcefully about the spreading corruption in the government and the unscrupulous use of firepower by some units that resulted in the death of innocent victims and destruction of their homes. He told us that his eldest son had been killed by our troops in an operation a long time ago, and that a VC death squad executed the second son a few years later, leaving him his grandson, who picked the coconuts. Neither of his sons had been collaborating with either side.

His change in political attitude proved to be very helpful. Many of his villagers, who held him in high regard, became friendlier. Some secretly gave us valuable information concerning VC activities. A few others persuaded VC soldiers to defect to our side. One of the villagers disclosed to us the local cell of the *kinh tài* (economic-financial) network after we agreed that we would not kill or arrest the VC *kinh tài* cell leader, who was his relative. *Kinh tài* was the most important branch that procured money and material support for local VC activities.

We passed all such information on to the local military and police officials and to the 199th Brigade. I heard later that the information was processed successfully with extreme care for the safety of the tip providers, especially ones who disclosed information related to the *kinh tài*. As a rule, the VC "security" branch listed villagers as well as their defectors who disclosed to our intelligence agencies information on communist *kinh tài* networks as "number one traitors" to be executed. Those who provided destructive military information only came in the second line of the list. The Communist Party gave *kinh tài* the supreme authority and called it the Party's "main artery."

A National Police report asserted that the communist underground *kinh tài* agency in Định Tường province collected a large amount of money nearly equal to the provincial government's taxation revenue, but it did not have to pay for public expenses (social services, health care, education).

It took my men nearly three months to win the sympathy of just one octogenarian. But his influence carried his opinion to other villagers. That's what we were looking for after several previous failures.

FOREIGNERS' COMPREHENSION OF THE WAR

While the war effort against the communists in Việt Nam was under fierce attack from many in the American media and from war protesters, the Chiêu Hồi program didn't bear the brunt of their disapproval. It seemed that they could find no significant target in the program at which to direct their criticisms.

During my three years in the program, I was assigned the most difficult and unpleasant task of receiving foreign visitors, including politicians, journalists, scholars, delegations of official and private organizations, and a few tourists. Many of their questions were dismaying; most foreigners, including our American friends, both war protesters and supporters, lacked basic knowledge about the true nature of the Việt Nam War.

One of the private visitors was a doctor from Germany who had spent two decades in communist prisons. His experiences in jails would provide valuable advice to me when I was incarcerated after the war.

Besides briefing visitors, every Saturday for two months in 1967 I was invited to talk to an orientation class of about 100 incoming Americans. They were military officers from captain to full colonel and U.S. government officials of similar rank. I was there to tell the class about the Chiêu Hồi program, but I often had to explain other matters. With respect to the war, I would tell the class my own opinion as a military officer.

The class was scheduled at the worst hour when class members were tired after a week of being crammed with topics presented by many agencies and speakers and when they were about to have lunch before relaxing into the weekend. Moreover, my English was not rich enough to explain complicated points of view, and I was often confused by the Americans' accents. The classes stopped after the Tết Offensive.

Trying to keep the class from falling asleep, sometimes I cracked a joke. To my surprise, when I expected the least response, the audience burst out laughing as I invited them to visit my Chiêu Hồi Center and drink cold "33" beer with us "in the morning." Drinking a glass of beer with ice in the temperature of 90-plus degrees F before noon was nothing special to a Vietnamese in Sài Gòn, but it was unusual to an American.

A similar unexpected response occurred when I welcomed a delegation of four members of the British Parliament to my center. The briefing went smoothly, but I didn't think it was a good one. To conclude my presentation, I apologized to them for my *English with an American accent*. To my surprise, my honorable guests responded to my apology with a half minute of laughter. A few days later, I received a thank-you letter in which the distinguished MPs only said something like "Thank you for the joke." That was how the British MPs expressed their appreciation.

Many American visitors complained that before the trips to Việt Nam, they had visited the Vietnamese embassy in Washington, D.C., looking for publications about Việt Nam and the war, but few were available to them. I reported their complaints to the Chiêu Hồi minister, and he brought it up in the weekly meeting of the cabinet.

As Minister Nguyễn Xuân Phong told me later, President Thiệu asked the two responsible ministries, Foreign Affairs and Information, for an explanation. It was later reported that our national budget had allocated funds for publishing introductory books in several languages on a variety of topics regarding Việt Nam and the war. However, the books had been sitting in a warehouse for a year because no money had been allocated to send the books overseas.

At a meeting with Information Ministry officials to draw up the 1969 budget of both ministries, I found out that the national budget for 1969 provided only VN$23 million (equal to US$160,000 at official rate) for propagating information abroad, VN$16 million of which was for office rent and personnel salaries. Only VN$7 million was for propaganda and information materials. Meanwhile, sources from the RVN intelligence service estimated that North Việt Nam was spending millions of dollars each year for its propaganda publications overseas.

The Soviet Union, China, and the communist parties of many other countries were actively supporting Hà Nội on the propaganda front, particularly in the United States. According to friends of mine living in the States, publications supporting the communist side were smuggled across the Canadian and Mexican borders.

To make the situation even worse, there was inadequate effort to welcome and provide special assistance to members of the foreign press corps in Việt Nam. How could we get their support if we did not give them a warm welcome and considerate assistance? The Information Ministry and the Armed Forces Psywar agency may have had great ability, but with very little money their effort was blunted. U.S. direct aid to the Information Ministry was skimpy, and no government leader would agree to cut the budgets of other programs, such as education and health care, to provide more support to information and propaganda activities.

During the Việt Nam War, most foreign reporters proved their exceptional courage and professional spirit. But they preferred to accompany U.S. units into combat. Images of the GIs would attract larger U.S. audiences. They might find little or nothing worth reporting in operations of the ARVN soldiers because they couldn't speak their language. I believe this was the reason heroic fighting by many ARVN units was generally unknown in America and elsewhere. If sometimes an event regarding the ARVN was reported, it usually depicted the defects, lack of ability, or cowardice of the ARVN.

A good example was in the battles of Khe Sanh. While the American public was well informed about the U.S. Marines fighting NVA divisions, very few Americans knew that the ARVN Thirty-seventh Ranger Battalion took part in the defense of the base at the southwest perimeter. The Rangers fought and suffered with the U.S. Marines, but their presence was not appropriately acknowledged.

In my opinion, the insufficient concern on the psychological front and underestimating the power of the press corps by both Washington and Sài Gòn wasted the opportunity to underscore the positive achievements that over 58,000 Americans and 260,000 South Vietnamese had died for. The mass media, journalists in particular, had a strong aversion to the U.S. government and everything associated with the U.S. executive branch. And the U.S. and RVN governments' policies for improving public relations with the press corps during the war were thoroughly clumsy and detrimental to the cause of a free and democratic Việt Nam.

A FAKE COMMUNIST HERO

Although the South Việt Nam side could afford only limited resources for psychological warfare, its counterpropaganda once achieved a triumphant victory. In 1966, the Communist Party and the government of North Việt Nam launched a campaign honoring their "Martyr Nguyễn Văn Bé" with ceremonies and with publications distributed around the world.

According to propaganda materials from Hà Nội, the young man Nguyễn Văn Bé, a member of a VC local guerrilla group in South Việt Nam, was taken prisoner by the ARVN in an ambush. He was carrying ammunition to the battlefield, including a directional antipersonnel mine. On May 3, 1966, while the ARVN officers and American advisors gathered to watch Bé demonstrate how to use the mine at their request, Bé set off the mine, killing himself and sixty-nine of his enemy soldiers, including twelve Americans.

In February 1967, by some chance, South Vietnamese authorities found out that Bé was actually alive and being held in a prison camp in Mỹ Tho. In fact, he had been captured in an ambush, and some of his comrades in the squad had escaped. There was no mine demonstration, and no Vietnamese or Americans had been killed. The communist local commanders thought Bé was dead and felt free to make up the story. With active support from JUSPAO (formerly USIS), our side launched one of the largest counterpropaganda campaigns in Việt Nam, the States, and many other countries. Bé appeared at many public meetings and interviews and told his true story. The local VC guerrillas at his village area ordered Bé's parents to deny the government's claim and not to recognize him. The old couple had to flee to the government-controlled area.

The Chiêu Hồi National Center had to provide Bé's parents with shelter and a food allowance as no other ministry's budget was more appropriate to the case as Bé was awarded the Chiêu Hồi status. The old couple told me about their experiences going with their son to public meetings held around the country. In the meetings, Bé and his parents were under security protection by the police.

Communist propagandists denied the Sài Gòn version, saying that "the Nguyễn Văn Bé who appeared in the public meetings held by the RVN authorities was another person whose face was operated on by U.S. plastic surgeons to make him resemble the real Bé." Communist agents in the South cited the *Mission Impossible* series on the U.S. Armed Forces television channel in Việt Nam to support their argument. The series regularly showed disguised agents undergoing facial surgery to impersonate some bad guys in secret operations. Some Hà Nội's newspapers called for the assassination of "the faked Bé."

Many people believed the VC's allegations, until Bé's parents were introduced to the audience in many meetings. Bé's mother told me her simple argument against the VC's claim. In response to a question from the audience asking how she could know for sure that Bé was her real son, she said, "I am not a propaganda cadre, so I don't argue with you on complicated matters. Simply, I can be sure he's my dear son by just *smelling* him. The body scent *is* of my dearest Bé. Besides, he can tell everything that was known only between him and me. Even his daddy never knows our secrets. How could the Americans teach that to their faked Bé, even if they could make his face resemble my dear son's?"

The old mom's argument was a marvelous success, much more effective than any leaflet, poster, or radio comment. The "cosmetic surgery" theory faded away. Hà Nội silently canceled the scheduled ceremony to unveil a life-sized statue of Nguyễn Văn Bé that was to be presided over by Hồ Chí Minh. Meanwhile, the RVN prime minister awarded Bé a special favor by recruiting him in one of the field police companies in Sài Gòn.

HỒ CHÍ MINH GONE

On September 4, 1969, Sài Gòn media reported the death of Hồ with front-page commentaries. Some dignitaries predicted the weakening of the communist ruling power under his successors, but many others didn't think so.

Defectors who had been NVA high-ranking officers had a different opinion. They argued that Lê Duẩn, the VCP general secretary, and Lê Đức Thọ, the chief of the Organization Bureau (in charge of personnel affairs), had been holding supreme power since the early 1960s. Hồ Chí Minh's death would not affect Lê Duẩn's course of action significantly, they said. Võ Nguyên Giáp's position was not high enough to dream of further advancing in power after Hồ Chí Minh died, although he was the VCP's second most idolized leader. Moreover, he suffered harsh criticism and was held partly responsible for the NVA's heavy losses in the 1968 Tết Offensive in the South.

I respected Hồ Chí Minh as a devoted and persistent communist leader with energy, especially with firm resolution and high endurance in a time of despair, a talented politician with numerous skilled plots and counterplots to survive failures, to prevail, and to fool his enemy. He was firstly faithful to communist ideology. His patriotism, if any, came in second. I didn't see him as a hero but as a person who was one-third Machiavelli, one-third Tsao Tsao in the

Chinese "Three Kingdoms," and one-third skilled propagandist. In fact, his wily tricks, demagogic schemes, and self-idolizing histrionic acting outperformed not only Machiavelli and Tsao Tsao but possibly all other dictators, too.

Ho was the only king of Việt Nam who employed many rascals, rough and ready uneducated persons, even robbers and murderers in leading national jobs, in addition to faithful and devoted revolutionaries, at all levels of his party and government. Some of those were his confidential ministers. He achieved great success in forming a group of subordinates who faithfully carried out his schemes, particularly his idolization. His great skill of propaganda was undeniable. He was behind the deaths of thousands of his opponents and landlords, but he always passed the blame on to his subordinates. He was the unmitigated Sinophile who followed Mao's teachings to the letter.

For me, one of the worst things he did was write a book under a pseudonym to praise himself sky high: *Những Mẩu Chuyện Về Đời Hoạt Động của Hồ Chủ Tịch* (Stories about President Hồ's Active Life), 1948, reprinted many times since.[1]

One of the key successes of the Việt Nam communist front of propaganda must be the deification of Hồ Chí Minh. The clever scheme to praise him was generated right from the start of his rule over Việt Nam and carried out with the greatest effort and by every means of instruction. It won a large number of the Vietnamese hearts, including mine until I was twelve years old. I feel lucky to have expelled that idol from my heart soon enough.

THE DEGRADING IDOL

After Hồ Chí Minh passed away, General Giáp's position started going down-hill. He was the NVA idol, second only to Hồ in the VCP propaganda pecking order. Other VCP leaders enjoyed limited glorification. The communist propaganda machine succeeded in its effort to build up his international reputation after the battle of Điện Biên Phủ in 1954. It praised him to the sky until he was dismissed from the powerful VCP Politburo.

However, there are many questions concerning this legendary communist military leader that should be reconsidered. Although he was commander in chief of the North Việt Nam Army, he did not hold the full responsibility of a supreme commander to conduct the war. Unlike a western-styled military institution where the army had to do almost everything to confront the enemy, the communist army relied largely on the party's personnel, logistic, psychological, and intelligence support. His power as a commander in chief was significantly reduced. Besides, all-important strategic decisions were made by the collective Politburo, not solely by Giáp and his staff.

Chinese Communist generals played the decisive role in the battle of Điện Biên Phủ in which Giáp had only a supporting role. Giáp was successful as the

NVA commander in chief in dealing with his subordinate commanders, inspiring them to perform to the best of their ability, and winning their respect. Commanders at regiment level and higher adored him. His colleague, General Nguyễn Chí Thanh, won the sympathy of many NVA officers who did not favor Giáp.

Nothing actually proved that Giáp was a talented strategist. He was well known for exchanging huge loss of life for victories, even the ones of very little military value. I think sacrificing a large number of soldiers in exchange for battlefield achievements does not make a war leader a military genius. He did not have formal officer training, so he didn't have the appearance and manners of a military commander. People could easily notice his gestures and his salute in his pictures that looked very unmilitary. He appeared more like a political cadre than a soldier. But he was very arrogant while he was still in power.

In a 1969 interview with Oriana Fallaci, the famous Italian journalist, Giáp strongly denied his responsibility for the failure of the 1968 Tết Offensive. He said the National Liberation Front was to blame. He knew better than anyone else that people were well aware about his decisive authority over the NLF and that all communist strategic operations in the South were planned and decided by his headquarters in Hà Nội. He should not have passed the blame on to anyone else. In the interview, he also corroborated the American military figures that communist dead totaled about 500,000 men. But he denied that he did try a second Điện Biên Phủ at Khe Sanh, despite the fact that North Việt Nam's state-controlled media and the propaganda machine had asserted that "Khe Sanh will be the second Điện Biên Phủ."

He lost the Politburo's favor after 1968, reportedly because he was blamed for the NVA's great losses in the Tết Offensive. In 1982, he was dismissed from the Politburo and then from the VCP Central Committee. In 1983 he became absolutely powerless in the job of chairman of the Family Planning Committee.

We used to say that if Võ Nguyên Giáp had exchanged jobs with South Việt Nam General Cao Văn Viên, he would have done no better and probably would have suffered an even more tragic defeat.

POOR RELATIONS BETWEEN THE GIS AND THE PEOPLE

In the war, relationships between American fighters and Vietnamese people were minimal. American soldiers in Việt Nam did not seek to create favorable relations with the common Vietnamese. Both sides had very little friendly and reciprocal contact in which to learn about each other's culture. The Vietnamese often witnessed drunken GIs fighting each other, necking with girls in barrooms, and sometimes refusing to pay taxi fares.

Bars and nightclubs frequented by GIs were separate parts of the local communities or, as you might call them, the "nameless diasporas" in Việt Nam where people spoke a mixture of Vietnamese and English, with more dirty words and little grammar. To my knowledge, more GIs from logistic support units than from U.S. combat units showed up at the bars and nightclubs.

Once in 1969, the 173rd Airborne Brigade in Lâm Đồng province sent a captain and an enlisted man to a two-day temporary duty in my directorate for some matters related to the Kit Carson Scouts. The two GIs had a problem with transportation to and from my national CH Center if they stayed overnight at Tân Sơn Nhất MACV barracks. No U.S. military bus line ran near my directorate location. So I asked the two young men if they felt fine with two small bedrooms reserved for visiting officials from provincial Chiêu Hồi offices. The rooms were clean but not equipped with furniture and other conveniences even by Vietnamese standards. They accepted our offer happily.

They told me that they had not talked to a Vietnamese family since they were sent to Việt Nam. They had arrived at Tân Sơn Nhất one evening three months earlier, and the next morning they had boarded a plane to Lâm Đồng, then went on to fight in the dense jungles around that highland province. They had never been to any bars or clubs either. I felt sad to see the way Americans were sent to war without the slightest bit of knowledge about the people they were supposed to help fight for their freedom. The former U.S. advisors had been much better trained.

I invited both Americans to my family dinners. During the meal, they asked many questions, and I was happy to take the time to explain almost anything they wanted to know. At 7 PM, the two GIs asked me to show them Sài Gòn at night. I told my driver to guide them on a tour in my civilian jeep. I didn't forget to sign a travel permit for my jeep and its driver, which also bore the names of the two Americans so that they could stay out beyond the MACV curfew time at 10 PM and before the Vietnamese curfew at 12 AM.

Three hours later, at 10:30 PM, two American MPs in a jeep with the two 173rd GIs appeared at the gate of the Chiêu Hồi Center. They just came to have my office corroborate the travel permit. What seemed strange to the MPs was that they had never seen any American soldier riding in a civilian jeep with a travel order signed by a Vietnamese army commander. After my American liaison officer, who happened to be at my compound drinking beer with me, gave his explanation, the MPs withdrew without causing any trouble to the two sons of the 173rd. The two continued enjoying a Sài Gòn evening until midnight.

I almost forgot the story until a few months later. On a trip accompanying the Chiêu Hồi minister to visit Lâm Đồng province, I met the two 173rd Airborne soldiers again. After Minister Nguyễn Ngọc An and I arrived at the provincial guest house, the province chief asked the minister for my thirty-minute absence so that I could visit the 173rd Brigade as invited by the brigade executive officer. What a pleasant surprise! I followed an American major who welcomed me to the VIP parking nearby. The captain and the PFC who had dined with my family greeted me beside a sedan sent by the 173rd HQS. I met with the executive officer, an elegant and brilliant colonel on behalf of the commanding general, who was on a trip away from the base camp.

The 173rd gentlemen asked me what I needed from their units. I didn't know what I should ask for. At last, they said they would provide soft drinks and beer for the annual Chiêu Hồi rally held by the provincial Chiêu Hồi Center that evening with the estimated 500 participants. They also provided a lot of captured M-16 rifles for my armed propaganda company in Sài Gòn. The armed propaganda troops were equipped with carbines, and they always yearned for the lightweight and highly effective M-16. They knew quite well the NVA weapons, so they preferred the M-16 to the AK-47.

I've always believed that if only one-fourth of the half million GIs serving in the Việt Nam War each year had been treated kindly by our Vietnamese, we would have won many objectives of the war. But there were some high-ranking Americans who did not favor such mutual relations. I had a feeling that some Americans did not favor the friendship with Vietnamese closer than what they thought necessary, maybe to maintain a safe margin for future relationship problems.

My policy was that a friendship between the Americans and the Vietnamese in any aspect would bring many advantages to the two peoples. However, I couldn't help reacting when an American acted incorrectly in front of me.

Once, an American lieutenant from the U.S. Army Eleventh Armored Cavalry Regiment came to my directorate with some matters relating to the Kit Carson Scouts. He did not salute me, and he talked to me curtly through an interpreter, not the way he should have behaved to a field grade officer. I asked Ytzaina to show him to the gate and ask the Eleventh Cav staff section to send a polite lieutenant instead.

That afternoon, an American major from the regiment and the said lieutenant came to see me to apologize for his manners. The major asked me if I recommended that the regiment officially reprimand the poor boy. Of course I said no. His apology was enough.

To the extent that they had relations with the Vietnamese, most GIs behaved rather well. They respected local authorities. In the 1946–54 war, a Vietnamese district chief was nobody more than a common peasant to the French soldiers. Many daring Americans in defiance of imminent danger bravely landed their choppers under enemy fire to evacuate seriously injured civilians. Did such acts of courage and humanity ever appear on American TV screens?

One afternoon in 1969, I was riding in my jeep from Biên Hòa to Sài Gòn when the traffic was heavy. The car right in front of me driven by a middle-aged Vietnamese businessman in shirt and tie collided with a big truck coming from the opposite direction. The big truck broke open the sedan's left side door and hit the driver's head. I quickly ran to him, but he died instantly. His wife was slightly injured, and his two sons suffered a few scratches. The traffic was stopped completely.

His briefcase full of money at his side had broken open. A hundred 500-piaster bills were blowing all around the car. Passengers on nearby buses, cars, and some three-wheeled vehicles rushed in to snatch the bills. Right at the scene was a military truck with about twenty soldiers of the First Infantry Division under an American second lieutenant. I called the lieutenant and asked if he could help stop the looting. With a loud "yes sir," he ordered his troops to jump down from the trucks to surround all the looters with joined hands in about fifteen seconds. Most looters failed to escape the circle of the Big Red One GIs. The troops acted quickly. Two Vietnamese policemen arrived, retrieved the money, and handed the bills back to the victim's wife. The crowd cheered when the GIs left. If only the scene had been recorded and reported in the mass media.

PROPAGANDA AGAINST AMERICAN GIS

Communist propagandists, as I have noted more than once, were very clever. The most forceful propaganda was aimed at the Americans' presence in Việt Nam. U.S. involvement in the war was the most vulnerable weakness on the nationalist psywar front. Basically, the Vietnamese were jingoistic. They didn't like foreigners.

Among many South Vietnamese, images of peasants killed by American bombs in their rural shelters strengthened unfavorable opinions about the Americans. It was not easy to prove that the Americans had come to fight for the interests of the South Vietnamese in these cases.

Hà Nội's principal tactic was to convince common people that the plight of the South Vietnamese was similar to what Vietnamese people had suffered during the war with the French. North Vietnamese people (and South Vietnamese peasants who had never met the GIs) naturally saw no difference between the American GIs and the French soldiers: the same "big-nosed, pale-skinned, blue-eyed, and fair-haired" soldiers who had raped and killed whenever and wherever they liked in the 1946–54 war.

With the same tactic, the communist propaganda created the image of the RVN government and army as faithful valets of the "American imperialists," portraying the local South Vietnamese authorities as cruel wicked lords and the ARVN soldiers as brigands who raped women and killed children at will. The people in communist-controlled areas saw no difference between the RVN and the pre-1955 Bảo Đại regime, which had very limited competence under the French domination and its nationalist soldiers who looted and mistreated innocent villagers.

It was in such an environment that the massacre at Mỹ Lai was revealed.

THE MỸ LAI MASSACRE

Mỹ Lai was a hamlet of Quảng Ngãi province. In March 1968, a platoon under Lieutenant William L. Calley executed a large number of Mỹ Lai's villagers; most were old men, women, and children. The number of victims varied by sources, from about 350 (RVN) to 500 (communist government). Some ARVN officers and people in the area I met months later estimated that the number of victims may have been over 350 but certainly not 500.[2]

When the story became public in November 1969, the event was a shock to the public. During the 1946–54 war under the French soldiers' guns, there had been dozens of cases in which hundreds of innocent civilians were slain in retaliation for French losses. But since the French quit and the ARVN was reorganized in 1955, no mass killing had been committed. In particular, the American soldiers were known for their discipline. The killing was a surprise to many Vietnamese.

Any unscrupulous killing must be interdicted and punished. However, my friends and I had a feeling that the U.S. war protesters and government critics were exploiting the massacre for partisan politics more than for humanitarian and justice purposes. Apparently the controversy went beyond impartiality and fairness.[3]

As for my friends and me, atrocities in war like the Mỹ Lai massacre should never be pardoned. There was nothing wrong with the mass media's extensive reporting on the killing of innocent peasants in Mỹ Lai. The problem was that the reports were not made with comparisons to other war crimes committed by communist soldiers. Making loud noises about the Mỹ Lai incident without due concerns about the Huế 1968 massacre of about 5,000 civilians by the communists must be considered an act of accessory to their crimes.

In December 1967, the Dak Son hamlet, a community of about 2,000 ethnic Montagnards seventy miles northeast of Sài Gòn, was under a communist attack. After taking control of the hamlet, NVA soldiers killed more than 250 villagers, most of them old men, women, and children, and then they burned their houses to the ground. I do not know of any report covering the Dak Son massacre by the Western media.

I felt sorry that the Sài Gòn government did not react properly to the scandal. President Thiệu and his cabinet should have acted appropriately to bring justice to the victims and to show the government's responsibility in protecting its people. The RVN should have appointed an attorney representing the victims in any U.S. court trying the case. The RVN local authorities could have performed a more accurate investigation than American politicians and reporters, who were noisily taking advantage of the massacre on the victims' side.

In late 1965 after I left the Twenty-second Division, I heard that some Korean battalion on an operation massacred more than 100 inhabitants of a

Vietnamese hamlet in a coastal province along with 100 enemy troops. The killing was done after the Koreans gave the noncombatant villagers a short time to move out of the village, but communist soldiers held villagers as human shields, threatening to gun them down if they left their places. The Koreans killed all the women and children and all communist soldiers after they controlled the objective. A Korean officer told me that such "iron hand" rules had been applied in the 1950–53 Korean War, too.

Vietnamese killing one another was horrible enough. That foreign troops were killing our compatriots even if they were communist soldiers gave us a different feeling, more bitter and sad. I felt more indignant when our government kept mum, saying not a word about the bloody incidents to assert our sovereignty and to calm the people in the country. The RVN local authorities at the district and village levels should have been the most competent voice on the matters regarding the killings and the victims. But their voices seemed to be ignored.

In the ARVN, individual soldiers sometimes committed unscrupulous slayings of prisoners and wanton killing of civilians. Most such acts were done in remote areas, often out of the officers' sight. Many soldiers committing war crimes were brought to courts-martial and punished, but the verdicts rarely appeared in newspapers except for a few lines in short news columns. The government often failed to inform people what it had done to bring justice to the innocent people, a serious shortcoming on the psywar front.

There was never any report of unscrupulous killings by the Australian or Thai combat soldiers.

As far as a soldier's psychology on the battlefield is concerned, I didn't accept any atrocity under any circumstance. However, I could see how combat soldiers might get extremely mad on the battleground when suffering heavy losses. They might easily vent their anger on anything and anybody they thought to be responsible for their fellows' death. The fright of war and the pressure of inimical circumstances affected the soldiers' mood immensely. They could have reacted as if they were in their second personality or a demoniac. But it was their good-natured immediate superiors—company and platoon leaders—who could prevent such crimes owing to their close relationship and exemplary leadership.

I once was ready to kill when my power and honor were challenged. It was in 1964 when a civilian official serving one of the thirty-six New Life Hamlet teams acted against my order and intended to leave the hamlet without my approval while the area was under enemy pressure. He was a troublemaker, causing many problems to the team's operation and creating personal conflicts among the team members.

After my friendly explanation and my request that he return to the hamlet for duty, he talked back in an impolite manner, arguing that he was not a "lifer" so he wouldn't carry out my order. At last he even barked dirty words at me. By the legal power vested in provincial government, the province chief had signed a decree appointing him to the job in the team. The decree also made him a team member under my command and under the jurisdiction of the Court-Martial and Martial Law.

I got extremely upset. Unable to accept such humiliation, I loaded my M-2 carbine and said to him, "You have ten seconds to walk back to the hamlet with your team. After I count to three, if you still resist my order I will blow out your dirty skull." The coward stepped back to the ranks of his team members, his face turned pale. He might be extremely scared by my words and my flaming eyes, especially when he heard not a word was spoken in his defense by the fifty soldiers and civil servants standing around me.

Later, when my assistant asked me if I really would have shot him, I said that I would have shot at his leg if he kept acting against me. It was my hot temper that urged me to show my power to the team members who came from many different services and lacked discipline. The extreme anger totally controlled my action. But later on, I felt lucky not to have resorted to such fatal measures to restore order. I should have had recourse to other ways for that purpose. I regretted it.

THE BLACK PAJAMA CONFUSION

In war as well as politics, leaders at the top levels are usually more concerned about big matters. In my opinion, many issues that seem trivial could build into serious problems. One such matter has been the image of the enemy.

In 1957 when I was schooling at Fort Benning, the "enemy troops" in the combat exercises were played by GIs in uniforms and helmets specially designed for the imaginary army of the "aggressors." At the time, the USSR and the Red Chinese armies were the two possible threats against the United States. But the "aggressors" did not resemble either of the two.

Meanwhile, in military training in North Việt Nam and China, targets for marksmanship training were carton boards with images of U.S. soldiers and presidents as well. Fake enemies in combat training were depicted as American imperialists. They just didn't care. But the Americans didn't want to insult anyone; that's what an instructor explained to us.

Since GIs in combat units began fighting in Việt Nam in 1965, the "enemy" they were trained to fight were the "Việt Cộng." In many training centers including Fort Benning and Fort Bragg, the faked VC wore black pajamas and conic hats. In spots shown on U.S. armed forces TV stations in Việt Nam, we could see the same black pajamas and conic hats on those playing the Việt Cộng. The same image appeared in American commercial movies.

In fact, almost all of the South Vietnamese peasants wore black pajamas and conic hats. Farmers in North Việt Nam wear the same style clothes but in a dark brown color.

In the first phase of the war (1955–60), the guerrillas in South Việt Nam wore black pajamas but without conic hats, which would have hindered their movement and fighting. Since 1960, after the communist uprising and the founding of the National Liberation Front, known to the Americans as the "Việt Cộng," Việt Cộng gunmen wore their distinctive uniform: pale green or black shirts and trousers and sleazy cloth hats. Their comrades, the North Vietnamese Army soldiers, wore olive green fatigues with pith helmets. *Never were they clad in black pajamas and conic hats.*

In many occasions I was talking with American privates, I found out a horrible consequence of such images. Some confessed that they had mistaken a civilian for a VC when they first joined an operation. They asked me how to tell the difference between a VC and a member of the rural development team who also fought the VC and wore black pajamas. (In the trial of Lieutenant Calley for the Mỹ Lai massacre, one of the enlisted man also mentioned his confusion.) I am unable to guess how many innocent civilians could have been killed by such confusion.

The lack of minimal perception of the country and the people many times brought about some complicated problems. In the first few years after Americans began fighting in Việt Nam, many GIs stopped peasants suspected of being VC members, asking the suspects to show ID cards and arresting those who failed to do so. The suspects were then transferred to the POW camps under ARVN control. The Korean soldiers were doing the same thing.

In paperwork it was not easy to release citizens from POW camps. The ARVN/GPWD and JGS/J-1 received many letters of complaint from people whose family members were detained by mistake. It took some time to have their identity and background verified by their home village officials.

THE MOLES

In the first years of the Chiêu Hồi program, many people viewed the defectors with skepticism. They were afraid that the communist side might have sent the defectors to our side to infiltrate our armed forces units and agencies to work as spies or moles. But realities proved the contrary.

According to our survey in late 1969, there had been no more than two or three dozen who were trained for that purpose and sent to our side as fake defectors to act against the Chiêu Hồi program, not to spy in the military or the administration. The communists had many ways safer than the Chiêu Hồi channel to plant their secret agents in government and military agencies by regular recruiting procedures.

During my three years serving the program, the Chiêu Hồi agencies discovered eleven cases of defectors sent to the them as communist spies. A dozen other former defectors were arrested and charged with working secretly for the communists by the police all over the country. Of the eleven cases, our security offices at the Chiêu Hồi centers detected six. In the other five cases, the moles confessed themselves, including one who asked to see me one night to disclose his secret mission.

I was startled to hear him tell the whole plot of blowing up the main building of the National Chiêu Hồi Center with TNT. The charges were to have been placed in a ground floor corner next to my office and right below my bedroom on the second floor. According to the plot, a secret VC agent would hand him about ten pounds of the explosive piece by piece at various places in the market area 200 yards from the center. When enough explosive was ready, he would blow up the building by order of the secret agent.

I tried to keep my composure and asked him why he didn't carry out his mission. The young man with an artless countenance told me that he had been trained in North Việt Nam for three months. Besides demolition technique, the instructors brought him and his three classmates to see many bombing victims and pictures of South Vietnamese and American soldiers executing innocent peasants to imprint on their hearts the "Americans' and their puppets' war crimes." The young boy's older brother had been killed by an American bomb in an air raid in Nam Định City.

"However," he said, "I was received by the U.S. Marines and transferred to a South Vietnamese military unit, then to the Chiêu Hồi centers. The Americans or Vietnamese I met treated me so kindly and civilians were happy talking to me. Nothing proved that what I was taught in North Việt Nam was true. I cannot do anything harmful to those new friends and to you and your family."

I had the investigation office under my command and the police take care of the case. All investigators confirmed my observations. So I approved their proposal to close the case. He enlisted in an ARVN infantry unit and was killed in action the following year.[4]

A NARROW ESCAPE

In my nineteen years in the army, I faced many dangers, but none was as deadly as one on November 7, 1969, when I was almost killed in an attempted grenade attack. I still remember the details. What saved me was incredible.

Some members of the Chiêu Hồi security agency that was not under my control were closely watching Nguyễn Văn S., a defector allegedly identified by a counterintelligence network as a mole. To have concrete evidence for prosecution, the said security members had one of their informers pose as a communist secret agent to approach S. Security was the responsibility of another directorate of the Chiêu Hồi Ministry.

Acting as if he were a secret communist cadre, the informer gave S. an M-26 hand grenade and ordered him to attack the guests at the November 7 graduation ceremony. It was a routine indoctrination and orientation class of about 100 defectors who had completed the processing and training stage.

I was informed of the security agents' scheme about an hour before the ceremony, which Dr. Hồ Văn Châm, the Chiêu Hồi minister, was to preside over. I had my assistant warn the security people, "*This is my shop,* not a place for anything that foolish." But they assured my assistant that the detonator had been removed from the M-26 and that their informers would watch him closely and catch him before he could even pull the grenade out of his pocket. At last I said I didn't want them to play such a deadly game in my front yard. I was so busy that I only instructed my assistant to take care of the case. I didn't report the foolish plot to the minister, lest it should bother him unnecessarily.

The ceremony went smoothly, and I invited Dr. Hồ Văn Châm and our guests to take a look at the exhibition of some dozen large caliber antiaircraft guns of all types captured by the ARVN thanks to accurate information provided by some of the newly arrived defectors.

While I was talking in front of the classroom building to Dr. Châm, a U.S. Army colonel, and two Vietnamese ladies, an M-26 was thrown from the group of spectators outside a low fence. It rolled to within three feet of Dr. Cham, our guests, my six-year-old son, and me.

I was not frightened because of what I had been told earlier, but my guests ran away in panic and plunged into every corner for their lives. Two of Dr. Châm's bodyguards quickly pulled him down and covered him with their bodies. Many guests fell and suffered minor cuts and sprains. The military band from the First Airmobile Division was playing a piece of music. The musicians dropped their instruments and fell flat on the floor for cover. The small yard turned into a mess full of broken glasses and soft drink bottles, trumpets and saxophones and clarinets and drums.

People took half a minute to calm down. I picked up the grenade and found out that the safety lever was still in place. A one-inch piece of metal had broken off from the safety pin stuck in the lever holes, thus preventing the lever from being released. Probably a defect in manufacturing or because the suspect pulled the pin too forcefully was the reason the pin broke and got stuck at the lever. My bodyguard carefully secured the grenade with a makeshift safety pin and many rounds of metal wire he found on the fence to keep the safety lever from being released. I handed the grenade to my assistant, Captain Bảy, for further investigation along with the security agents. A few minutes later, my assistant ran to me, his face was pale and tense. He reported to me that the grenade detonator had not been removed as I had been assured. *The detonator was still there.*

My breath stopped, and I could hear my heart thumping. In a second I felt anger rising in my burning face. I would have punched the security agent's face if he were nearby. But I was busy explaining the incident to the guests with our apology for the danger and hurt they suffered. Following the minister's directive, I admitted the responsibility of the ministry without disclosing the true details. The security agent who was in charge of the task, out of either stupidity or fear of the grenade, had not removed the detonator. He assumed that whenever the suspect thrust his hand into his pocket, his security men would have plenty of time to stop him. Actually, the mole acted faster than the security men could move.

The incident scared me much more than any gunfire I had encountered and escaped in a close call. The pin breaking, a probability of one in a million, saved the minister, many of my guests, my son, and me from being torn into a pile of bloody flesh and bones.

The minister did not blame me for anything that took place that morning. But I had to blame myself for the incident, as I was the head official of a government agency. I was responsible for protecting its personnel and its property. I should have acted more resolutely to stop the stupid action of the security agents. Without a miracle, I would have paid for my weak reaction with my own life.

HAPPY RELIEF

In December 1969, I left the Chiêu Hồi Ministry. The new minister, Dr. Hồ Văn Châm, was a high-ranking member of the Đại Việt, a nationalist party as strong as the Việt Quốc. Naturally, he would need vacant positions to fill with his comrades, and it is common to do so in every democratic country. One of his close aides let me know that the minister's staff would offer me an equivalent post if I stayed, but I was too tired from three years of working like a horse, so I politely replied that I would not accept the goodwill offer. Furthermore, my mother and my wife both said to me that the grenade incident was an omen foreboding that my three years of luck could be over. And I believed their words. I was somewhat superstitious.

Before leaving, I reported to the minister, and he affirmed that I had not been corrupt or committed any major mistakes. Dr. Châm also did me a favor. He asked me to submit a formal letter demanding my return to the army so that in the decree ending my attachment to the Chiêu Hồi Ministry he could state that I was returned to the army "by personal wish" instead of "by service requirement." In administrative procedures, that was equal to "honorable removal" from an office.

I always feel grateful to Dr. Hồ Văn Châm for the way he treated me, even though sometimes I disagreed with his policies.

LEARNING ABOUT LIFE IN THE NORTH

My time with the Chiêu Hồi program taught me the best lessons of all kinds, especially concerning the communist regime. I would frankly admit that although my responsibility was to train the defectors, I actually learned from the defectors as much as I taught them. Meeting and exchanging opinions with thousands of North Vietnamese defectors greatly enhanced my knowledge of the communist regime, living conditions, and problems of its people and its society.

Realities of life in the North in accurate details could be discovered more by friendly and casual chats than by interrogations, interviews, and polls. So I devoted much of my spare time to talking with them.

Food Stamps and Rations

The defectors explained to me the effective system of food rationing, which was controlling every single one of the North Vietnamese populations and every kilogram of rice to mobilize human and food resources to serve the war. The system was incredibly effective, out of a researcher's imagination. The system also helped me understand why they could march the Long Mountains Trail with so much hardship and danger and fight so hard against the U.S. and South Vietnamese firepower.

Human resources mobilization for war efforts in North Việt Nam was under the general population control policies of the Việt Nam communist regime. Once a citizen was drafted for military service or mobilized for other tasks—people's labor, socialist labor—or transferred to another job at another location, his or her name was removed from the list of food stamp allocation. Without a food stamp, no one could buy as little as 100 grams of rice, even at the agricultural cooperative where he or she was a member. Because of the stomach-controlling system, a local Public Security office could keep track of every person living in its territory.

There were a very small number of draft dodgers. They could hide out somewhere, but no one, not even their parents, could share with them their food because the ration was already too scanty.

As a privilege, while serving in the army, an NVA soldier was given the highest ration: 21 kg/month of rice only. The other categories were of rice mixed with sweet potato or manioc: a heavy industrial worker was allocated 18 kg/month, light industrial worker 15 kg/month, and a farmer 13.5 kg/month. So an NVA soldier was very pleased with such a privilege. It was reasonable to say the 350-gram meal of full rice to the NVA soldier had a psychological impact equal to a feast of Chinese food and Maotai wine, or an American Bonanza steak dinner with red wine to an ARVN soldier. That privilege somehow boosted their endurance to withstand hardships and dangers.

They were already frightened by the brutal, relentless disciplinary measures in the army. However, if they lived to return to their home village but had committed any act violating party or military rules, misbehavior, or disobedience, they would have to pay for it with a high price. They would live as outcasts with bottom-listed starving jobs, maybe for the rest of their lives. Their faults might even cause problems to their parents, wives, and siblings.

Land Reform

From informal interviews, I discovered many untold facts about life in North Việt Nam. One was about the Land Reform Campaign, the largest genocide in the history of Việt Nam. Most people knew only that after the bloody campaign that came to an end in late 1956, Hồ Chí Minh and his men overtly admitted errors and launched a new campaign called Rectification of Errors.

Many researchers knew that the second campaign was no more than a staged play to ease the people's resentment. In the Rectification, the Communist Party and its government admitted the errors but contended that there was nothing wrong with the policy and that only the executing cadres committed errors.

During the Rectification Campaign, Communist Party local committees, government, and military authorities were ordered not to intervene to protect the Land Reform cadres and their collaborators who were in danger of being retaliated against by the Land Reform victims. Many cadres were attacked because of their excessive brutality and false accusations against innocent landlords. Thousands of the accusers-turned-victims lost their lives in the last three months of 1956.

Some denunciators volunteered, but most were compelled to do the job by the Land Reform team cadres. They had to show up first at the Land Reform People's Court and to accuse the landlords of the most serious crimes. They had to do the job vehemently with their wildest imagination to avoid merciless discipline measures from the Land Reform team if they failed to act as ordered. Consequently, denunciators were bearing the brunt of the revenge of the angry victims in the Land Reform bloody savage purge. Defectors from Nghệ An and Thanh Hóa provinces said they had seen several dozen corpses of the Rectification victims floating in the Mã River every week for a month during the time.

In his 1968 book *From Colonialism to Communism*, Dr. Hoàng Văn Chí asserted that "Rectification of Errors" was an integral part of the well-planned Land Reform and a bluff to pacify the angry people and calm down the consequences of the killing of faithful but stubborn party veterans. From casual talks with the ethnic North Vietnamese defectors, I found concrete evidence of the trick that could prove Dr. Chí's opinion. More than 100 North Vietnamese defectors who had witnessed the two campaigns reported that in their villages, there were landlords sentenced to death and executed from one to seven days before official letters commuting their sentences reached the village Land Reform team. The Land Reform committees of the province, on behalf of the Central Committee with ultimate competence on the decisions, issued the final verdicts. Provincial cities usually were not more than twenty kilometers from the remote villages. Land Reform authorities laid the blame on the postal service's tardy delivery for such unjust executions. Hundreds of such cases proved that it was a trick to cover up the party's responsibility for the systematic homicides.

In the Rectification of Errors campaign, local authorities held ceremonies to reinstate the victims' honor and party membership. Many of those were patriotic landlords who had contributed greatly to the war of resistance, but the party considered them enemies in order to get rid of them in its class struggle. Outspoken veterans were often criticizing the party for various policies and so constituted serious obstacles to the party's way to communism.[5]

Since the late 1990s, many high-ranking communist officials and Hồ Chí Minh's confidants in the central party committee (Đoàn Duy Thành and Hoàng Tùng, among others) revealed classified information about the decisive role of communist Chinese advisors to the North Việt Nam Land Reform committees. Many times Hồ turned down petitions from his subordinates requesting that death sentences of certain patriotic landlords be commuted, saying that he couldn't talk to the "comrade advisors" because they had already decided.

Loudspeakers for Air Defense

North Việt Nam in war needed sophisticated equipment from outside. But the highest priority may have been given to importing public address components. The communist regime lived partly on its propaganda warfare, which needed powerful broadcasting systems.

Loudspeakers were installed everywhere in city wards and villages. Ward or village information offices broadcast news and editorials, especially at 5 AM and 9 PM—the best times to instill propaganda materials into the human subconscious, according to a cadres handbook—and repeated them many times a day at highest volume. A baby growing up in the harping sound of propaganda articles was stuffed with prefabricated thoughts day and night.

Public address systems were also used to alert local people to run for shelter when U.S. bombers were coming. But local military commands used it as the key network to direct small-caliber antiaircraft guns and machine guns—even rifles—against low-flying U.S. fighters. By voice command sent through loudspeakers, thousands of gunners could concentrate their fire at a certain enemy aircraft, creating a dense wall of projectiles that increased the chance of direct hits. Loudspeakers were easily available and could send voice orders directly to gunners in a second, much faster and more effectively than radio transceivers.

Communist Fanatical Low-Ranking Commanders

Serving the Chiêu Hồi program also gave me a deeper comprehension of the fanatical low-ranking communist cadres. They were unprivileged youngsters of the social bottom class, usually with little education and living in poverty. They were easily tempted by promises of a better life and personal powers in a communist state. They were intensively indoctrinated and crammed with revolutionary ideals along with patriotism since kindergarten to become members of the Communist Party.

They soon became extremist leading party members, executing the party's directives to consolidate their positions. In battles, they were very authoritarian troop leaders, and many fought courageously. Sometimes I met communist prisoners who were very stubborn and who fiercely resisted our interrogators, and I was not surprised at that. Such fanaticism combined with iron discipline constituted a strong army that was difficult to defeat by conventional strategy alone. The anticommunists needed to have patience and a sagacious strategy in psychological warfare to prevail.

THE STORIES TO REMEMBER

During my nineteen years and seven months serving the RVN Army, the three years in the Chiêu Hồi program left so many unforgettable feelings in my heart and my memory, in which some stories might be typical for one of the many aspects of the Việt Nam War.

A Surprise Reunion

In 1968, many more former North Vietnamese soldiers reported to South Vietnamese and American units and were sent to the National Chiêu Hồi Center under my command. I used to hold informal friendly talks with them at their dormitories. The talks usually covered jokes, memories, personal stories, and every topic we could think of.

Once I told them about my last day in Hà Nội on August 11, 1954. When I recalled the time I spent at Lake Hồ Tây (West Lake), one of the new defectors jumped to his feet and grasped my hands firmly, saying, "It's you, *thủ trưởng* (boss, NVA term). I've never thought of meeting you again." He admitted that he had been the pro–Việt Minh boy who had been rude to my friends and me that August afternoon. As if to assure myself that he was the same boy from fourteen years ago, he related exactly what I had told him. I still remembered what I had said: *"You'll see for yourself what the Việt Minh really are after a few years living under them."*

He said things after 1954 happened exactly as I had warned him the afternoon before I left for Sài Gòn.

Another Surprise Reunion

One of the newly arriving NVA in late 1968 resembled the male nurse Nguyễn Văn Linh, who was working in the dispensary of the National Chiêu Hồi Center. Linh had been a North Vietnamese military practical nurse who defected to the American First Airmobile Division in the battle of Plei Me in November 1965. In 1966 the Chiêu Hồi Ministry hired him.

Many people in the Center notified Linh of one of the new defectors who looked a lot like him. In the afternoon while I was drinking beer with Ytzaina, a few American civilians, and a reporter in the canteen, Linh came in with the boy resembling him and some of their friends. The boy's name was Lâm. The two and their friends sat around a table next to mine and chatted. Lâm told his story first.

He was brought up as the only son of a middle-class landlord family. In 1955, his parents fell victim to the bloody Land Reform Campaign. The Land Reform group had enormous power overriding village and district authority. Its cadres revealed to him that he was just the landlord's adopted child. They ordered him to denounce his adoptive parents as a wicked landlord and landlady with whatever crimes he could fabricate.

The landlord confirmed to Lâm that he had adopted him in 1945 when Lâm was four years old from a poor couple who were not his biological parents. Lâm had changed hands several times during the 1945 famine. The landlord and his wife had no children in their twenty years of marriage. After the famine and the war that followed, the landlord was unable to track down Lâm's birth parents.

The landlord persuaded Lâm to do what the Land Reform group commanded in order to save Lâm from the unrelenting policy against the landlord class and its offspring under the communist regime. "We will be doomed whether you stand against us or not, so please do anything you can to save yourself," the landlord and his wife insisted.

However, Lâm refused to accuse his adoptive parents of crimes as the Land Reform group instructed him. He said he could never do anything against his adoptive parents. "They have brought me up with their great love and care, and I'd rather die than betray them," he testified. Consequently, after his adoptive parents were executed, he was given a three-year term in a reeducation camp. After being released, he was a laborer before he was drafted in 1964.

Linh's story was simple. He was from a peasant family, and he was the elder of the two sons. In 1943, his parents were too poor to raise both children, so when a rich family asked to adopt the younger boy, they accepted. After the war ended in 1954, they tried many times to locate their younger son, but all failed because their son had been readopted many times after 1945.

When Linh enrolled in the NVA in 1960, his mother reminded him of his younger brother. As a soldier, he would travel and meet many young people, she said. She asked him to look for her beloved younger son. "You can easily identify him. On his left chest, there is an oval reddish scar the size of a thumb. Once while playing with other kids, he fell over and a sharp stone hit him hard, leaving the reddish scar."

To everybody's surprise, Lâm unbuttoned his shirt, showing the scar on his left chest, the reddish scar that Linh described. The brothers hugged each other and cried for minutes. Everybody in the canteen cried, too.

With help from Linh, Lâm joined the ARVN Ranger Corps and got married. In 1970 he was promoted to corporal and then to sergeant after many fierce battles.

To Die Not a Coward

Bùi Thanh Quang was an ethnic North Vietnamese communist sergeant who defected to our side in Pleiku in early 1966 and was resettled in Phượng Hoàng village near Sài Gòn. In 1967 he followed his girlfriend to her village nearby, where he suddenly noticed that he had no way to escape the trap of VC gunmen surrounding him. They brought him to the boondocks.

After using him for a month as an eyewitness for propaganda against the Chiêu Hồi program, the communist local unit put him in an underground dark hole, with his legs locked in wooden stocks. Two months later, the U.S. First Infantry Division found the underground bunker with a Việt Cộng flag at its entrance, intended to prompt the soldiers to throw hand grenades into the hole. The kind-hearted soldiers, with help from a Vietnamese interpreter, rescued Quang and returned him to my center.

When the necessary investigation concluded, Quang was free "to think it over," as my investigation section proposed. No discipline was imposed, but I didn't talk to him when I visited the dormitories. Once meeting him, I told him concisely that I would like to see him do something to make up for his wrongdoing.

At the same time, an old rich widow adopted Quang. The childless widow had lived in a village next to his in the North before she moved to Sài Gòn in 1954. He promised to come live with her and take care of her as his mother after he found a good job.

A good job he liked turned out to be a soldier. One day, he volunteered to a special force unit operating beyond the northern and northwestern national borders. When he left for Đà Nẵng to begin training, he asked to see me and said, "Good bye, sir. You will see how I respect you. I'll try my best to please you and to prove I am not a coward."

He was sent to target areas beyond the national boundary several times. In the last mission before his scheduled honorable discharge, his team detected about twenty North Vietnamese field grade officers moving south toward the DMZ (demilitarized zone).

The team launched an ambush, killing many NVA officers, but in an instant Quang and his fellows were unexpectedly charged by a communist rifle company. A bullet hit Quang, breaking his thighbone, and he was unable to move. The only one alive beside Quang was another former defector.

Quang urged his friend to escape before the enemy closed in, while Quang diverted the enemy with his rifle. His friend reached the beach in darkness and returned to Đà Nẵng safely in a rubber boat. Within days he came back to Sài Gòn, and the first thing he did was tell me the whole story.

Quang's friend cried when he related Quang's last words. "Before I left him, Quang asked me to do only two things in his exhausted and choked voice, very short because we had very little time. 'If you get back safely, tell my adoptive mom that I'm very sorry not to come back to take care of her as I promised, and tell the Major how I am fighting to death and I'm not dying a coward.'" The defectors often called me "the Major."

I cannot keep tears from welling up in my eyes as I am writing these lines. The years in the Chiêu Hồi program left me with a deep empathy toward the young men coming from the other side of the war. Thousands of defectors knew me and talked to me, and many became my good friends. The dependents of those who served the National Center became close to my wife and my mother, who had helped them. Until April 30, 1975, when the RVN collapsed, many of them were visiting with us frequently. After I was released from reeducation camps, those who still lived around Sài Gòn often dropped by to see me. That was the greatest reward I've ever had.

The ARVN Desertion

Many foreigners may wonder how many soldiers of the South Vietnamese armed forces deserted to the communist side. The answer could be instant and certain. There were ARVN defectors who served the communist forces. But the number was too small to be significant. The simple reason was the communist commanders were rather dubious about their enemy deserters and rarely employed the ARVN defectors in their units.

Two ARVN captains changed sides after the failure of the coup against the Diệm government in November 1960, joining the communists to fight against the ARVN. In March 1972, a lieutenant colonel commanding the Fifty-sixth

Regiment surrendered his unit to the NVA. In the last days of South Việt Nam, an RVN Air Force pilot joined the communist side and conducted bombings of the President Palace and the Tân Sơn Nhất Air Base. The communist leaders used to assign ARVN deserters propaganda tasks or technical jobs. As far as I know, only a few hundred ARVN deserters actually served the communist side.

There were also communist moles within the ARVN officer corps. A dozen communist spies in ARVN intermediate and high positions were detected and court-martialed. After April 30, 1975, a dozen more spies among ARVN officers emerged.

The number of deserters recorded in ARVN personnel documents may have reached nearly 70,000 per year. But the actual story was different and was unknown to many researchers.

I attended many routine briefings at personnel offices from division level and higher. The deserters were usually those who went AWOL (absent without leave) after going on leave and remaining home for a few months. They could have fled the units during the rest and recreation time after days in combat operations. Most of them returned to their units. Many others reenlisted in other units after a few months at home under the same or a different identity. The post-recruiting check of the personnel branch had no difficulty in detecting their backgrounds. But the illegal practices were connived at for the sake of wartime convenience. There were very few true deserters who quit the army for good. But there were no public reports on these "returning deserters."

PEACE TALKS

The last month of 1969 saw favorable territorial security all over South Việt Nam. Thanks to the relatively effective pacification operation and military counteroffensives in the remote areas, security was reestablished in many parts of the country previously under communist influence. Safe land and water communication routes were extended and thus enhanced the economy.

However, the military achievements were not enough to tip the scale. The loud voices of the war protesters almost drowned all major successes on the battlefields. On the psychological front, we suffered critical failures.

The Paris peace conference didn't bring any hope for a quick and just solution. We saw both sides of the negotiation table were not ready for any covenant. The two sides wasted years arguing about the shape of the negotiating table.

Hà Nội took advantage of the lingering peace talks for propaganda. Intelligence reports confirmed that Hà Nội sent about forty tons of propaganda materials in all kinds of publications by airlines to Paris. It must have cost Hà Nội a lot of money that Sài Gòn could never match.

At the negotiation table, on the psywar front, and in its military strategy, the communist side never dropped its basic strategy of considering the nationalist Vietnamese, not the Americans, as its archenemy. According to some communist leaders, the "American imperialists" were extremely dangerous in certain situations, but it was the anticommunist Vietnamese who posed unyielding threats and deadly obstacles. "'American imperialists' will go home someday, but the 'puppets' stay here and are not easy to be eradicated."

* * *

More than a year after the communist Tét Offensive, many people asked my fellow officers and me why our soldiers were fighting so heroically and winning so many major battles, yet Americans continued to protest fiercely and build up a powerful pro-communist battleground right in U.S. cities.

The year 1969 was full of events that became deeply imprinted in my memory. First was the Vietnamization declared by President Nixon, which gave me hope for an early conclusion to the war. Second was the successful moon landing of Apollo 11. I was really surprised at the great achievement when watching the astronauts take their first steps on the moon's surface on July 20. One of my officers said to me, "The Americans know very well about a pebble on the moon surface, but they remain ignorant on issues concerning the Hà Nội communist leaders and their tricks."

TWENTY-TWO

The New Phase

The communists had the upper hand in espionage on RVN government and military installations. A spy scandal broke out in the last months of 1969. A high-ranking RVN government official, Huỳnh Văn Trọng, was arrested and charged as a spy. He was accused of working for the communist side ever since 1954. Two Chiêu Hồi Ministry employees were detained because of their personal associations with him. One of the two was working as chief of training in the Reception Directorate when I was serving at the ministry, but he was found innocent of all charges.

In 1970, I met several key people in the intelligence and counterintelligence community serving the Ngô Đình Diệm regime, including the famous spy hunter Dương Văn Hiếu and the legendary secret service chief Dr. Trần Kim Tuyến. As confirmed by other sources, Hiếu and Tuyến and their associates had successfully detected and captured an incredible number of spies during Diem's nine years in power. These spies were among about 400 high- and medium-ranking communist agents who had been sent from the North as "special envoys" to take charge of intelligence networks in the South. Among the captives were an important official serving the Communist Party Politburo, some NVA colonels, and hundreds of NVA majors and captains or political cadres of equal ranks.

Hiếu's special operations team, an unofficial creation, was surprisingly small and simple with only eight members and a driver. Local police and military-related services supported this team as required.

Hiếu had a sixth sense for counterespionage, according to those who knew him. People who were against the Diệm regime called Hiếu the "Devil of Central Việt Nam," saying that he had killed many innocent victims. Hiếu's admirers praised him as a born genius, a detective who frightened the communists and even stubborn nationalist opponents.

Hiếu's team had been created by President Diệm's brother, Ngô Đình Cẩn, Central Việt Nam's "viceroy," and like other counterintelligence agencies during the 1954–63 era, it was successful thanks to support from the supreme leader, President Diệm. Diệm's successors did not provide their spy hunters with similar support. Hiếu's team may have committed some abuses of power that were subjected to a punishment after Diệm's regime collapsed. But his team's mistakes must be evaluated with impartial consideration of his achievements to ensure national security. Most of the spies caught by Dương Văn Hiếu were released when the November 1, 1963, junta assumed power. Some said the communists bribed some generals for the release; some thought the generals mistook those communists for nationalist dissidents.

The case of ARVN Colonel Phạm Ngọc Thảo is worth mentioning. Thảo was an engineer and a high-ranking member of the VCP, serving the Việt Minh before 1954. After the Geneva Peace Accords, he defected to the nationalist government. Archbishop Ngô Đình Thục welcomed him and introduced him to President Diệm. He was commissioned as an ARVN captain and appointed to key jobs in the government. In 1957, he was promoted to major and appointed province chief of Kiến Hòa, an area seriously infested by VC rebels. He was successful in reducing VC activities and restoring security to remote roads and hamlets. In late 1963, he sided with the movement in the coup that overthrew Diệm.

After Diem's death, Thảo continued to hold important positions in the ARVN and took part in several attempted putsches. In February 1965, he was given a death sentence in absentia after he masterminded a failed coup. He was arrested in May while hiding out in a village in Biên Hòa. He died in a military security detention room. According to a rumor, he was killed by order of the military junta.

Since the early 1960s, many people had suspected that Thảo was a communist spy. They were concerned about the liberal and peculiar way he acted in dealing with the insurgency. Many others did not agree. Dr. Trần Kim Tuyến told me in 1970 that, because of Thảo's crucial strategic contributions to the RVN side, he believed that Thảo was not a mole. "But who knows?" Dr. Tuyến said to me. He also remarked that each side of the dispute had its reasons.

After April 1975, Hà Nội officially honored Phạm Ngọc Thảo as its secret agent and promoted him posthumously to brigadier general and reinterred his remains in a decent grave. The communist propaganda agency also produced a movie about Thảo, *Ván Bài Lật Ngửa* (The Cards Were Put on the Table). Hà Nội's decision certainly lends support to the argument that Thảo was a communist agent, but I don't believe it. The communist leaders used to play similar propaganda tricks to fool the public. In many cases, they got rid of their unwanted subordinates, including their unmasked spies, then supported the victims and awarded their families the posthumous honorable title "Martyr's Family."

Dr. Trần Kim Tuyến was Ngô Đình Nhu's most trusted lieutenant in charge of intelligence activities in foreign territories. He told me that South Việt Nam planted a number of spies in several top-level communist agencies in the North. His agency got support from the CIA under an agreement with specified terms and conditions.

According to Dr. Tuyến, the South Vietnamese side sometimes went beyond the agreed limits of the operation. He disclosed how Sài Gòn's spies had operated deep inside Cambodia, even managing an attempt on the life of Prince Sihanouk. Fortunately, an unexpected visit by a foreign delegation stopped Sihanouk from opening a package full of explosives disguised as a gift minutes before it exploded, killing his uncle. Another failed attempt was directed at Laotian premier Souvana Phouma. Similar incidents by Sài Gòn's secret operation that encroached on the Americans' area of responsibility resulted in the breaking of the bilateral agreement on intelligence cooperation.

According to my friends who served the counterintelligence agencies, many communist spies in the government agencies and military units were not volunteers. They were coerced into communist espionage by blackmail and various threats against their own lives and the lives of their parents, wives, and children as well.

LAND TO THE TILLER

In February 1970, the RVN Congress passed the bill for agrarian reform. The new law was an active policy to address one of the most sensible matters concerning poor farmers. In 1955, the Diệm government had introduced the agrarian reform program, but it failed to attain favorable results because the regulations were weak. They allowed landlords to retain large acreage (100 acres) and required farmers to pay in installments for the allocated rice lands. Only a small number of farmers got help from the program.

As land reform was a necessary part of the fight against the communist insurgency, the government of Nguyễn Văn Thiệu promulgated the so-called Land to the Tiller Act to address the land matter, replacing the failed 1955 reform program. The bill was meant to distribute five acres of land free of cost to each farming family. The most popular clause of the act "legalized the ownership of farmers' lands that had been distributed by the Việt Minh authorities before 1955 in the South in the Việt Minh areas." Farmers were awarded legal titles for their lands. The United States provided a small fund for the program.

The reform was far more successful than Diệm's program, although its achievements were modest. I met many poor farmers who praised the new law and some villagers who complained about corruption and red tape.

In 1970, on trips to some Mekong Delta areas, I met with many farmers who were living under easy circumstances on the five acres of rice land. A farmer with his wife growing rice on a five-acre field earned an income higher than an army second lieutenant's salary. They told me that what they got from selling straw and thatch was enough to pay for all kinds of taxes.

VETERANS' PROTEST

After leaving the Chiêu Hồi Ministry, I came back to the General Political Warfare Department and was appointed chief of its Study and Research Division. I also was a member of the Standing Committee of the Interministerial Committee for Disabled Veterans as representative of Lieutenant General Trần Văn Trung, our GPWD commanding officer.

The committee chairman was General Phạm Văn Đổng, minister of veteran affairs. At the time in most cities of South Việt Nam, disabled veterans were protesting every day, demanding help from the government for better living conditions. The scenes of the protest and the veterans' tactics may have somehow resembled the Bonus March on Washington, D.C., after World War I. The protest began with four disabled veterans released from the rehab center with little help from the government. Their protest drew more veterans. Within a week, hundreds had joined the movement, and after two weeks, thousands of protesters had gathered in front of the Veteran Affairs Ministry and the Independence Palace to voice their anger.

Disabled veterans built huts on sidewalks, small parks, private and public lawns, terraces, and large urban and suburban plots reserved for new construction projects.

The government was slow in dealing with the crisis. We had a feeling that President Thiệu was waiting for the protests to reach a stage that no government could accept. That would be when the protests turned violent or when the public became impatient with the movement, which had created social disorder and intolerable nuisances. Our prediction came true. One afternoon we received a secret order to be prepared for the crackdown, which the police field force would carry out. The raid started at midnight, and thousands of disabled veteran squatters' houses were knocked down.

The disabled veterans' "housing march" brought them unexpected success. Each was given an apartment in the newly built low-cost projects. Moreover, a new law was quickly passed by the Congress with supplementary payments to be made to the disabled veterans higher than the legislation bill proposed by the president.

The national budget would have had to put aside a very large amount for disabled veterans, widows, and orphans. If the RVN still existed, I don't know how it could bear such a financial burden for years to come. The new law even allowed full pay to a disabled RVN veteran who still worked and earned a full salary as a government employee.

The best thing the law brought the veterans was the reduction of red tape. From then on, an application for a newly disabled veteran or a war widow had only four or five justification papers instead of ten to twelve. Besides, the system of disability evaluation was reformed with an updated list of injury categories compatible with new weapons, military equipment, and techniques that were in use or would be used in war. Since the war broke out in 1960, this was the most important law ever, granting the war's invalids, widows, and orphans such benefits.

The problems with veteran affairs showed how ineffective the administrative system in the RVN was, especially in supporting the war effort, although there had been many important administrative reforms since 1955.

THE YOUNG WAR WIDOWS

There was no place in Sài Gòn where the tragic outcome of war could be seen more clearly than at the Ministry of Veterans. At any given moment, visitors might run across a dozen disabled veterans who had lost arms and legs, as well as war widows and their orphans with white bands around their heads. From Monday through Friday in 1970 after the ARVN invasion of Cambodia, hundreds of war widows came to the ministry to complete paperwork for a government supplement.

At first glance, a visitor might feel deep compassion for the children who had just lost their fathers. But to people working there, the most profound empathy was toward the young widows with or without children. Many of them were around twenty years old, pretty, and healthy. Some had already signed certificates of marriage, but the groom had been killed before the traditional wedding could take place. Some had been married just a day or two before becoming widows. Many spent only a few weeks or months in happiness as a wife. Some had children.

Looking at their lovely faces, I could read their hidden sorrow, loneliness, and despair. A young widow would have to work hard to raise a child, but she had something to hope for and to console herself with. A childless widow without a chance to remarry had nothing.

Many times in the countryside, I saw three-wheeled motor vehicles carrying coffins covered by the national flag. Sitting beside the coffins were young widows with their eyes reddened and dried, their faces pale, haggard, and lifeless. In some cases they were also holding their sleeping toddlers. Along with the sight of dead bodies on battlefields, these scenes deepened my feeling against war.

The military commands often did their best to recover soldiers' remains and bring them back to their families for the funeral. The task required a lot of effort and resources from the RVN side, whereas the communist side just didn't care much about its fallen warriors.

WHEN THE AMERICANS GOT TIRED

In April 1970, Vietnamese and American troops launched the incursion into Cambodia at Mỏ Vẹt area. (Parrot's Beak area, along the border between Tay Ninh province and Cambodia, is a piece of land resembling a parrot's beak.) Contrary to many media reports saying that the invading troops found only empty VC bases, my friends joining the operations witnessed the enemy's heavy losses of weapons. The arms losses were confirmed only after a few days of searching, but the media seldom published a new report with more accurate information.

The first Western journalist who crossed the border into Cambodian territory and reported on the ARVN-US operations there may have been a brave lady, a freelancer, and also my friend, Roxanna Brown from Chicago.

The allied troops won many major battles in the first few months of the initial phases. After strong opposition to the incursion by war protesters and the U.S. Congress, U.S. troops withdrew from Cambodia and ARVN units continued fighting there.

In April and May, many ARVN commanders were rather optimistic. Cases in which ARVN troops committed war crimes and looted were reported to the high command. Some that went unpunished were used as evidence by communist propaganda to vilify the South Vietnamese soldiers. To some extent, the communist propaganda gained certain advantages.

Right before the invasion, hundreds of Vietnamese nationals living in Cambodia were massacred. Their bodies were thrown into the Mekong River. The incidents prompted retaliation from a few ARVN small units.

The Cambodian incursion should have been launched many years earlier. Every Vietnamese knew that if the communist forces had not been allowed to set up logistics bases, hide troops, and maintain supply routes on Cambodian soil, the war would have ended much earlier and in favor of the South.

At the end of 1970, the enemy gathered strength and conducted fierce counterattacks against ARVN units. In a few months, ARVN units were widely assailed by North Vietnamese and Cambodian communist soldiers and lost many strongholds and suffered heavy casualties. NVA reinforcements continued moving unchecked into Cambodia from Laos.

In 1972, all ARVN units withdrew from Cambodia, leaving it in the hands of the stronger Khmer Rouge guerrillas. The Việt communist troops freely returned to rebuild their former bases in that country, but their heavy losses caused by the ARVN incursion limited their war potential in Cambodia. They could not exert the powerful offensive effort in the ARVN Third and Fourth Corps/Military Region that had been anticipated.

SCAG

In 1970, the RVN authorities launched the first large-scale crackdown on the drug traffic as "scag" began ruining a significant number of Vietnamese youth. Scag, slang for heroin, and other drugs including marijuana had been sold in South Việt Nam since 1965, initially for American GIs. It was easy to say that the number of drug addicts among GIs was soaring. I could see GIs smoking drugs at many bars and nightclubs in the cities and at shabby thatch-roofed beer stands near U.S. base camps in the fields where I was visiting.

Within a short time, many young Vietnamese began to fall victims of the scag business. Families in my neighborhood were greatly concerned when a dozen teens were caught smoking the white substance. Before the GIs came in large numbers, there were a few drug addicts. They smoked opium if they had money, and the poor got intravenous shots of spent opium residue concocted in boiled water.

When the American high command began phasing out U.S. units, drug dealers turned their efforts to luring young Vietnamese as their easy targets. They failed to attract ARVN soldiers because the South Vietnamese troops did not have the tendency for drug addiction. The National Police conducted routine searches and made a half dozen arrests in my neighborhood. The campaign minimally reduced the number of drug addicts.

There was palpable evidence that the communist North Việt Nam and China were involved in the drug campaign. In 1970, Chou En-lai, prime minister of China, stated that his government was supplying the American troops in Việt Nam with heroin in retaliation for the Western Opium War against China at the end of the nineteenth century. Besides, ARVN units in operations at many communist bases found packs of heroin that cost several hundred thousand dollars each.

Evidently, Chou En-lai was not kidding, and Vietnamese communist financial agencies did not store scag for nothing. However, I haven't heard of any intensive report or study on the topic of Chinese and Vietnamese communists employing scag as an effective weapon against U.S. troops .

THE FORSAKEN SPIRITS

In the first month of the Year of the Pig (1971), while I was going on temporary duty for a week in Hué City, several friends invited me to their home services commemorating victims of the 1968 Tét Offensive massacres. Most Buddhist families in the city were doing the same.

Commemorating deceased ancestors and family members has been a tradition in Việt Nam since time immemorial. On the date of their death on the lunar calendar, their families hold services at home or sometimes at pagodas. The tradition also extends beyond the limit of family members and ascendants. On the fifteenth day of the seventh month of every lunar year, Vietnamese Buddhists conduct more elaborate rites at pagodas. The congregation prays for the dead in general, particularly for the dead without offspring, soldiers killed in action, and war victims. The rites lasted a week or even fifteen days in the prewar era. It is called *Cúng Cô Hồn*, or Service for the Forsaken Spirits.

The tradition is the same in Hué City. Hué people, however, have two more *Cúng Cô Hồn* to do for the war dead. In the Fifth Moon each lunar year (in late June and early July), Buddhist families in the city holds *Cúng Cô Hồn* services to pray for innocent civilians killed by French invaders in the late nineteenth century. On the twenty-third day of the fifth month, the year Ất Dậu (or the Year of the Rooster, 1885), French forces conducted a fierce attack against the Việt Nam Royal Army defending the capital city. Unscrupulous French artillery shelling killed between 2,000 and 3,000 people, mostly city residents. Although the date is the twenty-third day of the fifth month, people are free to hold services for the dead on any date at the family's convenience, providing that it is within the fifth month. If you visit someone in Hue during the fifth month, you will certainly be invited to such services. You could be invited every day if you have a lot of friends and relatives living in this beautiful ancient city.

Buddhists in Hué held similar *Cúng Cô Hồn* services every first lunar month for the 5,000 victims of the Tết Offensive. The Hué Buddhists tacitly agreed upon the first month *Cúng Cô Hồn* as a pure religious tradition for the forsaken spirits in general. Therefore, after 1975, communist authorities found no good reason to interdict the practice. However, the first month services are the irrefutable incrimination of the horrible 1968 Tét carnage.

VIETNAMIZATION

In 1969, after Richard Nixon took over the White House, Washington announced an initiative called "Vietnamization" of the war. I appreciated the idea because the Americans would not be able to fight the war for us forever. What I personally hoped was that South Việt Nam would take care of itself as South Korea was doing with one or two American divisions positioned south of the 17th parallel as a deterrent force.

Sometime after the Tét Offensive, the ARVN military deployment underwent major changes. The four corps tactical zones became military regions, as they had been before 1962. The four army corps commands were placed in charge of the four military regions. The division tactical areas were deactivated, so that the ten infantry divisions could be relieved from territorial responsibility to resume full mobility.

Our troops' morale improved with the new aid of sophisticated weapons and equipment from the United States, and ARVN units were given intensified retraining to replace the U.S. forces that had been phased out.

Several times I represented the GPWD in the Joint General Staff (JGS) workshops on military aids to the Vietnamization plan. The Pentagon approved a large quantity of army equipment and sophisticated weapons. However, what we requested to augment our air force capability, such as the F-4 Phantom, was denied. Only the F-5A Freedom Fighters were provided. Everyone in the workshops understood that Washington wanted to limit the VNAF range of operations and in the air space defense of South Việt Nam only. Moreover, long-range fighters like the F-4 Phantom required larger technical support and maintenance facilities that would substantially increase the aid budget.

As if to prove the ARVN capability to check communist expansion in Southeast Asia, a large-scale operation of multiple divisions was launched across the border with Laos. The invasion of the ARVN task force of nearly 18,000 soldiers into Laotian territory began in the first week of 1971. We closely watched the battle reports with great hope for a victory. This operation involving multiple divisions was the first ever conducted by a Việt Nam Army high command beyond its borders. The United States supplied limited support from combat aircraft and air transportation. The operation was named Lam Sơn 719.

ARVN forces, including the two elite Airborne and Marine divisions, invaded Laos in a multipronged effort along the Long Mountain Trails to destroy NVA logistic depots and combat units that were being readied for a large-scale offensive inside South Việt Nam. The objectives were in an area from the border to Tchepone, a Laotian town twenty miles across the border from Khe Sanh.

The battles became bloodier every week. Both sides suffered heavily, but as in other battles in the war, human losses on the communist side were from three to five times higher than the ARVN with losses of about twice the amount in equipment and weapons. In the war where large numbers of North Vietnamese lives were sacrificed for every objective on the battlefields, such a ratio didn't constitute a true victory for the NVA.

The withdrawal of our armor units and convoys of motor vehicles met fierce attacks from NVA units. By the first week of April, all ARVN units had left Laos. According to reports compiled by the JGS/J-3 and GPWD, our ARVN units suffered more than 3,000 KIAs while communist HQS in Hà Nội boasted that its forces had eliminated 16,000 SVN soldiers. Reliable sources received by my office claimed NVA loss at nearly 10,000.

Lam Son 719 was the first conventional operation at army corps level conducted by an ARVN command. In the JGS, it was believed that the information about the operation had been leaked to the NVA command before the D-Day, which enabled Hà Nội to have time to prepare for the encounter.

Military critics directed their attacks at the high- and intermediate-level headquarters and their commanding generals. It was apparent that ARVN/JGS along with ARVN First Corps HQS and MACV underestimated the enemy strength, which had outnumbered the ARVN task force by three to five times and its armored vehicles capability. Evidently, only after the NVA armored task forces appeared on the battlefields did the ARVN First Corps command order its mechanized battalions to send for their 106 mm recoilless rifles stored in warehouses for years and install them on their M-113 personnel carriers in operation.

In the end, Operation Lam Sơn 719 did not constitute a decisive victory for the ARVN, but Washington and Sài Gòn both declared the operation a great success. The two capitals asserted that the Vietnamization could stand the test of battle and proved that it was on the right track.

It was apparent that ARVN units in Lam Sơn 719 fought the fiercest battles. Under unfavorable conditions and on rough terrain, the troops once again showed their endurance and willingness to fight. Except for a few strong points overrun by an enemy force five times larger as at Fire Base 31, other units inflicted heavy losses on the communists. Many soldiers died heroically, but few reports of their stories were made public. One of them, Captain Nguyễn Văn Đương, commander of a paratroop artillery company, fought to the last minute. He refused to surrender and was executed by NVA troops beside his howitzers.

But some of the mass media seemed to seek only tidbits and images that could be used to defame our army, such as a picture of some cowards who clung to the skids of a helicopter to get away from the battlefield. Every army in every war has such cowards, and the picture was not more shocking than some scenes of allied soldiers fighting each other for seats on boats in the Dunkirk evacuation I had watched in a WWII documentary. Sometimes I felt it was not only the Communist Politburo in Hà Nội but also the newsrooms in New York that precipitated the fall of Sài Gòn.

NVA LOGISTIC BACKBONE

Operation Lam Sơn 719 had key objectives on the NVA principal line of logistical support along the Trường Sơn, or Long Mountain, known to the world as the Hồ Chí Minh Trails. These were indispensable to the communist war strategy against the South.

Those who know the terrain along the west side of the Long Mountain are well aware of the enemy's ability to move trucks through the old forests. When serving in the Twenty-second Division, I flew low several times along the border and had a chance to observe the terrain of Laos and Cambodia. My knowledge of the southern portion of the trails included studies on maps and aerial photos.

Most of the west side of the Long Mountain consisted of gentle slopes. Old trees grew far apart with obstructive undergrowth that could be cleared by war laborers to make trails for trucks. Most streams could be negotiated without much hard work. There was no sizeable river. In many sections, the trails consisted of dirt roads lying in parallel up to a quarter mile wide. Such conditions enabled enemy personnel and vehicles to disperse in a large area to minimize human and material losses from bombing. Communist postwar statistics admitted tens of thousands of trucks had been destroyed on the trails while replacements from China seemed in endless supply.

The main trails for trucks ran along the common border with Laos and Cambodia and on the territory of these two neighboring countries as far south as to the area opposite to Tây Ninh province, not inside Việt Nam. At several places, the main trail branched off into many footpath groups where supplies were transported by war laborers far into the inner districts.

Many officers in our army believed that only infantry could stop the enemy's line of logistic support and personnel reinforcement. A plan devised by Secretary of Defense Robert McNamara resulted in the construction of a line of outposts manned by strike forces along the 17th parallel. The plan included an electronic alarm system in Vietnamese territory right below the DMZ to stop the enemy movement from the North. But the NVA main route to send troops and supplies into the South was via the trails in Laos and Cambodia. Infiltration crossing the 17th parallel in Việt Nam territory was a secondary effort.

The McNamara plan only established a barrier of mines and airstrikes directed by electronic sensors on the trails in Laotian and Cambodian territories. The plan worked, I believe, but not well. Bombs, sensors, and mines were unable to cause significant loss to enemy troops and trucks on the trails. Artificial rains could only obstruct trucks to a certain degree, but would not affect war laborers.[1] Logistic supplies lost to bad weather and mishandling was high but still within NVA capacity due to the enormous aid from China.

If the Americans' top effort in 1965 had been to establish a barrier of ground forces from the Quảng Trị seaside across Laos halfway to the Mekong River and leave pacification and the destruction of the enemy inside the RVN to the ARVN soldiers, Sài Gòn and Washington probably would have won the war in less than three years.

We believed that such a strategy would require no more than three divisions employed as a line of defense and a smaller backup force. The forces would have to resist fierce attack, but they could deliver deadly blows to the enemy and also reduce American losses. Such a line of ground forces would have completely stopped the NVA's supply of war materials into the South.

The special operations group in Laos helped destroy enemy logistic warehouses and convoys, but it was only successful on a small scale. The trail area was so vast, with enemy widely dispersed in small bases, warehouses, and field medical posts, that mass bombing did not have the required impact.[2]

In two to three years without considerable logistic support, we estimated, the enemy would have disintegrated or retreated to the North. Of course, there were always other factors kept secret at top levels in Sài Gòn and Washington beyond our comprehension that affected the Pentagon's decisions on U.S. troops invading Laos, but we still thought that such a solution was the best option.

Eventually, Operation Lam Sơn 719 was able to destroy only a part of the enemy logistic capacity and thus delayed the NVA plan of a large offensive, but it could not entirely stop the NVA line of human and material support for its troops in the South.

"U.S., GO HOME!"

The year 1971 saw American units leaving Việt Nam one after another at a higher rate. Businesses providing services to the GIs were dwindling fast. Other allied troops from New Zealand, Australia, Thailand, and South Korea followed suit.

On my trips away from Sài Gòn, I had a strange feeling when driving through areas with abandoned GI barracks. U.S. Army camps and Air Force bases at Evans, Phú Bài, Qui Nhơn, Đông Tác, and Tháp Chàm were no longer busy and noisy and crowded as in my last visit in late 1969, and some were even totally deserted of GIs. Little shanty houses that were once bars and nightclubs frequented nightly by GIs now were abandoned and in ruins.

The booming businesses related to the American soldiers' personal services slowed down. The six years of the American troops' presence in Việt Nam left their clear traces everywhere. For the first few years, the common Vietnamese were discontented with social problems resulting from relations with the GIs. They blamed the GIs for the soaring cost of living, the increase of prostitution, family breakups because of wives leaving home to live with American soldiers, Vietnamese teens addicted to drugs, and traffic accidents caused by U.S. military vehicles. When U.S. troops started to leave in 1971, people got a better look at the GIs and began to express some sympathy for them.

The high spirit of ARVN soldiers, boosted by the heavy enemy losses in the Tét Offensive, was fading away when news reports about waves of protests reached Việt Nam every day. In 1971, things worsened when some leftist activists tacitly connived with the RVN government to voice their anti-American, anti-war opinions right in the heart of Sài Gòn. They held many protests, accusing the U.S. and RVN governments of maintaining the war that caused the death and destruction of property of innocent Vietnamese. However, they avoided direct criticism of the military and never openly supported communist policies, although their literature smacked of pro-communist rhetoric.

In the view of many of us officers, such public protests were expressions of a cheap tactic initiated either by the RVN government or on the advice of the Americans in the embassy or in Washington to demonstrate that there was freedom of expression in Sài Gòn. But to the soldiers, this sort of free expression was a sign that the United States was about to give up South Việt Nam to the communists. It was not far from the truth to say that the RVN was sacrificed for the billboard of Freedom and Democracy raised by the Americans.

Many young Vietnamese protesters saw the war their own way, depending on information they were fed and following in the steps of their comrades in America. Behind them, there was only a very small number of communist agitators the police found impossible to detect. Sài Gòn police cracked down on protests that were not peaceful, but with measures far less harsh than the police in the United States at the time, despite the fact that Việt Nam was at war and under the immediate threat of enemy subversion.

In my view, the protesting students were not my enemies. I knew they were ill informed and ignorant about communist matters. They only reacted to the horrors of war as they saw them in newspapers and on the TV screen. They were acting as urged by their conscience. Antiwar literature, songs, and slogans were inspired by sights of war destruction, bomb and shell craters, blood, and burned houses. They had their reasons, but they did not have access to the gory scenes of civilians, including old men, women, and children, assassinated by communist terrorists that might have corrected their view of the war.

I didn't blame the Americans and other foreign protesters either. They reacted rightly to the scenes of war on TV, in pictures, and in books on our side, whereas the media cameras were not able to record what was actually happening on the communist side to help them make an impartial comparison. I never took them as my enemy but only as gullible, ignorant friends.

Although I was not an American citizen, I was offended when learning from TV and radio reports that many GIs returning from Việt Nam were humiliated and called "baby killers" by their compatriots. We knew better than those shortsighted Americans that the GIs were fighting to protect Americans' interests and freedom.

A special aspect of the peace movement in South Việt Nam concerned antiwar songs. During the war, hundreds of songs were freely produced. A great many had artistic value, particularly love songs. However, there were dozens of songs protesting the war with lyrics portraying the death, sorrow, and devastation. As they became top hits, national and military television and radio allowed them on music programs, and so did private music halls, clubs, and theaters. The antiwar music production peaked in 1971. Military commanders strongly protested, claiming that such songs might have a negative effect on their troops, many of whom owned small shortwave radio sets. The GPWD agreed, but failed to convince the authorities at higher levels and the public opinion as well that such songs should not be aired. Many soldiers contended that such songs were the kind of freedom of expression we were fighting to protect.

Songwriter Trịnh Công Sơn had produced famous antiwar pieces since the mid-1960s. His melodies carried distinctive nuances and sensational lyrics. His songs enthralled young men and women. He was inspired by scenes of houses burned, corpses scattered in rice fields, mothers searching for their sons' remains, and children crying beside their dead mothers. Destruction and death were tacitly ascribed to ARVN and U.S. artillery and air attacks. Only some of his songs depicted killing done by the communist guns and knives or made reference to the 1968 Tết massacre in Huế. Government supporters described Trịnh Công Sơn's antiwar stance as pro-communist, a betrayal of the fighting soldiers and the nationalist cause. They said his songs undermined the troops' morale. The Sài Gòn government restricted, even banned circulation of, some of his songs.

As for many of my friends and according to my studies, I came to a different conclusion. To a degree, the antiwar literature, the songs in particular, incited sorrowful feelings in a number of our troops and the youth as well. The undesirable effect could have been slow and indirect, but it did not play a key role in fostering anti–Sài Gòn sentiment. A great number of fervent anticommunists liked antiwar songs, probably because they gave them the images of the destruction of humans and villages by war, but their conviction against the communists remained the same. From a different perspective, we noticed the apparent psychology of romanticism in the young soldiers who were in the field. All the songs from radio gave the troops some kind of comfort after enduring battlefield dangers and hardships. My own experience was that many troops who loved romantic music with an antiwar theme showed great willingness to fight and to endure battle hazards courageously.[3]

On October 3, 1971, South Vietnamese voters elected President Nguyen Van Thiệu for his second term in the one-candidate election, with Trần Văn Hương as his vice president after the two others, Dương Văn Minh and Nguyễn Cao Kỳ, withdrew from the race. I didn't cast my vote because I had the same feeling I had had during the January 4, 1946, election when I witnessed overt fraud at the polling booths in my village and elections under the Diệm regime. However, I held the old man Trần Văn Hương in high esteem, as he was an outspoken incorruptible celebrity of the South.

Under Ngô Đình Diệm, in many villages and even in Sài Gòn, local officials instructed voters whom they must vote for, and elections in some districts were rigged. At many polling booths, soldiers in plainclothes were sent to vote with unregistered names to support the government's candidates. Since Nguyễn Văn Thiệu had ascended to power, most voters in cities were not following officials' instructions, and there were cases of rigged elections in remote villages that observers were unable to reach. According to my research, I thought less rigging was practiced under Thiệu than under Diệm.

It was easy to understand that Sài Gòn had no way to make sure that all voters would vote for candidates selected by the leaders as the communists were doing in North Việt Nam. If the RVN government had controlled its voters the way the communists did in North Việt Nam, it wouldn't have had to rig the results but just tell voters whom they were to vote for. In 1969, President Thiệu founded the Democratic Party as his political base. Its members were government employees and civilians, but it did not target the military. The party rallied a large number of members, but I saw in it no real power, just a face value.

As American forces were phasing out of Việt Nam in 1970 and 1971, the U.S. government began providing the RVN armed forces with better military equipment, from flag jackets in small sizes to fit the Vietnamese and M16–A1 rifles to M-48 tanks and 175 mm guns, all a result of the Vietnamization plan introduced by the Nixon administration. The huge aid had a great material value, but its morale impact failed to reach the expected level. It had come a little late.

I was certain that Washington was trying its best to support South Việt Nam. But many South Vietnamese, including those in the military, were not aware of some facts they should have known. One was that the Popular Force, or villages' militias in South Việt Nam, were equipped with brand-new M16-A1 rifles while U.S. Army units on the U.S. continent, in Europe, and in South Korea were not. ARVN company officers were driving brand-new quarter-ton M-151A2 jeeps long before the battalion commanders in the States ever saw one. The ARVN even received the M-48 tanks, whereas Israel and South Korea did not.

However, what the aid failed to achieve reminded me of the third-grade lesson: "He gives twice who gives quickly." Besides, although the better weapons did heighten troop morale a little, the stronger effect of our adversaries' psychological warfare was strengthening our warriors' pessimism.

FREEDOM OF SPEECH

In March 1971, I left the Interministerial Committee for the War Invalid Affairs to resume full charge of the Research and Study Section of the General Political Warfare Department. My section received all kinds of information, copies of reports and statistics from all levels of the armed forces, as well as some secret documents from J-2 and J-3 related to political warfare, including compiled news reports and analysis from the world media. My section also received comments and complaints from civilians and soldiers on matters relating to political warfare. We made related information into research documents and provided them to the political warfare offices at all major staff levels, including the general inspection branch, and performed general planning tasks. Sometimes my section sent selected teams to low-leveled units to do specific research required for evaluation and planning. The job broadened my perspective on the military affairs and also allowed me a little time to write for some newspapers.

The unlicensed *Thái Độ* magazine had finally closed. After the Tết Offensive, our group's activities diminished to infrequent meetings around dinner tables. Besides the new political and war atmosphere, the fact that many of the group's members had been drafted called a halt to the magazine's publishing activities. So, in early 1971, I contributed many articles to the *Diều Hâu* (The Hawk), a private weekly publication whose editors were military officers. I wrote editorials and *phú*, a kind of poem, the verses of which were sets of parallels, usually dealing with sarcastic themes. The board of editors decided that our objectives would be supporting the honorable fighting of our soldiers and doing a whistleblower's job against corruption. The *Diều Hâu* viewpoints were appreciated by a large segment of the officer corps. At the same time, I was writing commentaries for the *Diễn Đàn Chính Đảng* (Political Parties' Forum), a weekly magazine edited by Trương Vĩnh Lễ, former speaker of the National Assembly under Ngô Đình Diệm.

Beginning in 1964, military officers could write and publish editorials, commentaries, installments, novels, short stories, poems, and songs if they were officially permitted. Though many of us did not have written permission, we were tacitly allowed to write books and newspaper articles, provided that our writings would not be pro-communist. Sometimes we dared to touch on sensitive subjects such as the shady businesses of some generals.

Once I contributed an article to the *Diễn Đàn Chính Đảng* titled "The Republic of Vietnam Armed Forces Will Disintegrate in Five Years," in which I urged the military leadership to be more concerned about keeping the armed forces in good shape regarding personnel management, economy of forces, proper implementation of the psychological warfare strategy, and the probability of a large reduction in military aid. Mr. Lễ asked me to change "five years" into "fifteen years" so that the article appeared less offensive to the generals. I reluctantly agreed to his request. Actually, I just gave a wild guess of five years without any logical calculation. I did not expected that my guess would come true on April 30, 1975, four years after my article was published.

General Trung, my big boss, was told that it was my article. In a planners' meeting, he asked me, "Why are you so pessimistic?"

I replied, "Sir, every patriot must be as pessimistic as I am." I showed him how army commanders accepted graft. He talked to me softly and listened to my explanation. At last he agreed with me. I left his room while he looked sad. To me, General Trung was one of the incorruptible and capable generals, but he had little power to do what he should have done. To his subordinates, he was open and tolerant.

For many years, medal citations were awarded promiscuously, thus lowering the value of the decorations. When medals lost their value, high-level headquarters resorted to promotion to reward soldiers. There were so many battlefield promotions exceeding the reasonable limit. Hundreds of officers were promoted after major battles for reward without proper considerations of their true capability and conduct. Promotion lists were made with illogical standards. The mismanagement resulted in less respect in the military ranks.

* * *

At that time, war protesters in the United States and other cities in the world somehow succeeded in portraying the Sài Gòn regime as a dictatorship denying freedom of speech and plagued by briberies and embezzlement. Other writers in academic circles and the media simply took the charges for granted.

From 1954 to 1975, the South Vietnamese were not living under a full-scale democracy. Under Ngô Đình Diệm, there was not complete freedom of speech, and the government played roughly with the opposition. However, the Diệm regime was no worse than any other in South and Southeast Asian countries, even many in the third world. Ngô Đình Diệm was a kind of dictator, but his regime was much less oppressive than Hồ Chí Minh's tyranny. Under Diệm, some newspapers and magazines were closed, and there were taboos protecting government officials and military generals from media attacks and criticism. However, private publications were allowed to publish a wide range of articles and information. Diệm's successor, Nguyễn Văn Thiệu, was not strong enough to be a true dictator.

The successive post-1963 governments under the generals ruled the country with much softer hands. Freedom of speech was respected to a certain degree, not as free as in Western democracies, but certainly better than many of the developing countries, including those of American allies.

Was there any country at war that allowed criticism against the government so fiercely, even sometimes in articles smacking of leftist rhetoric? How many third world countries permitted journalists to publicly denounce corrupt ministers and generals and to severely castigate the president for almost everything he was doing without fear of being arrested? Although freedom of the press was limited, the South Vietnamese press corps had a voice against corruption and despotism, strong enough in fighting many cases of abuse of authority.

* * *

The military leadership was not better, either. When military sovereignty was recovered from the French, the new armed forces of the Republic of Việt Nam were organized with the officer corps from the Nationalist Army of the Bảo Đại government. A number of these officers formerly served with the French Colonial Army. Those who later became high-ranking military leaders may have been talented officers in pure military domains and conventional warfare, but they seemed unfit to conduct the war against the enemy that was fighting with everything it could employ in addition to conventional weapons. They considered fighting the communists as a mission against rebels illegally opposing the government, but they did not commit themselves to any anticommunist ideology.

Although ARVN generals were sharply criticized for corruption, and it was true that some generals engaged in shady deals to earn illegal money, those who ruled South Việt Nam after Ngô Đình Diệm did not constitute a militarist tyranny. South Việt Nam did not have any general who ruled the country with an iron fist and possessed an enormous ill-gained fortune, as do many generals of some dictatorships in Asia, Africa, and South America.

A group of us young officers who had served in different units had several private discussions concerning military leadership. We concluded that of our nearly 100 generals, about 20 were commanders of high morality and capability. General Ngô Quang Trưởng was in the top 5 percent of the list, beside Nguyễn Viết Thanh, Nguyễn Đức Thắng, Nguyễn Văn Hiếu, and others. Most of the rest were not excellent but had committed no serious wrongdoings. Ten generals were notorious for corruption and incompetence. The top government leaders were not strong and decisive enough to discharge the corrupt top brass.

THE YOUNGER OFFICERS

There were times I revisited the Đà Lạt Military Academy, the dearest place that had led me to a military career. I felt happy to see the young cadets in better physical condition, learning better lessons in a training program that included four years of college science education, and living in well organized and attractive buildings. They showed a great willingness to serve the country and to fight the enemy. But I still worried that the training seemed not enough to strengthen their capability to fight and to lead the troops in the war of ideology and against the enemy that was using propaganda and terrorism as the most effective weapons.

The Political Warfare University founded in 1967 had an excellent academic curriculum and practical subjects of anticommunism. But the organization of the Political Warfare branch was not suitable to the formation of polwar officers who graduated as experts of the multifaceted ideological conflict in which the country was engaged.

My original concept when I was doing studies and preparing documents for establishing the Political Warfare University in 1966 was to reorganize the Đà Lạt Military Academy into a larger one with the same military training program but with two baccalaureate curriculums: the existing bachelor of science and a new bachelor of arts program specializing in psychological warfare and human studies. The graduates would be assigned to appropriate jobs in the polwar branch, as well as to other branches and services of the armed forces, or to command positions in combat units. Thus personnel distribution of the officer corps could be effectively managed.

My idea was not welcomed. In 1974, some trouble in the employment of polwar officers emerged. As the lieutenants moved up to higher ranks, there were no polwar jobs awaiting them. A directive from President Thiệu required the ministries of defense and education and the JGS to submit plans for restructuring the two institutions into one. But it was still on the desks of the big wheels when the RVN collapsed.

Following a tradition maintained by the graduates of the Đà Lạt Military Academy, I used to favor my alumni, the juniors in particular. But I also felt sorry to see so many of those younger guys, elegant, full of energy and courage, falling on the battlefields when they were too young. The nineteenth VNMA class (1964) graduated at the peak of the enemy's offensive waves. By 1975, among thirty-one classes of the academy, this class suffered the highest human loss: of the 395 graduates, 112 were killed in action.

Young officers who graduated from Thủ Đức Reserved Officers School fought with no less determination. Although they were draftees, many served combat units with great willingness to fight and courage second to no "lifer."

The generations of young officers were constructing a new military spirit and enhancing the performance of the ARVN several times better than their seniors.

TWENTY-THREE

The Fiery Summer

THE BATTLES IN QUẢNG TRỊ

Richard Nixon's visit to Red China in 1972 was the most important event of the time. The new relations of the two adversaries apparently worried both North and South Việt Nam.

In Sài Gòn, we officers were greatly concerned about the Nixon-Mao meeting, from the state dinner to welcome the Americans with *maotai* wine to the joint communiqué in which for the first time the Beijing leaders called South Việt Nam government "the Government of the Republic of Việt Nam" instead of other insulting terms such as "the Sài Gòn Puppet Regime." In Hà Nội's radio broadcast and newspapers, there was not a word mentioning Nixon's visit. My research subsection found just one vague comment on the Beijing summit in the Communist Party's *Nhân Dân Daily*. It said something like, "The world powers have no right to impose their will on other countries."

Before the Beijing summit, there had been indications of a large-scale offensive about to be launched. Secret information from top intelligence agencies sent to my office in February 1972 indicated that communist units were preparing a general offensive. Reports from the U.S. Air Force confirmed a number of NVA tanks had crossed into South Việt Nam border areas. They were aiming at Quảng Trị province (below the demilitarized zone), and Kontum and Tây Ninh. Later, the enemy launched massive attacks at Quảng Trị, Kontum, and An Lộc instead of Tây Ninh. We were not surprised but were concerned at the fall of Camp Carroll, in the northernmost line of defense in late March, where the Fifty-sixth Infantry Regiment of the ARVN Third Division surrendered to the NVA multi-division force.

General Trung told me to go to the First Corps Headquarters at Huế City to reinforce its political warfare staff. It was April 2, 1972, three days after Camp

Carroll was overrun. It had been a firebase of the U.S. Marines. The ARVN Fifty-sixth Regiment took over the camp after the Marines withdrew in 1971.

The fighting in the Đông Hà area ten miles south of the demilitarized zone in summer 1972 appeared in every aspect to be true conventional warfare. Combat units of the two sides faced each other across a determined front line, conducting attacks under artillery support. In most places, the two sides were so close that our air force fighters found it impossible to strike without hitting friendly troops.

After years of fighting on all-direction battlefields, the South Vietnamese forces were fighting on a directional battle area and a controlled rear area. There were no enemy activities—of guerrillas or regular troops—behind the Đông Hà front line and in adjacent districts to the seashore. No bridges were blown up, so there were no troops guarding most of them. There were only ARVN troops fighting in the 1972 campaign without participation of U.S. ground forces. However, the U.S. Army and Air Force still provided effective air support.

At night, only a few kilometers away from the front line, troops could find several kinds of food and drink, especially beer and some booze. The "bomb-crater peddlers," mostly women, sold food and drinks on discarded military cartons and wooden crates set at the bottoms of wide craters created by artillery shells and bombs. They made big money. People felt safer traveling at night around many villages behind the battle areas. The two sides seldom conducted night operations.

Attacks began at sunrise and stopped at sunset. They didn't shell us at night because flashes and reports from the guns could be easily detected and pinpointed. Precision rockets and bombs from our fighters would destroy their artillery pieces with higher accuracy. The counterbattery was much more effective at night than during the day.

Life near the battle areas looked so inert in daylight but was somewhat lively at night without fear of communist guerrilla attacks. The fact was that the Phượng Hoàng campaign had largely eliminated local VC infrastructure. Besides, the loss of guerrillas since 1968 was so heavy that local communist leaders failed to enroll new recruits. The campaign proved to have been a great success, greater than I had thought in 1968 when I took part in its founding phase. Until then, I had never dreamed of a countryside area where I could travel freely without fear of mines, sniper fire, or ambushes. Previously, communication in most countryside areas was largely unsafe except for Long Xuyên province, homeland of more than a million Hòa Hảo Buddhists, the most ardent anticommunist people.

Although enemy artillery fire was heavy, a great number of NVA 130 mm shells exploded into only a dozen fragments and left a lot of unspent explosives. That saved a lot of our soldiers. The really deadly things were the 82 mm mortars, which could hit targets with high precision.

Enemy shelling was successful in destroying our resupply facilities. Many times enemy shelling turned camp Ái Tử, one of the two forward supply dumps, into flames beneath columns of dense black smoke, blowing up thousands of gasoline barrels and tons of artillery ammo, along with C-rations and other supply items.

It seemed to me that our commanders and their staffs at division level and higher, for unknown reasons, did not take the best advantage of the favorable territorial security situation when the areas behind the front lines were so safe. Colonel Phan Phiên, the chief of I-Corps' political warfare block, and his staff once suggested that gasoline, C-rations, and ammunition be kept at smaller dumps in villages with reliable militia defenses along Highway 1. We needed to accept a certain loss and trouble in managing so many small storage sites, which would require more personnel and complicate management in order to ensure logistic support. Unfortunately, only deaf ears received the suggestion.

The 130 mm and 122 mm guns were emplaced in a wide area to the north. The most effective tactics against the enemy guns were commando raids. A group of armed propaganda troops of Huế Chiêu Hồi service volunteered for a bold operation. The sapper squad of fourteen armed propaganda troops, specially armed and equipped for the mission, slipped into the communist-infested jungle areas in Quảng Trị and Thừa Thiên for a ten-day commando raid. They pinpointed several locations of the enemy's 122 mm and 130 mm guns during the day and conducted flash sapper attacks to destroy the guns at night. They even took a few pictures of some blown-up 130 mm cannons.

On the way back, an ARVN front line unit mistook them for communist soldiers by their disguised uniforms and by errors in password challenges. They opened fire, killing half of the AP team before they were recognized as friends. Receiving the bad news, I stopped by to see the survivors. Most of them had known me in the National Chiêu Hồi Center. Trần Văn Thủy, the company commander, hugged me and cried.[1]

THE RETREAT

On April 20, I returned to Sài Gòn to report to my commanding general about the critical situation on the Quảng Trị front, which was deteriorating. The shortage of artillery ammunition played a deadly role in undermining our troops' morale. For years since the war escalated, with stronger enemy regular units and more support for South Việt Nam from the Americans, our troops had become more dependent on artillery and air firepower.

By the end of April 1972, the allocated rate for each gun was down to three shells a day. The Army Corps I zone was depending on ammunition resupply from the Thành Tuy Hạ general depot near Sài Gòn. In the last days of April in Quảng

Trị, a large convoy of more than 100 trucks transporting artillery ammo was hit by enemy artillery attack, and it exploded outside of Quảng Trị City. Every hope of holding fast to the strip of territory in northern Quảng Trị evaporated.

The enemy had prepared the 1972 offensive for many years. It was estimated that hundreds of thousands of war laborers had been moving artillery ammunition to the jungle areas along the common border with Laos since 1970. A two-person team would carry just one 130 mm shell from the northern DMZ into Quảng Trị province and leave it at one of the numerous storage sites. The enemy's ammo supply actually outnumbered ours.

On April 30, General Vũ Văn Giai, commanding officer of the Third Infantry Division and also commander of the Northern Theater of Operations defending the Quảng Trị territory, officially ordered the retreat to the new defensive line some ten miles south of Quảng Trị City, or twenty miles south of the previous front line.

The withdrawal itself was justifiable, but General Giai was sacked and later court-martialed. Many people accused him of losing the battle to the enemy. But I sided with others who supported him. He made the right decision to retreat before his troops were totally routed. How could he hold the line with such a shortage of artillery ammunition?

Friends of mine serving in the Third Division told me that General Giai acted properly when he decided on the retreat plan, and his command post moved out along with the last mechanized unit at 5 PM, as scheduled in the operation order. Controlling chaos along the withdrawal routes should have been the responsibility of commanders of his subordinate units.

In the world of military history, retreat was always the most difficult operation, several times harder than defense or offense. There are always problems in maneuvering the retreating units in good order as planned while maintaining discipline. Just one element of the retreating force failing to act as planned could provoke waves of panic leading to chaos.

That was what I saw on April 29 when I came back to Huế. Many units were moving south in disorder. ARVN Marines Brigade 147 deserved high praise, as they were retreating in good order, with very few stragglers, and the commanders could still perform their duties rather well.

There were some infantry battalions that proved their high spirit. One of the defeated Third Division battalions moved on foot from the Gio Linh area with about 510 soldiers, fighting along the way of retreat. A few days later, they reached Huế with 505 men, 5 missing. In such a situation, it was an excellent feat, but it was not made known to the public!

Civilians, most of them women, old people, and children, were moving in an endless stream from Quảng Trị to Huế and to Đà Nẵng, followed by civilians from the Huế area. They made the trip on foot and in every available means of transportation—cars, trucks, carts, bikes, motorbikes, and even wheelchairs. The long line of war refugees filled Highway 1, turning it into one-way traffic. From the air, I estimated the line to be as long as two miles. It took my jeep an hour to cover eight miles from Phú Bài Airport to Huế City, crossing many dry rice fields beside the highway.

All of those in the slow moving line I spoke to were talking about the bloody massacres and the mass graves in the 1968 Tết Offensive that frightened them greatly. They dared not stay, although they were not closely related to the RVN government or military. The risk of death by bombs and artillery was frightening them, too, but it was not as horrible as the possibility of barbaric executions by the communists.

On the way from Quảng Trị to Huế, hundreds of military and civilian cars and trucks with thousands of passengers got stuck in the traffic jam at the Trường Phước bridge, about ten miles south of Quảng Trị City. Although 90 percent of the crowd were women, old people, and children, whose appearance was easily discernible, the communist force launched a fierce artillery shelling and a company-sized infantry attack, killing most of the crowd and destroying cars, trucks, and motorbikes. The one-mile segment of HW-1 at Trường Phước was named the Đoạn Đường Kinh Hoàng (Road of Horror), as people in Quảng Trị still call it today.[2]

Huế looked like a lawless city; the small number of police and military police were unable to control the mass of refugees and soldiers. There were robberies, lootings, and car hijackings. Half of the Huế population had fled to Đà Nẵng along with people from Quảng Trị.

Beside the main roads, many straggling children from toddlers to early teens were crying and watching the flow of people moving by while looking for help. I saw a boy about twelve years old holding his brother of about three years old leaning on a roadside tree. Walking without shoes, their feet were bleeding and swollen. The older one was holding a piece of letter-sized paper on which he had scribbled, "We are children of Mr. Xuân in Quảng Trị. Can't find our parents. Please help us." A family living nearby brought them home to help. With assistance from the police, other local families helped gather other stray kids to take care of them.

The shocking scenes of war were not from fighting only. No foreign reporter could notice hundreds of short messages scribbled with chalk or charcoal on the walls of any building that refugees found available. Some were written in pencil on pieces of paper and glued onto tree trunks using cooked rice. Many read like these: "To PFC Nguyễn Văn Ba, 1/57th Btn. The children and I are moving to Auntie's home in Đà Nẵng" or "Corporal Bảy 3/2 Inf. to wife: I'm alive and fighting. Buddha blesses you and our kids!" The message that moved me most was on paper: "Wife Hoa to husband Sgt. Trường RF-Quảng Trị. VC mortar killed our baby girl yesterday. The boy is safe with me. Don't worry and don't go AWOL."

An order from Sài Gòn gave me full authority to control the Huế TV and radio stations while the city was in crisis. The first thing I did was to procure a small stock of food (rice, sauce, dry meat, and fish) to make sure the remaining staffers at the two stations would not be left starving. Only a very few had fled to Đà Nẵng with their families.

In such a hopeless situation, the young principal announcer of Huế radio station proved her courage. At a meeting of all members of the station, I allowed her to go to Đà Nẵng with her six-month-old son for safety because Huế could be attacked at any time. I would have some WAC noncommissioned officers replace her temporarily.

She said with tears and an assertive tone that she wouldn't leave the station if I allowed her to stay. According to her, people in the region were so familiar with her voice that if it stopped and was replaced by a new voice, however much sweeter, it would cause unfavorable psychological effects at a time when we must do everything to elevate morale.

"I would like very much to share danger with you. Everybody dies sometime," she insisted. At last, the station chief agreed with me that we should let her stay. Despite the tense atmosphere hovering over the imperial city, her voice on air was calm and hopeful as if there were not a single threat of war. In the following weeks, she received many letters of appreciation; a lot of them came from the villagers.

One of my few orders as the emergency situation required was to have the two stations run a special program several times a day to help people and soldiers locate their families. Hundreds of families highly appreciated the broadcast.

The next day, General Ngô Quang Trưởng assumed command of the Corps/Military Region I. He was well known as one of the most incorruptible and capable generals of South Việt Nam. His reputation apparently deflated the tension and pacified the public.

After Huế returned to normal, I spent a lot of my time seeing reporters, typical soldiers, and POWs. On visits to four infantry battalions and an armored unit, I was alarmed by some information relating to their American advisors. In 1972, many ARVN soldiers in the area heard that there was an order from some American headquarters instructing that when a Vietnamese unit was at risk of being overrun, its American advisors must be picked up by helicopter.

The rumor spread far and wide. Many soldiers believed that whenever an American chopper landed at the command post to evacuate American advisors, it would be the last hour of the unit. Some expressed their bitterness toward the U.S. high command, saying that the order was a clear sign that the U.S. government was betraying South Việt Nam. Some of them went even further, saying that the advisor evacuation would be performed whenever there was a decision from the American side to put the fate of a Vietnamese unit into the hands of the communists after an agreement between American and communist field commanders. To most officers, the rumor was unreasonable and unfounded. But to many troops, it was psychologically damaging. At least ten soldiers let me know there were some fellows in their units who vowed to shoot down any helicopter that came to evacuate the advisors. ARVN military security services were aware of the plot.

Until the last day before the RVN collapsed, nothing like that ever happened, only because—so far as I know—very few U.S. advisors in ARVN combat units agreed to be evacuated.

The war protest movement in the States was gaining strength, despite the fact that the ARVN had gained credibility after its 1968 Tét Offensive victory. The protests delivered painful blows to troop morale in 1972 when there were more and more indications that the Americans would abandon Việt Nam soon. Also, in February 1972, the majority of South Vietnamese soldiers were informed of Nixon's visit to China. The events in Beijing added to the ARVN troops' discontent. On the other side of the battle line, no North Vietnamese Army troops knew about the summit.

However, despite the imbalance on the propaganda front, ARVN troops in other regions were fighting and maintaining control over their areas. Communist forces were unable to conduct large or medium-scale attacks, except in the U Minh marshy area in the vast Mekong Delta.

Foreigners might be unable to understand why, though operating under the adverse psychological effects from negative rumors, most ARVN soldiers still fought bravely until 1975. It may have been the fact that ARVN troops while serving the RVN military service had experienced the stark realities of the communist regime, which urged them to keep fighting under such hopeless circumstances. The troops' resolve could be noticed in the popular force units in the three northernmost provinces of the RVN where there was a large number of VNQDĐ and Đại Việt party members. In the areas of Thừa Thiên-Huế and Quảng Nam, Việt Quốc members made up the majority of popular force platoons. They kept the large populated areas under their protection. A great number of provincial and city councilmen in the area were Việt Quốc and Đại Việt members. They also won a score of seats in the National Congress. In Sài Gòn, the Việt Quốc was present along with other nationalist parties; all had strong voices in the national political arena but were weaker at the provincial level.

During the darkest days of the 1968 Tét Offensive, more than 300 Việt Quốc members were massacred along with 5,000 victims in Hué. In 1972, the Quảng Trị Popular Force troops suffered heavy losses when the regular forces withdrew from this province.

SOME REMARKABLE ASPECTS OF THE 1972 BATTLES

As I noted earlier, the 1968 Tết Offensive and the 1972 Summer Offensive caused despair in a segment of Vietnamese high society and in the United States. But in all walks of life in Việt Nam, it created a more favorable attitude toward the nationalist cause than in previous years.

Beside the fact that more volunteers joined the infantry units before their draft age, the government and the military received more cooperation from common people, especially poor farmers. But at the same time, the antiwar movement and rumors that the Americans would soon pull out left South Việt Nam's better-educated segment of society greatly demoralized.

Some of the lightly armed regional force units in the Huế area proved their willingness to fight, even in defense against the better armed North Vietnamese regulars. In late April, I had a chance to watch a regional force company under a young first lieutenant attack a NVA company and regain control of a hamlet about a mile from the main battle line at Quảng Trị in two hours without air or artillery fire support.

On the enemy side, the NVA soldiers were displaying degeneration in their capability and willingness to fight in the Quảng Trị battles. For the first time since the war began in 1955, communist troops from the North were using truly conventional warfare in the South. Tactical maneuvers of NVA battalion-size units showed they were not very familiar with conventional maneuvers.

Once in mid-April, I watched a clip taken by a brave reporter of the Huế TV station at the front line. On the screen, one of the first NVA combined armor-infantry task forces was advancing near Đông Hà. NVA infantrymen moved in one block behind the column of five tanks instead of following each tank to provide mutual protection. A single 90 mm high-explosive antitank shell shot by an M-48A1 of the Twentieth ARVN Armored Battalion knocked out a Soviet T-54 tank at the range of about 2,000 meters. The destruction of the leading T-54 caused other enemy tanks to turn around, and the infantry company retreated in disarray.

In another part of the front line, an NVA battalion marched uphill toward an ARVN defense line. The NVA infantry unit launched three attacks that day, but did not reach the defense line closer than about 300 yards when they were met by a barrage of fire from several ARVN 105 mm and 155 mm artillery battalions. The attacks failed at last.

The NVA fought more successfully in keeping close contact with their enemy, usually under 200 yards, but were forced to conduct piecemeal attacks.

NVA artillery fire was slow and imprecise. Their guns were heavy, resulting in limited mobility. However, communist artillery batteries made up for the shortcomings by sending observers well forward into the target area, sometimes to within a few hundred yards from the targets to adjust fire. In many cases at Quảng Trị battles, communist forward observers—or "artillery reconnaissance observers" in NVA terminology—were sent beyond the ARVN front line, disguised as peasants or war refugees.

I met scores of POWs and defectors from various North Vietnamese units and learned of some changes in the new generation of communist soldiers from the North. They were younger than those I had been familiar with in 1969, my last year in the Chiêu Hồi Ministry. Most of them were eighteen years old, but many were only seventeen. I could guess how North Việt Nam's human resources were depleting.

Many of the pre-1968 NVA soldiers fought with higher determination and endurance. Eliminating a cell of resistance held fast by a small number of them was not an easy task. Some showed bold resistance when taken prisoner and interrogated.

The rate of NVA deserters in the North before they reached the South was much higher than in 1968, due to weaker communist control over North Vietnamese peasants when the household registering system and the labor management at village level suffered great failures as a result of great food shortages and people's passive reaction.

As far as combat basic training was concerned, most of the 1972 NVA soldiers fighting in Quảng Trị spent seven to fourteen days in district boot camps before departing for the war zone. Many had never shot an AK-47 live round before arriving in South Việt Nam. They showed little hostility and no great fear of being mistreated. It seemed that they were too young and were not stuffed with much propaganda, as were their older brothers. Poor boys!

From captured documents and talking with NVA prisoners, I realized some important information. Most NVA small unit commanders—platoon to battalion—were young with fewer years in service and with no similar experiences with their predecessors just five years older. Heavy losses had greatly decimated the communist corps of subaltern officers.

COUNTERATTACK AT QUẢNG TRỊ CITY

In late May and June, ARVN units were busy preparing for counterattacks, reorganizing and completing replacement of personnel and materials. In the inner circle of the corps HQS, people were talking about the possibility of invading North Việt Nam to cut its forces in the South off logistics supports from the North. Some ARVN Marine battalions were isolated for secrecy and highest readiness. But the red alert was lifted a few days later.

Tanks, armored personnel carriers, cannons, infantry weapons, and equipment poured in by air on hundreds of flights from Sài Gòn and Okinawa. And at the end of June, the large-scale operation for retaking Quảng Trị City started with a massive artillery concentration to clear terrain for the advancing units of Marines.

The Tenth Polwar Battalion was responsible for protecting and receiving civilian refugees who fled their villages in the districts north of the Mỹ Chánh River, the line of departure. Villagers were held in their villages by communist units as human shields. As people ran out of the villages on the dirt roads, despite communist troops' yelling and firing to stop them, ARVN troops directed their machine-gun fire and artillery shelling along the two sides of the strip of dry land to protect streams of old people, women, and children swarming out of the tree lines to the ARVN side. Communist fire killed a few civilians.

A young woman of about twenty gave birth to a baby right outside the village. She carried her newborn son with the help of two older women who were trying to tie a string of cloth torn from her garment to stop blood from the baby's umbilical cord. She fainted upon reaching the low dyke where the first ARVN soldiers were taking position. She had run half a mile under scorching sunshine, which burned the baby's exposed skin to light purple.

Next on the "Road of Horror," reoccupied after nearly two months, the ghastly sight of war atrocities glowed bright under the summer sun. There were hundreds of cars, trucks, bikes, and motorbikes riddled with communist bullets and shell fragments, some burned to ashes. Human skeletons lay scattered along the roadbed. Many ARVN soldiers' coffins, under half burned national flags on military trucks, had been riddled with bullets fired at close range. Several dozen wounded soldiers had been killed inside ambulances that bore gaping holes caused by B-40 rockets. The image that sent a wave of compassion through my heart was a tiny skeleton of a child about two years old inside a large aluminum wash basin. A tiny pair of rubber sandals lay beside the mother's remains.

The battle lasted for many weeks, claiming thousands of lives on both sides. The ARVN side, the Marines in particular, suffered more than 3,000 KIA in the fighting to reoccupy the Quảng Trị Citadel, in exchange for more than 16,000 enemy soldiers killed. The brave Marines did their marvelous task. But most buildings inside the old citadel were destroyed.

For the last years of the war, the two ARVN elite divisions—the Airborne and the Marines—bore the brunt of the fighting. They were stretched thin all over the country and suffered huge losses when the supreme command stagnated their battalions in major battle areas, instead of just assigning them missions as mobile national general reserves and as strike forces.

THE BEGINNING OF THE END

After three months of temporary duty at Huế, I was called back to Sài Gòn to resume my principal job. I made a long report to General Trần Văn Trung on the general situation in the First Corps Military Region. I concluded by noting that our soldiers were still good fighters. They were even better in critical times. But a number of our officers did not perform their duties well enough; among them, the younger seemed the better.

For years, combat soldiers were not treated as they should have been. Low pay and continuous operations left them little time to recover from the hardships of war. Most officers were incorruptible and endured the unfavorable living conditions. Only a few who had the opportunity committed embezzlement and corruption, rewarding themselves with ill-gotten money as if to compensate for their hardships. When a corrupt officer committed wrongdoing, his subordinates sometimes felt free to do the same and paid him no more respect.

The officer corps, with higher education, was easily affected by biased news reports and by the war protest movement in the United States. In 1968–69, officers' morale reached a higher level than their troops; they suffered stronger blows from the 1972 battles. Even the slightest rumor regarding less support from the U.S. military dealt a destructive punch to their determination. The impact on the troops' morale was as strong as that from communist propaganda. But their resolution to fight suffered the weaker damage, probably owing to their fighting experiences and the comradeship in their units.

A young captain met me on his way to the front line with his battalion, saying, "Sir, I don't think we could expel the enemy from the present line, and they even might break our defense in a few weeks. I heard from the Division G-3 DTOC that the Americans now approve only four or five out of our ten air support requests. Last year, we got eight or nine out of ten. It is the Americans' intention to give up South Việt Nam to the Chinese communists." I tried to explain the way the Americans were working to prove that it was our willingness to fight that counted and played one of the key factors that shaped Washington's policies in Việt Nam. He didn't comment, but his eyes told me that I didn't convince him.

During the withdrawal from Quảng Trị City, only soldiers in units whose commanders abandoned their CPs fled the position in disarray. Commanders who stayed and retreated at the time specified in operation orders saw their troops fight until the last minute. We had numerous heroes, but one coward could nullify what nine heroes had gained.

News from other battles in Kontum, especially the defeat of the ARVN Twenty-second Infantry Division, produced very unfavorable effects on the soldiers at other fronts. However, communist forces failed to seize Kontum City.

The heroic defenders of An Lộc, however, earned praise from their fellow fighters far away. The division-sized force defending An Lộc fought under a shower of several thousand communist artillery shells a day. However, ARVN troops knocked down a dozen enemy T-54 tanks and stood fast. It was in the battle of An Lộc that an ARVN Ranger corporal, leader of a T-54 hunting team, invented the famous antitank technique. He arranged four soldiers together—two kneeling in front of two standing. They fired four M-72 rockets at the same time. They killed two T-54s on a hunting mission. The U.S. Army Ordnance Corps developed his initiative to manufacture the XM-202 antitank rocket unit, which consisted of four M-72 tubes put together in a single trigger mechanism. I learned this story in my course at the U.S. Infantry School, 1974–75.

In other areas, communist regular units conducted separate attacks to maintain military pressure. They often launched short-range rockets, the 122 mm Katyusha, against the cities. All of the rockets hit only civilian homes but did little to disrupt the daily lives of the people even in a district town.

In the battles of Quảng Trị, the communist side gained a great advantage for the first time when the Soviet Union armed North Vietnamese combat units with antitank wire-guided AT-3 missiles and antiaircraft infrared-controlled SA-7 missiles. The sophisticated Soviet missiles frightened pilots and armored soldiers for a week or so, until they successfully used flares to jam the guiding system of the missiles.

The Americans quickly sent their wire-guided antitank TOW missiles. Officers who participated in the battle test of the TOW told me that it was accurate and powerful, but too heavy to move around by hand.

THE FEMALE WARRIORS

During the war, there had been many women of great courage serving both sides. The communist side mobilized larger efforts and resources to glorify its military service women for propaganda purposes. The South Vietnamese government and military spent a much smaller budget on this underestimated but crucial front. So many South Vietnamese heroes and heroines have been left in oblivion or given insufficient acknowledgment.

On the communist side, there was no special women's army corps. The communist military employed women in almost every support unit and in a few combat units as well. The female soldiers served and lived alongside their male fellows.

In the ARVN, Women Military Corps members served in two separate branches. The Social Assistants from sergeant to full colonel under the ARVN Department of Social Services, which belonged to the General Political Warfare Department, took care of the military dependents' welfare, health care, and education. The others were regular female soldiers at ranks from private to full colonel serving as technicians, operators in technical services and support units, clerks in offices, and nurses in hospitals. They were not assigned to combat missions.

In Quảng Trị I saw something beyond my expectation regarding the brave women serving the RVN side. So far, the communist side had many courageous combat platoon and company female leaders. Our side had many heroic examples, but the difference was that our courageous women were seldom acknowledged in news reports. One was Corporal Nguyễn Thị Nguyệt, a soldier who served in the supply section of a company of the Tenth Political Warfare Battalion. This was one of the five polwar battalions assigned to the four corps/military regions and one in general support. While the battle was going on in Đông Hà, a polwar company was supporting the front line units and its forward command post located at Camp Ái Tử, an army forward logistic base. Corporal Nguyệt stayed with her company CP in an underground bunker, taking care of food and almost all of the supplies for the operating teams. At the time, the camp was undergoing heavy enemy shelling, with about 500 to 800 rounds from 130 mm and 122 mm guns every day. But the brave five-foot woman showed no sign of fear under the earth-shaking explosions close to her bunker.

When her battalion commander said that she should come back to work in the battalion CP lest she should be in danger of ground attack, Corporal Nguyệt assured him with a smile that with her patience and skill in cooking she was doing helpful tasks that would have required two male soldiers to complete. As to the enemy shelling, she said if a man could stand it, why couldn't she? "Under enemy fire, men and women are equal," she quoted someone as saying. During the chaotic withdrawal from Quảng Trị, Corporal Nguyệt jumped onto an M113 APC and directed the driver to search the division CP for a dozen straggling military servicewomen and bring them to safety.

Another remarkably brave woman was the wife of an artillery sergeant major who was missing in action in the first battles of the 1972 communist Summer Offensive. When the ARVN forces withdrew to the new line south of Quảng Trị, his wife, Thạch Thị Định, and her many children were unable to flee their home village, La Vang, near Quảng Trị City. For more than a month living under communist control, she secretly sheltered a dozen ARVN soldiers, WIAs, and stragglers who had lost their way when their units moved south. She hid them in a small underground shelter and fed them with whatever she could procure. It was a dangerous task that could have cost her her life if the communists had discovered what she was doing.

When ARVN forces launched the counteroffensive two months later to retake part of the lost territory, the hidden soldiers were anxious to leave. But the dauntless woman decided when would be the time. She estimated how far from her village friendly troops might have reached by listening to reports from the ARVN guns—the 105 mm and 155 mm—and explosions at the target areas. Only when she heard the departing sound move closer to her village and explosions shift further up north did she venture out of her village to make contact with the advancing ARVN units and lead her soldiers to safety.

She was awarded a medal for outstanding services supporting the military. When asked how she could estimate the battle situation, she simply explained that during years of living with her husband in several artillery units, she had learned a lot of artillery techniques. "I am no heroine. Many artillery soldiers' wives could do much better than I," she said.

I told her that it was her courage that counted, and she still denied my compliment. "No sir. I just help the men because they wore the same field dress as my husband, and it's a very little help I could offer."

In twenty years of war, there were nearly 100 examples of brave wives of ARVN soldiers, the Popular Force and Regional Force in particular, who were fighting beside their husbands and were killed or wounded. A typical case involved Phạm Thị Thàng, wife of the assistant platoon leader, the Popular Force platoon defending Giồng Đình outpost, Gò Công province. One day in October 1965, a communist battalion attacked the outpost. She helped her husband to defend the two bunkers after the other two had been seized by the attackers. With artillery support requested and adjusted by Trần Thị Tâm, the wife of the seriously wounded radio operator, they caused the enemy to withdraw before dawn. Phạm Thị Thàng was killed along with her two children after hours of fighting with a M-2 carbine and throwing sixteen hand grenades at the communist soldiers, killing many of them.

In July 1971, a Montagnard woman, Ksor Amreng, wife of a Regional Force PFC, stationed in an outpost of Phú Nhơn district, Pleiku province, became a heroine when she was helping her husband operate a machine gun. She replaced him when he was wounded, holding off the enemy attackers and saving the RF company from heavy losses.

*   *   *

The most devoted groups of civilian women in the Việt Nam War must have been the Chính Huấn (political indoctrination) team members. They were called Nữ Huấn Đạo (women political instructors). I heard about them many months previously, but I had never expected that the young girls could perform their tasks so marvelously.

Once, a Chính Huấn team was working with an armored unit in its reserve position in the Hải Lăng district south of Quảng Trị City. About 300 soldiers sat in a half circle in a roadside field. The team consisted of four girls in uniforms of light blue shirts and dark gray trousers and a young man with a guitar. One of the girls was the team leader. The team was leading the troops to play games like that of Boy Scouts, interlaced with songs and short briefings. When the troops were most enthusiastic, a volley of enemy shells whizzed over their heads, followed by deafening explosions. The shells hit several places about 300 yards to the south.

A few seconds of panic passed, then it died down as the team leader's voice was heard from the megaphone in her hands. "Are Armored Corps soldiers frightened by communist artillery? Are you, or are you not?" she asked calmly. The troops yelled, "No, no! Never!" (Who would say yes in this situation?) At that she continued with a pretty smile, "Will we run for shelter, or will we stay to go on?" The troops yelled even louder, "Go on, go on!" So the activities went on while a few more rounds hit farther south before the shelling stopped. As I learned later, the team leader was the daughter of a high society family. She dropped out of college to join the Chính Huấn program.

A western reporter who witnessed the scene told me that what he saw moved him deeply. He compared the team leader to the U.S. Army band captain who braved Nazi V-1 or V-2 rocket attacks to keep on conducting a musical program in a London square during World War II. Other foreign reporters even told me later that if all the ARVN commanders could motivate their troops as well as the girl team leader was doing, the ARVN would defeat the communist forces in a few years.

I rarely praise someone as a hero or heroine, but I had to honor the Chính Huấn girls. They were mostly from middle-class families, some from high society. They were pretty high school graduates who would have had an easy life with nice rich husbands. But they left all that behind to join the group, which consisted of some forty members in ten teams under the Department of Political Indoctrination, one of the four departments under the General Political Warfare Department. Similar teams were under the political warfare blocs of the four army corps. They were paid as unskilled day laborers with wages not higher than a street sweeper's. In principle, they wouldn't be treated in military hospitals, and their relatives wouldn't be paid if they were killed in action. They received no temporary duty pay, of course.

While on field trips, a self-imposed regulation required them to always travel in pairs. Flirting during the trips was strictly prohibited. Of course, they could do so when they were off-duty and not at their office. But none of them had a bad reputation. They showed people that they were not professional singers or any kind of wanton. However, their voices and songs were excellent, especially songs arranged for quartets. Strict discipline was imposed in daily professional training when they were not on field trips—about ten to twenty days a month.

To be recruited, the girls had to pass an examination in which they were to answer questions concerning singing, musical theory, and politics; deliver a short speech after a few minutes of preparation, discuss a political or social issue; and conduct group games and tell jokes. Only about forty of the hundreds of applicants passed the exam and were enrolled in the Chính Huấn.

The girls truly represented the strong surge of patriotism of the wartime generation—hearty anticommunists and fervent patriots who were unknown to the outside world in the midst of lies and biased news reports. Their appearance with new songs promoting patriotism and high spirits in the units and on TV had some positive effect on the general audience.

There were other women in the South who did their part in the war effort. They were outnumbered by women in the North Vietnamese Communist Army and security forces, but they were no less courageous. I had few chances to meet them, but their stories are always clear in my memory.

They were the Rural Development cadres, members of RD teams. Along with male members, they were serving thousands of hamlets all around South Việt Nam, facing death every day in remote areas. They served as teachers, health care and information workers, and even specialists in agriculture.

Another very small brave group whose fame was not well known in the last years of the war was the Thiên Nga Special Group (nicknamed "the Swans"). They belonged to National Police Headquarters and served in covert operations gathering intelligence about criminal gangs and communist secret cells. They infiltrated the targeted gangs as common saleswomen in the market, curbstone dealers, peddlers, or unskilled workers. Little was known about those female detectives, as they had to hide their identities. Their thrilling activities and marvelous successes were never fully disclosed. Some of them were imprisoned after April 1975 and suffered badly in communist prisons. Some fled Việt Nam and are living in the United States, and only parts of their suspense stories were made known to the public.

THE TWENTY-SECOND INFANTRY DIVISION IS OVERRUN

While I was in Huế in 1972 during the hottest days of summer, the battle in Kontum drew my deepest concern. The Twenty-second Division and the land of Kontum were parts of my life where I devoted years of my youth to serve my country. When I returned from Huế on April 20 to report to General Trần Văn Trung, the Twenty-second Division was under waves of attacks in the Dakto area. On April 24, the division HQS at Tân Cảnh base camp, south of Dakto district, was overrun. The division commanding officer was missing, and many of the staff members were killed or captured.

On April 29, General Trung asked me to continue my work in Huế when the ARVN units withdrew in disorder from Quảng Trị. I took a flight to Huế that cloudless morning. The plane flew on an air route high over the area of the Twenty-second Division fallen CP in the Tân Cảnh base camp. With a pair of binoculars under bright sunlight, though with flickering tiny images, I could see the regimental base camp I used to frequent years ago.

I imagined a field around the tall flagpole scattered with bodies of my friends and the enlisted men who had been working with me and were still serving the division. Only a few months before Tân Cảnh fell, some of them who had served the division for ten years could still recognize me on the phone when I said: "Hello, give me number Xung Phong-xxx" (telephone code name).

UNEXPLOITED ADVANTAGES

Similar to the Tết Offensive, the 1972 Summer Offensive saw young South Vietnamese crowds gather at the gates of recruiting offices to enroll in combat units. Soldiers were killed by the hundreds every week, and the deadly communist shelling seemed to incite boys of eighteen or nineteen to volunteer for military services before being drafted. Since 1968, the war had changed its appearance.

In 1972, the communist side lost much of the South Vietnamese people's credibility they had had in the 1950s. Our propaganda, though lacking strength, did some effect, which was consolidated by realities of the conflict. Besides, our efforts to eradicate communist infrastructure produced considerable successes.

Since 1969, the Communist Party infrastructure and guerrillas in most areas had suffered heavy losses. In many villages under communist control in the summer 1972 offensive, there were no more volunteers to replace those who had been killed or captured. Local communist leaders had to do as their comrades in other areas did: appoint ethnic North Vietnamese regulars to be guerrillas, who often failed to build good relationships with villagers.

The National Police at Quảng Trị and Huế were successful in eliminating a great number of VC infrastructure and intelligence networks as well as moles in the administration and the armed forces in 1970 and 1971.

In the areas north of Mỹ Chánh River (Quảng Trị province), after our troops withdrew in April 1972, communist guerrillas and regular soldiers failed to set up the communist village and hamlet provisional government as they always did in their newly controlled territory. The Phượng Hoàng Campaign had detained almost all of those who had been collaborating secretly with them and their party members. During the three months of their occupation, the communists were unable to name village chiefs, let alone recruit guerrillas. Besides a lack of collaborators, the communists also failed to persuade the remaining people to accept jobs. The communist propaganda effect had been weakening since 1968.

The most important change in communist policy happened in 1972. Communist doctrine asserted the basic iron policy: "Wherever liberated, the Phát Động Quần Chúng (people's motivation) must be launched." Carrying out the policy in many locations in Lộc Ninh, Sa Huỳnh (Quảng Ngãi), and Gio Linh (Quảng Trị), communist political cadres conducted sessions of đấu tố (denunciation in lynch type summary trials) immediately after communist troops seized control of an area. Đấu tố, an exact copy of the 1953–56 Land Reform in North Việt Nam, frightened the population in areas adjacent to the communist-occupied territory.

But sometime at the end of 1972, the đấu tố stopped. The RVNAF Joint General Staff J-7 (Electronic and Radio Communication Warfare) sent my office a copy of a secret message from Hà Nội to Communist Party provincial committees in South Việt Nam after the agency's cryptography section monitored and deciphered it. The message ordered a complete halt to all forms of "people's motivation." It did not give an explanation. The policy had brought death to a dozen South Vietnamese in each area in 1972 before it was suspended.

Previously, communist lessons always asserted that "there will be no revolution if people's motivation is not performed." Various communist teachings also stated, "People's motivation is a *must*."

This event should be recorded as one of the turning points in the history of communism in Việt Nam. The step backwards from communist dogmas meant something very important in the ideological aspect. This event has never been treated properly in most studies of the Việt Nam War.

*   *   *

The communist 1972 offensive had been the second largest in the Việt Nam War. The communist leaders waged the offensive with all their might. They exchanged heavy losses to establish symbolic control of the two areas in Quảng Trị and Bình Long provinces. They could mobilize a large number of combat forces while leaving the ground defense of North Việt Nam to the paramilitary forces and the 250,000 soldiers of Red Chinese Army stationed there.

The ARVN units fought their enemy with a ratio of about 1:5 in strength and in losses. Most of the troops did their jobs well. There were heroes and cowards, as in any other army. Even so, foreigners knew more about some regimental commanding officers who failed to act as military commanders. One surrendered while his troops were still able to fight; another delivered a long speech over communist radio after being captured, accusing RVN leaders of war crimes. Some other officers of all ranks acted similarly.

But many other officers did not surrender so easily. My friend Colonel Vi Văn Bình, assistant commander of the Twenty-second Division, former G-3 of the same division in 1965 when I was G-5, was captured after the division was routed at Tân Cảnh, Kontum. In his radio message to his family made under the enemy's coercion and reported on VC Radio, he said only this: "I'm Colonel Vi Văn Bình, assistant to the commander of the ARVN Twenty-second Infantry Division, being held prisoner of war. I am fine without injuries and am treated well."

More than 3,000 ARVN Marine troops and officers died courageously in the battle retaking the Quảng Trị Citadel.

TWENTY-FOUR

Hope Draining

One day in December 1972, an air raid of several B-52s began bombing many targets in North Việt Nam. Unlike tactical air raids that were aimed at small targets, B-52 bombings couldn't avoid killing civilians. I had experienced bombing since I was ten years old. I knew how the civilians in North Việt Nam were feeling under the thundering and highly destructive firepower raining down on them.

At the same time, the blockade of major North Việt Nam seaports that started on May 11, 1972, was having an extremely powerful impact, denying most of the crucial imports that were necessary to continue the war. Hà Nội had to rely on a fleet of nineteen merchant ships from China to provide limited supplies to the panhandle area, north of the 17th parallel. The Chinese ships were anchored away from the American mine cordon along the coast. Military supplies and food for the NVA and for the area population, packed in large watertight plastic bags, were dropped on the sea. They were driven ashore by floodtide and wind, although a large number of bags drifted away with the southward current. Hundreds of fishermen in the area south of the 17th parallel made money by hunting for floating supply bags—mostly rice, combat rations, military small equipment, and medicine. Every day, an intelligence report compiled by the ARVN/JGS/J-2 sent to my office estimated the amount of rice and equipment released on the sea by each of the nineteen Chinese Hồng Kỳ (Red Flag) cargo ships. However, the Hồng Kỳ fleet could not provide all of the food and other supplies required.

According to military and media sources, the earthshaking raids in 1972 around Christmas, combined with the sea blockade, had unendurable effects that forced Hà Nội leaders to compromise with the Americans and sign a cease-fire agreement. If the blockade had been conducted much earlier on a more powerful scale, our side would have prevailed in the war, I believe. Seaport blockades were much more effective than bombing in breaking the NVA's logistical backbone.

The U.S. high command did not have recourse to seaport blockades earlier, probably because of Washington's self-restrained policy to avoid possible direct confrontation with the communist powers. More likely, they considered such measures only as a last resort.

In October 1972, Hà Nội and Washington intended to sign a peace agreement, but they failed to do so on the last day because of strong objections from Sài Gòn. A part of it was released to the press. It greatly disappointed our troops. Washington meant to give up too much to the communists in Hà Nội, while South Việt Nam would win almost nothing.

READY FOR A NEW PHASE

Most South Vietnamese anticipated that the cease-fire would be signed sooner or later and that there might then be a general election. We needed to do something before it was too late. The Prime Minister's Pacification Office and the General Political Warfare Department joined in a civic action campaign to approach the peasants all over the country in order to prepare the ground for a "postwar political struggle" in the immediate future.

The armed forces branches and services as well as the JGS general departments were providing their best effort to support the campaign. I was a member of the campaign's Board of Planning and Operation. All cadets of the four training institutions—the Việt Nam National Military Academy, the Political Warfare University, the Reserve Officer School, and the Officer Candidates School—were to join the operation. The total strength amounted to more than 2,000 cadets. The cadets were to live with peasant families for weeks to learn about their actual aspirations and to keep them informed of the general situation. The last thing the cadets had to do was to win the peasants' hearts and minds by explaining the RVN policies, national objectives, and achievements.

Contrary to the suspicion at its beginning, the campaign was a success. The cadets with young elegant faces, polite manners, and the appearance of intellectuals won the people's confidence. Most people in the countryside adored the young cadets and showed true sympathy to the government side. Peasants in communist-influenced areas felt easy and safe when speaking to the cadets without fear that the cadets were actually communist secret agents. The peasants frankly complained about corruption and bribery in local governments to the cadets because they knew the information would not be leaked to invite retaliation from corrupt authorities.

Cadet units reported the attitude of many peasant families whose sons and daughters were fighting in the communist ranks, including those who had fallen. Many of the families contributed accurate intelligence information and constructive suggestions for the local administrations. The campaign provided facts that assured me about a possible victory if general elections were to be held with effective international supervision and control.

In an orientation session for the Thủ Đức ROS cadets before the operation was launched, I was one of the five field grade officers who shared with them our experiences and general knowledge related to the campaign. One cadet raised a question about how to explain to the peasants the fact that the RVN negotiators at the Paris talks had taken a secondary role to the Americans, while the North Vietnamese had a negotiating position equal to the Americans.

Answers that merely repeated official statements did not satisfy the young cadets. But an explanation using simple and realistic arguments did. According to the explanation, the negotiation proceeded as in a play. On the allied side, the director (American) did not trust his partner (South Việt Nam), so he appeared himself on the stage as the leading actor. On the other side, the directors (Soviet Union and China) put absolute confidence in their partner (North Việt Nam), and so they let him (NVN) appear as the leading actor while they stayed behind the scenes to pull the strings. The fact supporting the argument was that NVN chief negotiator Lê Đức Thọ visited Beijing and then Moscow for directives on each of his eleven trips from Hà Nội to Paris. So the question was: between Hà Nội and Sài Gòn, who was the foreigners' more faithful puppet?

The nearly 1,000 Thủ Đức cadets yelled their approval. Later in the campaign, the argument proved successful in many targeted villages.

In the lower Mekong Delta provinces, a cadet battalion of the Thủ Đức Reserve Officers School ran an investigation into corruption practices by interviewing villagers. The information was evaluated and compiled into a general report in which the cadets submitted a people's proposal for the prosecution of four district chiefs and special rewards to the other five. The government approved their proposals, but the punishment was just an administrative reprimand, and the reward was a little pat on the back. The success of the campaign, however, contributed greatly to the people's morale, though not enough against the adversarial political atmosphere that besieged the RVN.

FIGHTING CORRUPTION

I am sure that corruption exists more or less in every country all the time. But in South Việt Nam, it played a critical role in ruining the war effort.

Under the precolonial Vietnamese Kingdom, corruption was common at district and village levels, but none was committed on a national scale. It continued in the colonial era under the French as a privilege awarded to local authorities. From 1945 to 1954, it was not a big problem in the Việt Minh–controlled regions because there was almost nothing worthwhile in the government assets that the officials could claim for their own. After 1954 in North Việt Nam, corruption was spreading wider, but the bribes were not very large because most people were living in extreme poverty.

In the South under President Ngô Đình Diệm, corruption was a legacy of the colonial era. However, he could check its expansion to a certain degree, owing to his personality and his prestige. His successor did not have the same power. I felt certain that he was incorruptible, based on what I had heard from my friends who were very close to him. There were rumors about his relatives' shady businesses. But I think that if the rumors were true, all of their alleged ill-earned assets put together probably would not have amounted to more than a few million dollars, which is extremely small compared with a corrupt Communist Party provincial leader's fortune nowadays.

As the war escalated after 1965, corruption spread. South Vietnamese patriots desperately called for an effective measure to eradicate the most dangerous social evil that was threatening the stability of the republic. The critical situation after 1969 heightened the threat.

When the respectable statesman Trần Văn Hương became vice president in late 1971, many people hoped that he would somehow be successful in fighting corruption. He was then appointed chairman of the Anticorruption Committee. He and his committee members, including General Nguyễn Văn Hiếu, were doing their best to solve the problem. But after months of endeavor, Hiếu admitted failure. The cancerous corruption had already metastasized.

Government and military leaders after Diệm's era accepted the idea that, as necessitated by war effort, government officials and military officers in charge of crucial positions—performing difficult tasks, enduring dangers, and suffering hardships—should be indulged if they made some ill-earned money. Ogden Williams once told me that the American side sanctioned the concept.

The policy of "limited connivance" actually helped mitigate some national finance problems that did not permit decent salaries for public servicemen and soldiers. However, no one was content with what he had already stolen and always tended to acquire more money through corruption. The practice soon became uncontrollable. When corruption expanded, it involved more key persons in the government and the armed forces. Actions against one violator would cause repercussions for many of his conspirators, some of whom held powerful positions.

In the South, although corruption was a crime, it had its own rules of conduct. Those who engaged in corruption made illegal money from almost every government fund, material, service, and expenditure, but most of them avoided taking money away from basic aid to war victims and the poor, health care, and emergency relief.

My job as director of the Directorate for Reception gave me opportunities to take bribes and other illegal profits; the largest of them was the construction fund of the Chiêu Hồi centers. Everyone likes money, and I was no exception. However,

I didn't put a finger in the pie, because I would have had to do many things contrary to my nature and to associate with persons I didn't trust or respect. Besides, I didn't have a reliable connection for my safety. My bosses would support the way I did my job but would not provide me such protection. Everyone in the corruption business must have at least one competent protector to lean on.

I could keep my hand out of shady affairs thanks to my wife, who never talked me into corruption. Like my mother, she always reminded me to stay away from anything dishonest that might be harmful to my military career.

Ironically, because I didn't join them, the corruption gang that had approached me for collaboration then threatened me by sending letters to the Inspectorate charging me with a dozen misdeeds. All were fabricated to accuse me of authoritarianism, applying military discipline to defectors, and using government cars and telephones for personal purposes (my legal privileges as a director)—but not a single one accused me of accepting bribes. After a formal investigation, I was cleared. Minister Nguyễn Ngọc An supported my innocence.

Corruption in South Việt Nam during the war was so common that the public took it for granted that everyone whose work related to money was corrupt. Actually, only a few who had some competence in public expenses or power to decide on people's legal interests or to award them certain rights would engage in embezzlement or accept bribes.

In the South under Ngô Đình Diệm, no policeman dared accept bribes for not citing drivers for traffic violations. In the early 1970s under Nguyễn Văn Thiệu, such a practice was widespread, and I often saw it overtly done on Sài Gòn streets. However, even in the last years of the war when everything was at its worst, corruption in the South was still contained due to relatively effective financial regulations and procedures and the strong voice of the press corps. Moreover, pre-1975 Sài Gòn cops didn't get bribes from the poor, such as cyclo drivers and peddlers.[1]

After April 1975 under the communist regime, corruption became much worse.

THE CÔN SƠN "TIGER CAGES"

Côn Sơn Island had the largest prison in South Việt Nam. This prison was famous during the colonial era and the wars. High-risk felons and political prisoners served their sentences on Côn Sơn Island, also known as Poulo Condore.

A great many revolutionaries—communist and nationalist—who were struggling for Việt Nam's independence under the French colonialist regime spent some time there after sentencing by the French courts. French authorities ran the prison with an iron fist. Torture and execution were used to maintain discipline. The prison was notorious for its horrible methods of punishment.

Once the Ngô Đình Diệm government was in power, the Côn Sơn prison changed significantly. There was no more barbaric torture, and "gang colonies" no longer ruled the wards. But in the early 1970s, the western media began investigating rumors of mistreatment. Reports on the treatment of political prisoners drew great concern from human rights activists and humanitarian institutions. The RVN government was harshly criticized.

The reports described with many sensational details the "tiger cage" as an inhuman tool being used to punish stubborn prisoners. Two friends who visited the prison on many working trips gave me descriptions that I had no reason to doubt. My mother, who had worked there a few times, confirmed their observations.

They asserted that the tiger's cage was nothing more than a concrete compartment of about five by eight feet wide and nine feet high, down from the floor level, with the top covered by a metal grill. A 200-watt electric bulb burned day and night. A plastic box was used for a toilet. One or several prisoners held in the compartment were allowed to go out once a day to wash and empty his toilet container. The punishments might include denying the caged prisoners water. With very little water, they suffered terrible thirst. Some had to drink their own urine. The tiger's cage was used to punish very stubborn prisoners who acted against jail regulations and had committed acts dangerous to others. Naturally, this kind of imprisonment under the strong light and in such a narrow space was in no way humanitarian. But in every aspect, it was no more savage than in many countries, including the ways the U.S. military treated Iraqi rebels in the early 2000s.

In South Việt Nam, communist insurgent prisoners might be subjected to torture when the special police detained them. The interrogators might rely on torture to wring out confessions. After the men had been sentenced and transferred to the prison, there was no more interrogation by the police, except for special cases.[2]

When foreign reporters and human rights investigators paid surprise visits to Côn Sơn Island, the South Vietnamese authorities allowed them to see every nook of the prison and talk to prisoners without limitation despite the possibility of some prisoners telling fabricated stories about ill treatment by the jailers.

By 1973, South Việt Nam had six POW camps with about 60,000 captured soldiers of NVA and VC local units. There were nearly 100,000 civilian prisoners—criminals, communist activists, rebels, and terrorists—not covered by the Geneva Convention, held at four national and forty-two provincial prisons. The largest of these were the Central Reeducation Center at Chí Hòa, Sài Gòn, and the Reeducation Center at Côn Sơn Island.

THE PARIS AGREEMENT

In the wake of the extensive B-52 bombing campaign, Hà Nội leaders at the Paris Peace Conference finally accepted a peace plan. On January 26, 1973, President

Thiệu called a closed-door meeting with all generals in key posts from the Joint General Staff, corps and division commanders, some ministers, and all province chiefs. Five field grade officers in charge of research, study, and planning from JGS/J-2, JGS/J-3, JGS/J-5, and the General Political Warfare Department, including me, also attended.

President Thiệu stepped into the conference room with the attitude of a man whose heavy burden had just been lifted. In a friendly tone, he told us that the peace agreement would be signed in Paris the next day. He sincerely recounted to us what he had been undergoing: not the nagging North Vietnamese demands and requests, but the highhanded pressure from Washington. He honestly admitted that as far as the White House was concerned, he could act only as a second lieutenant to his regiment commander. As the lieutenant, he had to advance to attack the assigned objectives without arguing. He had no power to argue except for suggesting that some changes of approaching routes be allowed so that his troops could avoid a dangerous area, such as a hazardous water body, before reaching their objectives.

He showed us a short letter from the American president, in which Nixon promised appropriate responses to any breach of the peace agreement by Hà Nội. His words were the last hope we had from Washington, D.C.

Thiệu gave oral orders to the generals and province chiefs to launch decisive full swing operations within hours to occupy and defend strategic sites such as Cửa Việt, the firth of a river in Quảng Trị province, or a portion of the Sài Gòn–Đà Lạt Highway where the enemy often ambushed or conducted sniper fire, before the agreement took effect the next morning.

I felt exceptionally disappointed with the agreement.

First, as anyone should have expected, Washington, Sài Gòn, and Hà Nội were to have officially announced the agreement at the same time, as had been previously scheduled. But in the last hours, President Thiệu was asked to make his announcement "fifteen minutes later than Nixon." That request from Washington greatly hurt our feelings. I thought some American politicians enjoyed humiliating Thiệu and the RVN, but that attitude toward their closest ally, however bad it might be, gained nothing worth mentioning for the American people. It only earned Washington distrust from other allies. I must call it a very stupid course of action.

Second, the text of the agreement was written with Vietnamese terminology, imported from Chinese communists, that was only used in North Việt Nam. Anyone reading it would have the same notion of how Sài Gòn was treated so badly by its closest ally when the Vietnamese copy of the agreement apparently had been drafted or translated by Hà Nội without Sài Gòn's knowledge. The Americans should have known that, during the war, the communists had made use of every single word for their propaganda purposes. This was another fatal blow to the South that U.S. officials may have been too ignorant to understand.

The most controversial clauses in the agreement concerned the presence of NVA units in South Việt Nam. Everyone in Việt Nam and all U.S. combat soldiers had no doubt about that. It was beyond question that the NVA must go back to the North. But Washington conceded to Hà Nội on the issue; there was not one word in the agreement directed at the NVA withdrawal. I couldn't imagine how the United States, the supreme power in the world, would agree to a loss of face like that.

Right after the secret meeting at the palace, I got a draft copy of the agreement from the Foreign Ministry. By order of my commanding general, the Psywar Department Printing Office had the printing machines set up, ready to produce several thousand copies of the agreement to distribute to every ARVN unit and agency, especially the front line combat companies and outposts. The printing shop expected to complete its printing a few hours after the agreement had been signed in Paris. Two C-130s in Sài Gòn and scores of helicopters and small planes at the four military regions' headquarters were standing by to deliver the agreement copies to the lowest level units within four hours.

All our effort was nullified when the Information Ministry claimed its right to print the document. Its copies only ran out of the contractor's printing machines about five days later. My office had to ask the American embassy to provide hundreds of the limited copies it produced to send to headquarters down to regiments and provinces, three days later than we had planned.

Meanwhile, only a day after the pact was signed, our Popular Force in villages and troops at outposts or at defense positions were faced with the enemy's tricks of harassment. The communists showed their version of the agreement requesting our troops to respect their rights of movement and passage across our areas as well as other clauses they made up but that did not exist in the agreement. Our troops didn't have copies of the document to verify the clauses until the third day.

POW EXCHANGE

Implementing one of the clauses of the Paris Agreement, POWs were exchanged. The South Việt Nam government released to the communist side not only all of the more than 60,000 communist POWs but also all communists who had been arrested as fifth columnists, criminals, or terrorists but not soldiers.

However, there were hundreds of RVN soldiers captured by the communist forces who were not released. The communist delegation bluntly refuted our request for investigation and for full implementation of the POW clauses in the agreement.

In February 1973, the Joint Four-Party Commission was activated, mainly to discuss issues of POWs and MIAs. My office compiled a long list of our Biệt

Kích (special commando) soldiers who had infiltrated the North for special operations. Their cases were authenticated by reports published in many issues of Hà Nội's *Nhân Dân Daily* since 1960. We suggested that the RVN delegation put the issue on the commission's agenda and demand that North Việt Nam release all those brave warriors.

The communist representatives on the commission couldn't deny the *Nhân Dân* reports, but they claimed that the soldiers had been doing espionage work. Meanwhile they insisted that our side release all their men arrested while conducting terrorist attacks and fighting the unconventional war. Finally, the U.S. delegation refused to act. We guessed that the Americans disagreed with our proposal because they were too worried about the fate of their prisoners in Hà Nội to do something that might displease the communist leaders.[3]

As we had expected, the communists in Hà Nội disappointed the U.S. government. They didn't provide full information concerning American POWs and MIAs as requested. The issue has been lingering since, and we have reason to believe that Hà Nội is still holding back secret files concerning the fate of hundreds of American MIAs.

Along with the American pilots released in Hà Nội after the Paris Agreement, there was one South Vietnamese Air Force officer. The American team refused to receive him, saying that he did not serve in the U.S. Air Force and that he was a South Vietnamese citizen. He was Aspirant (below Second Lieutenant) Ngô Trọng Đạt. The South Vietnamese delegation attending the releasing ceremony in Hà Nội was not expecting the event and welcomed Đạt after awaiting a decision from Sài Gòn for an hour. Đạt came back to Sài Gòn and had to report to the South Vietnamese Air Force personnel office every day waiting for a decision regarding his status. He got no word from the national and armed forces top leaders until the U.S. ambassador forwarded a formal letter from the Association of the Former American Hà Nội Hilton Prisoners of War, inviting Đạt to their reunion.

In a mission over North Việt Nam, Đạt was brought down by North Vietnamese antiaircraft fire. He was locked up in Hà Nội's Hỏa Lò Prison along with the Americans. The Hỏa Lò jailers had Đạt help with some trivial tasks such as typing the prisoners' lists and sometimes acting as an interpreter. He was secretly providing the American prisoners with good information he had collected while working at the jail office. He helped the Americans exchange verbal messages and even set up a secret code of communication by knocking on the walls between some Americans. The letter reached President Thiệu's desk a week before the scheduled reunion. The letter with Thiệu's endorsement prompted a rush in the related services and offices. The air force quickly worked for Đạt's promotion to captain. The Ministry of Foreign Affairs immediately issued his passport. The army uniform factory completed his dress uniform within three hours—only twenty-four hours before his departure.

I was to brief Đạt about the political and military situation in Việt Nam, the RVN national policies, and how to deal with the America media. As he was extremely pressed for time—he had just twenty-four hours to do a lot of paperwork and money exchange—I talked to him briefly and handed him a bunch of related materials, including the latest military and economic reports. Đạt was enthusiastically welcomed to the reunion, and he traveled around the States. After he returned to Việt Nam, the ex-POWs at the Hà Nội Hilton sent him a nice sedan in gratitude for his assistance during their time of extreme hardship.

In April 1975, when Sài Gòn was in its last days, the American POWs association helped evacuate Đạt and his greater family out of Việt Nam. He has lived in northern California ever since.

THE WAR ONLY PAUSES

According to the agreement, both sides had to respect each other's territories. The National Liberation Front's mask, known as the Provisionary Revolutionary Government of the South Việt Nam Republic, controlled only the northern part of Quảng Trị province, the jungle area north of Kontum, Lộc Ninh district, and small parts in some Mekong Delta provinces.

The common Vietnamese were happy to see the war ending with no more clashes and no more people killed. But only a short time after the cease-fire was announced, sporadic skirmishes were reported daily. Intelligence information confirmed that NVA logistics support routes were exceptionally busy with convoys transporting men and weapons into South Việt Nam. Very few Vietnamese believed either side would respect the peace agreement.

The International Committee for Control and Supervision with four teams from Canada, Indonesia, Hungary, and Poland was formed to replace the former committee activated by the 1954 Geneva Accords, which consisted of three teams from India, Canada, and Poland. The new ICCS was actually powerless and could do nothing better.

On a Sunday afternoon, my ten-year-old son had a small get-together with his classmates at my home. I overheard my son say: "They are saying that the war did not actually stop. In that case, in ten more years we will be drafted in 1983 if we fail to enroll in the university." The kids were preparing their minds rather early for the war from which they saw no exit. One of my son's friends stood up, saying that if he served in the military, he wouldn't accept a desk job but would elect to fight in an infantry unit as a man and a patriot should. All the boys yelled approval.

I asked myself, would the bloody conflict ever cease to throw the youngsters into the inferno of war?

As most South Vietnamese expected, the war continued on right after the Paris Agreement was signed. However, in 1973, there were not many major battles.

The two sides used the time to reorganize their forces and to prepare their ground and war resources. Several small-scale clashes were reported almost every day.

According to classified information my office received from JGS/J-2 and J-7, communist forces overtly built fuel pipelines along the Long Mountain Trails and consolidated the existing truck routes without fear of U.S. air raids. Movement on the trails was much busier than before the agreement. RVN air forces were unable to go beyond the 17th parallel to attack the convoys. Dwindling U.S. aid caused logistical problems, especially a shortage of ammunition and spare parts.

It was under these circumstances that Henry Kissinger and Lê Đức Thọ, the two chief negotiators, were awarded the Nobel Peace Prize. Most educated Vietnamese knew the two reached the Paris Peace Agreement not really expecting to arrange a cease-fire and to end hostilities in Việt Nam. Many people said, "If only the members of the board of Nobel prizes would come and live in Việt Nam countryside for three months."

SOUTH VIỆT NAM SOCIETY IN 1973

The Paris Agreement led South Việt Nam to a half-war/half-peace situation. The communist forces had seized two districts (Đông Hà and Lộc Ninh) and several patches of the jungle since the 1972 Summer Offensive. But the South Vietnamese government controlled most of the remaining territory. Guerrilla activity shrank, and territorial security was enhanced. Land and water communications were improved, thus elevating economic and trading development to a degree. Interprovincial bus transportation could be available at night on most highways.

However, security was only superficial in many areas where communist insurgents temporarily withdrew to their hideouts. Some even managed to live as legal residents in government-controlled villages to work as underground agents.

Many fence-sitters foresaw communist victory, and the possibility of the communists' complete control over South Việt Nam scared them away from the nationalist side. Popular support for Sài Gòn dwindled quickly. Many people who had sided with the government now began supporting the communists.

There were more and more protests by leftist activists and university students criticizing military operations and corruption and demanding more social assistance and health care. The government firmly cracked down on violent demonstrations and publications that blatantly supported the communists. But to the last days of the republic, the media were free to denounce government officials and ARVN officers who committed violations and moral corruption. Some books and musical works with antiwar themes were banned for form's sake, but they could be found and bought without trouble in bookstores or sidewalk stalls.

Smuggling was booming along with corruption. Everybody seemed to rush for any kind of business legally or not before the good chances would possibly end in the unpredictable future. Social evils were thriving. Prostitution, once booming thanks to the presence of GIs, subsided a great deal in 1973. Prostitutes laid off by nightclubs, bars, and restaurants became streetwalkers. Teenage drug addicts filled rehabilitation centers. Economic troubles greatly affected military families and government civil servants. We could notice their unpleasant plight by observing their partly empty refrigerators or pantries, mine included.

Cultural life progressed, though at a slower pace. The public could still find inexpensive novels, poetry, and music while the publication industry was focusing on making quick money.

Daily skirmishes created instability that scared away prospective foreign investors. I participated in several meetings with their representatives to prepare for cooperation in some joint ventures and projects. But such plans failed because security conditions did not look promising in the coming years.

Like many of my friends in 1973, my hope that the RVN would be able to stand on its own feet was flickering a little. But we still clung to the idea that Washington would continue to aid Sài Gòn at the 1973 rate for three to five years and that the RVN would certainly survive the war.

THE ALLIED TROOPS PULL OUT

After the 1973 Paris Agreement, all allied military forces quit Việt Nam. The half million U.S. soldiers had left deep marks on the South Vietnamese society, both good and bad. Their illegitimate children with Vietnamese women made up a special large group of the population that had to immigrate to the United States on a scale that had never happened in previous wars.

In the memory of my generation, the rank-and-file U.S. soldiers appeared as innocent young men, noisy with four-letter words but not prone to criminal acts. In combat, they were effective, abiding by military discipline, though they were not all class A warriors.

Most GIs behaved well toward the Vietnamese, contrary to communist propaganda that likened them to the French soldiers in the 1946–54 war.

Personally, I heard of cases of promiscuous killing by GIs. I asked a dozen ARVN officers and NCOs who served as liaisons officers and interpreters in U.S. combat units if there were rapes committed by U.S. soldiers. None of them had known a single case in their years of serving with the GIs.

All U.S. advisors I knew in units and agencies I served behaved well to their Vietnamese counterparts. There were some whose unfriendly attitude may have earned antipathy from the Vietnamese. I also have heard of advisors who went beyond a reasonable limit to impose their will on the Vietnamese counterparts. But during my years of ARVN service, I never met any U.S. advisor of that type.

South Korean combat units were formidable fighters especially in close combat. Vietnamese civilians living in the ROK forces areas of responsibility were fearful of the Koreans. A single violation of their rules of movement at night, without light, for instance, would bring a sure death. Besides, peasants were not bothered or harassed unreasonably. People living outside the Koreans' responsible areas might have disliked them much more. The 1966 massacre of an entire hamlet in Central Việt Nam earned the Korean soldiers a bad reputation.

Rumors about the Korean troops' atrocities seemed bigger than what actually took place. We heard rumors of rapes, but most were unconfirmed. Actually, the Korean Forces Command brought several of its soldiers to its court-martial for war crimes and condemned some to death. My assistant representing the Chiêu Hồi Ministry attended one of the Korean courts-martial of a soldier who had raped and killed a nineteen-year-old girl at Ninh Hòa (near Nha Trang). He was executed by a firing squad on the spot where the victim was killed. The case was reported in a few lines in newspapers and on radios that reached fewer people.

Credible rumors ran that Korean troops were stealing guns of any model from any source, mostly from the Americans, and handing them over to the Korean ships anchored at South Việt Nam ports for some money. A cheap World War I pistol, an M1 Garand rifle, or a modern M-16 rifle would sell for a good price to ship managers who would resell them to the government in Korea. People even said that some Korean officers advised their Vietnamese counterparts to do the same to build a reserve of material for the country's industry, but we didn't have strong and willing leaders like the ROK big wheels to perform similar deeds.

The Australians received the highest sympathy from Vietnamese people, civilian and military. They had the most discipline in using firepower, were skillful in antiguerrilla operations, and inflicted casualties on the enemy with the highest loss ratio. In eight years of fighting, nearly 500 Australian soldiers fell on the soil of South Việt Nam in exchange for about 10,000 communists killed by the Australian forces, a reliable figure.

The 1966 battle at Long Tân in Phước Tuy province east of Sài Gòn showed the Australian soldiers' capability in combat. The Australians suffered 18 casualties, whereas the communist battalion left 254 bodies. The Long Tân battle proved that there was at least one way to fight the war of insurgency successfully with conventional forces.

Dozens of defectors who had served in communist units in the region and defected a year after the Long Tân battle confirmed with me that after suffering the heavy losses, the communist regional military command sent a directive to its units, instructing them that no unit was allowed to attack, especially to ambush the Australian soldiers, without specific orders from the communist top regional commander.

The Australians were doing nothing that invited aversion from the Vietnamese population. They employed very few Vietnamese workers in their barracks, but they succeeded in several civic action projects.

The Thai soldiers did not have any special reputation, although they came in two divisions, nor did the 2,000 Filipinos and the 500 New Zealanders.

HUMAN LOSSES ON BOTH SIDES BY JANUARY 1973

During the war, people on our side often claimed that the communist losses reported by the ARVN and the U.S. forces were exaggerated. In public relation matters, the Americans were making serious mistakes. In its press releases, MACV in Sài Gòn stressed body counts and achievements with rhetoric that had long become tasteless to the already skeptical U.S. public. The RVN had made similar mistakes. Only twenty years after the war ended was the truth revealed, but it did not reach the general public. The truth was communist KIAs in the war reported by U.S. military (more than 900,000) was lower than the figure released in 1995 by the Hà Nội office of veterans' affairs (1,100,000 KIAs and 300,000 MIAs).

In February 1973, my Research and Planning Section compiled general statistics concerning human loss on both sides based on classified statistics of ARVN/JGS J-2 and J-3. The figures were no different from other allies' sources.

I was certain that the figure of U.S. casualties was relatively accurate, and so was that of the allied forces (South Koreans, Australians, Thai, and New Zealanders). The ARVN loss differed in sources, but I believed 260,000 deaths were close to reality. In 1970 when I worked in the Interministerial Committee for Disabled Veterans Affairs, I found out in the Ministry of Veterans Affairs records that there had been more than 80,000 dead soldiers who had wives and about 140,000 KIAs who were single.

Civilian victims of communist terrorist assassinations amounted to more than 50,000 and may be up to 100,000. These were unarmed local government officials, common people accused by communists as being "reactionaries" or government informers and their family members. There were no credible figures of victims of unintended bombing, shelling, and other firearms on both sides. I thought a half million in the South was a reasonable figure.

ARVN/JGS estimated that by 1973, about 1,300,000 communist soldiers had been killed, while the MACV showed a figure of more than 900,000 communist KIAs. Western media didn't accept those numbers, accusing MACV of lying in the so-called body count.

Press agencies AFP on March 3 and AP on March 4, 1995, quoted a report released by Hà Nội's Ministry of Labor, War Invalids, and Social Affairs in which it confirmed that 1.1 million NVA soldiers were killed in the 1955–75 war in the South. Hà Nội's figures did not include the NVA 300,000 MIAs it had claimed since the early 1990s.

The Hà Nội ministry also reported that 4 million civilians (2 million in the North and 2 million in the South) were killed. This figure appeared to be widely exaggerated. American bombing over North Việt Nam did not cause great losses of life.

The Hà Nội's claim of its 300,000 MIAs is questionable. All of the ground battles since the commencement of hostilities to 1975 were in South Việt Nam. Most—if not all—of the bodies of fallen communist soldiers were left on the battlefields in the South. A very small number of them were buried hastily by their fighting fellows when they had time and it was safe to do so. Other communist KIAs were buried by allied troops. Technically, more than 90 percent of the 1.1 million communist dead claimed by Hà Nội should be classified as "missing in action" instead.

Before departing for the South, NVA soldiers had to discard every ID card or any piece of paper carrying their names, birth dates, and origins. Most of the dead NVA troops had no personal identification. The retrieval of their identified remains, therefore, was mostly impossible.[4]

Total losses during the war of the South Vietnamese armed forces compiled from reports by Hà Nội's *Nhân Dân Daily,* the official newspaper of the Communist Party (from 1958 to January 1973), amounted to more than 3 million, about twelve times our actual losses.

That was how Hà Nội media covered war news. For example, in a report published on communist-controlled newspapers, Hà Nội said its forces eliminated 15,000 South Vietnamese troops in the three-month campaign of 1972 in U Minh area, the southernmost tip of Việt Nam. Our troops—all of the uniformed and armed personnel in the area—totaled fewer than 15,000.

However, all during the war, the *Nhân Dân* had never reported any communist losses: not a single troop killed or wounded.

After the war, the communist authorities in Hà Nội could not lie to their people anymore. They admitted that besides losses in battles, a great many NVA war deaths had resulted from exhaustion and the lack of protection against hostile climatic conditions along the routes of infiltration into the South. Nowadays, on the sides of several major rivers across the infiltration routes, there are many cemeteries with thousands of unmarked graves of NVA soldiers who were too weak to cross the streams.

When a soldier was too weak to go on, his fellows would collect his weapon and leave him at the riverside with a canteen full of water and a pouch of rice. Those who recovered later had to join the other units on the infiltration route. The weaker soldiers died without medical care and would be buried by fellows of the next coming unit if their remains still existed.

COMMUNIST ACTUAL STRENGTH

Another matter that has long been misreported was the communist strength fighting in the war as compared with the ARVN.

In 1968, the United States had more than 550,000 soldiers and the ARVN had more than 437,000 soldiers in the regular army and 393,000 soldiers in the Regional Forces and Popular Force. In 1972, regular forces increased to 516,000 soldiers, and 532,000 regional and popular forces; ARVN totaled 1,040,000 soldiers. The RVN police force had 147,000 members.

According to American sources, the communist side reportedly had about 100,000 local forces and about 300,000 North Việt Nam regulars. Numerically, we had a ratio of 3:1 or 4:1. But that figure did not reflect the realities of the war.

The larger part of ARVN regular soldiers, the main force facing the NVA, were doing supporting tasks. Only about 40 percent of the 516,000 regulars were real combat troops. The Sài Gòn government did not conscript its citizens to serve in labor forces for military logistic support.

By contrast, Hà Nội employed a very large number of civilians as laborers on a compulsory or voluntary basis. In North Việt Nam, the largest force of dân công, people's laborers, or conscripted laborers (Hà Nội's translation) contributed the greatest labor strength serving the war. In fact, they were "war laborers," the term I use in these memoirs. The number of laborers was incredible. According to reliable sources, the figure may have been more than 1 million. Besides conscripted laborers, Hà Nội recruited more than 143,000 members of the Thanh Niên Xung Phong (Youth Volunteers) to support frontline soldiers.

To conscript peasants for war laborers, communist authorities at the district level decided a quota of men and women that each agricultural cooperative had to provide. The term and area to serve of each laborer was up to his or her family burden and decided by the cooperative board of managers. Most laborers were women. Most were serving in their provinces. Only a few were sent to serve in the faraway fields, on the Long Mountain Trails, and in South Việt Nam.

The laborers' tasks depended on the demand of the areas. They might be building roads or dykes for flood protection and irrigating canals or building military fortifications and carrying supplies to the battle areas. On rough terrain, they carried supplies with bamboo poles. On level trails and paths, they secured loads onto bicycles to push along. In North Việt Nam, groups of war laborers were attached to Chinese and NVA combat engineer units at each major bridge to repair it or prepare a bypass after bombings. At each sizable bridge, there might be hundreds of war laborers standing by.

The dân công were fed but received no wages.

Rearline war laborers serving each division in a combat area may have reached 1,000. They made up a long line of resupply from ammunition and food dumps behind the operational area for the division troops.

The Young Volunteers Brigade consisted of many companies with about 100 young men and women each. The Young Volunteers were serving one to three years and were exempted from the draft. They were not armed but working under military discipline.[5] Youth volunteers were deployed to serve in rear areas to transport military supplies to the front line and to construct combat defense fortifications and temporary camps. Other companies stayed in readiness in base camps in North Việt Nam to provide emergency support. Along with the war laborers, youth volunteers also had to provide manual labor to repair bridges, roads, public buildings, military barracks, and antiaircraft positions damaged by bombs. When the situation required, youth volunteers had to serve on the front lines, and a number of youth volunteers could be enlisted on the spot and armed to fight as soldiers. Therefore, they were called unarmed or rankless troops.

Like the war laborers, they received no salary but were provided with generous rations of food items such as rice, salt, and sugar beside cigarettes, soap, clothes, and footwear. There were no official statistics, but it was estimated, and recently confirmed by Hà Nội reports, that tens of thousands of war laborers and youth volunteers were killed in the war. The hundreds of thousands of youth volunteers and war laborers supporting NVA forces should have been included in the total combat strength of the communist forces in South Việt Nam.

The North Việt Nam large force of war laborers and youth volunteers extended to the front lines enabled the NVA divisions to engage their enemy with full-strength combat troops. Eventually, the ratio of direct combat manpower of the NVA to the ARVN was no less than 3:1 and, in some major battles, 5:1.

Besides, territorial forces in North Việt Nam consisted of large paramilitary regional units under the provincial and district governments, village militias, and the Armed Public Security Force (Field Police), which included Coast Guards and Border Guards. The total strength of these forces was estimated at more than 1 million.

In addition, a reportedly large number of Red Chinese troops (some 250,000 in sixteen infantry divisions and scores of engineer battalions), Soviet antiaircraft missile battalions and pilots (over 2,000), and North Korean combat pilots (200) were deployed to reinforce North Việt Nam's defense.

With such large paramilitary and foreign forces taking care of the North, Hà Nội leaders could send their largest number of combat soldiers to South Việt Nam. This may have been much larger than the 300,000 as being estimated in Sài Gòn and Washington.

GPWD ASSESSMENT

Right after the Paris Agreement, branches and services of the RVN armed forces made various evaluations of their war efforts. The General Political Warfare Department held some small conferences for the assessment of twenty years of war and for drafting general plans to deal with future situations. My Study-Research-Planning section was organizing the conferences and keeping records of the discussions. Participants were officers seasoned by years in service at company level and higher coming from various related corps, branches, and services. Psychological activities were the most important topics.

Established in 1965, when Sài Gòn and Washington began to lend greater support to the RVN, the GPWD assumed the role of "leading the psychological warfare." That was supposedly a great task, as important as the military side of the conflict. But the GPWD failed to achieve its principal goals. The national and ARVN leadership did not assign adequate power and responsibility to the department.

People in the army easily noticed that many of the ARVN generals didn't like the idea of strong polwar elements, under and above their commands, that might affect, even interfere in, their freedom of actions, good or bad. Besides, many military commanders were extremely allergic to anything that resembled "Communist Political Commissar" order—and even to the nationalist Chinese polwar institution. Some commanders even took polwar staff as a sheer office for entertainment with shows and ceremonies. The large military institution supposed to conduct crucial psychological warfare tasks could only perform some secondary missions such as raising funds for gifts and entertainment supporting combat soldiers. It was also conducting passive propaganda operations. Plans to boost morale were implemented without the commanders' enthusiasm.

At many unit headquarters I was visiting, the political warfare offices looked like recycle bins. ARVN psywar leading personnel were not selected from the most competent and talented government officials and officers but mostly from those who were not given important jobs whether they were not in favor with the bosses or simply because of their lack of skills. Many chiefs of the polwar blocs were simply figureheads.

From 1968, hundreds of second lieutenants were graduated from the University of Political Warfare. They were well trained for psychological warfare and were ready to perform their complicated tasks in the ideological front. However, the armed forces senior leaders did not have proper interest in their job, their performance, or their necessary supports.

On the communist side, political tasks were assigned to the chief of the party committee in a government agency or a military unit. It should be mentioned that an NVA unit had two commanders: a military commander and a political commander; the latter held greater power. Therefore, psychological tasks were implemented by the Communist Party system with full power.

TROOP MOTIVATION

Like in any army in the world, living conditions were greatly influencing the spirit of ARVN troops. Their salary was among the lowest in the free world militaries. Those married with children suffered badly, much worse than the manual laborers. There was a question, Should the military have been smaller, and should combat troops have been paid considerably more? I thought they should have. Apparently, Washington and Sài Gòn selected quantity over quality.

The NVA did not encounter this problem. Military units occupied barracks with no soldiers' dependent quarters. The Hà Nội government did not support a soldier's wife and their first child; additional children were each paid NVN$5. A private's salary was NVN$26, equal to the North Việt Nam workers' minimum wages. He had to pay $NVN21 for his meals provided by the unit kitchen, and only got NVN$5 as pocket money. A kilogram of rice cost NVN$ 0.4. His all-rice meal was the highly appreciated privilege.

Communist units had the advantage on the battlefield. A communist combat soldier carried only a very simple outfit. On his head was a pith helmet; in his rucksack he carried a set of field dressing, a nylon poncho used as tent and raincoat, boiled rice rations, and—the most indispensable—some spare pairs of straps for rubber tire sandals. Because each soldier carried less than twenty pounds, including an AK-47 and five magazines, an NVA company could spread out over a wide terrain in a few minutes and regroup in a similar time, thus effectively minimizing human losses by ARVN and U.S. bombing and shelling.

The combat outfit of an ARVN soldier weighed about 1.5 times as much. GI field gear was even heavier.

In political indoctrination, communist troops and government employees had to attend compulsory sessions of political lessons even in time of rest after work or operations. Students at low levels were asked to learn the lesson texts by heart. For instance, a flying crew of the commercial Việt Nam Airlines had to cancel a scheduled flight to attend an unplanned political indoctrination session. When an event took place or a new directive was promulgated, every soldier, public servant, and party member had to learn intensively. Every cheap political anecdote fabricated by the central agency for cultural and political instruction and taught in indoctrination classes could be repeated verbatim by any soldier or party member.

The RVN side acknowledged the importance of the same field, but troop indoctrination was not actively exercised and boosted by compulsory measures. The national and military leaders were not active in this field. Before the South fell on April 30, a large segment of ARVN troops including officers did not know much about life under the communists in the North.

As to the attitude of the Vietnamese troops of the two sides toward the war, thanks to uncensored information by radio broadcast and newspapers, our common soldiers were aware of our sorrowful situation when the two Việt Nams were killing each other on our own lands selected as the outposts of the capitalist and communist worlds and for the interests of those two blocs. The communist soldiers were not. They did not realize that they were also "lackeys" of the two communist powers when they called us American "puppets."

We didn't expect similar actions from the U.S. commands with the GIs as far as the American way of life, tradition, and war concept were concerned. But at least some form of orientation should have been carried out to inform GIs why they were serving in Việt Nam.

PSYCHOLOGICAL OPERATION

Only one psywar campaign directed at the communists scored significant success: that was the Chiêu Hồi (Open Arms) program. The fact that a large number of communists left their ranks to join the nationalist government side was undisputable. Although Sài Gòn and Washington did not give first priority to the psychological front, the limited efforts on the Chiêu Hồi program rendered a surprising outcome. I haven't known of any other war where troops who deserted one side to join the opposite side reached 150,000 in fifteen years of fighting.

Communist psywar efforts to persuade ARVN soldiers to defect had little success. The number of ARVN troops who deserted to the communist side was relatively insignificant.

In the South, most cultural works of an anticommunist nature were created by free writers and poets. Literature of political propaganda and songs supporting the war produced by the government took up a very small portion.

South Vietnamese government and military adopted the concept of "freedom wherever possible." Besides the restriction highly necessary for war, no leader would like to impose a strict limit on domains such as speech, writing, and music. Except for newspaper articles and books tacitly supporting communism, antiwar publications were not censored.

The South Vietnamese press corps had been allowed a wide range of freedom since the ARVN generals assumed power. Dissenting opinions and leftist arguments were appearing in newspapers and magazines without sanction. The government sometimes banned songs and confiscated newspapers that it charged for "supporting the communists" or "expressing ideas that undermine the anticommunist struggle." However, most of the banning orders were not fully implemented. Banned antiwar songs were still circulated and presented at public rallies without being interrupted by the police.

Late 1973 saw a hard blow to the press corps. After years of not-too-strictly-limited freedom of the press, President Thiệu imposed a new regulation. He set stricter limits on the publishers that actually strangled many newspapers. It required each newspaper a deposit of many million VN$ for a publishing permit. Several rightist papers had to discontinue along with several leftist papers.

Cultural activities supporting the anticommunist fighting and the troops achieved some favorable outcome. The general psychological front, though not as powerful as that of the communists, gradually received more people's support.

THE PARACELS INVASION

While the general situation was deteriorating, the Paracels battle with the Chinese communists dealt another painful blow to Sài Gòn. On January 19, 1974, ships of the Red Chinese Navy engaged in a sea battle with the Republic of Việt Nam Navy task force, which included two cruisers and two destroyers. After a long day of fighting, one South Vietnamese ship and one Red Chinese ship were sunk, and the RVN Navy task force had to withdraw with seventy KIAs. Beijing sent a squadron of MiG fighters to reinforce its troops. The RVN Air Force F-5 interceptors could not reach and stay for a time to fight in the area. At last the Chinese captured forty-eight members of a South Vietnamese Regional Force platoon along with some meteorology team members and a U.S. advisor. The Chinese suffered equal human losses including a general officer.

Before President Nixon visited Beijing in 1972, U.S. Navy planes flew over the Paracels once every day to make routine security checks. When the Chinese routed the RVN Navy, not a single diplomatic action was taken by the U.S. government to support the RVN. Even when the RVN Navy appealed for help to rescue drifting sailors, the U.S. Pacific Command did not lift a finger.

Beijing refuted all recorded evidence supporting the RVN's argument including agreements between the Chinese Ching Kingdom and the French government asserting Việt Nam's sovereignty over the two groups of islands, the Paracels and the Spratlys. The RVN would have won the case in the international court if Beijing had not refused to have recourse on the tribunal.

North Việt Nam kept silent even after an appeal by the RVN National Congress for a joint effort of both the North and the South to voice protest and to demand that Beijing withdraw its troops, probably because in 1959, Hà Nội had publicly recognized Beijing's claim over the two island groups of Paracels and Spratlys.

Even worse, in documents and maps issued since 1954, the communist regime in Hà Nội dropped the names of Paracel and Spratly in Vietnamese:

Hoàng Sa and Trường Sa. The two names had been used for hundreds of years. But Hà Nội followed Beijing, referring to them in Vietnamese as Tây Sa and Nam Sa—exactly after the Chinese terms Xisha and Nansha.[6]

Strangely enough, since Nixon's visit in 1972, particularly after the Paracels incident, Beijing began referring to the South Vietnamese government as "the government of the Republic of Việt Nam" instead of its usual derogatory "American puppet" or "American imperialists' servant." The polite form also appeared in Beijing's declaration on the release of forty-eight South Vietnamese Regional Force soldiers captured by the Red Chinese Army on the Paracels.

There was a remarkable event regarding the relations between Chinese Communists and the National Liberation Front (also called the Provisionary Government of the Republic of South Việt Nam). Sometime before the Paracels crisis, my office received a transcription of Radio Beijing, released by the ARVN-JCS/J7. Radio Beijing reported that the two ministers of foreign affairs of the People's Republic of China and the Provisional Government of the Republic of South Việt Nam had signed an agreement permitting citizens of the one country to travel to the other country without visas of entry or exit and regardless of quantity, purpose, time length, profession, or locations. Was Beijing preparing some kind of invasion in South Việt Nam, as rumors were running in March and April 1975?

Along with the Paracels crisis, the U.S. Congress cut some aid to Sài Gòn and passed a bill forbidding the White House to engage in any war action in Indochina. The news strengthened our pessimism, but we still believed that without U.S. intervention, the RVN could resist the communist invasion if U.S. aid at the 1972 level were maintained.

FRUSTRATION

In the political arena, President Thiệu failed to build more credibility. That he won the presidential one-candidate election caused frustration among nationalists. He lost much credit he had received in his first four-year term. His visit to the United States, Great Britain, and the Holy See also proved his painful failure. All of those combined to inflict serious damage on the people's morale.

And worst of all, the economy suffered heavily from the continuing war when corruption became more and more intolerable at lower levels. Buying lucrative seats in the government and the army was a common practice after the fall of Ngô Đình Diệm.

The drug business was blooming when GIs were spending their time and their bucks at bars, nightclubs, and brothels. Now that they were all back in the States, our indigenous youth became the drug dealers' only targets. In 1973 and 1974, South Việt Nam police conducted a campaign to control drug traffic with some success, but it was impossible to completely control drug addicts, although public opinion strongly supported the move. When the district police arrested a "scag" dealer in my alley and beat her badly when she stubbornly resisted and fought back, people in the neighborhood refused to protect her, saying she deserved such a beating.

However, smuggling was on the rise. A notorious smuggling case was detected when a convoy of trucks transporting tax-evading goods with Military Police escort was caught on its way to Sài Gòn. People believed that it was a conspiracy of some ARVN general officers and government officials.

Protesters found it a good time to rally in antigovernment demonstrations with the obvious intention of creating social and political chaos. Meanwhile, living conditions for the military and civil servants' families were getting worse and worse. My salary in 1974 bought only half of what it had in 1969.

TWENTY-FIVE

America 1974–75

From 1968 to 1972, I devoted an hour or two every week to studying aspects of life in North Việt Nam. In the first year serving the Chiêu Hồi program, I realized that much of what we had known about North Việt Nam was wrong. There were some Vietnamese scholars who were specialists on the Vietnamese communists, but without sufficient support, their works were not published and propagated appropriately. Besides, their studies were mostly concerned with high-level information and theories, not with day-to-day life except for such books like Dr. Hoàng Văn Chí's *From Colonialism to Communism*.

I had an urgent desire to publish my study to tell readers about what life in the northern half of our country was really like. It could partly answer the question as to why the communist leaders were able to stand against the powerful U.S. and South Việt Nam military and were so largely supported by the North Vietnamese peasants. Without basic knowledge about the communist regime from the food ration system to the political security machine, such questions would never be answered accurately and sufficiently.

From about 500 such interviews, I compiled the reliable information, confirmed by printed materials published in Hà Nội, into a manuscript of more than 600 pages. When I applied for a publishing permit at the Information Ministry, I was turned down without any explanation. I believed that by denying the publication of my book, the censure section only applied certain directives from some high-ranking officials: "Don't mention anything good about North Việt Nam." In my manuscript, I frankly appraised what I thought Hà Nội was doing for the better life of the North Vietnamese people. I always believed that telling the whole truth is the best strategy for fighting psychological warfare.

Late in 1973, I applied for the Infantry Officer Advanced Course (IOAC) at Fort Benning, Georgia. General Nguyễn Bảo Trị, my boss when I served the

Twenty-second Division and the Chiêu Hồi Ministry, was now head of the ARVN General Training Department. He advised me to go to Fort Leavenworth instead. He said, "With your eighteen years of service and the jobs you've had, you deserve such high-level military instruction. I have full authority to help you." But I explained to him why I wouldn't accept his favor.

The reason I preferred Fort Benning was simple: The Ytzainas, my dear friends, were in Fort Rucker, Alabama, only 150 miles from the Infantry School, so I could have had some help from them to publish my study in the United States. I could even enroll in some postgraduate courses on evenings and weekends at a nearby university to earn some credits toward my master's degree in criminology, which I planned to complete later at Sài Gòn University, where I had graduated Licentiate at Private Law. Unfortunately, the Ytzainas had moved to Paris about thirty days before I departed for Fort Benning. He was unexpectedly appointed to a new job at the headquarters of MAAG/France. My plan failed.

While I was applying for my passport and visa, friends who had been attending the IOAC-5/74 at Fort Benning since February 1974 wrote me long letters telling how a lot of Americans were showing their unfriendly attitude toward the Vietnamese around Columbus, Georgia. Sometimes the situation was too hostile to stand. When one of them asked an American who was a visitor from Columbus for a ride in her car on her way to the local airport, she refused. The woman just said no. He asked "How come?" and she coldly replied, "'Cause you're a Vat'nese." The woman must have had strong dislike for the South Vietnamese to behave so crudely. My friends advised me to be prepared for the hostility.

On May 24, 1974, I arrived in San Francisco and stayed overnight at Travis Air Force Base before boarding a Delta flight to Atlanta and an extension flight to Columbus, Georgia.

I was amazed at the great changes in America. Streets and cities were looking much better than in 1957. Nice cars filled the streets, and Chinatown sidewalks were cleaner. But people, the young Americans in particular, looked less friendly and were not as polite as their older brothers and sisters had been seventeen years earlier.

FORT BENNING

The Infantry School had changed a lot, too. The wooden buildings 1525 and 1526 where I lived for nine months in 1957 had been dismantled. The school headquarters and classrooms were moved into the new five-story building. I saw the new hospital and the huge PX building. But the roads and some BOQs were not as clean as they had been in the late 1950s. I felt something sad, a kind of nostalgia when looking back at the old days. Old days are always more beautiful, especially when war makes everything of today look worse than yesterday.

The first month in Fort Benning went smoothly. Although the general attitude against South Việt Nam was noticeable everywhere, our American classmates were treating us nicely. There were 77 among the 152 Americans in my class who were willing to sponsor the 5 Vietnamese. Ninety percent of my American classmates had served the Việt Nam War.

We Vietnamese knew better than anyone else that the hostile attitude emanated from slanderous reports and insufficient information provided by the American media. It was difficult to make Americans change their view in a short time. But as patriots we had to do something for our country, large or small, successful or not.

My class was the Infantry Officers Advanced Course 7/74 (IOAC-7/74). By then, it was one of the largest regular advanced classes in the school's history (195 students) with the highest number of foreigners (43 officers from 16 countries).

My closest classmate was Lawson W. Magruder III, a brilliant officer ten years younger than me. He showed an excellent capability in his military career and was appointed class leader. He retired in 2001 as a lieutenant general.

His wife, Gloria, was a pretty lady from Maine. Once talking about the role of an officer's wife, I quoted some famous American general (General Douglas MacArthur, if I am not wrong) as saying that an officer's wife is like the tail of a kite. If it is too heavy, the kite can't fly high, but if it is too light, the kite won't be stable.[1]

We Vietnamese were active in joining assemblies of the class or groups, making friends with all classmates, and doing anything helpful. We also offered our assistance to the school as the situation required.

Five of us often attended social activities such as class parties and section potlucks. I felt ten years younger while playing college games with my handsome American friends and their lovely wives.

During eleven months at Fort Benning, I had many good friends from Africa, the Middle East, Latin America, and Europe. Many of them were misinformed about what really had happened in Việt Nam, but I found that it was easier to make them see the truth about the Việt Nam conflict than the American war protesters.

On many occasions outside Fort Benning, I met people who were against "Thiệu's despotic regime," but some of those were unable to say where Việt Nam was exactly on the map, and many others could not specify what made them think Thiệu was a dictator. I told them that Thiệu might have been involved in corruption, allowing his faithful subordinates to accept bribes, or he was an incapable president who relied on tricky schemes to consolidate his throne. But he was not a dictator. "I wish he *were* a dictator so he could do something better to fight the communists," I said to them.

Once I ran across a lady about sixty years old in a middle-class neighborhood in Columbus. She asked me to come and visit her home. In the living room,

I happened to see a small altar on which was the portrait of a young soldier. She told me he was her only son, who was killed in Việt Nam years ago.

I stepped to the altar, saluted the soldier's portrait, and turned to the mother. "I believe you are proud of your son, a respectable hero. As a Vietnamese officer, I would like to express our grateful thanks to your noblest contribution to the freedom of our Vietnamese people."

She cried and held my hands tight, speaking between sobs. "I have been waiting years for a word from the Vietnamese government honoring my son's sacrifice of himself for your country."

I have long been against the policies of the leaders in Washington in conducting the war and the way they dealt with our national affairs. They appeared simply as global authoritarians who imposed their decisions on the small developing countries, but they were easily bluffed and intimidated by international rascals. However, I have always felt grateful to the young Americans who sacrificed themselves and suffered hardships for the freedom of half of my country, even those who later protested the war.

One day I was invited to be guest speaker at a lunch of the local chamber of commerce. After fifteen minutes of my speech about our armed forces, a businessman asked me about my salary. I said, "About 45,000 piasters a month (equal to about US$80), which is a little less than the income of a cyclo driver or an unskilled strong worker." He said he was our supporter, but he felt surprised that ARVN officers' salary was so low. "How could a soldier fight with that starving salary?" Probably the South Vietnamese military servicemen received the lowest salary in the Free World countries.

Another day I was invited to talk to a group of Boy Scouts. After my short presentation on Việt Nam history, a dozen boys raised their hands for questions. The most emotional question came from a twelve-year-old. "As my parents told me, all American soldiers have withdrawn from Việt Nam after the peace agreement. But the two sides in Việt Nam are still fighting each other. When you kill the Vietnamese on the other side, do you feel sad? And do the communists do the same when they kill your men?"

"Yes, we do, at least most of us do. Maybe some of the communists do, but their superiors taught them not to," I told him. I had met hundreds of foreign reporters and visitors, discussing the war with them. But no one had ever asked me questions that moved me so deeply.

Even many Americans who were fighting in Việt Nam didn't apprehend the stark realities of the war. On the RVN National Holiday, November 1, 1974, we showed some documentary movies and news reports about our armed forces to a 200-plus audience—my classmates and a few dozen guests. One of the reels was about the mass graves unearthed a month after the 1968 Tét Offensive around Hué. Another reel recorded the battles of An Lộc, Quảng Trị and

Kontum in the "1972 Summer Offensive," or "Flaming Summer," as coined by our Vietnamese journalists.

The third reel reported the military parade on June 19, 1973 (the RVN Armed Forces Day). It was the first parade held in Sài Gòn since 1966. The pompous military ceremony and large-scale march drew tens of thousands of spectators lining both sides of Trần Hưng Đạo Boulevard.

After the shows, many Americans—scores of colonels—who had served as advisors in Việt Nam, told me they had never known that the 1968 Tết massacres were so horrible and that the number of victims was so high. What they had known was from a few short news reports at that time, and they had thought there were only a few hundred victims. In fact, of the people missing in the Tết Offensive in Huế, only 5,000 were found in two dozen mass graves.

Dozens of other American officers, some with tears filling their eyes, shook our hands and said that if they had been fully informed about the savage killing of so many unarmed civilians, they would have fought the war with much stronger determination. The course of events could have been much different.

The fighting in An Lộc won high appraisal from the audience. It showed the thrilling scenes of combat against the enemy tanks and the enemy's heavy artillery shelling. The heroism of the ARVN units fighting in An Lộc couldn't be denied, although the film narration, like others made by the Information Branch in South Việt Nam, carried a light scent of propaganda. Of course, it contained much less boasting rhetoric than those made by North Việt Nam.

Still many other American field grade officers who had been in Việt Nam for more than a one-year tour showed their surprise when watching the parade, especially when they learned that the marching Marine, Airborne, Regional Force, and Infantry battalions were real combat units. "They marched so perfectly that we think they were recruits freshly graduated from peacetime boot camps," they said. "The U.S. combat units were not able to drill so well in World War II or in the Korean War."

I welcomed their remarks with a reluctant smile. Deep in my heart, I felt very disappointed to see how the brave, patriotic American officers were so poorly informed about the Việt Nam War. Without such basic knowledge of their enemy and their Vietnamese combat fellows, how could they assert the right cause they were fighting for?

ACHIEVEMENTS

My four Vietnamese classmates urged me to study hard every weekend, particularly the day before a test. They said I had to prove that we Vietnamese officers were not ugly cowards, as war protesting activists were striving to brand us, or "puppets of the American imperialists," as the Việt communist propaganda called us.

I did get high scores from the start. Some friends of mine praised my achievement, but I was not sure if I deserved it. I had been familiar with U.S. military activities, tactics, and military terminology and jargon. Moreover, I had learned to read and write English rather well due to some experiences in military operations, whereas my classmates from other countries had not. Grading instructors may have felt more comfortable with my papers, and so they gave me more points.

On Saturdays and Sundays, I held classes where allied classmates came to review lessons and other materials before examinations. By telephone, instructors helped clarify any issues that we felt difficult to grasp. At times, some Americans were attending as well. I was assisting them with topics I comprehended rather well such as insurgency and guerrilla warfare.

The results were quite encouraging. We were highly appreciated by General Thomas M. Tarpley, commanding general of Fort Benning, General William Richardson, deputy commanding general, Colonel Russell W. Weathersby, senior faculty advisor, and many instructors. Some American friends said to me, "You should be at Leavenworth, not here," to which I quipped, "Don't you mean the long course?" They didn't know why I preferred Fort Benning to Fort Leavenworth.

General Richardson, former deputy commandant of the Infantry School wrote me a personal letter when he had left Fort Benning to be the U.S. commander in the Panama Canal Zone. He highly appraised our Vietnamese in classes IOAC-5/74 and IOAC-7/74: "Since you came here, people walking into my office began saying something good when they talked about 'the Vietnamese.'" Richardson had been an advisor to Long An province for three years.

In relations with the Americans and other allied classmates, I always felt easy and friendly. I haven't forgotten my many American classmates besides the Magruders—the Brosnans, the Kims, the Croneins—and many allied students—Dawuni, Dyarea, Adomokai, Funk, Razavi, and others. Also, some instructors became good friends, including Major Lee, Colonel Ford, and Major Kinnard. They understood Việt Nam better than many others.

AN ANGRY AMERICAN

But not everyone sympathized with the ARVN officers. At least one I knew: a U.S. Army major who had served two tours in Việt Nam. From the beginning of the course, he would never speak more than a few words to us. He said nothing unfriendly, but his eyes and facial expression betrayed his true feelings.

At a field exercise in September 1974, he came to me while I was eating my lunch under a big tree. He sat down and asked me if I knew why he hadn't behaved warmly toward Vietnamese officers. I said I really didn't have any ideas, and so he told me his story.

He was a true American patriot. He volunteered to go to Việt Nam and was serving as an advisor to a combat battalion. He was proud of being a member of the ARVN unit, and he greatly sympathized with the troops and their commander.

At the beginning of his second year, he was assigned to another advisory team. He admired the Vietnamese field grade commander of the new unit, praising him as a hero, a peerless patriot. But his Vietnamese hero was soon investigated for a wily plot of corruption relating to a project that was supposed to help poor peasants. The probe discovered that his hero had played a role in the dirty scheme, which allegedly brought him and his superiors a few million pilasters.

Without knowing the dirty plot of the Vietnamese commanders, the U.S. advisory team did their best to support the "civic action operation" with trucks and air cover for transportation of illegal products. Some Americans were investigated, but no one was charged.

The scandal was too much for the American major. He felt cheated by the Vietnamese, whom he had held in such high esteem. Becoming too uneasy to work in such an unfavorable environment, he asked to be transferred to the American Division, where he spent his last months of the second tour, trying to cool down his bitter experience.

He admitted that after the scandal, he was wrong to see every ARVN officer as having corrupt money in the pocket. I told him I understood his feelings and also admitted that although reports on corruption were usually exaggerated, the existing corrupt practices were more than enough to sabotage the fledgling democracy in war.

NIXON RESIGNS

In August 1974, President Richard Nixon appeared on national TV to announce that he had decided to resign. After months of confronting his opponents' attacks on the Watergate scandal, he looked gloomy and tired on the color screen. Many of my American classmates were sad while watching his speech. We five Vietnamese felt it in a different way. We were worrying that the new president, Gerald Ford, would be in a weak position, as he became the chief of the executive branch not based on the people's votes. My American friends all predicted that Ford would not act with the full power of an elected president if the situation in Việt Nam became critical, especially under the War Powers Act of 1973.

Three months after Nixon resigned, allied students of my class toured Washington. The school staff faced a difficult problem. A few African officers insisted that they wouldn't share hotel rooms with the other Africans, who were not their compatriots. It meant that three more single-bed rooms would be required for the four-day tour. However the budget was very tight, and there was no way to pay for a few more rooms. The matter was very delicate, and the school officials found it difficult to deal with.

We Vietnamese officers volunteered to help. Each of the five of us would share a double room with one of the five African classmates. The Thais and the Laotians also would join us if necessary. The African gentlemen happily agreed. I shared a room with Major Joe E. Dawuni from Ghana. The crisis, though very small but very difficult to solve, was settled at last.

We visited the Capitol, the White House, the Pentagon, the State Department, and historic sites. At the State Department, a ranking American official who was a Việt Nam "son-in-law" received us seven Vietnamese as a single group. The other visiting officers were welcomed in groups of regions (South America, Africa, Europe, and Asia)

The official talked to us in perfect Vietnamese about many topics concerning Việt Nam, particularly on the U.S. aid and the oil reserves in Việt Nam. At the time, reports of possible large oil wells raised some of our hope. But he frankly warned us of Việt Nam's difficulties from the military situation, including troubles from "having oil."

On the tour, I visited Dr. Hoàng Văn Chí in Bowie, near Washington, D.C. He was a Vietnamese scholar, author of *From Colonialism to Communism,* the best study of the 1953–56 bloody Land Reform in North Việt Nam. I held him in high esteem in many aspects. In 1954, he escaped the Việt Minh region where he had served the War of Resistance with a full heart. He was serving the government of President Ngô Đình Diệm for a few years before he fled to live in France because of his dissent with the regime. In 1974, he was teaching at the school of the international development agency in the U.S. State Department.

For hours, we discussed the gloomy situation in Việt Nam. He had a profound knowledge of world affairs and the communists. I learned a lot from him. I still remember his opinion about the fate of the free South Việt Nam. According to him, Kissinger and Nixon were seeking a shameful exit from Việt Nam by selling out their poor friends in Sài Gòn. Two of his predictions turned out to be true. He said that Washington leaders were going to provide some aid to keep Sài Gòn surviving for two to three years so that they could say that the RVN was fully responsible for its collapse when the Americans had granted an enormous amount of military aid and successfully trained the ARVN. He also predicted that sooner or later the communist leaders in Việt Nam would take sides with the Americans to replace current leaders in the South and become the more obsequious and more faithful American puppets.

VIETNAMESE GI BRIDES

There were about ninety Vietnamese women living in the Columbus area. They were all GI brides, except for two university students. The 1975 Tết or Vietnamese Lunar New Year was celebrated by at least five groups of them, separately.

They all wanted us five ARVN officers to attend, and we had to be at all five or none. As the five in IOAC-5/74 had returned to Việt Nam, we five in IOAC-7/74 had to show up at all five Tết parties, arranged consecutively from lunchtime to 9 PM so that we could have time to digest the food.

That night I stayed up late chatting with my friends in one of their rooms because of my full stomach. Minutes after I returned to my room, I threw myself on the bed and quickly fell asleep. In a dream I saw myself as a third-grader walking past skinny corpses of the 1945 famine victims along both sides of the road to my school. Only the ones who have suffered from hunger and poverty can properly appreciate the happiness of being rich and well fed.

At the time, GIs' Vietnamese brides constituted a special community. They were scattered all around the United States. Several large groups were living on major military bases, such as Fort Bragg, Fort Benning, and Travis AFB. For the first time in the history of Việt Nam, tens of thousands of Vietnamese women were married lawfully to decent foreigners. Their husbands were soldiers from private to colonel and many who served in civilian jobs in government departments, particularly the State Department, where scores of them were high-ranking officials.

In the 1946–54 war, many women lived with soldiers from France and her African colonies, but only a very few married and joined their spouses in France or Africa. Moreover, the average level of education and social status of those women was far lower than the Americans' wives twenty years later.

Most of those Americans treated their Vietnamese wives so affectionately and submissively that if they had lived in Việt Nam they would have been dubbed henpecked husbands.

They also had profound affection for Việt Nam. One of them said to me that he took Việt Nam as his second homeland, the motherland of his wife and his children. He believed that a large number of those Americans who were and would be high ranking in the U.S. military and foreign affairs services would favor Việt Nam when related matters would come to their areas of competence.

OMINOUS NIGHTMARES

After 1975 Tết, bad news began taking up larger segments on TV screens and newspaper front pages. Reports on the fall of Phước Long (30 miles northwest of Sài Gòn) made me unable to sleep for more than four or five hours a night. I had a presentiment that the Phước Long battle would mark a point close to the end.

In early March after final exams, my score was 913 out of 1,000 points after being adjusted on the bell curve. I was in the top 10 percent of the 192 graduates, along with Bernard Funk from France. He outscored me by one point. At last it was the best thing I had ever done in honor of my country. The graduation ceremony took place on March 13, 1975, when many communist divisions launched an all-out offensive, first at Ban Mê Thuột.

At the farewell party for the allied students from sixteen countries, General Tarpley introduced me to about 300 guests with praise that I still think that I did not deserve. He said, "In the IOAC number 7, this ARVN officer has done well in his two roles: as a student and also as an instructor."

During my last days at Fort Benning, I had mixed feelings of sadness about leaving the school where I had been trained twice and fear of the possible collapse of the democracy to whose construction I had eagerly devoted my very little part. It was not a perfect regime that I was dreaming of, but it was far better than the communist dictatorship. Its collapse would certainly bring havoc and perils from the fanatical and brutal communist leaders upon the 19 million South Vietnamese.

I left Fort Benning on the morning of March 16 for Washington, D.C., on a Greyhound bus, along with my two classmates, Lê Văn Lễ and Nguyễn Đình Hà. We were staying a week at the home of Dr. Hoàng Văn Chí. At Dr. Chi's home the following evening we heard a special TV news report saying that our Twenty-third Division had withdrawn from Ban Mê Thuột, some 200 miles north of Sài Gòn. My heart sank; my head was heavy. Dr. Chí and the others in his living room suddenly became silent, deep in thought. I felt as if I were in a funeral home at midnight, although the sound of the news broadcast was still on.

Mr. Chi wanted to introduce me to Douglas Pike and Kenneth Quinn and asked them to help me publish my study on North Việt Nam. I failed to see Pike, as he had to go to Việt Nam on a few hours' notice. I met with Quinn at his office (the Việt Nam desk) in the National Security Council building close to the White House.

I was a friend of the family of Quinn's Vietnamese wife in Sài Gòn. He was eager to help, asking the translators pool under Lou Broddock of the U.S. embassy in Sài Gòn to assist me in translating my manuscript. They were about to start the translation when Sài Gòn succumbed on April 30.

FROM HEAVEN TO HELL IN THIRTY DAYS

The next day, I went to see old Mrs. Mulhall in Phoenixville, Pennsylvania, whom I often called "Mother." Her daughter, Elizabeth, and son-in-law, Raymond Ytzaina, had been my close friends since 1967.

While Mrs. Mulhall and I were visiting Valley Forge, an old friend of hers working at the George Washington Museum told me that I would have to surrender to the North Vietnamese communists.

"You should not say so to my son," Mrs. Mulhall protested. "He has been serving in the South Vietnamese Army for nineteen years, doing nothing wrong. He will be fighting the enemy to his last minute."

The old man apologized. I felt ashamed, however, that even though I was doing nothing wrong, I had not done as much for my country as I once promised to do at the graduation of my class at the Việt Nam Military Academy.

Before I left Phoenixville, Elizabeth and Raymond talked to me from Paris, sobbing, "We'll pray for you." Choked by tears, they could talk no more.

Two days later, my Greyhound bus to San Francisco stopped in the early morning in Omaha, Nebraska. On a stand, some newspapers covered the front page with nothing but a diagonal black stripe and short headlines that stunned me for a moment. An old woman bought the paper and, holding it against her chest, cried bitterly after a quick glance at the huge headline: "HUE FALLS! DA NANG NEXT?"

"My son was killed in Hué in the 1968 offensive. He died for nothing. How can the city fall so easily?" she moaned.

I couldn't help telling her I was a Vietnamese officer on my way back to Việt Nam. A man whose son had lost a leg in Việt Nam shook my hand. "May God bless you, my friend," he said. "If you fight when you get back there, remember to shoot two more rounds for the old lady and me each time you shoot ten of yours."

The night I arrived at Travis AFB, I dreamed that Việt Nam communist red flags were streaming on every house and public building in Sài Gòn, and communist solders were taking all of us ARVN officers prisoner. I woke up sweating. I could not sleep again and stayed up until dawn.

The next morning, I went to the bus station to check out my luggage, which I had sent on Greyhound lines direct from Columbus. When I opened it in my room to reorganize it for the trip to Việt Nam, I was stunned to find that the trophy of an infantryman I was awarded by the school was broken. Its right arm with a rifle was severed from the trunk. My roommate sighed, "A farewell to arms!"

While waiting for the flight to Việt Nam at Travis AFB, I saw TV reports of shocking scenes of soldiers and civilians swarming Đà Nẵng's harbor and airport to find ways to flee the area. One of the clips showed a Boeing 727 hobbling at low altitude back to Sài Gòn after being attacked by hand grenades; the back door was open with passengers falling from it. Other reports were about holdups, looting, and even rapes on ships evacuating refugees and soldiers from Đà Nẵng.

Many U.S. commercial airlines responded to the appeal from the U.S. airlines association to help evacuate hundreds of thousands of Vietnamese from Hué and Đà Nẵng. They would be sending dozens of large planes to Phú Bài and Đà Nẵng airport, but the local RVN governments' inability to maintain order at the two airports frustrated the evacuation plan.

All Vietnamese I knew in the States were extremely nervous. Some of them advised me to stay. I thought about it, but could not make up my mind.

On March 31, twelve hours before my scheduled flight to Sài Gòn, a friend of mine, a rich Vietnamese American whom I had known for six months, called me from Alabama. She suggested that I stay in the States. She promised to pay for a bribe of less than US$3,000 through a connection she had in the Sài Gòn Interior Ministry to get exit visas for my wife and children. She said my family would be in the States with me in no more than two weeks.

She promised to lend me $50,000 without interest to help us make our living in America. She only asked me for a "little" favor. That would be to look after the education of her ten-year-old daughter, so that her child would be as successful in American society as possible.

Her voice was intimate and honest, but I told her I was sorry not to accept her great favor. I concluded the matter with my grateful thanks to her and switched to a different topic. When she insisted on the suggestion, I told her: "People say, forsaking parents, spouse, and children is difficult, but forsaking the fatherland is much more difficult, even impossible. I'm grateful to your offer, but I can't accept it now. Please understand."

I had my family including my mom and my aunt to take care of. And I had many friends, Vietnamese, Americans, and those from other countries, who might have considered me a deserter if I fled the country when Sài Gòn was in its last hours. That was scaring me more than the possible communist victory followed by bloodshed.

On April 1, I boarded a USAF chartered plane back to Sài Gòn along with three of my four Vietnamese classmates; one had decided to stay. Good-bye calls from my American and Vietnamese friends were full of sobbing. I didn't know why I told Lawson Magruder and his wife, Gloria, that I felt strongly I would return someday. Gloria cried a lot on her phone at Fort Lewis, Washington.

No country could survive the fierce attacks, not only from the North Vietnamese communists but also from the entire communist bloc and from our unfriendly friends, without full assistance from the U.S. government. Meanwhile, the communist forces could leave North Việt Nam undefended to concentrate their might and main to overrunning South Việt Nam.

In the last three years of the war, the Soviet Union and China increased military aid to the Vietnamese communists. Besides small infantry weapons, cannons, ammunition, and medicines, many new kinds of antiaircraft and antitank missiles, radios, clothes, boots, combat rations, and even rice were provided.

On our side, since 1974, military supplies of every class had been extremely low. Even batteries for radios at battalion level were allocated for only ten days a month, let alone artillery ammunition and the most effective weapons, the M-79 grenades and Claymore mines. No army could fight and stand fast with such a shortage of supplies.

450 · *Victory or Defeat*

Our plane approached Sài Gòn at a high altitude, and the pilot made a steep dive to land, apparently to avoid possible ground fire. An American sitting beside me pointed to the ARVN National Cemetery appearing below where graves formed parallel slanting lines. Combined with other constructions, the whole complex had the figure of a soldier bee. Soldier bees died after attacking their enemy. I said, "The thousands of brave men lying there sacrificed themselves for their country but have never expected there would be an unhappy ending like this to come."

TWENTY-SIX

The End

DARK APRIL

When I stepped out of the plane at the Air America terminal in Tân Sơn Nhất, the Vietnamese girl who checked the manifest asked me, "Why do you come back? Đà Lạt fell last night." I said nothing, because it might have taken a few hours to explain what I was thinking to one who had never been a soldier.

I didn't go on leave traditionally given to those just coming back from schooling abroad and went on to work at the GPWD. That was one of the longest months in my life. There were too many events that frightened everybody. My superiors were all nervous and so busy that they did not remember to complete the last simple paperwork to make my promotion to lieutenant colonel official. As for me, I didn't like to ask them to act. So I could claim myself a major or a lieutenant colonel as I liked.

The American plan to evacuate a number of Vietnamese heightened panic in Sài Gòn. U.S. Air Force C-5A flights were evacuating Vietnamese orphans out of the country in the "Baby Lift" operation. Other U.S. flights moved Vietnamese who were related to U.S. citizens. Then a large number of Vietnamese began to seek ways to leave Việt Nam.

The death of General Nguyễn Văn Hiếu moved me deeply. General Hiếu died by a pistol shot in Biên Hòa on April 8 when I had just returned from the States. Some said he was shot by a corrupt general's underling; others said he accidentally killed himself when he was cleaning his pistol. Among my bosses in my years serving the ARVN, General Hiếu had been my favorite. He had impeccable manners and was a brilliant commander. His death aggravated my despair at the survival chances of the RVN.

The situation deteriorated greatly when an ARVN Air Force pilot who had deserted to the communist side flew an RVNAF jet fighter and tried to drop a bomb on the Presidential Palace. He missed. The A-37 had been captured by the communist forces weeks earlier in Central Việt Nam.

On April 17, the anticommunist regime in Cambodia under President Lon Nol was overthrown. Its prime minister, Sirik Matak, refused the U.S. ambassador's offer to evacuate him and died bravely at the hands of the Khmer Rouge. The last words of his letter to the ambassador read, "I have committed the mistake of believing in you, the Americans." Most Vietnamese nationalists like me did not believe in the American leaders either, but we found no better friend to rely on.

The fall of Phnom Penh seemed to precipitate the fate of Sài Gòn. I felt that the end was coming closer.

The deadliest blow came when the U.S. Congress refused to allocate more military aid to South Việt Nam. Many people sought help from American friends or bribed officials to flee the country by American air transportation; some even managed to have their children registered in the list of orphans to be flown by the "Baby Lift."

Every day, more friends left the country with their families. A few of them let their families go first while they stayed. I felt such a solution acceptable, but my wife firmly rejected it. She said she and the whole family would be beside me and share with me everything that might happen to me whether I decided to go or stay.

Many times in my dreams, I saw myself dialing my office telephone to get through to my friends at long-distance area codes 957 or 958 or 964 in Phú Bài, Đà Nẵng, Qui Nhơn, and elsewhere. These areas were under control of communist forces.

In the second week of April, I met Ogden Williams at the home of Mr. Buss, who was an advisor to the Rural Development Ministry. I just asked them about the possibilities of defending South Việt Nam. Williams had been a good friend to Việt Nam since 1955. He was trying to do something to help. He was working on the idea of asking Iran for military aid.

I hated to ask any of them to help my family, even Lee Broddock in the U.S. embassy. Kenneth Quinn had introduced me to him for the translation of my study on North Việt Nam. Lee had my address and telephone number. I was unable to contact him in the last hours.

I was living the last days of Sài Gòn with a lonely feeling when my friends fled one after another. My best friends who could help were too far away.

On April 23, President Gerald Ford announced that the Việt Nam War was "a war that is finished." Along with Congress's failure to pass a supplemental aid bill for Vietnam, Ford's statement destroyed our last hope.

Then President Thiệu resigned and was replaced by Vice President Tran Văn Hương. A few days later, Hương resigned. Power was shifted to General Dương Văn Minh, whose ascent to power had not been provided for by the RVN constitution. The political solution was only hastening the already irrecoverable panic among the people and soldiers.

French statesmen and diplomats were trying to negotiate a peaceful solution to the conflict. Their failure to do so only aggravated our despair. In that situation, I couldn't decide what to do. I knew for certain that I would be in danger at the hands of the communists, but I also hesitated to flee. The feeling of being a "deserter" while the majority of my fighting fellows were still there was too great for me to make a final decision. So I had to wait until the last minute.

I heard a rumor that some groups of army soldiers and officers were planning to bring down any airplane of former president Thiệu and former prime minister Trần Thiện Khiêm if they fled the country. However, the two leaders quietly left for Taiwan five days before Sài Gòn collapsed without any trouble. General Cao Văn Viên, joint chief of staff, followed suit.[1]

Another rumor circulated that some ARVN major units would fight U.S. combat forces if they entered Việt Nam to evacuate 1,000 American civil and military personnel. Anything was possible in a chaotic situation. But the rumor did not come true.

On April 28, a second VNAF fighter from the communist-controlled area attacked Tân Sơn Nhất Air Base. The bombing stopped most air traffic in and out of Tân Sơn Nhất. On April 29, only a few fix-winged planes took off. A communist missile hit and destroyed a VN Air Force cargo C-119. After that, only military helicopters were seen in the sky.

By the early morning of April 29, Sài Gòn's main streets were jammed with traffic. People were nervous. They were heading for the quay areas and Tân Sơn Nhất Airport/Air Base to seek ways to escape the imminent disaster.

In that hopeless situation, on the front line in Xuân Lộc, Long Khánh, north of Sài Gòn, the ARVN Eighteenth Division still held its ground, fighting to stop the enemy. According to some news reports, the ARVN Air Force attacked the advancing communist force in Long Khánh, using a powerful bomb (either a CBU-55, cluster bomb unit, or a BLU-82 "Daisy Cutter") that wiped out an NVA regiment. The news flashed a thin ray of optimism, but it was not bright enough to become a torch of hope.

Many friends of mine had a plan to withdraw their units to the Mekong Delta if there was an order, or even an appeal, from some leader to establish a new line of defense of a smaller republic in the "rice bowl" of Việt Nam. There was no such order or appeal as no leader had power and credibility enough to rally a disintegrating army. The new joint chief of staff had no way to assume full control of his armed forces.

The nationalist parties were too weak to do anything in such a desperate situation. My Việt Quốc comrades in Military Region II, especially in the provinces of Quảng Trị, Thừa Thiên, Huế, and Quảng Nam, suffered heavy losses after the area fell into the hands of the NVA divisions. The Việt Quốc strength in other parts of South Việt Nam was not strong enough to affect the situation.

Late on April 29, many of my men did not report to my GPWD, a noncombat service. At 4 PM, I stopped by my home for a quick dinner. "Kids! Should I stay home with you or go to my barracks?" I asked my children.

"The sergeant and the corporal down the street went to their units half an hour ago," my fifteen-year-old daughter said. "You are a field grade . . ." I knew what she meant. I told my wife to take care of the family, jumped into my jeep, and nodded to the driver to go without looking back.

Since early in the afternoon, American Jolly Green Giant helicopters and their brother UH-1Bs had been picking up Americans and Vietnamese at several places—the Defense Attaché Office (DAO) landing zone, the U.S. embassy, and the top floors of many tall buildings. High in the sky, several U.S. jet fighters returned after more than two years to protect the evacuation.

At 9 PM, General Trần Văn Trung, who decided to stay until the last minute, called General Nguyễn Hữu Có, the defense minister newly appointed by President Dương Văn Minh. General Trung asked me to listen to their conversation on an extension phone. From them, I knew that the general situation over most of the Mekong Delta provinces was quiet. At least two infantry divisions with full strength were available for reinforcement to Sài Gòn.

But the JGS Operations Center, the key instrument to coordinate all movements, operations, and supports, ceased operating because only a few officers and NCOs were present. General Trung told me that even if the two divisions were in Sài Gòn that very minute, they could only extend the fate of the capital city for a few more days or a week when aid was cut. He looked tired, and I could tell how he was feeling lonely by his voice and his eyes.

That was my sleepless night, and the roaring of a dozen helicopters evacuating people from the U.S. embassy only 100 yards from my barracks terrified me. I asked the guards to patrol around the block, warning them that bomb attacks were possible. Standing on the street corner beside the barrack, I could see thousands of Vietnamese stuck fast to the fence of the embassy. I tried to reach a U.S. Marine sergeant and ask him to let the two American reporters in, but no luck, as no one was allowed in or out after about 7 PM.

I felt paralyzed by despair. However, I was calm enough to deploy the guards platoon to maintain order around the barrack and around the embassy in coordination with the police. I had my men clear people away from the Thống Nhất Boulevard in front of the World Vision Building on the left side of the embassy so that a Chinook helicopter could have a safe place to land, put a group of refugees aboard, and then fly away. A big tree in the embassy backyard broke under the strong wind of the Jolly Green helicopter, thus hindering others from landing in the backyard. After that, only the Hueys (UH-1) landed on the top floor.

That night, for the first time in my life, I drank half a bottle of Jim Beam bourbon without getting drunk.

At 6 AM, General Trung went to the JGS meeting. He told Colonel Lương and me, the two field grade officers still present in the last minutes, that we must follow the order of the supreme command, which actually was the president's office. About an hour later, the general's sedan stopped at our front gate, dropping off his bodyguards. The driver took him to the Navy HQS. He kept his word that he would stay to the last minute. The last minutes were tickling slowly.

At about 8 AM, Captain Sơn, a French-language translator in my office returned after a trip along with the retired General Vanuxem (former commander of French Army Vietnam/North Southern Zone, who managed the June 1954 retreat from the five provinces south of Hà Nội). During the 1955–75 war, Vanuxem was the strongest French supporter of South Việt Nam. The general needed Sơn as an interpreter on his tour around Sài Gòn to look at the defense system. Sơn's pale face startled me when he stepped through the gate. He said that Vanuxem was totally disappointed.

"The general is certain that the soldiers who are still in defense positions will fight to the death. But we could stand no more than three days. When the communists move their heavy cannons closer, they will reduce this capital city to rubble. They will accept any price for the conquest of Sài Gòn. It is estimated that several thousand Saigonese will be killed. He said 'adieu' to me when he stopped by the Presidential Palace to advise General Minh to surrender," Sơn said.

I had the same opinion. At the time, Sài Gòn was prepared for a major battle. Food and fuel stock was enough for the population of 1 million people, and there was enough medicine for the many hundreds of injured a day to last at least one month, according to a classified report from the JGS. But we could be defeated sooner than one month, perhaps in a week, because we had no more ammunition or other military supplies.

Although the troops in Sài Gòn were serving supporting units and they were rather dejected, I was certain that most of them would fight fiercely before they were routed. A flame always flares up before dying out.

The blue sky over Sài Gòn was clear and ominously quiet. On a regular day, Sài Gòn airspace used to be filled with the low rumbling of all kinds of airplanes, military and commercial. But that morning, the unusual silence heightened the people's fear. At about 7 AM, the last two U.S. Chinook helicopters circled around downtown Sài Gòn and headed east toward the sea.

Sài Gòn was in its last hour. Loud explosions of communist shelling were heard all around the city's northwest region and more from the Tấn Sơn Nhất Airport.

At about 10:30 AM, General Dương Văn Minh, then president, announced his decision to surrender. Although I had expected it, the order to drop weapons shocked me. My eyes ached. The visual angle of my eyes seemed to shrink narrower, and everything around me looked as if it were shrouded by a veil of gray mist.

The thought of suicide flashed through my mind and seemed attractive. I held my pistol against my temple, thinking of what would happen if I stayed alive and suffered from my enemy's atrocity.

My jeep driver rushed in. "Don't do that, please, I beg you," he said. His cheeks were smeared with tears and oil because he was checking the jeep engine. He held my arm and stuttered, "If you decide to end your life to go down there in the Netherworld, let me go along with you and I will keep being your driver." He was a devoted Buddhist.

He was a stammerer. When getting excited, his words were jostling hard to get out of his throat. I couldn't help laughing at his words and his countenance. His funny acts somehow calmed me. I told him that I did not decide anything but would wait and see.

"Pet Soldiers"—those who paid bribes or got help from high connections to be assigned noncombat jobs around Sài Gòn—were still present in my barracks. Many of them said they would rather fight to death than surrender and refused to go home when I told them that they were allowed to leave the barracks if they would because I didn't consider them fit for combat.

A company of ninety paratroops under a captain, drifted from the front line, asked me to let them join the suicidal last battle. A group of about fifty police officers—half were field police—in a station nearby asked me to join as well. Three of the police who had been protecting the embassy the previous night said, "Sir, we've done our best to protect the people who have a good chance to be evacuated by the Americans, and we have wished them good luck. There must be some who stay for those who go. Now it's our next thing to do. That is to fight."

I reported their request to the assistant commander, Colonel Nguyễn Văn Lương, a brave and honest anticommunist veteran since 1945, then the highest-ranking officer present in my unit, the General Political Warfare Department. He ordered me to tell the troops that their willingness to fight was highly appreciated, but that they had to abide by the order of the president.

With eyes full of angry tears, he said, "Your suicidal fight, however heroic it could be, will not be mentioned by even one single word in the now unfriendly western media. Your self-sacrifice will be for nothing. You see, even thousands of unarmed civilians' remains found in mass graves around Hué in 1968 were ignored or reported with only a few short sentences no longer than a notice for a lost pet dog, let alone your 300 lives. Furthermore, there are your parents, wives, and children. Just do as we are required by the order."

I stepped out into the front yard. The Airborne troops still sat on the roofs and the surrounding walls. Some were crying. Some took their weapons apart and threw the parts away when I told their captain the colonel's final order.

My heart sank when I realized the stark truth: the armed forces of a million soldiers with the formidable Airborne and Marine divisions; the Air Force of nearly 1,200 airplanes, including 800 rotary wing planes, the fourth most powerful on the list of the world air forces; the Navy with strong coastal and river force; the National Police of over 150,000 members—all were defeated so easily by the enemy, which was weaker in strength and in sophisticated means of war but had faithful allies.

It was like a lengthy nightmare.

A BROKEN COGWHEEL

In my last minutes as an ARVN field grade officer, I was filled with sorrow about my service and the goals I had failed to realize. I had served the RVN Army for nineteen years, six months, and twenty-five days. Who could easily put behind such a long career?

The unforgettable minute came at last as nobody could guess what would happen next. When the communist troops of a battalion along with their commander entered the barracks, Colonel Lương calmly received them. Their commander talked to the colonel politely, addressing him as "Colonel." After handing over control of the installation to the communist commander, the colonel told him he must pay a farewell salute to the flag. The two guards slowly lowered the red-stripes-on-yellow banner, then folded and placed it on the table of the gate security office. We then left for home.

I realized later that the communists didn't behave so considerately in other areas out of the capital city. In many provinces, they detained officers and seized their homes, looting and even killing a lot of civilians who were labeled "reactionaries" not long after the surrender took effect.

I changed into civilian clothes and returned home. The streets around my neighborhood where the ARVN forces and the Self-Defense Corps held the last line of defense were littered with discarded tanks, weapons of all kinds, flak jackets, helmets, and field uniforms. The scene would never fade from my memory.

I would never forget how my mother and wife looked at me without a word when I stepped in. I took my Vespa scooter to go watch the enemy advance into Sài Gòn. My mother decided that my wife should go with me.

Not far from my street, the first NVA troops from the front on the west of the city were moving in. I could tell that it was a battalion by the Chinese-made radios and by its commander rank—captain—marching in formation of three rifle companies. However, it had no more than about thirty soldiers in each company. Information from J-2 intelligence reports in early April was proved correct. Personnel strength of the NVA units ran very low in the last battles.

The NVA troops were moving cautiously, their faces tense, while people along the streets were quietly watching from behind half-opened windows and doors.

Following the communist troops at a distance were thousands of disarmed ARVN soldiers from different units and the boot camp west of Sài Gòn. They were also marching into the city. Their talks made the air noisy, while coffee shops, restaurants, and houses that had anything to drink or eat opened their doors and invited the defeated soldiers to come in and served them beer, soda, coffee, soup, noodles, rice, and even cigarettes, almost everything for their refreshment, and free of cost.

Only long after that did pro-communist figures show up on the streets in downtown Sài Gòn along with a few hundred spectators, welcoming the incoming NVA units. A group of young men called the people to cooperate with the victorious army on the airwaves of Radio Sài Gòn. Most of the city homes and businesses were closed. The communist army units were not welcomed as warmly as they might have expected.

Five doors from my home lived an army major and his family. The major, Đặng Sĩ Vĩnh, his wife, and seven children committed suicide after a big lunch. Each drank some kind of sleeping drug and laid down, side by side, on the floor. The major shot his wife, the children, and himself in the head with his .45 pistol. He had scribbled a note: "Dear neighbors, my family can't live under the communist regime. We have to end our misery this way. Please forgive us and help my relatives bury us. In our safe there is a little money. Please use it for our burial expenses. Thank you and farewell!"

All around the capital, privates, sergeants, officers, civil servants, doctors, and statesmen committed suicide. Former minister Trần Chánh Thành also ended his life. Police Lieutenant Colonel Nguyễn Văn Long shot himself with a pistol in front of the Lower House Building on Tự Do Street.[2]

Days later we heard that four ARVN generals who were known as incorruptible, talented commanders, Nguyễn Viết Thanh, Lê Văn Hưng, Nguyễn Văn Hai, and Phạm Văn Phú, had taken their own lives. The brave province chief of Chương Thiện, Colonel Hồ Ngọc Cẩn, fought to his last minute and was executed by the communists in front of 100 compelled spectators.

Rather than frightening me, their deaths tempted me. For the first time, I knew why people took their own lives when they were in extreme despair. It took me two long days to recover from the desire for a painless death.

I found out later that my mother secretly had my children take turns watching me in case I did "something unusual." She and my wife hid all the knives, razors, drugs, and ropes.

The way my family took great care of me was one of the many factors that calmed me. Moreover, my mother said in her choked but energetic voice: "They defeated you, but they do not win the total and eternal victory. They can't do all that they want to destroy us."

That afternoon while I was upstairs, completely in despair and waiting for the worst thing to come, I heard my mother talking to some young man and inviting him in. I overheard him telling my mom that he was a corporal in one of our Eighteenth Infantry Division combat units.

He had been wounded in his left foot a week before and was in the Cộng Hòa Military General Hospital when the surrender was announced. He was kicked out of the hospital along with his other wounded and sick fighting fellows by the first NVA unit that occupied the hospital.

He had not a penny in his field dress pockets. Hesitantly, he asked my mom for a little money, together with what was given by other families in my neighborhood, to help him go back to his home in Cà Mâu, the southernmost province of Việt Nam 150 miles from Sài Gòn.

My mom called me to come downstairs. He asked my mother if I was her son. My mother thought he would be pleased when she told the poor corporal, "Don't worry, he is an army major."

Stepping downstairs, I saw him in his field dress, spotted with blood, the light blue pajamas of the hospital on his left arm. At my mom's last word, he instinctively jumped up but failed and dropped again to the tile floor, as his painful wound didn't let him stand up. "Oh, no. I can't see him," he stuttered. "He will call me down badly. A soldier goes begging for money. No, he won't wink at it."

I quickly stopped him. "Stay there. I'd like to talk to you." He tried to stand up once again, this time pulling himself up with one hand on the doorknob, the other leaning on a crutch. He tried to raise his right hand to salute me, but stopped before his hand reached his brows.

I felt like laughing but held back and said to him, "Our republic is no more. Our armed forces have collapsed. I am no more a major, and you are no more a corporal. Why do you care?"

The young corporal looked straight at me. I could read a muted protest in his eyes. After a moment of silence, he said with a voice articulated but monotonous in deep thinking, "No sir. I don't think so. Despite what the communists are saying, our people will never forget that you are a major and I am a corporal whenever you or I do anything good or bad."

At last, he accepted my mother's gift of VN\$2,000 (\$4 at the time). The money he was given by my neighbors amounted up to about VN\$10,000, enough to pay for the bus and boat fares to his village. One of the cyclo drivers in my neighborhood volunteered to drive him to the bus station where all bus owners offered him and soldiers like him free rides to their home provinces. It was one of the cyclo drivers down the alley from my home who had picked up the corporal on the street in front of the military hospital and brought him to our neighborhood so that he could get help.

Those cyclo drivers and other witnesses recounted that within minutes of taking over the Cộng Hòa Military General Hospital, the communist soldiers received orders to kick all 1,000 ARVN patients out onto the streets, even those who were on operating tables. Seriously wounded soldiers, whose limbs were torn and bleeding, some even with stomachs cut open and intestines exposed, were pulled out to the terrace in front of the hospital gate. Many died in a short time. I had never imagined that such barbarism would happen.

"Word spread quickly," said the cyclo drivers in my alley. "In half an hour, hundreds of cyclos rushed into the streets around the hospital and offered the wounded soldiers free rides to wherever they wanted to go. Most were heading for the cross-country bus stations." He added, "Many cyclo drivers not only gave them free rides but also bought them food. Some even brought them to their homes for nice meals before driving them to the bus stations."

It was quite a surprise to me. But that evening, the cyclo drivers and some poor workers in the alley made me much more surprised when they came to see me and an army captain, a block from my home.

"You should stay home, particularly at night," they said. "If VC knock on your door to see you, don't let them in until we come to stand by you. You'd better call us from your second floor windows. We sure can hear you."

I shook their hands with sincere thanks. One of them reassured me, "You may have thought I was a VC . . ." He did not go on, but I could guess what he meant to say.

"Aren't you afraid of being in trouble because of me?" I asked. One of them shook his head and said, "You can't reason with them, but we poor workers can. They have to rely on us to exist unless we do something really big against them."

My family home was in a suburb of Sài Gòn where middle-class and poor families had lived together peacefully for many decades. During the war, many peasants from Central Việt Nam provinces moved into Sài Gòn suburbs to avoid the war. Their home villages were under severe communist influence. Many people in Sài Gòn were looking at them dubiously.

They earned their living by menial works including driving cyclos. They used to complain about the government. Their language always made me more convinced that they might have been VCs or at least that they sympathized with the communist side.

On that day, many of my neighbors also admitted that we had been seriously wrong. Many facts in war were too complicated and abstract to understand, even to us Vietnamese, let alone foreigners.

* * *

Many ARVN units were fighting to the last minute beside the ARVN Eighteenth Infantry Division in Long Khánh, north of Sài Gòn. The bold resistance of 100 junior cadets of the Junior Military Academy in Vũng Tàu was remarkable. Two cadets from my neighborhood came back and recounted the story of their short fighting.

There were more than 100 of the junior cadets, most of them twelve to fifteen years old, who stayed at the academy while the others were spending the early summer vacation at home. The advancing communists met fierce resistance from the cadets for a few hours. At last, after accepting a truce, the young boys stood at attention to strike the national colors. Then they snuck out the back gates and into the nearby neighborhood. Communist forces had no choice but to let them go.

THE FIRST MONTH UNDER THE COMMUNIST REGIME

Only two or three hours after NVA forces took over Sài Gòn, many communist field grade officers were fighting one another over the possession of luxurious homes whose owners had fled the country. In some cases, troops under the contending officers were fighting with AK-47 rifles to seize their properties. The most favored targets were beautiful villas around Tân Sơn Nhất Airport.

Ten miles away, communist officers and officials evicted most of the owners from their private villas in the Thủ Đức University Village on short notice and allowed them only to take their clothes and personal articles.

On highways and local roads, our soldiers were robbed of their bikes, especially motorcycles and personal valuables. Besides, several military and police officers were murdered in villages around Sài Gòn and in the provinces in the first three days; many were killed after being robbed. A lot of local government officials and army officers were evicted from their own homes at ten minutes' notice, leaving behind all their possessions.

Sources from Huế alleged that several hundred Việt Quốc and Đại Việt members were assassinated in the first weeks of April when Huế fell. Most of the other members were sent to reeducation camps with others who had been serving the RVN government.

Fortunately, there was no bloodbath in Sài Gòn but only single cases of covert executions and kidnappings, possibly because the presence of many foreign observers and reporters hindered them.

In many small Mekong Delta provinces where communist guerrillas' activities had almost been insignificant for years before 1975, no communist official or officer showed up to take over the province until twenty-four or even forty-eight hours after President Dương Văn Minh announced the unconditional surrender.

In those localities, only a few dozen VC guerrillas appeared in the province capital cities to accept the surrender. They had to wait several days until ranking communists were appointed to assume their responsibilities.

THE LONGEST WEEKS

On the first day controlling Sài Gòn, the communist city military command called all former RVN officials and officers to report to its many offices and to register their names and addresses. Everybody was thinking of similar procedures that communist forces had applied in Huế during the 1968 Tết Offensive a few days before 5,000 victims were slain and dumped into mass graves. They were frightened at what might become of them, but they had to wait and see without any way to react or resist.

Daily radio programs were filled with arrogant commentaries and boasting news reports. Stories about invented crimes of the former regime were repeated day and night. Communist leaders broke their promises and asserted, "There will be no reconciliation and concordance with civil and military members of the puppet regime."[3]

The arrogant conquerors seemed to enjoy humiliating the former Sài Gòn regime, not excluding its fallen soldiers. A few days after April 30, communist authorities destroyed monuments honoring the RVN war dead (front gates, memorials) in many ARVN cemeteries around the country. In some places, they even destroyed their graves. In Sài Gòn, they vandalized the Gò Vấp ARVN Cemetery and displayed a signboard that read, "Here lie the Americans' puppet soldiers after they have paid for their crimes." Not long after that, they bulldozed the entire cemetery for their government building construction.

The large ARVN National Cemetery near Sài Gòn-Biên Hòa Highway was still there, but many graves were vandalized. The famous statue "Thương Tiếc" (The Mourning Soldier) at the front of the cemetery was destroyed.

May 1975 saw great and chaotic changes in Sài Gòn. Communist army drivers, who used to conduct military trucks only on the jungle trails, drove Molotova trucks wildly without any idea about one-way streets, traffic lights, and signs. They caused many fatal accidents.

The first swarm of communist cadres from North Việt Nam rushed to Sài Gòn and other cities in the South. Many of them carried clothes, earthenware pots, low-grade enamel bowls and spoons, chopsticks, and even rice as gifts to their South Vietnamese relatives living in Sài Gòn. They believed that their relatives in the South were suffering a great shortage of cooking utensils, clothes, and rice because the Americans had confiscated all consumer goods produced in the South for their American markets. They realized in no time that they had fallen for Hà Nội's fabricated stories.

North Vietnamese who came to the South later learned the good lessons quickly. They visited with their relatives who settled in Sài Gòn and asked for anything available: mostly clothing, tools, utensils, chinaware, medicines, or some expensive appliances such as electric fans, radios, cassettes, and TV sets.

The former capital of South Việt Nam looked like a patient just released from the hospital. Only small stores were open. Day and night, long military convoys were transporting everything from the occupied South to the North—guns, rifles, jeeps and trucks, military equipment, medicines, furniture, luxury goods, bikes, motorbikes, motors, engines, rice, and almost everything else.

Right after occupying Sài Gòn, communist local leaders quickly installed their ruling machine. People in the neighborhoods had to attend ward meetings three or four nights a week. Lecturers were mostly abecedarian secret agents who had formal educations no higher than second grade.

In some areas, communist local authorities ordered all sewing machines owners to work in co-operatives. In others, they organized villagers into an agricultural co-operative. At some wards in Sài Gòn, communist cadres set up "people's courts" to try criminals with the attendance of about 100 people at each court. They asked the mob to vote for a sentence after a brief denunciation of the suspects' crimes. In some extreme cases involving murders, the communist cadres proposed death sentences and insisted on approving votes, but people objected vehemently to the communist cadres' verdicts.

In the first weeks after April 30, there were orders overtly issued from top-level authority to eradicate every cultural and educational work in the South. Public security cadres coming from the North and newly recruited members searched houses, bookstores, and libraries that they suspected of having many "counterrevolutionary" materials. They confiscated all kinds of publications, disks, and tapes. They burned them or sold them to recycling plants for a little money. Many families and libraries lost their rare and valuable collections of literature, music, and technical publications. Of course, political materials were the first targets, particularly anticommunist papers.

Fortunately, the national library was spared. Besides, many families were somehow aware or had experienced the communists' cultural policies. They successfully hid their favorite books, tapes, and disks.

In North Việt Nam after the 1954 Geneva Accords when the Việt Minh took control, a campaign was launched to eliminate all noncommunist cultural materials, literature, music recordings and scores, and art. All were confiscated and destroyed.

The trade of discarded papers in the South after April 30, 1975, was prosperous. Novels, documentaries, scientific works, magazines, thesauruses, encyclopedias, textbooks, and collections of poetry in Vietnamese and foreign languages were sold by panicky owners at dirt-cheap prices. Tons of police fingerprint cards and birth, death, and marriage records were sold by communist occupying units to paper mills for recycling.

The first North Vietnamese government and party officials following the front line soldiers to take over military and civilian installations were surprised to see that everything in the South was far different from what they had been taught. Some of them I met frankly admired South Việt Nam's progress in science and technology compared with what they observed in the Soviet Union.

But some North Vietnamese specialists with limited technical knowledge couldn't understand modern technology. North Vietnamese doctors assigned to take over the largest military hospital in Sài Gòn refused the use of the most advanced blood test machine. It was the first sophisticated digital tester recently invented and installed by American specialists at the ARVN Cộng Hòa Military General Hospital that could produce test results in a much shorter time.

According to a friend of mine, a doctor working at the ward, the new communist boss stated that the machine was made by the American Imperialists to kill the Vietnamese patriots slowly but certainly. He then ordered workers to dismantle it.

Other better-educated North Vietnamese doctors were honest. Those from Hà Nội who took over Hùng Vương Maternity Hospital in Sài Gòn said to the South Vietnamese doctors who were serving in the hospital, "We are sorry to tell you that in North Việt Nam, uterine perforation occurs in 7–8 percent of cases of uterus curettage. You must be prepared to work under such conditions." They said so in the handover meeting when the South Vietnamese doctors reported that among medical malpractices in South Việt Nam, uterine perforation in curettage procedures rarely if ever occurred.

Most of the Saigonese was surprised when they met communist cadres and soldiers. The communists, the officers in particular, were unmitigated boasters. There were stories recited by thousands of them with the same version. Perhaps they learned them by heart from the same texts at their political indoctrination classes.

One typical lie was that North Vietnamese MiG pilots often lay in ambush by *hovering* inside large banks of thick clouds, waiting for hours to take down the U.S. warplanes. Another was that a North Việt Nam operator was conducting a single antiaircraft SAM missile in such a way that brought down seven American B-52 bombers: "He was manning the SAM to approach each B-52 so close that he forced the crews to bail out from six of them and finished off the seventh by detonating the missile," they said.

One of the anecdotes propagated in the NVA political indoctrination classes was about Henry Kissinger's secret trip to Hà Nội to begin his negotiations with communist leaders. The story ran that when Kissinger visited the War Museum, the first thing he saw was Hồ Chí Minh's statement "There is nothing more precious than Independence and Freedom" on a large board above the main entrance. The words scared Kissinger into profusely sweating, and he quickly accepted Hà Nội leaders' conditions for a peace agreement.

The fact that so many North Vietnamese soldiers and educated people believed such impossible stories was incredible to the foreigners' ears, but it was the moral strength of the North Vietnamese Army.

South Vietnamese people on first contact with the communist forces were somewhat startled about corruption in the NVA units. Right on the first day in Sài Gòn, all of those in charge of buying food and goods for their units openly proposed fraudulent deals to storekeepers and other vendors. They would pay the amount of money on the vendors' invoice while the actual quantity of merchandise they received would be about 50 percent. The two sides would divide the overpayment.

Before April 1975, most South Vietnamese believed that under the iron fist of the communist regime, corruption wasn't able to exist in the North. After meeting newcomers from the North, South Vietnamese learned that right since 1954 when the communists took over Hà Nội, corruption was spreading all over North Việt Nam. In the land where people were living in extreme poverty, bribes for a job in a factory could cost an applicant a month's pay, which was similar to what a South Vietnamese had to pay for being hired as a secretary in an office. According to the North Vietnamese, most officials and officers managing the financial or logistic offices were rich, several times richer than their counterparts in other branches.

FORMER RVN CIVIL SERVANTS AND SOLDIERS

As I mentioned earlier, on May 1, all former South Vietnamese soldiers, civil servants, and members of political parties were to report to the dozen communist security offices in Sài Gòn. We were told to register our name, address, rank, job, and unit or agency in which we served. Then we were told to go home and await further instructions.

Despair turned me to extreme pessimism. From then until forty-five days later, when we were imprisoned, I always wore clothes bought in Fort Benning with colorful patterns and styles that were seldom found in Việt Nam. In 1968 at Huế, where hundreds of victims were buried in mass graves, their relatives quickly identified only remains clad in garments with rare colors and patterns.

The new communist authorities didn't do anything brutal against most of us former RVN officers in Sài Gòn. Killing, torturing, and looting occurred in the countryside.

We were not considered citizens of the new regime, nor aliens, nor professed prisoners. We just stayed home and might visit with friends within the capital city.

In the first few months, the Communist Military Administration had only a limited number of security agents while communist army units were able to take care of military matters. Without enough security agents, the communist authority could not keep close watch over former RVN government and military members. Therefore, most of us were not harassed. The communist political security agencies' efforts were directed at those who were key persons in RVN intelligence agencies and especially the CIA informants. Many of them were detained or interrogated for intelligence information. Many arrests were made at night.

THUS THE VIỆT NAM WAR STOPPED

My stories of the war should have ended here. However, the consequences of the war have been lingering endlessly since April 30, 1975. I am one of the millions of Vietnamese on both sides who bear scars from the sixty-year conflict. So my memories should go on with what happened to me after my fellows and I were incarcerated until the day I moved to the United States. Events in South Việt Nam after the communist takeover basically defined the cause of war.

Stories of life in Vietnamese communist prison camps could take up a few hundred pages in a separate volume. Therefore, I will only describe the most remarkable events in the following pages of this memoir.

Years after "Black April," as Vietnamese refugees called the month when Sài Gòn fell, I only regret two things: I did not fight to the last minute as Mrs. Mulhall said, and I did not fire any round for the old lady and the old gentleman on the Greyhound bus as they had requested.

PART V

After the War

TWENTY-SEVEN

Prisoner

JUNE 15, 1975

What we were waiting for came at last. On June 9, the communist military governor of Sài Gòn announced his decision to call all former RVN field grade officers and ranking civil servants, including elected legislative officials, to report for "reeducation." Everyone knew the rhetoric meant "incarceration" or, to be more exact, "incarceration in a concentration camp." The ARVN NCOs and enlisted men in the Sài Gòn area had been ordered to attend the three-day reeducation class at the wards in late May. They were then released to live with their families.

Communist authorities in the provinces acted differently. In most areas, military officers, civil servants, and other notables were detained right after April 30. The NCOs and troops were subjected to "local reeducation" and released. In other areas, they were sent to serve the unlimited terms in forced labor projects that included clearing land mines left from the war.

On June 15, 1975, I left home for the reeducation camp.

The announcement was composed with words selected to make people think the course might last for one month. It said, "Each must bring an amount of money for one month's food." Many of us thought we would be free after thirty days in the camps. I didn't think so, but I avoided sharing my opinion with my family members lest they should be worry too much about me. I tried to appear carefree but was unable to hide my true feelings from my wife. As if reading my thoughts, she only held me tight and said, "I feel it'll be long, but be brave, our lives will be brighter someday."

So I began my long journey to an unknown destination.

THE FIRST CONCENTRATION CAMP

Those who were supposed to be "reeducated" by communist authorities re-ported to several places depending on their residence. In the small hours of June 16 they were sent to dozens of concentration camps around the areas of Sài Gòn, Biên Hòa, and Xuân Lộc.

I was detained in the former base camp of the ARVN Fifth Engineer Group in Hóc Môn, seven miles northwest of Sài Gòn. The camp held about 1,500 majors, captains, and lieutenants. Officers lower than major reported to the camps a week after I did. We were detained in groups, each of about fifty officers of the same rank. The headquarters of a communist regiment with only an NVA company ran the camp like other camps all over South Việt Nam. Each of the twenty groups in turn prepared rice and food for a 150-man bloc. My camp had more than 800 men in six blocs. A civilian contractor provided raw food in the morning.

Communist political officers delivered ten political lessons about great achievements of their regime and "the war crimes of the American imperialists" as main topics. We laughed a lot at the made-up allegations and tall tales, but most of the time the "instructors" kept lecturing. We had to write an autobiographical sketch that filled one or two pages. No interrogation or cross-examination was carried out.

CHRISTMAS 1975

On December 23, the camp command informed us that we would be allowed to celebrate Christmas. But on the afternoon of December 25, we were ordered to conduct religious practices inside houses, not in the yard, as we had requested.

At 9:00 PM, ten of my friends and I, all Buddhists, set up a team guarding a covered nook where two Catholic military chaplains were hearing confession. One of my team members acted as monitor, giving a sign to each of the waiting men when his turn came. The task went smoothly, and confession ended at 11:30. Then at midnight, Catholics at each house sang two popular Christmas carols in unison. Communist soldiers stayed outside, watching.

During the last months of 1975, we were idling away the time, doing very little work except for tasks that served ourselves. Around the camps in Hóc Môn area, there was no farmland available for the prisoners to work on. We spent time learning and teaching one another everything we could (English, French, music, Chinese characters, Chinese horoscopy), and playing cards.

Many of us with dexterity spent time making small artworks, such as carving pictures on duralumin plates or making combs decorated with tiny drawings. Other fellows were successful in making metallic xylophones and various objects.

I spent twenty days making a guitar and a chromatic flute with five-semitone keys. Owing to a great amount of equipment of all kinds left by the Fifth ARVN Engineer Group in the large warehouses, we could procure lots of materials for different works: brass and duralumin tubes, aluminum sheets, stainless steel plates.

NVA soldiers broke to pieces expensive machines such as bulldozers, levelers, and dump trucks to take their component parts just for fun, out of their ignorance of the value of heavy equipment that cost several hundred thousands of dollars. After they started the destruction, we were free to search the machines for materials we needed.

RVN officers and government officials confined in scores of camps in the provinces were not as lucky as their fellows in Sài Gòn. From the first days, prisoners in most provincial camps did forced labor, working in rice fields, digging irrigation canals, making fish and shrimp farms, and lumbering. At some places, they worked from eight to ten hours a day, seven days a week. In other camps, they were forced to clear land mines with spikes and bayonets and suffered a number of deaths. There were even cases of executions upon the decision of the communist camps' authorities. Women Army Corps (WAC) Second Lieutenant Nguyễn Thị Kim Lang was sentenced to death and executed at the Gò Công City soccer field on July 15, 1975, while she was pregnant, after she voiced her vehement protest against the communist policies. I only knew the information when the first relatives of my prisoner group were granted permission to visit in April 1976.

TẾT 1976

An order from the Communist Military Administrative Committee permitted our families to send Tết gifts to us. All wives and mothers did their best to send something to their husbands and sons for the most important holiday. Among candies and traditional gifts for the Lunar New Year celebration, my wife sent me an English-Vietnamese dictionary and half a dozen books, including Mark Twain's *Life on the Mississippi* and John Steinbeck's *Grapes of Wrath*.[1] The camp allowed the Bible and literature works in foreign languages. Many other camps did not.

In the first months of 1976, I continued running an English class to help my many fellows speak and write better English, which they had learned years ago when they were high school students. Among materials used as textbooks was the Bible. One day we came to Luke 23:34 in the New Testament, relating the story of Jesus Christ on his way to the Skull where he would be crucified. To the followers about the soldiers who tortured and insulted him, Luke 23:34 reads, "And Jesus said, '*Father, forgive them, for they know not what they do.*' And, parting out his garments, they cast lots." Suddenly the words shed a new light in my mind. The great Jesus did forgive the soldiers who inflicted extreme pains on his body because they didn't know what they were doing (only by orders of their superiors). So why would we not forgive those communists who, also carrying out their superiors' orders, were finding every way to humiliate and torture us, even to kill us, when there was a good reason? They "don't know what they are doing." We should not bear animosity to them but have compassion for them instead.

When Luke 23:34 came to me, I attained a profound perception of forgiving, not only from the Bible but also from the Sacred Books of Buddhism.

We were allocated food at average rations in the first weeks, and then the rations decreased in the following months. But the lowest was still as high as a South Vietnamese farmer's meal. Corruption ran wild. NVA supply officers stole from the food allowance by sharing illegal profits with civilian food providers.

Sometime we asked communist officers when we would be released, and most of them responded with ambiguous answers that came to nothing. Only one communist lieutenant colonel said bluntly, "As soldiers of a regime, you are not guilty of anything. The party herds you into the camps just for political security concerns, not for reeducation, because there is no way to reeducate you or me. When the party feels it's safe to let you go back to your areas, you'll be freed." We knew he had told us this of his own accord. Once a group of about fifteen communist colonels came and met with about twenty of us who had been selected by background, including me. They asked each of us to write an essay about the attitude of the poor South Vietnamese toward the new regime. The group's leading officer said, "When we came to newly liberated areas, we expected that the proletarians in the South would be happy to welcome us. But most of the poor workers and farmers are giving us the cold shoulder. Some even refused to repair our bikes, sell us merchandise, or give us direction of way around."

We said we would carry out the task on condition that there would be an official written order from competent communist central authorities. After a week they returned without producing any kind of paper we asked for, but they discussed the topic with us. We only gave them our general ideas without going into details lest they could use them for some unpredictable tricks against us. We said the southerners lived in a society where they could have information from any source and always be free to express their ideas and that they were fed up with propaganda from both sides. That greatly affected their attitude and manners.

THE FAILED ESCAPE

One night at 11:30 PM, we were awakened by gunshots on the west side of the camp. Two fellows, Quách Hồng Quang and Nguyễn Văn Thịnh, had failed an attempt to escape. They were shot at the middle of the barbed wire fence. Quang was hit in the leg and groaned in pain. An NVA lieutenant who was in charge of barrack security shot him three or four times with his K-54 pistol. Quang died instantly. Thịnh was wounded but shammed being dead. When it was discovered that Thịnh was alive, the communist camp commander refused to move him inside for first aid. We strongly voiced protests, and Thịnh was brought to a dispensary for first aid. He was then held incommunicado in a metal container known as a U.S. Army "connex" for several months until he was executed in April 1976.

CAMP TÂN HIỆP

March 1976

All the 800-plus ARVN majors in Camp Hóc Môn were moved to Camp Tân Hiệp, south of Biên Hòa. It had been a former communist POW camp of the ARVN Military Region III. Camp Tân Hiệp consisted of five adjacent annexes; each held about 1,200 former ARVN officers. When we arrived, nearly 6,000 prisoners had already been moved there from different places around Sài Gòn. We had to do a little farmwork. Food rations were the same as in previous months.

More than twenty ARVN generals were in one of the annexes, including one imitation general. He was a loony young guy who had escaped the local asylum. He had been loitering around Sài Gòn markets for months before the city fell wearing a tattered dirty green uniform with three paper stars glued on each of his shoulder strap. He called himself "Lieutenant General Nguyễn Huệ, commander of the Quang Trung Army Corps." Nguyễn Huệ was the true name of King Quang Trung, the Napoleon of Việt Nam. Almost everyone in Sài Gòn knew this insane person and knew that there was no army corps of that name. But communist authorities believed that he *was* a CIA general officer. So they locked him up as a general. Only after several months was he released.

In Camp Annex 4 where I was, there was a nine-year-old boy prisoner. A year before 1975, he led an airborne unit to a site in his village where he had seen a communist agent hiding some weapons. He was rewarded with a little money for the information. After April 30, the boy was imprisoned as a "CIA informant." He spent almost a year in the camp.

Many of us bribed some NVA guards at the camp for secret communication by short letters to our families. From these sources, we were informed of events outside. The news about the gunfight between a group of resistance activists and the communist force at the Vinh Sơn church in Sài Gòn did not bring us any hope, but we all admired the great courage of the Vinh Sơn militants. The fighting lasted a day, and most of the militants were killed or taken captive. At the end of 1976, three of the militants—two of them were Catholic priests—were executed.

Camp Tân Hiệp did not allow our fellows who were doctors to treat us when we got sick. In Annex 4 where I was, an NVA corporal, who had graduated as a medic after a six-month course in the jungle, was in charge of treatment of prisoners. He examined patients and gave prescriptions. A prisoner who had been a surgeon and medical corps lieutenant colonel commanding the ARVN Seventy-second Medical Group was appointed "assistant" to the NVA medic corporal. Every morning, the lieutenant colonel carried a set of syringes and related equipment with him to do the task of injection following the NVA corporal's prescription.

One day the colonel objected to the corporal's Rx, stating that the remedy would pose fatal risks to the patient. The corporal got upset, saying, "All of you Puppet Army doctors were paying bribes for graduation at the medical school. I can do better than all of you doctors in medical treatment." He pointed his AK at the colonel, threatening to blow out the colonel's brain. The colonel, in an unexpected reaction, boldly stood up and said, "If you dare, shoot me, but I can't kill the patient with this medicine." The "physician-corporal" gave up only when his NVA first lieutenant intervened.

THE SPECTACULAR WHIRLWIND

In early June 1976, three coffins were specially delivered to Camp Tân Hiệp. A few days later, the three prisoners who had been locked up in the three connexes for months were given haircuts, baths, and new clean clothes. They were Major Nguyễn Văn Thịnh, Major Tống Viết Lạc, and Major Trần Văn Bé. All three had attempted to escape. They were recaptured and locked up incommunicado. Nguyễn Văn Thịnh was the one who had failed to escape Camp Hóc Môn when I was there.

According to information we collected from a bribed communist sergeant, each camp around South Việt Nam had been ordered to select three names to be sentenced among the ARVN officers who attempted to escape and were caught. Two days before the scheduled trial, the sergeant told us that by a new order from the high command, there would be only two death sentences in each camp. At last, Thịnh and Bé were brought to the so-called court-martial, whereas Lạc was released from his connex back to the regular barracks with us.

I am sure that most former prisoners at the five sub-camps in Tân Hiệp still remember what happened in front of their eyes that afternoon.

The two court sessions began at 10 AM and 4 PM. Twenty-five prisoners from the five annexes were selected to attend the summary trials presided over by a communist lieutenant colonel. A friend whose sleeping place was next to mine described the court sessions to me after he attended the trial.

The procedures in the morning session were very simple and lasted less than thirty minutes. The court prosecutor was a communist lieutenant. He read aloud an accusatory document telling how the defendant, Major Trần Văn Bé, had snuck away while working at the camp's manioc field. He was caught twenty-four hours later. The NVA lieutenant's document included interrogation records and the defendant's background, citing his parents' biography to prove that he was "incorrigible." When the lieutenant concluded, the judge announced the death sentence following some questions he put to the defendant.

Bé protested, but the two NVA soldiers gagged his mouth with their hands. In ten seconds they pulled him into the front yard, pushed him against a wall of sandbags, loaded their AKs, and shot him. The two bursts of AK fire warned the prisoners of the fate of their comrade-in-arms.

The afternoon session was for ARVN Major Nguyễn Văn Thịnh, who had failed in an attempt to run away from Camp Hóc Môn. The prosecutor read a similar document. Again, the judge accepted the prosecutor's proposal and sentenced Thịnh to death.

Right after the judge's last words, the two guards wrestled Thịnh down on the floor, using a chopstick to force a piece of cloth into the defendant's mouth to prevent him from yelling protests against the communist regime as Major Bé had done that morning.

The rough hands of the guards made Thịnh's mouth bleed profusely. He was immediately pulled outside. In a corner of the yard only ten meters from the door, he was pushed against the wall of sandbags where Bé had been executed in the morning. The guards stepped back a few meters; then one of them riddled the victim with a burst of his AK that was followed by a finishing stroke.

At about 4:30 PM, I was eating a small bowl of rice when the burst of fire from the AK resounded throughout the rows of sheet metal houses. We knew what had happened. The AK report sounded like the one after the first trial that morning. My throat choked and I tried to keep me from throwing up. I stepped out to the yard.

Suddenly, all of us in the yard were stunned by a spectacle. At the place where Thịnh was just executed, about 100 yards from where we were standing, a small whirlwind was building up. It became 50 yards high, drawing dust and trash into a gray column that traveled slowly through all the five sub-camps before it disappeared at the gate to the west. The ghostly scene is still imprinted in the memory of everyone who was at Camp Tân Hiệp at the time.

In a camp in Long Giao, Biên Hòa, there was only one officer who ran away and was caught a few days later. The second officer picked out to be prosecuted had only written a message he intended to sneak to his wife, telling her of his intention to run away when he had a chance. The message fell into the hands of a communist officer. Because there was only one prisoner who had actually tried to escape, the other man was prosecuted on the charge as "having intention to escape." So two officers were sentenced to death as the communist high command required.

Later in the month, some NVA soldiers we bribed disclosed that the same thing had happened in every other camp. In case a camp had a large number of escapees, only the two that communist authorities decided were the most serious cases were pronounced guilty and executed.

How lucky were the others on the death lists.

July 1976

The so-called National Liberation Front, known as VC in Western media, along with its Provisional Revolutionary Government of the Republic of South Việt Nam, ended its existence in June 1976 after a short vote of hands in the Hà Nội Congress Hall. Thus the reunification of Việt Nam was declared. Then fifteen minutes later, by a similar vote, the Democratic Republic of Việt Nam was changed to "Socialist Republic of Việt Nam."

In the first year of securing rule over all Việt Nam, communist leaders' arrogance could be unbearable. Lê Duẩn, the party general secretary, once said in a formal speech that "after the next two or three five-year plans, Việt Nam will develop to be as strong as, or even stronger (in all aspects) than Japan and France." Some other Việt Nam communist leaders repeated his statement.

We all wondered why the top communist leaders who had been pragmatic revolutionaries in their struggle could blindly believe in such a utopia.

MOVING NORTH

In the second week of July, the first groups of former RVN servicemen incarcerated in South Việt Nam were moved by ship to prison camps north of the 17th parallel. The transfers continued until the end of the year.

The first group from Tân Hiệp departed with about 1,000 prisoners. I was in the second group of about 1,200 men, from Tân Hiệp and other camps in the region, to be moved to the North on June 26, two weeks after the first.

One afternoon, about a third of the prisoners of each camp annex on a list were ordered to gather in groups at the large yard of the camp with all our belongings. Communist officers rummaged through our bags and rucksacks. Except for dictionaries, other books and novels were labeled "reactionary materials" and were confiscated.

We were brought to Sài Gòn New Port at night on Molotova trucks. We boarded the ship by walking on an aluminum ladder placed at an angle of 30 degrees from the ground. It was difficult to hold the steps and to keep balance as its flat rungs were turned vertically with the thin edges up. The ladder had been made for use at high angle against walls, not as a walkway.

My friend, Major Phan (...) Tuân, with a heavy rucksack on his back, slipped at the middle of the ladder about two yards above ground and fell onto the concrete edge of the quay. I was the third in line from him, waiting to step to the ladder about ten yards away. The second fellow was at the first rung of the ladder. A communist soldier standing about five yards from me ran to my side, unbuckled his rifle strap, and motioned with his head for me to give him a hand to keep Tuân from falling into the river. He didn't ask the second fellow who was trying to keep his balance on the first few steps of the ladder. But the communist lieutenant in charge of my group stopped the soldier and me and said, "Stay back, comrade, it's not your business." He turned to me and pushed me back, saying, "Don't move out of your line." Tuân sank slowly as the slow current drifted him away in front of us.

When it was my turn to board, I felt as if I were walking a tight rope in a circus. Fortunately, no one else fell, as those who were already on the ship held each other's arms to reach their fellows and help them one by one walk on the narrow, slippery ladder.

We were crammed into one of the cargo holds that was too narrow for 300 prisoners. No one could lie down. A fifty-gallon fuel barrel was placed at a corner as a makeshift latrine. Five unlucky fellows had to sit around the barrel, which leaked. They had to suffer all the worst in life from other friends who roosted on the thin edge of the rusty barrel to discharge their bowels, and their clothes became soaked with leaking liquid wastes. No one was benevolent enough to share their horrible suffering. They exclaimed as if they had been under the dangers on the battlefield: "No complaining. Fate wills it so." Yes, everyone has his own destiny.

On the second day, one officer—later identified as ARVN Marine Major Nguyễn Văn Nhiều—committed suicide by taking a large dose of some drug. Fellows around me all prayed for him silently.

When some of our fellows raised a question of how the ARVN had done in moving communist prisoners back and forth from the prison camps on the islands of Phú Quốc and Côn Sơn, a former military police captain asserted that though the best convenience couldn't be provided to a large group of prisoners, what the RVN authorities had done in similar transportation was decent enough and not as barbaric as the communists were doing to us.

For three days, until we landed at the northern port of Hải Phòng, I didn't eat but drank little gulps of water each morning. Then we were loaded onto a train of cargo wagons pulled by an old steam engine over narrow gauge railways, similar to trains from the U.S. Civil War era. Fifty prisoners on each wagon shared one toilet barrel as in the ship. Some died from lack of air in the narrow wagon, which had only two small openings. On the way to the northern mountainous areas, young kids and even adults attacked us with rocks that wounded some prisoners and some of the communist escorting troops as well.[2]

At last, the next morning we arrived at a campsite deep in a forest on a hillside covered by low brushes. It was in a mountainous district of Hoàng Liên

Sơn (formerly Yên Bái) province, twelve miles from Yên Bái provincial town and fifty miles northwest of Hà Nội.

Prisoners from various camps of the South were shuffled into groups of fifty each and sent to scores of camps in the province. I was moved to Camp Hoàng Liên Sơn 4, about twelve miles northeast of Yên Bái town. It was one of nine camps under the NVA 776th Regiment in the east side of Hoàng Liên Sơn province.

One hour after our arrival, we had to start working hard to build the camp with bamboo and thatch we cut from the forest. That night, we 200 prisoners had no sleep. We just sat and stood under raincoats or anything large enough to cover our heads from heavy raining. Within a month, two fellows committed suicide. One was an ARVN surgeon.

CAMP 4 HOÀNG LIÊN SƠN

November 1976

In this camp, we had to work full-time seven days/week including Sunday morning. Little farmwork and most of the time we were assigned tasks in the forest including lumbering. In the first month in the North, we still were given 15kg/month food allowance (rice plus manioc), higher than that of light-working farmers. From the second month, our ration fell to 12 kg/month. Each prisoner was given 100 grams (about four ounces) of meat or fish once a month.

We were supposed to receive 200 grams of sugar and three packs of bottom-class cigarettes a month. But each of us actually got from 80 to 100 grams of sugar. The total remaining was allocated to the forty communist officers and soldiers, although they already had 500 grams of their own. The same stealing happened with rice and meat rations.

A dozen prisoners ventured to escape, but no one succeeded, and none of them were brought to court for trial, probably because of pressure from international public opinion after the summer 1976 executions.

In the camps run by NVN Army, prisoners went to work outside from 6 AM to 6 PM, under guard if working in groups, or going freely if working individually in the forests. At night we had to stay inside the thatch-and-bamboo shelters.

In this camp, my friends and I had many chances to meet local people. From them, we learned many facts of life in North Việt Nam that were new to most of us.

Right on the first day in this camp, I noticed the evident reduction of the bird population in the region. In 1954 when I was still in the North, a summer morning had been filled with birds twittering in rice fields. But in 1976, in the forests around the camp and the nearby villages, there were remarkably fewer birds and foxes, hares, and other small wildlife. While working on rice fields, we did not find many worms and insects. The local farmers said that because of the excessive use of quicklime for insecticide and the DDT in the last ten years, worms were largely eradicated, thus seriously minimizing the population of insectivorous species and others. Similarly, the fishermen told us that the heavily contaminated overrun water from rice fields greatly reduced the size of the fish population in the river that seriously affected the fishermen's life and probably the people's health as well.

We were somewhat surprised to see the extreme poverty of people in the area, which was beyond our imagination. They told us that their meals were nothing more than 10 percent rice, 90 percent sweet potato or manioc, and sometimes green papaya growing everywhere in the forests and their small gardens in case of shortage of potato and manioc.

We prisoners suffered badly from unmitigated hunger. Men of small size like me felt the hunger less torturous than corpulent fellows. Satisfaction of the stomach haunted everybody day and night. While working in the forests or the fields, we looked for anything eatable. Grasshoppers, locusts, bird eggs, frogs, rats, little fish, wild fruit, bamboo shoots, manioc, and batata were in the list of favorites. Many suffered food poisoning that resulted in death.

Back in 1967, a doctor from West Germany (I don't remember his name) had visited the National Chiêu Hồi Center. He told me how he had survived his twenty years of forced labor in many prison camps in Siberia under Stalin and in northern China under Mao Tse-tung. He said that the majority of prisoners died in communist prison camps for two reasons. First, under extreme hunger, they might eat something that caused a deadly digestion disorder or food poisoning. Second, they might perish from extreme despondency, lack of spirit and confidence that led to mental collapse and body endurance break down. According to him, doctors and clergymen had a greater chance of surviving after long terms in communist prisons. Doctors were well aware of dangers from careless food consummation, while clergymen had a strong spiritual life to maintain high endurance and to control the way of eating. His story greatly helped me bear my hardships during my long years in the Việt communist prisons. I owe him my deepest grateful thanks. I hope he will read these lines and accept my thanks.

The majority of Vietnamese were smokers. Besides food, we all were feeling extremely hungry for a smoke, cigarette or "*thuốc lào*," a Vietnamese tobacco for hookah, which were not supplied for three months. The first time each of us was allocated one cigarette, I inserted one-eighth of it into a bamboo hookah and drew a long whiff. Unexpectedly I fainted and fell on the ground. Some of my friends had similar experience. The longtime thirst for a smoke intensified its effect.

In October, our families were allowed to send us gifts. Because of the ambiguous clauses in the announcement, each post office permitted gifts on a different basis: some accepted pencils but not pens, summer clothes but not

winter garments, sweets but not salty foods, footwear but not headwear, cigarette lighters but not flints, and vice versa.

In the parcel my family sent me there were a few pencils along with a small
pencil sharpener which children in the South and remote hamlets of other poor
countries were using since their first grade. A squad of NVA soldiers including
a second lieutenant of the camp rejoiced at seeing the "machine." They asked
me to let them try it and showed their great surprise at the simple tool. Only
three inches of the seven-inch pencil remained after their trials.

Most of the peasants did not believe us when we told them that in the South,
a pig usually weighs 80 to over 100 kilograms (175–220 pounds) and some might
reach over 200 kilograms as in Australia, the United States, and other developed
countries. To these farmers, a 60 kg pig was miraculous enough.

When each of our groups was to form a team of singers to participate in the
Tét celebration, I led a ten-man team. We tried to set up the cultural presentation with patriotic songs composed before 1954, praising the heroic fighting
against the French, the war that most of us had participated in one way or another. This was the only common ground in music enjoyment between the
communist jailers and my fellow prisoners, although that kind of song had not
been favored since 1951 in the communist areas.

IN AN NVA PRISON CAMP

Sometimes I was given the task of repairing different gadgets of the camp such
as simple electronic and mechanical appliances. Once when I was working on
a portable radio of the camp office, alone in a storage room, I overheard the
communist regiment political commissar talking to a dozen communist officers
in a political refreshment class. They were in the next room, separated from the
storage room by an earthen wall.

The commissar said in his instructions, "You should never feed prisoners
full. We can control them effectively if we keep them hungry all the time. Our
party and government won the war mainly because we have successfully implemented the food ration system." Half a minute later, I quietly slipped away before they might notice my presence.

According to a peasant who was friendly to us, in their routine political
class sessions, party members, police, and military officers were taught, "In the
two world wars, the American army and its allied forces killed most of the Axis
prisoners of war to save a large budget for keeping them in POW camps. Only
the Soviet Union held the POWs and fed them, out of humanitarian concerns.
They were given compulsory work to do so that they could be productive for the
benefits of the humankind."

Many schoolchildren and local officials said that from political lessons, "Prisoners do not have human rights. They might be killed, and their relatives have no right to complain or claim." Actually, they showed us hatred, sometimes even refused to reply to our questions or greetings.

From these experiences along with the stories of "ambushing and chasing the B-52s," we realized the incredible power of the systematic political propaganda lies.

After about six months, however, local people's attitude changed. They covertly helped us, although they were so poor. Occasionally they gave us fruit, vegetables, sweet potatoes, and even boiled chicken.

A twelve-year-old student and his younger brother met me at a hillside road. They asked after my health, then gave me two of their six sour balls they had just bought from the marketplace. They said they had saved one week's allowances from their parents to buy the six cheap candies. They must have had great hearts to give away one-third of their treasure.

When I asked him why he sympathized with us, the older brother said, "My dad and mom told me that I should respect the officers from the South, that you are well learned and benevolent, not war criminals or American henchmen." His words surprised me and also moved me deeply, especially when he stressed that his parents had no relatives serving on our side.

On another hot summer day, my group-mate and I met an old man with a Russian bolt-action rifle who stopped us in an unfriendly manner: "Are you stealing my manioc crops?" We sternly denied it. "We've never touched the smallest root of people's manioc. We've only taken what belongs to the camp."

The old man laughed. "Don't you mind! I'm just kidding. I am serving as the deputy chairman of this village's people's committee. I have been watching many of you for the last two weeks. When you cross the unclaimed field on the hillsides, you've never trampled on our vegetable seedlings. This proves that you are gentlemen, not wicked American puppets as the communist propaganda labeled you. I used to listen to Radio Sài Gòn, and I know rather much about life over there. If you violate people's rights, there are Upper House, Lower House, and Provincial People's Committees who are ready to bring you to the court of justice. You were promoted to higher ranks because of your ability and behavior, not because you are faithful to a party."

He added, "You have democracy, but you relied too much on the Americans and tolerated corruption beyond reasonable limits." It was another surprise: a North Vietnamese farmer who had a profound perception of life in South Việt Nam. He then told the two of us—as later he also told many others—to feel free to dig manioc in his field when we're hungry. He knew how we were treated in the camp.

One rainy Sunday morning, the camp officer in charge of labor ordered us to go collect fire wood for the camp kitchen. When we were about to depart, a group of some twenty women of over sixty years old stopped by the gate. Many of the old moms called the camp officers and argued in their loud voices, "You have to treat the prisoners with humanity. They shared the same blood with you. You're so heartless as to send them working under this heavy rain on the slippery mountain sides."

It was the first time we witnessed how the oppressed people under the communist despotic regime reacted against inhumanity. They dared to voice their protest because they were from the Tày tribal community, the outspoken minority tribe in North Việt Nam, and because they were old women. The camp commander immediately canceled the order.

We 350 prisoners had a lot of medicine when we reported to the first concentration camp. A month after we came to Camp Hoàng Liên Sơn 4, the camp command confiscated all of the medicine, which included more than 10,000 antibiotic pills. The camp officers and soldiers sold them to villagers, collecting big money for their own. When many of us suffered from illnesses as fatal as dysentery, we had nothing to treat the disease. In a month, about twenty prisoners in five camps around my camp died from the epidemic.

The camp's political deputy commander always found ways to inflict hardships on us. He punished prisoners for trivial violations that used to be tolerated by his boss.

The camp commander, a senior NVA captain, treated us humanely, imposing light labor requirements. Sometimes he sang along with me songs of the Resistance era. The logistic deputy commander was a good man like the commander, too. But in late 1977, the camp commander was relieved because he was friendly to prisoners, according to some communist officers of the camp.

In mid-1977, we were ordered to prepare grounds for one more camp on the side of a hill nearby. We heard that the other camps in the North were building new camps for all political prisoners still in the South to be moved north by the end of the year. But later in September 1977, the half-completed project was canceled. According to some civilians in the district town, it was because of the conflict between Chinese and Vietnamese communists over the common border.

During the year in this camp, I suffered two accidents: one little finger crushed under heavy lumber and my left knee joint sprained when I fell on the hillside. I received no medical treatment and relied only on my fellows who were practicing acupuncture.

In October 1977, prisoners in my camp were moved to Camp Phú Sơn 4, Thái Nguyên province, forty miles north of Hà Nội. After that, we were no more under the communist army's control. Later, all of us prisoners in one NVA camp after another were handed over to a score of camps like Camp Phú Sơn 4 under the authority of the Ministry of Public Security. Since then we actually became semiofficial "political prisoners."

UNDER PROFESSIONAL JAILERS

Under the Ministry of Public Security, professional jailers kept the camp in strict obedience to the rules and regulations of a typical prison under the Việt Nam communist regime. We were given prisoner ID numbers and wore clothes with large printed letters, "PS-4," on the back. Rations were reduced to the category of a second-rate farmer, which was 12 kg/month or 400 grams/day.

Phú Sơn was the model of prison camps under the Department of Prison Management, Ministry of Public Security. It had an "Emulation Board" consisting of three or four selected prisoners. The board members carried out orders of the camp command, aiding the camp command in keeping good order and implementing the camp's directives, namely, representing the prisoners.

In prison camps under nationalist or communist regime, a matter of everyone's concern was the role of the informers. The public security cadre in charge of a prisoners group, the security officer of the camp, and the camp commander each picked prisoners to serve as informers. An informer had to secretly report to camp officials everything happening in his ward.

Most informers did their assigned tasks reluctantly; only a very small number of these guys were actively collaborating with the jailers. They reported everything going on around them, apparently in exchange for some favor from the camp supervisors and from the regime. Usually their information could result in some disciplinary measures for their victims, such as a few days or weeks locked up in dark cells. In extreme cases taking place in some camps, their victims were tortured to death. In the only case ever revealed, it was a prisoner, chief of a camp's Emulation Board, who beat another prisoner savagely until the victim fell dead on the spot.

In general, it could be said that 95 percent of the RVN prisoners after 1975 had not morally submitted to the Việt Nam communist regime. Most of the RVN prisoners quietly endured the hardships unless being pushed into the corners. Most prisoners avoided resisting camp rules. Young officers tended to complain and voiced their dissatisfaction more than the aged.

According to many communist jailers who had been serving in various camps in the war, our ARVN fellows who had been commandos in special operations in North Việt Nam and prisoners captured before 1975 showed a dauntless attitude toward communist jailers. They refused to work outside when it was raining or under very low temperatures or on risky tasks. They refused to attend communist political indoctrination, acting in solidarity, ready to argue against treatment that not in accordance with international POW conventions.

Each group of forty prisoners was under a public security cadre who watched everyone closely. The most insignificant violation such as stealing a handful of peanuts in the field would cost a man and his group mates dearly.

Almost six nights a week, all group members had to attend sessions reviewing the day's work, reading newspapers, and criticizing themselves. A violation would be a topic for one-hour discussion and the violator would suffer painful criticism from his group mates by order of the PS cadre in charge. The entire group had to endure the whole tiresome evening because of a trivial violation of just one fellow. That kind of punishment scared everyone from doing anything, however small, against the prison regulations. No one could stand harsh reproof or even angry curses from his own friends who had to suffer for what he did.

In case of a serious breach of the prison rules, one would be confined in solitary for a day to several weeks with one or two legs locked in stocks. Political prisoners were not beaten except for those who escaped the jail and were captured. But criminal prisoners took beatings as their routine hardships.

In Camp Phú Sơn 4, there were 1,200 political and 200 criminal prisoners. Criminal inmates stayed and ate in different wards. Under the communist regime in North Việt Nam, prisoners convicted of voicing dissidence, protesting, or acting against the rulers were sentenced as offenders of social order or public security and incarcerated as criminals, not as political prisoners. That was why communist spokespersons always say, "There are no political prisoners in our prisons."

The communist authorities did not mingle us with criminal prisoners, probably because there were so many of us. Keeping us in the same wards with criminal prisoners would have caused serious security problems.

I still remember my uncle explaining to me in 1953 why communist authorities always lock up political prisoners along with criminal inmates. "They wanted to humiliate them on one hand. On the other, they believed that the criminal's bad nature would ruin the political prisoner's good mentality, personality and dignity after living beside them in one room, sharing the scanty ration, and vying with each other for shoddy scraps of food," he said.

Before every important event such as the Party National Congress, national elections, introduction of a new policy, and (during the war) prior to a military major campaign, large numbers of unfavorable young people convicted or suspected of committing larceny, illegal trade business, hoodlums' activities, or incurring the disfavor of local authorities were detained by decision of the local public security chiefs without any trial in the court of justice.

When we were transferred to Camp Phú Sơn 4, North Vietnamese prisoners detained during the 1975 Spring Campaign overthrowing the Sài Gòn government were still held in all prison camps around North Việt Nam. A camp official told men privately that the population of those prisoners may have come to many tens of thousands.

Among the 200 criminal prisoners, there were 20 whose terms had ended, but they were still waiting for release paperwork for a year or more. One of them, a sixty-year-old man waited for such paperwork for more than twenty years, and he finally submitted a petition to stay in the camp when the release paper came. He had been sentenced to twenty-five years for committing rape. He was too old to return to society and to reintegrate into any community. Local authorities refused to have him back in his village.

Another special case was a fourteen-year-old boy. When he was eight, he had fought with a girl of his age; the girl stabbed him with a pair of scissors and wounded him slightly. He hit her head with a glass bottle, and she died a few hours afterward. Village authorities sent him to prison without trial and refused to have him back. So he was growing up in prison without an education. He was a normal boy with no sign of physical or mental disorder. Until 1979, when we moved to another camp, the poor teen was still there. His mother visited him once a year with gifts of about five kilograms of rice and sometimes a half-kilogram of brown sugar, as he related to us.

The prison ward where my group of forty-two prisoners and another group of forty were staying had been designed for forty inmates. Each shared a space of twenty inches wide. One hardly rolled over without waking up the two fellows beside him. Camp Phú Sơn 4 had about fifteen wards; most of them were built in 1954.

The toilet compartment inside each ward allowed only three users at a time on three fecal discharge containers. A rowdy race lasted for half an hour every early morning. Ones who suffered from constipation dared not join the long line whereas those with diarrhea would fight their way for the first place without waiting in line. Ill smells tortured the unlucky fellows who occupied the spaces close to its entrance.

The guardian in charge of my group once told us that the writer Thụy An, a famous lady in Hà Nội before 1954, was incarcerated in my ward after she joined the Nhân Văn opposition movement and was sentenced to a prison term in 1957. According to him, one day Thụy An used a sharp object, supposedly a honed bicycle spoke, to gouge out an eye in protest. "She said she wanted to keep one of her eyes from being soiled by the filthy sight of this regime. Years later, she died in prison," he related.

To criminal prisoners, beating was a daily experience. We were amazed to see how the poor creatures could stand flogging, kicking, and punching but were up and around not long after the torture. The jailers applied such measures to a criminal prisoner sometimes only because of his stealing a fist-sized potato. And many times when a PS guard was beating one, other guards passing by would join the sadistic sport by hitting the victim with anything on hand.

Required working norms were very high. Prisoners were doing farm work and other menial tasks to produce compound revenue to finance a part of the total expenditures to maintain the prison camp. Every kind of work had a detail norm. A prisoner had to break soil in preparation for a planting season at about 2,000 square meters (22,000 square feet) a day and higher. The cadre in charge of a group might fiercely criticize ones who often failed to meet the requirement or even reduced their daily ration for days or months.

The jailers in charge of prisoners' groups were ordered to force them to fulfill the highest norm. A fellow in my ward who graduated with a PhD in chemistry at an Australian university was a victim of such a forced labor practice. As an active patriot, he refused to stay and teach in Australia and came back to serve South Việt Nam as a professor at Cần Thơ University. He was locked up at the same time with us. In Phú Sơn 4, he served his term in a construction group next to mine.

One morning, he was told to climb a ladder to bring bricks to the bricklayer on top of the wall. Because of his severe acrophobia, he asked the jailer to give him another task instead of climbing to a four-meter height. The jailer scolded him with strong words and threatened him with a week in a dark cell if he did not carry out the order. After a few steps up on the ladder, the poor fellow fell down on the ground buried under bricks and wood. His brain suffered serious damage. He lost his ability to speak and one leg was paralyzed.

A public security cadre in charge of a group was always ready and pleased to have the chance to run self-criticism sessions. You might guess that was because he was given a kilogram of manioc as overtime pay for each evening session he presided over.

Criminals who were parents and children were not permitted to call each other "Daddy" and "Son" or "Daughter." Camp regulations decided that a convicted person was deprived of the rank in his or her family. So they had to address each other *anh* or *chị* (brother or sister, used between equals in age, rank, or position).

The beasts of burden in the camp also suffered atrocities. Buffalo refusing to obey orders were beaten until they bled. Some of them working along with my group were the most recalcitrant. Every day when the clanging sound was heard at 5 PM ending the day's work, some of them immediately stopped pulling farming equipment—harrows, plows—and categorically refused to go on despite brutal beatings. And they always won. They never mistook the clanging sound of the 4:30 PM feeding time at the fowl farm nearby for the 5 PM signal. We called them our "dauntless beasts."

The beasts of most prison camps had to work eight hours a day but were allowed to graze only three hours in poorly grown grass fields. Their stubborn behavior probably resulted from the way they were treated.

An ox pulling a big cart in Phú Sơn 4 may have been the most intelligent bovine. He would only do his task if the prisoner in charge loaded the cart with the weight to a limit he felt precisely. With loads weighing more than five kilograms, he would protest by stomping his feet and not moving. But with a reasonable weight, he would pull the cart to and from any of the subcamps A, B, and C when his boss spoke clearly in his ears the words, "To camp B," or C, or A. And he would do just that.

"Only a communist prison could have such a miracle," we concluded.

Since we were moved to a brick prison, we were victims of the armies of bedbugs. They hid in every tiny nook in the walls and in the seam lines of our mats and mosquito nets. At night, they marched in hundreds across our mosquito nets toward the fellow beside. Bedbugs did not like the blood they had already relished but were always searching for new flavors, sometimes traveling several meters away from their nooks, crossing many sleeping men.

One night a fellow in my group claimed his championship in killing bedbugs: nearly 300 the first night when we moved to another ward. Bugs liked new victims. After a few days, he completed the slogan by Hồ Chí Minh, "Không có gì quý hơn Độc Lập, Tự Do" (Nothing is more precious than independence and freedom), written on the whitewashed wall with blood from the bedbugs. Consequently, he was thrown into a dark cell for seven days after the guards discovered his ghastly work.

In spring 1978 we were ordered to write our personal biographies. We were asked to account for everything we had done in our life in great detail. The task lasted more than a week. The public security cadres read our reports at the end of each day and asked for more details or clearer explanations. We had to write down details concerning the smallest things in our lives, such as why our parents gave us our names, the reason one's father died, or why a mother moved to a new residence in March 1965 . . . or how we had met and married our wives . . . including extramarital affairs, if any.

It was a tricky game that might have produced some political intelligence information from unimportant persons, but it seemed not successful to some of our real big wheels in the top circles. As for me, it meant only a form of torture. Some of us had to write more than 600 pages as required by the PS cadres in charge. They had to answer scores of questions concerning things that they had never known. We spent days racking our brains to have something to write down, including some white lies.

In mid-1978, a foreign delegation visited the camp. They came from many countries. Jail officials said one of them came from Cuba and some from the capitalist world.

Each of the fifteen brick houses, about six by twenty-four yards, held seventy or more prisoners. To clean up the camp to welcome the visitors, only about twenty prisoners were left at a house so that a prisoner could share a large space. The others were moved with all their tattered belongings to a field far from the camp and only returned after the visitors had left.

The camp dispensary housed about twenty very sick inmates. They were evacuated to subcamp B for the same purpose. The poor fellows had to walk, many with walking sticks and on crutches, almost three hours to reach camp B just a mile away. The camp had at least five trucks that could have been used for the movement. Those "real" patients were replaced by the healthy substitutes clad in brand-new blue pajamas of the dispensary. On each night table there were books, newspapers, an orange, and a can of sweetened condensed milk.

The fake patients were told that things on night tables were for display only, not gifts for them. But a bullheaded one of them casually opened the milk can and consumed half of it at a few gulps when some visitor asked him why he didn't enjoy the gifts. When the camp official in charge threatened to lock him up in the dark cell, he said, "If I didn't open the can and take a few gulps from it, the visitors would feel certain that these luxuries were just make-believe. I did actually help you, didn't I?" Of course the inmate won the little game.

The communist regime paid a lot of attention to cultural activities, most of which were singing and staging plays. Every village, factory, state farm, military and police unit, and prison camp had a cultural group. There were many local talents as North Vietnamese had a tradition of playing folk music and performing stage plays. Unfortunately, those talents were permitted to play and sing only works that directly served communist propaganda goals.

At Camp Phú Sơn 4, there was a cultural group of more than twenty criminal inmates before we were moved in. So in Tết 1978, we political prisoners founded our separate choir and prepared for the show. I was the leading voice of the bass section.

As usual, we selected songs of the anti-French era, and the camp cultural section chief accepted them, requiring our choir to sing just one song, "The Glory Communist Party of Việt Nam," to praise the party "according to the rule," he said. He then added, "As the war has already ended, one 'red' song is enough. I dare not approve 'golden music,' but a little 'bluish' is OK."

Although it was a part of the prisoners' body, the cultural group had a lot of expensive equipment—violins, guitars, accordions, trumpets, drums, stage lights, flood lights, and large backdrops and curtains that cost a lot of money. As a tradition of the regime, singers and musicians won special favors from the leadership.

THE DEVASTATING DELUGE

In autumn 1978, most parts of Việt Nam, the North in particular, suffered devastating flash floods. Half of the Camp Phú Sơn 4 annexes on the hillside were inundated. We had to endure low rations but suffered no casualties. Some camp officials disclosed to us that at Camp 5 Thanh Phong, Thanh Hóa Province, no food supplies came during the flood or for many days afterwards. About five prison guards and ten prisoners died from serious malnutrition after they had nothing but water spinach to eat for three long weeks.

Whether or not the step back in the economy aggravated by the deluges affected the Communist Party's policies, Hà Nội treated us more kindly. There were lower norms of forced labor, and we suffered fewer peevish complaints by the jailers.

Camp Phú Sơn had a large growing land where we were toiling all summer. We still had contact with civilians from surrounding villages. One morning in December 1978, an old woman of about seventy was wandering in the manioc field that belonged to the camp, where we prisoners were harvesting. The old woman said she would wait for our completion of the day's harvesting so that she could glean some leftovers for her family.

I asked why she was still working hard at her age. She said she had to feed two grandsons of five and seven years old whose fathers—her sons—had been killed in South Việt Nam and their mothers had left them to her care before remarrying and fleeing the village.

Before leaving the field in late afternoon, we told her not to dig up all around but only at places we marked with two twenty-inch twigs that made an X, where we left many manioc roots untouched.

The next morning while we were working in the field next to the one of the previous day, the old grandmother wandered close to us within earshot. Before we could react, she kneeled on the ground and kowtowed three times toward us. She said, as if praying in front of the altar, "Our lenient and benevolent captains and majors and colonels, please accept my kowtow on behalf of my two grandsons. Thanks to your help, for the first time in their lives their stomachs are full. With your help, I have gleaned 20 kilograms of manioc yesterday. Buddha bless you!"

We couldn't hold our sighs, and I saw some of my fellows crying.

* * *

In 1978, while I was imprisoned in Camp Phú Sơn 4, a high-ranking communist official from the Hà Nội's Ministry of Interior (also known as the Ministry of Public Security) interrogated me about the Chiêu Hồi program. One of the questions was "If our defectors went to your side mostly because of falling into a desperate situation, hungry, thirsty, or lost as you said, why did many of them become so faithful to you and fighting so hard against us? Did you pay them a lot of money? Or did you brainwash them?"

As he insisted that I tell the truth, I frankly explained: "We have never bought their faithfulness with money or material profits. Only a few of them got rewards for significant contributions such as turning in a lot of weapons or accurate intelligence information leading to significant military successes. We won their fidelity solely by treating them fairly without discrimination, taking good care of them, sometimes as if they were our brothers. And the common people also did the same spontaneously, without being compelled by the government. As to brainwashing, we've never done it."

The official looked at me intensely. Finally he said in a thoughtful manner, "My leaders wouldn't believe that when I told them the same thing. But they will if you do. Would you sign this transcript of your own words?" I said I would and signed the paper.

In November 1978, my sister was allowed to see me for half an hour under close surveillance. She had no official permit, but her husband's brother, who was a North Việt Nam Army Medical Corps senior colonel with many good connections, tried his best to help. She cried a lot when seeing my emaciated face and calves swollen from beriberi. She brought me good news: her husband had fled Việt Nam by boat and arrived safely in Indonesia.

MOVE TO CAMP 6

It was at this time the Chinese army launched the first attack across the northern border of Việt Nam. The camp command isolated some of the prisoners from the South who were Chinese Vietnamese for security concerns. In the last week of February 1979, we were reorganized into groups of about thirty-five each to fill a cross-country bus. In the next few days, political prisoners were all moved to the three camps south of Hà Nội possibly to avoid being under the Chinese direct military threat.

Before departure, I wished that I would be sent to Camp 5 (Camp Thanh Phong) in Thanh Hóa Province, where my father died in 1951, so that I would spend some time near his soul. But I was not satisfied. My group along with the other four reached Camp 6, Thanh Chương District, Nghệ An province in the poorest region of Việt Nam. Camp 5 was 100 miles away. More than 1,000 prisoners from other military camps had been transferred to Camp 6 the previous year.

A few days later, a group of about 100 criminal prisoners from a camp in Lai Châu province near the border with China arrived in Camp 6. Before the emergency evacuation, Camp Lai Châu command announced a decision of the Public Security Ministry to release about 50 percent of the camp's inmates. Paperwork would be done in the new camp, and the remaining would be freed in the next few weeks, camp guardians assured them. Then they began their march on foot in a 150-mile journey to Camp 6.

After arrival, the inmates were waiting for release paperwork, but nothing happened. When they asked for it several times, the camp officials explained that for safe evacuation, the decision of the Ministry of Public Security was just a faked document to calm them and keep them in good order.

Some of them told me that "in this land of the liars, we have been cheated many times, but we are always ready to be cheated once again."

We were allowed only a tiny ration. The daily meal was 90 percent sweet potato or manioc and 10 percent rice along with spinach and water spinach. Meat or fish could be seen once or twice a month. Each time a prisoner received a piece of meat or fish, it measured about two square inches.

However, we felt pleased that camp officials here didn't care much about our anticommunist irony. They cared even less about the South Vietnamese songs that some of us were singing. We thought they didn't treat us roughly because "both sides" of the camp were hungry. Moreover, information reaching us through visiting relatives proved that the situation here was almost the same in other camps.

After the short but bloody battles between the Chinese and Vietnamese communist armies and we were moved to Camp 6, the security measures in concentration camps were tightened. A dozen political prisoners who were considered reactionary elements who might become troublemakers or master-minds of protests and revolts were locked up incommunicado in March 1979. Those included former ARVN officers of Chinese origin. Cardinal Nguyễn Văn Thuận was held incommunicado for ten years.

Each was held in an insolation cell measuring only seven by ten feet. He could be allowed to walk around a few hours a day in the adjacent small yard measuring ten by fifteen feet. The prisoner was spending time alone in the narrow space surrounded by thick walls with a low sleeping platform and a sedge mat, but he was not locked in stocks.

For punishment, the camp used dark cells to detain prisoners who seriously violated regulations. A typical dark cell in the communist prison was about four by seven feet on a cement floor. A prisoner had to lie on the floor without a blanket when it was cold, with one or two legs locked in iron stocks. He had to urinate and defecate, without being unlocked, in an earthenware large bowl. He was allowed to dump the waste and clean the bowl every morning. Sometimes prison guards on their night patrol would pour dirty water or urine on the prisoner just for fun.

The communist dark cell was in a way much more torturous than the so-called tiger cages in the prison at Poulo Condore Island in South Việt Nam, which were a topic of fierce criticism against the RVN's human rights violations in the early 1970s. After April 1975, as if to make a higher record in torturing techniques, several communist prison camps in the South used old connexes that had been discarded by U.S. and ARVN military units as dark cells to punish prisoners. In 90 degree heat, prisoners were really barbecued inside the infernal metal boxes.

After June 1976, when we were sent to North Việt Nam, the camps held political classes only once in a while when it rained too hard for prisoners to work in the field. Most jailers were smart enough to know what was in our minds, so most of the time they did not eagerly perform the task of instructor. They ran the classes reluctantly, just trying to keep the class in order. But Camp 6 went further than that. The camp jailers did not care a dime about holding political classes, even though we were locked up under the label of reeducation.

* * *

In mid-1978, after three years with very few of our relatives permitted to visit us, a directive from the Public Security Ministry decreed that our relatives and friends might see us for fifteen minutes (up to one hour for those who were evaluated high on the scale of "progressiveness") once every three months. Relatives might supply us with food and other items of limited categories and quantity according to regulations. They could slip in some money, an act against camp regulations that was usually ignored by the camp cadres and guards as they would gain a little profit from our spending.

So trading and corruption became common among the camp guards and officials. In Camp Nam Hà, sixty kilometers southeast of Hà Nội, the security guards even brought cooked foodstuffs and small sundry items to sell in the wards. In Camp 6, guardians in charge of prisoner groups might allow us to visit markets to buy anything permissible, sometimes even rice wine. A jailer in charge of a group was paid no less than 10 percent of the total payment made at the market each time he checked out a team of a few prisoners to go shopping.

One day, it came my turn to go to the nearby village open market to buy various items for my group along with another fellow under a guard's watch. The guard sat at a beer seller's and let us shop around the market. At a little hut of a middle-aged woman, my companion bought one kilogram of brown sugar in a cheap earthenware container. After paying the price, he scooped up some sugar to taste. He felt something unusual, so he pushed the spoon deeper into the container, only to see that below two inches of sugar was all sand.

When he complained, she said, "You don't check the content before paying. It's your fault, not mine." An older woman selling rice and beans in the adjacent little stall said to us, "It's the way of life here. Once you have paid for an item, you won't have your right to argue, however much you are cheated."

Turning to the woman selling sugar, she said, "These gentlemen come from the South. They don't know the way we are doing business here. I suggest that you refund him." The sugar dealer responded with a smile, refunded the money, and took back the sugar and container.

An old man selling candy next to her little hut said to us: "Don't be surprised. This practice is common everywhere in the North nowadays." The friend beside me said, "There are cheats in the South, but they are not so brazen and shameless."

Our prison life became more endurable thanks to the friendly attitude of communist cadres in the camps. The three years after the defunct of Sài Gòn regime seemed enough for the communists to see the truth about us.

The local people were unfriendly at first, but later on, they sympathized with us. Thanks to supplies from our families that included a lot of medicines, we could help many sick peasants with some of our drugs. It was actually a civic action task we were doing on behalf of the conquered army. Due to the extreme scarcity of medicines for many years in North Việt Nam, a small dose of a drug could produce a marvelous effect. Sometimes they received from us aspirin and Tylenol for treatment of pain, but at home they administered the medicines for their children who had serious sicknesses such as dysentery, typhoid, or even scabies. And strangely enough, the diseases were cured. It was really a spectacle.

While we were in Camp 6, we had lots of chances to deal with civilians living around the camp, thanks to the easing control of the guards.

Many times I heard ten-year-old schoolgirls saying very dirty words, so dirty that it sounded as if they had been old filthy whores. I never dared to repeat their words verbatim when relating the story to someone. Before 1954 in the North, ill-educated children said dirty words, but much less dirty and at much older ages.

At many schools near the camps we had a chance to visit, a lot of fifth-graders had only small blackboards and chalk to write; they never had notebooks and pens. That tenth-graders in the ten-year high school system were unable to do a sixth-grade math exercise was very common. In newspaper reports, however, no school graduated less than 98 percent of its students every year.

People told us that the New Life Movement launched in North Việt Nam in 1957 did not approve the tradition of "male yielding seat on bus and trains to female." Since the first days in kindergarten, children hadn't been taught to say "thank you." Many times when we said "thank you" to communist cadres, they readily responded like a prerecorded lesson: "Under the light of socialism, it's not necessary to thank anyone for anything. People are performing the obligations of a citizen, not for thanks."[3]

When working outside Camp 6, I gave a group of five children of about seven to ten years of age some sourballs and chocolate M&Ms candy that my family had just sent me. They had been very friendly to us all the time since my group was in charge of growing manioc on this field.

To my surprise, all of them refused my goodies when they knew the gifts were made in the United States. They said, "Sweets made by the Americans cause death. They mix poison in candies to kill children." When I explained to them that it was just a lie by propaganda, they didn't believe me at first. Only after my intensive reasoning and demonstration did they accept the little gifts. Of course, they changed their opinion almost immediately.

Only at that time did my fellows fully understand why so many people could believe fish stories and cheaply fabricated propaganda anecdotes such as MiG fighters hovering behind clouds and how one SAM missile could bring down six B-52s.

Hà Nội made the best use of cultural activities on the propaganda. Poets, composers, and novelists were mobilized to create works that described imaginary crimes of the Americans and the Sài Gòn regime. With skillfully versed and well-employed rhetoric, the themes of those works could be effective beyond imagination.

In one of the books for elementary school students, a story ran "How Diệm scares every toddler when someone calls his name." Another anecdote was about how President Diệm was having an affair with Madam Nhu, his sister-in-law. A poetic version of a story was telling how a squad of South Vietnamese soldiers trampled on the belly of a pregnant woman until the embryo was forced out of the victim's womb.

A dozen such stories and poems stuffed the heads of millions of people every month in political indoctrination classes held weekly or monthly in villages, government agencies, laborers' groups, and army companies and platoons. Participants were expected to learn these by heart so that they could answer the instructors' examination questions. The lesson content was from the unique text compiled by the central office of indoctrination. Therefore, when the first NVA troops were in Sài Gòn, we heard thousands of them relating the same fabricated stories, which they apparently believed. The effect of that blatant propaganda was greater than what any citizen of a democratic country might have guessed.

A THIN RAY OF HOPE

In late 1979, five of our ARVN prisoners, one major and four captains, escaped after many months of careful planning and preparation. When they had crossed about eighty miles of jungle and reached the Mekong River on the Laotian side, they were captured and returned to the camp. All suffered daily beatings until the major died of injuries to his intestines.

While we were in the camps, more and more South Vietnamese fled the country every day. News about waves of boatmen leaving Việt Nam for lands of freedom despite high risks on stormy seas and in wild jungles elevated our spirits and heightened our concerns. We knew the greatest event in the world history of refugees was ongoing.

In autumn, my wife and my youngest child visited me and supplied me with dry food, medicine, and lots of sweets, thanks to gifts sent by my sister's husband, who had fled the country by boat one year earlier and resettled in San Jose, California. My wife had to bribe local officials to get a travel permit so that she could buy train tickets and be allowed to see me in the camp. Citizens' travel out of their provinces was still strictly controlled in 1979.

She told me how she had managed to overcome every difficulty to take care of our family. She was running a small business of trading vegetables as a cover in which she hid other consumers' goods that were under government monopoly between Sài Gòn and Đà Lạt. She had to use the best of her intelligence to hide the smuggled items. She earned a meager income to feed the family. If her goods were discovered and confiscated, she had to bribe the police or else accept a reduction of the family's meals.

When I left home for the communist prison camp, my wife had $900 on hand—no gold, and no savings. She worked hard, and sometimes she was exhausted after using her strength to move the heavy goods quickly to avoid having them confiscated by the police. The tiresome work left her weak. Fortunately, my sister's husband was sending gift parcels and money to help; my wife's hardship was relieved and my children had some fancy sweets to relish. That was how my wife and children had to share the consequences of my war.

She asked me to permit my children to flee the country when there was a chance. I said okay. My mother, my aunt, my wife, and my sister all agreed to let them risk the trip for a better life in freedom.

My wife said, "I can endure any hardship while waiting for your return home. But your sister and I feel that our children must get as good an education as possible. As you've always told me, we prefer intellectual assets to riches."

Only twenty days after my wife and our son returned from the visit, my aunt died from pneumonia. Upon returning from the trip visiting me, my wife gave the whole family her account of the visit. Talking to my aunt, my wife lied about my health. The lies somehow alleviated my aunt's worries about my safety before she departed for the Eternity. My eldest daughter wrote me, "A few minutes before her last gasps, Grand Auntie still asked if you were coming back soon." Her death dealt a painful blow to my heart. She had taken care of me since I was a toddler, even when I was middle-aged. I cried for her several nights.

A month later, I had good news. In a letter to me, my sister used a South Vietnamese slang to let me know that my eldest daughter and son had safely reached a refugee camp in Thailand after a four-day boat trip.

At that time, there was a new directive from communist education authorities to bar all children of former RVN officers and officials, civilian dissidents, and bourgeoisie families from enrolling in tenth grade and the university. The policy met strong protests from every side; the strongest was from many renowned former members of the so-called communist National Liberation Front.

The new rule was canceled silently, but it still caused much concern to my family. Communist leaders often restored their intended measure after the first attempt failed, usually with more wily tricks. That caused my family to work faster for the escape of my two oldest children.

Thanks to the food my wife brought me, I recovered part of my health. I wrapped a thin thread around my bicep and marked the circumference with ink. Each day my muscle grew a quarter of an inch. In thirty days, I regained fifteen pounds.

We knew a criminal prisoner who was locked incommunicado for eight months, with three small bowls of food and half a liter of water a day. In the summer, the temperature reached 90+ degrees. Suffering from extreme thirst, his muscles shrank. When he was released from the dark cell to the rice field where we were working, he snatched the water jug of a fellow inmate and guzzled long swigs in thirty seconds. Half an hour later, we witnessed a miracle: his biceps had noticeably expanded.

TROUBLESOME VISITS

Every prisoner longed for visits by relatives. But there were visits that caused troubles. That was the case of some polygamists.

A fellow in my same group had two wives, one legitimate and the other just a mistress. One day, the two women who hadn't known each other took the same bus and sat side by side on the trip to visit him. After minutes of chatting, they realized both of them were cheated on by the same gentleman, an RVN Air Force pilot and a lady-killer. They appeared together to see him at the camp visitors' house. Of course, he was harshly scolded.

Fortunately, after the unwanted confrontation, the generous wife did her best to help the mistress and her child move to Sài Gòn to join together in a small business. She said the loss of the country was the greatest pain. She wouldn't want to make another woman who also loved her husband suffer any more. The two women in turn made a trip every three or four months to visit him. I don't know how long the peacefully arranged triangle wedlock lasted after I was moved to another camp.

Other fellows in a similar situation were not so lucky. Many of the wives resorted to divorce.

And not all relatives' visits were welcomed. As mentioned above, there were many RVN officers whose fathers had joined the Việt Minh communists in the North in 1954, leaving them to the care of their closest relatives, usually their mothers. Many others fled to the South in 1954 while their fathers and siblings stayed in the North.

I've personally known about ten officers whose fathers came back from North Việt Nam, including an NVA general. After April 30, 1975, when all of us were detained in communist prison camps, some of the fathers went south to see their children and grandchildren. But many others would not do so; probably they were afraid of being accused by their superiors as having a "passive attitude" about the "friends/foes" viewpoint. Most of those RVN officers refused to see their fathers and even cut short the visits and returned gifts that the old men brought to them. One of them, a captain in an ARVN combat unit, was in the same prison ward with me for two years.

One day his father, who was an NVA full colonel, visited him. He happily welcomed him at first. But after half an hour of conversation, the captain said to his father, "Please don't preach such communist lessons again. I'm fed up with communism, and that's why I joined the South Việt Nam Army and fought against the communists with all my heart."

When the poor father kept talking the way of a communist cadre, my angry friend got up and left the "guest room" after telling his father not to come again. He refused the old man's gifts (sugar candy, cigarettes, and rice cakes) and was ready to confront any action the camp's guards might take against him. The father tried once more three months later, and the son refused to see him. They never met again.

WHEN VILLAGERS BEGGED PRISONERS FOR FOOD

The devastating deluges in late 1978 caused great harm to the economy, which could be seen clearly from the prison camp. In agricultural cooperatives of the villages near the camp, the backbone of the ruling system that was controlling the rice production and manpower, peasants refused to do their farm work, leaving the cooperative rice fields unattended. Hà Nội leaders had to give in, applying the new policy called *khoán sản phẩm* (production piecework), allocating land to farmers for their private farming with rent based on productivity.

The Việt communist regime suffered a new setback. Flooding in Thanh Hóa province had resulted in a serious shortage of food for the peasants. Village officials had to sign travel permits (as dictated by the rule regarding citizens' travel out of their provinces) to allow villagers to go anywhere out of the province to earn their living. Many of those hungry peasants from an area fifty miles away came to the fields belonging to Camp 6 to glean manioc, batata, and corn left after prisoners were done harvesting. Many became beggars, wandering far away, even to the South, to earn a living.

With the guards' tacit consent, we gave a group of them a lot of each produce. They thanked us, saying that it was beyond imagination that farmers were begging prisoners for food. One of my fellows remarked with a dab of irony, "We are doing a better civic action operation here than we did in the South years ago."

CRIMINAL PRISONERS

Before 1975 we had read some books about the communist prison life in the Soviet Union and mainland China. But we only realized how close to reality those stories were when we saw with our own eyes the life and the treatment of criminal prisoners in North Việt Nam while we were in Camp Phú Sơn and especially in Camp 6.

Every evening in Camp 6, guardians in charge of criminal groups punished criminal prisoners who violated the camp's rules in the day. The guardians often ordered the prisoner who was appointed leader of the group to carry out the punishment.

The bamboo stick was a simple tool, with which beatings were done with brutality far beyond our imagination. During my years in North Việt Nam prison camps, I witnessed hundreds of beatings in which one died at the scene and a few passed away days later.

Once in 1980 in Camp 6, a criminal about twenty years old whose weight was no more than ninety pounds stole a pumpkin and the prison guard in charge of his group caught him red-handed. On the way back, about a quarter mile from the camp, the guard beat him continually. When they reached an orchard, the guard kicked the boy until he fell into a ditch.

The ditch was about two yards deep and three yards wide with bamboo spikes planted at its bottom. It ran beside a bamboo fence around the orchard to protect it from thieves. Some spikes slashed the victim's calf and buttocks. The guard didn't let him climb up, just kept on scolding him with bad words until we prisoners working nearby yelled loudly in protest.

When we returned to the camp, we saw the guard continuing to beat the criminal at the gate area. A female public security nurse was passing by. After the guard told her that the poor boy had stolen pumpkins many times, she hit the boy's shins three or four times with her metallic ruler and laughed heartily while the boy shrieked in pain. Seeing his bleeding shins, I felt pain in my own tibias.

The guardian in charge of my ward explained that a criminal prisoner was considered the waste of the society. The camp was to exploit the criminals' last working capability to help feed them. Some guardians openly said that there was no simple way to keep the stubborn prisoners obedient to camp regulations; only cane beatings could be effective. The camp was not responsible if the death rate was not higher than 2 percent a month, they asserted.

In North Việt Nam prisons, criminal prisoners treated each other with unthinkable brutality. Many of them killed their rivals for trivial reasons, such as cheating for a small amount of money. Whenever possible, they cheated other inmates even for a five-inch piece of potato or a small ear of corn.

One among the criminal convicts was an NVA lieutenant with a good education and schooling in Russia who used to talk to me when he was working close to us. He was serving his life sentence after his soldiers in an NVA signal company attacked a public security checkpoint, killing some of the PS officers who were beating an old woman black and blue for some trivial violation. He behaved well with remarkable manners in the criminals' society. He assigned himself a task of leading his fellow convicts back to honesty and a good way of living. In a way of speaking, he obtained a little success.

Once discussing with me the excessive cheating habits of the criminal prisoners, he said, "Honesty does not exist in the criminal inmates' society. For so long, a promise had no value to a large number of the population in this backward and starving North Việt Nam countryside."

The prison has become an instrument of the communist regime to deter law breaking and scare away opposition. But at the same time, the communist prison policy engendered a class of incorrigible social evildoers. They got in and out of prison many times and spent more time in prison than in society. They were ready to endure the most painful methods of torture for their wrongdoing and cared little about life or death. A bout of beating that could end a strong American wrestler's career was within the endurance of an emaciated criminal prisoner in a North Việt Nam camp.

In turn, the prison camp's authorities had to apply more and more brutal punishment to subdue them.

A PRACTICAL VIEW OF THE NVA SOLDIERS

A young geologist trained in Moscow working at a site close to the field where we were growing rice flatly criticized us for our lack of knowledge of the communist regime. When one of us asked him why NVA soldiers from the panhandle area (the northern part of Central Việt Nam) could fight boldly against our terrible firepower, he explained in a low and compassionate voice:

"The poor boys in this area have suffered from extreme hunger since they were born. They have never enjoyed a full meal of rice. They are used to seeing life switched to death beside them. They don't care much about life the way we do. You and the Americans have at least something to be concerned about: wife, children, a civilized lifestyle, and your good jobs. Naturally you don't like to waste all of that for nothing.

"Furthermore, the young men here are afraid of being persecuted at their home village because of bad conduct while fighting the war much more than death on the battlefield. Besides, while serving in the battle areas they were fed full with 100 percent rice, a special favor from the communist government they had never dreamed of at their villages. Marching by foot for hundreds of miles on the Long Mountain with a pair of rubber sandals and a second field dress in the rucksack was just fine, no worse than doing hard work in the cooperatives' rice fields back home."

The geologist concluded, "A communist soldier had no choice but to charge forward with a hope of survival; otherwise, he would face a sure punishment by his commander and be an outcast in his village for the rest of his life if he came back safely from the battlefield."

MORE LIGHT OF HOPE

Prison life became less torturous after we were moved to Camp 6. My fellows often voiced their criticism of the communist regime without being punished. The jailers acted as if they had not heard the dissenting remarks or the ARVN martial songs that called for fighting communists.

My sister visited me in December. She was surprised that the camp officials were friendlier toward visitors, more considerate than before.

Visiting relatives brought us some good news about several humanitarian and human rights organizations in the world that were calling for our release from the communist prison camps. Although many rumors seemed to be baseless and too optimistic, they actually raised our spirits.

According to information shared by our relatives and confirmed privately by some friendly jailers, there was a plan by the communist central authorities in 1977–78 to resettle us prisoners after we ended our prison terms. If it had gone on as Hà Nội was planning, we and our families would have been sent to state-controlled farms along the common borders with Laos and China to live for the rest of our lives. Many sites were picked and primary preparations for the project were made before the Chinese forces invaded the northern border provinces in 1979. The invasion may have been one of the reasons that brought an end to the project.

Tết 1980 in Camp 6

The cultural shows presented by our prisoners' choir attracted an audience of about 700 people, many of whom had ridden twenty miles by bicycle to attend the show. This time we played songs of North Việt Nam as required by the camp. The audience cheered us to the echo, saying, "Them South Việt Nam officers sing better than the professionals in our district's and province's cultural troupes."

The next evening, the cultural group of the camp's public security unit held a show with costumes and stage decorations full of colors and lights, but there were only 200 people attending, including a score of children.

Several villages near Camp 6 sent letters to the camp inviting our choir to perform, and the choir would be paid more than the Nghệ Tĩnh provincial cultural group had been previously. The camp approved, but the Ministry of Public Security turned down the requests because of possible unfavorable influence, a friendly jailer told us.

One more thing we had not been aware of before April 30, 1975, was the ruling system established at the infrastructure level in North Việt Nam.

The above-mentioned geologist engineer explained to us: "To replace the old-time landlord class dominating the rural life for thousands of years, the communist regime has founded its village government system with the 'neo-red wicked lords,' who are given unlimited authority over poor peasants, much more brutal than wicked lords under the French colonialists."

Although these wicked lords were successful in maintaining social order and political security, they were incapable of local economic and administrative management. Thousands of development projects ended up in complete failure, wasting a large chunk of the national budget and the contributions of the people, the young engineer asserted. He pointed to a nearby hamlet and said, "That hamlet has been moved to new locations five times during the last twenty-three years. A new village party committee might decide on a different land allocation map and people had to move and build their new shelters without any assistance from the local government."

He alleged that those red-lords ran their political security business much more effectively than their pre-1945 predecessors at the cost of hardships falling upon the necks and shoulders of the toiling villagers. On behalf of "the Revolution," local communist leaders—especially the public security—were ruling the countryside with an iron hand, being much more atrocious than the wicked village lords in colonial times. The typical scene of a twenty-five-year-old public security officer scolding a sixty-year-old woman with abusive language when she got caught in an illegal trading of clothes or food was not uncommon in many villages.

Heavy agricultural taxes and another half dozen compulsory contributions were imposed on the peasants and collected to the penny. Tax collectors along with public security officers would search the homes of those who failed to pay sufficient income tax (in rice) in time to seize everything in their homes that had some value, including a rudimentary bed, a sedge mat, an altar, cheap earthenware pottery, bowls, and chopsticks.

BACK TO THE SOUTH

In October 1980, some prisoners in Camp 6 were moved to Camp Z-30C at Hàm Tân, in the former province of Bình Tuy, South Việt Nam. I was in the first group of about 400 prisoners to be transferred.

On a roadside in front of Camp 6, about twenty local people waved farewell to us. I saw some wiping tears from their cheeks. They lived near the camp, and we often helped them with medicines and bought their goods, paying them generously.

After moving by truck for two hours from Camp 6, we boarded the southbound trains at Vinh City. At the railway station, we were all sitting in a half dozen passenger cars, every two of us sharing a pair of iron handcuffs. At the long platform there were a few teenage boys and girls peddling their wares. A girl of about twelve years old seemed surprised at our presence on the train while she was selling brewed raw tea. She disappeared for a minute, then came back beaming. She poured hot tea from her portable kettle into the cup of everyone who was asking for it.

She was busy serving us, saying that we should pay her later as she had to fill all the two scores of cups before the station security guards might interfere. The public security troops escorting us were gathering in two groups and chatting noisily at the two ends of the trains.

When every cup was filled, she withdrew to the platform of the adjacent line and refused to collect our money. After we insisted many times, she said, "My mom tells me not to take your money."

One of my fellows asked her: "Why? Do you know who we are?"

The skinny little girl nodded while wiping her wet cheeks. "Yes, we do, my uncles." We were moved deeply by the attitude of a little girl in this panhandle area of North Việt Nam, which had long been strongly influenced by communist propaganda.

On the way to the South, we received many other signs of sympathy and respect, particularly after crossing the Bến Hải River (at the 17th parallel, which once divided the two Việt Nams). From Quảng Trị to Hàm Tân, many groups awaited our railway cars near the stations. As the trains reduced speed, they threw food, candy, and cigarettes to us through car windows.

At last, we returned to the South after four years in four prison camps in North Việt Nam.

*   *   *

Camp Hàm Tân—in a location also known as ARVN Fire Base 6—had three subdivisions: Annexes A, B, and C. My group was locked up in Annex B.

We quickly realized the big difference between the camps in the North and those in the South. Here in the South, criminal inmates behaved much better than those in the North: honest, less brutal, and more humane with each other. Communist guards and camp officials, all from the North, were treating prisoners with more consideration. Probably the environment and the social atmosphere in the former free nation largely influenced them.

One day in my first week at Camp Hàm Tân, a prisoner working close to my group drew our attention. He was emaciated; his skin was pale after fourteen months locked up incommunicado in a dark cell. He was working laboriously under the hot sun. When he stopped for a minute, one of the two jail guards asked him to continue and he didn't answer. After the guard repeated his order several times, the young prisoner became upset. He said, "You stupid ass! Every guard in this camp knows how hard I am working for years. I stop when I feel tired. Shut up your lousy mouth!" The angry guard was about to beat him when the other guard stopped him, saying that one should not argue with that "mad prisoner. Just leave him alone."

At break time, he told me his story.

He was brought up in an orphanage and worked hard for a high school diploma. At twenty years old, he was drafted and trained at the Thủ Đức Army Reserve Officer School. He was serving in combat units until April 30, 1975, when he reported to the communist authorities for "reeducation" with the rank of second lieutenant. He was sent to a prison camp in Phước Long province, seventy miles north of Sài Gòn.

A few years later, four young wives of four lieutenants imprisoned in the camp came to visit their husbands. Arriving in the late morning, they were told to stay overnight in the reception house while waiting to meet with their husbands the next morning. That night, several communist soldiers in the camps raped the four women, then killed all of them with bayonets. The soldiers looted all of the victims' belongings.

"When I went with a dozen fellows to bury the young ladies, the gory sight dealt me a great shock," he said. "I will never forget the ladies of about twenty-some, lying naked on the dirt floor and soaked in blood from stabs, apparently riddled by AK bayonets on their unclothed bodies.

"The camp officials refused to investigate, just declared that there was no evidence that connected the camp soldiers to the crimes, although civilians didn't live within five miles of the camp," he related. (I learned from friends who had been in Camp Gia Trung, thirty miles east of Pleiku city from 1976 to 1985, that five or six prisoners' wives and daughters were raped and killed by NVA troops of the camp and no investigation or prosecution was ever conducted.)

After the event, he attempted to seize rifles from the guards to fight them but failed. He was thrown into the dark cell for weeks. When he was released, the camp security officer asked him if he had changed his attitude, to which he said, "Yes, I have changed. I am much more anticommunist now. I regret not fighting harder in the war. I also regret treating communist prisoners with great compassion and soft hands. As a Catholic, I may not commit suicide. If you kill me anyway, I will appreciate your good help. If not, please don't release me because once I am free, I will exchange myself for as many communists as I can."

The dark cell failed to scare him after fourteen months, and the camp officials reluctantly released him to the working prisoners' ward.

When I asked him the reason that urged him to act, he said, "An officer must act accordingly to his rank and age. I am a second lieutenant, so I must act as a lieutenant, tough and unyielding, and I should not act the way of a major. You have the dignity of a field grade, so you should not act the way of a lieutenant because you are not supposed to have actions that are rude and too fanatic."

He added, "Some said that my acts against the communist regime that is consolidated and is holding powerful authority are futile. But I assert that we must act against the tyranny in Việt Nam whether our efforts are large or small. Our fight would obstruct some of the little communist plots against the interests of our people."

In Camp Hàm Tân, I met many young men; some had been ARVN soldiers who were captive members of the Phục Quốc movement (Nation Restoration). The Phục Quốc was formed after the RVN was overthrown as an armed group operating in Sài Gòn and the provinces. Its objectives included elimination of the communist regime. In the late 1970s, the communist security forces launched an all-out effort to eradicate the movement. Those young men still maintained their high spirits in prison.

PRO-SOVIET CULTURE

Nearly a year had passed since the short but bloody war between Hà Nội and Beijing. We could tell how the war between the two previously close-knit communist parties was demoralizing the communist party members. Every time we heard commentary on communist Radios Hà Nội and Sài Gòn attacking the Chinese aggressors with the most insulting language, I felt as if it were a joke.

For one year there had been no political indoctrination class. The guards and other jailers did not talk to us as they used to about how good the Chinese had been to their Vietnamese comrades.

In December 1980, Hà Nội promulgated its new constitution. Its lengthy preamble strongly criticized the so-called Chinese hegemonic aggressors. Imitating the Soviet Union terminology, the 1980 constitution changed its formerly called prime minister into chairman of the Council of Ministers. Songs that smacked of Chinese tunes were played no more. Chinese Vietnamese continued to flee Việt Nam to Western countries and to mainland China.

A PLAN TO ESCAPE

Since 1976, there had been strong protests by prisoners in several reeducation camps. The prisoners raised their voices against cruel treatment, calling on the communist leaders to respect human rights and to abide by international conventions on prisoners of war. I heard of such events at some camps in many provinces such as An Điềm (Quảng Nam), Xuân Phước (Phú Yên), Xuân Lộc, Long Giao (Long Khánh), and Tân Hiệp (Biên Hòa).

In summer 1981, a large protest flared up in Camp Z-30D (also called Camp Thủ Đức) located at the former ARVN Fire Base 5, next to Camp Hàm Tân. Because a guard beat a prisoner, all 1,000 inmates joined a hunger strike for a few days in protest. The camp HQS reacted softly, treating the prisoners with smooth hands to restore order while sending for an armored platoon along with hundreds of soldiers ready to crack down on the prisoners. A few days later, public security authorities picked out many prisoners from a list of could-be leaders of the protest and sent them to other camps.

We were fed better and forced to work less than in the previous years and received supplies more frequently from our families owing to their shorter trips to see us. In a month we looked healthier with higher spirits.

In a visit shortly after I moved to Camp Hàm Tân, my mother and my wife brought me good news. My two children had been resettled in San Jose, under the sponsorship of my sister's husband. He had been giving great assistance to my family during the long struggle to rebuild our lives in America.

It was the first time my mother had seen me since I was locked up in June 1975. She was among the millions of unfortunate Vietnamese women whose husbands underwent painful hardships in prisons of the two sides when they were young wives, and their sons suffered the same way when they became old grandmothers.

In April, a communist army colonel came to see me for information related to some former high-ranking communists who had defected to the SVN side in the war. I provided him with information that was too old to do any harm to anyone. He thanked me and said, "I tell you this, even if I were your own brother, I wouldn't be able to get you out of jail a day earlier. Those who approve the list of prisoners to be released don't care about your prisoners' records and don't care much about what you're doing in the camp unless you do something really important, committing murder or setting fire to the camp, for instance." That might be why during my prison years, a half dozen prisoners on the lists of those to be released had been found dead or missing or had already fled Việt Nam.

I kept teaching English to young fellows who were eager to learn, using instruction sheets enclosed in medicine containers as teaching aids. Sometimes prison security agents asked me if I was running an English class. I replied that I was only explaining how my fellows should use the medications.

I also continued to work on my personal project to compile the book of Vietnamese-English synonyms. In 1980, I bribed a jail guardian to buy me Vietnamese-English dictionaries printed in Hà Nội. Besides a dictionary my wife sent me in 1975, the newly bought dictionaries helped me spend every hour of my spare time listing all possible English synonyms corresponding to a

Vietnamese word. I planned to work with some English-language professors to publish a book of Vietnamese-English synonyms that would assist users in looking up terms in dictionaries.

I was working industriously on that in order to stay busy and to keep myself from worrying about my family, as well as maintaining my normal mentality. If I had been in jail for five more years, I would have completed my project.

In summer 1981, my group was moved to Annex C, a mile farther into the forest. A new public security guardian came to take charge of my group. It happened that he was from a family who had received some help from my family during the 1945 famine. He silently did me some little favors that were within his power. One day when there was nobody around, he showed me a report in my file made by a jailer of the camp where I had stayed in 1978. The report concluded, "This prisoner has been fostering an extreme reactionary ideology, often doing covert anticommunist propaganda. An incorrigible element that should be watched closely."

I thought I would spend my lifetime in the communist prison.

I asked my wife and my sister to plan my escape. On the following visit, my wife told me that a family of farmers, friends of ours who lived close to the area where we prisoners were often working, had agreed to help me run away. That family would hide me in their secret underground shelter and also arrange my trip on a fishing boat to flee Việt Nam. Ten solid gold taels was the price. My family could afford it as my sister's husband had a good job in the Silicon Valley, and he was eager to help.

A fellow next to me in the ward was a Special Forces captain. He escaped in 1978, and when confronted by armed troops, he seized a Russian-made CKC rifle to fight back. He did not surrender after firing both magazines. Out of ammunition, he continued fighting with his bare hands. He was detained incommunicado and suffered savage torture for months. The friendly guard said that the similar report of the captain's case stated that he was an extremely dangerous prisoner. He also had no hope of early release, so he also had a plan to escape.

"REEDUCATION"

All former officers of the RVN military and government class A employees like myself had been imprisoned since June 1975, as had many artists, novelists, writers, poets, journalists, politicians, nationalist activists, and civilians suspected of being CIA informants.

According to information we learned after our release from our fellow officers who had been working in the Joint General Staff/Adjutant General Department, we could estimate that about 80,000 ARVN officers were incarcerated in communist prison camps: 32 of the total 112 generals, some 350 to 600 full colonels, between 1,700 and 2,500 lieutenant colonels, 5,500 to 6,500 majors, and 72,000 to 80,000 captains and lieutenants, including Woman Army Forces Corps officers. About 90 percent of these prisoners were younger than fifty in 1975.

The communist leaders did not imprison all of the nearly 1 million ARVN noncommissioned officers and enlisted men. These men had to attend the three-day reeducation classes at village level conducted by local communist authorities. Most were allowed to live with their families under the close watch of the public security as second-rate citizens. A small number of them were sent to reeducation camps along with the officers, while many others and their dependents were resettled in remote "New Economic Areas." In some districts they were compelled to serve in the land mine clearing groups.

There were approximately 200,000 nonmilitary prisoners. Blacklisted civilians including writers, poets, artists, songwriters, and members of nationalist parties were incarcerated months later than government officials and officers. Properties—the real estate of businessmen, entrepreneurs, and of large and small firms and factories—were confiscated and the owners were locked up for "reeducation" under the 1978 Commercial and Industrial Reform policy.

Actually, we were imprisoned under the status of half-POW, half-political prisoners. The communist authorities never officially recognized us as either of the two. In written paperwork, they referred to the North Việt Nam National Congress Resolution 49 in 1961 as the legal basis for sending us to "reeducation" camps. In fact, we had not been citizens of North Việt Nam.

In mid-1976, about half of the incarcerated RVN officers and civil servants (some 40,000 prisoners) were sent to one of perhaps 100 camps throughout the mountainous areas north of the 17th parallel. More than 40,000 were kept in South Việt Nam. In 1978, a camp official said to my friends and me there were around 170 national and provincial prisons in Việt Nam, including the Hỏa Lò Central Prison known as Hà Nội "Hilton."

It should be noted that the communist governments of many southern provinces had their different solutions to the problem of political prisoners. Provincial authorities from Quảng Trị to Nha Trang did not send their RVN prisoners to the North. The communist governments in Đà Lạt and Tuyên Đức did not permit prisoners' relatives to visit them, but allowed their families to send food, gifts, and medicine once every three months at seven kilograms each instead of five kilograms in other provinces.[4]

We were compelled to do manual labor six and a half days a week and eight hours a day, which might be more like ten hours/day in some camps, rain or shine. We were allowed a food ration of a farmer, the third in the five food-ration classes in North Việt Nam. In camps around the South, prisoners were fed at a little higher ration—only a little more but significant as nutrition is concerned—due to the region's higher productivity. As a result, the death rate in those camps was lower.

Thousands of former officers and civil servants of the RVN died of accidents, sickness, and malnutrition in the first five years. There was no official statistic, but as we exchanged information in later years, we could reach some general figures of death in more than 100 camps. Camp Tân Lập in Phú Thọ Northern Province was at the top of the list: of about 2,000 prisoners, there were more than 400 deaths in the first three years. In other camps, an average of 5 to 8 percent in three years was common.

There is no official figure of South Vietnamese prisoner deaths in reeducation camps. Given a death rate of 5 percent, the total deaths of former RVN officers and officials may have been more than 10,000. The death rate of criminal inmates must have been higher.

Most of the dead were buried carelessly in shallow graves with pieces of wood bearing their names scribbled in ink. No full record was kept. Every twenty years or so, communist authorities cleared the cemeteries, disinterred the remains, and discarded them in streams or rivers to make space for new dead prisoners.

A communist colonel told us in 1975 that when sending us to the concentration camps, the top communist leaders didn't really mean to "reeducate" us but were locking up all of us for political security concerns. "Reeducation" was just rhetoric for propaganda purposes. So during time in the coops, the prisoners' principal task was forced labor.

In the first few years, each camp had a few recalcitrant prisoners or fanatic anticommunists who openly attacked the communist policies, refused to endorse communist principles, and denied communist slanderous propaganda against the RVN. They were punished brutally, but most of them remained unbendable. In the end, most communist jailers gave up and left them untouched, except for cases of brutal beatings that ended with the prisoner's death.

There were numerous instances of barbarous treatment, ferocious torture, and unscrupulous executions of prisoners in many camps, particularly in the Central Việt Nam coastal areas. In many others, prisoners were compelled to work to exhaustion. Some camps even forced prisoners to clear minefields and unexploded bombs and shells with their bare hands and simple tools (bayonet, shovel). Persecution and torments also depended partly on the camp commander and his staff. Communist leadership traditions vested power to a subordinate unit or agency. Such power sometimes overrode the superior's directives.

Camp A-20 Xuân Phước in Phú Yên province and Camp An Điềm in Quảng Nam province were at the top of the list of infamous prisons in the South where jailers treated the prisoners with ruthless and cruel discipline. But the most ruthless treatment of prisoners must be in Camp Cổng Trời or Heaven Gate, twenty-two miles north of Hà Giang, the northernmost province, six miles from the China–Việt Nam common border. The camp received direct orders from the central committee, as most prisoners of the camps were stubborn dissidents who were the regime's archenemy. The most barbarous torturing measures were exerted. That included the execution of death row inmates by leaving them lying naked in a locked cell without food or water until death.

* * *

In 1976, when many of our fellows were running away from the camp, communist authorities issued an order to give the death penalty to the escapees. The order resulted in two fellows of each camp receiving the death penalty. Single death sentences were given to prisoners who voiced protest against the regime, including an ARVN female second lieutenant, Nguyễn Thị Kim Lang, on July 15, 1975, while she was pregnant with her first child. Communist authorities only notified their relatives of their execution after a few months.

However, after 1977 when they moved half of us to North Việt Nam, there were dozens of prisoners who escaped and were recaptured. But the communists brought none of them to court, at least in the North, to my knowledge.

Until 1995, when most RVN prisoners were released, no more than ten of the thousands of escapees safely reached the lands of freedom, as far as I have heard.

My friends and I sometimes agreed that if the communist leaders hadn't put us in jail but had treated us with a less inimical policy, we could have somewhat submitted entirely to their authority. If they had dispersed us all around the country, assigning each to a work at low and intermediate jobs, I thought that our anticommunism would have diminished to an insignificant degree. But no one thought the communist top leaders would keep their promises to treat us as brothers without any plot for vengeance and oppression.

We believed that communist leaders wouldn't buy that idea because they were unmitigated skeptical fanatics. They were afraid that former RVN officers resettled in a village would prove to villagers they were a group of persons with better education and better conduct compared with the communist counterparts. We could have undermined the communist authority and caused unpredictable troubles to the Communist Party.

THE FATE OF THE CHIÊU HỒI DEFECTORS

After April 30, 1975, the communist regime seemed to have no consolidated policy on the former defectors even though they had been considered its worst enemies.

During the first few days after the communist forces occupied South Việt Nam, many defectors were executed. It was impossible to have any reliable figures. I estimate that the communist security authority at local levels put to death no less than 1,000 and no more than 10,000 defectors. Ex-NVA Lieutenant Colonel Phan Mậu was detained on May 5, 1975, and was executed not long afterward.

All other defectors were to report for incarceration. A number of them were thrown into regular prisons and military prison camps. Many others were sent to reeducation camps to stay along with us RVN officers and officials. Many were tried at courts-martial as deserters and traitors and given specified sentences. Many others were released from reeducation camps after years without being formally convicted and sentenced.

Only a few former North Vietnamese officers, including Lieutenant Colonel Lê Xuân Chuyên, former 66th NVA Regiment CO, and ex-Senior Captain Phan Văn Xướng, serving the NVA Armor Corps, a specialist on the Red Chinese T-54 tanks, were overtly sentenced to death by a communist court-martial. Xướng's sentence was commuted owing to his wife's continuous faithful services to the communist cause in her home village in the South.

Most of those who had been communist regular soldiers (North and South Vietnamese) were handed prison terms from three to fifteen years. My former bodyguard (when I served the Chiêu Hồi Ministry), who had been a VC squad leader from South Việt Nam, got nine years instead of six years because, as a VC judge decided, he must have been very faithful to our side to have been employed as a bodyguard.

Other defectors who had been common guerrillas were to attend an indoctrination course of a few days or weeks and then were allowed to come back to their families. Communist authorities were busy with other security concerns such as building and operating the so-called reeducation camps to imprison hundreds of thousands of former South Việt Nam government officers, employees, nationalist activists, writers, journalists, and artists. They were incapable of dealing with the huge number of more than 150,000 defectors.

Their fate when they returned to the home villages largely depended on the local party authorities' decisions. Some of those local leaders were tolerant, and some weren't. However, all were classified as third-rate citizens. Their children were facing discrimination. A small number of the defectors fled and immigrated to the United States, Canada, and Australia by taking risky boat trips or going through the Orderly Departure Program.

After Sài Gòn collapsed, evidence from the communist side proved Chiêu Hồi a very effective strategy of the psychological warfare with the highest humanitarian spirit.

THE LESSONS WE ACTUALLY LEARNED

In fact, communist leaders failed to teach us anything if they had intended to do so. Ironically, during our incarceration we learned many unexpected valuable lessons from the common people we met while working outside the camps. The lessons we learned best were realities under the Communist Party's regime.

Before 1975, military and common people in South Việt Nam had a vague notion about the North. The new lessons taken from real life gave me not only wider knowledge but also deeper feelings. Most of my fellows said that if they had learned the truth about life in the North under the communists, they would have acted differently in war.

What made me feel sad was the fact that by 1976, North Việt Nam had declined in almost every aspect. For years, young compatriots in the North had been taught to hate instead of to love. General education was extremely poor. They were prone to play very brutal games, one of which was throwing rocks at passenger cars on railroads. A large segment of the youth did not care about social etiquette, and crude manners, vulgarity, and violence prevailed. They were ready to cheat and lie to earn even a petty profit. Children were not taught to be honest.

However, it was amazing to see how communist leaders achieved great success in exerting obscurantism for harnessing their people's thoughts and actions. Cramming political teachings and lies into the people's heads since childhood proved very effective. It helped motivate the youth's morale, although overstuffed political teachings resulted in severe unfavorable social psychological behaviors such as the tendency to lie and be hypocritical.

It was easy to notice that the retarding impact of the 1955–56 Land Reform Campaign, which had taken the lives of more than 200,000 landlords and prospective antagonists, was still noticeable in every hamlet and village. The "Machine of Terror" was still horrible, much more threatening than we had thought. It helped communist authorities keep the peasants under control, dampening every spark of opposition.

The war left unmistakable scars on the poor and surprisingly backward society. In every village we had a chance to visit, the number of war widows was incredibly high. We could easily notice the apparently reduced population of young men of the 1945–55 generation. In talking with us, villagers said that there were many women who received more than two "Martyr's Wife" status certificates. In some villages, the champion of them might have gotten as many as four certificates: four husbands killed in the war whose bodies had never been recovered. I don't know whether there has been any other country where the value of human life was so low.

*   *   *

On the brighter side, the society of North Việt Nam had some good aspects under the communist regime.

I believed in the statistic claiming that 95 percent of the population could read and write, but most children living far from the cities went to school past second grade. It takes a Vietnamese child only 12 months to learn how to read and write relatively well. Rudimentary general knowledge helped more effective propaganda and political teaching. It reminded me of George Orwell's *Animal Farm*, which I had read years earlier. If Orwell had lived a few months in North Việt Nam, he would have added at least one more chapter to his book on the *Animal Farm Annex in Việt Nam*.

The public health care net covered most of the population, but the government medical budget was too small. A great number of villagers had to rely on primitive herbal medication.

Women—particularly in cities—enjoyed more rights and decency and suffered less brutal oppression from their husbands while they participated more and more in political and social activities. However, in the countryside, there were many men who were living with two wives; some even had three.

Being not party members, the common people were equally poor and suffered equal hardships.

*   *   *

What really reeducated us came from some North Vietnamese people who harshly criticized us for our shameful defeat. One of them said to my group in absence of the guards, "For twenty years since 1954, we have been waiting for you to march north to liberate us. But you come here at last as prisoners. You are shameful! It's because you didn't fight hard enough, you tolerated corruption, you enjoyed too much. You have betrayed us."

Those of us who were scolded quietly swallowed the stinging words as a punishment we deserved. Our fellows at every other camp were receiving the same bitter cup of rebuke from many people they met, and they also silently drank it all.

To many of my fellow officers and me, the years of mental torture and hard labor in the communist prison camps helped us reform ourselves. Getting rid of certain bad habits, asserting more reasonable opinions about mistakes and errors our side had committed, and having a clearer vision of the communist side and of the war all resulted in the radical renovation of our minds.

UNEXPECTED SYMPATHY

Communist leaders may have thought that North Việt Nam would be a safe place to lock up South Việt Nam's officers for some time. But our presence in the North produced effects they could never have anticipated.

In our first weeks, we were facing the inimical attitude of many people living around the camps, especially the young men. Several times villagers we met on rural roads called us "You American puppets" or traitors or even uttered curses upon us. Others refused to help or to talk to us. It hurt our feelings a great deal.

Months later, things had changed. More than half of the villagers around the camp areas treated us as friends. Many even showed their sympathy to us openly in front of communist officers. North Vietnamese city people who had been resettled in these remote villages since 1961 greatly sympathized with us. The camp authorities were unable to stop us from seeing villagers, simply because they had to have us work in open fields to grow food as required by their Public Security Ministry.

When we were moved to the other camps nearly every year, many villagers were waiting to see us off and to give us food and gifts along with tearful farewells. We had never expected such profound sympathies from them.

Sometimes communist cadres of medium and high rank showed us their goodwill, too. The retired district party committee's secretary of a village east of Camp 4 met us when my group was going to work and invited us into his home for tea, disregarding protest from the escorting officer of the camp.

The retired party chief of the village next to Camp 6 met my two fellows and me at a rice field and shared with us secret information that we would be moved to the South in a month. He reminded us, "You are now prisoners, but someday you will rebuild our country. We wish you luck. Take care of yourselves and preserve your virtues and dignity so that you will become unblemished builders of the new Việt Nam." His words elevated our morale, but I felt that I did not deserve his appreciation and expectations.

After incarcerating us for long years, Hà Nội failed to win over our hearts and minds. Its prisons only hardened our anticommunist determination. On the contrary, South Vietnamese prisoners had converted hundreds of communist cadres as high as colonels to Catholics, Protestants, and Buddhists, and especially had made them secretly relinquish Marxist-Leninism. The late Cardinal Nguyễn Văn Thuận proselytized four communist officers who were in charge of guarding him while he was held incommunicado for over ten years.

I knew many communist prison guards secretly sided with us, telling us their dissenting opinion and helping us whenever possible. They made our life in prison since the sixth year gradually more agreeable without the use of bribery.

WHAT IF SOUTH VIỆT NAM HAD WON THE WAR?

Some friends of mine from North Việt Nam asked me: "If your side had won the war, how would you have treated the Communist Party members, its officials, and its officers? Would you do the same as they did to you?"

My answer was prompt: "In that case, we would not have sent all communist officers and ranking party cadres to concentration camps except for the central top leaders. There would possibly be some personal revenge, even killing, that would be out of central authorities' control, but not as rampant and systematic as what the communists did to us in 1975. There certainly would be no discrimination against their children either. What we did before 1975 in the Chiêu Hồi program justifies my assertion.

"We would have maintained all cemeteries of fallen communist soldiers, and continued to pay pensions to communist disabled warriors and war widows," I said to him. After the 1954 Geneva Accords, the South Vietnamese government did not destroy the cemeteries of the Việt Minh war dead. On the sites of major battles, French and Việt Minh troops' scattered remains were gathered in graves on which solemn memorials were built with the inscription "In memory of the Vietnamese and French fallen warriors in the Indochinese War, 1949–54." Many of those were raised along the Mang Yang Pass on National Highway 19 from Pleiku to Qui Nhon.

"Former communist officials serving the government and the armed forces would have been retained to do their jobs. Communist medals and public heroic feats would have been preserved and recognized. Communists who gave their lives in the struggle for independence of Việt Nam would have been remembered, except for Hồ Chí Minh and top communist leaders who were responsible for spreading communism in Việt Nam and waging the devastating war. But all schemes to revive the Communist Party would have been firmly eradicated."

I related the stories of the U.S. Civil War when the Confederate army surrendered to the Union forces. General Grant accepted the surrender of General Lee with great respect. The Confederate soldiers were free to return home with personal gear including their horses and were living as any other American citizens without being humiliated, retaliated against, or ill treated.

THE BRAVE ARVN BRIDES

I also have to highly honor the wives of the post-1975 South Vietnamese political prisoners. Most of them had great courage and patience, working hard to stay on their feet and take care of their families and to supply their imprisoned husbands with food and medications as well. They were facing a lot of trouble in the new regime that included a chaotic economy and the discrimination system against the South Vietnamese in general and members of the former regime in particular.

Under such narrow circumstances, most wives were trying their best to travel as far as 1,000 miles to visit their husbands and supply them with food and medicines. Their trips to many camps were not easy on lonely rough roads where they had to walk many miles through jungles. Some of the brave women were robbed and killed before reaching the camps. However, it was the hardships and dangers they endured that earned them deeper love from their husbands that wouldn't have been attained if the RVN hadn't fallen on April 30, 1975.

A lot of ARVN officers' wives were evicted from their homes and compelled to move to the "New Economic Areas" in remote virgin lands, in mountainous or marshy districts with little or no food or financial assistance. Most fled the areas illegally to come back and lived in shabby huts erected on pieces of unclaimed land in the suburbs.

When both husband and wife were military officers and were locked up in the reeducation camps, they suffered many more hardships, especially when they had young children. If they had no close relatives or good friends to get help, the fate of the kids was miserable.

Other brave women must have included the wives of ARVN enlisted men and NCOs. Most of their husbands were not incarcerated in concentration camps. But compared with the officers' wives, they suffered as many if not more hardships. The most unfortunate cases were the wives of the ARVN disabled veterans, who were paralyzed or who lost their limbs in war.

LIFE IN THE OUTER PRISON

I spent eight years and nine months living in Sài Gòn with my family after I was released from a prison camp and before I immigrated to the United States in October 1990. Those years helped me gain a deeper insight into the communist regime.

The most remarkable evil in the communist regime is corruption. Before April 30, 1975, most South Vietnamese thought that communist cadres and leaders were fanatical and authoritative, even bloodthirsty, but they never expected that those "revolutionaries" would have been so greedy and corrupt.

During the two wars, corruption was the most critical weakness of the nationalist side that the communist propaganda always exploited successfully. Meanwhile, few people had ever known that after the 1954 Geneva Accords, corruption in the North Việt Nam government was just as serious. The only difference was that in North Việt Nam the state-controlled media never reported it. After 1975, it grew faster, larger, and almost overtly into an incorrigible social evil.

In Sài Gòn of the 1980s, I often saw traffic policemen taking graft from curbstone dealers, cyclo drivers, and other poor people every day. Graft might have been as cheap as a cigarette or a glass of soft drink. Under the pre-1975 regimes, corrupt police officers would take bribes from well-off violators at an amount that was worth the risk but would never deign to accept a graft of such small value from the paupers.

I believed that corrupt high-ranking officials in the communist government had ill-earned illegal incomes several times larger than their counterparts in the former South Việt Nam regime. The Red Bourgeoisie built up their assets at a rapid speed, and their wives and children spent money recklessly.[5]

Communist ranking members appointed to leading jobs at state-owned firms and government offices appeared to be inept but authoritarian. Because of their low education, their orders and directives were usually impracticable and revealed their ignorance. Public assets were squandered away.

National education was degrading, social values were declining, and morality was deteriorating. The poor suffered more hardships and inequality than in the colonial era. I found it impossible for the communist regime to lead Việt Nam into prosperity and an advanced economy in democracy.

TWENTY-EIGHT

Release

FREE TO LIVE IN A LARGER PRISON

On January 10, 1982, while I was waiting for the escape information—time, place, and password—I was informed that I was on the list of eighty-eight prisoners to be released on January 21. That was far beyond my expectation.

In January 11, the release decision was read at Annex C large yard. My name was about the tenth on the list. To my surprise, the name of the Special Forces captain was called near the end of the list. He was stunned and shocked, staggering to join the group of to-be-released inmates. To him and me, it was far beyond our hope.

A dozen others classified as "slow progressive and reactionary" prisoners were also released. Meanwhile, some who collaborated with the camp guards as informers and those whose parents and siblings were ranking communists were not on the list. Many of them stayed ten to thirteen years in prisons without the least idea why their close relatives' faithful service to the communist cause had failed to help them get out of jail earlier.

Before leaving the camp, I went looking for a public security sergeant to say good-bye. He tacitly sided with us, allowing us rest more than compelling us to work whenever it was his turn to guard my group working in the fields. I shook his hand and thanked him for his kindness. After half a minute of silence, he said to me with a sad tone:

"I am sure many of you do understand me. I was very sorry I have not been able to help you more than what I could." Then without smiling, he shook my hand, wished me good luck, and said, "You are leaving the *smaller* prison and will begin to live in the *larger* prison with me and our 70 million compatriots." The expression was not new, but it was a surprise to me when it was said by a thirty-year-old communist, son of a hardcore communist district leader in Thanh Hóa province, North Việt Nam.

After a ten-day fattening period, as is often done in communist "reeducation camps" when prisoners to be released were fed with higher rations, on January 20, 1982, at 1 PM, I walked past the camp main gate, ending the long term of six years, seven months, and five days in the "smaller prison camps."

Like other released fellows, I lost no time walking away from the barbed-wire gate a few seconds after a jail clerk handed me the release certificate, not waiting to receive the bus ticket fee from the financial office. Many prisoners who had been in Camp Hàm Tân since 1977 advised us to leave the camp as soon as possible after walking out of the gate. They said that one day in 1978, more than 100 prisoners of that camp received release papers and were lining up waiting for bus ticket fee. When half of them received the money and walked out of the gate, a telephone call from somewhere ordered those who were still inside the gate to give back their release papers and return to the wards. Those who were already outside the main gate went home without any trouble. The unlucky guys remained in the camp for more than two years before being released in 1981. No reason was given, even to the jailers.

So I was released four days before Tết 1982. The communist authority freed thousands of prisoners in camps all over the country during that week.

At a small rural hamlet beside Highway 1 to Sài Gòn about a mile from the camp, two farmer families invited everyone of the released group into their poor houses built with thatched roofs and earthen walls and treated us to a special dinner. The two old men asked us to stay to enjoy their homemade rice wine and pork noodles. They said they had killed two hogs for the "happy and well-wishing occasion."

About twenty of us joined the families at their dinner tables. The others just dropped in for cups of tea and thanked the families for their friendship, but they had to catch the earliest bus for a long trip home far away in the Mekong Delta.

One of the old men said, "We didn't care much about you before 1975, even hated some of you. But now we realize that you really had been good members of the former republic's army. We feel a true happiness when seeing you released from the camp. This dinner is a sign of profound sympathy to all of you. Please drink a toast to the good health of all of us."

I stayed with the old men for an hour, then got on a small bus to Sài Gòn. All of the bus owners offered us a free 100-mile ride to the capital of South Việt Nam. I arrived home at 5:30 PM. The kids who were old enough to know me when I left the neighborhood on June 15, 1975, cheered loudly when I stepped down from a cyclo in front of my home. My wife and the children met me at the front door, whereas my mother came about a half an hour later from my sister's home.

I had a strange feeling at my home. It took me an hour trying to reconnect with my past, even with my mother, my wife, and my children, trying to fill the gap of 2,411 days' memories.

It was a fancy coincidence. We had been married on the same lunar calendar date nineteen years earlier, on January 21, 1963. When my wife and I were alone at last, I held her tightly in my arms, and we had the longest kiss since we first met in 1962. Time passed in a happiness that seemed greater than on our nuptial night, which had also been four days before Tết 1963. Half an hour later under the dim light of the bedroom, my lips felt tears on her cheeks.

"You're crying! How come? Aren't you happy to have me come back?" I asked. She turned to me, holding me against her and said, "I'm happy. But I also begin to worry about how you will live safely under *them*." I knew a new period of my life would begin tomorrow.

During my incarceration in three camps in South Việt Nam and three camps in North Việt Nam, I underwent all kinds of hardships imposed by the communist regime. In fact, the so-called reeducation camps were simply forced labor concentration sites where cunning retaliation was carried out on a calculated scale.

A THIRD-CLASS CITIZEN

The next morning I reported to the ward public security office and registered as "temporary resident" at my own home and family. I then started my life in the "larger prison" under the communist regime without legal citizenship. I had to get the public security office's permission when traveling outside of Sài Gòn.

A week later, on January 27, three days after Tết, the respectable notable Trần Văn Hương passed away peacefully at his home. He had served as Sài Gòn's mayor, twice as RVN prime minister, and as president of the republic after President Thiệu resigned and before General Dương Văn Minh, the last president of the South. I held him in high esteem for his character. He was a brave, outspoken old man who refused to be evacuated from Việt Nam in April 1975. When the communist government offered to restore his citizenship, he categorically refused.

I was living without citizenship and didn't have the citizen's identity card until 1987. We were admonished that we would be expelled from Sài Gòn if we did not abide by the communist laws and regulations. Many of my fellow officers were sent to work at the construction sites of the Trị An hydroelectric power plant project near Biên Hòa and to join the teams clearing land mines and unexploded shells around the pre-1975 allied and ARVN base camps.

I had to report to the ward public security office every Sunday, telling the PS officer in charge of my neighborhood what I was doing, where I was visiting, and whom I met. Six months later, the report was requested every three months. I was living as a temporary resident, not qualified to buy food at official prices, but I had to contribute money like any other citizen for "Socialist Labor," a kind of poll tax once applied in Việt Nam under the French colonialist regime.

So we had to buy rice at higher prices in the "gray market," which was tacitly allowed by communist authorities and managed mostly by ranking communists' dependents and those who had good connections with them. However, it was illegal to carry rice from one province to another. A dozen checkpoints in the Mekong Delta would seize any amount of rice as little as one kilogram carried by a passenger without a written permit signed by a local food control agency, which was rarely awarded to commoners.

In 1982, the waves of people who fled Việt Nam for free world countries were still high. My wife and my sister urged me to venture for a boat trip. But none of the boat trip organizers convinced me of their navigational expertise and safety arrangements.

In my neighborhood, about one in every five people was attempting to flee Việt Nam. Only two or three of ten were lucky to reach the land of freedom on the first trip. The other four were caught and jailed, and three or four died and were missing on the way to escape. A great number of the boat people had not been working for or related to the former RVN.

An old couple living ten doors from my home sent their six children on three consecutive boat trips. Thai pirates killed two children on the first trip. They had their other two children follow, and they drowned on the high seas in a violent hurricane, according to a few survivors. Not much later in 1980, they sent the last two. They never heard from them again. Whenever I met the couple on my alley, I saw the inconsolable sorrow in their countenance.

From 1977 to 1980, local communist officials exerted their power to organize the so-called semi-official boat trips for people fleeing Việt Nam. Boat people had to pay the organizers in solid gold, commonly 10 *taels* per passenger. Owing to the local leader involvement, many rich Chinese found their way to the free world after the Hà Nội–backed anti-Chinese campaign, especially after the Private Industrial and Commercial Reform in 1978.

Semi-official boat trips ended when Hà Nội was harshly reprimanded for "exporting refugees." Each local communist leader allegedly earned many thousand gold *taels* after contributing a share of the earnings to the Communist Party budget.

In 1980 when my two children fled, a boatman had to pay between 3 and 5 *taels* to the private boat owner. My family paid eight *taels* for the two kids, thanks to $1,000 dollars my sister's husband sent from San Jose, California.

After more than six years under communist rulers, Sài Gòn was no longer a pleasant city. The busy downtown bore the appearance of a sick body. Most big stores and shops were closed. The brutal Private Industrial and Commercial Reform campaign had deprived the city of its living potential. The former capital of the republic seemed to be under foreign occupation and was looted of its opulence. The reform campaign turned South Việt Nam from a prosperous society where a business system had been consolidated and well coordinated into a disintegrating economy that was driving people into difficult living conditions. Local governments and public services were finding their own ways to make money.

Many people said that things were getting more unbearable than during the war. Although the Mekong Delta was a great granary of Southeast Asia, the agricultural co-operative program met passive protest from farmers, causing serious problems for rice production.

The hasty socialist reform of South Việt Nam turned out to be a disaster, negatively affecting every sector of the part of land that could have been a powerful economy.

Communist local leaders were ruling the districts and the wards as if they were the old-time mandarins. Their authoritarianism under the label of socialism and patriotism was worse than under the pre-1945 colonialist regime.

Red tape was hanging heavily over the population. The least important paperwork must bear the red seal of the village or ward public security to be valid. Applicants had to pay a small graft to get it. It took people a week to get a certified copy of a birth certificate.

The local public security agents had the authority to go into any home at any time, day or night, without a search warrant to check the household members' identity, to inspect every corner of the house, and to detain anyone suspected of breaking laws and regulations.

According to the communist officials I knew personally, there were about 600,000 public security officers all over Việt Nam, more than army soldiers. The city ward where I lived had 6,000 residents. It was under the control of twenty-five public security officers. Several hundred public security members served in the city and district agencies that supervised the sectors of political security, economy, social order, cultural activities, publication, and traffic control. Those were uniformed officers, not including several hundred plainclothes agents operating in every corner of the city—restaurants, coffee shops, *phở* houses, public parks, movies theaters, marketplaces, and on buses and trains. They were trailing after the suspects, noting every unusual behavior of common people—the trading of controlled staples, the business input of stores, restaurants—and reporting any irregularities to the agency for action.

Communist Party members held key jobs in most major economic and public institutions, especially the highly lucrative firms and businesses. Most of those new bosses were ethnic North Vietnamese.

Since the Black April, there were many radical changes at schools. All principals were Communist Party members. There were junior high school principals who had dropped out at second grade before joining the VC ranks and serving communist various services, many as guerrillas. After 1975, they were to attend special high school courses with simplified curriculum to be awarded a high school diploma after two years. It meant they would complete nine grades from third to twelfth in two years (four grades per year). They were appointed principals without having had any pedagogic training.

A great many directors (chief executive officers) of state-run enterprises had the same background. This simplified curriculum was called a "supplementary course," including some college classes. Its sole purpose was to give the "directors" an appropriate title, not a real education level.

In the scientific, educational, medical, and cultural domains, the faithful party members held most of the top posts, although their training, expertise, and capability were far below par. Even today, the new ruling class from low to high ranks has brought about the deterioration of writing and speaking the Vietnamese language. With the exception of people from the pre-1954 middle class who had a relatively better education, most communist cadres, officials, and common people are speaking Vietnamese in casual dialogues with political terms and complicated phrase construction as if they were delivering a philosophy lesson or addressing a political summit. Even worse, many of the terms are spoken in an improper obscure context, thus critically impoverishing the Vietnamese language.

I was more concerned about the education of my two children, who were still in Việt Nam. The quality of education in high schools was far below pre-1975 South Việt Nam standards. In physics and mathematics, lessons were taught of "what and how" to do but not "why." So the volume of work students had to accomplish became quite onerous because they needed to learn almost everything by heart, even solutions to the problems and writing task models. Therefore, I devoted much of my time to coaching my children to enhance their knowledge and creativity.

Many of my children's classmates were from families of communist party members, cadres, officials, and guerrillas. When some of them failed the semester tests, their parents came to see the teachers and used the threat of force that they must pass the tests and be given bonus marks to advance to the next grades. All teachers had to comply with the "revolutionaries'" demands.

Since the RVN fell into the hands of the communists, South Vietnamese learned more facts about the new regime, one of which was the behavior of children of communist leaders.

In the RVN before 1975, some ARVN generals' children were known for their bad conduct. They joined street gangs or became drug addicts, but none of them committed felonies. Youngsters from families of lower-ranked officers and civilian government officials could find no protection from their parents to participate in outlaw activities, as their parents had no power over the law enforcement officials.

This changed in 1975. Many communist chiefs of villages and city wards did not hesitate to defend their children who acted against laws and regulations. The second son of a former ward People's Committee chairman living 200 yards from my home joined a scuffle between teenagers in the neighborhood to support his younger brother. When his side was about to be beaten up, he picked up his father's pistol and killed a boy of the opposite gang. Within half an hour, the district public security office helped him by sending a truck to move all valuable household items and the four pigs for safekeeping at a friend's house. He was afraid of possible attacks at his home by angry mobs who were infuriated by the killing.

The public security forbade the victim's family to hold a funeral service and denied their request to have the dead boy returned to his home for burial preparations. So his funeral was performed with a simple ritual and was attended by a few family members at the hospital morgue. The case was closed after the victim's family received a small sum of money for compensation. The killer disappeared without being investigated or prosecuted.

The teenage sons of the chairman of a ward next to mine were intimidating all the children of his neighborhood. When they clashed with other boys, their father intervened, sending self-defense troops to crack down on his sons' enemies.

In a high school, my friend who was teaching mathematics once got into troubles. A male twelfth-grader brazenly squeezed the breasts of an eleventh-grade girl in front of their schoolmates. When the teacher stopped him, he fought him madly and called him names. The teacher, a black-belt Judo graduate, fought back and knocked him down easily. The naughty boy's father was a communist lieutenant colonel. He asked the school discipline board to fire the teacher and acquit his son. By voting, the school council of teachers (two-thirds had been serving under the former RVN regime) opposed the suggestion. The boy's behavior was beyond tolerance, severely infringing on moral and ethical conduct. The council decided to dismiss the boy from high school and found the teacher not guilty of any charge.

The communist colonel had his underlings attempt to murder the teacher, who fled to a Mekong Delta town before taking a boat trip to leave Việt Nam for a refugee camp.

Everywhere, people were complaining about the communist leaders' authoritarian attitude. A village chairman was more authoritative and wielded a lot more power than a pre-1975 province chief. Owing to their parents' great fortunes acquired by personal power, their children thus became junior lords at school and on the streets, standing behind gang activities such as motorbike and car races on crowded avenues, fighting, drinking, betting on sports events, prostitution, robbery, and fraud.

* * *

Since my return home, many of my remote relatives from the North had come to visit my family and me. After April 1975, the 1954 North Vietnamese refugees living in the South received hosts of relatives and friends from the North. The visitors felt happy with almost everything they could collect in the visited households.

Some of my neighbors felt bothered by the guests from their old villages, but my family did not mind treating our villagers kindly. We knew they were too poor. My mother often said to us that if we had stayed in the North after the 1954 Geneva Accords, we would have been acting like them and possibly being even more bothersome.

After the communists took over the South, most of the key jobs in every branch of the government, industrial, economic, commercial, and educational sectors were assigned to Communist Party members coming from the North. Ethnic North Vietnamese really dominated the South. Therefore, a great many former communist faithful party cadres and warriors in the South were excluded from the distribution of authority after the victory.

To the VCP faithful members who were serving the party, the army, and the government, the party leaders had to reward them with homes as they had promised. The available houses that could satisfy the large demand were the homesteads of the former RVN officers and other political prisoners.

According to classified directives of the real estate authority, the homestead of a family having one or more members serving the former republic and released from the camps or a businessman having served a term in the 1978 Industrial and Trade Reform was put under communist government control. I planned to sell my house, but the Land and Home Agency would not allow this.

A week after April 30, 1975, homes that belonged to RVN officers and civil servants serving in the provinces were confiscated on short notice. But that measure was not carried out in Sài Gòn, except for the cases where the homeowners fled Việt Nam illegally.

As for Vietnamese who were permitted to immigrate to Western countries, their properties were "put under the government management" upon their official departure in the Orderly Departure program. In fact, it was nothing other but confiscation. Their houses were given to privileged communist officials. After a decade, they were resold for large profits during the boom in the real estate market in 1990s.

In a typical case of my friend who was to immigrate to America under the Orderly Departure program, communist armed troops of a NVA colonel seized the home hours before the family left for the airport. With the home under his troops' control, the communist colonel headed off the real estate agency in a fait accompli. The agency had no choice but to issue approval paperwork legalizing the usurper's ownership.

* * *

More and more young soldiers died in Cambodia. The VCP army had been stuck in Cambodia since 1978. Some wounded soldiers coming back from the battles told me that the Vietnamese communist army units were using gas bombs against the Khmer Rouge troops in small-scale attacks. The gas attacks stopped when there were big noises in the world about them.

After being released from prison, I met several South Vietnamese former communist security agents who told me what the Communist Party had intended to do to former members of the RVN and the ARVN after the 1975 Dark April. Those once-faithful party members were excluded from the ruling class. They were feeling indignant and aggrieved.

According to their accounts, right after Sài Gòn fell, Communist Party leaders had their army and public security set up large-scale plans to move about 500,000 to 1 million RVN government civil servants and military soldiers along with their dependents out of Sài Gòn and major cities. The plans would have had to be completed within six months to build economic development centers in areas bordering Cambodia and Laos. The plans also proposed the similar movement of North Vietnamese 1954 refugees from their two large settlements in the Sài Gòn suburbs. The two areas would have been leveled for large construction projects.

They didn't know for sure why the plans were dropped. They guessed that the horrible genocide in Cambodia or high pressure from worldwide public opinion had dissuaded communist leaders from carrying out the giant projects. I trusted their disclosures, which were confirmed by many other medium-ranking communist cadres like them. Besides, in 1977 and 1978, there was an overt plan by the communist central authorities for the resettlement of prisoners and their families in border areas after we were released from the camps. This plan corresponded with the above-mentioned disclosures.

* * *

Many of the released political prisoners believed that it was because the majority of South Vietnamese people still sympathized with our former RVN officers that the communist leaders must use harsh measures against us. Nine out of ten common people were very friendly to us. Though now and then they had been against the former Sài Gòn government, they showed high regard for many former RVN officials and officers. Many peasants in the Mekong Delta covertly displayed the small portraits of the late ARVN Lieutenant General Nguyễn Viết Thanh on their family altars to worship him as a saint. General Thanh had been a commander of the RVN Military Region IV (Mekong Delta) and was the most popular general in South Việt Nam. He had been killed in a helicopter accident in 1970.

* * *

The talks between Washington and Hà Nội on the Americans missing in action reached favorable fundamental agreements. The news of the negotiation prompted a business of searching for information on the missing American soldiers and their remains. There were thousands of Vietnamese buying unidentified sets of human remains along with dog tags with a hope of being awarded official immigration to the States. Several people even paid a large sum of money for information concerning living American soldiers hiding somewhere in the remote areas. Most of the cases were fraudulent, as far as I knew.

THE DIM FUTURE

Beginning in April 1975, the communist regime tried to depopulate South Việt Nam's cities. The New Economic program was activated. Local authorities strived to resettle city people in remote New Economic areas by persuasion or by coercion. A large number of families of former RVN officers and civil servants who were in concentration camps were the targets. The program was a failure. By 1983, many of the resettlers left the areas to move back to cities and lived wherever they could, including in cemeteries. They could not stand hunger and hardships in the New Economic areas when the government starving subsidy ended. The Montagnards were not an exception. Along with the campaign to fight the Phục Quốc, who were still operating in small groups in the highland jungles, communist authorities forced hundreds of highlander hamlets in remote lands to move to locations nearer to the road with little help.

I was given a teaching job by the English Center of the Patriotic Intellectuals Association. It was one of the two largest English centers in Sài Gòn. Public security agents attended class in order to watch the teachers. However, some of the agents admitted to me their covert missions and assured me, "You should go ahead with your ironies and sarcasms. Don't worry about me. Just don't do anything really big."

At the same time I began an English class at my home and other classes at students' homes with permission from the local authorities. Since 1980, there were many people trying to flee Việt Nam and others who were on the waiting list for legal immigration to Western countries in the so-called Orderly Departure program. They prompted a large demand for English teaching facilities.

Sài Gòn education authorities operated many English evening courses for more than 10,000 students. Many other thousands were attending private home classes. Only 1,000 students attended French classes, a few hundred were learning German, and there were nearly 150 in the three Russian classes. It was a large student population, whereas capable teachers were limited. So nonprofessional teachers like me could have grounds to earn a living.

Most of the 135 English teachers in my English Center were former RVN officers. A smaller number of them were teaching mathematics and sciences. A fellow teacher who came from the North once said to me, "You South Việt Nam officers became capable high school teachers after being released from prison camps. Our NVA retired officers could only make a living by working in rice fields or doing minor repairs on bicycles on street corners."

We teachers wouldn't use English language textbooks from the state publishers in home classes because we found in them many serious errors. I had to look for pre-1975 textbooks sold in sidewalk bookstalls. Books of all kinds except for anticommunist texts could be found there. A large number of old-book hunters came from North Việt Nam to look for the pre-1975 books, particularly the pre-1954 works that were banned in the North. Thanks to the old-book dealers, many valuable publications were saved from 1975–80 cultural purging campaigns.

When teaching advanced English classes, I couldn't procure any appropriate instruction material. So I had my students buy collections of short stories translated and printed by some Hà Nội publishers. I assigned them pages of the translation along with the original for homework, in which they had to find common mistakes. The best students could pick out 90 percent of the mistakes, while ones at the bottom could detect 50 percent of the errors. The worthless books thus became successful teaching tools.

The income from teaching English could help me earn a somewhat meager living, but thanks to gifts once in a while sent by friends and relatives in the United States and France, my family could lead a good life without much trouble. Moreover, I earned a lot of grateful thanks from the students and their families, especially ones who were successful in interviews for resettlement in English-speaking countries and those who made good progress in universities abroad after leaving Việt Nam.

Among the highest rewards I received during the eight years I lived in the "larger prison" were letters from my students who achieved success in the States, Canada, and Australia, owing partly to my teaching them English. They are now well-paid engineers, pharmacists, businessmen, and teachers. Most of them were the age of my children; I loved them as if they *were* my own sons and daughters. They had never known how happy I was whenever one of them reached the various refugee camps safely and how I was crying silently when some were reported lost at sea or on the Cambodian trails crossing the border with Thailand.

* * *

After eight years living under the communist regime, most South Vietnamese were still unable to get used to its ways of ruling the society. Communist propaganda called for revolutionary ethics, but the communist government tended to act otherwise.

City and district governments ran most of the luxury restaurants with halls or open floors modified for dancing. Dancing was promoted as a source of money for the government budget. To boost the movement, local authorities held evening dance courses and urged young government employees, including woman teachers, to attend for free.

Many district governments even stood behind the prostitution business in state-owned hotels. In the dependents' quarters of the NVA unit at the former ARVN/JGS, many communist field grade officers ran mini theaters in their homes, showing pornographic movies and videos. When the first videotape players and camcorders were imported, a rule of the customs offices permitted only communist officials to receive and operate them at home.

Almost all final scores of sports matches, soccer in particular, winners of contests, competitions, and other games including primary school TV puzzles were decided beforehand by the party cells of the related organizing agencies.

As local and central governments were greatly in need of cash, they were finding every possible way to collect the most money from the people. Tax officials were terrible devils to all kinds of businesses. At checkpoints along highways, communist tax collectors inspected every piece of travelers' luggage—and sometimes their bodies—for hidden controlled merchandise.

Stores, shops, and stall owners were the easy targets of Sài Gòn City's tax assessors, who were also tax collectors. They had arbitrary power to decide the tax rates. Sometimes they revisited targets that had been taxed to reassess them at higher rates and collected the difference, saying that the previous assessments were incorrect.

At Tân Sơn Nhứt Airport, customs officers ran meticulous inspections, looking for valuables inside passengers before they boarded overseas flights. Passengers were required to change their garments into thin pajamas and undergo strip searches. Once they tried to insert a forceps into the private parts of a seventeen-year-old virgin to look for gold and jewels before her departure to the States in the Orderly Departure program. Her mother protested so fiercely that the inspector had to surrender. The dirty practice, which had been done routinely, was stopped after the incident.

DISCRIMINATION

My second daughter passed the entry examination for the Sài Gòn Teachers College. She was an excellent student in math and natural science. She wished to become a doctor or an engineer. But she knew she would never be admitted to the medical or engineering schools.

Directives for admission in college and university listed children of former members of the RVN government and military as the lowest priority of fourteen categories. Highest priorities were for top party leaders' children. So a large number of children of party members could enroll in highly aspired universities (medical, polytechnic, foreign trade).

Many children of district party committee members were admitted into such universities with scores of 40/100 to 50/100. Meanwhile, children of my three friends passed the entry exams for the medical school and the polytechnic university with scores as high as 93/100, ranked top 1 percent of the passed candidates in three consecutive years. But all were denied enrollment only because their fathers had been ARVN lieutenant colonels.

Only three years after admission, my daughter was thrown out of the college because a teacher, also a party member, saw a copy of the Bible in her school bag. She was accused of bringing religious material into the class, although she didn't let anyone read the book. In my family, my wife and I were Buddhists, whereas my two daughters were Catholics.

Political background discrimination was much worse in many provinces. Children of many friends of mine living in towns away from Sài Gòn were not admitted into the tenth grade and higher only because their parents had served in the former RVN government and armed forces.

A medium-ranking communist cadre once told me that "the Communist Party tells us that if every student were enrolled in universities and colleges and admitted in government jobs without political family background considerations, the former American puppet regime would reclaim the ruling power again in a peaceful progressive anticommunist revolution within thirty years."

THE ORDERLY DEPARTURE PROGRAM

My youngest son reached the conscription age. If he were drafted, he would be sent to the battle areas in Cambodia as a labor soldier without being armed. I couldn't stand seeing my dear son sent to the battle as cannon fodder without an inch of steel on hand facing the Khmer Rouge's bloody machete. In my neighborhood, a dozen draftees fighting in Cambodia were wounded, some were killed, and their remains were never recovered.

To be sure that he would be draft exempted, he enrolled in the Teachers School. He passed the entry exam with no difficulty, as he was brilliant in high school and mainly because the job of teaching elementary grades after graduation was not attractive to children of Communist Party members.

One of my cousins, who was my mother's adopted daughter, arranged a boat trip for her two children, my son, and me to flee at the first opportunity. The other members of my family would stay waiting for the ODP official immigration. She would pay half of my part; one of my wife's sisters would pay for the rest. Everything was going fine with the most favorable conditions as planned. But an unforeseen incident occurred that spoilt the attempt. The boat owner and also pilot fled before the coast guard police could have arrested him for a charge of smuggling, leaving behind all prospective travelers, except for his four-man crew.

After the failed attempt, my left knee sprain from an accident in 1977 returned. Pain caused by certain movements of my left leg prevented me from running fast and from swimming—I was a bad swimmer in any case. Therefore, I gave up any plan of fleeing the country by boat or by foot.

In spring 1984, the world mass media broke the first official news about immigration to the United States by former political prisoners who had served the RVN. I applied for official immigration in the Orderly Departure program office in Bangkok and for an exit permit in the Communist Foreign Affairs Ministry. Because of our applications, my son was discharged from the Teachers School. The official information brought real hope to my friends and me. We saw the bright light rising in the distant horizon.

The Orderly Departure program, founded by the High Commissariat for Refugees in 1979, provided assistance to applicants in Việt Nam to immigrate to Western countries under the sponsorship of their relatives. By 1984, a number of Vietnamese who were of ethnic Chinese origin left Việt Nam as official immigrants instead of risking their lives as boatpeople.

Mai Chí Thọ, the top leader of the Sài Gòn Communist Party Committee in 1984, said to a German reporter that he endorsed the plan to allow former political prisoners to immigrate to Western nations. He was quoted as saying, "New York City is the best place to keep them," as political security was concerned.

He explained, "If they remain in Việt Nam, it will be rather difficult to control them. But once they are resettled in America, they would not risk a comfortable life over there to return to Việt Nam to do anything anticommunist. Besides, they would save their money to help their relatives in Việt Nam."

The ODP also provided support to the "Amerisans," children of American soldiers and Vietnamese women. They were awarded entry permits to resettle in the United States. Their relatives, birth mothers, or adoptive parents accompanied them to America. They had lived the outcasts' lives after 1975. The programs saved them from extreme misery. They began to gain some consideration from people around them and their relatives.

Sometimes I received written documents of dissenting groups in Sài Gòn. They called for democracy and pluralism. A close friend of mine had direct contact with at least three of these groups. We secretly supported their activities until 1988, when I had the first signs of Parkinson's disease. A short time later, all three were disbanded or arrested after they were detected by the communist political security agency.

ECONOMIC CRISIS

The year 1985 began with the execution of Trần Văn Bá and his two comrades on January 8. Bá and twenty members of his resistance group were captured as they infiltrated Việt Nam one after another from France.

By 1985, almost half of the political prisoners had been released. For the rest, life in the camps was not so oppressive as before. Less work and more foods were allowed, possibly by bribes paid to jailers. Many wives were allowed to visit for twenty-four or even seventy-two hours with their husbands in private rooms in the camp reception houses. Consequently, some of the young wives had to explain intensively to friends and relatives to prove that their newborn babies belonged to their legitimate husbands in prison.

That is one of the Việt Nam communist regime's prison regulations that were worth appraising. Another regulation permits good criminal prisoners who were serving light to medium terms and living by the rules of the camp to go home for a week to a month. The public security system proved its effectiveness in controlling the country people.

In spring 1985, there was news that official immigration from Việt Nam to the United States, Canada, Australia, and France of former RVN political prisoners had been negotiated between Hà Nội and Washington. Hundreds of rumors circulated among the would-be candidates about when and how they would be departing.

I definitely abandoned my attempt to escape by boat in summer 1985 also because of a reliable source from my good neighbor, the brother of Vũ Đình Liệu, a retired communist government deputy premier. He disclosed that Hà Nội leaders would certainly let us immigrate as many as possible because such a policy would render more benefit than harm to the regime.

They took advice from the Soviet Union and Cuba that, according to the source, releasing the former political prisoners and their close relatives to the West would cleanse the country of a mighty unarmed opposition that might one day become dangerous to the Communist Party. Moreover, the former prisoners would send an important amount of valuable foreign currencies to help their relatives in Việt Nam, thus pumping millions of dollars a year into Hà Nội monetary reserves.

We former political prisoners released from concentration camps were under close watch and some kinds of harassment, and we were also threatened with the possibility of being sent to the New Economic Areas. We had to find work, however cheap and toilsome, a condition that would allow us to stay in Sài Gòn. But in mid-1985, local officials stopped using the "New Economic Area" threat.

The communist authorities in Sài Gòn celebrated the tenth anniversary of their April 1975 victory with a parade. People, especially the kids, were not eager to attend the celebration as they had seen the pre-1975 ARVN military review and parade many times. The communist troops were not marching in straight lines in rhythm with martial music. Their gestures were awkward. For an air show, a group of six commercial jet airplanes flew over the parade ground at low speed and at a distance of about 100 yards from each other. The spectators laughed wildly. Most of them had seen much more fantastic acrobatic airplane presentations made by ARVN and allies' air forces.

The communist military and police officers' uniforms looked ugly in the eyes of the people in South Việt Nam. The caps were carelessly made and deformed. Police officers conducting the traffic brandished their clubs clumsily, which made them look like marionettes. Military honor units welcoming foreign VIPs looked similarly awkward.

The most important event in 1985 in Việt Nam was the currency reform in September. The new *đồng* was to replace the old ten *đồng*. But new bills of smaller denomination—smaller than 50 *đồng*—were not issued. The ill-planned reform caused a great shortage of small change bills and unpredictable trouble to everyone. Every day my wife would spend less than 50 *đồng* at the market for items at prices of 1 to 10 *đồng* each. Buyers and sellers were in much trouble when they did not have small bills for change. It was like the U.S. currency without bills smaller than $100.

Besides creating galloping inflation that dealt a hard blow to the economy, the failed reform precipitated successive economic crises that compelled basic changes in economic policies in the following years.

For the first time since 1945, the communist regime promulgated its criminal law. For forty years, communist judges had been free to give criminal convicts sentences that were based on government directives and administrative regulations instead of a criminal code passed by a legislative body. People were telling one another hundreds of stories of the communist court rulings as jokes and satirical anecdotes.

In Mỹ Tho, forty miles south of Sài Gòn, a truck driver killed two people and wounded two others in a traffic accident. The judge of the city court sentenced the driver to two years in prison. After a week, one of the wounded victims died at a hospital. The judge reconvened the court session for an additional ruling and gave the defendant a new term of three years of imprisonment, saying that in this manslaughter case, he decided that the convict had to serve one year in jail for each death.

There were waves of tourists from communist countries, the Russians in particular, visiting Sài Gòn, a former capitalist big city that still smacked of capitalism, where they could easily be granted exit permits by the Soviet authorities to travel in order to see an exhibit of American technology. The Vietnamese were reluctant to talk to them because public security could investigate them with offensive questions afterwards. I met some of them, but I only exchanged a few words with them, such as to give them street directions.

Right after April 1975, many Russian technicians came to do research in Sài Gòn factories, industrial and technological institutions, and military installations. They told some of my friends who were working beside them that the American technology was way ahead of the Soviet Union. They had to learn much more from Sài Gòn.

One of my subordinate officers once introduced me to his younger brother, who stayed in the North after 1954. He was an engineer graduated from a Soviet university. After a few days talking to each other, he became less reserved and frankly admitted that in technological training, "the Russians taught us North Vietnamese only from A to F while the Americans taught you from A to X if not to Z."

WAITING FOR A BETTER FUTURE

In June 1986, my sister, her two children, and my mother departed for San Jose, California. My brother-in-law sponsored them under the Orderly Departure program for a family reunion. My mother was happy to see my two children again in America, but she missed my other two still in Sài Gòn. Along with my sister and her husband, my mother saved some of her money from social welfare to help us in Việt Nam. Life appeared to be a lot easier.

About half of my students in English home classes had departed for the States, Canada, and Australia in the Orderly Departure program by 1986.

The Communist Party initiated the so-called *đổi mới* (perestroika, renovation). People started their small private businesses on a limited scale. The cities began to recover some of their living appearance. We former political prisoners were under less rigid control. However, a great many of us were not awarded legal resident's status in our own home. Without our names being in the household registry, we were not given full citizenship.

The halfway economic reform brought a new pleasant face to Sài Gòn and other cities. More goods and services were provided at brightly decorated stores. New houses and buildings appeared more and more on busy streets. The change could be seen everywhere, but the communists' social behavior remained intact.

Most government employees directly serving patients at hospitals and the customers at various public services, including administrative offices, often treated people curtly, rarely smiling. Their unrefined manners may be noticed even in the today's Việt Nam.[1]

We were still living under the direct watch of the village or city ward and the district governments. Under the communist regime, district and village authorities are the most powerful rulers. To some extent, they might ignore directives and even laws promulgated by the central authority. When one of my friends brought a letter from the city government approving his demand to be awarded citizenship to the officials of his ward, one of them refused bluntly, saying, "This is my ward, and it's me who decides. Even if the chairman of the City Party Committee is right here and now, I will say no to his approval."

The head of my district financial office once told me that he had to continue importing thousands of motorbikes against the decree of the prime minister banning the imports. He said, "If the prime minister were running my job for one day, he would do the same. Without imports of articles of high demand, where could I make enough money to pay a thousand employees working under the district government?"

The party leaders in a village or a city ward wielded the most effective instrument to exert their power on the population. It was the household registry. A family had to swim through a lot of paperwork and meet many criteria to be granted legal resident status in the household registry. Most of the applications were denied. The strict procedure was a source of corruption.

In Sài Gòn and other cities, there were hundreds of thousands living in shabby makeshift shelters and in cemeteries without citizenship. They had been ousted from the cities and resettled on a compulsory basis in the New Economic Areas. After the New Economic campaign's great failure, they found their way back to the cities to lead a dog's life.

They were not admitted to any public hospital or dispensary. Their children were not enrolled in schools. They wandered like shadows in the cemeteries at night. They received no help and were completely forgotten by the communist rulers.

PRISONER RELEASE

News about resettlement of former political prisoners in Western countries gave us hope. Released prisoners gathered almost every day in front of the Sài Gòn City Foreign Affairs Office for information. Rumors true and false spread far and wide.

The Public Security Office in charge of exit approval was playing psychological games with us. Every month, it issued a news line on the board of notice with vague sentences concerning departures that offered faint hope of early immigration, but nothing was certain. That made the public frantic.

A lot of former RVN officers and public servants were released from camps. Fewer than 1,000 remained imprisoned near Sài Gòn.

Many of us who had been released in the previous five years were awarded citizenship and officially listed in the family household registry by local communist authorities. Additionally, communist district authority awarded us our ID cards. Consequently, we didn't have to report to the public security office anymore.

My wife and I felt impatient with the Orderly Departure program. Months had passed since 1984, when the immigration of former RVN officers and civil servants was negotiated, but there was no sign of progress. My daughter and son, who were still in Sài Gòn with me, were growing older and older. They should not waste their time in Việt Nam without higher education. So we began arranging to have them flee the country as soon as possible.

In 1988, Southeast Asian countries were planning to close the camps. People who planned to flee were trying to make the trip in time. For more than ten years, refugees had disappeared before reaching lands of freedom. Many people estimated that up to 400,000 people were missing in the South China Sea. The lowest estimate claimed that 200,000 had perished on the high seas, a little less than the number of ARVN soldiers killed in the twenty-year war. Most of their boats were small; many were only fifty feet long without instruments for sea travel and powered by old, sloppily rebuilt engines.

Horrible stories of death at sea and in jungles were reported in letters from the camps and on radio airwaves. Victims were raped, drowned, and stabbed after being robbed by barbarous pirates—actually Thai fishermen. The communist coast guard killed others. Many died from running out of water and food after many weeks of being lost at sea and landing on uninhabited small islands. There were several cases of cannibalism. Most of the others were just missing after departure from Việt Nam.

Terrible death and danger lurking on the journey to freedom seemed not strong enough to dissuade ones who were looking for a way to flee Việt Nam. Being too frustrated and too disappointed in life under the new regime caused them to take risks, although the Vietnamese were not an adventurous people.

One of my students said to me, "I was not an anticommunist before 1975, and they did not cause me any trouble. But I hate seeing ignorant stupid communist bosses of most government agencies and businesses, the way they act and speak. I can endure physical hardships and hunger, but I cannot live without freedom under this oppressive regime. That overcomes my fear of possible bad luck."

My mother, my wife, and my sister all were afraid of allowing my two younger children to take the boat trip. The stories of victims perishing at sea were too much for them. But after many months of pondering the matter and at my son's insistence, we all decided to allow him to take the risk.

After two failed attempts, on March 12, 1988, my son left Việt Nam. Before the trip, my wife and I married him to his girlfriend, to make sure that in the refugee camps, they would be resettled together. It was a well-prepared trip with a good boat. We had money just for him, so my daughter had to wait for the next chance if any.

Two weeks after they departed, we were so worried about their safety that we could not sleep. On the fifteenth day, a telegram from my sister in San Jose, California, brought me the big news: they had arrived safely on the Malaysian island of Bidong. They telegraphed their safe arrival in Bidong to her hours after they reached the refugee camp.

In a letter three weeks later, my son recounted how he and 100 people on the twenty-one-meter boat had suffered from lack of water and food for fourteen days drifting on the high seas after the boat engine broke down. A Malaysian police coast guard patrol rescued them just as pirates were about to attack.

I had the first signs of Parkinson's disease. Diagnosis examination and initial treatment seemed inaccurate. At the hospital, several Hà Nội graduated neurologists examined me. But only one who had graduated from a medical school in Czechoslovakia seemed to be really capable of treating me. The others showed their obvious lack of medical knowledge. The three who took my case didn't have adequate comprehension about common drugs for the disease, according to what I learned from the instruction sheet attached to the pill containers.

According to the son of my first cousin, a communist captain working in the city public security office, three-fourths of the medical doctors and two-thirds of the engineers who graduated in the South before 1975 had fled the country. Their escape created a great shortage of capable physicians and technologists. Doctors and engineers who graduated in Hà Nội were very undependable. Some of them were so notorious that people bribed hospital officials for their relatives *not to be treated and operated on* by those ill-trained doctors.

A friend of mine who was a surgeon introduced me to the old respectable Dr. Đặng Văn Chung. He was one of the only five *"agrégées en médecine"* who graduated in France and were serving in Việt Nam before 1954. *Agrégée* is the highest title in the French medical hierarchy. In 1954, he elected to stay in Hà Nội instead of leaving for Sài Gòn. He was honored by the communist leaders and was a renowned professor of the Hà Nội Medical University. In the mid-1980s he retired and worked as a volunteer at the An Bình Hospital, Sài Gòn, where I sought treatment.

After many visits, he became more open to me. Once I asked him whether he regretted his decision to stay in Hà Nội. I added, "If you had come to the South, you would have made great progress in your medical career and contributed much greater assistance to our people."

He looked deep in my eyes, slapped at my shoulder, and laughed in a way that seemed not like a laugh. He said, "You are among the thousands of people who have asked me that question. I could tell you only that everybody makes one serious mistake in his or her life."

I said, "Doctor Chung, I know there are many respectable medical professors of your caliber at Hà Nội Medical University. But why are so many doctors who graduated since 1954 so incapable with very little comprehension of their career?"

He replied, "Before 1954 in Hà Nội and before 1975 in Sài Gòn, a professor always had to spend most of his time explaining the lessons and his students had to take notes as fast as possible. Otherwise, they could not follow up the teaching after leaving the classroom. In Hà Nội since 1954, a lot of students of every class had never passed tenth grade. A number of them even were fifth-grade dropouts. They were admitted to the university only because of their services to the Communist Party or their families' background. I had to dictate the text, and they were writing it down very slowly. The dictation took up half of every period. The other capable students had to wait. With the thirty minutes left, I could do very little instruction. So the dumb students existed at the expense of the brilliant. And by the end of a school year, the education authorities required 99 percent students to be graduated. That's why."

He added that, since 1954, he had no new medical books and publications or magazine articles on the medical profession from Western countries to update his knowledge. The same was true of his fellow professors.

DISSIDENCE ON THE RISE

What used to be claimed to be unfounded rumors became realities. After numerous talks with Hà Nội, the United States accepted the immigration of former political prisoners from Việt Nam. My friends and I were waiting for that good news for many long years. In October 1989, the first group of more than 100 former RVN officers departed for the States.

The Immigration Service in Hà Nội approved immigration of applicants for the Orderly Departure program as former political prisoners in special lists starting with H-01, H-02, ... to H-10 ... H-30. "H" did not stand for anything, but many credulous people thought it meant HO-1, HO-2, and guessed it was the abbreviation for "Humanitarian Operation," which has never existed.

I dearly loved my father-in-law. He was bedridden for a month before his last breath. It was when communism began disintegrating in Eastern Europe.

He was so happy with the news about the successful struggle of the Polish Solidarity from Radio BBC in the last days of his consciousness. Whenever I visited him, he would ask, "When will the Soviet Union be next?" He died on the last day of October 1989.

My youngest son and his wife were granted resettlement in the United States. They were transferred to Palawan Island of the Philippines for preparation training and processing for a few months. They lived in my brother-in-law's home and enrolled in the universities.

Realities under the communist regime changed the opinion of many people in all walks of life. Voices of discontent were heard everywhere, and the poor peasants who once gave assistance to the VC insurgents were the most fearless critics.

In 1988–89, there were more celebrities who voiced their dissenting opinions about communism and Hà Nội's policies in the war. Many of the pre-1975 activists who were anti–Sài Gòn, anti-American, pro-communist popular leaders turned against Hà Nội only a few years after the war.

A pre-1945 doctor who graduated in the medical school in Hà Nội told me: "In South Việt Nam before 1975 there were 5 million pro-communists, 5 million anticommunists, and 10 million fence sitters. After 1975, pro-communists were down to 1 million, anticommunists rose up to 15 million, and the rest were staying in the middle."

A typical case emerging in 1989 was the renowned dissenting female writer Dương Thu Hương, author of the best-seller *Thiên Đường Mù* (Paradise of the Blind), who experienced the same reality.

As an NVA devoted female soldier, not long after Sài Gòn was overrun she visited the capital of South Việt Nam. Sài Gòn was not a bit like what Hà Nội had taught her. She has become the fiercest outspoken dissident who is attacking the communist leaders with the strongest language. She has been imprisoned several times, but nothing has changed her convictions.

The late 1980s saw scores of writers, artists, former communist high-ranking members, and communist army officers including one general who boldly voiced their dissent, in disregard of the communist government's oppressive measures. Many books and magazine articles, even some movies, directly or indirectly criticizing the communist regime appeared more often.

The 1980s dissenting voices paved the way for the movement advocating democracy and human rights in Việt Nam in the following decades. Thousands of dissidents joined the movement in the 2000s, including communist high-ranking members, army generals, famous veterans, intellectuals, and writers.

After the communists took over South Việt Nam, I felt sorry for the former warriors and cadres of the communist side who were discharged and forgotten, leading a poor life with starving retirement pay.

I met three of them in North Việt Nam and another ten in the South after I was released in 1982. Many of those openly voiced their protest against communist authorities without fear of being in trouble. There had been so many false promises made to communist warriors. Many of them were respectable patriots who had been serving the Communist Party faithfully, but at last they were discarded like broken household utensils.

Tens of thousands of ARVN disabled veterans were also living a crippled dog's life without any help. I couldn't alleviate my sorrow for those who had lost their limbs or their eyesight, moving with what was left of their bodies around the wet marketplaces. They were begging for food and money in wheelchairs and on crutches, and some were crawling along dirty alleys and muddy sidewalks on what remained of their amputated limbs.

They deserved the best humanitarian assistance. But who cared? Did the manufacturers of war materials and those in the media industry who made great fortunes owing to the Vietnam War ever have a second to think about the disabled warriors?

Many times I met communist NVA disabled soldiers in ARVN uniforms. They said that in Sài Gòn and the South they were given far less if they wore their NVA uniforms.

One of the smart inventions must have been what I called "reconciled beggar teams." In pairs of crippled veterans, one ARVN and one NVA, going side by side in wheelchairs, they shared one piece of cardboard that read, "Please help us! We are victims of the same war." People said their little "cooperatives" earned them bigger money.

The sights moved many hearts and reminded me of other remnants of the war. Many families I visited displayed portraits of their close relatives—their sons in some cases—who had died fighting on both sides. I wondered if their souls would ever reconcile in the Netherworld.

One condition for receiving exit permits was that I had to give up ownership of my house to the communist Land and Property Authority. It had been built with savings by my family after years of hard work (my mother, my sister, and I, plus contributions from three of my mother's adopted sons and daughter, who were successful in their various businesses).

FAREWELL TO VIỆT NAM

My wife, my daughter, and I were awarded visas of exit by the Việt Nam communist authorities in April. On October 12, we boarded Việt Nam Airlines for Bangkok. The sky was blue and full of white clouds after a light morning rain. I walked to the plane, looking around to memorize the last images of the land I had vowed to serve with my best.

There was nothing special. Trees and buildings were lifeless. On the other side of the runway stood a line of concrete hangars that had once sheltered the Việt Nam and U.S. Air Force jet fighters, the subdued symbols of the war.

At the last sight around Tân Sơn Nhứt Airport before the plane took off, I mumbled a farewell to my fatherland. Sài Gòn grew smaller and smaller under scattered white clouds. It gave me a strong feeling of loss.

When we were flying over the common border area with Cambodia, I saw the green rice fields of the Mekong Delta with bunches of bomb craters in the border lands and the blue Mekong River winding through the southern delta provinces.

Suddenly the sight of the rural life moved me deeply. It reminded me of my years working and fighting for the lofty cause of serving the highest interests of the poor peasants. All had evaporated. The long, bloody war left with images of bomb craters and burned houses and terrorists' dismembered victims that would never fade from my memory.

After a week of entry paperwork processing, my family and I left Bangkok for the States. We arrived at San Francisco International Airport on October 19, 1990. My eldest daughter and son met us, with tears in their eyes after fifteen years. They had not seen me since June 15, 1975, when I was locked up in the first concentration camp. My youngest son and his wife, both resettled in San Jose after one year waiting in two refugee camps in Malaysia and the Philippines, also met us there along with my sister and her husband.

I am one among tens of thousands of former RVN officers who were given asylum and resettled by generous assistance of the American people and government. But I think that the nearly 1 million RVN noncommissioned officers and enlisted men—the disabled in particular—and their close relatives deserved such help more than we officers did.

Thank God for the safety of my great family—my sister's and mine. At last we reunited and were no more under the communist oppression.

So I began my new life in my new home. The love of Việt Nam and the memories of the war will be with me forever. My family and I were among more than 2 million Vietnamese who fled the communist regime for the lands of freedom.

The number of refugees who fled Việt Nam from April 1975 through 1995, as compiled by overseas Vietnamese community humanitarian organizations, based on reports of the refugees' camps in Southeast Asia, was as follows:

More than 130,000 evacuated out of Việt Nam as of April 30, 1975;
More than 900,000 fled Việt Nam by boat and more than 42,000 on foot;
From 200,000 to 300,000 perished on the high seas and jungles on the
    way of escape;

About 500,000 left Việt Nam officially in the Orderly Departure program, including 100,000 former civil servants and officers of the
RVN released from reeducation camps, along with their families.
This figure does not include thousands of civil servants and officers
who fled Việt Nam by boat after being released from the camps.

There are about 2.5 million Vietnamese refugees now living in North Amer-
ica, Australia, and Europe. Among them, according to the 2005 survey by the
American Community Survey/U.S. Census Bureau, 1,521,353 resettled in the
United States.

The bureau estimated that 18.2% of Vietnamese Americans had earned a
Bachelor's degree, compared to 17.2% of the American population as a whole.
Other reports state that among the 2.5 million Vietnamese living overseas, there
are over 300,000 graduate professionals (doctors, engineers, scientists).

Most of those nationalist Vietnamese now living in the western countries
constitute a strong overseas anticommunist political front opposing Hà Nội's
dictators. They firmly support the struggle for freedom and democracy in their
fatherland against the communist tyranny. The struggle seeks similar patriotic
objectives of the pre-1975 era, but with different and non-violent approaches.

PART VI

Epilogue

TWENTY-NINE

On the Việt Nam War

THE NATURE OF THE WAR

The war from 1945 to 1954 was initially a war of independence when Vietnamese patriots of all dispositions were fighting to liberate their nation from French domination. The Việt Nam Communist Party's campaign to eradicate political opposition drove the anticommunist Vietnamese patriots to the other side. So the war of resistance became mingled with the communists' long-range scheme to consolidate their ruling power. Beginning in 1951, the Red Chinese were involved in the conflict, providing aid and military and political advisors to the Việt Minh side, and the United States began providing assistance to the French, elevating the war to a new level, turning it into a conflict of influence between the international communist bloc and the capitalist world.

After the 1954 Geneva Accords, the nationalist Vietnamese gathered in the South, founding an anticommunist regime backed by the United States. Millions of Vietnamese like me picked up arms to fight communism because we would not live under communism. We trusted the invincible power of America to defend the democratic and free South Việt Nam. Prior to April 30, 1975, I had never imagined a day when the U.S. government would accept an inglorious defeat.

Actually in every aspect, the Việt Nam War was not an armed conflict just between the United States and the Hà Nội regime, or an anticolonialist war between the neocolonialist imperialist Americans and the Vietnamese people, as the communist bloc strived to make the world believe, a characterization that was both slanderous and utterly misleading.

After the war, many people outside Việt Nam debated on how wrong the U.S. involvement was in Việt Nam. They refuted the so-called Domino Theory as a justification, arguing that after April 30, 1975, no Asian country other than the three Indochinese nations fell into the hands of the communists. Few of them have ever sought reasonable answers for the question, "What could have happened if Washington had done otherwise?"

My view is that if the U.S. military hadn't intervened in Việt Nam in 1965, South Việt Nam might have collapsed no later than 1967. In such a case, hundreds of thousands, if not millions, of South Vietnamese would have been massacred and other millions tortured in labor camps, not much less than what the Cambodians suffered ten years later under the Khmer Rouge. Most Vietnamese were aware of how belligerent, fanatical, and arrogant North Việt Nam communist leaders were at that time.

We nationalists knew that if the Việt Nam communists had conquered South Việt Nam and all Indochina in 1967, Beijing's power would have threatened all of Southeast Asia. Bangkok would have become the next objective after Sài Gòn. Singapore and Kuala Lumpur would have been in much trouble before long, and even Indonesia would have suffered one way or another

My belief is based not on intellectual research and official information but on sources from North Việt Nam's high-ranking army officers who were once involved in the plot to support armed insurgency in Thailand. They disclosed the secret to people in the South after 1975, as the plot had been revoked in the early 1970s and it was no longer strictly classified information. I had my reasons to believe their disclosure, which I trust much more than any other sources.

I think that the least accomplishment of the allied forces in the Việt Nam War was to have reduced Hà Nội's military potential, which would have been exerted outside Indochina as the vanguard for the expansion of Red Chinese power in Southeast Asia. At least the Việt Nam War bought plenty of precious time for Thailand, Singapore, Malaysia, and other neighboring countries for their development.

I also think that in some way, the Việt Nam War contributed to the Free World's cold war triumph.

We were fighting on the American side only because we believed that the American policies in South Việt Nam were obviously less harmful than the Soviet and Chinese ideological dominion over North Việt Nam. We were well aware of the fact that no nation would support and protect another nation without actual interests. We also knew that America was not a perfect republic, with several problems concerning human rights and crude foreign relations. However, between the two evils, we had to opt for the less detrimental.

In fact, Việt Nam was the battleground where the two Việt Nams were fighting each other for the ultimate interests of the world powers. Moreover, the two communist powers, the Soviet Union and the Communist China, provided North Việt Nam with a huge amount of war supplies. The aid might have cost them not far less than the American budget for the Việt Nam War from 1961 to

1972, if relative national productivity was taken into account. If the two communist powers had ended their military aid to the NVA in 1975 as Washington did to Sài Gòn, the war might have stopped and Hà Nội would have gained little more than what it had in 1955.

RESPONSIBILITY

The controversy about the reasons for the defeat of the South Việt Nam side has not ceased since April 30, 1975. Many American leaders laid the blame on the South Vietnamese armed forces, arguing that the ARVN soldiers were not fighting, that the RVN government was corrupt, and many other reasons. South Vietnamese nationalists claimed that the loss of South Việt Nam was the consequence of fundamental mistakes made by the Americans.

I think both Washington and Sài Gòn should be blamed for the tragic end of the war. However, I simply think that Washington was responsible for the larger part of the defeat.

U.S. leaders could not deny that responsibility. They intervened in Việt Nam with a promise to defend the free South Việt Nam. To deny the Americans' responsibilities by laying the full blame on the RVN troops is both unreasonable and cowardly. The ARVN human loss (260,000 killed in action and nearly 1,000,000 wounded in action) in twenty years of fighting a stubborn enemy speaks for itself.

Although the Americans held the supreme war making policy, the Vietnamese government and military leaders still retained full authority in certain domains. The ARVN supreme command made independent decisions on military management and operations concerning its responsible areas.

Looking back at the twentieth-century history of my country, I conclude that both sides in the 1945–75 conflict were guilty of conducting the fratricidal war. The communists started the war. The nationalists did not wage the armed struggle, but they were blamed for excessive reliance on U.S. assistance and for failing to lead their people actively and efficiently to defend their freedom. However, the nationalists did not cause significant harm to the national culture, morale, and social integrity as their rivals did in the North after 1954 and in all Việt Nam after 1975.

THE WAR LEADERS

The two Vietnamese sides of the conflict fought each other with very different war machines.

On the top of the machine in Hà Nội was Hồ Chí Minh. The communists were successful in making him the idol of many Vietnamese. He was the spiritual leader of the North Việt Nam Army. However, recent disclosures show that for the last nine years of his life (1960–69), he yielded the supreme ruling power to the Party General Secretary Lê Duẩn. Lê Duẩn remained in the general secretary's seat until his death in 1986.

Lê Duẩn was a fanatical leader who relentlessly pursued the war to occupy the South and stood behind merciless policies toward the conquered South Vietnamese even after the war ended. He had three legitimate wives, living in three mansions in Hà Nội, Sài Gòn, and Hải Phòng.

In fact, the actual ruling power was vested in the VCP Politburo, the circle of the most active and energetic communist leaders. Its prominent members included Trường Chinh, Lê Đức Thọ, Phạm Văn Đồng, and Võ Nguyên Giáp. Every top-level policy was decided by the Politburo. However, the general secretary was the actual commander in chief of the NVA. General Võ Nguyên Giáp had the title of supreme commander but without full power.

Under the top leaders, the backbone of the VCP war machine was the corps of communist intermediate and infrastructure leaders. They had little general education but were extremely faithful to the Communist Party. They were granted special ruling power and privileges they would not have dreamed of if they had not served the Communist Party, in commanding positions that they would endeavor to consolidate. That made a communist leader authoritative and dogmatic. He or she eventually became an aggressive boss or commander who propelled the subordinates to do their best in fighting and working.

Before April 30, 1975, although I was a fervent anticommunist, I still had some respect for the Vietnamese communist ranking leaders. After April 1975, my opinion changed. Most of them had been brave warriors, but after their party took over all of Việt Nam, they were incapable of running public key positions given to them as rewards.

They were not the first-rate patriots or revolutionaries they had been cracked up to be. Once they climbed higher on the power ladder, they became more arrogant and authoritarian, and that made them greedy. They have been founders of the ever-expanding and uncontrollable corruption that is at least many dozen times larger than that of the nationalist officials in the pre-1975 South. I believe that most VCP leaders have been suffering from megalomania. They were victims of their own propaganda.

In South Việt Nam, President Ngô Đình Diệm was a capable leader in economic and administrative matters. He was not a military leader or thinker, nor was he a skillful politician. He was not interested in propaganda, and he was not a demagogue. However, he was a religious man who stuck to ethical principles. He didn't play a decisive role in national defense. His personality and his authoritative manners made his leadership powerful. Most members of his government and military generals held him in awe. I saw many civilian and military bigwigs who dared not look at his face when standing in front of him.

South Việt Nam was not under the rule of a strong regime. The central government was relatively weak in both the First Republic under Ngô Đình Diệm and the Second Republic under Nguyễn Văn Thiệu. The RVN had a sizeable elite in administrative operations, including many good ministers and generals, but they seemed to be highly capable only in a peacetime government and in conducting conventional warfare. Except for Ngô Đình Diệm, other central leaders in Sài Gòn were not praised, let alone idolized, by the government propaganda like their counterparts in Hà Nội.

The ARVN officer corps, the executive body of the RVN armed forces, was well trained and well educated, but it was not aggressive. Officers did not cling to military posts, as no special privilege was granted, and they could always secure good jobs in the civilian sectors when they were discharged from the military.

In action, Hồ Chí Minh and his subordinates tacitly supported the theory that "all's fair in love and war" and "the end justifies the means." They obviously applied the *pa tao* ruling doctrine (the Way of the Lord), as opposed to *wang tao* (the Way of the King), according to old Chinese political teachings. (With *pa tao*, the rulers impose oppressive measures, brutal policies, and tricky schemes as well as deception to control and motivate the people and to keep the country in good order. *Wang tao* is the way of ruling with peaceful manners, abiding with ethics and morals, humanity, honesty, tolerance, and farsighted concerns.)

The South Vietnamese leaders were not willing to endorse the *pa tao*, and even if they had, they were not smart and daring enough to exercise it as effectively as their rivals in Hà Nội.

About the ARVN general officers, I agree with some U.S. military leaders. The ARVN had many heroes, a large number of brave, devoted, and talented young officers commanding small units from platoon to regiment. But there were few brilliant strategic thinkers and commanders who could do farsighted planning and make decisions that required complex coordination and the power of anticipation. Therefore, ARVN operations larger than division scale did not achieve great success.

The RVN leaders did not give proper attention to training and promoting military science geniuses. We had several "George S. Pattons" but no "George C. Marshall," and we needed both plus a "Napoleon." The younger generations were not being groomed ahead of time to assume high-ranking positions, although there were many prospective excellent leaders. If only the RVN had stood fast for five more years, younger military and political talents might have led the country, and South Việt Nam would have had a happier ending.

After President Diệm was slain in the 1963 coup, the generals assumed the national ruling power. Like military leaders in many third world countries, they became targets of bitter criticism. It was undeniable that Diệm was a strong leader whose prestige could have prevented his men, military officers, and civil servants from dipping their hands too flagrantly into shady affairs. When Diệm's power ceased to exist, many of them felt free to act.

WAR SUPPORTING MECHANISM

The communist war effort was made by all means that nationalists in the South could not and dared not employ. To consolidate their power and to fight the war, the communist leaders ran the "Machine of Fear." In the North, they extinguished every spark of dissent. That system helped control all sources of basic staples (grain, salt, cloth) to the last measure and thus mobilized the largest number of North Vietnamese to help in the war effort and to endure incredible hardships.

In the South, the communists ran that machine to keep the people living in remote areas under their control in absolute obedience. They relied on terror along with deceptive propaganda to mobilize peasants into supporting subversive movements, especially to recruit insurgents, to collect monetary and food contributions, and to run their intelligence networks. South Việt Nam did not impose and enforce a strict law to squeeze extra public contributions to the war effort (food, labor) besides comparatively light regular taxes. Therefore, people living under RVN government control lived rather normal lives. Well-to-do civilians enjoyed the luxuries of urban life protected by the armed forces but contributed little to the war effort without worrying about the danger and hardships that the soldiers and the peasants were undergoing.

In the pre-1975 South Việt Nam, there was no food rationing system or other strict measures to control the people. Residents were required to register in the household registry, but no harsh rules were imposed by local authorities. South Vietnamese citizens were free to travel anywhere in the country, even in disputed areas, while the North Vietnamese were allowed to travel outside their provinces only with local authorities' permission.

CONDUCTING THE WAR

The U.S. forces in Việt Nam fought with conventional military strategies and tactics, whereas the Việt Nam Communist Party conducted an all-out war effort with everything they could manipulate. The communists called their war the "People's War," and they compelled every citizen to contribute.

U.S. troops were sent to South Việt Nam as part of an enormous war machine. Nobody expected that their primary mission would be to fight the guerrillas. However, with earthshaking fire support, they performed their tasks perfectly, causing heavy losses to the enemy regulars, which indirectly eliminated many of the guerrillas. Unfortunately, fire support also killed innocent villagers.

As for the ARVN, the task of fighting guerrillas was the principal responsibility of the village militia and district regional forces so that regular army units could handle the larger battles. But that required great capability of local commanders and enormous resources to support the troops physically and psychologically.

In fact, before the Tét Offensive, not many ARVN military territorial HQS effectively practiced antiguerrilla tactics. After 1968, the fighting to contain guerrilla activities proved successful in many districts. The guerrilla attacks and harassment were no more a major concern thanks to the pacification effort and the more active operations of local territorial forces.

As far as territorial security was concerned, the ARVN high commands deployed regular combat units to the fullest extent to control the population with little reserve force. Those units were stretched thin and had to conduct operations to safeguard the area when local regional force units failed to fight off the enemy. The regular forces had little time to rest, and combat soldiers seldom got leave. That seriously affected their spirits. The national general reserve (Airborne, Marine, Ranger) were sent into battle after battle and were even tied to territorial defending missions. Therefore, the ARVN regular units seriously lost their mobility.

Along with Sài Gòn, Washington relied too heavily on military power and the military state of the art. But firepower was only highly destructive against enemy unit concentrations. In fact, the communist troops' capacity for quick dispersion saved them from total annihilation by the shower of bombshells. Communist troops were allowed to carry only a few items in their rucksacks beside their rifles. Their safety and health were sacrificed for military advantages of high mobility.

The bombing over North Việt Nam was several times more powerful than in the other wars. But the objectives to be bombed were not of great importance to top Communist Party leaders. They would survive, and their ruling power would not be endangered because of the destruction of the few dozen old-fashioned industrial installations and bridges, trucks, and boats. It was the common people, not the leaders, who suffered.

Apparently, the leaders in Sài Gòn and in Washington underestimated the high endurance of the poor North Vietnamese people who were under a ruling system with absolute control power that left them only one way forward.

As the basic strategy, the communist command in Hà Nội accepted very high human losses in exchange for military feats and to cause the heaviest injuries to the U.S. forces. The communists resorted to the largest available manpower from the overpopulated North Việt Nam.

But North Việt Nam human resources were not unlimited. After each large-scale campaign, Hà Nội had to wait for a few years to re-man its divisions. This could not be done in a short time. After the 1968 general offensive, they could only launch the next campaigns in 1972, then in 1975, at three-year intervals.

South Vietnamese officers said that the U.S. forces should have been deployed on an infantry blocking line across Laotian territory to stop communist war supplies from the Long Mountain Trails, the logistical backbone of Hà Nội military power in war, into South Việt Nam. Bombing could not do the task effectively enough to cut off the flow of supplies, which were moved and scattered over wide areas.

The ARVN and its U.S. ally should have acted even more aggressively to neutralize other communist war-supporting bases in southern North Việt Nam provinces close to the 17th parallel (to avoid a clash with the Chinese communist infantry near Hà Nội), Laos, and Cambodia with ground forces, and to blockade all North Việt Nam seaports earlier in the war in particular. But we thought that Washington would never have taken risks to accept such courses of action in full for fear that they would lead to a larger military confrontation with Red China. Washington would never win a war without destroying the enemy's war potential, while electing an overly cautious policy of self-restraint.

In the military intelligence domain, ARVN and U.S. intelligence was not very effective. Territorial tactical intelligence operations were successful, especially in the Phượng Hoàng Campaign. The last effort to eliminate the communist infrastructure in the South, the Phượng Hoàng Campaign, proved to be on the right track. It was one of the most successful strategies of the South Vietnamese. Unfortunately, Sài Gòn and Washington failed to exploit its achievements to the largest extent possible.

Communist spies infiltrated RVN government and military agencies and units at all levels. RVN counterintelligence agencies detected many important enemy espionage networks and individual moles, but only during the Ngô Đình Diệm era.

Little was known about intelligence activities in the North. Only the military intelligence service's high-ranking officers had a clear image of the top-level espionage. I heard from some reliable sources that South Vietnamese spies were working at several North Việt Nam central agencies.

FIGHTING PSYCHOLOGICAL WARFARE

The conflict was of an ideological nature. The communist regime founded its struggle on communist dogma. Communism's religious-like teachings were charming poor people into supporting the proletarian revolution. Skillful propaganda schemes, well coordinated with terrorism, effectively boosted and coerced the North to support the party's war policies.

On the nationalist side, no specific ideology was imposed. In the government's messages, key national objectives were depicted in general terms solely as "freedom, democracy, and economic development," which were vague and not very convincing.

Therefore, ARVN soldiers were not fighting for any specific ideology. But they held their ground longer than expected and many times won battles despite extremely unfavorable conditions, poor leadership, and a negative psychological environment. Our soldiers' willingness to fight and their endurance were generated more by their personal experiences that spontaneously led them to a conviction to fight against the communist dictatorship and its brutal and merciless rule and immorality, much more than by indoctrinated ideals of freedom and democracy.

The nationalist government in South Việt Nam was facing numerous adversary conditions on the psychological front. One was the power of "street rumor." In a country where most of its population does not have access to the impartial media, rumors, especially malicious rumors, play a significant role. It is human nature to be interested in sensational tidbits.

The communists put much effort into compiling fake information, skillfully mixing prevarication with truth to serve their propaganda purposes. The nationalists were defeated at last on the ideological front. Even if they had employed similar communist propaganda tricks, they would not have prevailed over the communists because they were not trained and were compelled to employ such lying techniques in the psychological warfare they were fighting. The war occurred when Washington was under fierce protest and criticism from all over the world by the anti-American movement that was on the rise. South Việt Nam was the easiest target for the war protest, and Sài Gòn became a scapegoat for the powerful media campaign against Washington.

The important role of psychological warfare in the Việt Nam War in which propaganda was the communists' principal tool should be treated in a separate volume. However, the communist psychological strategies and tactics have not been sufficiently evaluated by the academic circles and the mass media in Western countries. Generally, the communist side was using propaganda as a major weapon beside conventional warfare and terrorism, and U.S. forces were not. The international communist front contrived skillful plots in propaganda strategies to defeat the United States right in the heart of America, while facing very little resistance from the U.S. side. It even drew a large number of Americans to support its psychological offensive against their own nation.

Our war leaders in Washington and Sài Gòn did not endorse the principle that "offensive is the best way to defend" in the psychological warfare. Washington and Sài Gòn should have directed a strong propaganda offensive at the vital spots of the communist center of ideological power along with military efforts.

Active assistance was given by ARVN and U.S. military Psyops and Civil Affairs units only at a tactical level. The strategic psywar missions performed by the U.S. information services and radio station were successful to some degree but proved to have insufficient support from the U.S. government.

POSTWAR PSYCHOLOGY

Even without a large propaganda effort, the U.S. presence and aid along with Western countries' assistance have slowly gained more positive appreciation from the people in the RVN government-controlled areas. Washington was winning the hearts and minds of more and more South Vietnamese people when it began phasing out its troops in 1970 in the face of deteriorating morale.

The Vietnamese sympathy with the Americans in general surfaced bright and clear in the postwar era. After April 1975, most South Vietnamese and many North Vietnamese realized that during the war, the Americans also brought to Việt Nam something better, not only bombs and shells and Agent Orange. Large-scale assistance in rural development, economy, health care, education, highway construction, technology, and culture had changed the lives of the South Vietnamese people in every domain and sector for the better, although not to the best expected. Washington has never strived with proper effort to make that known to the world.

Realities of life in South Việt Nam also produced a powerful impact on the many North Vietnamese, from common peasants to intellectuals, when they visited the South for the first time, not only because this part of the country had been much more prosperous but also because of the freedom and civilization the southerners had been enjoying.

I am certain that this changed sentiment has resulted in the friendly attitude of the common Vietnamese toward American visitors nowadays.

WHAT IF THE REPUBLIC OF VIỆT NAM STILL EXISTED?

I doubt that the final victory on the battlefield to end the war in our favor would have brought permanent and perfect peace to Indochina. It might have stopped communist forces from conquering the RVN or minimized communist subversive activities against South Việt Nam, Laos, and Cambodia. But the Việt Nam Communist Party still could have maintained guerrilla warfare at the lowest degree in the South for a long time, at least until 1991 when the Soviet Union disintegrated. In such a case, unstable rural security in remote districts would have limited the full potential economic growth of the South.

Besides, it was very improbable that the American policy makers would have changed their foreign policies concerning developing countries in that era. Washington would continue supporting foreign dictators who were backing American interests in the region. Việt Nam could not have been an exception. Consequently, there would not have been democracy to the degree that many

Vietnamese had wished for, but economic and politic development would have still been the strongest in Southeast Asia.

COMMUNIST MANAGEMENT

Before the war ended, I sometimes wished that if the communist leaders won the conflict, they would, in their way, bring something good to our poor Vietnamese. If the communists took over the ruling power, should we nationalists let them do it their way, even help them attain the ultimate interests of our beloved compatriots?

The answer after April 1975 was no. I have been totally disappointed to see that the communist rulers were incapable of governing the country. Their inability, plus greed for personal wealth, held back progress. They often ascribe their economic problems to the consequences of war, whereas Việt Nam has rich natural resources and an able labor force, and it has received generous aid from United Nation institutions and rich countries.

However, since the introduction of the so-called *đổi mới* (renovation), Hà Nội communist leaders have practiced market economy. But they still cling to "socialism" as a label to justify their despotic ruling power. In fact, the "socialist-oriented market economy" is virtually an economy without an appropriate regulative system, with laws and regulations that are often vague and conflicting.

Right after taking over North Việt Nam in 1954 and South Việt Nam in 1975, the fanatical and dogmatic communist leaders imposed a policy to annihilate all cultural works of national value contributed by nationalist authors and to disclaim all achievements in sports, academic, scientific, and other sectors made by noncommunist citizens and institutions. Their policy failed at last. The soul of noncommunist culture, the expertise of South Vietnamese technologists and management, survived and prevailed.

Social evils grew much worse than in the pre-1975 South. Since 1990, Hà Nội leaders have tolerated all types of recreation, social evils, corruption, and superstitious practices to pacify the common people—particularly young city dwellers, the most politically sensitive population—and to consolidate the party members' support. Prostitution is at least ten times more prevalent now than in South Việt Nam in the late 1960s when a half million U.S. troops were present. Many world demagogic leaders have resorted to similar connivances to ease political tension.

The most critical deterioration is in the education system, from first grade to postgraduate studies, as asserted by Hà Nội state-controlled newspapers. It takes a few decades to correct political errors, but ethical depravity could hardly be cleaned by 100 years of endeavor.

The "red bourgeoisie," the new upper class of rich communist cadres, has adopted excessive foreign ways of life, despite communist ethos they have preached for eighty years and breaking all common social ethical morality. This ruling class has encouraged incurable immorality and corruption.

The communist leaders conquered the South militarily, but they failed in other domains, bringing nothing worth mentioning to the people. Singapore's former prime minister Lee Kuan Yew noted in his book *From Third World to First* (HarperCollins, 2000) that in 1975, Sài Gòn was equal to Bangkok, but the former capital of South Việt Nam lagged twenty years behind Bangkok in 1992.

Some statesmen in South Việt Nam once said, "Only the communist leaders' total victory over South Việt Nam could definitely defeat them." Similarly, a British journalist remarked in a BBC Radio report in mid-1980 that communists in Việt Nam began their downfall when their tanks crashed through the main gate of Sài Gòn's Independence Palace on April 30, 1975.

THE PRICE OF WAR

The war between the communists and the noncommunists from 1945 to 1975 claimed the greatest loss of human lives and properties in the history of the nation. Casualties have been estimated at 58,000 Americans, 260,000 South Vietnamese, and 1.4 million North Vietnamese. Civilian war victims were estimated at 500,000, mostly in South Việt Nam. They were slain by terrorists and by firefights on both sides, It does not include 200,000 "boat people" who died fleeing Việt Nam and political prisoners who died in concentration camps. These figures may also include victims of the 1945–49 political purges and the 1953–56 Land Reform Campaign.

In the war, tens of billions of dollars of property was destroyed.

Had Việt Nam developed under communism to be a free country with true democracy and the highest prosperity in Southeast Asia after thirty-three years of unification under the communist leadership, we would have had to accept the bloody Việt Nam War as a good price to pay.

Looking into actual consequences of the Việt Nam conflict, I maintain that despite the fact that the Vietnamese communists won the earth-shaking war against the world's top superpower, their war to unify the country under their rule has been nonsense. It reminds me of some stories about Genghis Khan. His thirteenth-century army invaded China, Europe, and Persia with swords, horses, and iron discipline. But in the end, they were absorbed into the conquered societies, and their Mongolian Empire left few contributions to civilization.

THE JUST CAUSE

The defeat of South Việt Nam on April 30, 1975, was the fall not only of a government but also of a society, a civilization, a sovereign nation with its own identity in educational, judicial, economic, financial, business management, effective law enforcement, and administrative practices.

While facing the destructive war, South Việt Nam still maintained good schools, free health care for the poor, science and technological advances second to no other Southeast Asian country, and an economy strong enough to endure difficulties by war and, with U.S. aid, to withstand economic sabotage by communist insurgents.

The RVN armed forces were a well-organized entity with recognized laws and regulations, a system of discipline, an independent spirit, and an ideal to serve. Although defeated, they contributed a lot to national science and technology, education, culture, music, arts, and sports—besides fighting the war. Their contributions must not be ignored.

Moreover, the loss of 260,000 soldiers killed, 1 million wounded, thousands of heroic acts, and the fact that our common soldiers showed their willingness to fight even though they were under Sài Gòn's questionable leadership concretely affirm that the RVN armed forces performed the assigned tasks to serve their nation well. They were not fighting for money, nor were they compelled by iron measures. History should not forget their lofty spirit and respectable motivation.

The total failure of the economic, social, and cultural policies in North Việt Nam before 1975, and in all Việt Nam after 1975, the current mismanagement of the country, and the more than 2 million refugees who have escaped the communist regime all prove that we were fighting for a just cause.

I am certain that I served on the right side in the nationalist/communist conflict in Việt Nam.

MUTUAL RECONCILIATION

Deep in my heart, I don't bear any animosity against the Communist Party members and soldiers. My resentment, if any, is only against the Communist Party leaders who brought communism into Việt Nam and waged the political purging campaign leading to the thirty-year bloody war that made Việt Nam one of the bottom ten developing countries of the last sixty years.

Though many nationalists are not fostering animosity or seeking revenge, it's unreasonable to tell them to forget what the communist regime has done to their country and their compatriots. Who could forget a beautiful lost love? Who could forget the deadly and painful bite by a mad dog? One who can do so is acting against human nature. Wounds may heal, but scars rarely disappear. Similarly, I accept the fact that people on the communist side who suffered from actions of war by our side will not forget their painful feeling toward the nationalists.

I believe reconciliation is vital after a war. But it requires mutual goodwill from both sides. I wish that war victims on the communist side would have the same opinion as mine. Mutual understanding should be built without interference by any power. Peace of mind in all of us will come sometime in the bright future of Việt Nam.

To serve my fatherland, I would accept the risks in war: death, losing parts of my body, being captured and tortured. Hundreds of my friends and acquaintances have been lost, and their spouses and children are still searching for their traces with a tiny flickering glow of hope that they will learn about their fate. Thank God I came out unscathed.

In reminiscence of my years serving the RVN military before April 30, 1975, my deepest regret is that I had not done my best to the ultimate interests of my Vietnamese people before I lost my war at last. I was thirty-eight years old when the RVN collapsed. The span of life from thirty-eight to sixty years old should have been my best time to serve my people at the highest capability along with millions of men and women like me.

During my years of military service, I did not record any achievement that was worth mentioning, nor did I receive any special reward from the government or the ARVN. I only believed that my service may have contributed some small part to the assertion of our right cause.

THE UNDYING WAR MONSTER

Some dignitary once remarked, "No one knows the values of peace better than the soldiers do." And especially the soldiers at bottom ranks, I believe.

On the battlefields and in remote hamlets, bones, flesh, and blood from torn-up bodies killed by bombs, shells, daggers, and machetes taught me better than lessons at school about how human life is priceless.

As poverty, injustice, exploitation, and oppression exist, there is no way to eradicate all the roots of war. But even a war for a right cause always invites unpredictable, harmful consequences that bring the entire society to unavoidable hardships and sorrow.

As a supporter of the nationalist revolution, I once fostered the idea of exercising violence to bring better changes to society. However, the war and the years in prison followed by time living under the communist regime have changed my view. Violence may help shorten the road to victories, but it tends to become excessive and to build greater obstacles against the ultimate objectives of the revolution.

I was a war protester by nature, but I was forced to support the war; I had no other choice.

Human nature contains both love and hatred. By provocation of faith, ideology, hatred, animosity, greed, and ambition, a tyrannical ruling power can wield terrorism and skillful propaganda to incite millions of innocent people to enter into an unjustified war, to kill and to be killed. The cost of such a war is always fathomless and usually much higher than the gains it makes.

However, peace activists, religious leaders, educators, and an impartial and honest mass media could join in the effort to alleviate the causes of war and promote understanding between the adversaries and restraint from inciting hatred.

The Việt Nam War was one of the contemporary world's most painful experiences, but from it we can learn invaluable lessons that should be taught accurately and sufficiently to every generation to come.

THIRTY

Ever in My Memory

THE ROD OF MY TEACHER

I entered second grade after the long summer vacation of 1943.

My teacher, Mr. Kinh, was a devout Buddhist and a severe educator. He seldom smiled, or to be more exact, he sometimes smiled with his fellow teachers but almost never with his pupils. Moreover, he did not talk much, using gestures instead of voice whenever possible.

He was my favorite, and I hated him as well. His voice, low but powerful, and his eyes, stern and murderous, are imprinted deeply in my memory. But the image of his rod, hung on one side of the blackboard, always appeared clearer and livelier in my mind whenever something turned on the high-definition images stored in the picture file of my brain.

During the colonial era, we had to learn French in the first grade. It was rather difficult to learn a new language that appeared to have nothing in common with our mother tongue. I tried my best but was unable to memorize the gender of a noun and the difference between an adjective and an attribute despite my teacher's efforts to simplify his teachings.

Once a week in the second half of second grade, Mr. Kinh gave us a simple "orthography" in French. He would write a text on the blackboard in beautiful handwriting. The text usually contained three or four short sentences, each containing two or three new easy words taken from a French textbook that he had already explained to us in detail.

He let us read and memorize the chalk lines on the blackboard for five minutes without taking notes. Then he covered the blackboard with a cloth before reading aloud the dictation and we began writing. When the dictation was over, I gathered all notebooks and brought them to his table to be graded.

His rule was one lash of his rattan rod for each mistake a student made in the dictation.

In the fifth month of the school year 1943–44, Mr. Kinh appointed me the "rod keeper," but later our classmates called me "đao phủ" (the executioner).

The procedures went on routinely once a week for the four months of our second grade. When the teacher began grading the notebooks, I stepped to one side of the blackboard and took down the rod, which was nearly three feet long and about a quarter inch in diameter. As Mr. Kinh was reading and making corrections on the notebooks, I stood beside his desk with the rod in my hand, my face tense and my eyes looking straight at nowhere, awaiting his *ruling*.

After having graded a notebook, he put it to his right hand side and announced the "verdict," very clear and always with only a three-word clause in French, for example, "Hoàng, trois fautes!" (Hoàng, three mistakes!). My classmate Hoàng would say, "Yes, sir," then walk to the teacher's desk to pick up his notebook. Then he would step to the blackboard, which rested on a wooden horse, obediently bend down, and put his neck under the lower side of the board.

I would lash his buttocks three times with the rod. Hoàng would happily stand up after the third lash without waiting for an order, because teacher Kinh did not require us to do so, and returned to his seat. Hoàng would smile as if thinking, "It could have been much worse."

A pupil would be extremely happy if the *verdict* was cut short to a single word, only the pupil's name, without the other two words stating his mistakes. Our classmates dubbed it *acquittal*. The lucky pupil would quickly approach the teacher's desk and turn back with the notebook, a radiant smile, and a face blushed by happiness. Some could not resist boasting, "You see how good I am."

Among my classmates in the first quarter, fifteen often had one mistake or none, the other fifteen or so frequently had one or two, and the remaining five frequently had two or three. As far as I can remember, no one always had "no mistake," and no one had more than three.

In the first few days on the job, I was unable to determine how hard I should "punish the convicts," because at that age, I did not have enemies to take revenge on. Moreover, we were rather friendly to each other, although many years later we would become enemies fighting on both sides of a long and bloody civil war.

The first time, I carried out my duty with a hesitating arm on a boy who had been sitting next to me since the first grade. Mr. Kinh suddenly stopped grading and looked at me—a dagger look that was much more threatening than the rod itself.

He slowly rose from his chair, walked to the blackboard, and snatched the rod from my hand. Mr. Kinh showed not a bit of anger, and his face was calm as usual as he said to me in a toneless voice, "Not hard enough. Let me show you how it must be." He motioned me to put my head under the blackboard. He lashed my buttocks with a forceful blow that I still remember. From then on, I dared not perform my task with light hands on any classmate.

There were six girls in my class. Girl pupils at the time wore black trousers with *áo dài* (Vietnamese female's dress) made of fine materials, smooth and thin. I never thought of lashing them with that fearful rod.

Fortunately, only one or two girls made any mistakes in the first month. Mr. Kinh scolded them instead of giving a rod sentence. After that, all of them always got "no mistakes." They might have been doing better than us boys in French, but probably the teacher felt uneasy seeing the girls endure the painful experience. So he always *acquitted* them even when any of them *"committed a crime,"* as we said in our jargons.

Then at last came my turn. My notebook always was the last to be graded by Mr. Kinh. This was the worst time in the sequence. He graded my dictation, then without a word, only ordered me by his head motion.

If he motioned me toward the pupils' tables, he meant that I had no mistakes. If he motioned me toward the blackboard, I would hand the rod to him instead of hanging it up. I would put my head under the blackboard and wait. Mr. Kinh himself handled the *execution,* and I never hoped that his lashing would be more lenient than mine.

A few days after starting my job, I made an unpredictable mistake beside the spelling errors. When he gave me two lashes, I was still bending with my head under the blackboard, waiting for more lashes. As he turned his back, he realized that my head was still under the board. He snarled, "You want more?" So I got one more.

From then on, while I was undergoing the punishment, I had to watch him by looking back through my two legs. If his feet turned to step toward his desk, I would stand up quickly to get my notebook and return to my seat.

What I suffered was much more painful than that of my classmates, but at the time, I was too young to analyze my feelings to tell my friends, who thought I must have been happy with my *powerful job.*

They did know how many lashes they would receive, so they could be certain when the painful suffering would stop. I was not so lucky. Before putting my head under the blackboard, I did not know how many lashes I would get, so the lashes seemed longer and more painful to me. The feeling tortured me so much that I did not feel relieved when I knew it was the last blow, and the time waiting for the last seemed endless. Fortunately, I never made more than two mistakes in a dictation.

At last, as we were beaten into learning the language, we made fewer mistakes. By May 1944, more than three-quarters of us often made "zero faute."

* * *

After the South Vietnamese republic collapsed on April 30, 1975, I was imprisoned along with hundreds of thousands of former members of the South

Vietnamese government and military, members of political parties, and anti-communist notables. We suffered a great deal from the treatment of the communist regime in the prison camps. However, most of us did not feel resentment toward the barbaric communist jailers. As for me, they were doing their job somehow similar to what I did with the rod of my teacher in 1943: beating hard in order not to be beaten harder.

We were quietly given terms of three years. The North Vietnamese National Assembly Standing Committee's Resolution 49 in 1961, which was applied to us, empowered the chief of public security at the district level and higher to give anyone unlimited three-year terms in prison without trial in a court. The prisons are called *laokai* in Mainland China and reeducation camps in Việt Nam under the communist regime. We were not told how many terms we would have to serve. So we did not know how long we would remain incarcerated.

Only a small number of prisoners of North Vietnamese origin were given definite sentences by the courts. Resolution 49 imprisoned the others under the clauses of the reeducation measures. Those prisoners did not know when their terms ended, either.

But during seven years in seven camps before I was released, I often recollected my feeling I had had when I put my head under the blackboard waiting for the last blow of my teacher's rod nearly forty years earlier. A criminal serving a determined sentence clearly announced by a court must be feeling happier than a political prisoner put in jail by Resolution 49/61.

"MY DIVISION"

During the time serving as the Twenty-second Division G-5, I had to perform some tasks not specified in any books or directives. Sometimes I had to deal with cases that might have best described my odds-and-ends job.

One day in April 1965, a battalion from the Forty-first Regiment/Twenty-second Division launched an operation in an area north of Highway 19, northeast of An Khê. During a clash with an enemy company, one VC surrendered with his rifle. Quickly he told the ARVN commanders that he had been serving the ARVN Fortieth Regiment of my division until a communist regional unit ambushed his company two years earlier and captured him. Under security regulations, the Division Military Security Office handled his case. I met him at his request.

The good-looking boy had been an actor in a small traditional theatrical troupe that was not known outside his native province. He fell in love with a girl, a supporting actress, and married her. Not long after the wedding, he got what some Americans at that time called a "greeting card," or draft card.

After basic training, he was assigned to the Fortieth Regiment in 1962. His wife followed him, living in the battalion dependents' quarters near his barracks.

After his draft term ended, he reenlisted and was promoted to corporal. When his company was ambushed and suffered a dozen deaths, he was among the missing-in-action.

After months of detention in a VC camp as a POW, he decided that he would free himself at any cost, but every attempt failed. At last he managed to win the confidence of the communist company commander. By skillfully pretending that he was "enlightened by the revolutionary ideals," he was allowed to join the VC ranks.

For several months, he fought beside the communist troops, who watched him closely. He had to prove his faith to the communist cause while fighting beside them in the coastal area. "I've faked fighting against our army units while waiting for a chance to meet ARVN fellows from 'my division,' the tough Twenty-second," he told me. "I pretended to be faithful to the VC. I was facing lots of danger while doing so and was almost killed sometimes, but I tried not to do anything that might have injured the ARVN soldiers out of *my division*." He confessed. "Day and night, I hoped to see my division's fellows for a long time. Last month the VC command promoted me to squad leader. A week ago, when I saw the advancing troops with the three-black-mountains and two-white-rivers on their arms, I was so happy. Disregarding imminent danger, I flew to our side. I am sorry for just one thing. I would have been much happier if it had been my company, my battalion, or my regiment."

He did well in the security investigation, proving his innocence through interrogations. His only request—to be reassigned to "his battalion" of the Fortieth Infantry—however, was not approved. So I talked to the ACoS-Military Security to propose the review. The chief of the Military Security Office agreed with me that although he was fighting in a VC unit, facts showed that he was honest and faithful to the division. Moreover, he provided accurate information on enemy activities.

That was enough to prove his honesty. But according to regulations, he had to be transferred to another unit. At last the military security branch agreed to send him to another battalion of his regiment. He was somehow pleased with the decision.

While he was staying in the division headquarters for administrative process, he came to ask me for a favor. He said his wife might still be in Kontum, and he wanted my help in learning her situation before writing a letter or even reuniting with her.

In meetings with me, he recounted his life as a traditional music artist. He had been traveling on many show tours with the troupe, falling in love with girls where the troupe was visiting. Then he met his wife, who made him change a lot. He described to me the beautiful time they had been together with a voice full of romantic emotion.

It seemed to me that he loved the military life and his unit as much as the sweetest songs he had been singing on the stage. He didn't care much about the nation, the government, or communism. What he loved most was his unit; the highest was *"our division."*

We easily located the poor woman. One of my NCOs said that when he gave her the news, she burst into tears. She told him that after two years without any information about her man, she believed that he had perished in the wild and dense forests.

Living in narrow circumstances and lonely without the least hope of her husband coming back, she decided to marry another soldier serving the Forty-first Infantry, only three months before her first man returned. She cried for days and asserted her unchanged love for the first husband, but didn't want to betray her second man. Finally she took our advice to just disappear from the sight of her beloved artist husband.

After a night of thinking, I decided against telling the brave soldier the truth. I told him simply that we had failed to locate her. Two years later, I learned from some who knew him and his heartrending story that he didn't remarry and was fighting with extremely high courage before he was seriously wounded and was given a desk job due to his health condition.

To him and soldiers like him, fatherland, country, and patriotism were too abstract. *"His Division"* seemed to him the loftiest entity he had to be faithful to.

In our war, many similar situations have occurred, and with their sentimental nature, no one could be sure which solution was the best. Anyway, I was not trained as a marriage counselor, but I acted as one in an unsuccessful case.

HE TALKS! (A TALE FOR THE MEMORIAL DAY)

Lieutenant Colonel Anthony J. Tencza arrived in our Vietnamese Twenty-second Infantry Division sometime near the end of 1961. He served as senior advisor of the MACV Team beside the division headquarters. I was then a young first lieutenant, twenty-five years old, with six years in service.

He was one of the best American friends to the Vietnamese in Kontum City. Behind the thick glasses, his eyes were always bright and pleasant, and he always smiled when he met anyone. I respected him more than any other American in the MACV Team.

As a liaison officer, I had to see him almost every day. He liked me probably because of my English—not very fluent but good enough to spare English listeners from confusion between fifteen and fifty, thirty and thirsty, or tie and time, or phrases like "If you go to the PX, please buy for me some booze." In 1962, the relations between Vietnamese military men and American advisors were still very close. I was about fifteen years younger than he, and Tencza treated me as if I were his younger brother.

In the early morning of Sunday, July 15, 1962, the division operation center let me know that a strategic hamlet armed with some fifteen to twenty rifles had been overrun an hour before by a VC company. The division CO, Colonel Nguyễn Bảo Trị, ordered his artillery commander, the G-2, and the commander of the reconnaissance company to join Colonel Tencza on a reconnaissance flight over the area.

I always liked to participate in such trips. I was given a special task by the division commander to study major battles, especially such enemy hit-and-run attacks, so I had been sent to several overrun outposts and hamlets as soon as the situation permitted, sometimes while fighting was still going on.

When I saw the G-2 that morning, I asked him to join the reconnaissance party. At first he said OK, but while waiting for me to get my pistol and put on my field gear in my BOQ room, Captain Phó Thịnh Trinh, the G-2, suddenly said to me, "You should not go." His face lost its usual composure.

"Why," I asked him. His voice was slow but firm, "I've just *bấm độn* [fortune telling by calculation based on some principles of Yi Ching, the classic *Chinese Book of Changes*]. It forebodes *very* bad luck."

When I insisted, he turned serious and refused adamantly. He said, "If I didn't *bấm độn*, I would let you go. But as I predicted bad luck, I can't put you on the plane with us. As a G-2, I must go. The colonel said you are allowed if you want to go, OK. But you don't have to. So you must obey me to stay home."

Captain Trinh loved fortune telling. His rate of accuracy was more than fifty-fifty like any other amateur fortune tellers. But that time, his calculation was correct.

Thirty minutes later, the Division Tactical Center called me and let me know that one of the two "whirly birds" had just crashed. Enemy fire took it down while it was circling over the hamlet, a small mountainous community of nearly 300 people of the Bahnar tribe, about fifteen miles northwest of Kontum City. On the downed ship were Tencza, Trinh, and Lieutenant Nguyễn Văn Hòa.

The other H-21 that followed at a distance soared into the air out of the enemy fire and landed at Polei Kleng, an outpost nearby. Major Đoàn Viết Liêu, division artillery commander, and an American officer were in this helicopter.

It took several hours for the reconnaissance company to reach the crash site. They rescued Lt. Hòa, the recon company commander, and an American pilot. Both survived the crash and hid in the brush. The VC shot Col. Tencza and Captain Trinh to death about ten yards from the H-21. The two crew-gunners were killed inside; one of them was Sergeant Harold L. Guthrie, whom I had met on some previous flights. The other pilot died hiding beside a small stream, as far as I can remember.

Late in the afternoon, the dead were brought back to Kontum. After examinations by the division surgeon, all of them were laid in the medical company morgue. In the morgue there were also bodies of about twenty Vietnamese Special Forces soldiers killed on a C-47 when it crashed while taking off at the Kontum airport the previous morning.

That evening, we Vietnamese officers kept vigil in one-hour shifts until the next morning, when a C-123 would fly the corpses to Sài Gòn. My turn was from 2 to 3 AM along with Lt. Trần Văn Đáng. Under the glimmering weak light bulbs, the morgue looked ghostly and dreadful, especially with an altar on which stood two red candles in brass holders and censers holding glowing incense sticks.

At about twenty minutes before our turn ended, I told Đáng to stay and I walked out to the latrine in the nearby building. I had not gone more than thirty yards than Đáng ran out, calling me in a frightened voice. I could feel horror in his tone.

"What's the matter?" I asked.

"He talks . . ." Đáng said. It made my flesh creep. I swallowed hard when trying to control myself and whispered, "Who talks? And how?"

Đáng spluttered: "A corpse." I tried to appear calm and bold, though my heart was thumping. "Someone in the middle of the room. I heard a voice, not a noise of an object," he said.

"We both go in to see, OK?" I said. A moment later, I gathered all my courage to enter the room with Đáng beside me. Both of us drew our pistols and cocked. We moved slowly along two rows of stretchers laid on trestles about three feet above the floor. Nothing happened.

When we were about to walk out to the door, we were startled by a voice, a human voice, as if it were from someone in his sleep. I was really frightened, but with all my strength I turned in the direction of the voice. Right then the voice repeated, and it was from Colonel Tencza.

That it was from the colonel restored my composure. I did not feel anything frightening from him. I knew what happened. Gas from inside rose through his throat and caused the sound.

Instinctively, I took off my field cap, holding it at my chest and prayed as I often did in front of the altar of my Vietnamese fallen fighting fellows. "Tony, you do know how we respect you, and I know you like me. I will pray for you and remember you all my life as my fallen Vietnamese fighting fellow."

A little blood trickled from the corner of his mouth. It reminded me of what the Vietnamese believed. It is said that a person who suffered a violent death would have blood trickling from the mouth when a close relative or friend arrived. His close relatives were on the other side of the globe. He may have considered me one of his friends, I said to myself. He had often called me his younger brother.

The next morning, we saw the dead off at the airport. Two Vietnamese and two American military servicemen carried each of the dead onto the C-123 cargo plane. The scene symbolized the true friendship between the Americans and the Twenty-second Infantry Division.

About a week later, I went to bed late one night. I turned my tape recorder on to listen to a tape of American country music that Tencza had copied and given to me that I had never played. A few seconds after putting on the stereo headset, my breath almost stopped when a voice rang in my earphones: "Hello, Luận." It was Tencza's voice.

My heart jumped as I threw the headset on the bed and sprang to my feet. It took me a few seconds to realize that the colonel had dubbed the tape from his original copy and said some words for testing.

Since then, whenever I have a service commemorating a deceased member of my family, Tencza is among the names of my Vietnamese fallen friends whom I always pray for.

A HERO OF THE KIT CARSON SCOUTS

Bùi Ngọc Phép had been a Việt Minh soldier in South Việt Nam before regrouping in the North after the 1954 Geneva Accords. He was trained as a sapper in mainland China, specializing in land mines. He was a lieutenant in the North Việt Nam Army when he was sent to the South. A few weeks after his arrival at the National Chiêu Hồi Center, he joined the Kit Carson Scouts serving in the U.S. Eleventh Armored Cavalry Regiment in Dĩ An, Biên Hòa province. He was named leader of the group of about thirty scouts.

What made him believe that the Chiêu Hồi policy was real and merciful resulted from a special case. On the night of January 31, 1968, when the Tết Offensive broke out in Sài Gòn, Phép was ordered to lay mines under the concrete bridge leading from an area beside the National Chiêu Hồi Center to the Sài Gòn Zoo across the Thị Nghè Canal. He laid waiting for an order to blow up the bridge when a communist battalion had crossed it.

While hiding behind dense brush and water lilies on the canal side, he was an uninvited listener to a conversation between an ARVN Marine and an armed propaganda soldier who was a former NVA. The two were guarding the fences of our two adjacent units close to the bridge.

It happened that the armed propaganda soldier was from a place not far from the village of the sapper Phép. The AP soldier told the Marine about his life, his decision to go "chiêu hồi," and the Chiêu Hồi program. It was enough for Phép. After the communist battalion failed to reach the bridge area, he retrieved the explosives and went back to his unit. A few months later, he decided to leave the NVA side.

The Eleventh Armored Cavalry Regiment highly appreciated his performance. His keen sense and well learned techniques helped him locate many antitank mines skillfully laid by communist sappers, and he saved many M-48s and other armored vehicles. One day he volunteered to join a major operation, although it was not his turn, because he was greatly concerned that many tanks were deployed.

Returning from the operation, Phép was hit in the bladder by a sniper's bullet and died in an American military hospital in Long Bình. Because of some confusion, the hospital discarded his corpse in the shabby morgue of the civilian hospital of Biên Hòa instead of returning him with honors to the Eleventh Armored Cavalry Regiment as requested by HQS.

By an agreement with the Vietnamese side, the regiment held a solemn funeral ceremony honoring Phép. His casket was put on an armored personnel carrier, followed by other M-113 APCs and an American platoon with white headbands, a Vietnamese mourning sign. The similar piece of white cloth was also wrapped around the lowered 90 mm canon of an M-48 leading the procession. Honor guards carrying the Eleventh Armored Cavalry Regiment flag beside the Vietnamese and American national colors, bugle sounding U.S. taps . . . all made many Vietnamese spectators think Phép must have been a general.

He had no relatives in South Việt Nam. If he had any, all members of the Eleventh would have contributed to the memorial fund for his relatives. The executive officer of the regiment representing Colonel Patton, commander of the Eleventh, attended the burial ceremony. He officially informed us of disciplinary measures taken against those responsible members of the American hospital for their failure to honor the official recommendation of the regiment regarding the treatment of Phép's body.

THE SKINNY GIFT DOG

One morning in March 1971, I got a telephone call from the wife of my best friend, Đỗ Tất Phú. She let me know in a choked voice that Phú had been killed after a bloody battle in the marshy land of U Minh, near the southernmost cape of Cà Mâu. He was one of my comrades in the VNQDĐ. We were like blood brothers since we sat next to each other in the sixth-grade classroom in Nam Định provincial city.

In 1953, he and I joined the ranks of the VNQDĐ. He was a zealous Việt Quốc party member, while his eldest brother was an ardent Communist Party medium-ranking member, serving the Việt Minh rank in the Việt Minh zone. Phú respected and loved his brother but not his brother's party.

After a reunion with his brother at their parents' home in Nam Định for a week following the July 20, 1954, cease-fire, he silently left home for Hà Nội and went aboard a military airplane along with my group to Sài Gòn. While I was in the military academy, he was attending college and serving as a teacher.

He was living in a suburban ward. In the neighborhood there were several gangs of thieves, swindlers, pickpockets, and hoodlums. He held several night classes for the gang members, teaching them the regular curriculum of first to fifth grades, free of tuition. He gained the respect and sympathy of a large number of the gang members. His good heart helped many of them return to a normal life.

In 1968, he was drafted and trained at Thủ Đức Reserve Officer School. After graduation he was assigned to a province in the Mekong Delta. In 1970, he was promoted to first lieutenant and appointed to command an infantry company. He was a brave commander and a devoted officer who took great care of his soldiers. He was a determined anticommunist, but his heart was full of kindness for the people and for the captured enemy troops.

In late 1970, on an inspection trip to the Mekong Delta, I stopped by an ARVN base camp to see Lieutenant Phú. His battalion had just come back from a monthlong operation. While we were drinking tea in his small company office, an old woman and an old man stepped in. Before we could say a word to greet them, both knelt down on the floor and kowtowed before my friend and me.

Phú and I quickly helped them up, telling them that they should treat us as if we were their children. The two poor peasants then told us the sad story that brought them to see Phú. He confirmed their accounts.

About a week earlier, his unit had been conducting a raid on a swath of uninhabited wetlands deep in the VC infested areas. In a short firefight, troops under his command killed four and captured one suspected VC. Phú's company suffered one KIA.

The young captive was wounded in the calf. He admitted that they were guerrillas in charge of supply transportation. Upon receiving the company's report, the ARVN battalion commander gave an order through the radio net to "get rid of him."

The young guerrilla was aware of his fate by overhearing the radio communication. He begged the lieutenant for one favor, which was to shoot him on the roadside or any high ground so that his family could identify him later. He prayed not to be shot in the water-filled rice field because his corpse would quickly discompose and be disfigured beyond recognition under the hot sun. Their relatives could hardly tell one body from another when they came to retrieve them for burial.

After giving him first aid, Phú told him he wouldn't carry out the order and would give him a sampan to go back to his family. The boy didn't believe Phú, but he had no choice. The lucky boy left on the sampan, rowing slowly at first. Apparently he thought that the lieutenant would play a trick on him, luring him on the sampan and then killing him on the water. After going far beyond rifle range and realizing that Phú had kept his word, the boy took off his black shirt, waved it, and yelled to thank the lieutenant and rowed away at full speed.

So that day the boy's parents had come to see Lt. Phú to show their gratitude. The old man said, "Lieutenant, you have given birth to our son a second
time. In my village, every young boy like my son has to serve the VC under the
threat of having his right hand chopped off or even immediate execution."

Phú and I felt sad, but the gift the old peasants gave Phú made me feel sadder,
although it sounds funny at first. Their gift was a skinny dog. The old couple said
their village, partly under communist control, was extremely poor. They had to
pay high taxes in rice to communist collectors and would raise no chickens or pigs
because of the taxes imposed on every product, even on a few eggs or a batch of
lemons. Besides, communist guerrillas did not allow dogs so that they could move
around without being detected by a dog's barking. The dog they offered to Phú
had been raised in their shelter below the ground. The old couple explained that
they had nothing more valuable than the dog. So they gave it to the lieutenant to
show their gratitude for what he had done for their son.

"Lieutenant," the old man said, "we heard that you men of North Vietnamese origin eat dog's meat. The dog is not fleshy to be cooked into a delicious dish.
But it's the best we have. Please accept it and use it anyway you like."

His remark made us laugh, but Phú's eyes were full of tears. Mine too,
naturally.

Phú said to me, "The reason I spared the young guerrilla was his wound and
his utter fear when seeing the four companions getting riddled with bullets and
falling down after a short firefight. Looking at his pale countenance and his
wound, I felt sure that he would no longer be a dangerous VC fighter. Furthermore, VC unit commanders would not employ those who had been captured
and then released by their enemy. So I let him go." Phú also asserted his belief
in the Việt Quốc spirit, saying, "There are things that a good VNQDĐ member
will never do."

Phú told me that he had informed the battalion CO about his decision to
disobey the order. Phú was ready to claim responsibility for setting a VC free.
Phú did not report the incident to the higher headquarters because this was the
first time the battalion commander had given such an order. Moreover, the CO
was Phú's good friend. However, the story reached their superiors. Both Phú
and his CO were reprimanded.

About four months after the incident, Phú was killed in a VC night attack.

At Phú's funeral, one of his platoon leaders gave me an account of Phú's last
minutes. Phú and his troops all volunteered to stay and fight against an enemy
battalion when Phú's battalion commander ordered his company to retreat to
the other side of a small river. He tried to buy time for the battalion to reorganize
its defense. He said if his company moved back, the enemy would advance and
concentrate their efforts on thrusting into the battalion command post. That
would certainly cause heavier losses to friendly troops.

At midnight, the enemy's last B-40 grenades killed Phú just before the communist unit withdrew.

As he had often requested before his death, both the national flag and the VNQDĐ banner covered his coffin. A young man joined the funeral on behalf of the former gang members Phú had been teaching in the night class years earlier. They also contributed some money to Phú's memorial fund.

The old couple who gave Phú the skinny dog attended his funeral at the last minute. News about Phú's death took time to reach the place.

After April 30, 1975, some local communists vandalized many graves of fallen ARVN soldiers in the regional military cemetery where Phú had been laid to rest. Phú's portrait on his headstone was partly destroyed by a pickaxe. After that, his wife had to reinter his remains in her family garden.

THE WANDERING STATUE

"He often appeared in this area at midnight after 1967. Many times he was just wandering about on the village roads for nothing and disappeared at a wink when somebody approached. He sometimes stopped by lonely homes straggling on the flat land beside the Sài Gòn-Biên Hòa Highway. He has never scared people, only asked for water, especially during the dry season when the climate usually reached 90 degrees Fahrenheit and higher.

"He wore field dress with jungle boots, a rifle, and bandoleers on his shoulders, a helmet in one hand and an empty canteen in the other. He looks exactly like the statue 'The Mourning Soldier.'"

That was a legend about the ghostly spirit of the soldier statue erected at the branch road leading to the RVN National Military Cemetery near Biên Hòa, South Việt Nam. The story spread far and wide, and many people who lived in and around the villages surrounding the cemetery believed it.

The apparition of the Mourning Soldier was seen a few years after the statue was erected. There were several tales about the soldier wandering at night. It was said that besides asking for drinking water, many times he showed up in time to protect young women from assault or rape by scaring away the attackers. A rural shop owner related that once the Mourning Soldier took the bag of a hundred loaves of French bread delivered every morning at the side of the statue before she could pick them up. She found out later that the loaves had been laid . . . one at each grave.

People in any country, particularly in Việt Nam during the war, easily accept such mystic tales. After decades of armed conflict, with death at their side every day, people have to rely on something, however superstitious it might be, to ease themselves from the horrors of war.

The story is associated with the National Military Cemetery, located on a gently sloping hill of more than 500 acres, midway between Sài Gòn and Biên

Hòa and close to the highway. Constructing a national cemetery had been intended under the administration of President Ngô Đình Diệm, who died in a
coup on November 2, 1963. The idea was translated into reality in 1965, and
President Nguyễn Văn Thiệu inaugurated the cemetery on November 1, 1966.

The cemetery is divided into rows of graves, laid out symmetrically on the
two sides of the main road in the center. Seen from the air, the large plot looks
like the abdomen of a giant bee: its head is the temple with a memorial situated
on high ground, and the 100-yard road from the temple to the highway is its
stinger. It is the image of the brave soldier bee "charging at the enemy despite
sure death," symbolizing the heroic actions of the fallen warriors.

On the corner, where the road leading into the cemetery links up with the
highway, was a large statue of a soldier. He sat on a rock, his M-1 rifle on his lap,
his helmet pushed a little up above his forehead. His sorrowful countenance
expressed his feeling, which was described as "mourning his fallen fighting fellows." It was a famous work of the sculptor Nguyễn Thanh Thu, who was also
an ARVN captain.

In 1965, Captain Thu was asked to create a statue memorizing the ARVN
fallen soldiers. It took him weeks to find a model before he caught a sight from
which he drew an inspiration. In a rural shop near the old military cemetery,
he happened to meet an airborne corporal who sat at a small table with two
cans of beer. The corporal was drinking and talking as if he were sharing the
beer with his invisible comrade in arms to whom he had just said farewell at
the funeral.

The sorrowful look and posture of the airborne corporal helped Captain
Thu materialize his inspiration. Upon Thu's request, the corporal, Võ Văn Hai,
became the model for Thu's work.

The statue was made of concrete first and unveiled on November 1, 1966,
when the memorial temple was first opened. In late 1969, it was moved to Sài
Gòn to be cast in bronze and returned to its place in 1971.

The statue was named "Thương Tiếc," which could be translated as Lam-
entation, or Mourning, or Sorrow.

Hours after Sài Gòn was taken over on April 30, 1975, the communists
pulled down the statue and destroyed it. To defame the ARVN fallen warriors,
they hung on the gate of the ARVN Gò Vấp cemetery, three miles from Sài Gòn
central, a board of notice that read, "Here lie the Americans' puppet soldiers
after they have paid for their crimes."

Many graves were vandalized, but the Biên Hòa cemetery was not leveled
or moved as were most of military cemeteries in the provinces. In a number of
regional ARVN cemeteries, common civilians were buried beside ARVN war
dead after everything relating to the ARVN was removed. Communist authorities forbade visits and maintenance of the graves until the early 1990s.

However, communist authorities have not approved formal petitions by overseas Vietnamese for overall cleaning up the National Military Cemetery. In 2006, VCP central government signed a decree regulating the cemetery area as property of the local district government.

During the Việt Nam War, South Vietnamese military and civilian authorities buried tens of thousands of communist soldiers in jungle areas, in POW camps, or near populous villages, towns, and cities. But none of the mass or individual graves was marked with such a humiliating sign.

In an English evening class in Sài Gòn in 1988, an eighteen-year-old student whose father rested in the cemetery asked her teacher, who was my friend, "Is it true that after the American Civil War in 1861–65, at some places in the United States, the federal government buried dead soldiers of both sides in the same cemeteries without any mark of discrimination?" The teacher, who had studied in the United States and was well read in history, could only say, "Yes, it is." However, he refused to discuss the topic further to avoid trouble with ubiquitous undercover political security agents.

NOTES

1. A Morning of Horror

1. Việt Minh is the shortened form of Việt Nam Độc Lập Đồng Minh Hội (Việt Nam Independence League). This was a revolutionary front founded by Hồ Học Lãm in southern China in the late 1930s. Hồ Chí Minh was a member. After Hồ Học Lãm died in 1941, Hồ Chí Minh claimed the League as his own. It consisted of the Indochinese Communist Party and some noncommunist parties as its satellites, led by the communists but under a nationalist cover.

Việt Minh seized power in August 1945 and established the government that launched a political cleansing campaign against the nationalists before the War of Resistance started in December 1946. To the French, anyone fighting against French forces in Việt Nam in 1946–54 was considered to be Việt Minh. To the Vietnamese, Việt Minh consisted of pre-1954 Communist Party members.

2. My Early Years and Education

1. The VNQDĐ became an active anticolonialist and anticommunist revolutionary party in 1945 and was declared the communists' archenemy by the Việt Nam Communist Party. In the nationalist regime after 1954, the VNQDĐ was in the opposition.

2. More than a decade later, several Koreans, Filipinos, and Taiwanese I met in Việt Nam and abroad seemed surprised to learn that the Vietnamese did not hate the Japanese as bitterly as they did.

3. In the colonial era, the French rulers divided Việt Nam into three parts. Each was an autonomous territory with different status as a state in the Federation of Indochina, which included Cambodia and Laos: Tonkin or North Việt Nam from the 19th parallel to the northern border with China; Annam or Central Việt Nam was from the 12th parallel; and Cochinchina or South Việt Nam was from the 12th parallel to the southernmost Cape of Cà Mâu at the 10th parallel. Under French dominion, Tonkin and Annam were "protectorates" where the king's government, down to villages, had some limited power, while Cochinchina was France's colony where the king had no power.

4. Discrimination by class and political background in examinations and school admission was instituted in North Việt Nam by the communist regime in 1955. No similar discrimination existed in the South prior to April 1975.

5. In this book, my family, as commonly understood in Việt Nam, sometimes denotes my grandmother, my parents and their children, my father's elder brother and his

wife, and my father's widowed elder sister. We all lived together as one unit with common possession of property and finances.

3. 1945

1. The Greater East Asia Co-Prosperity Sphere was imperial Japan's designation for an Asian block of nations that would share prosperity and peace, independent of Western control. The concept was used to justify Japanese expansion in East Asia and the creation of puppet governments to control local populations and send much needed resources to Japan.

2. Before 1945, the king's banner and other national banners had been a long red stripe on yellow. As described above, in 1945 under Japanese occupation, the national flag was three short red stripes with the middle broken on yellow. The nationalist government banner after 1949 was just the pre-1945 king's banner with the large red stripe divided into three smaller ones. The three red stripes on yellow represented the RVN after the declaration of the republic on October 23, 1955.

3. Đại Việt Quốc Dân Đảng, ĐVQDĐ, or Đai Việt was a revolutionary party advocating the struggle for Việt Nam's independence, led by Trương Tử Anh, a brilliant leader who was assassinated by the Việt Minh in 1946.

4. My father's account of the event was not far different from what I read later in books written by many honest nationalist leaders. Those books and reports alleged that the Việt Minh broke the promise given by Hồ Chí Minh to the Việt Cách for full cooperation with other nationalist parties whenever the joint command gave the order for a general uprising. One of the stories known to most nationalists concerned an important meeting between the nationalist parties on August 16, when there was reliable information indicating the Việt Minh was about to act alone. In the meeting, attended by two dozen nationalist leaders, the top representative for the VNQDĐ, Lê Khang (alias Lê Ninh), a renowned leader, suggested a plan of preemptive action to take over the national ruling power. All other committee members opposed his plan, as they were afraid of the possibility of a civil war. They also believed that no matter who fired the first shot, a coalition government would be established as the Việt Minh had promised. At the end of the meeting, Lê Ninh warned, "Your decision will bring havoc to you and me and the people very soon." Lê Ninh was right. He was assassinated a few months later during the communists' "cleansing" campaign, one of the many thousands of his comrades assassinated in 1946.

5. Nguyễn Văn Trấn, a member of the Communist Party/Tonkin Committee in 1945, asserted in his article in the *Lao Động Daily* (August 18, 2000) regarding the August Revolution: "When the revolution [forces] seized power in Hà Nội, Uncle Hồ was unaware of the event.... So the central leadership directed that we must have the Uncle back [to Hà Nội] as soon as possible." Nguyễn Văn Trấn wrote that he led one of the two teams sent out to look for Hồ Chí Minh. It was the other team led by Trần Đăng Ninh that met Hồ somewhere in a province north of Hà Nội. Hồ asked him if the revolution was already launched. Trấn recounted the story: "In the evening of August 25, the Uncle showed up at 25 Hàng Ngang Street, where he drafted the Declaration of Independence."

6. On August 30, 1945, Bảo Đại surrendered leadership of the country to Hồ Chí Minh and the Việt Minh. On September 2, Việt Minh leaders proclaimed the Democratic Republic of Việt Nam, with Hà Nội as its capital and Hồ as its president.

7. Nguyễn Hải Thần (1869–1954), real name Vũ Hải Thu, graduated the Tú Tài (second honor graduate of the King's National Examination in the ancient education system). He had fought the French in the anticolonialist movement for the national independence since the 1900s. He fled to China after a failed attack at a French outpost. He served

in the Chinese Nationalist Army as a two-star general and was once the deputy com-mander of the Chinese Wang Po Military Academy. He was highly esteemed by Genera-lissimo Chang Kai-shek and was a close friend of Sun Yat-sen.

He was the chairman of Việt Nam Cách Mạng Đồng Minh Hội. He returned to Việt Nam in September 1945, leading the nationalist coalition. Serving in the nationalist-com-munist coalition government as vice president since January 1946, he fled Việt Nam in July after the Việt Minh began an all-out offensive to eradicate nationalist parties. He died in China in 1954.

8. Nguyễn Tường Tam (July 25, 1905–July 7, 1963) was a senior editor of revolution-ary-minded magazines and books and founder of the Tự Lực Văn Đòan (Self-Strength Liter-ary Group), the elite in the cultural history of Việt Nam. Evading French arrest, he fled to China in 1940 and created the Đại Việt Dân Chính Party, later integrated into the Việt Quốc. He returned to Việt Nam in September 1945 and became one of its top leaders. He was foreign minister in the coalition government. Facing the risk of being eliminated by Việt Minh's cleansing campaign, he fled to China in 1946 and returned in 1949 to live in Sài Gòn and Đà Lạt and continue writing. He remained a spiritual leader of the Việt Quốc and sup-ported the opposition under Ngô Đình Diệm's regime. He committed suicide one day before he was to be tried at the Sài Gòn court-martial. His style and works are remarkable contribu-tions to the modern literature of Việt Nam.

9. "Hồ Chí Minh proved to be a talented actor," my father once said. Hồ could burst into histrionic tears at will. Many people recalled his crying trick, including Miec-zyslaw Maneli, chief of the Polish delegation to the International Commission for Control and Supervision after the Geneva Accords in Việt Nam, as recounted in his book *War of the Vanquished,* trans. Maria de Görgey (New York: Harper and Row, 1971).

4. On the Way to War

1. Vũ Hồng Khanh (1904–85), real name Vũ Văn Giản, was a teacher who joined the VNQDĐ and participated in the 1930 revolt as commander of the Kiến An town bat-tle. After the failed uprising, he fled to China, only returning to Hà Nội in September 1945, along with other nationalist revolutionary leaders. He was deputy prime minister in the coalition government of the nationalists and the communists. He fled to China in late 1946 and returned to Hà Nội in 1949. He served in the Bảo Đại cabinet as minister of youth (1953). He was chairman of the VNQDĐ from 1955 until 1975, when Sài Gòn fell. He died in Sài Gòn in 1993 after serving eleven years in communist prison camps and seven years under house arrest.

2. Vũ Thư Hiên confirmed this story in his memoirs, *Đêm Giữa Ban Ngày* (Dark-ness at Noon) (Stanton, Calif.: Văn Nghệ, 1997). He is the son of Vũ Đình Huỳnh, Hồ Chí Minh's private secretary.

5. Take Up Arms!

1. In this part, the Resistance denotes the Vietnamese side of the 1946–54 war against the French. Việt Minh denotes the communist government, which was leading the Resistance.

2. When I came back to the city in the spring of 1948, the first thing I did was to visit the bank building. To my surprise, the great hole created by the howitzer was only twenty inches in diameter and ten inches deep—half of the wall thickness as far as I could esti-mate. It was one of the first lessons about propaganda I learned from the war.

3. Few studies have ever estimated the number of nationalist parties' members who were massacred by the Việt Minh between 1945 and 1954. I think the Việt Minh cleansing campaign may have claimed at least 100,000 lives all over Việt Nam.

After arriving in South Việt Nam in 1954, I also learned that in 1947 and 1948, the Việt Minh had massacred thousands of followers of the Cao Đài and Hòa Hảo sects in the southern provinces. On a few trips to Long Xuyên province, I was surprised by the fact that each of a great many Hòa Hảo families had at least one relative killed by Việt Minh in 1947.

Local Việt Minh officials later admitted to the mass killing. They explained that it was caused by a mistake in the radio message sent by the Việt Minh government in the North to its local authorities in Quảng Nam, Đà Nẵng, Châu Đốc, Long Xuyên, and Tây Ninh, cities where a large number of Cao Đài and Hòa Hảo followers lived. The local Việt Minh officials explained that the original top-secret message from its central government in North Việt Nam ordered local authorities to *bám sát* (closely watch) the Cao Đài and the Hòa Hảo. In the text sent by radio, the letter *b* in Morse code was missing, so the word *bam sat* became *ám sát,* (assassinate)!

8. The Shaky Peace

1. Under the Bảo Đại government, the state of Việt Nam was organized into four military regions: South Việt, Central Việt Nam, North Việt Nam, and the Central Highlands. After the Republic of Việt Nam was founded in October 1955, South Việt Nam had four MRs: northern Central Việt Nam, southern Central Việt Nam and the Highlands, eastern South Việt Nam, and western South Việt Nam or the Mekong Delta.

2. Patriotic songs produced in cities under the French and nationalist governments were rare and did little to raise our spirits. However, romantic music thrived and would flourish later in South Việt Nam.

3. The ten-year system continued in the North until 1976 after the reunification, when Hà Nội reinstated the twelve-year system.

9. Bloodier Battles

1. "One point two sides" was a tactic of attacking military strongholds, base or outpost, with one "main effort (point)" to strike at the objective and with two (or more) "secondary efforts (sides)" to support the main effort. It is similar to a common military tactic but stated under a new name with Chinese rhetoric.

2. Recently, some Hà Nội publications have translated *dân công* as "conscripted laborer." In these memoirs, I use "war laborer" instead.

12. To Be a Soldier

1. Ever since the Việt Nam War reached a high intensity with the U.S. involvement, the U.S. military and foreign media have mistakenly used the term "Việt Cộng"—abbreviated VC—for the communist local military forces in South Việt Nam only. To the Vietnamese, "Việt Cộng" means "Vietnamese communist," which denotes communists from anywhere in Việt Nam, whether the North Vietnamese Army or its local units in South Việt Nam under the Communist Party's satellite, the so-called National Liberation Front.

2. A Land Reform group was made up of between thirty and forty faithful party members who were specially trained for the implementation of the Land Reform policy and were under direct command of the Land Reform district and province committees.

Each team operated in a designed area of several villages with full authority, replacing the dismissed village government. The group investigated everyone subject to the campaign—landlords, rich farmers, and anticommunist suspects—and coerced poor farmers into joining the denunciation session at the village people's court. A people's court had the authority to sentence citizens to death without appeal.

13. Progress and Signs of Instability

1. In 1967, the large slums near Khánh Hội again suffered a great fire, and U.S. Army helicopters rendered help by dropping fire suppressant chemicals to control the conflagration. However, that 1967 fire provided nothing that could have been used as evidence for such rumors, although the Americans' active help in the firefighting was not appropriately praised by the government information service and the mass media.

14. Mounting Pressure

1. Hà Nội publications and communist VIPs, writing after South Việt Nam collapsed in April 1975, publicly admitted the communists' leading role in the war right from the beginning. Since the end of the war, I haven't heard of anyone who had asserted that the Communist Party in North Việt Nam did not have an active role in the 1959–64 war in South Việt Nam step forward to admit his mistake.

2. It should be noted that although South Việt Nam imported a lot of movies and musical productions from the United States during the presence of a half million GIs, with thousands of nightclubs and bars serving them, American ways of life and cultural styles have not had a considerable influence on the Vietnamese life. The South Vietnamese culture, promoted by freedom and prosperity although in wartime, was strong enough to assert its place in the society.

15. The Limited War

1. During the war, the members of those agencies and units were very seldom mentioned, although they contributed some part to the war. After the war, American (and South Vietnamese?) military authorities deliberately abandoned them as if they had never existed.

2. FULRO is the abbreviation in French for "Front Unifié De Lutte Des Races Opprimées," the movement for political autonomy of ethnic minority people in the Việt Nam Central Highlands founded 1957. The uprising in 1957–58 was suppressed. Revived during the 1964 rebellion, the movement disintegrated after the second crackdown.

3. The Communist regime in the North was running a very similar resettlement program. According to my research based on reports in state-control newspapers from Hà Nội in the early 1960s, by 1963 there were 93 state farms (34 of them built by army regiments) and 70 state silvicultural farms all over North Việt Nam. Hà Nội resettled, on a compulsory basis, more than 200,000 people from populous cities and villages in the Red River Delta. State farms were government-owned firms where farmers worked as wage-earning laborers. Each farm employed from 2,000 to 5,000 workers growing cash crops such as tea, sugar cane, rubber, coffee, and tobacco, or in forestry and apiculture.

Hà Nội also launched the "Khai Hoang" (Reclaiming Waste Land) Campaign. It resettled people who were classified as unemployed workers and self-employed workers in trades that weren't allowed by Hà Nội's economic policy. They were sent to the highland provinces north of Hà Nội. The campaign carried the beautiful name "Xây Dựng Quê Hương Mới," (Building New Homeland). By 1964, about a half million people had been moved to their "new homelands."

The two campaigns helped communist local authorities oust the great many unwanted innocent families from their responsible areas including former soldiers, civil servants of the pre-54 nationalist government, and close relatives of those who had left for the South in 1954. Local authorities also sent away released convicts, students who failed to enroll in college, and anyone who had earned the disfavor of the local Party Committees, particularly individuals who often argued and were seen as stubborn, restive elements.

The resettled families of both kinds received very little initial support from Hà Nội, as compared to the similar programs in South Việt Nam. Their working conditions were horrible as recounted by people who had been workers in those farms and communities.

16. The Year of the (Crippled) Dragon

1. In 2001, Hà Nội started a project called Hồ Chí Minh Highway from South Việt Nam to the North along the common borders with Cambodia and Laos. It includes the existing Highway 14 from near Sài Gòn to the northern border of Kontum province that was constructed by the French before 1954. The French also prepared ground for an extending temporary road from Kontum to Ashau and Khe Sanh, negotiable by military trucks in dry season. Now Hà Nội has upgraded the old highway and given it the new name. This highway has no relation to the legendary Hồ Chí Trail, which also ran along the borders but far away on the territories of Laos and Cambodia.

2. The five coastal provinces—Quảng Trị, Thừa Thiên, Quảng Nam, Quảng Ngãi, and Bình Định—had experienced bloody fighting since 1945. The communists' terror campaign in 1945–48 decimated the Việt Quốc (and other noncommunist parties' members, in particular the Cao Đài sect followers in Đà Nẵng). The terror campaign was followed by the far less brutal vengeance by nationalist fanatics during the "Communists Denunciation Campaign" in 1955 after the Sài Gòn government took control of the region formerly under Việt Minh's rule. The last massacre of the war occurred in April 1975, when hundreds of Việt Quốc and Đại Việt members were killed after South Việt Nam collapsed.

3. Until April 1975, there were a lot of rice fields and homesteads in South Việt Nam belonged to Việt Minh followers who left for North Việt Nam in 1954. RVN laws protected their ownership. Their closest relatives were granted temporary usufruct on the estates that continued until April 1975, when the RVN collapsed.

4. For more information, see http://www.history.navy.mil/photos/sh-usn/usnsh-m/dd731-k.htm.

17. On the Down Slope

1. During the 1959–75 Việt Nam War, there were no suicide bomb attacks. Such attacks took place only in the War of Resistance (1946–54) against the French, an indication of the great differences between the two wars.

19. Sài Gòn Commando

1. The Taiwan delegation, however, kept offering advice until the last days they were in Việt Nam in late April 1975, whether the advice was welcomed or not.

2. Ironically, after April 1975, more Vietnamese appreciated the good help in psyops and civic actions the American units had provided them in time of war. People living in areas protected by American, Australian, and maybe Korean troops during the war would long remember the Medcap teams from those allied forces.

3. Prostitution in Việt Nam under communist rule increased rapidly during the late 1980s, probably five to ten times more than in South Việt Nam in the late 1960s, when a half million GIs were in Việt Nam. The number of illegitimate children of Vietnamese women and American servicemen was as many as 30,000, according to some sources. Vietnamese society treated them as degraded persons. After 1975, they suffered terrible discrimination under the communist regime until the early 1980s, when the U.S. government allowed them to move to the States.

4. Black propaganda is false information that purports to be from a source on one side of a conflict but is actually from the opposing side. It is typically used to vilify, embarrass, or misrepresent the enemy. In gray propaganda, the source is not identified. In white propaganda, the real source is declared and usually more accurate information is given, if also slanted or distorted.

5. For readers' convenience, the "*hồi chánh*" are referred to as "defectors" in these memoirs to avoid possible confusion, although both English translations of "*hồi chánh*" (defector and returnee) do not fully convey its meaning.

6. Ytzaina returned to the United States in April 1970. After his discharge from the army, he became a university professor in St. Louis, as he had wished when working with me in the Chiêu Hồi program. He died in 2004.

7. Combined with military achievements, the program helped consolidate control of the South Việt Nam countryside. After 1971, more and more highways and populated areas were made safe for traveling day and night, and terrorist attacks diminished considerably every month. The communist-controlled areas were reduced to a little less than in 1959, owing partly to the rural development program.

20. The Tết Offensive

1. After the event, Eddie Adams, the AP photographer who took the snapshot of the killing, expressed his profound remorse about the photograph that ruined General Loan's life. Adams wrote in *Time* magazine on July 27, 1998, ten days after General Loan died of cancer, "But photographs do lie, even without manipulation. They are only half-truths. What the photograph didn't say was, 'What would you do if you were the general at that time and place on that hot day, and you caught the so-called bad guy after he blew away one, two, or three American soldiers?' The photograph also doesn't say that the general devoted much of his time trying to get hospitals built in Việt Nam for war casualties." And he added, "There are tears in my eyes."

2. Years later, some authors in Western countries wrote that the NVA Supreme Command imitated the heroic King Quang Trung in his miraculous military campaign that smashed the Chinese invading army during Tết 1789. The great king ordered its troops to celebrate Tết one day earlier so they could launch their attack on Tết's Eve for an absolute surprise while their enemy was enjoying the New Year's rest and recreation. Some Western authors wrote that the Supreme Command in Hà Nội had its troops celebrate Tết on January 29 so that they could launch their first attack on January 30, 1968.

3. Years later, in 1972, the horrible images of 1968 mass graves drove many tens of thousands of people from all walks of life in Huế and Quảng Trị to take the route of war refugees. The press corps named it "voting with their feet." Panic evacuations from South Việt Nam's

northern cities happened once again more tragically in March 1975 before South Việt Nam fell. It was later apparent that people from Huế and the adjacent provinces made up a significant proportion of the Vietnamese boatmen fleeing Việt Nam after the RVN collapsed on April 30, 1975. After April 1975, communist authorities evicted a large number of close relatives of the 1968 carnage victims living in the Huế area and resettled them in remote "New Economic Areas."

21. Defeat on the Home Front

1. Although a lot of people knew who actually wrote it, it was not until 1985 that Hà Nội writer Hà Minh Đức disclosed that the real author was Hồ Chí Minh. He must be the only dictator to engage in such an ignoble, underhanded, and self-deifying trick that a self-respecting leader would never do.

Since the 1990s, many respectable personages serving the communist regime, plus information from secret records of the former Soviet Union in Moscow, revealed more and more facts about Hồ's true life. According to these reliable sources (former VCP Hà Nội city committee secretary Nguyễn Minh Cần, and the son of Hồ Chí Minh's private secretary, Vũ Thư Hiên, in his memoirs *Đêm Giữa Ban Ngày* [Darkness at Noon], 1997, and others), it was confirmed that Hồ had been living with at least three women as husband and wife, not including Nông Thị Xuân, who was selected to serve him as a sex partner until she was killed in an arranged car accident.

In *Viết Cho Mẹ Và Quốc Hội* (Written for My Mother and the National Congress), a book self-published in Sài Gòn in 1995, Nguyễn Văn Trấn, a former VCP central committee member in charge of the Propaganda and Training Office, recounted that at a meeting with the central committee, Hồ asserted that he "had no thought at all." He said, "Every ideal that needs to be brought forward has been taken up by Comrade Stalin and Chairman Mao. I have nothing to say."

The communist forces had a tradition of increasing their efforts to celebrate Hồ Chí Minh's birthday. On May 19 of each year since 1947, they conducted hundreds of actions such as attacking outposts, laying mines on roads, assassinations, and blowing up bridges and local government installations. Hồ was probably the only national chief of state in the world whose birthday was celebrated with so much blood.

2. Field reports gave the casualties as 128 Việt Cong and 22 civilians dead. The final U.S. government report on the incident notes "at least 175 Vietnamese men, women, and children" killed.

3. The highest figures of American and ARVN soldiers' war crimes alleged by the Hà Nội propaganda machine, though greatly exaggerated, were still much lower than in wars in other countries according to my best knowledge. Compared with the crimes of French troops in the 1946–54 war, those committed by the U.S. troops as claimed in communist reports were about twenty times smaller. There were more than 100,000 French soldiers in Việt Nam in 1953. The number of American GIs in seven years of the Việt Nam War reached 595,000 in 1968.

4. After April 30, 1975, it seemed that all of the moles in many areas stepped forward, admitting their roles in the war and got their rewards. In cases I knew, only a few were fake defectors serving in the Chiêu Hồi program. It was difficult to know how many secret agents had been working undetected in our Chiêu Hồi agencies. Two of them were members of the Armed Propaganda Company in the National Center from 1968 to 1975, as they frankly confirmed. After my release from the seventh communist prison camp in 1982, I met both of them. They greeted me with friendly and polite manners and said nothing about their clandestine works in the war. I didn't know whether they had done

anything significant against the program or anything against me. I think there could be some more like those two, but they did not make their stories public.

5. In the following years I went further into the study on the Land Reform campaign. I found more interesting information of the bloodiest genocide in the history of Việt Nam by searching through communist publications in the Psywar Department Library.

By the early 1970s, most South Vietnamese only knew that the Việt Nam communist Land Reform policy was to redistribute land to the tillers. Very few of them ever knew that the ultimate objective of the campaign was not to redistribute the lands but "to eradicate the landlord class, who was ruling the country and living on the expense of the poor and landless farmers' labor for thousands of years." An article in *Học Tập* (Cultivation) magazine, issue 6, 1958, asserted that the compulsory measures in running the "đấu tố" (denunciation session) was an intentional move to unify the poor farmers so that they would be hostile toward the landlord class forever without any chance of reconciliation. The article also stated that the sole "reeducation" of the landlord class was insufficient. I compiled my research into a special study over North Việt Nam in 1973 but failed to get a publishing permit from the RVN Information Ministry.

Since the mid-1990s, there have been publications (books, memoirs, documentaries) in Việt Nam that boldly recounted the macabre tales of the Land Reform and even discussed its fatal errors and their irreparable consequences. Such topics have been strictly prohibited under communist rule so far.

In a study I made in 1968–72, I estimated that about 50,000 victims were executed in the Land Reform. According to President Nixon in one of his books, the figure was 15,000. In Gerard Tongas's *L'enfer communiste du Nord Vietnam*, 1960, the figure was 100,000. However, *Lịch Sử Kinh Tế Việt Nam, 1945–2000* (Việt Nam Economic History) by the Institute of Economics, Hà Nội, 2002, claims that 172,008 victims were executed and that 123,266 of these were wrongly sentenced to death (2:85).

22. The New Phase

1. Artificial rain was a technique to seed the clouds using chemicals that act as nuclei for water vapor condensation in a small area. It was used in the Việt Nam War in an attempt to obstruct communist transportation of soldiers and military supplies on the Hồi Chí Minh Trail into South Việt Nam.

2. NVA troops did receive limited supplies from North Việt Nam by sea from 1962 to 1965. But it was not a big problem after 1966 when the U.S. and RVN navies could greatly minimize communist sea transport. Limited military supplies for communist forces in the Mekong Delta came by sea to Sihanoukville in Cambodia, then by war laborers into the deep southern provinces.

3. A short time before South Việt Nam fell, Trịnh Công Sơn joined the communist ranks and faithfully collaborated with Hà Nội. A few years later, he lost favor with the communists and incurred their disregard. Only after his death in 2001 did Hà Nội honor him and allow selected pieces of his 600 songs to be played. However, a great number of overseas anticommunist Vietnamese are freely enjoying Sơn's melancholy songs of love and war without much concern for his role in the war.

23. The Fiery Summer

1. The communists executed Thủy and many of his company members when they took control of Huế in March 1975.

2. On April 28, 2002, hundreds of Buddhist followers in the Quảng Trị region conducted a religious service in remembrance of the victims of the Road of Horror. Communist local authorities could not ban the services but played small tricks to discourage people from attending.

24. Hope Draining

1. Under the communist regime since April 30, 1975, corruption has not been equally restricted because of the lack of a unified financial management and control system. The situation is aggravated by the Communist Party's leadership, which tends to tolerate its high-ranking leaders. No effective law is carried out. Corruption in Việt Nam is booming out of control nowadays. Communist cops do not spare even the poorest citizens.

2. Most of the exhibitions by the communists in their post-1975 war museums denouncing Sài Gòn for its brutalities in prisons were forged or exaggerated.

3. Not until the late 1990s did the U.S. government recognize the existence of the RVN Biệt Kích, who had been left behind by the Americans in charge of the so-called secret war, and pay a humble compensation to those who already had reached the States in the Orderly Departure program.

4. Actually, both ARVN/JGS and MACV estimates of NVA losses were below Hà Nội's official figures. But none of those who had criticized Sài Gòn JGS and U.S./MACV has ever stepped forward to apologize and give the ARVN and MACV Headquarters credit.

5. According to the Đại Học Hà Nội web site (University of Hà Nội), an article reprinted from *Thanh Niên* magazine on June 3, 2005, asserted that the Young Volunteers serving from April 1965 to December 1975 in the "American war" amounted to 143,391 men and women, seventeen to thirty years old. The real number may have been much higher.

6. After the 1979 conflict with Beijing, Hà Nội reestablished the Vietnamese names used by Sài Gòn before April 1975. The action proved how the Vietnamese communists were the real "puppets" of the Chinese communists.

25. America 1974–75

1. In 1998 my wife and I visited the Magruders at Fort Drum, New York, when he was commanding the Tenth Division (Mountain). I told her, "You're an excellent tail of the kite. Believe me! If Mr. So-and-So could be secretary of defense, why not Lawson Magruder III?"

26. The End

1. After April 1975, a rumor circulated in Việt Nam and overseas that President Thiệu had seized all seventeen tons of gold reserves from the National Bank and transported it to a foreign country. But in the mid-2000s, a former official of the National Bank affirmed in an interview with communist-controlled newspapers in Việt Nam that he had handed over the gold to the communist government officials right after they took control of the bank. News stories did not disclose how the communists handled the gold after that. Rumors were that the gold was divided among the communist leaders as war booty.

2. In 1988, I met two neurologists who alleged that 2,000 people in Sài Gòn were suffering from incurable dementia, a direct consequence of the shock caused by the fall of South Việt Nam.

3. Before April 30, 1975, the Communist Party leaders were clamoring for reconciliation and concordance with the nationalists, a smart psychological tactic.

After April 1975, in their various statements, they referred to the Vietnamese refugees as "reactionaries, Americans' underlings who are living on imperialists' leftover butter and milk." Since the early 1990s, Hà Nội leaders' attitudes have changed, and they have always called them "the 1,000-mile-away consanguineous segment of our people's bowels." The 2 million overseas Vietnamese, most of whom were originally refugees, sent more than $3 billion/year to help their relatives still in Việt Nam, thus building up Hà Nội's strong currency reserves.

27. Prisoner

1. It was with this dictionary that I could refresh my English vocabulary during my years in the camps. The book helped me ward off possible adverse psychological effects and maintain a clear mind.

2. Initially we thought they were stoning us because we were former South Vietnamese officers. However, we soon learned that it was simply a sport for the kids living along the railroad tracks in North Việt Nam. According to a Hà Nội newspaper in December 1976, train passengers were killed or wounded each year by stones. As of 2005, the brutal game had not stopped but was spreading to the South and was upgraded by throwing dung at the passengers. In the early 2000s, a number of trucks and cars also were attacked on highways. "Is it a form of sadism generated by an oppressed society?" I have not read any answer to this question from competent experts.

3. In 1977, the communist ranking theorist Trần Bạch Đằng wrote in a newspaper article that the first communist cadres to travel to the South after April 30, 1975, were startled to see how children in the South were very polite and well behaved, far better than children in the North.

4. In 2005, Hà Nội confirmed there were 240,000 South Vietnamese people like us who had been concentrated in its "reeducation camps." Hà Nội has never disclosed the number of other types of prisoners from the South (prisoners of social evils, petty criminals) imprisoned after April 1975. It may have been another 200,000.

5. Based on rough estimates, the greatest loss to corruption in various government construction projects in pre-1975 South Việt Nam was 30 percent. In the 2000s, the similar estimate in Việt Nam reached 50 percent and higher, according to Đỗ Mười, a former Communist Party general secretary. In state-controlled newspapers in today's Việt Nam, there are lots of reports of cases of communist officials' shady affairs that can't be hidden. There were many cases involving brutal retaliations and threats to silence witnesses.

28. Release

1. According to many foreign specialists who were training Vietnamese marketers in Hà Nội in the early 2000s, trainees were quick to learn marketing techniques, but it was difficult to teach them how to wear a thank-you smile.

INDEX

Nguyễn Công Luận (pen name Lữ Tuấn) was born in January 1937 in North Việt Nam, near Hà Nội. He moved to South Việt Nam after the 1954 Geneva Accords and enrolled in the Republic of Việt Nam Military Academy, Class 12, in 1955. Luận served in the Army of the Republic of Việt Nam in various units, among them the Twenty-second Infantry Division, General Political Warfare Department, and the Chiêu Hồi Ministry. He graduated with a BA degree in private law from Sài Gòn University. After attending an advanced course in the U.S. Infantry School, he returned to Sài Gòn on April 3, 1975. Luận was subsequently incarcerated for six years and seven months in several communist prison camps. Released in 1982, he moved to the United States on October 19, 1990.